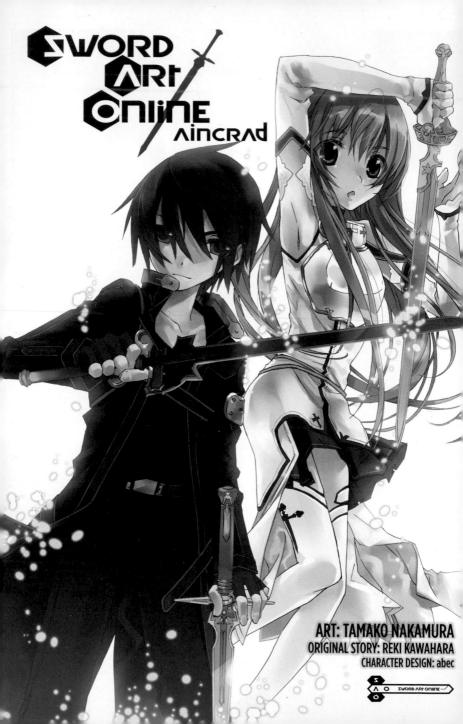

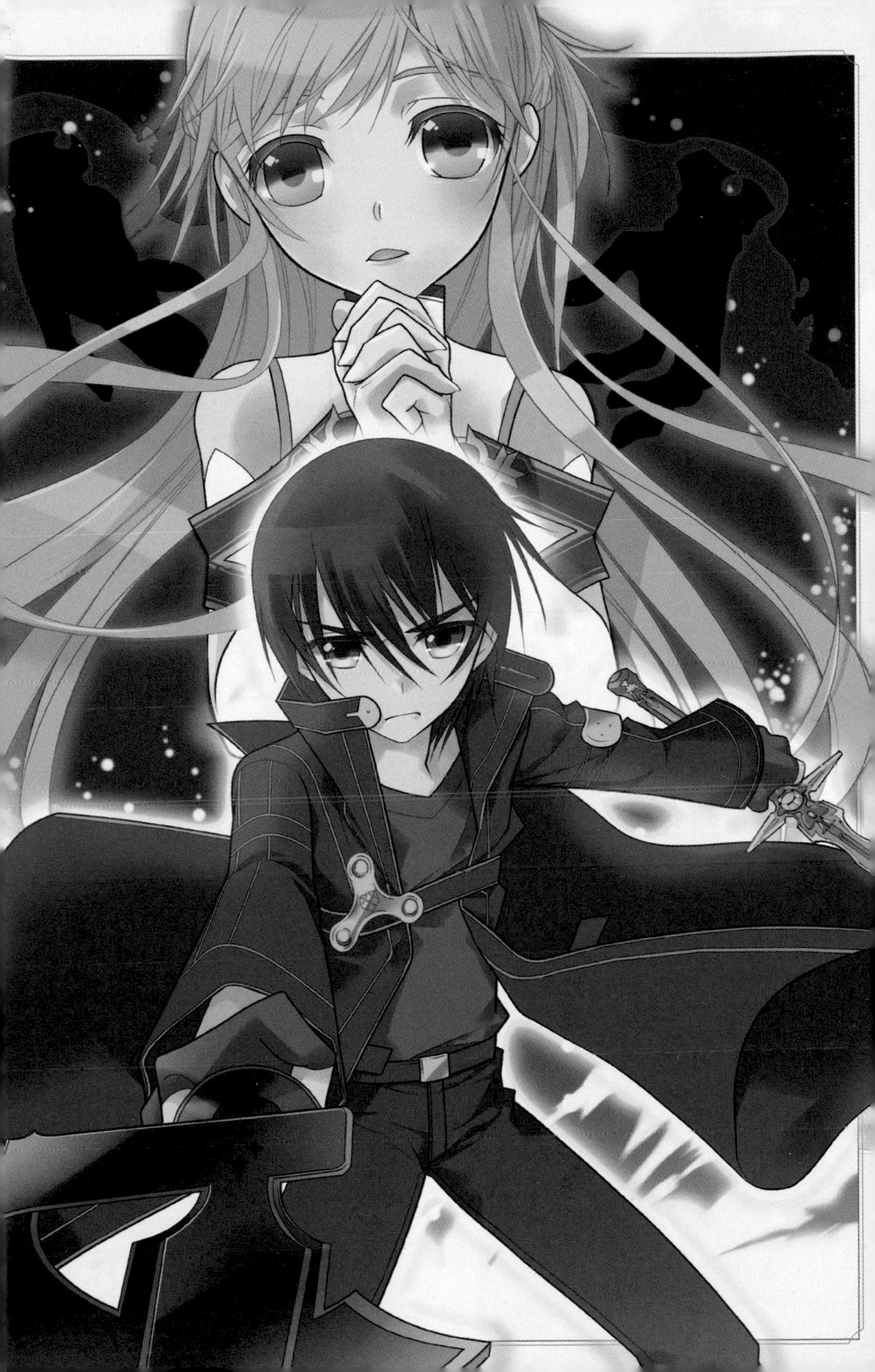

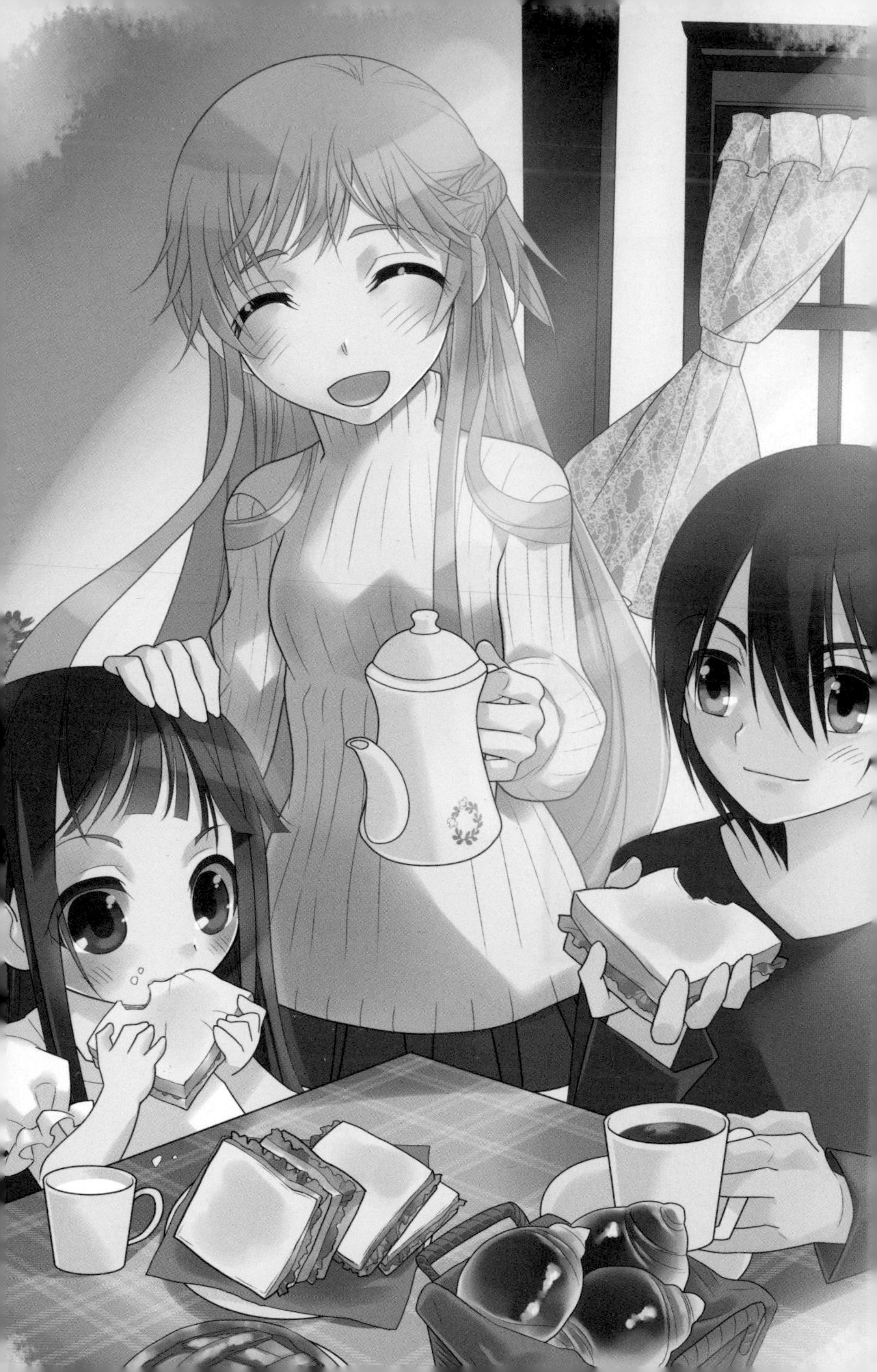

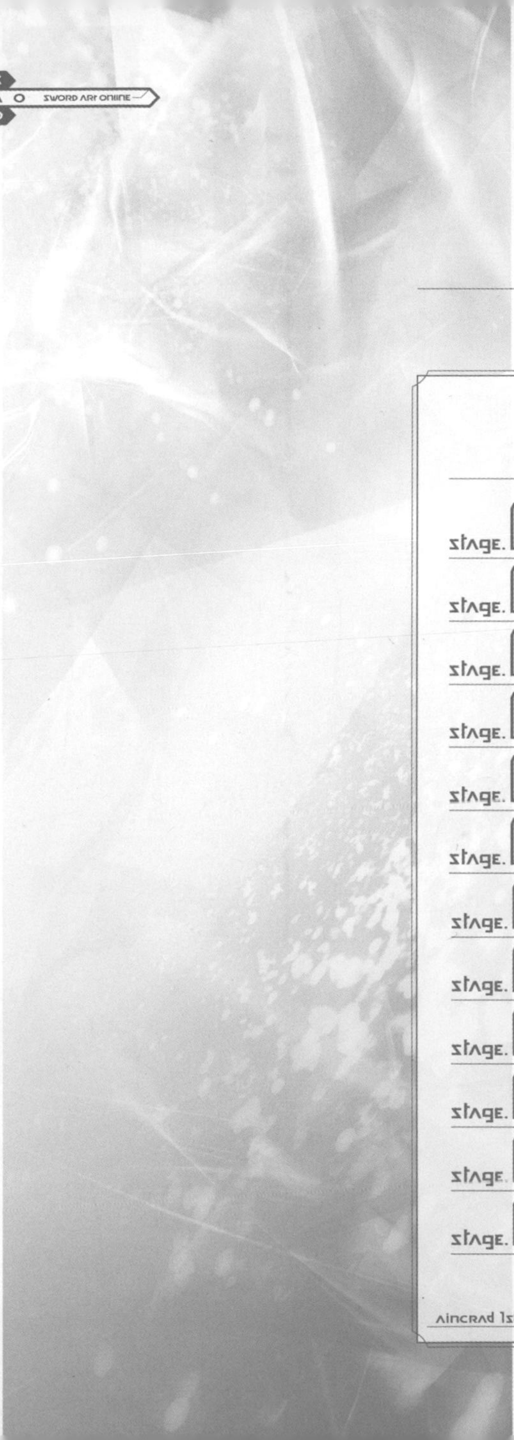

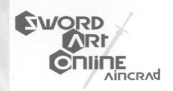

Sword Art Online
Aincrad

Art : Tamako Nakamura
Original Story : Reki Kawahara
Character Design : abec

contents

Aincrad 1st floor : the town of beginnings

Argus sword art online

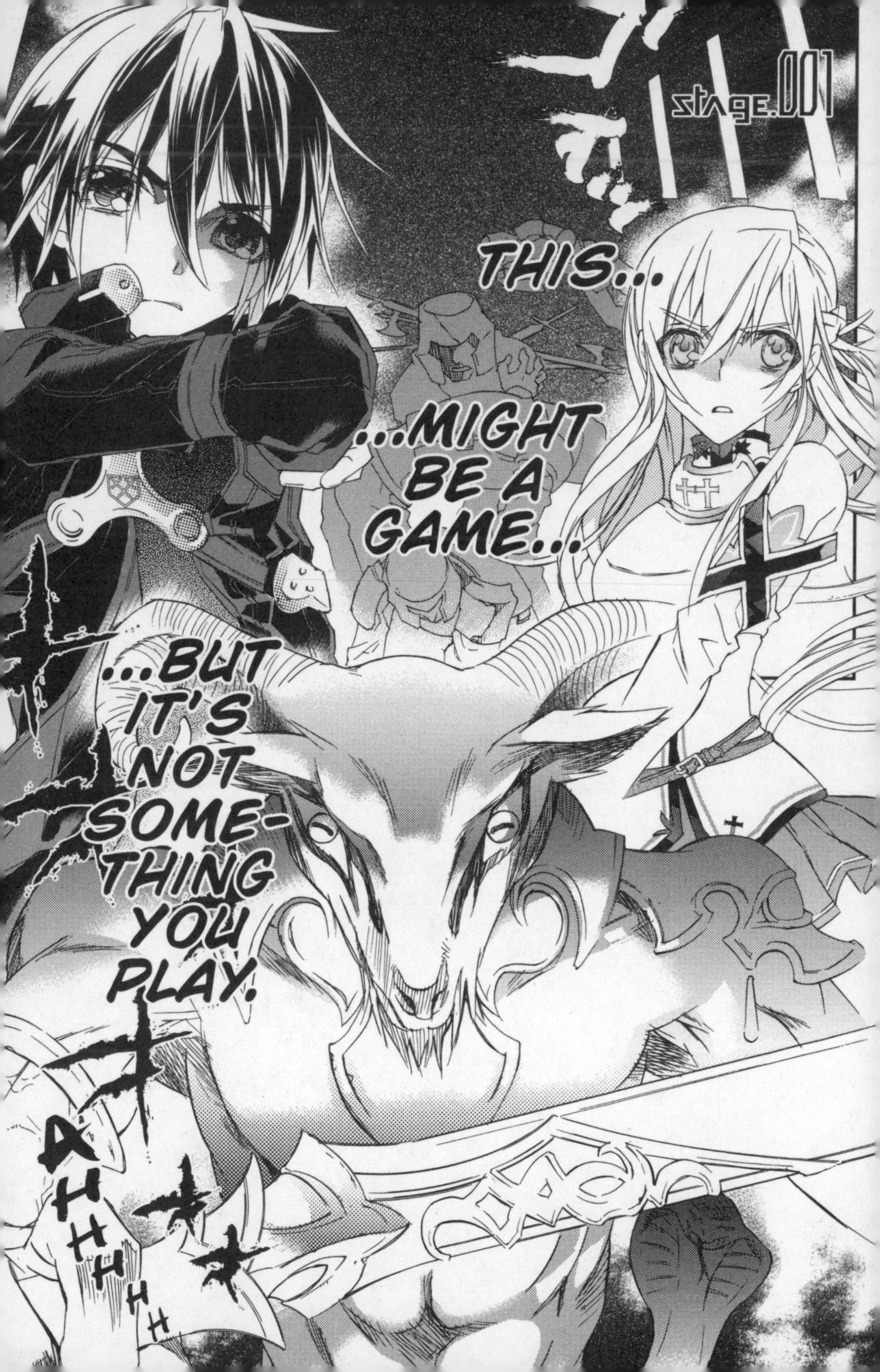
stage.001
THIS...
...MIGHT BE A GAME...
...BUT IT'S NOT SOME-THING YOU PLAY.
AHHHHHH

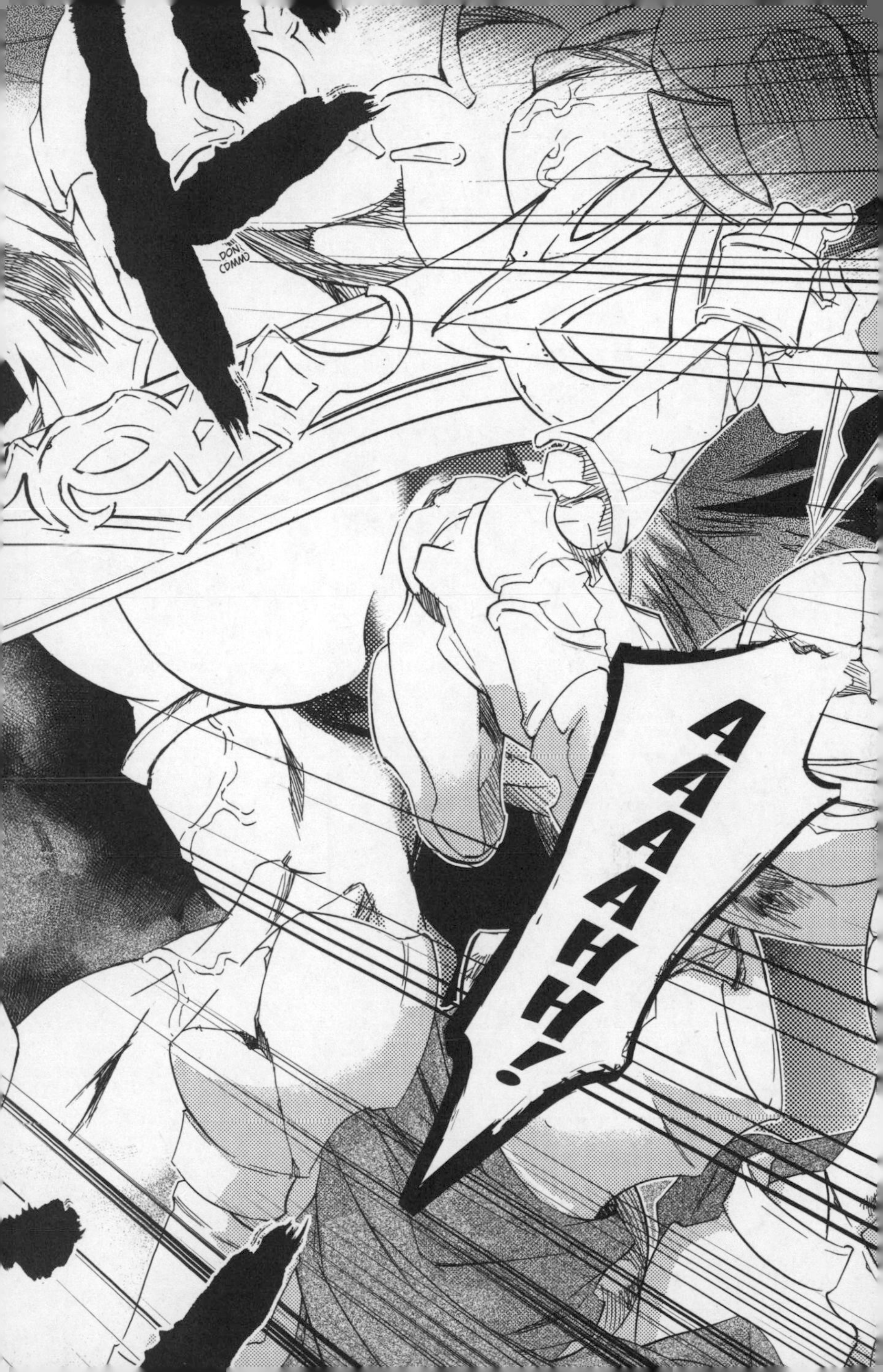
DON
(DMMM)
AAAAHH!

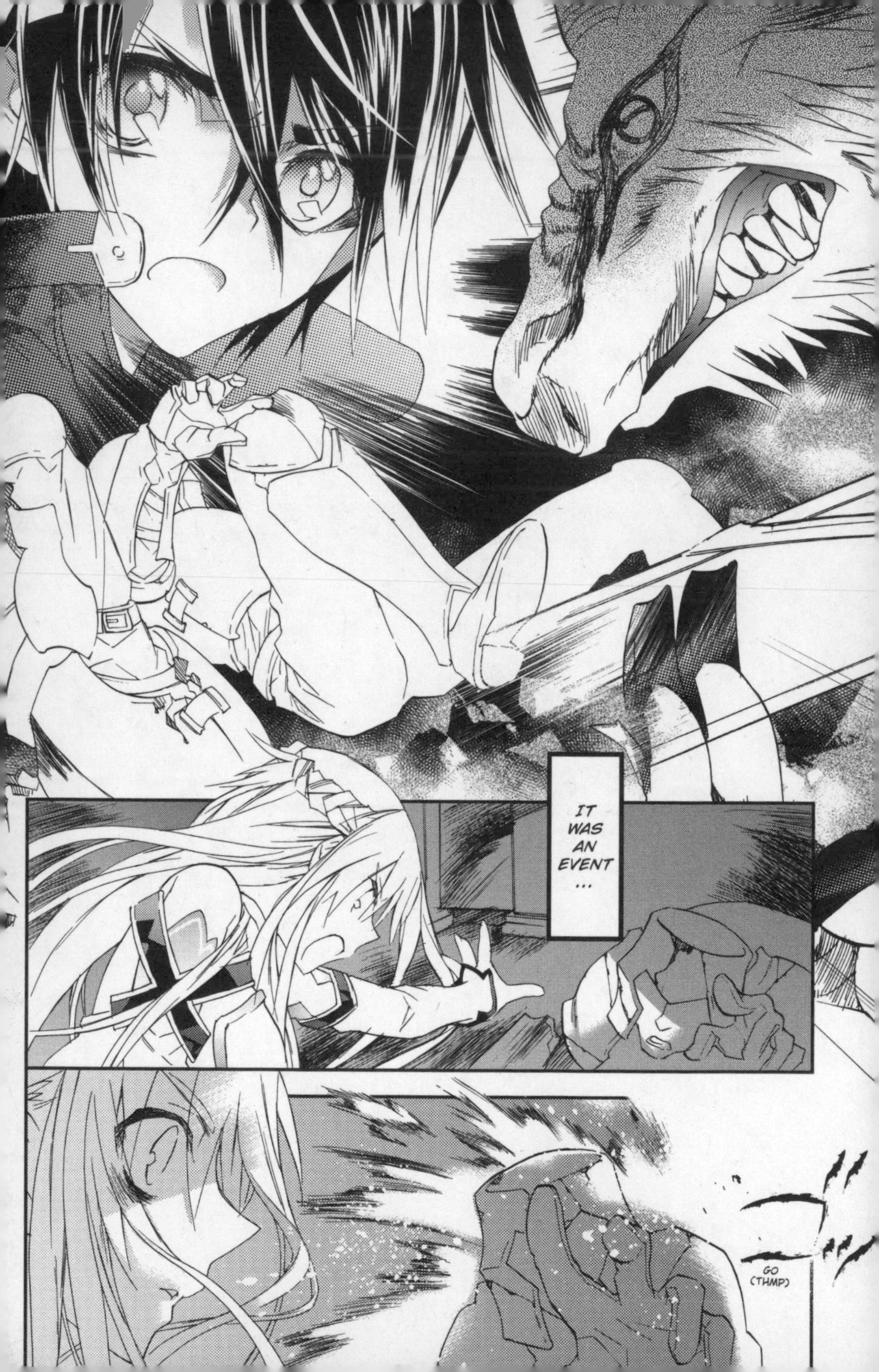
IT WAS AN EVENT...
GO (THMP)

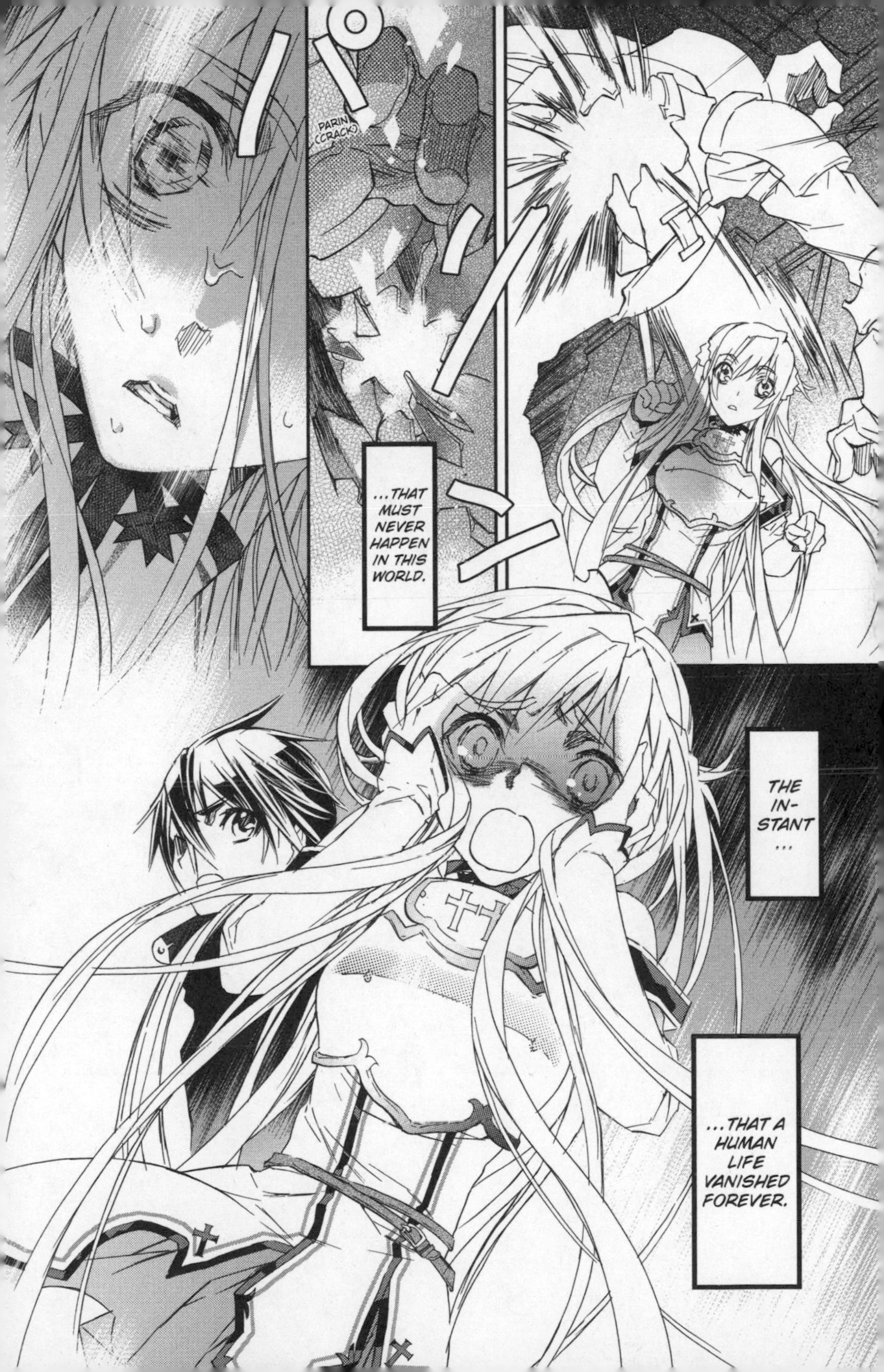
PARIN (CRACK)
...THAT MUST NEVER HAPPEN IN THIS WORLD.
THE IN-STANT ...
...THAT A HUMAN LIFE VANISHED FOREVER.

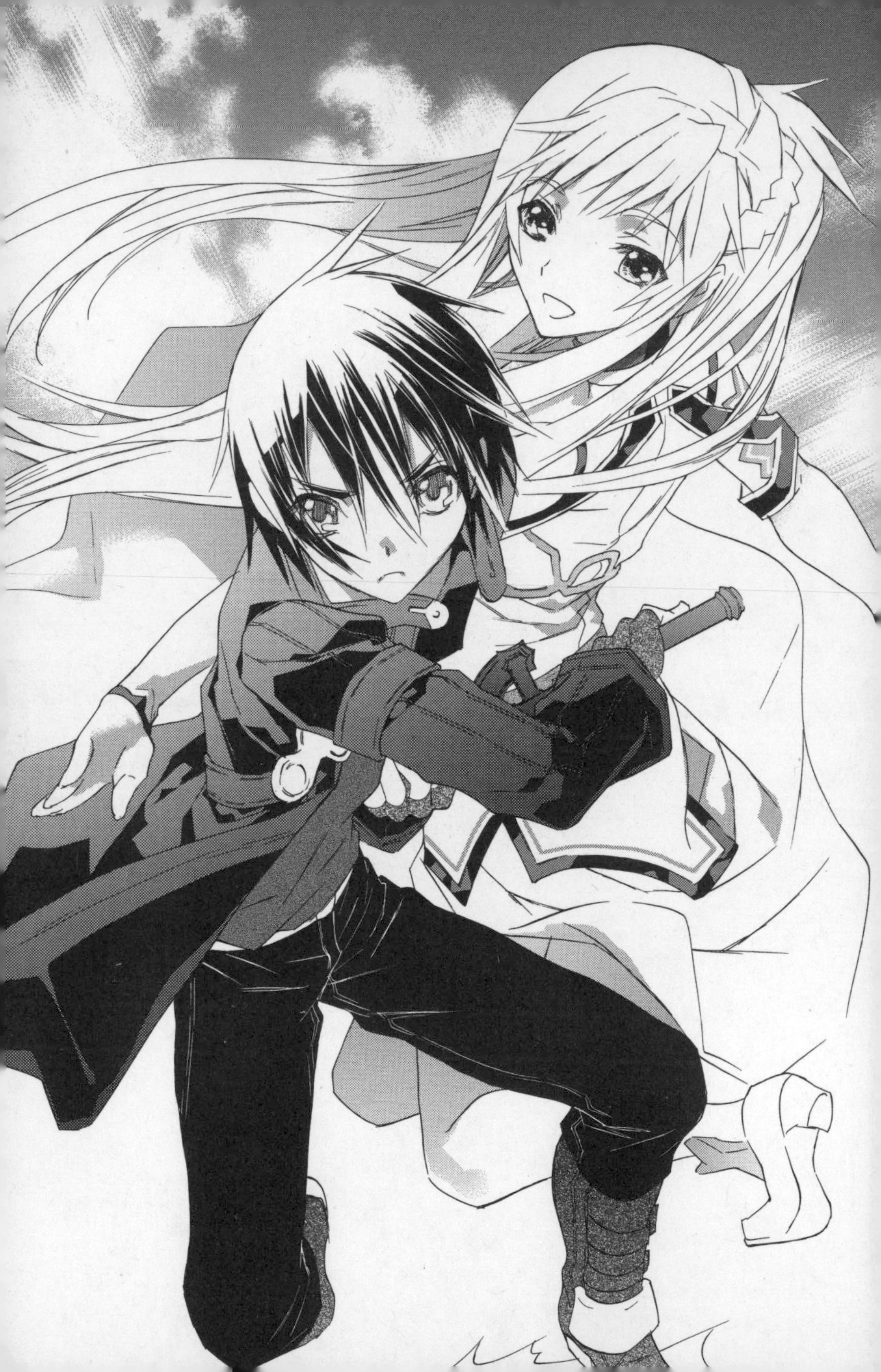

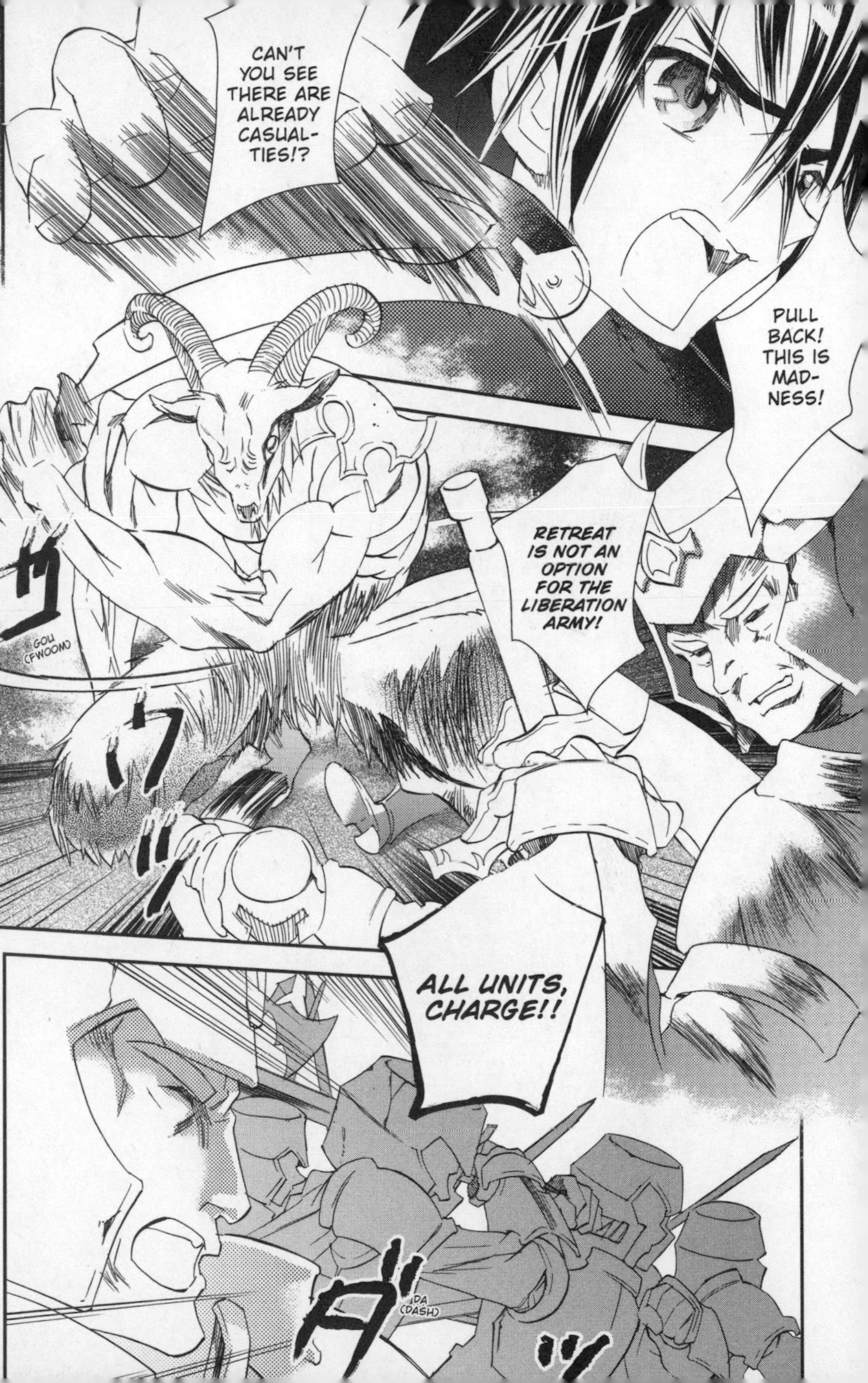
CAN'T YOU SEE THERE ARE ALREADY CASUAL-TIES!?
PULL BACK! THIS IS MAD-NESS!
RETREAT IS NOT AN OPTION FOR THE LIBERATION ARMY!
GOU (FWOOM)
ALL UNITS, CHARGE!!
DA (DASH)

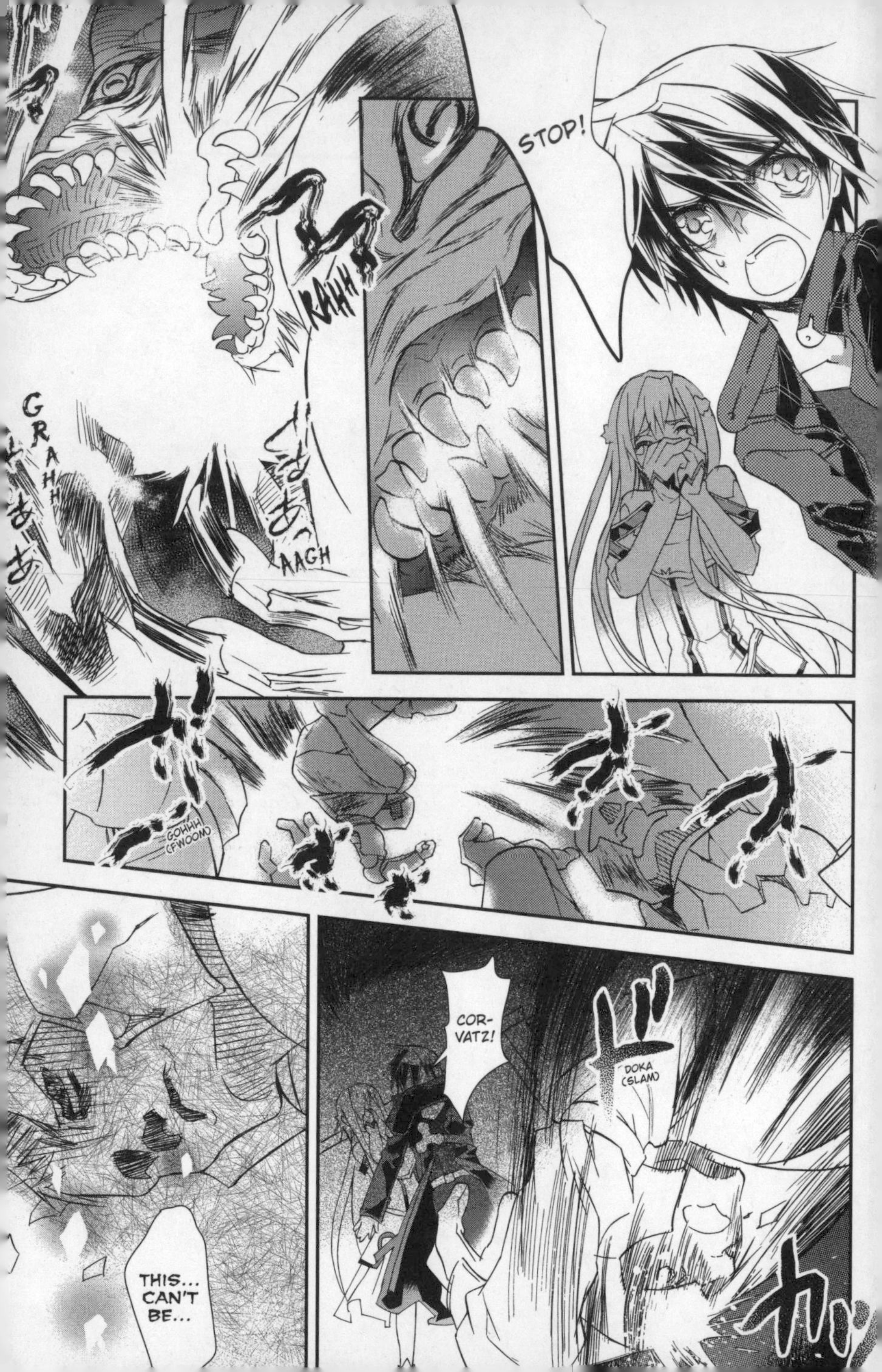

STOP!
RAHH
GRAHH
AAGH
GOHHH (FWOOM)
DOKA (SLAM)
COR-VATZ!
THIS... CAN'T BE...

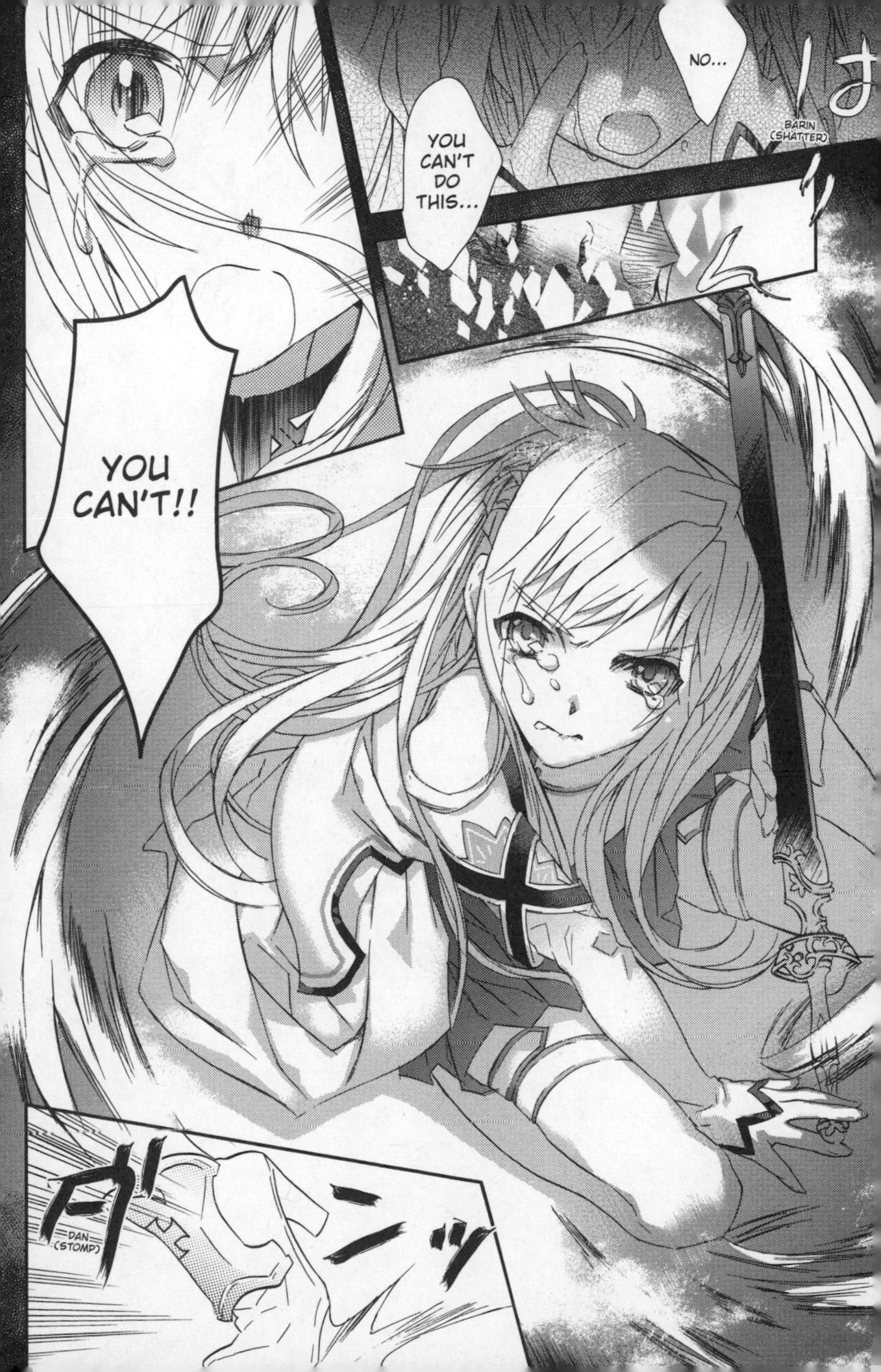
NO...
YOU CAN'T DO THIS...
BARIN (SHATTER)
YOU CAN'T!!
DAN (STOMP)

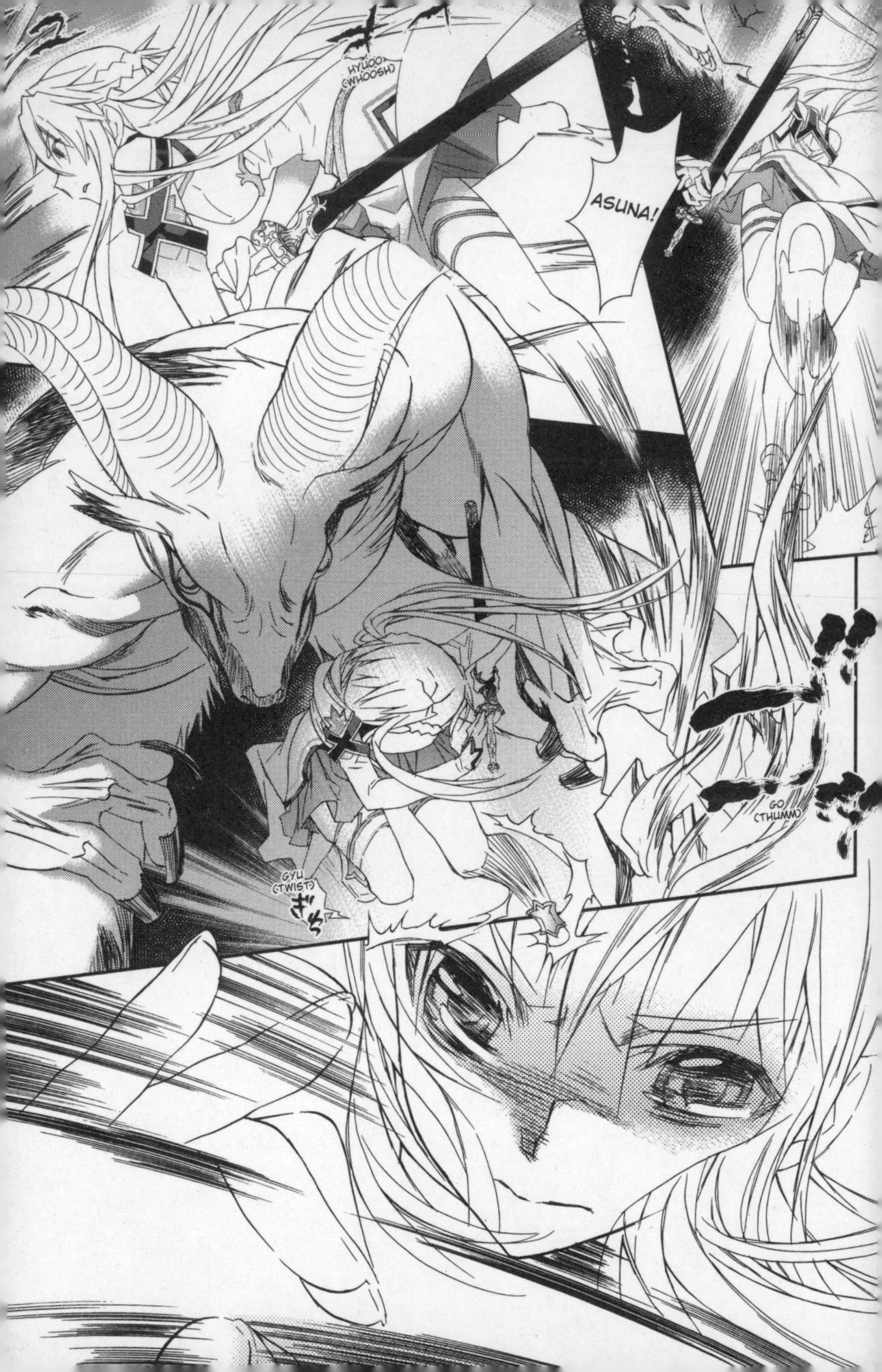
ASUNA!
HYUOO (WHOOSH)
GO (THUMM)
GYU (TWIST)
ぎゅ

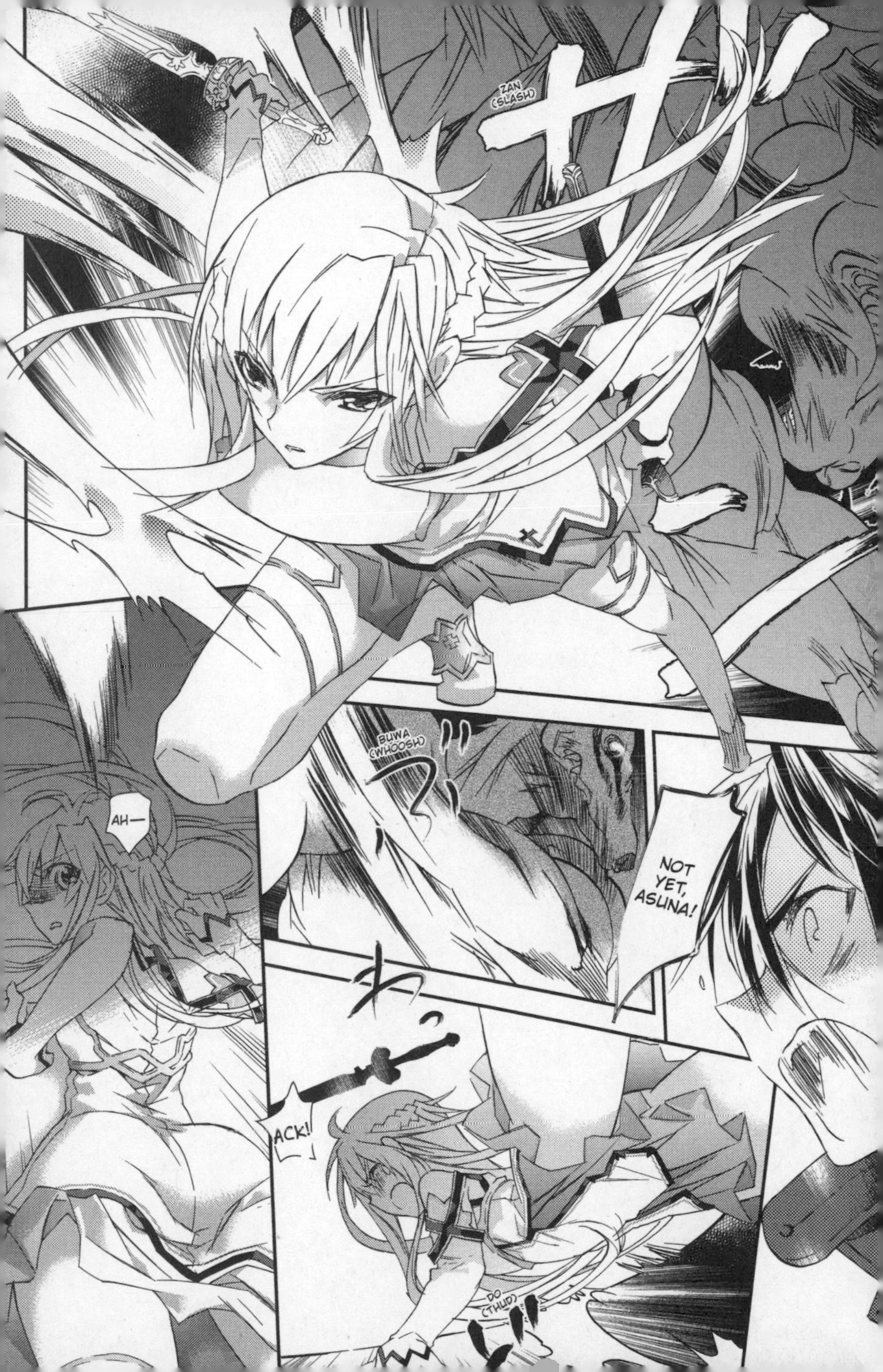
ZAN (SLASH)
NOT YET, ASUNA!
BUWA (WHOOSH)
ACK!
DO (THUD)
AH—

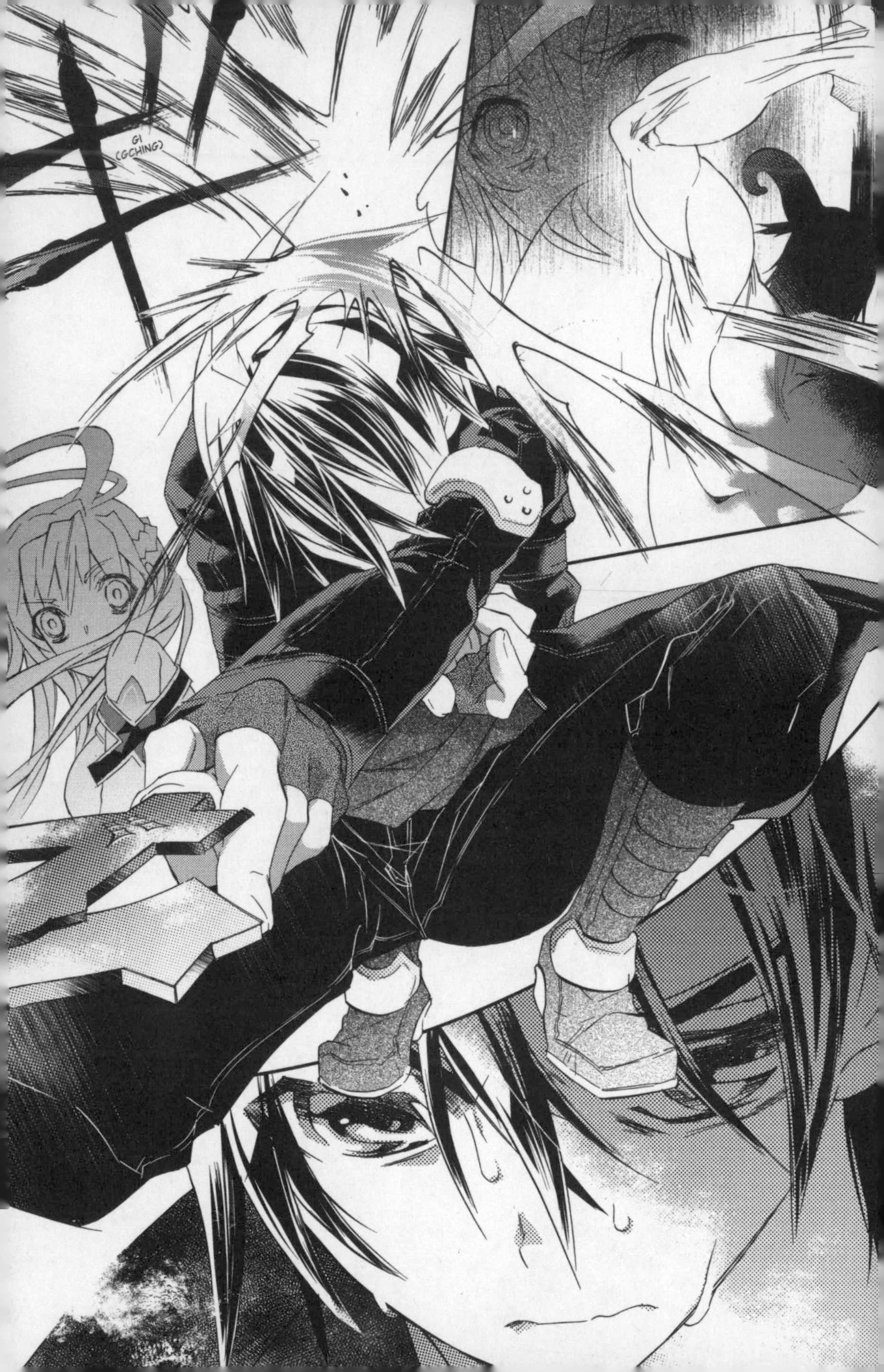
GI
(GCHING)

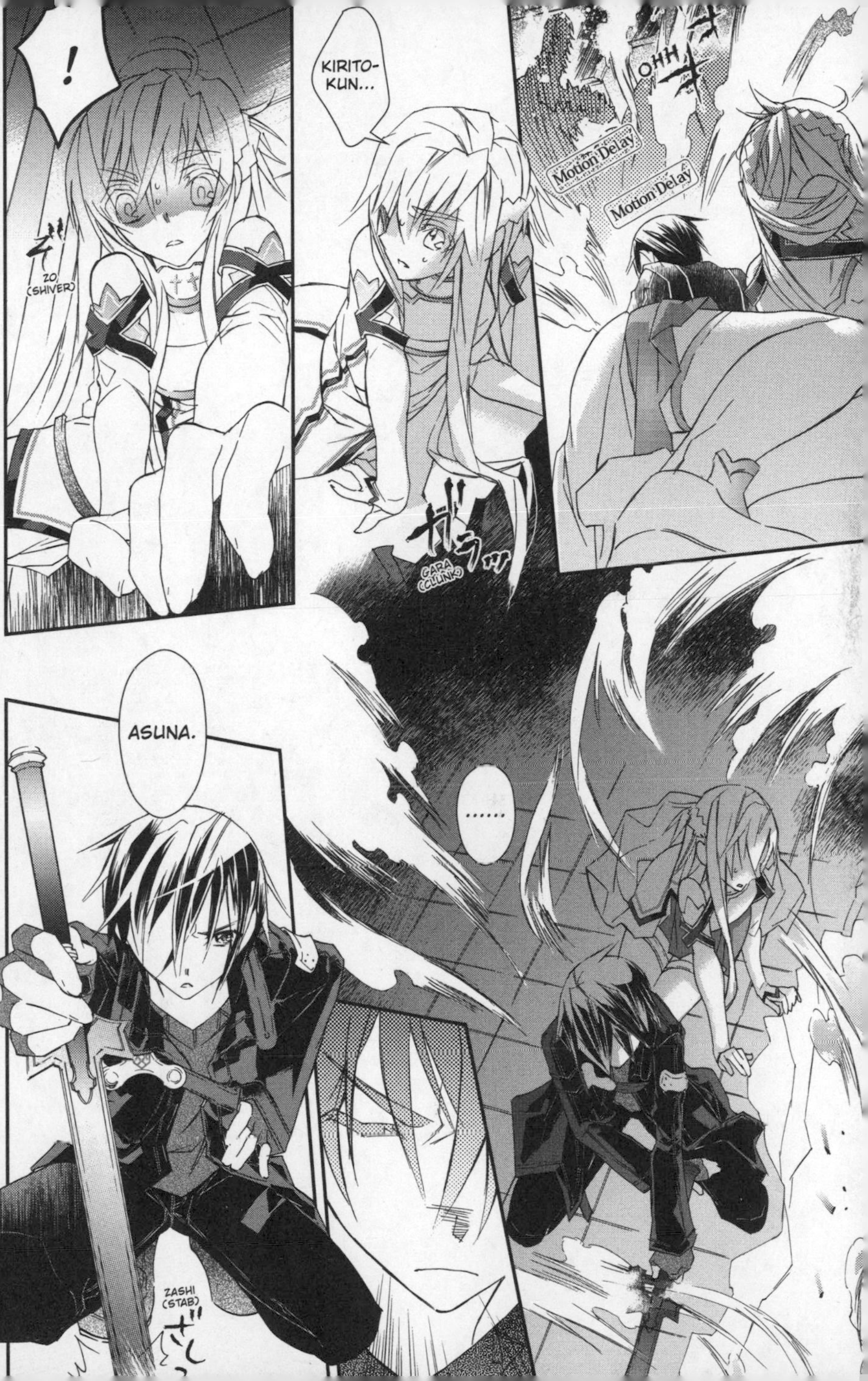
OHH
Motion Delay
Motion Delay
KIRITO-KUN...
GARA (CLUNK)
!
ZO (SHIVER)
......
ASUNA.
ZASHI (STAB)

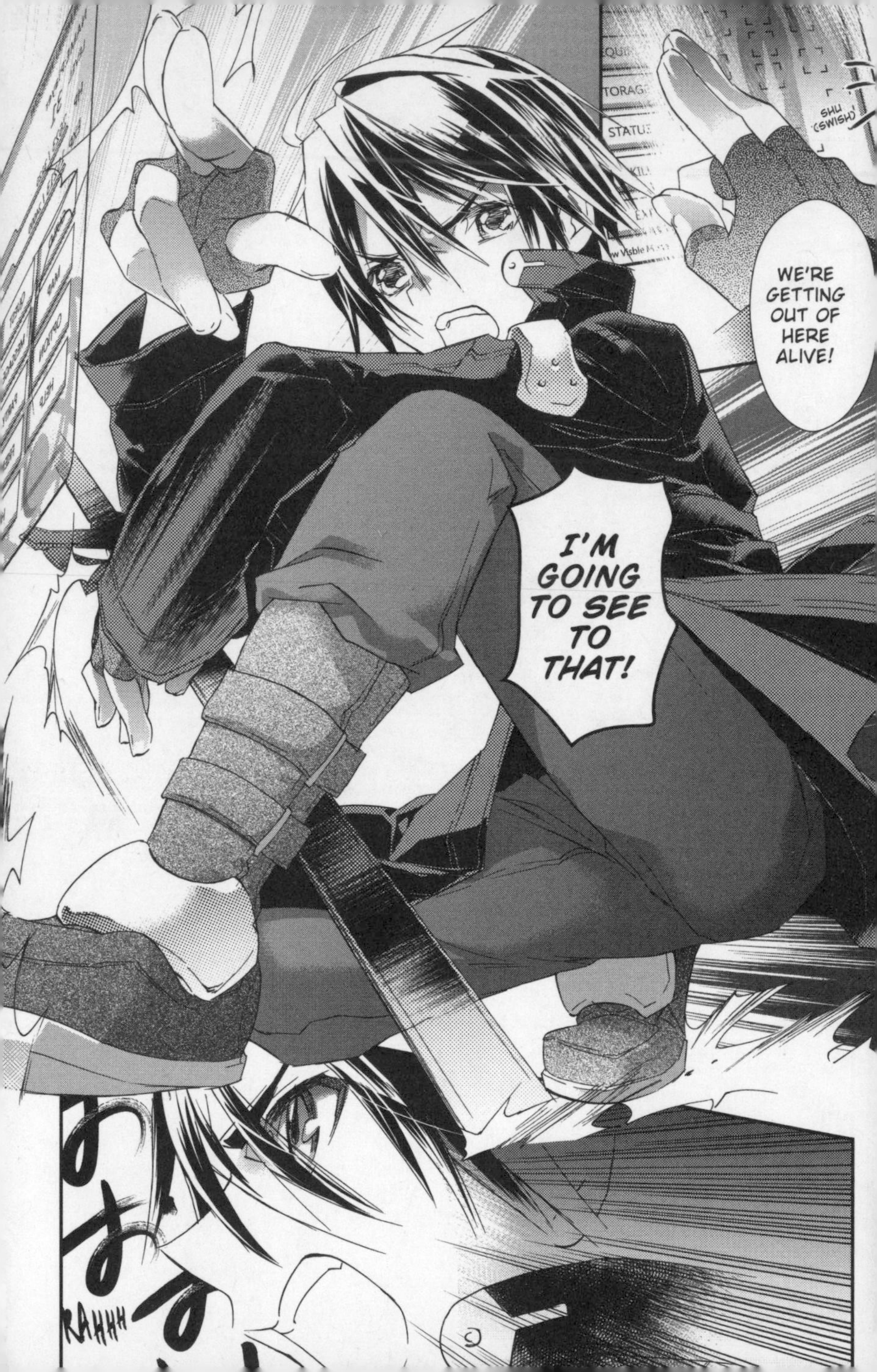
SHU (SWISH)
WE'RE GETTING OUT OF HERE ALIVE!
I'M GOING TO SEE TO THAT!
RAHHH

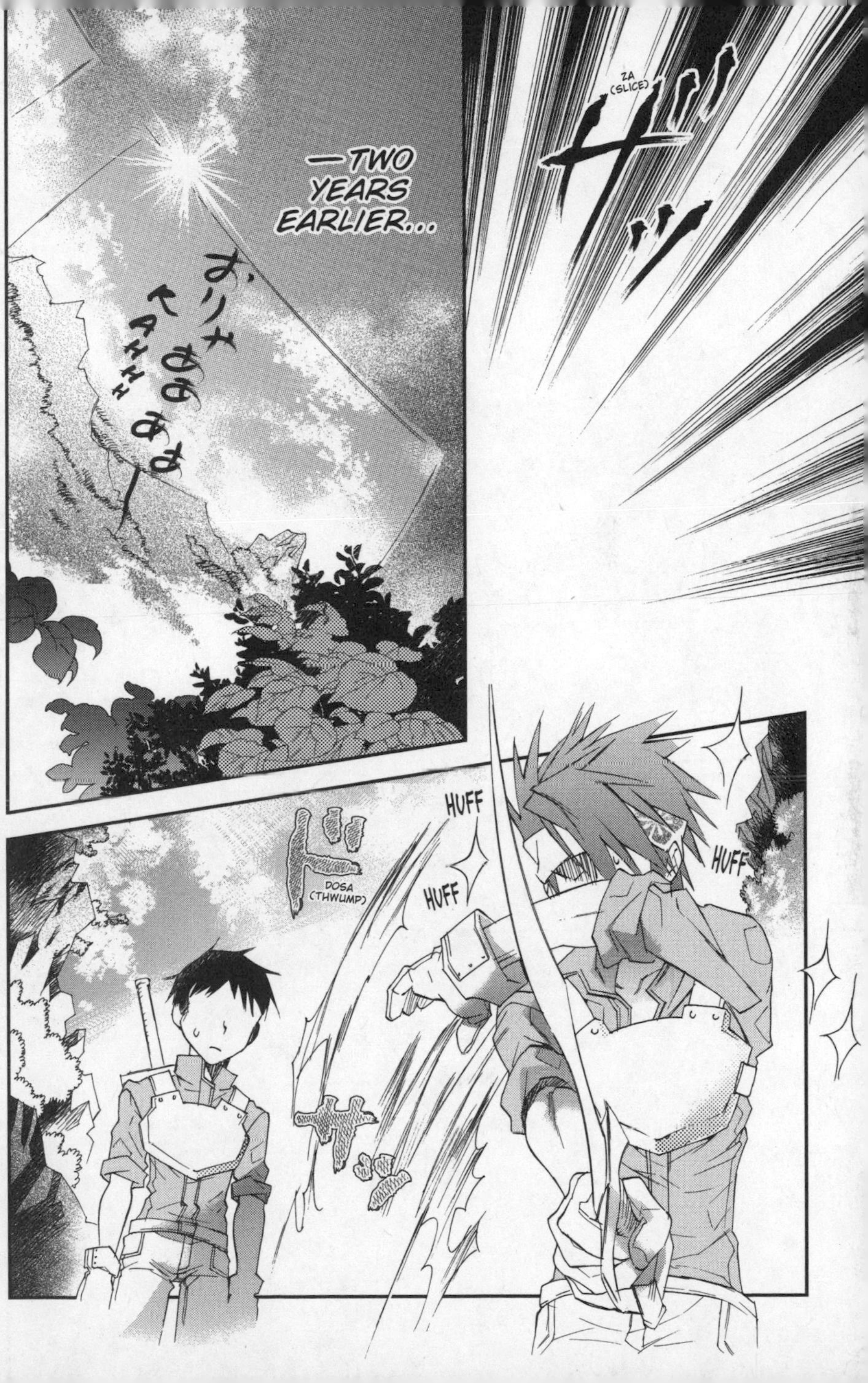
ZA (SLICE)
—TWO YEARS EARLIER...
おりゃあああー
YAHHH
HUFF
HUFF
HUFF
DOSA (THWUMP)

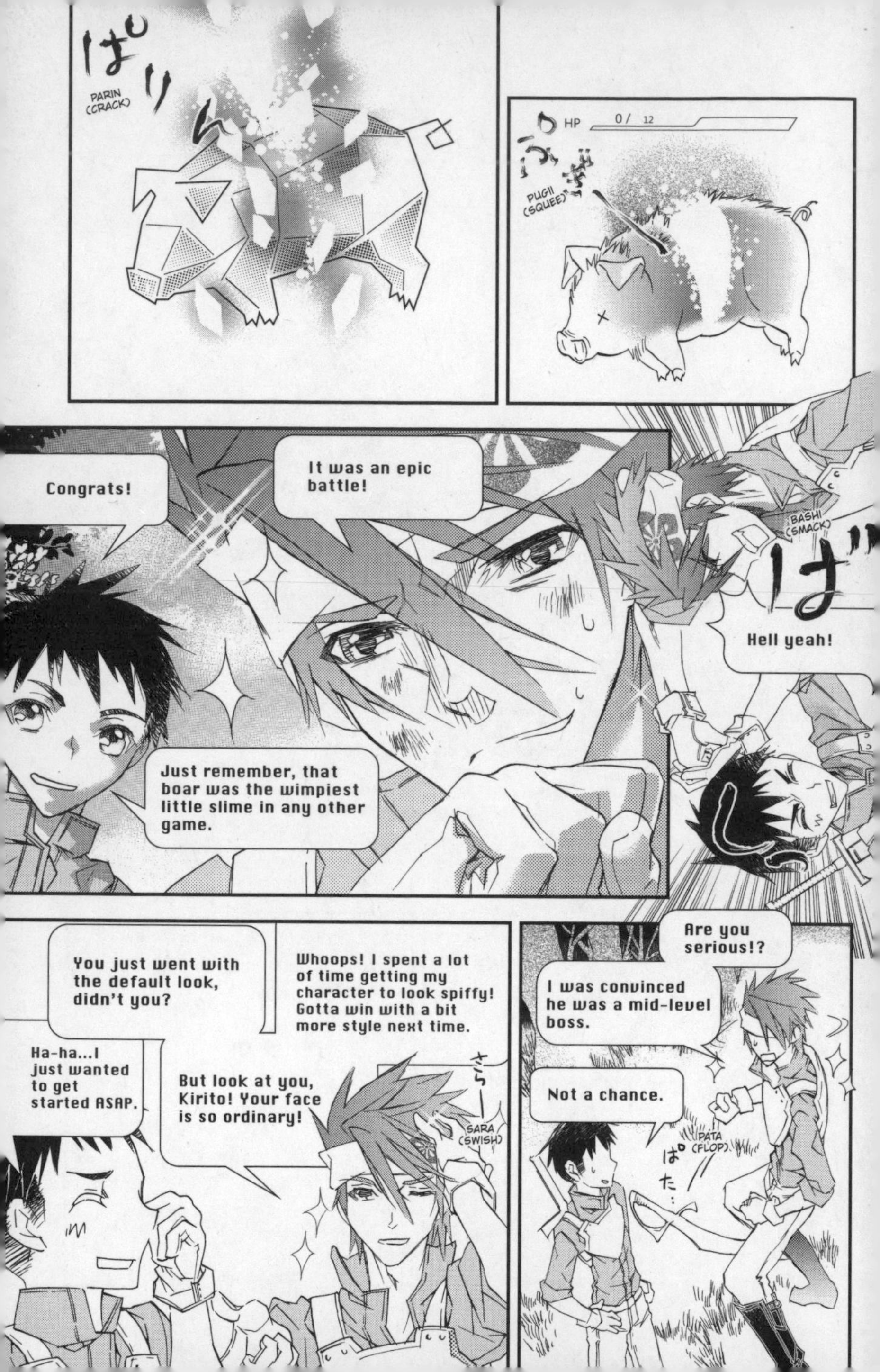
HP 0/ 12
PUGII (SQUEE)
PARIN (CRACK)
BASHI (SMACK)
Hell yeah!
It was an epic battle!
Congrats!
Just remember, that boar was the wimpiest little slime in any other game.
Are you serious!?
I was convinced he was a mid-level boss.
Not a chance.
PATA (FLOP)
Whoops! I spent a lot of time getting my character to look spiffy! Gotta win with a bit more style next time.
You just went with the default look, didn't you?
SARA (SWISH)
But look at you, Kirito! Your face is so ordinary!
Ha-ha...I just wanted to get started ASAP.

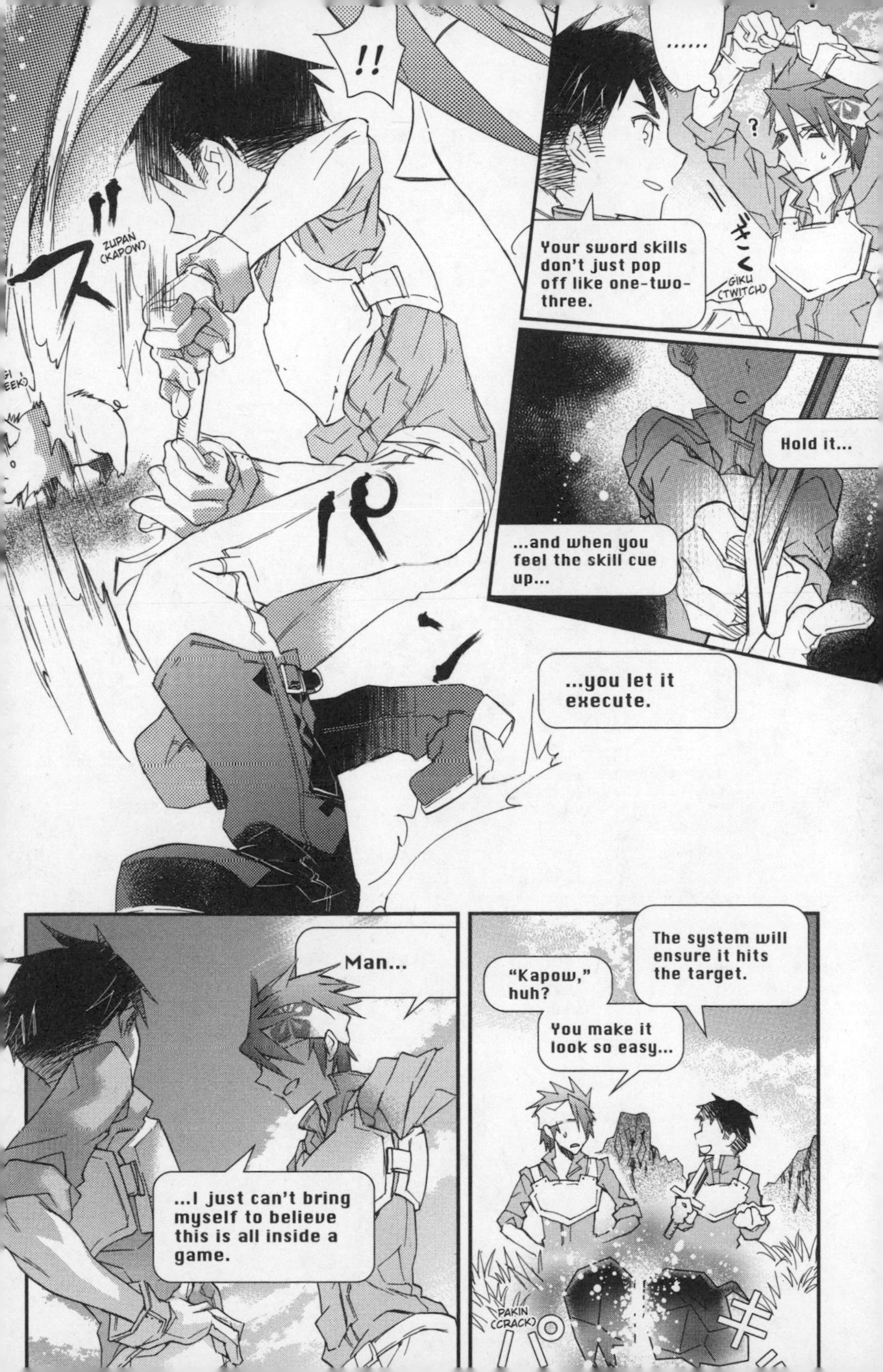
......
?
Your sword skills don't just pop off like one-two-three.
GIKU (TWITCH)
Hold it...
...and when you feel the skill cue up...
!!
ZUPAN (KAPOW)
...you let it execute.
The system will ensure it hits the target.
"Kapow," huh?
You make it look so easy...
PAKIN (CRACK)
Man...
...I just can't bring myself to believe this is all inside a game.

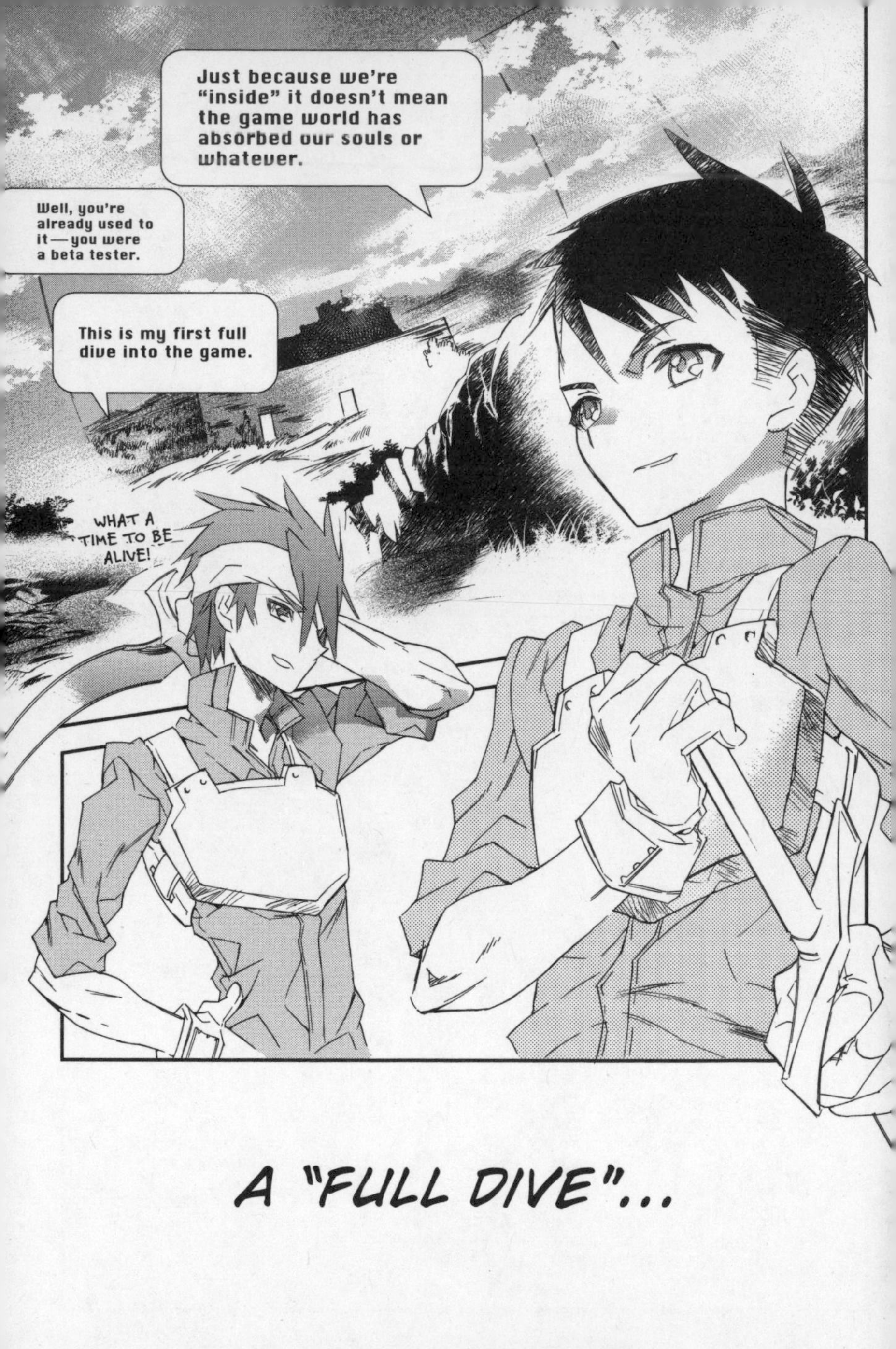
Just because we're "inside" it doesn't mean the game world has absorbed our souls or whatever.
Well, you're already used to it—you were a beta tester.
This is my first full dive into the game.
WHAT A TIME TO BE ALIVE!
A "FULL DIVE"...

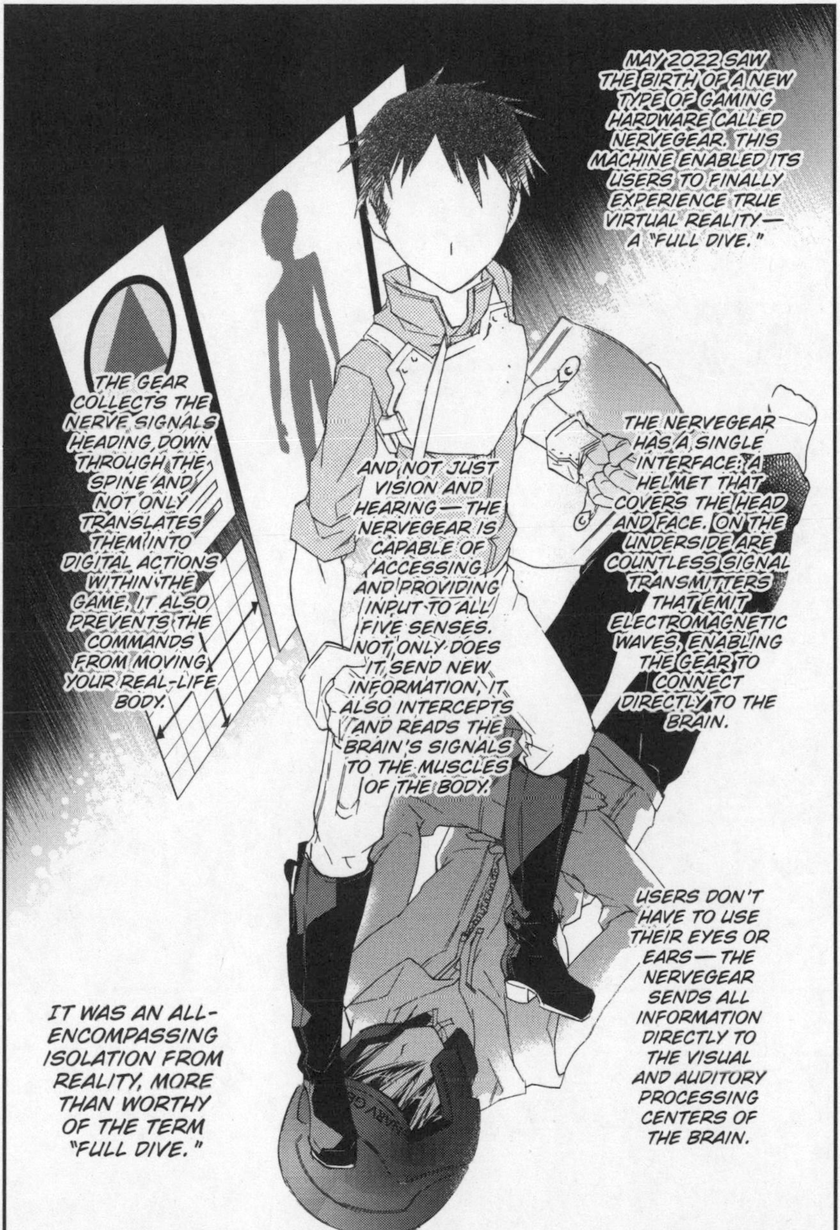
MAY 2022 SAW THE BIRTH OF A NEW TYPE OF GAMING HARDWARE CALLED NERVEGEAR. THIS MACHINE ENABLED ITS USERS TO FINALLY EXPERIENCE TRUE VIRTUAL REALITY— A "FULL DIVE."
THE NERVEGEAR HAS A SINGLE INTERFACE: A HELMET THAT COVERS THE HEAD AND FACE. ON THE UNDERSIDE ARE COUNTLESS SIGNAL TRANSMITTERS THAT EMIT ELECTROMAGNETIC WAVES, ENABLING THE GEAR TO CONNECT DIRECTLY TO THE BRAIN.
USERS DON'T HAVE TO USE THEIR EYES OR EARS— THE NERVEGEAR SENDS ALL INFORMATION DIRECTLY TO THE VISUAL AND AUDITORY PROCESSING CENTERS OF THE BRAIN.
AND NOT JUST VISION AND HEARING— THE NERVEGEAR IS CAPABLE OF ACCESSING AND PROVIDING INPUT TO ALL FIVE SENSES. NOT ONLY DOES IT SEND NEW INFORMATION, IT ALSO INTERCEPTS AND READS THE BRAIN'S SIGNALS TO THE MUSCLES OF THE BODY.
THE GEAR COLLECTS THE NERVE SIGNALS HEADING DOWN THROUGH THE SPINE AND NOT ONLY TRANSLATES THEM INTO DIGITAL ACTIONS WITHIN THE GAME, IT ALSO PREVENTS THE COMMANDS FROM MOVING YOUR REAL-LIFE BODY.
IT WAS AN ALL-ENCOMPASSING ISOLATION FROM REALITY, MORE THAN WORTHY OF THE TERM "FULL DIVE."

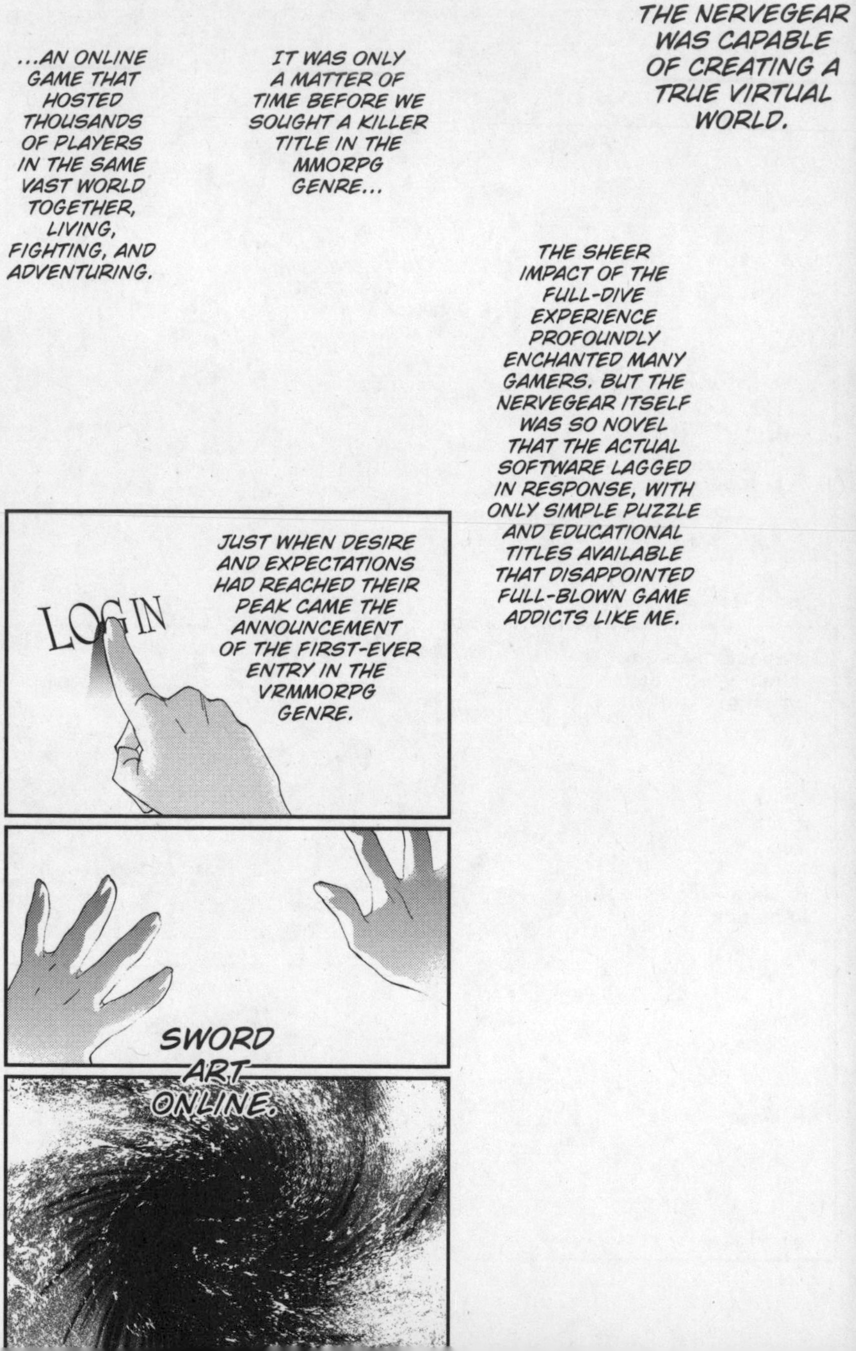
THE NERVEGEAR WAS CAPABLE OF CREATING A TRUE VIRTUAL WORLD.
THE SHEER IMPACT OF THE FULL-DIVE EXPERIENCE PROFOUNDLY ENCHANTED MANY GAMERS. BUT THE NERVEGEAR ITSELF WAS SO NOVEL THAT THE ACTUAL SOFTWARE LAGGED IN RESPONSE, WITH ONLY SIMPLE PUZZLE AND EDUCATIONAL TITLES AVAILABLE THAT DISAPPOINTED FULL-BLOWN GAME ADDICTS LIKE ME.
IT WAS ONLY A MATTER OF TIME BEFORE WE SOUGHT A KILLER TITLE IN THE MMORPG GENRE...
...AN ONLINE GAME THAT HOSTED THOUSANDS OF PLAYERS IN THE SAME VAST WORLD TOGETHER, LIVING, FIGHTING, AND ADVENTURING.
JUST WHEN DESIRE AND EXPECTATIONS HAD REACHED THEIR PEAK CAME THE ANNOUNCEMENT OF THE FIRST-EVER ENTRY IN THE VRMMORPG GENRE.
LOG IN
SWORD ART ONLINE.

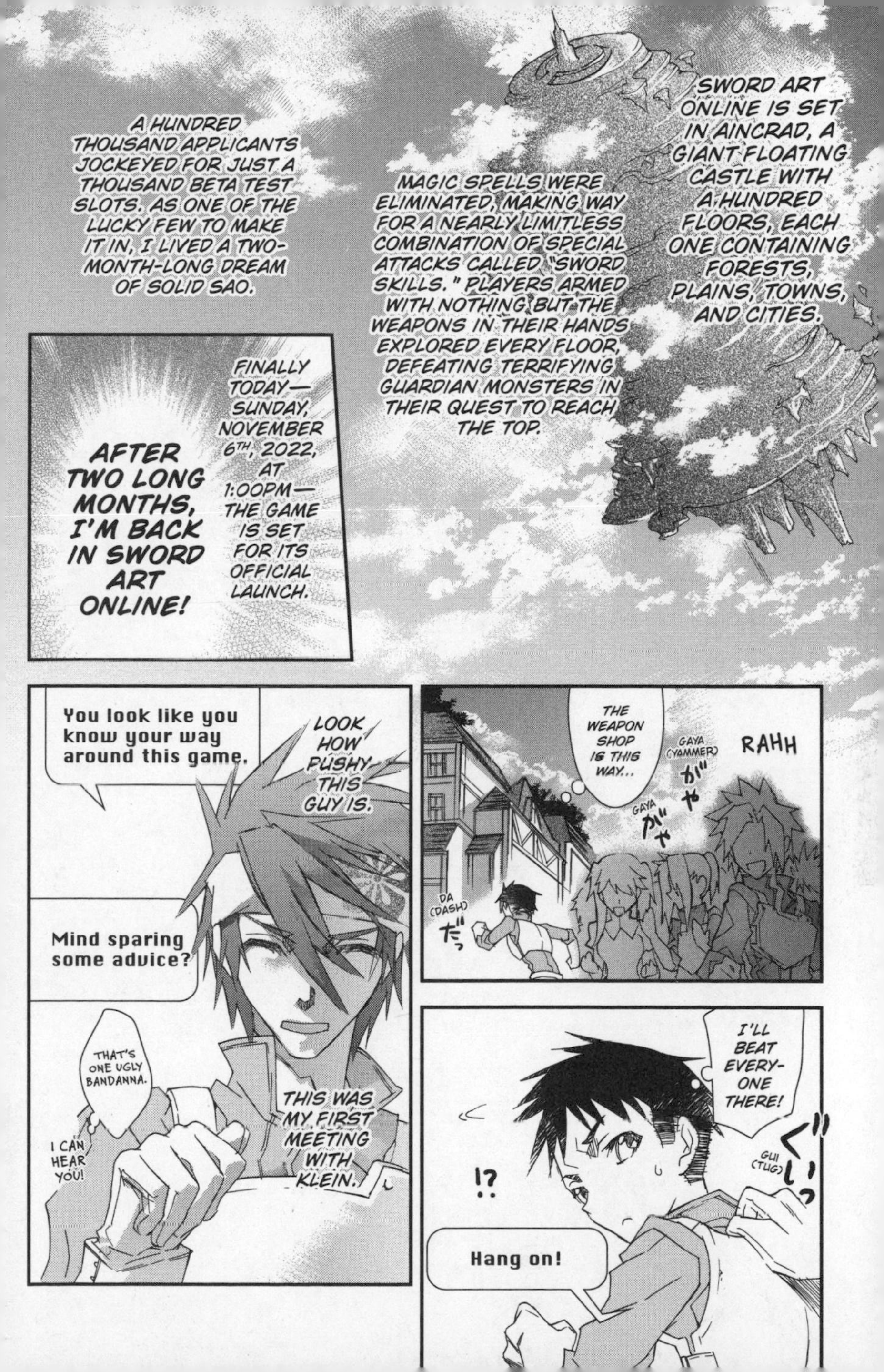
SWORD ART ONLINE IS SET IN AINCRAD, A GIANT FLOATING CASTLE WITH A HUNDRED FLOORS, EACH ONE CONTAINING FORESTS, PLAINS, TOWNS, AND CITIES.
MAGIC SPELLS WERE ELIMINATED, MAKING WAY FOR A NEARLY LIMITLESS COMBINATION OF SPECIAL ATTACKS CALLED "SWORD SKILLS." PLAYERS ARMED WITH NOTHING BUT THE WEAPONS IN THEIR HANDS EXPLORED EVERY FLOOR, DEFEATING TERRIFYING GUARDIAN MONSTERS IN THEIR QUEST TO REACH THE TOP.
A HUNDRED THOUSAND APPLICANTS JOCKEYED FOR JUST A THOUSAND BETA TEST SLOTS. AS ONE OF THE LUCKY FEW TO MAKE IT IN, I LIVED A TWO-MONTH-LONG DREAM OF SOLID SAO.
FINALLY TODAY—SUNDAY, NOVEMBER 6TH, 2022, AT 1:00PM—THE GAME IS SET FOR ITS OFFICIAL LAUNCH.
AFTER TWO LONG MONTHS, I'M BACK IN SWORD ART ONLINE!
THE WEAPON SHOP IS THIS WAY...
RAHH
GAYA (YAMMER)
GAYA
DA (DASH)
I'LL BEAT EVERYONE THERE!
GUI (TUG)
!?
Hang on!
You look like you know your way around this game.
LOOK HOW PUSHY THIS GUY IS.
Mind sparing some advice?
THAT'S ONE UGLY BANDANNA.
THIS WAS MY FIRST MEETING WITH KLEIN.
I CAN HEAR YOU!

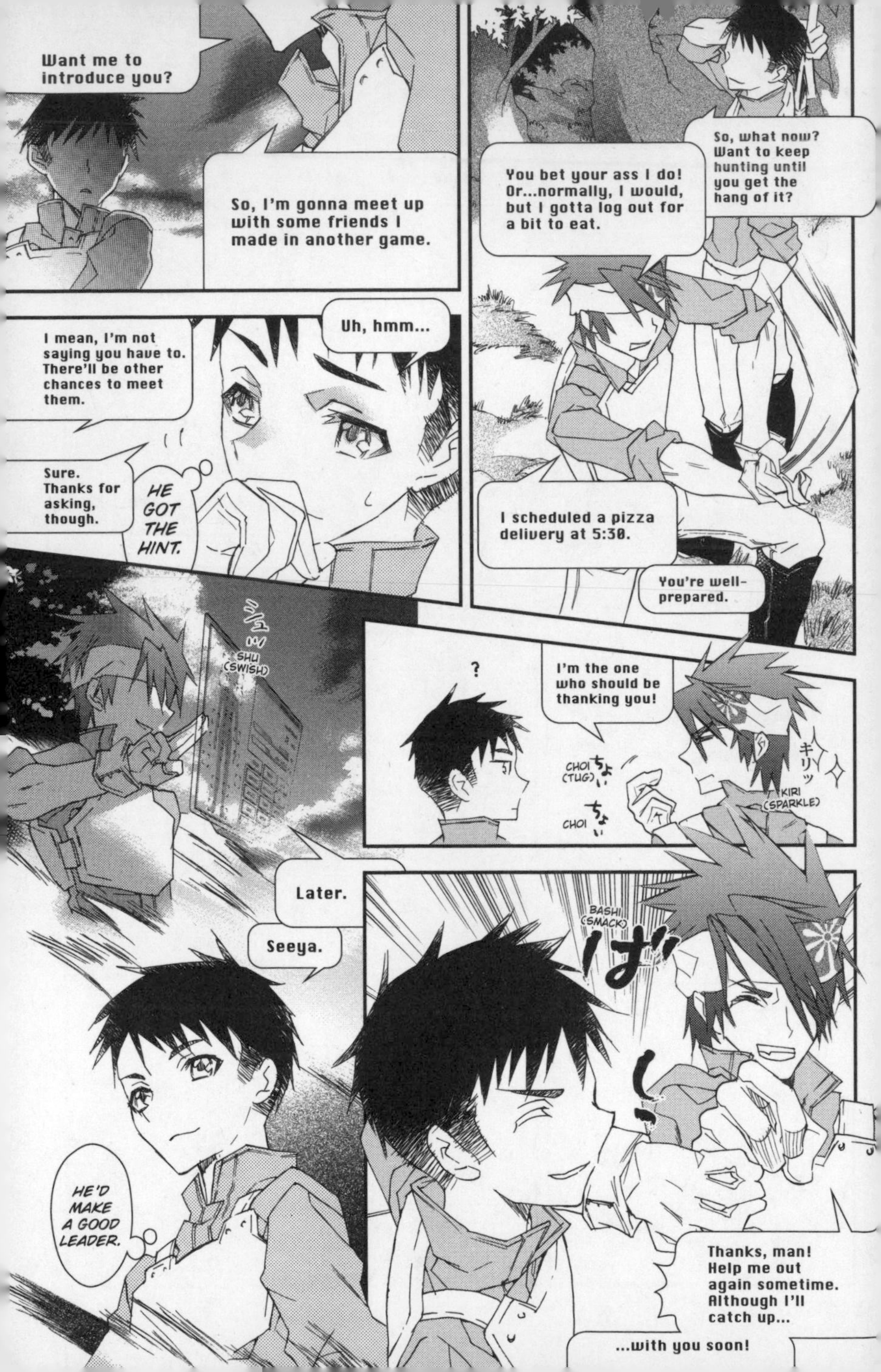
So, what now? Want to keep hunting until you get the hang of it?
You bet your ass I do! Or...normally, I would, but I gotta log out for a bit to eat.
I scheduled a pizza delivery at 5:30.
You're well-prepared.
So, I'm gonna meet up with some friends I made in another game.
Want me to introduce you?
Uh, hmm...
I mean, I'm not saying you have to. There'll be other chances to meet them.
Sure. Thanks for asking, though.
HE GOT THE HINT.
?
I'm the one who should be thanking you!
キリッ
KIRI (SPARKLE)
ちょい
CHOI (TUG)
ちょい
CHOI
ばしッ
BASHI (SMACK)
Thanks, man! Help me out again sometime. Although I'll catch up...
...with you soon!
シュッ
SHU (SWISH)
Later.
Seeya.
HE'D MAKE A GOOD LEADER.

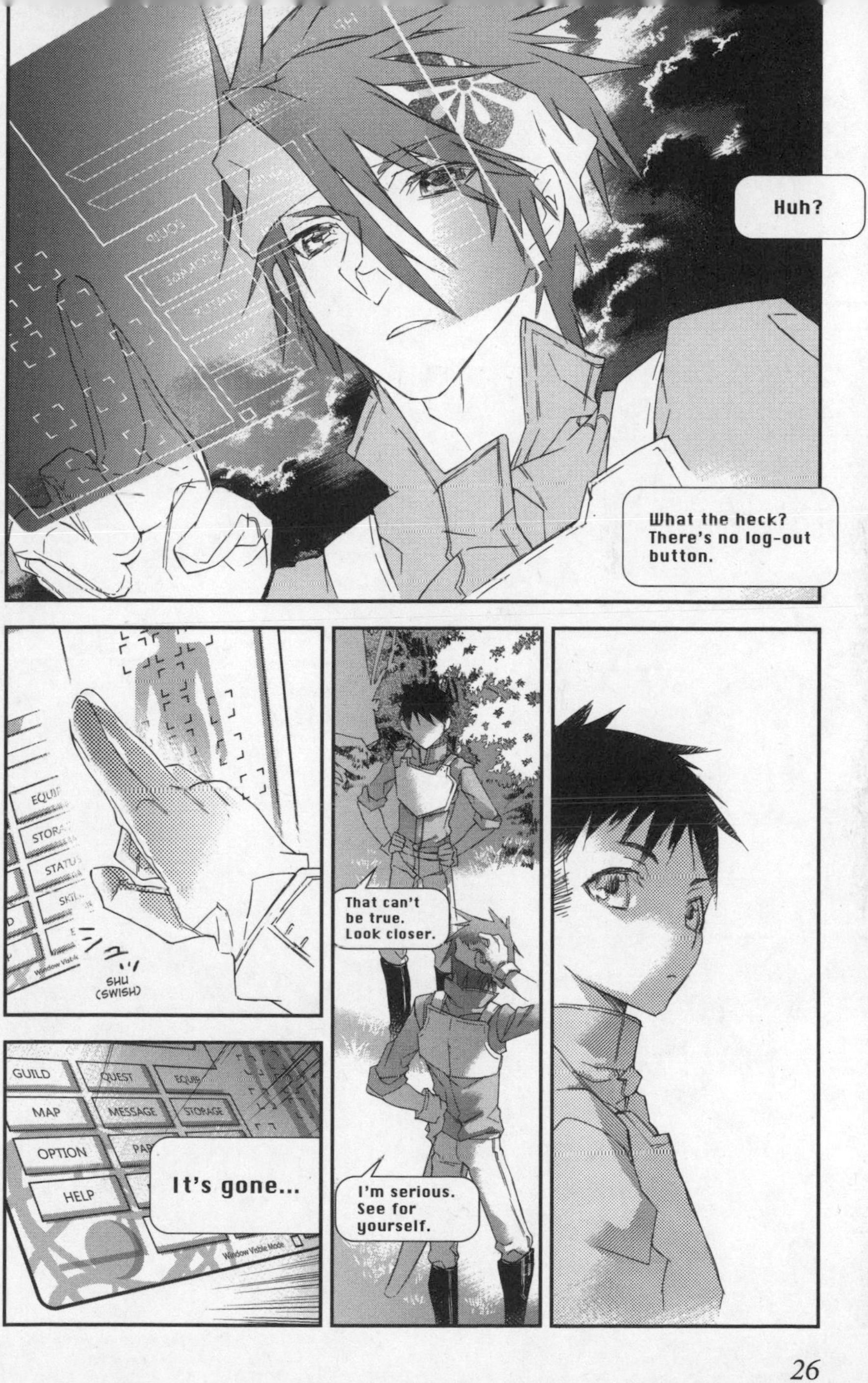
Huh?
What the heck? There's no log-out button.
That can't be true. Look closer.
I'm serious. See for yourself.
EQUIP
STATUS
SHU (SWISH)
GUILD
QUEST
EQUIP
MAP
MESSAGE
STORAGE
OPTION
HELP
It's gone...
Window Visible Mode

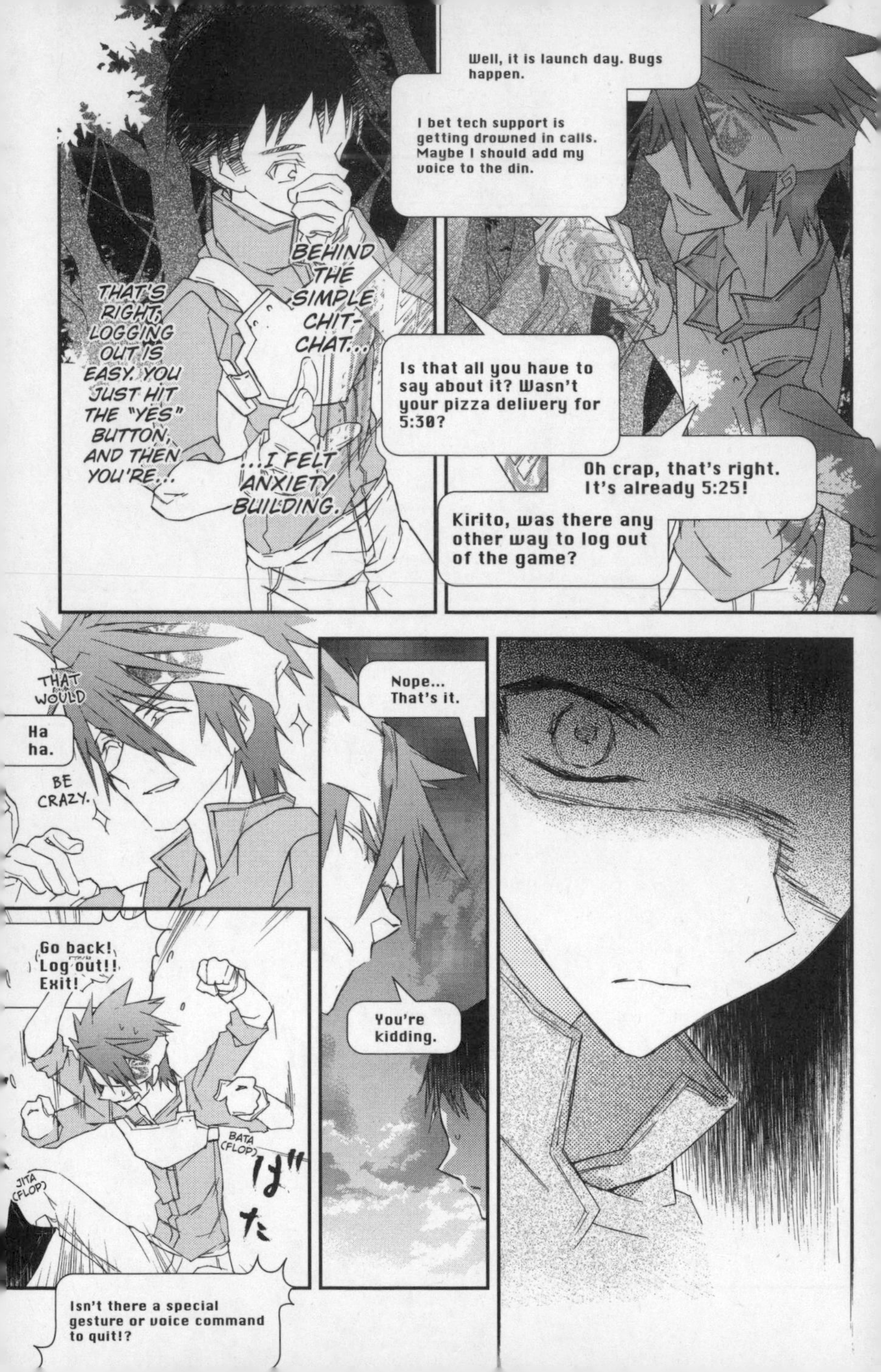
Well, it is launch day. Bugs happen.
I bet tech support is getting drowned in calls. Maybe I should add my voice to the din.
Is that all you have to say about it? Wasn't your pizza delivery for 5:30?
Oh crap, that's right. It's already 5:25!
Kirito, was there any other way to log out of the game?
BEHIND THE SIMPLE CHIT-CHAT...
THAT'S RIGHT, LOGGING OUT IS EASY. YOU JUST HIT THE "YES" BUTTON, AND THEN YOU'RE...
...I FELT ANXIETY BUILDING.
Nope... That's it.
You're kidding.
THAT WOULD
Ha ha.
BE CRAZY.
Go back! Log out!! Exit!
BATA (FLOP)
JITA (FLOP)
Isn't there a special gesture or voice command to quit!?

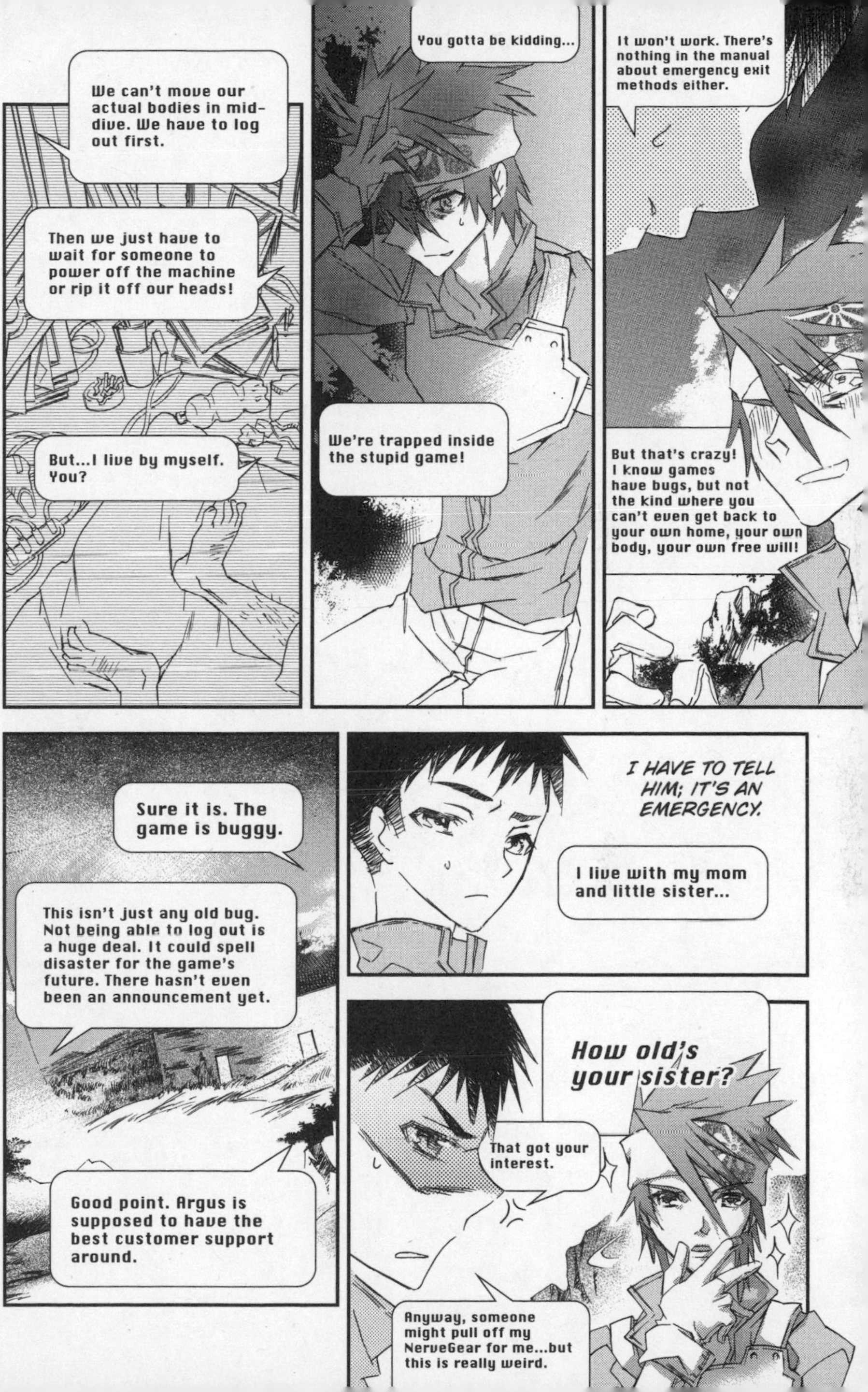
It won't work. There's nothing in the manual about emergency exit methods either.
But that's crazy! I know games have bugs, but not the kind where you can't even get back to your own home, your own body, your own free will!
You gotta be kidding...
We're trapped inside the stupid game!
We can't move our actual bodies in mid-dive. We have to log out first.
Then we just have to wait for someone to power off the machine or rip it off our heads!
But...I live by myself. You?
I HAVE TO TELL HIM; IT'S AN EMERGENCY.
I live with my mom and little sister...
How old's your sister?
That got your interest.
Anyway, someone might pull off my NerveGear for me...but this is really weird.
Sure it is. The game is buggy.
This isn't just any old bug. Not being able to log out is a huge deal. It could spell disaster for the game's future. There hasn't even been an announcement yet.
Good point. Argus is supposed to have the best customer support around.

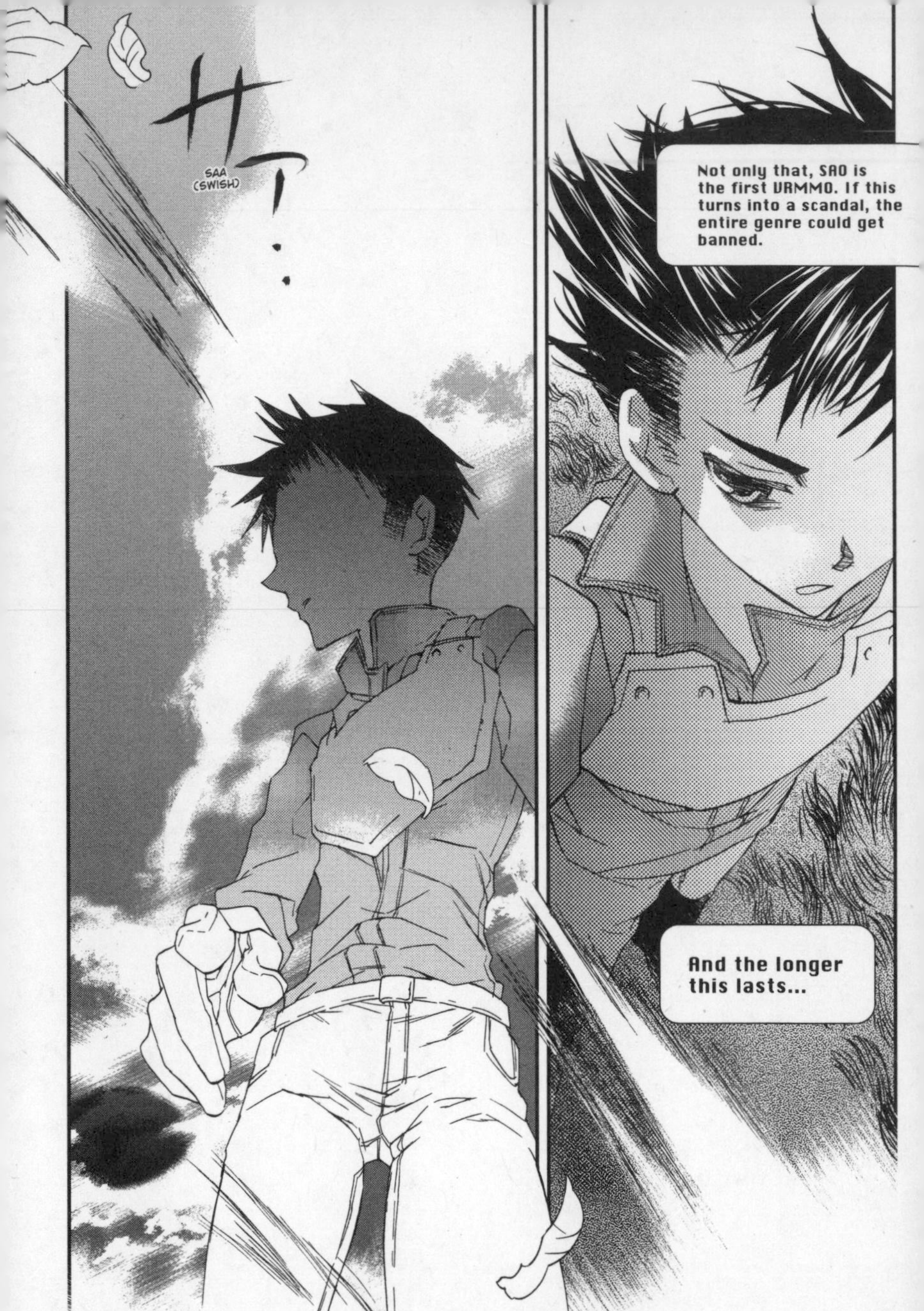
Not only that, SAO is the first VRMMO. If this turns into a scandal, the entire genre could get banned.
And the longer this lasts...
SAA (SWISH)

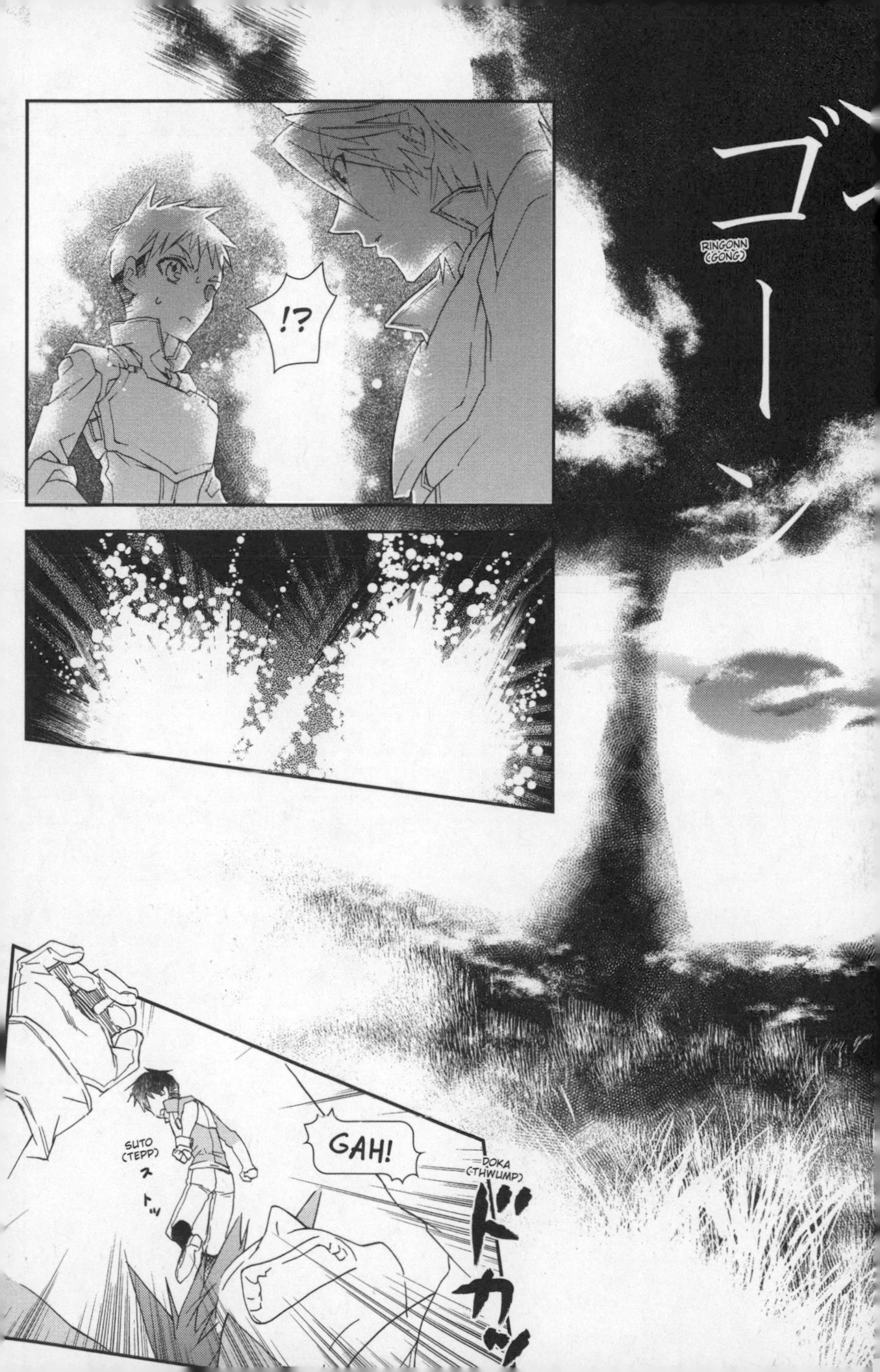
ゴーン
RINGONN (GONG)
!?
DOKA (THWUMP)
ドカッ
GAH!
SUTO (TEPP)
ストッ

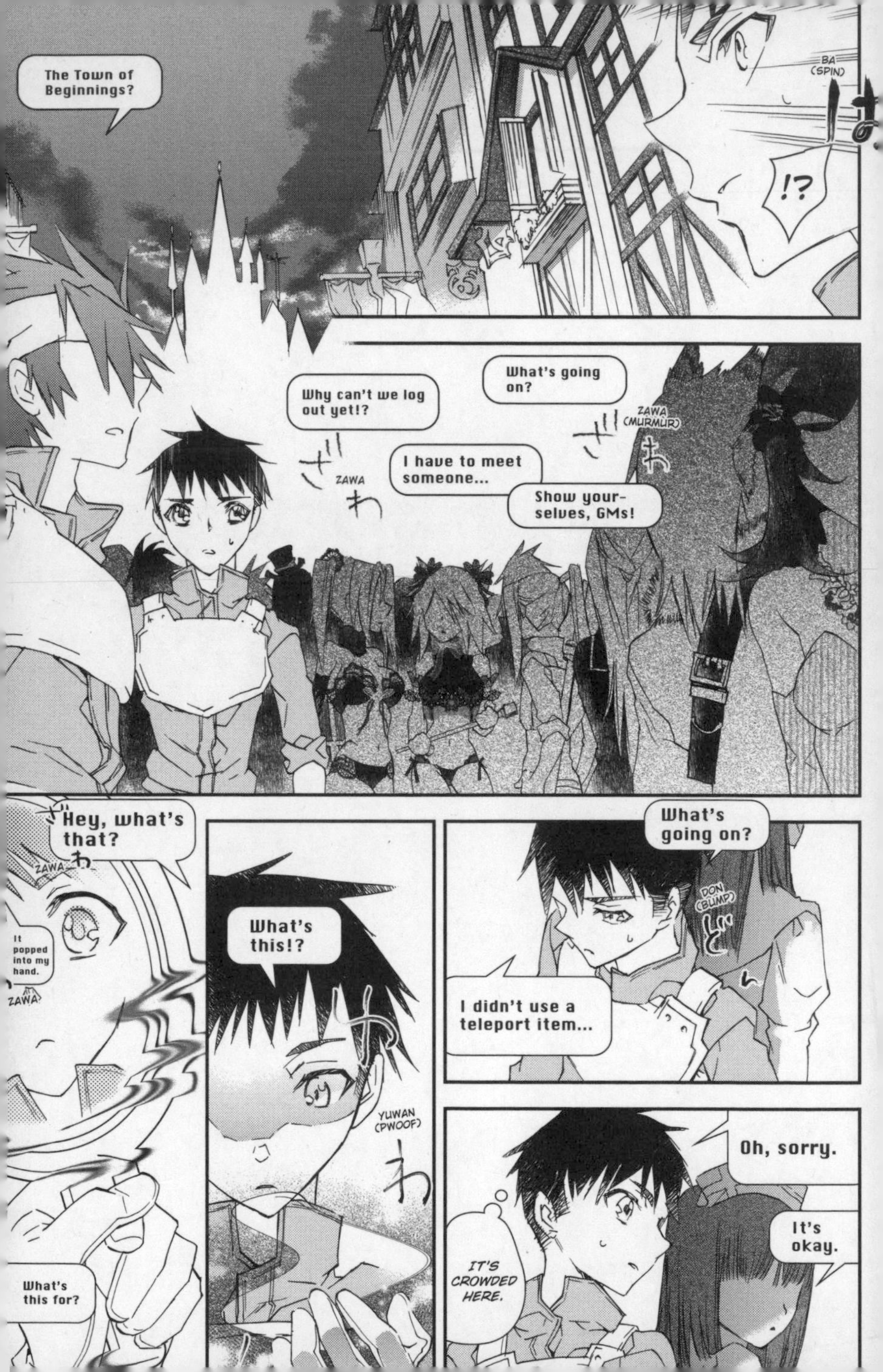

BA (SPIN)
!?
The Town of Beginnings?
What's going on?
ZAWA (MURMUR)
Why can't we log out yet!?
I have to meet someone...
Show your-selves, GMs!
ZAWA
What's going on?
DON (BUMP)
I didn't use a teleport item...
Oh, sorry.
It's okay.
IT'S CROWDED HERE.
What's this!?
YUWAN (PWOOF)
Hey, what's that?
ZAWA
It popped into my hand.
ZAWA
What's this for?

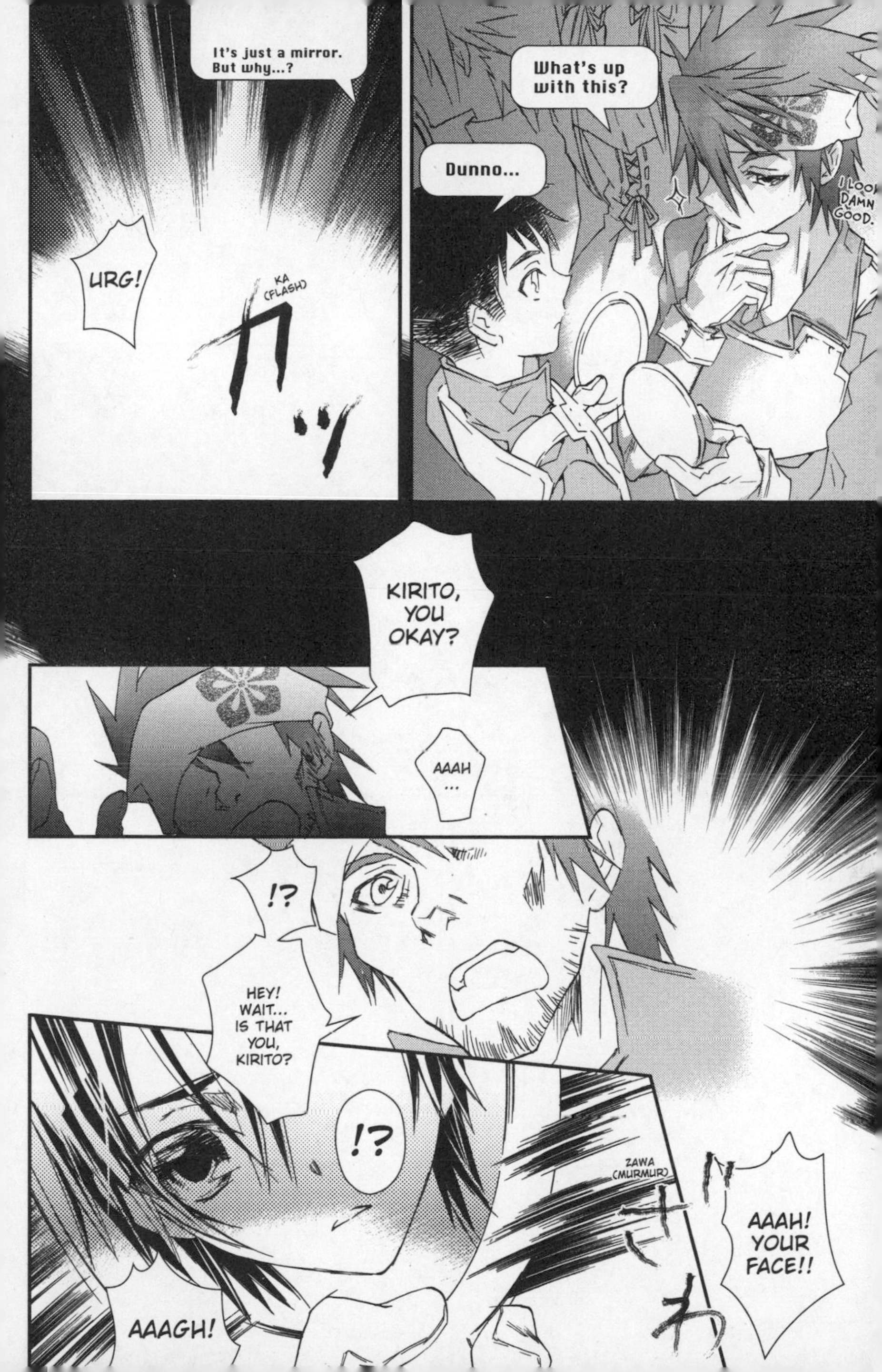
What's up with this?
Dunno...
I LOOK DAMN GOOD.
It's just a mirror. But why...?
URG!
KA (FLASH)
KIRITO, YOU OKAY?
AAAH ...
!?
HEY! WAIT... IS THAT YOU, KIRITO?
AAAH! YOUR FACE!!
ZAWA (MURMUR)
!?
AAAGH!

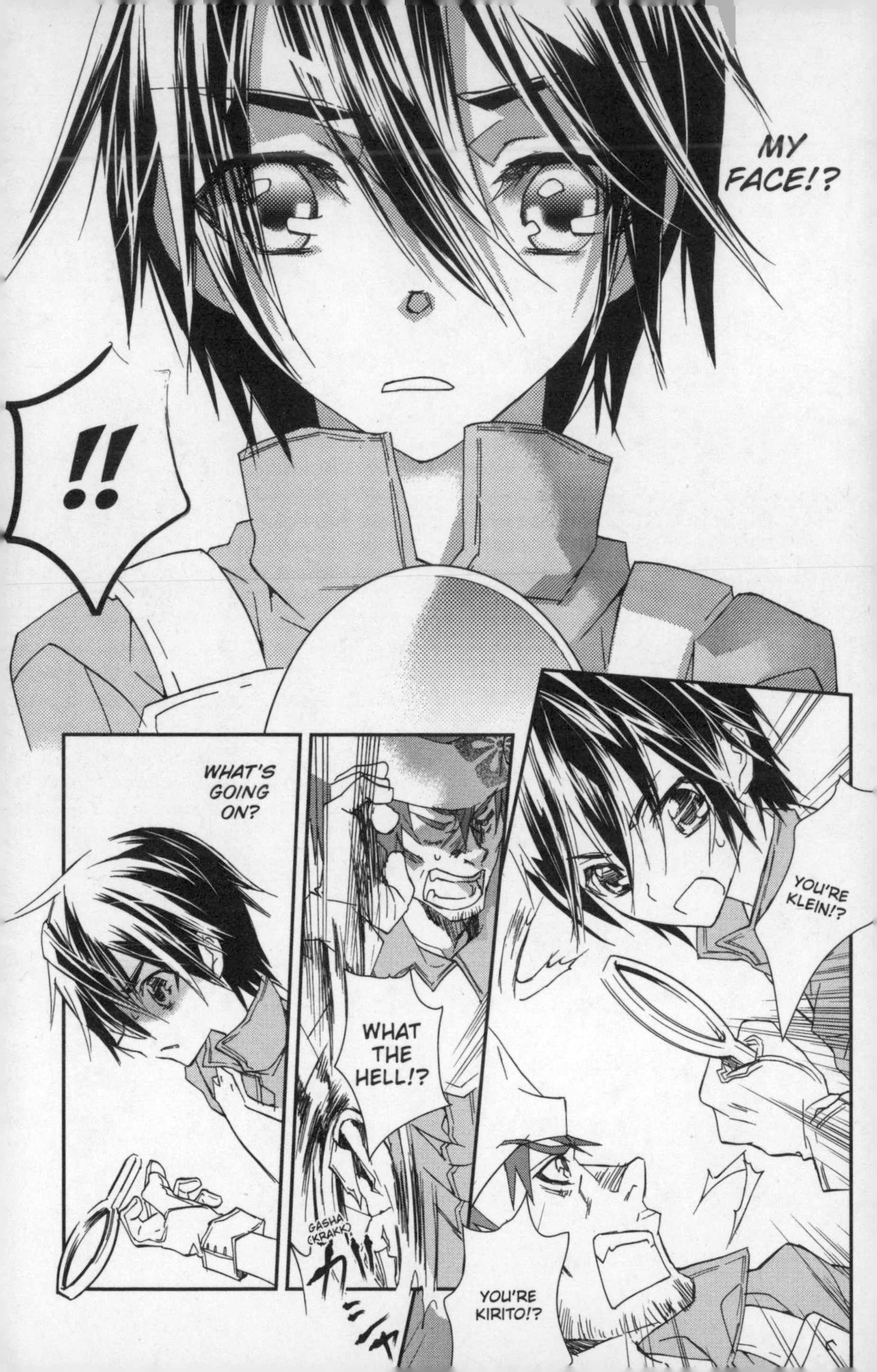
MY FACE!?
!!
YOU'RE KLEIN!?
YOU'RE KIRITO!?
WHAT THE HELL!?
GASHA (KRAKK)
WHAT'S GOING ON?

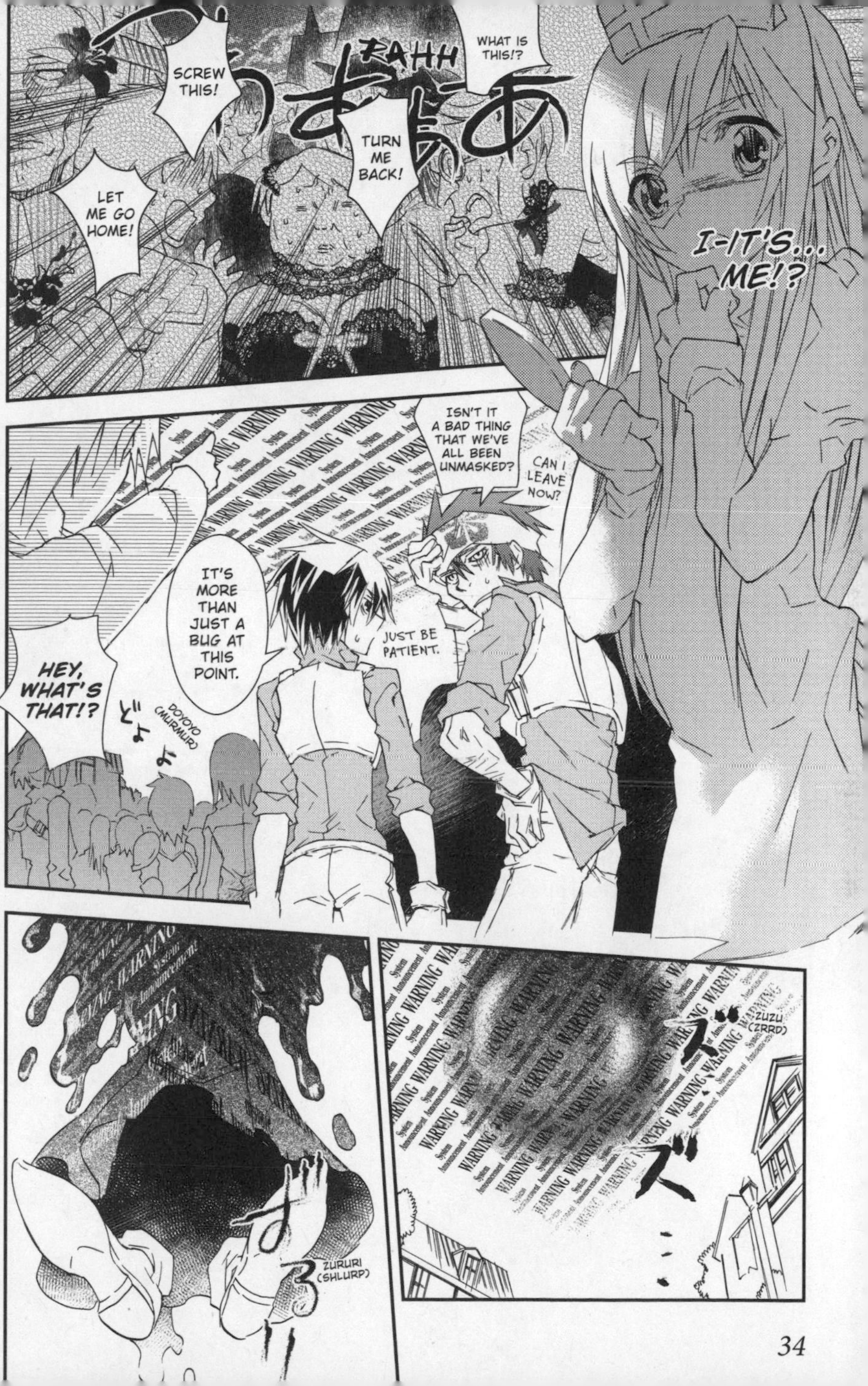
I-IT'S... ME!?
WHAT IS THIS!?
RAHH
SCREW THIS!
TURN ME BACK!
LET ME GO HOME!
CAN I LEAVE NOW?
ISN'T IT A BAD THING THAT WE'VE ALL BEEN UNMASKED?
JUST BE PATIENT.
IT'S MORE THAN JUST A BUG AT THIS POINT.
DOYOYO (MURMUR)
HEY, WHAT'S THAT!?
ZUZU (ZRRD)
ZURURI (SHLURP)

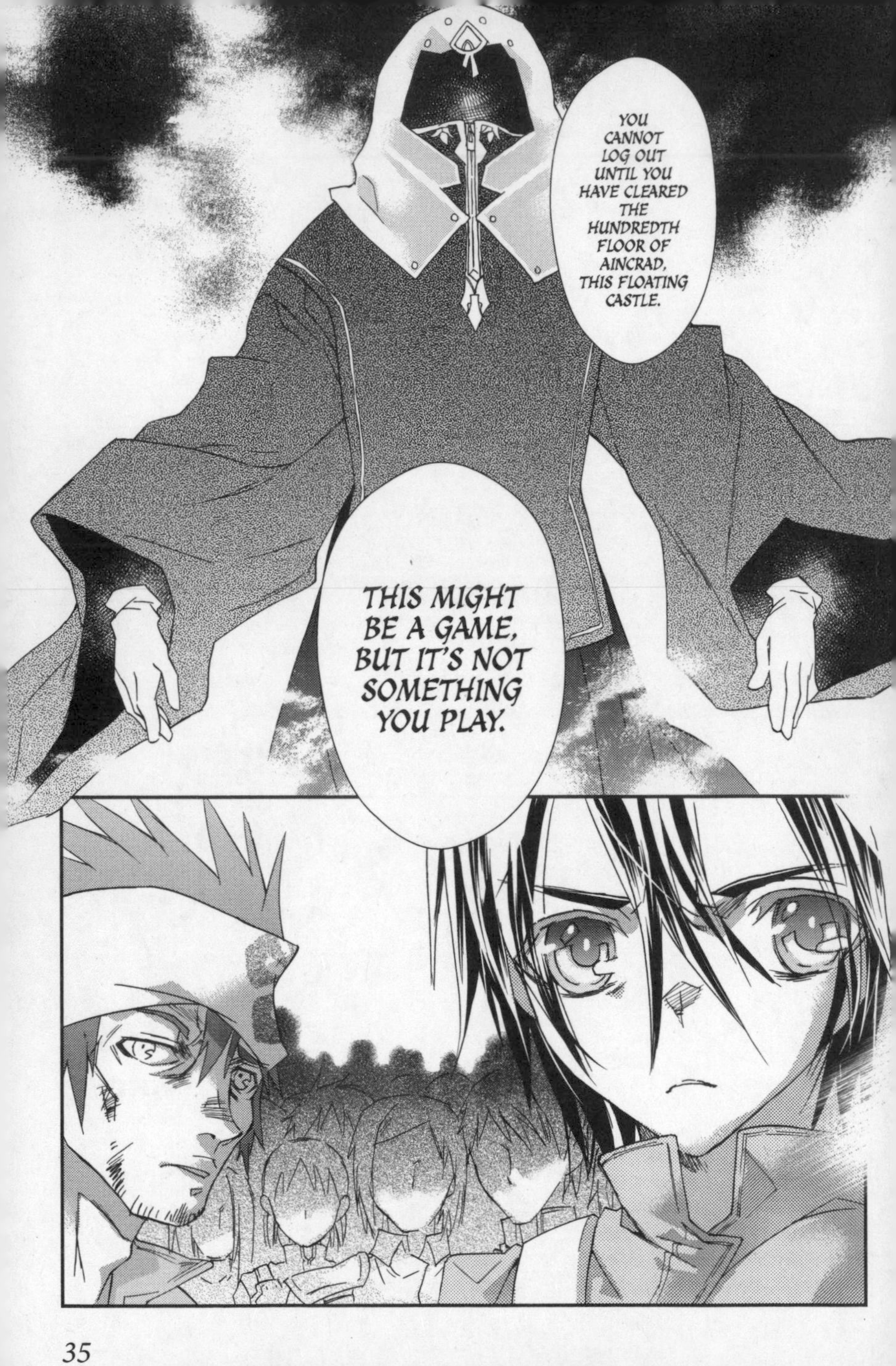
YOU CANNOT LOG OUT UNTIL YOU HAVE CLEARED THE HUNDREDTH FLOOR OF AINCRAD, THIS FLOATING CASTLE.
THIS MIGHT BE A GAME, BUT IT'S NOT SOMETHING YOU PLAY.

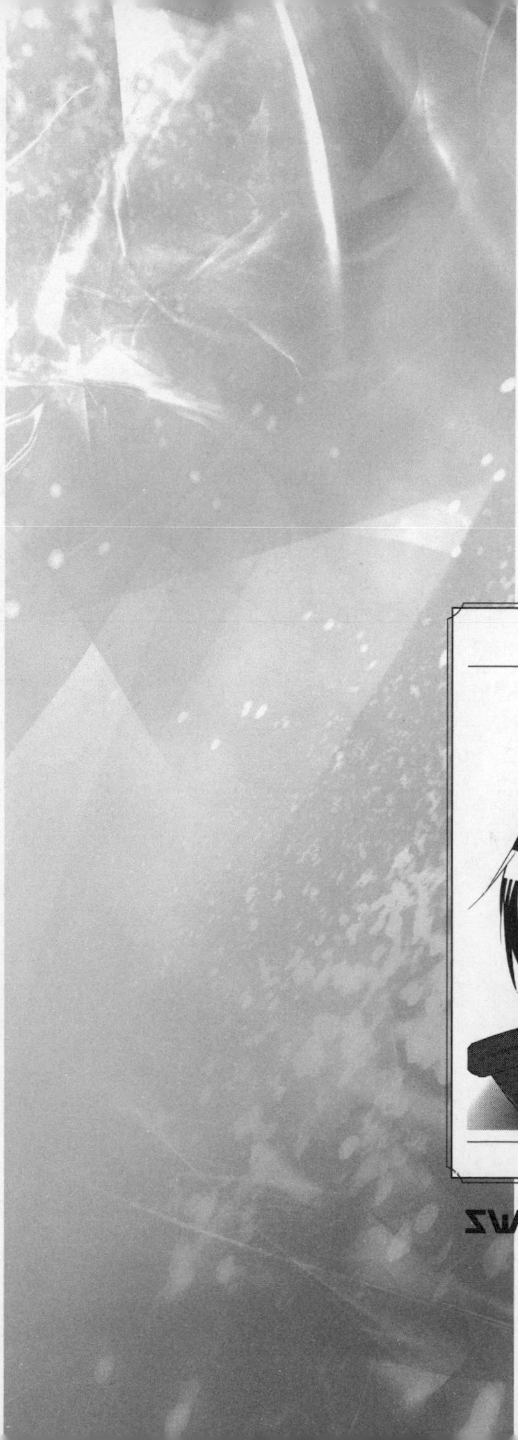

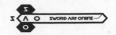

character

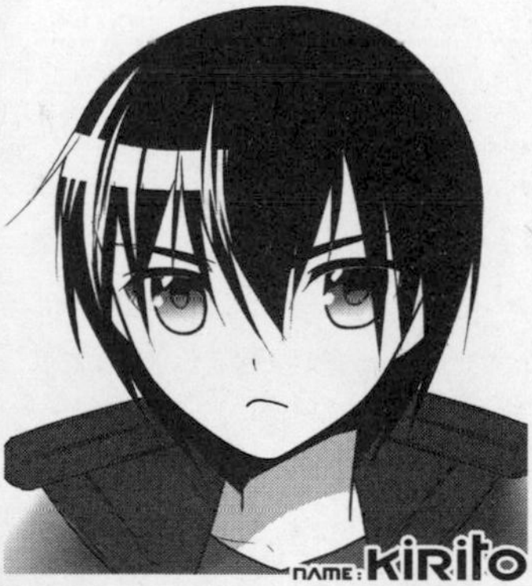

NAME: kirito

Affiliation: —

SWORD ART ONLINE
aincrad

stage.002

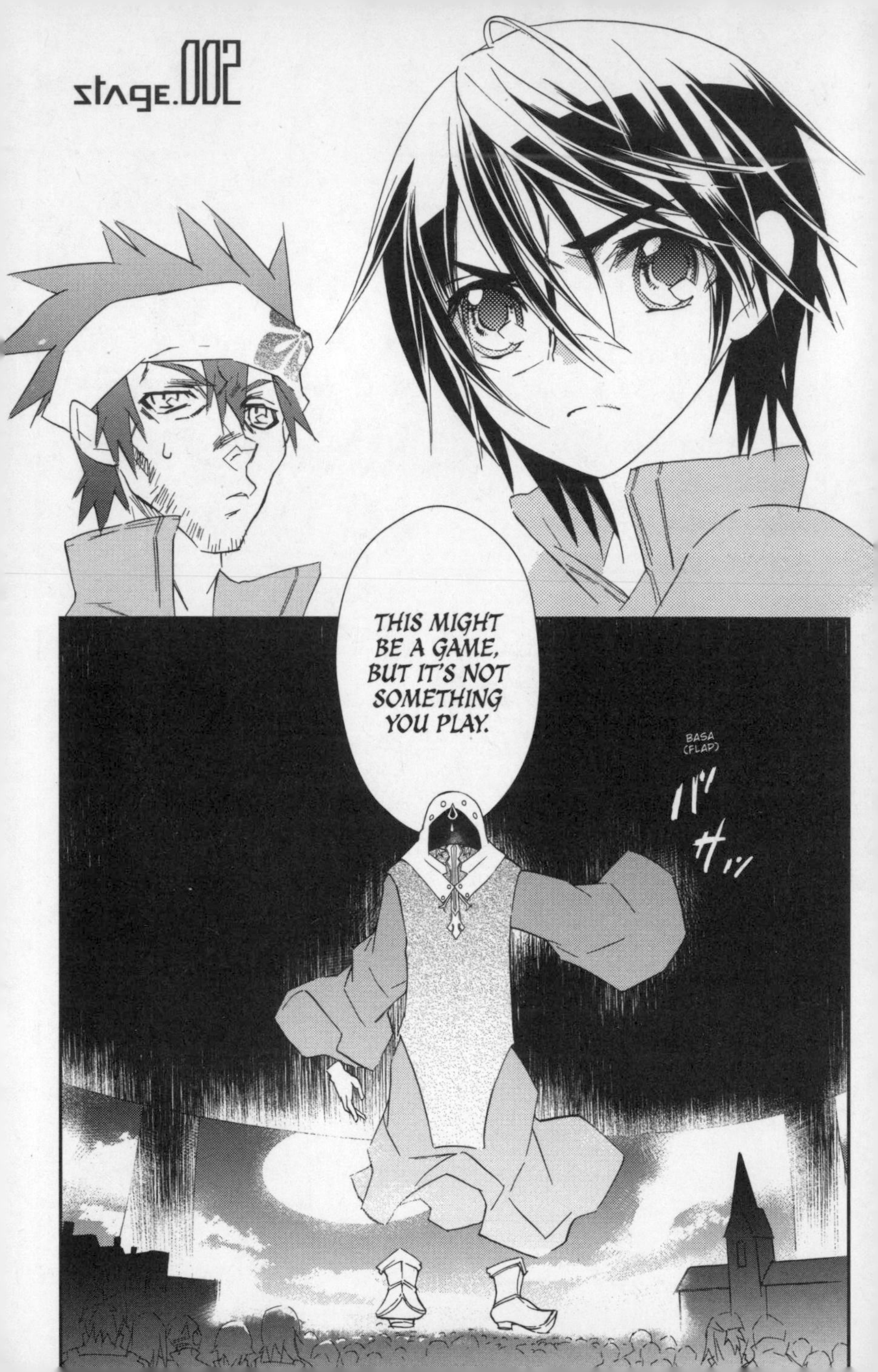
THIS MIGHT BE A GAME, BUT IT'S NOT SOMETHING YOU PLAY.
BASA (FLAP)
バサッ

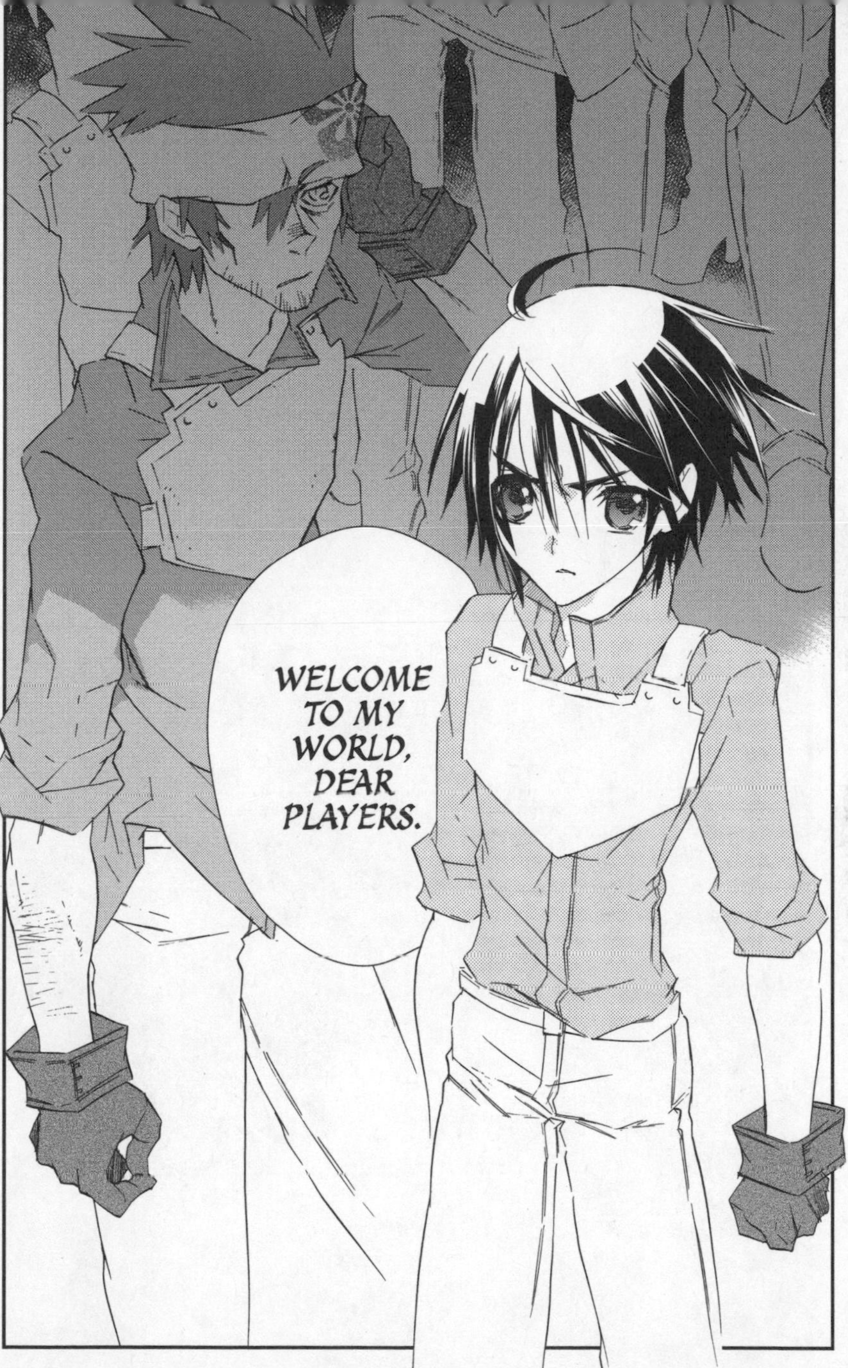
WELCOME TO MY WORLD, DEAR PLAYERS.

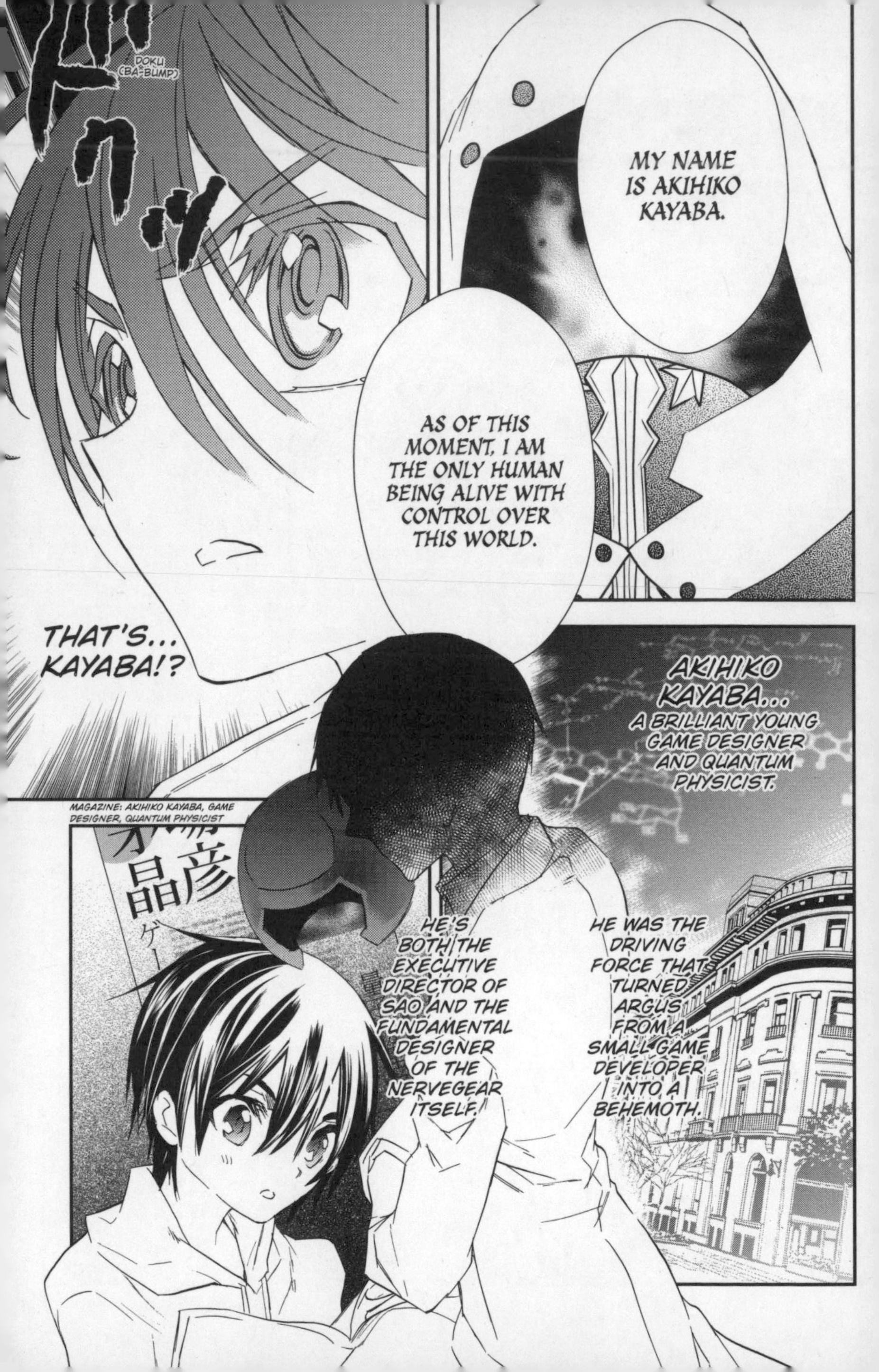
MY NAME IS AKIHIKO KAYABA.
AS OF THIS MOMENT, I AM THE ONLY HUMAN BEING ALIVE WITH CONTROL OVER THIS WORLD.
DOKU (BA-BUMP)
THAT'S... KAYABA!?
AKIHIKO KAYABA... A BRILLIANT YOUNG GAME DESIGNER AND QUANTUM PHYSICIST.
MAGAZINE: AKIHIKO KAYABA, GAME DESIGNER, QUANTUM PHYSICIST
晶彦
HE WAS THE DRIVING FORCE THAT TURNED ARGUS FROM A SMALL GAME DEVELOPER INTO A BEHEMOTH.
HE'S BOTH THE EXECUTIVE DIRECTOR OF SAO AND THE FUNDAMENTAL DESIGNER OF THE NERVEGEAR ITSELF.

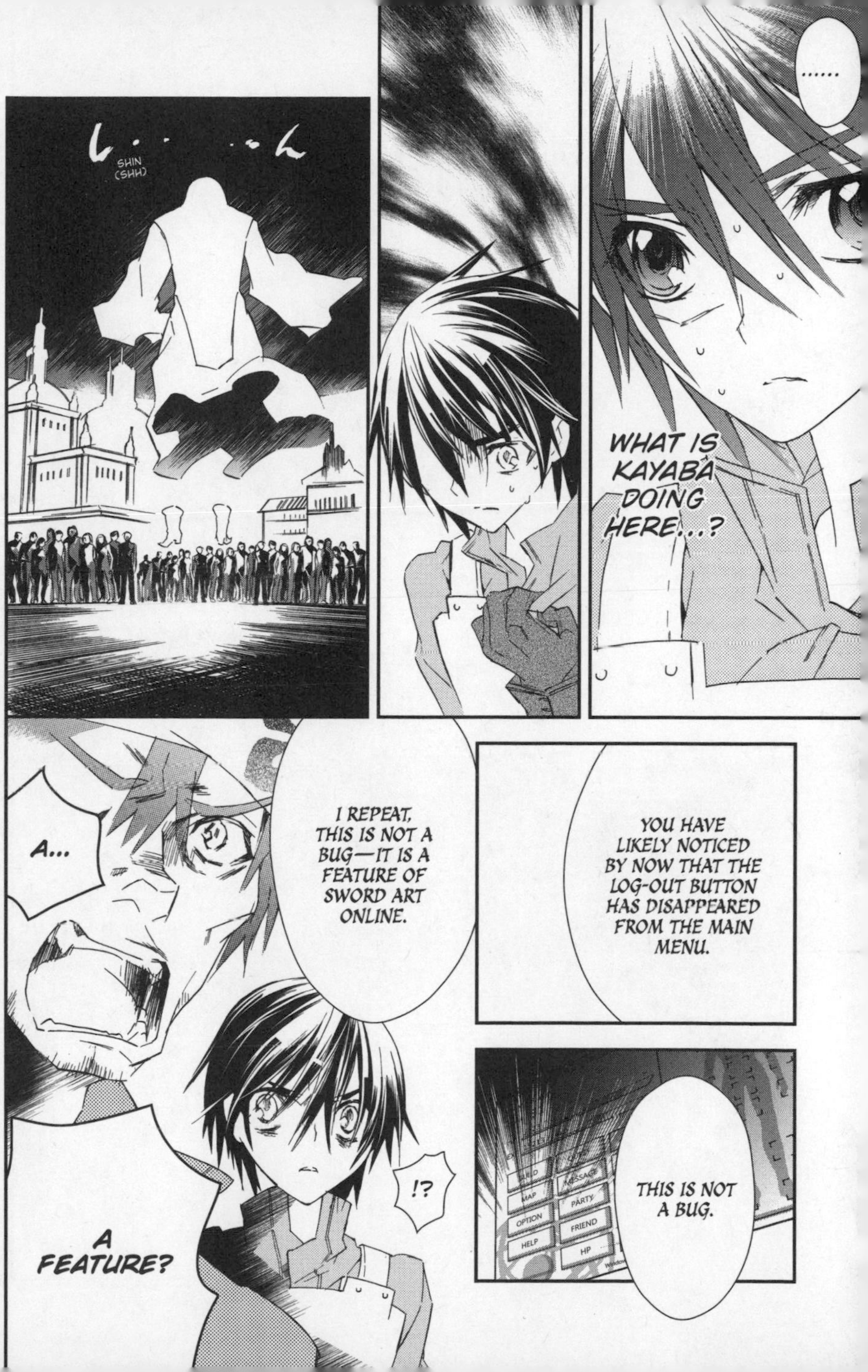
......
WHAT IS KAYABA DOING HERE...?
SHIN (SHH)
YOU HAVE LIKELY NOTICED BY NOW THAT THE LOG-OUT BUTTON HAS DISAPPEARED FROM THE MAIN MENU.
THIS IS NOT A BUG.
FIELD
MESSAGE
MAP
PARTY
OPTION
FRIEND
HELP
HP
I REPEAT, THIS IS NOT A BUG—IT IS A FEATURE OF SWORD ART ONLINE.
A...
!?
A FEATURE?

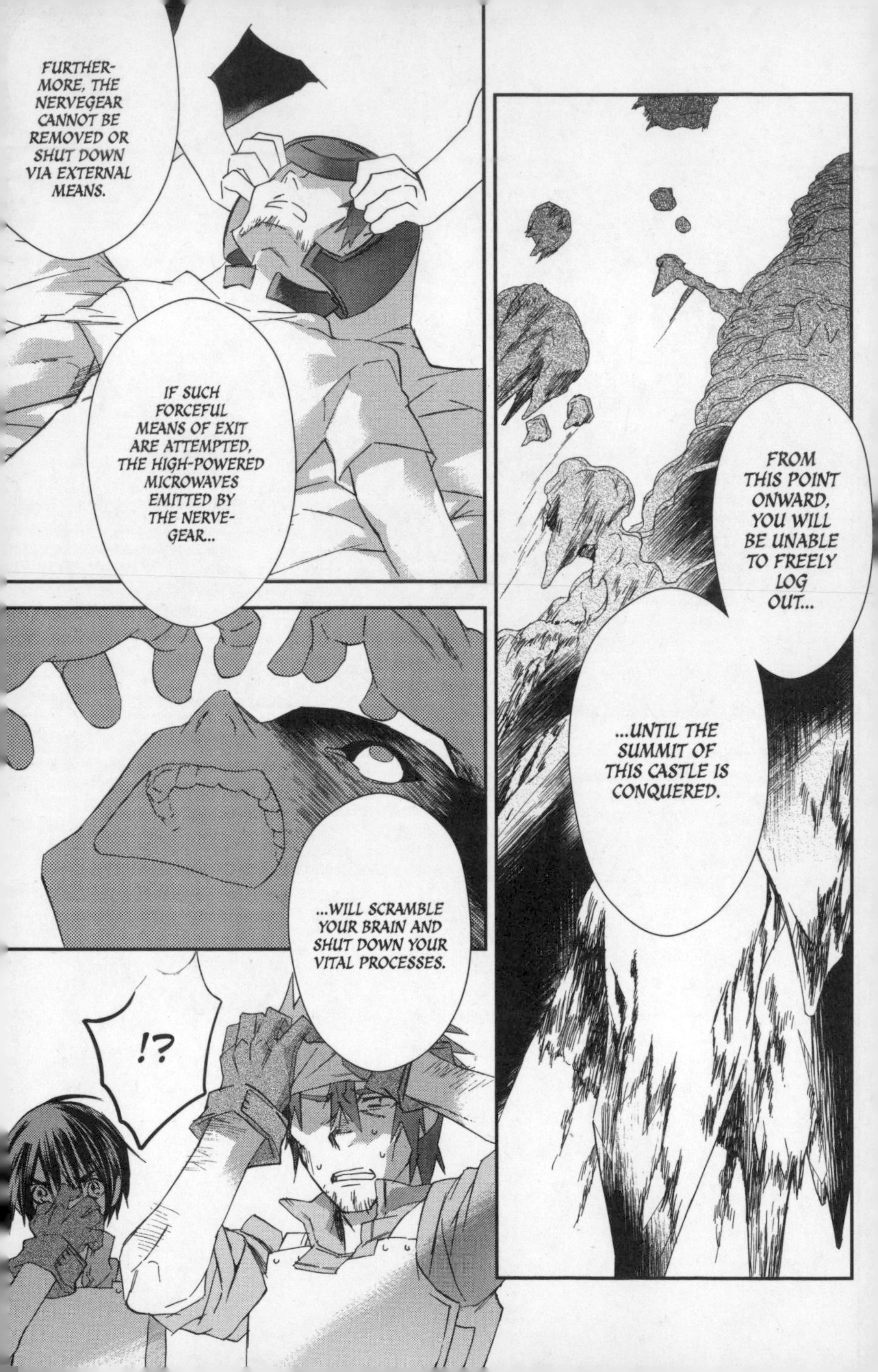
FROM THIS POINT ONWARD, YOU WILL BE UNABLE TO FREELY LOG OUT...
...UNTIL THE SUMMIT OF THIS CASTLE IS CONQUERED.
FURTHER-MORE, THE NERVEGEAR CANNOT BE REMOVED OR SHUT DOWN VIA EXTERNAL MEANS.
IF SUCH FORCEFUL MEANS OF EXIT ARE ATTEMPTED, THE HIGH-POWERED MICROWAVES EMITTED BY THE NERVE-GEAR...
...WILL SCRAMBLE YOUR BRAIN AND SHUT DOWN YOUR VITAL PROCESSES.
!?

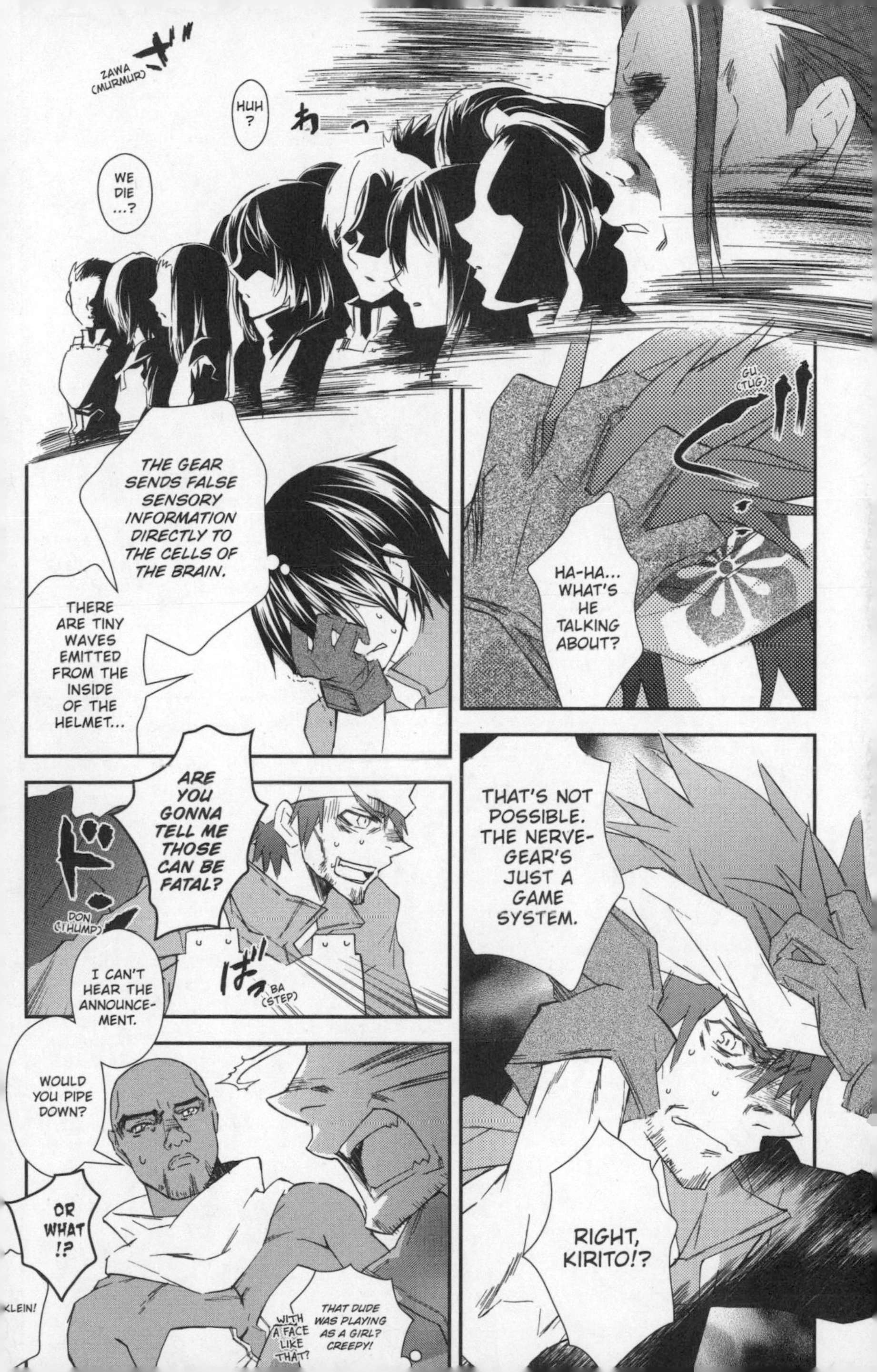
HUH ?
ZAWA (MURMUR)
WE DIE ...?
GU (TUG)
HA-HA... WHAT'S HE TALKING ABOUT?
THE GEAR SENDS FALSE SENSORY INFORMATION DIRECTLY TO THE CELLS OF THE BRAIN.
THERE ARE TINY WAVES EMITTED FROM THE INSIDE OF THE HELMET...
THAT'S NOT POSSIBLE. THE NERVE-GEAR'S JUST A GAME SYSTEM.
RIGHT, KIRITO!?
ARE YOU GONNA TELL ME THOSE CAN BE FATAL?
DON (THUMP)
I CAN'T HEAR THE ANNOUNCEMENT.
BA (STEP)
WOULD YOU PIPE DOWN?
OR WHAT !?
THAT DUDE WAS PLAYING AS A GIRL? CREEPY!
WITH A FACE LIKE THAT?
KLEIN!

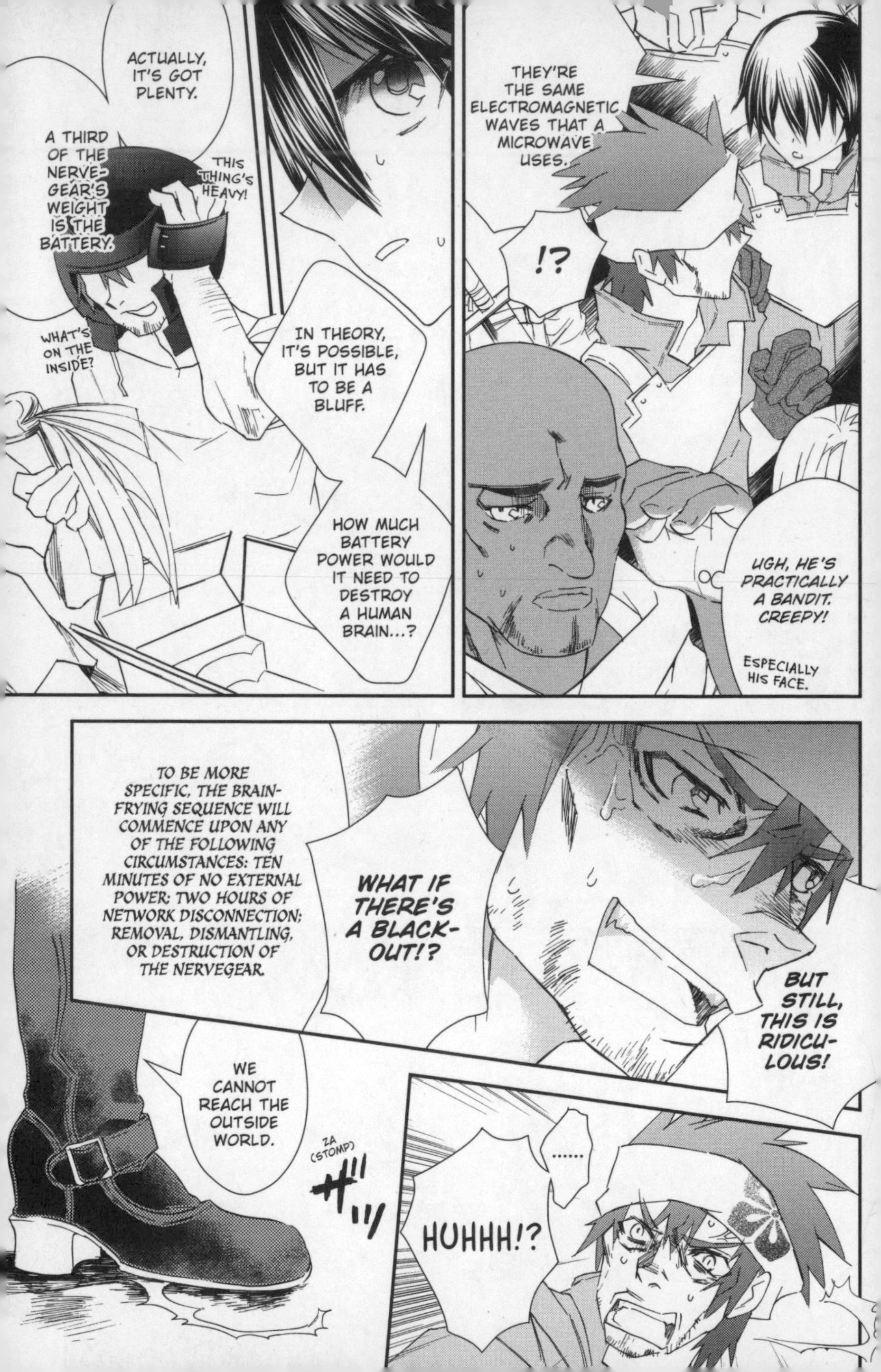
THEY'RE THE SAME ELECTROMAGNETIC WAVES THAT A MICROWAVE USES.
!?
UGH, HE'S PRACTICALLY A BANDIT. CREEPY!
ESPECIALLY HIS FACE.
IN THEORY, IT'S POSSIBLE, BUT IT HAS TO BE A BLUFF.
HOW MUCH BATTERY POWER WOULD IT NEED TO DESTROY A HUMAN BRAIN...?
ACTUALLY, IT'S GOT PLENTY.
A THIRD OF THE NERVEGEAR'S WEIGHT IS THE BATTERY.
THIS THING'S HEAVY!
WHAT'S ON THE INSIDE?
BUT STILL, THIS IS RIDICULOUS!
WHAT IF THERE'S A BLACKOUT!?
TO BE MORE SPECIFIC, THE BRAIN-FRYING SEQUENCE WILL COMMENCE UPON ANY OF THE FOLLOWING CIRCUMSTANCES: TEN MINUTES OF NO EXTERNAL POWER; TWO HOURS OF NETWORK DISCONNECTION; REMOVAL, DISMANTLING, OR DESTRUCTION OF THE NERVEGEAR.
WE CANNOT REACH THE OUTSIDE WORLD.
ZA (STOMP)
......
HUHHH!?

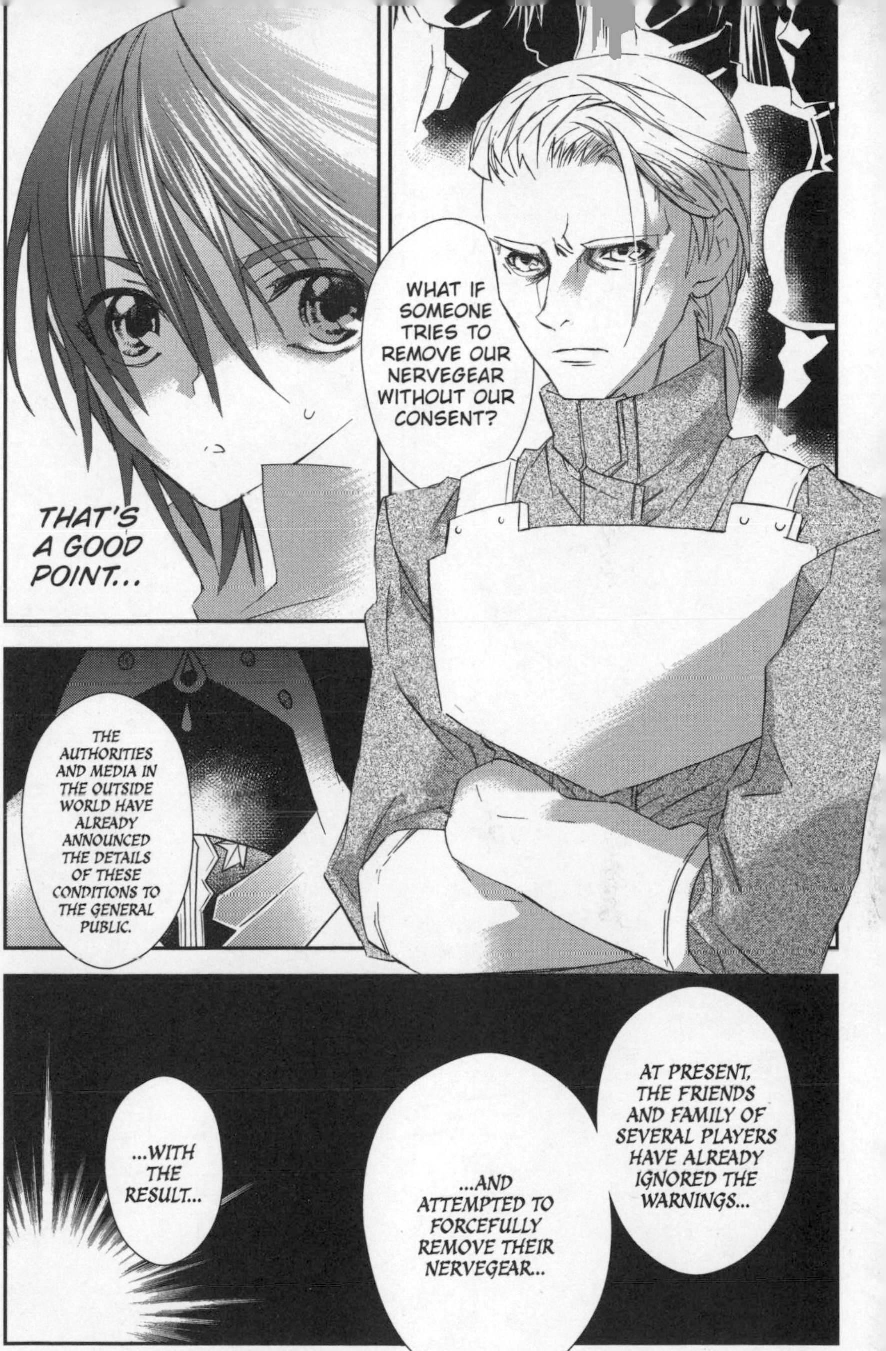
WHAT IF SOMEONE TRIES TO REMOVE OUR NERVEGEAR WITHOUT OUR CONSENT?
THAT'S A GOOD POINT...
THE AUTHORITIES AND MEDIA IN THE OUTSIDE WORLD HAVE ALREADY ANNOUNCED THE DETAILS OF THESE CONDITIONS TO THE GENERAL PUBLIC.
AT PRESENT, THE FRIENDS AND FAMILY OF SEVERAL PLAYERS HAVE ALREADY IGNORED THE WARNINGS...
...AND ATTEMPTED TO FORCEFULLY REMOVE THEIR NERVEGEAR...
...WITH THE RESULT...

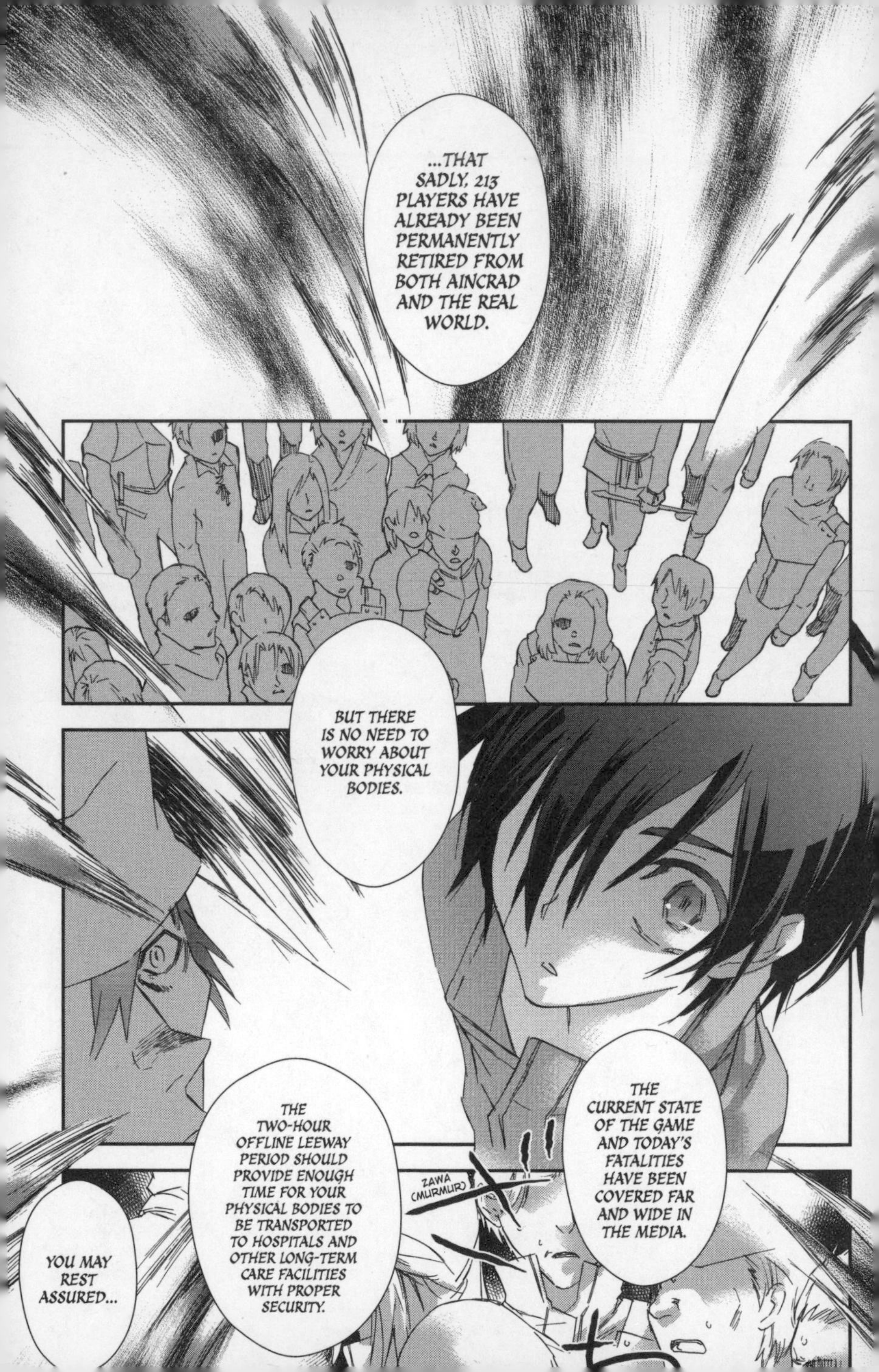
...THAT SADLY, 213 PLAYERS HAVE ALREADY BEEN PERMANENTLY RETIRED FROM BOTH AINCRAD AND THE REAL WORLD.
BUT THERE IS NO NEED TO WORRY ABOUT YOUR PHYSICAL BODIES.
THE CURRENT STATE OF THE GAME AND TODAY'S FATALITIES HAVE BEEN COVERED FAR AND WIDE IN THE MEDIA.
ZAWA (MURMUR)
THE TWO-HOUR OFFLINE LEEWAY PERIOD SHOULD PROVIDE ENOUGH TIME FOR YOUR PHYSICAL BODIES TO BE TRANSPORTED TO HOSPITALS AND OTHER LONG-TERM CARE FACILITIES WITH PROPER SECURITY.
YOU MAY REST ASSURED...

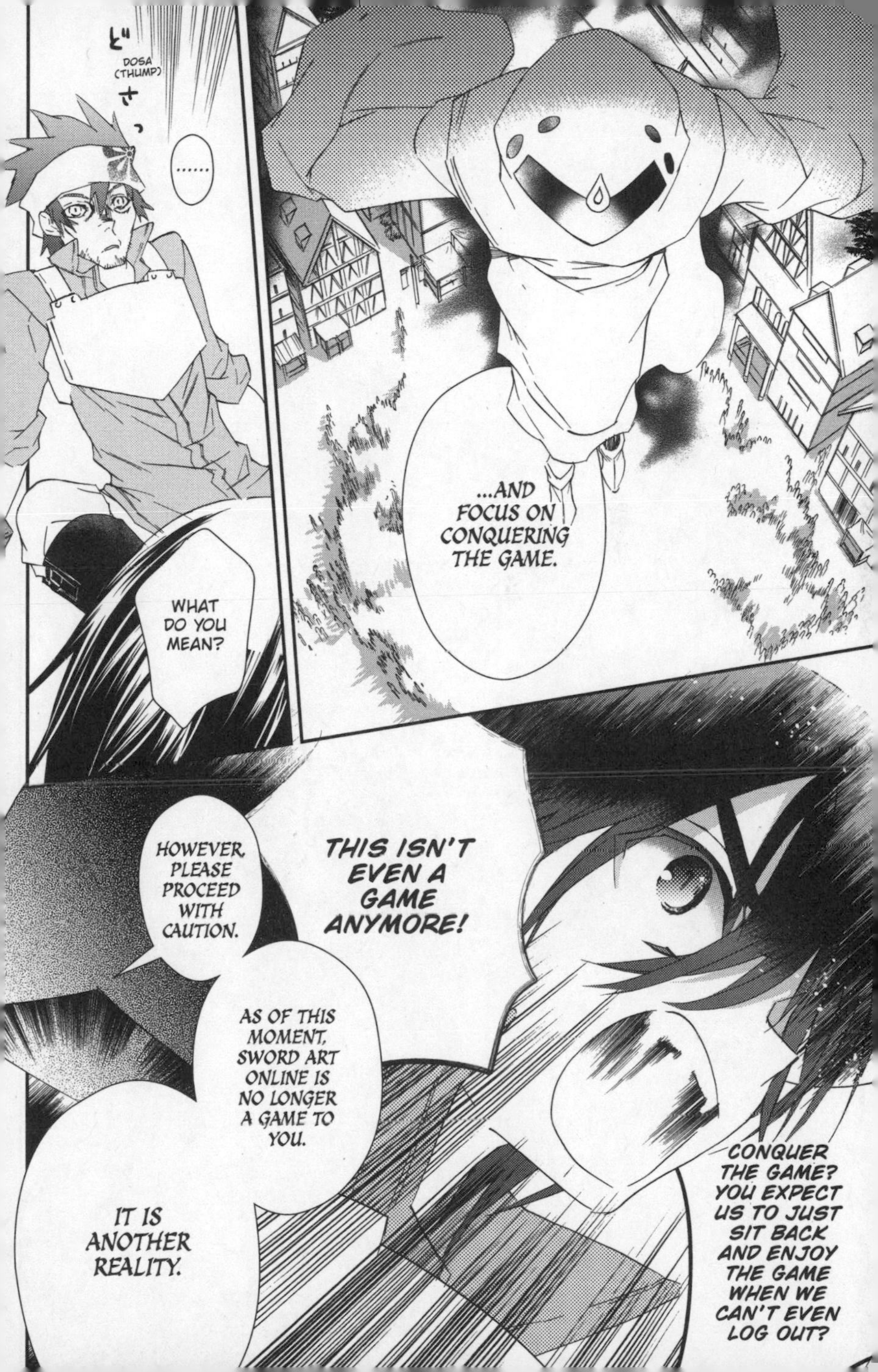
...AND FOCUS ON CONQUERING THE GAME.
どさっ
DOSA (THUMP)
......
WHAT DO YOU MEAN?
CONQUER THE GAME? YOU EXPECT US TO JUST SIT BACK AND ENJOY THE GAME WHEN WE CAN'T EVEN LOG OUT?
THIS ISN'T EVEN A GAME ANYMORE!
HOWEVER, PLEASE PROCEED WITH CAUTION.
AS OF THIS MOMENT, SWORD ART ONLINE IS NO LONGER A GAME TO YOU.
IT IS ANOTHER REALITY.

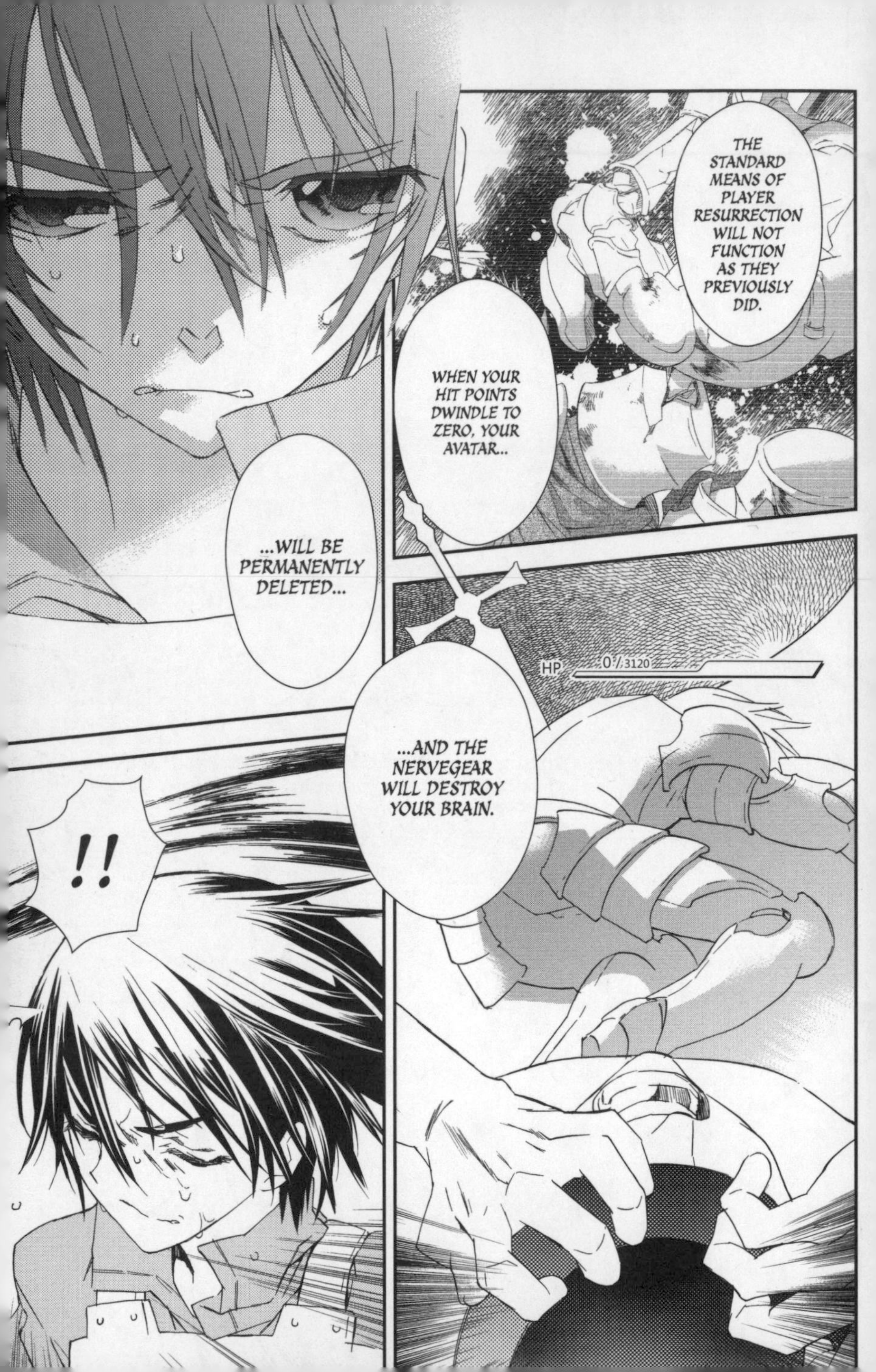
THE STANDARD MEANS OF PLAYER RESURRECTION WILL NOT FUNCTION AS THEY PREVIOUSLY DID.
WHEN YOUR HIT POINTS DWINDLE TO ZERO, YOUR AVATAR...
...WILL BE PERMANENTLY DELETED...
HP 0 / 3120
...AND THE NERVEGEAR WILL DESTROY YOUR BRAIN.
!!

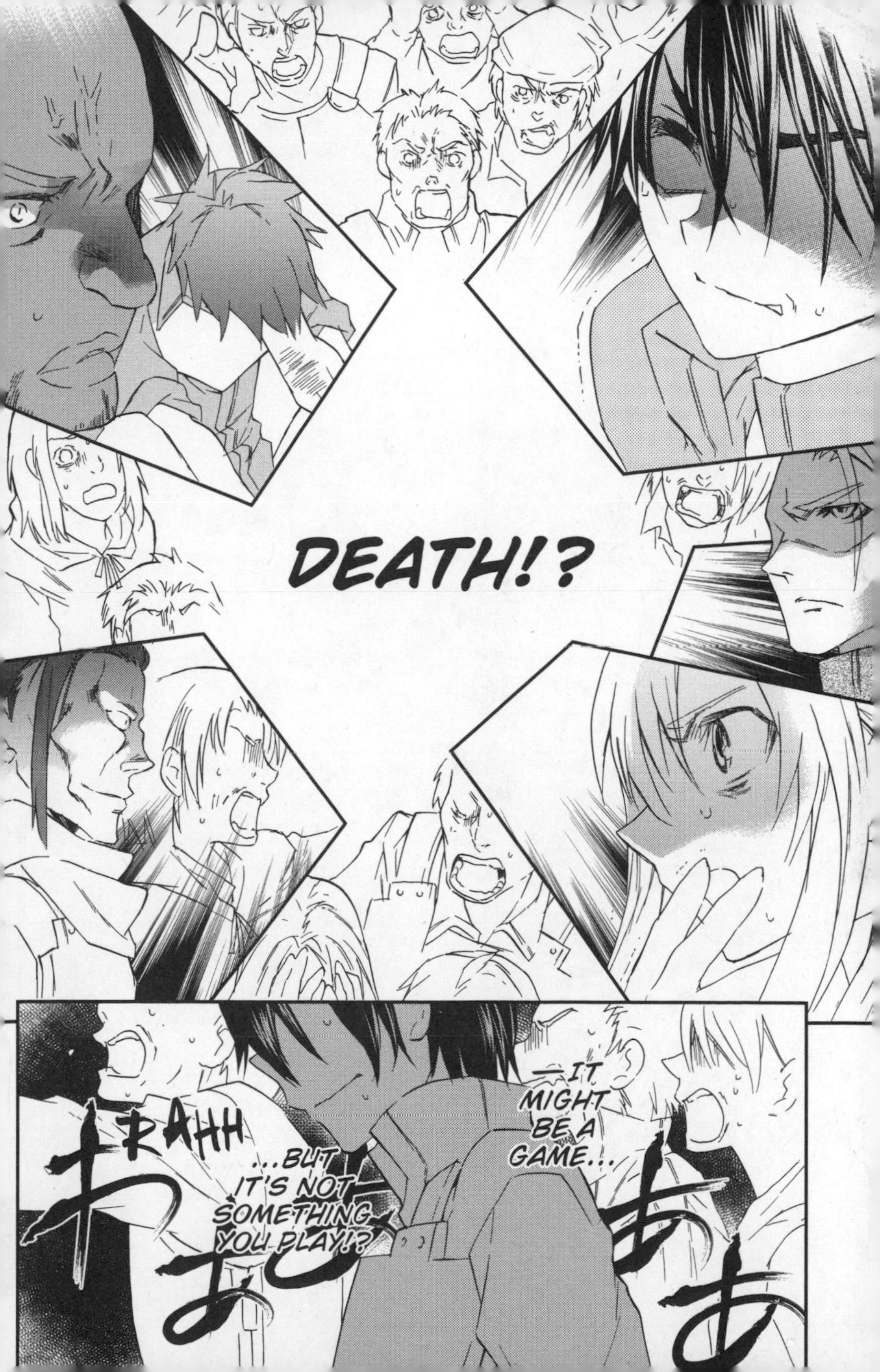
DEATH!?
—IT MIGHT BE A GAME...
...BUT IT'S NOT SOMETHING YOU PLAY!?
RAHH

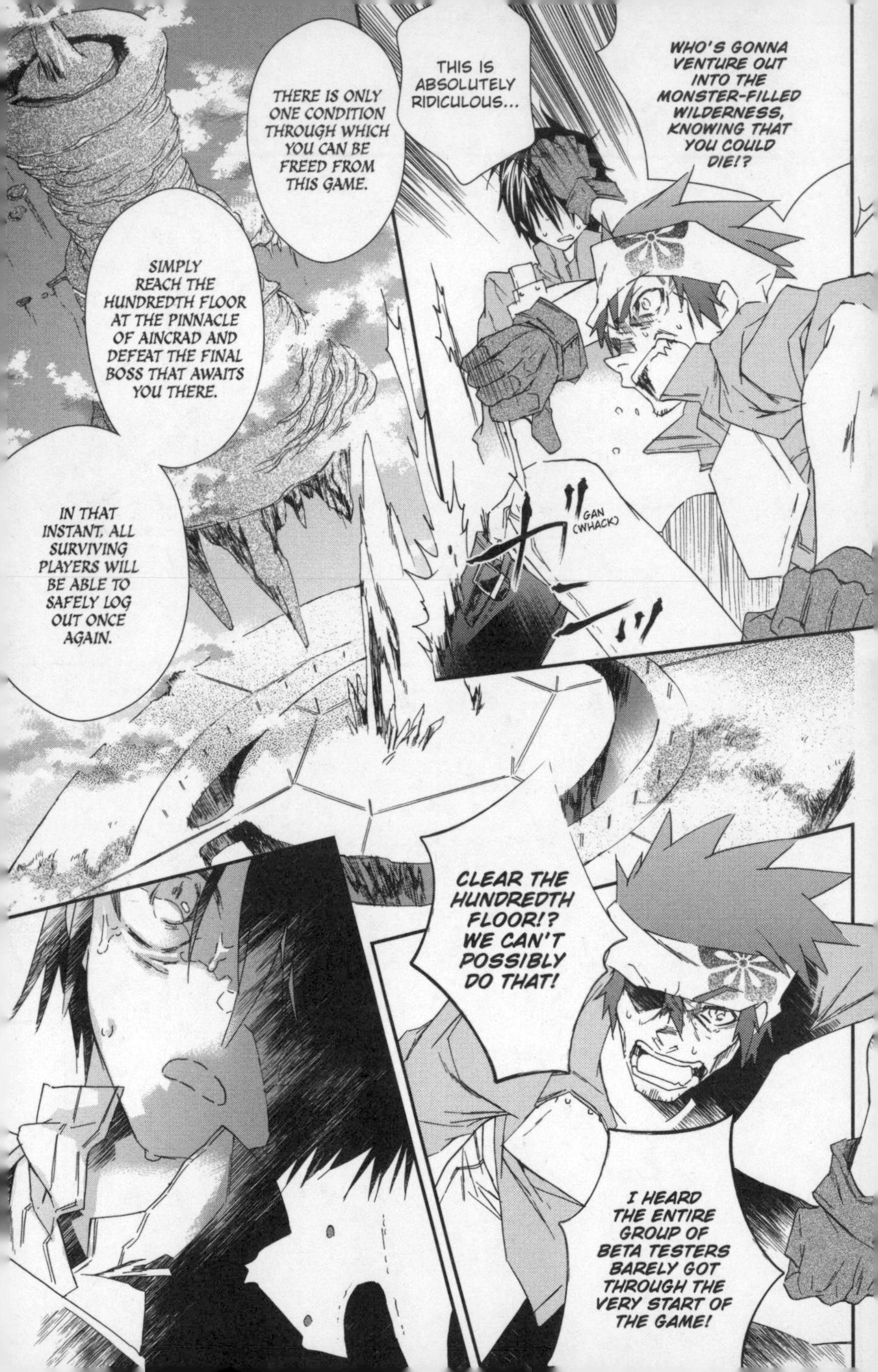
WHO'S GONNA VENTURE OUT INTO THE MONSTER-FILLED WILDERNESS, KNOWING THAT YOU COULD DIE!?
THIS IS ABSOLUTELY RIDICULOUS...
GAN (WHACK)
THERE IS ONLY ONE CONDITION THROUGH WHICH YOU CAN BE FREED FROM THIS GAME.
SIMPLY REACH THE HUNDREDTH FLOOR AT THE PINNACLE OF AINCRAD AND DEFEAT THE FINAL BOSS THAT AWAITS YOU THERE.
IN THAT INSTANT, ALL SURVIVING PLAYERS WILL BE ABLE TO SAFELY LOG OUT ONCE AGAIN.
CLEAR THE HUNDREDTH FLOOR!? WE CAN'T POSSIBLY DO THAT!
I HEARD THE ENTIRE GROUP OF BETA TESTERS BARELY GOT THROUGH THE VERY START OF THE GAME!

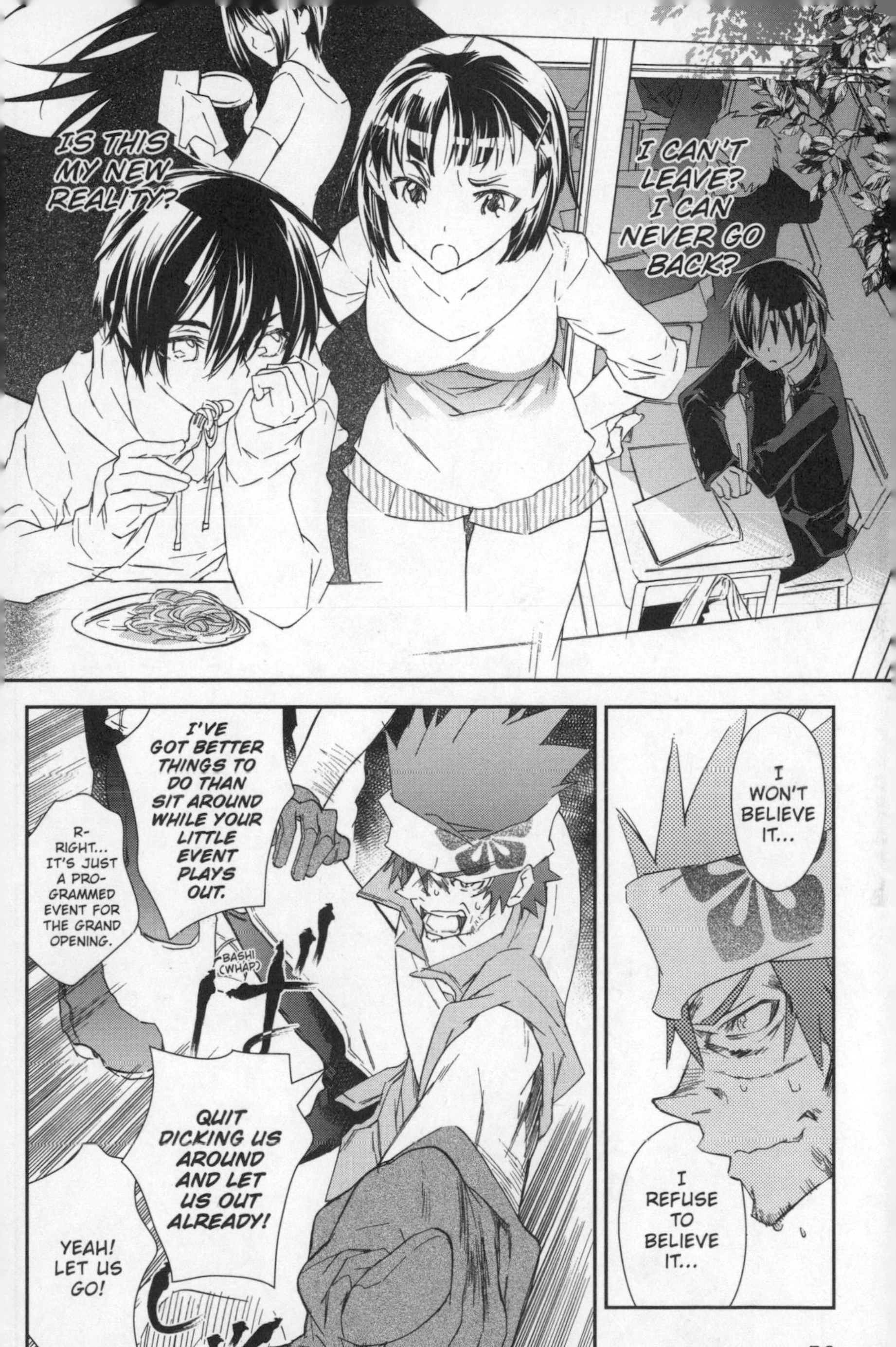
I CAN'T LEAVE? I CAN NEVER GO BACK?
IS THIS MY NEW REALITY?
I WON'T BELIEVE IT...
I REFUSE TO BELIEVE IT...
I'VE GOT BETTER THINGS TO DO THAN SIT AROUND WHILE YOUR LITTLE EVENT PLAYS OUT.
R-RIGHT... IT'S JUST A PRO-GRAMMED EVENT FOR THE GRAND OPENING.
BASHI (WHAP)
QUIT DICKING US AROUND AND LET US OUT ALREADY!
YEAH! LET US GO!

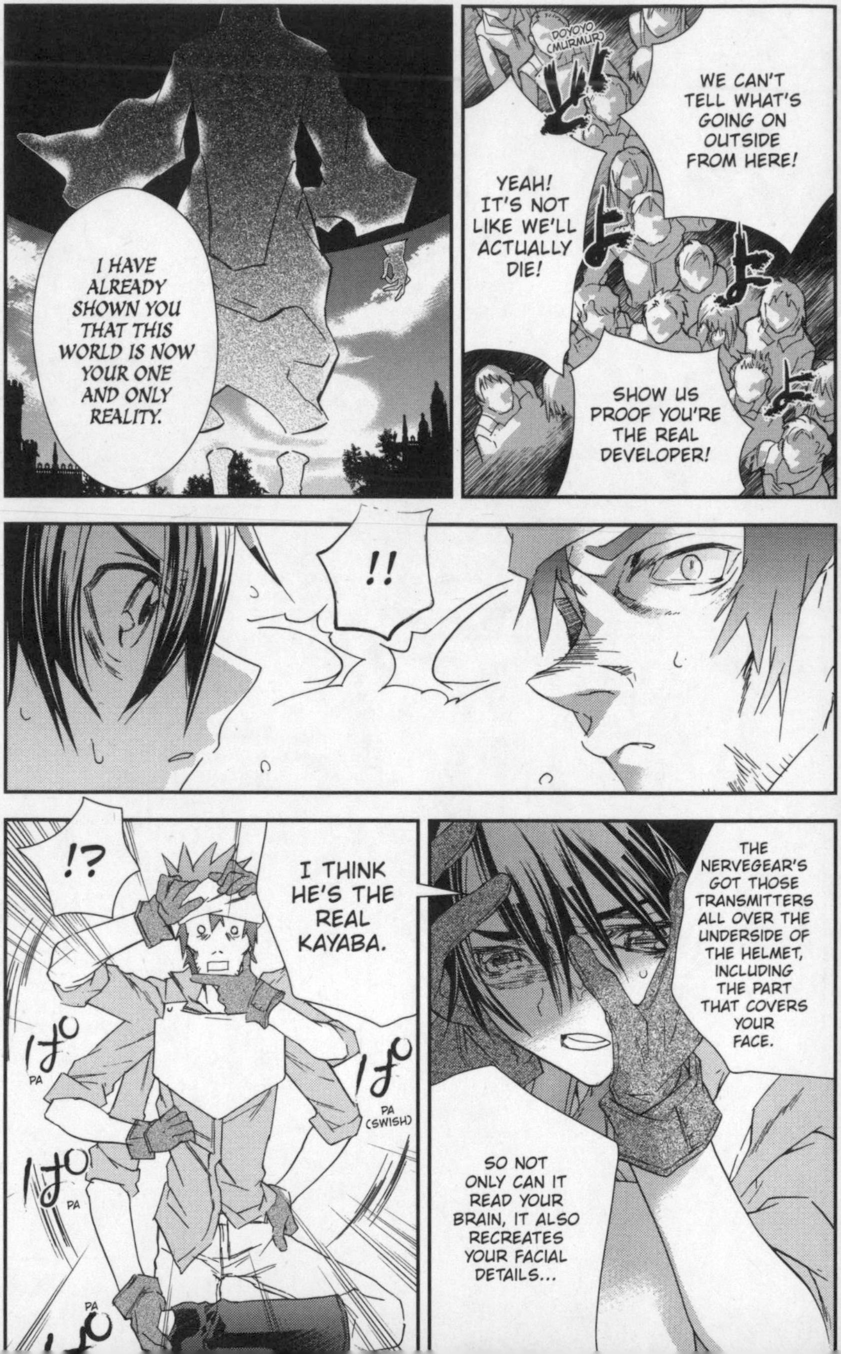
DOYOYO (MURMUR)
WE CAN'T TELL WHAT'S GOING ON OUTSIDE FROM HERE!
YEAH! IT'S NOT LIKE WE'LL ACTUALLY DIE!
SHOW US PROOF YOU'RE THE REAL DEVELOPER!
I HAVE ALREADY SHOWN YOU THAT THIS WORLD IS NOW YOUR ONE AND ONLY REALITY.
!!
THE NERVEGEAR'S GOT THOSE TRANSMITTERS ALL OVER THE UNDERSIDE OF THE HELMET, INCLUDING THE PART THAT COVERS YOUR FACE.
SO NOT ONLY CAN IT READ YOUR BRAIN, IT ALSO RECREATES YOUR FACIAL DETAILS...
I THINK HE'S THE REAL KAYABA.
!?
PA (SWISH)
PA
PA
PA

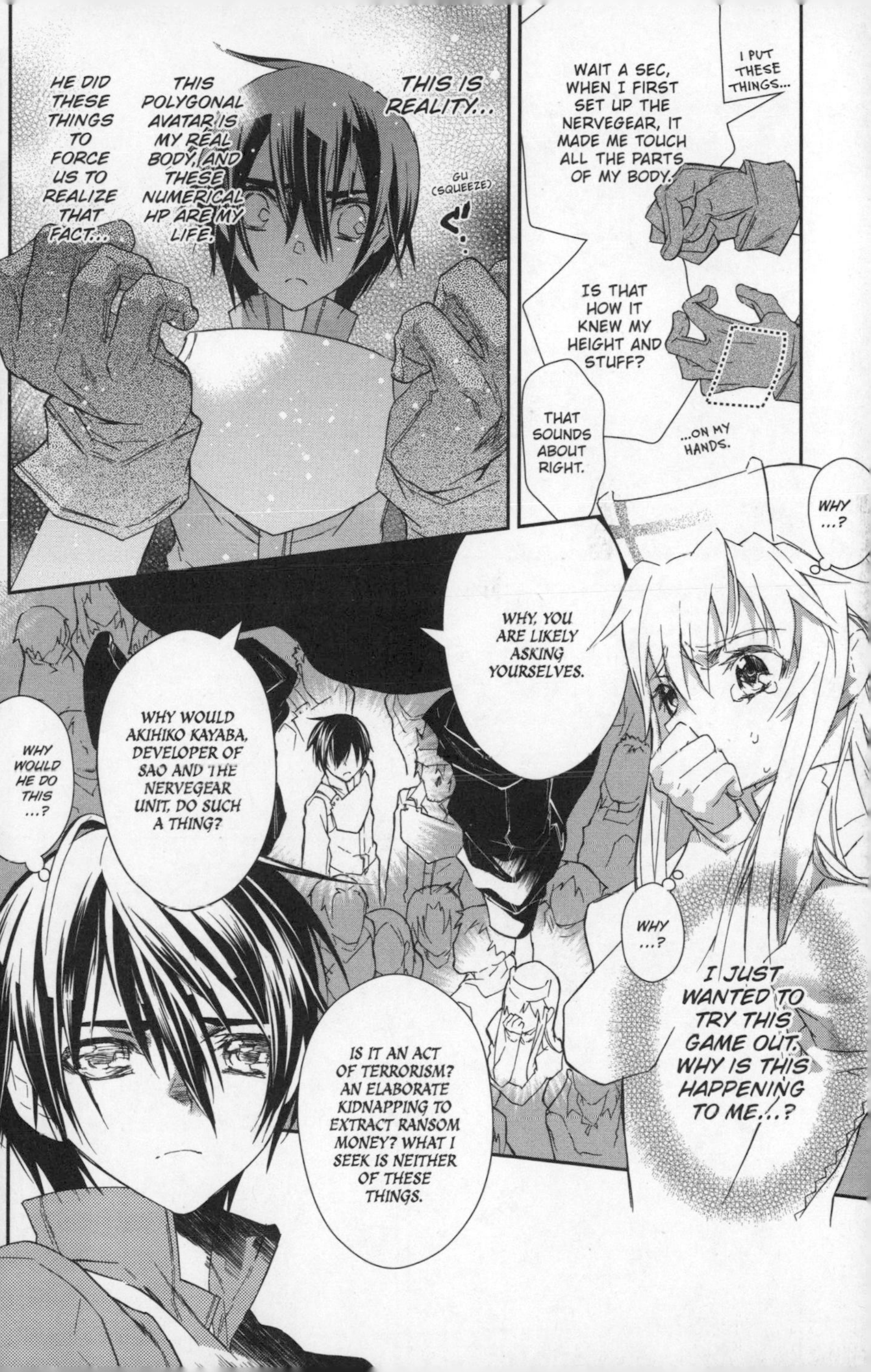
I PUT THESE THINGS...
WAIT A SEC, WHEN I FIRST SET UP THE NERVEGEAR, IT MADE ME TOUCH ALL THE PARTS OF MY BODY.
IS THAT HOW IT KNEW MY HEIGHT AND STUFF?
...ON MY HANDS.
THAT SOUNDS ABOUT RIGHT.
THIS IS REALITY...
GU (SQUEEZE)
THIS POLYGONAL AVATAR IS MY REAL BODY, AND THESE NUMERICAL HP ARE MY LIFE.
HE DID THESE THINGS TO FORCE US TO REALIZE THAT FACT...
WHY ...?
WHY, YOU ARE LIKELY ASKING YOURSELVES.
WHY WOULD AKIHIKO KAYABA, DEVELOPER OF SAO AND THE NERVEGEAR UNIT, DO SUCH A THING?
WHY WOULD HE DO THIS ...?
WHY ...?
I JUST WANTED TO TRY THIS GAME OUT. WHY IS THIS HAPPENING TO ME...?
IS IT AN ACT OF TERRORISM? AN ELABORATE KIDNAPPING TO EXTRACT RANSOM MONEY? WHAT I SEEK IS NEITHER OF THESE THINGS.

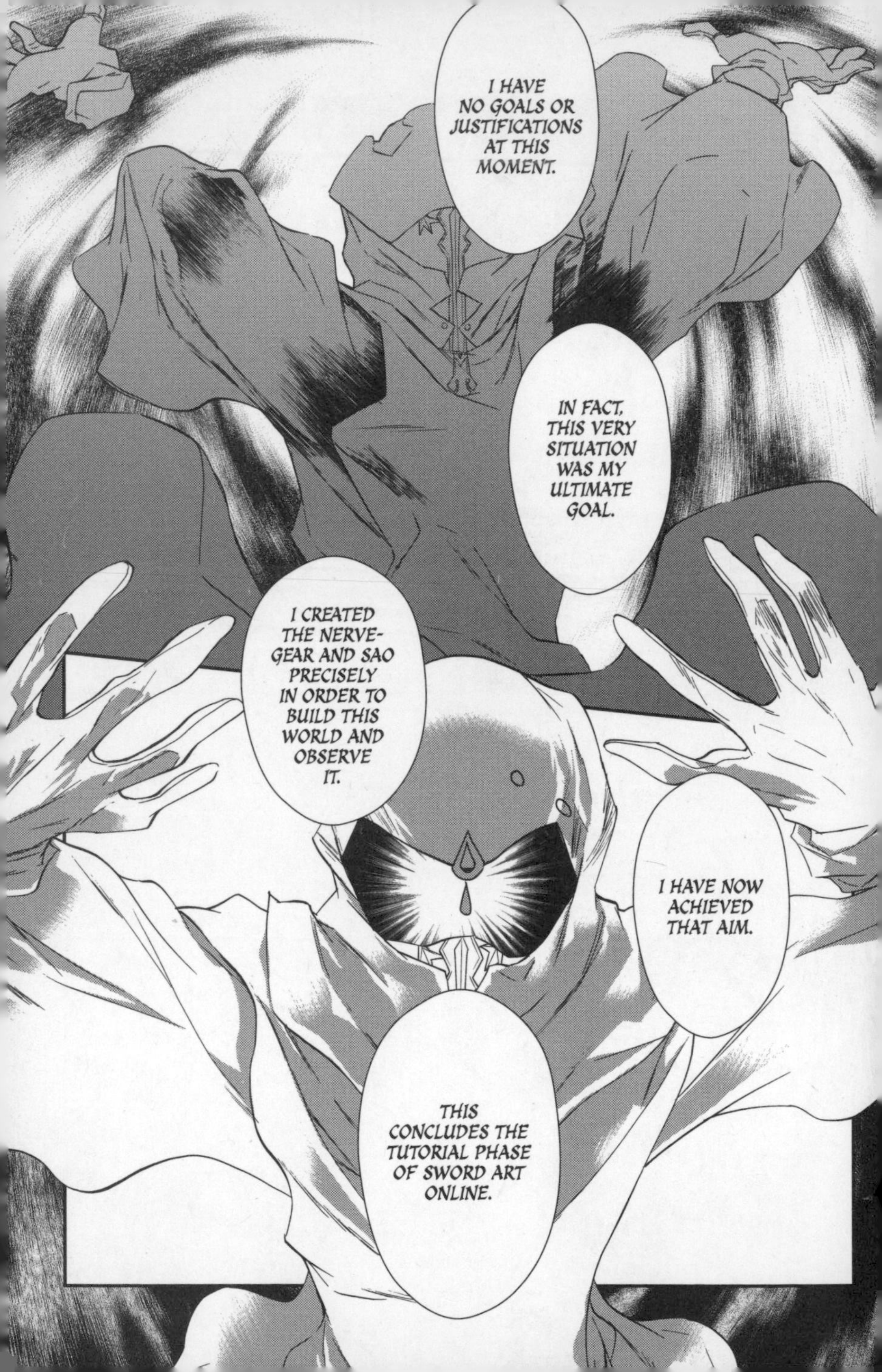
I HAVE NO GOALS OR JUSTIFICATIONS AT THIS MOMENT.
IN FACT, THIS VERY SITUATION WAS MY ULTIMATE GOAL.
I CREATED THE NERVE-GEAR AND SAO PRECISELY IN ORDER TO BUILD THIS WORLD AND OBSERVE IT.
I HAVE NOW ACHIEVED THAT AIM.
THIS CONCLUDES THE TUTORIAL PHASE OF SWORD ART ONLINE.

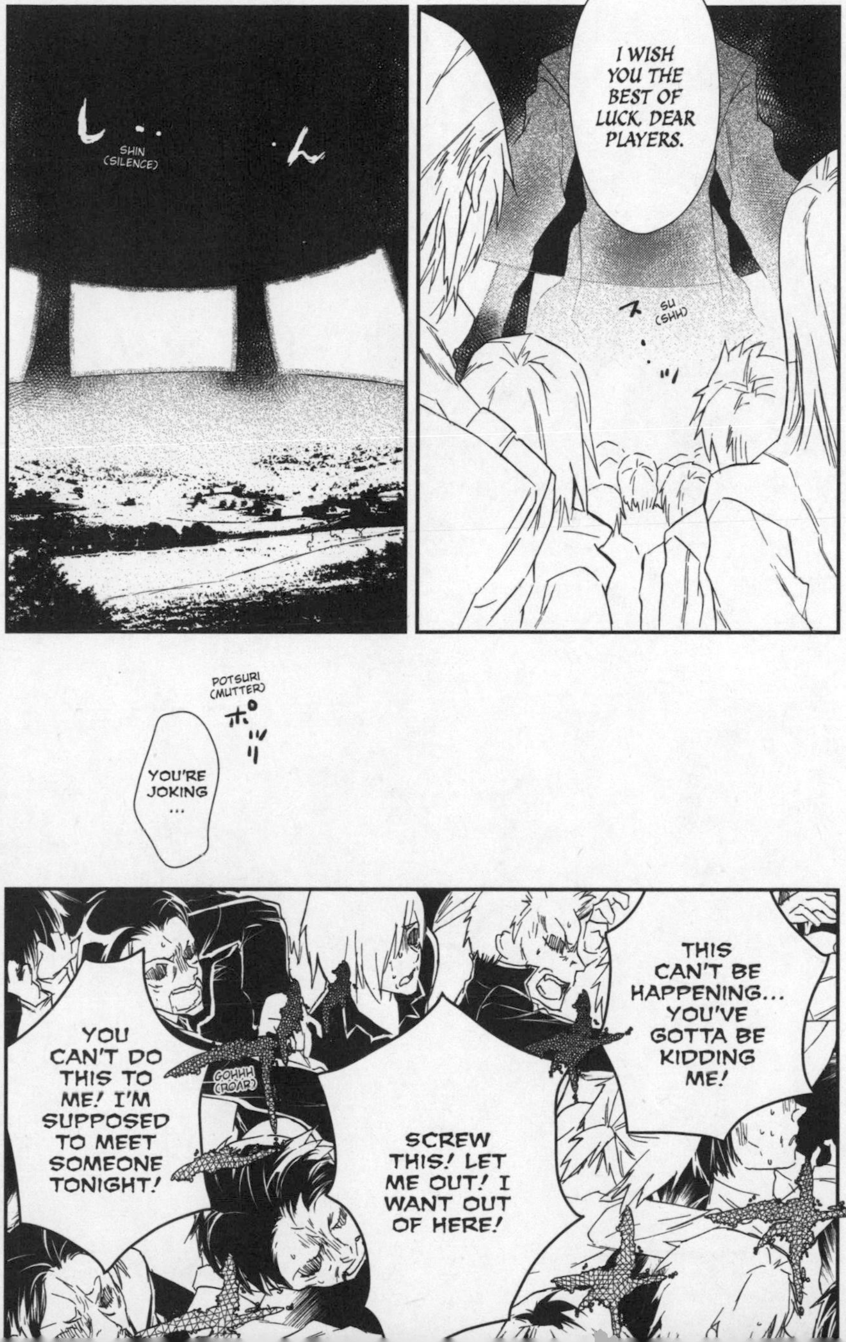
I WISH YOU THE BEST OF LUCK, DEAR PLAYERS.
SU (SHH)
SHIN (SILENCE)
POTSURI (MUTTER)
YOU'RE JOKING ...
THIS CAN'T BE HAPPENING... YOU'VE GOTTA BE KIDDING ME!
SCREW THIS! LET ME OUT! I WANT OUT OF HERE!
GOHHH (ROAR)
YOU CAN'T DO THIS TO ME! I'M SUPPOSED TO MEET SOMEONE TONIGHT!

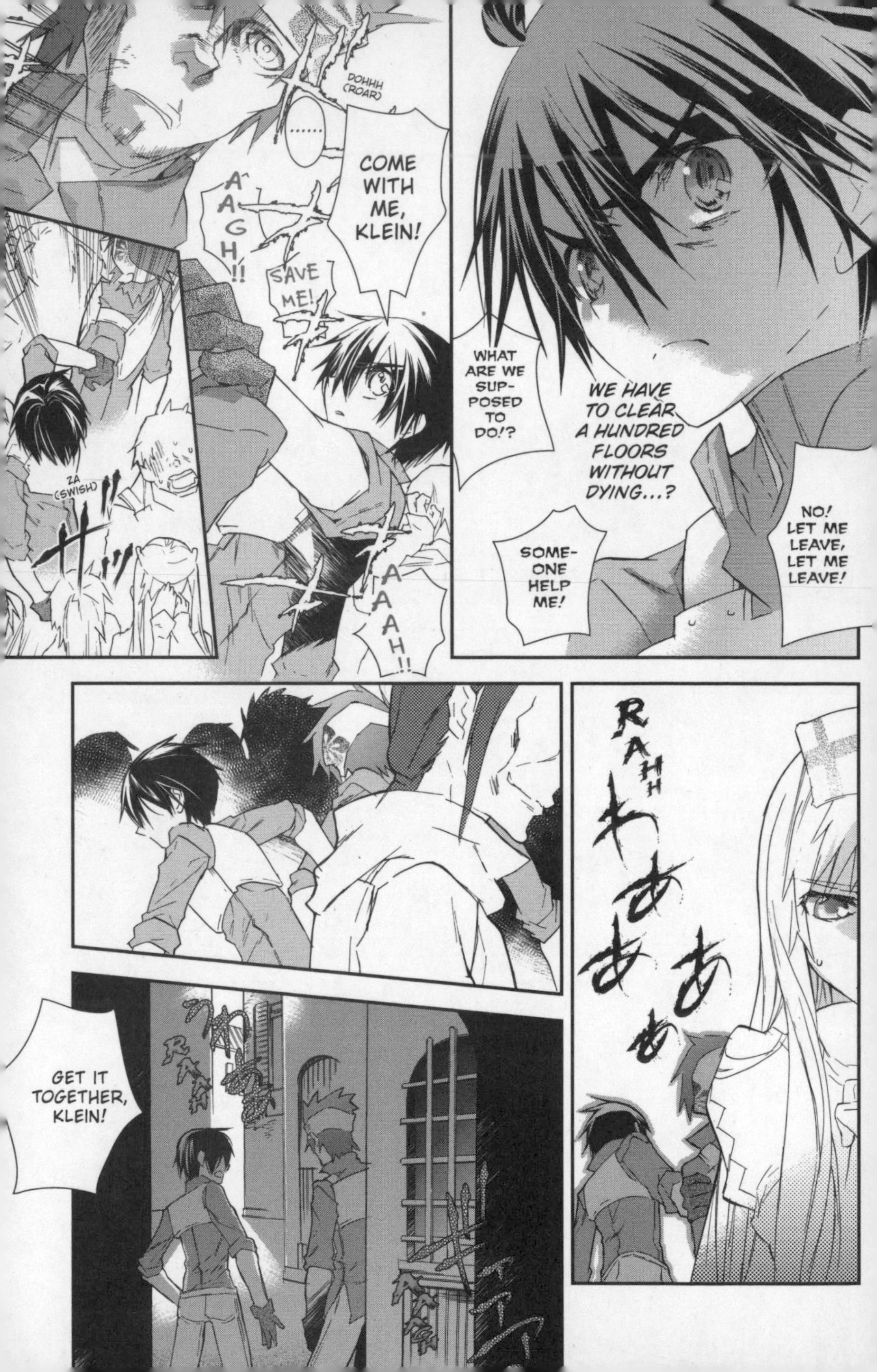
WE HAVE TO CLEAR A HUNDRED FLOORS WITHOUT DYING...?
WHAT ARE WE SUP-POSED TO DO!?
NO! LET ME LEAVE, LET ME LEAVE!
SOME-ONE HELP ME!
DOHHH (ROAR)
......
COME WITH ME, KLEIN!
AAGH!!
SAVE ME!
ZA (SWISH)
AAAAH!!
RAHH
GET IT TOGETHER, KLEIN!

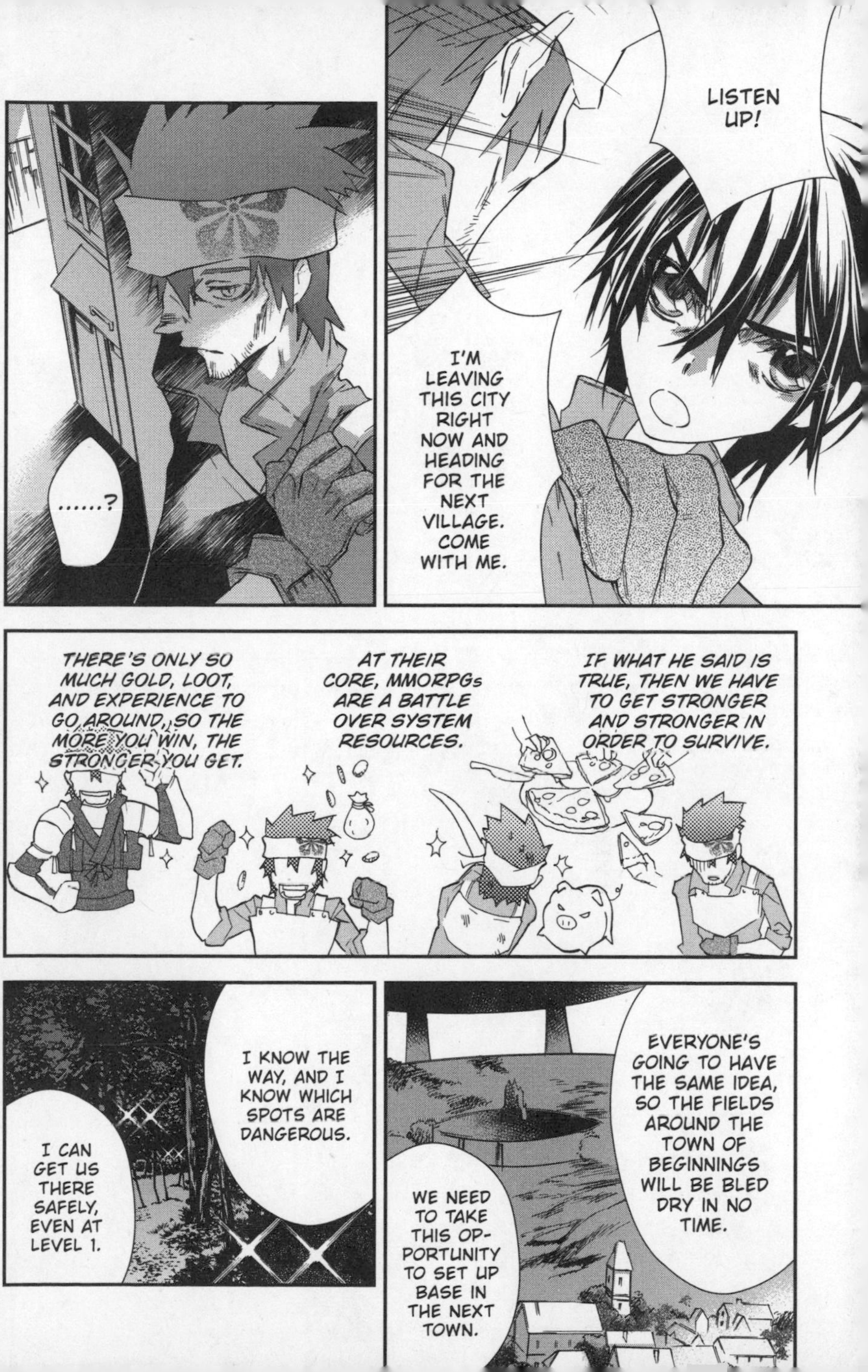
LISTEN UP!
I'M LEAVING THIS CITY RIGHT NOW AND HEADING FOR THE NEXT VILLAGE. COME WITH ME.
......?
IF WHAT HE SAID IS TRUE, THEN WE HAVE TO GET STRONGER AND STRONGER IN ORDER TO SURVIVE.
AT THEIR CORE, MMORPGs ARE A BATTLE OVER SYSTEM RESOURCES.
THERE'S ONLY SO MUCH GOLD, LOOT, AND EXPERIENCE TO GO AROUND, SO THE MORE YOU WIN, THE STRONGER YOU GET.
EVERYONE'S GOING TO HAVE THE SAME IDEA, SO THE FIELDS AROUND THE TOWN OF BEGINNINGS WILL BE BLED DRY IN NO TIME.
WE NEED TO TAKE THIS OP-PORTUNITY TO SET UP BASE IN THE NEXT TOWN.
I KNOW THE WAY, AND I KNOW WHICH SPOTS ARE DANGEROUS.
I CAN GET US THERE SAFELY, EVEN AT LEVEL 1.

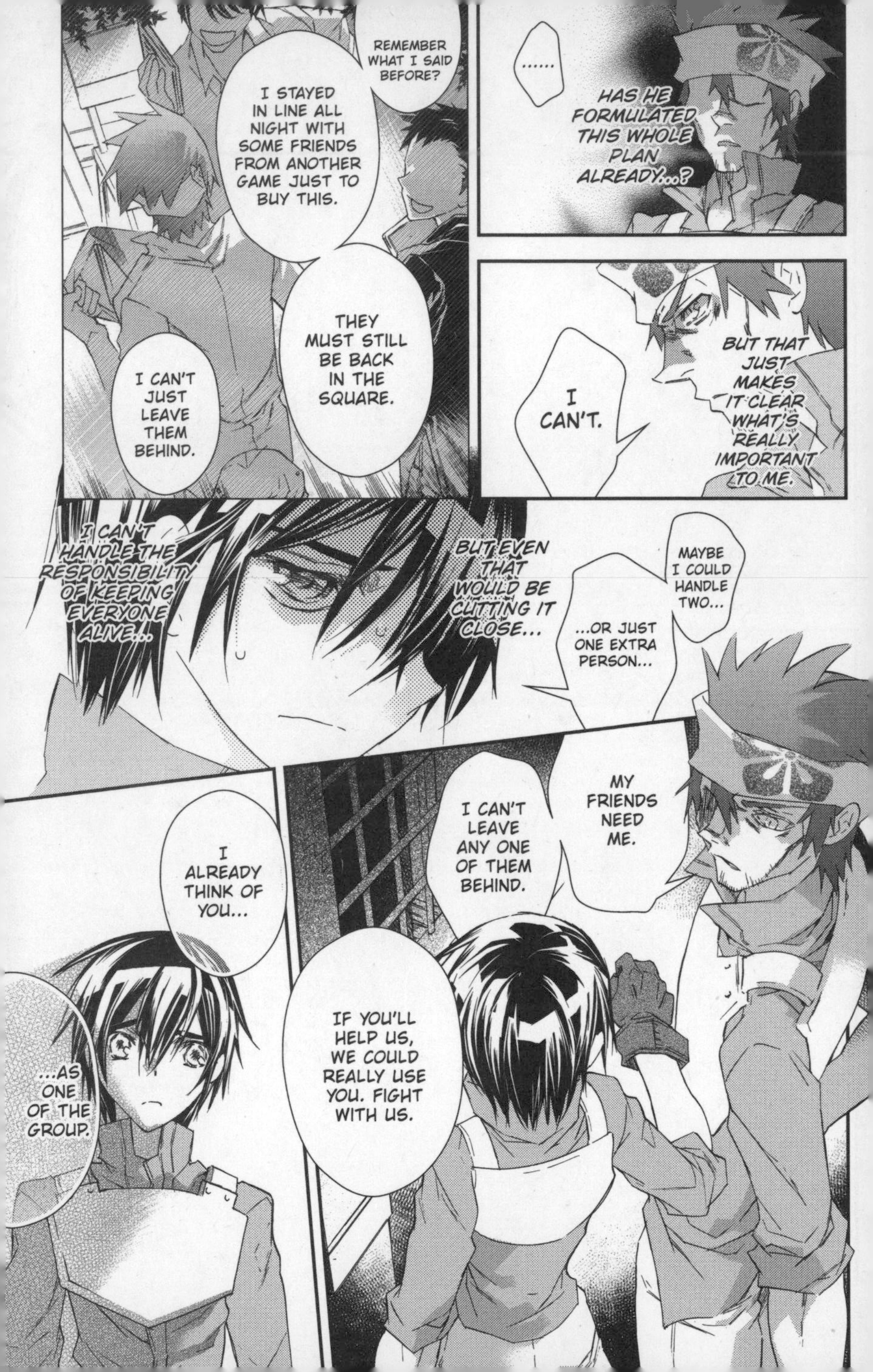
......
HAS HE FORMULATED THIS WHOLE PLAN ALREADY...?
BUT THAT JUST MAKES IT CLEAR WHAT'S REALLY IMPORTANT TO ME.
I CAN'T.
REMEMBER WHAT I SAID BEFORE?
I STAYED IN LINE ALL NIGHT WITH SOME FRIENDS FROM ANOTHER GAME JUST TO BUY THIS.
THEY MUST STILL BE BACK IN THE SQUARE.
I CAN'T JUST LEAVE THEM BEHIND.
MAYBE I COULD HANDLE TWO...
...OR JUST ONE EXTRA PERSON...
BUT EVEN THAT WOULD BE CUTTING IT CLOSE...
I CAN'T HANDLE THE RESPONSIBILITY OF KEEPING EVERYONE ALIVE...
MY FRIENDS NEED ME.
I CAN'T LEAVE ANY ONE OF THEM BEHIND.
IF YOU'LL HELP US, WE COULD REALLY USE YOU. FIGHT WITH US.
I ALREADY THINK OF YOU...
...AS ONE OF THE GROUP.

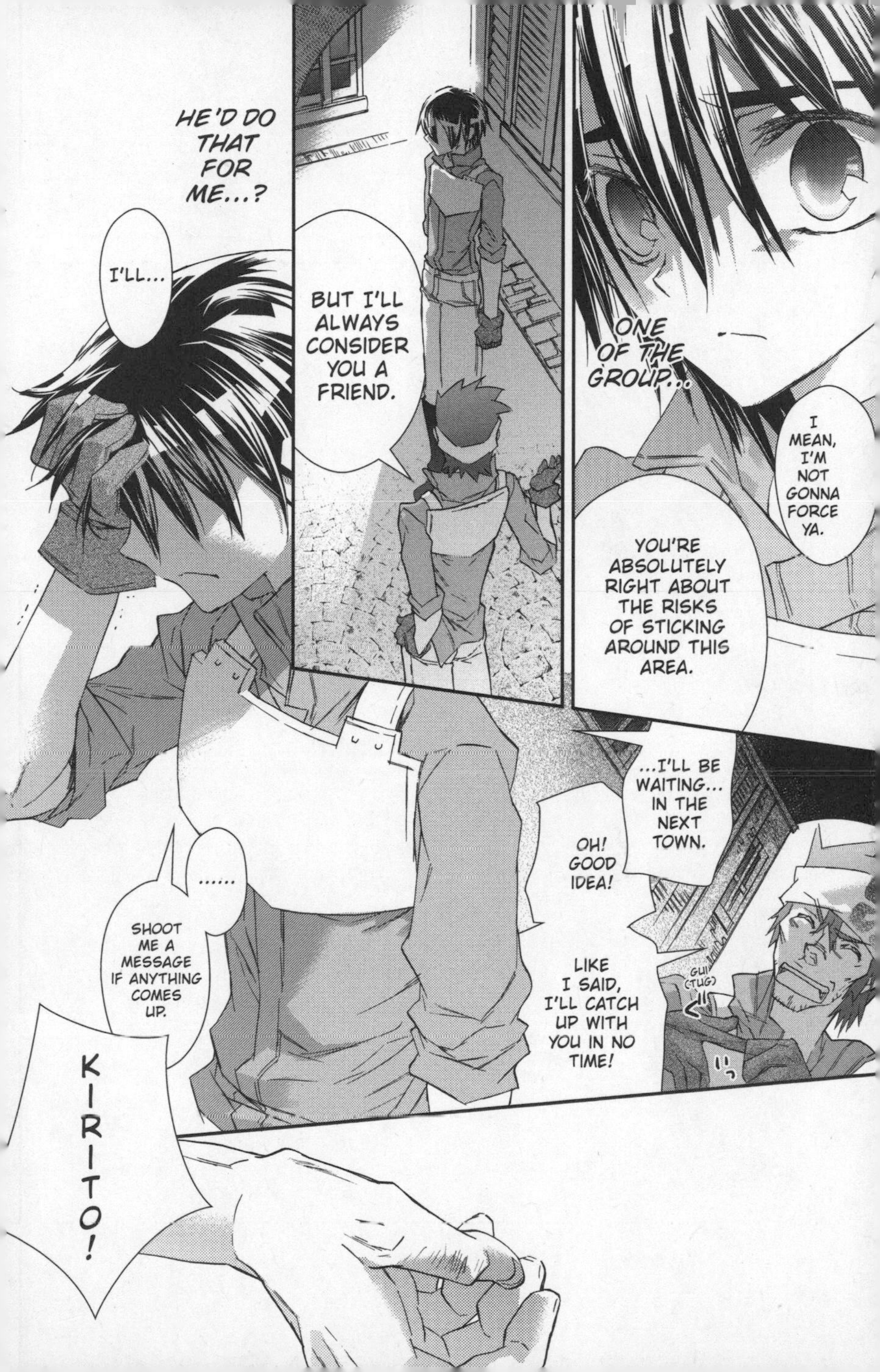
ONE OF THE GROUP...
I MEAN, I'M NOT GONNA FORCE YA.
YOU'RE ABSOLUTELY RIGHT ABOUT THE RISKS OF STICKING AROUND THIS AREA.
BUT I'LL ALWAYS CONSIDER YOU A FRIEND.
HE'D DO THAT FOR ME...?
I'LL...
...I'LL BE WAITING... IN THE NEXT TOWN.
OH! GOOD IDEA!
GUI (TUG)
LIKE I SAID, I'LL CATCH UP WITH YOU IN NO TIME!
......
SHOOT ME A MESSAGE IF ANYTHING COMES UP.
KIRITO!

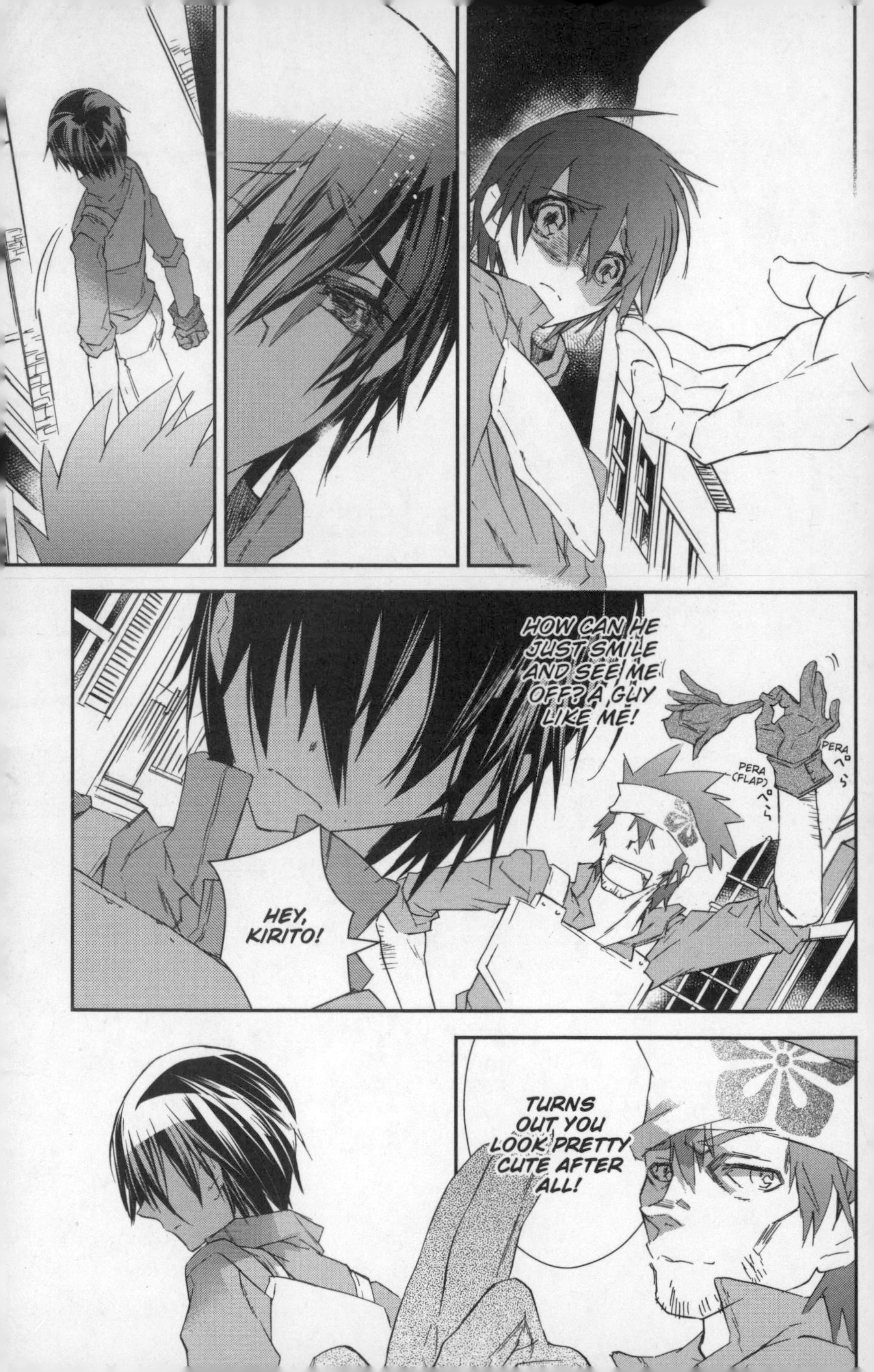
PERA
ぺら
PERA (FLAP)
ぺら
HOW CAN HE JUST SMILE AND SEE ME OFF? A GUY LIKE ME!
HEY, KIRITO!
TURNS OUT YOU LOOK PRETTY CUTE AFTER ALL!

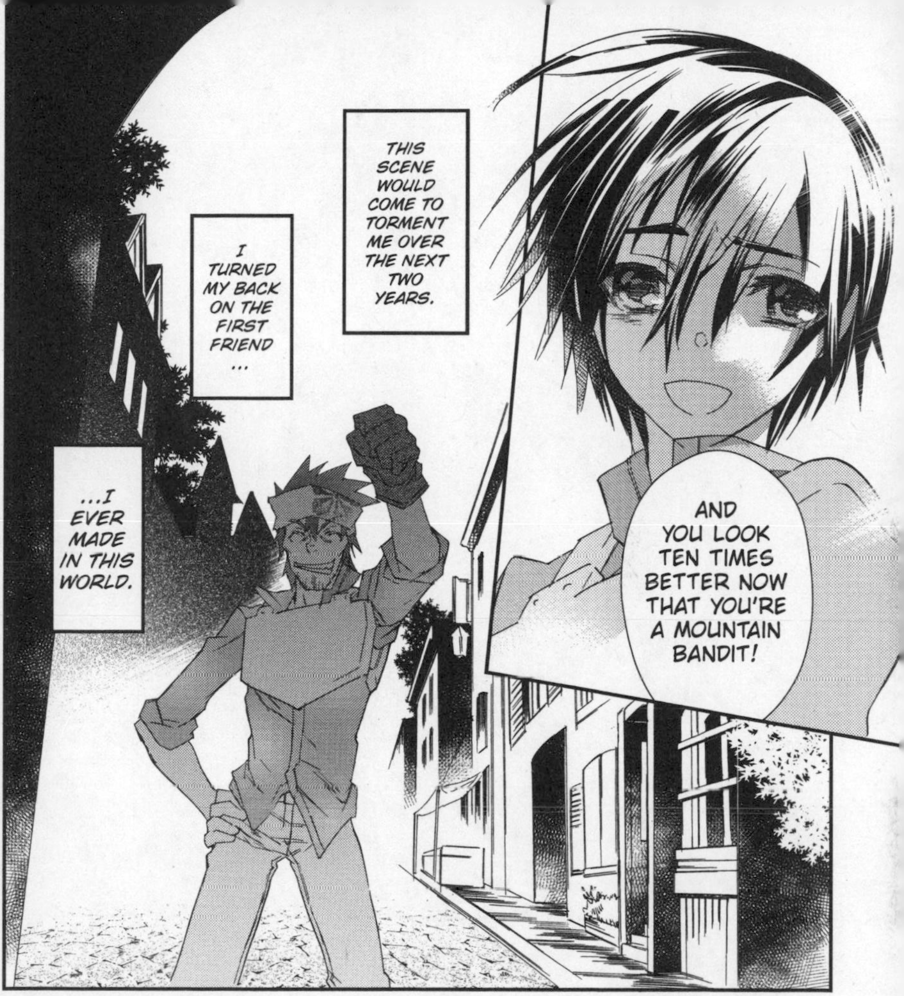
AND YOU LOOK TEN TIMES BETTER NOW THAT YOU'RE A MOUNTAIN BANDIT!
THIS SCENE WOULD COME TO TORMENT ME OVER THE NEXT TWO YEARS.
I TURNED MY BACK ON THE FIRST FRIEND...
...I EVER MADE IN THIS WORLD.

I DIDN'T STICK AROUND TO SEE IT, BUT FROM WHAT I HEAR, THE PANIC IN THE SQUARE THAT DAY WAS FRIGHTENING TO BEHOLD.

THE OUTSIDE WORLD NEVER MANAGED TO SOLVE OUR QUANDARY.

WITHIN A MONTH OF THE GAME'S RELEASE, TWO THOUSAND OF THE ORIGINAL TEN THOUSAND PLAYERS WERE DEAD.

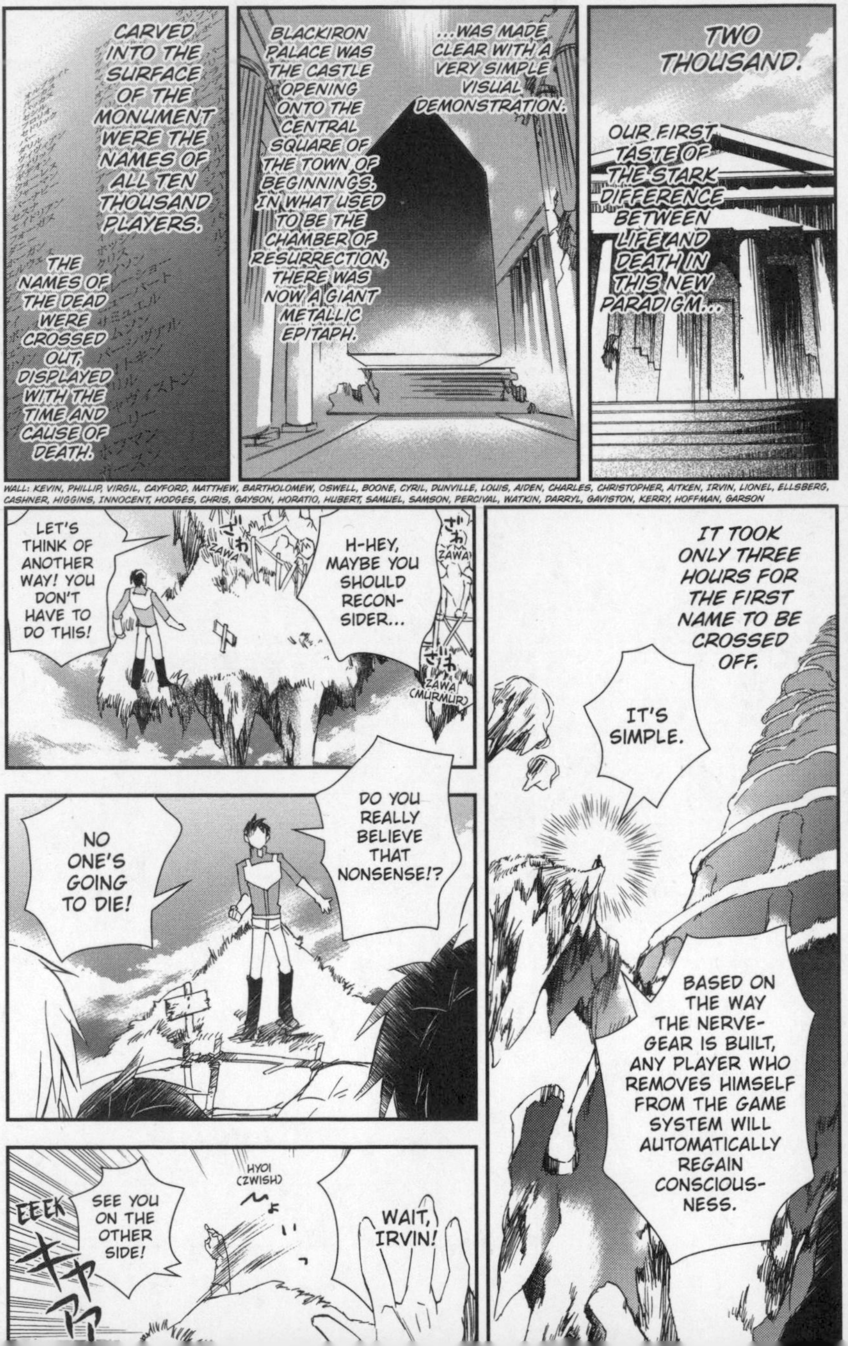
TWO THOUSAND.
OUR FIRST TASTE OF THE STARK DIFFERENCE BETWEEN LIFE AND DEATH IN THIS NEW PARADIGM...
...WAS MADE CLEAR WITH A VERY SIMPLE VISUAL DEMONSTRATION.
BLACKIRON PALACE WAS THE CASTLE OPENING ONTO THE CENTRAL SQUARE OF THE TOWN OF BEGINNINGS. IN WHAT USED TO BE THE CHAMBER OF RESURRECTION, THERE WAS NOW A GIANT METALLIC EPITAPH.
CARVED INTO THE SURFACE OF THE MONUMENT WERE THE NAMES OF ALL TEN THOUSAND PLAYERS.
THE NAMES OF THE DEAD WERE CROSSED OUT, DISPLAYED WITH THE TIME AND CAUSE OF DEATH.
WALL: KEVIN, PHILLIP, VIRGIL, CAYFORD, MATTHEW, BARTHOLOMEW, OSWELL, BOONE, CYRIL, DUNVILLE, LOUIS, AIDEN, CHARLES, CHRISTOPHER, AITKEN, IRVIN, LIONEL, ELLSBERG, CASHNER, HIGGINS, INNOCENT, HODGES, CHRIS, GAYSON, HORATIO, HUBERT, SAMUEL, SAMSON, PERCIVAL, WATKIN, DARRYL, GAVISTON, KERRY, HOFFMAN, GARSON
IT TOOK ONLY THREE HOURS FOR THE FIRST NAME TO BE CROSSED OFF.
IT'S SIMPLE.
BASED ON THE WAY THE NERVE-GEAR IS BUILT, ANY PLAYER WHO REMOVES HIMSELF FROM THE GAME SYSTEM WILL AUTOMATICALLY REGAIN CONSCIOUS-NESS.
ZAWA
ZAWA (MURMUR)
H-HEY, MAYBE YOU SHOULD RECON-SIDER...
ZAWA
LET'S THINK OF ANOTHER WAY! YOU DON'T HAVE TO DO THIS!
DO YOU REALLY BELIEVE THAT NONSENSE!?
NO ONE'S GOING TO DIE!
WAIT, IRVIN!
HYOI (ZWISH)
SEE YOU ON THE OTHER SIDE!
EEEK

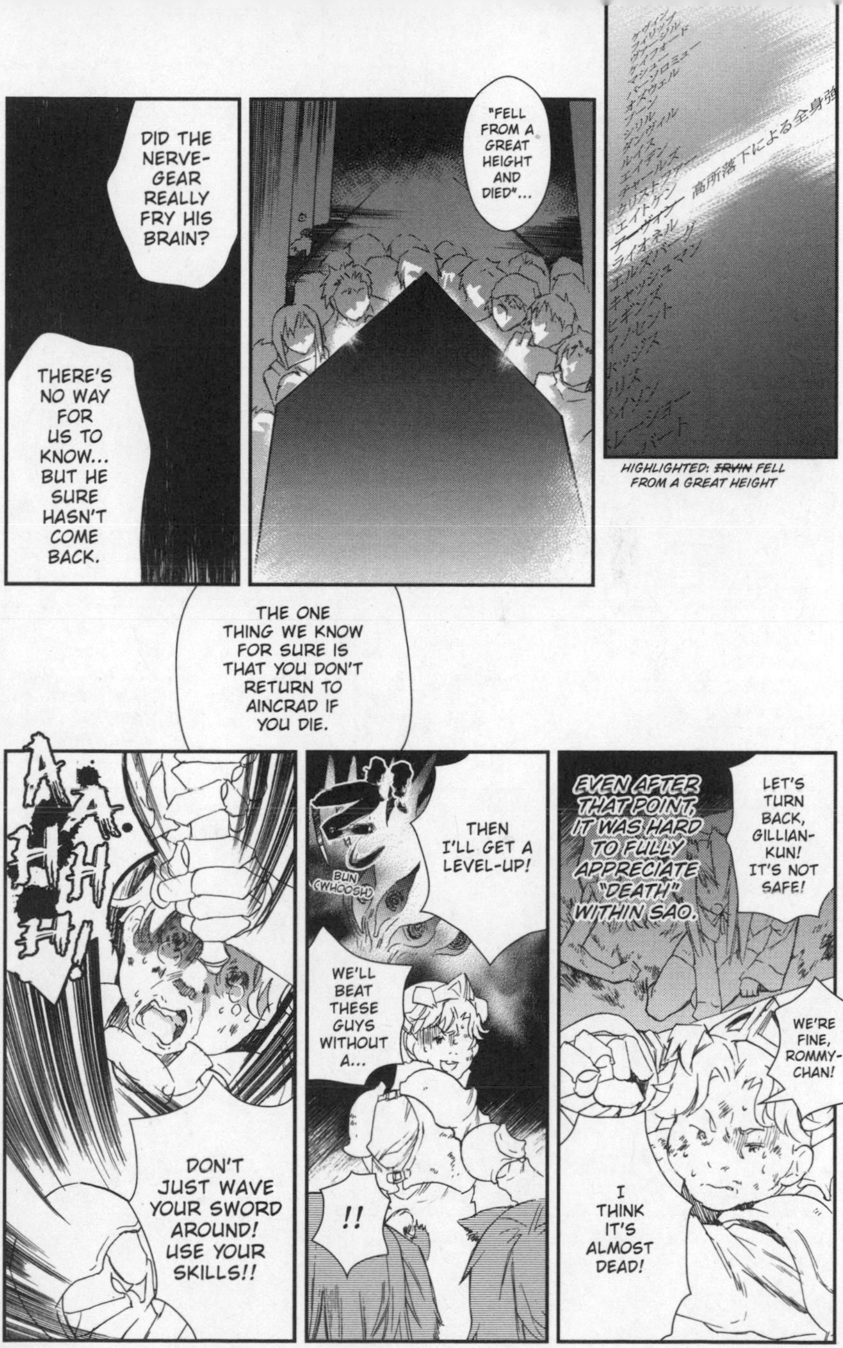
高所落下による全身強
HIGHLIGHTED: ~~IRVIN~~ FELL FROM A GREAT HEIGHT
"FELL FROM A GREAT HEIGHT AND DIED"...
DID THE NERVEGEAR REALLY FRY HIS BRAIN?
THERE'S NO WAY FOR US TO KNOW... BUT HE SURE HASN'T COME BACK.
THE ONE THING WE KNOW FOR SURE IS THAT YOU DON'T RETURN TO AINCRAD IF YOU DIE.
EVEN AFTER THAT POINT, IT WAS HARD TO FULLY APPRECIATE "DEATH" WITHIN SAO.
LET'S TURN BACK, GILLIAN-KUN! IT'S NOT SAFE!
WE'RE FINE, ROMMY-CHAN!
I THINK IT'S ALMOST DEAD!
THEN I'LL GET A LEVEL-UP!
BUN (WHOOSH)
WE'LL BEAT THESE GUYS WITHOUT A...
!!
AAHHH!
DON'T JUST WAVE YOUR SWORD AROUND! USE YOUR SKILLS!!

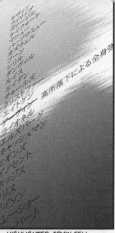

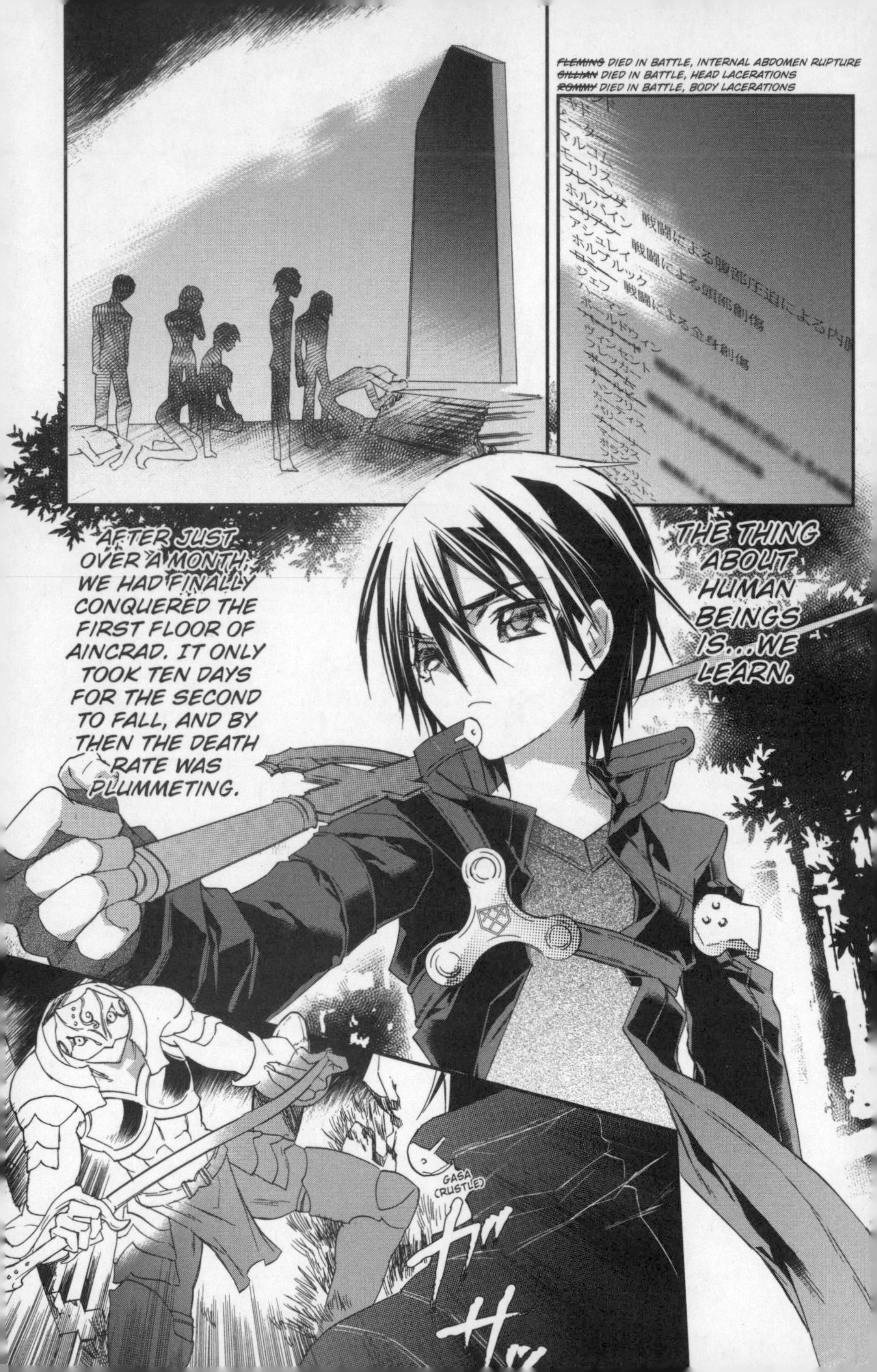
~~FLEMING~~ DIED IN BATTLE, INTERNAL ABDOMEN RUPTURE
~~GILLIAN~~ DIED IN BATTLE, HEAD LACERATIONS
~~ROMMY~~ DIED IN BATTLE, BODY LACERATIONS
THE THING ABOUT HUMAN BEINGS IS...WE LEARN.
AFTER JUST OVER A MONTH, WE HAD FINALLY CONQUERED THE FIRST FLOOR OF AINCRAD. IT ONLY TOOK TEN DAYS FOR THE SECOND TO FALL, AND BY THEN THE DEATH RATE WAS PLUMMETING.
GASA (RUSTLE)

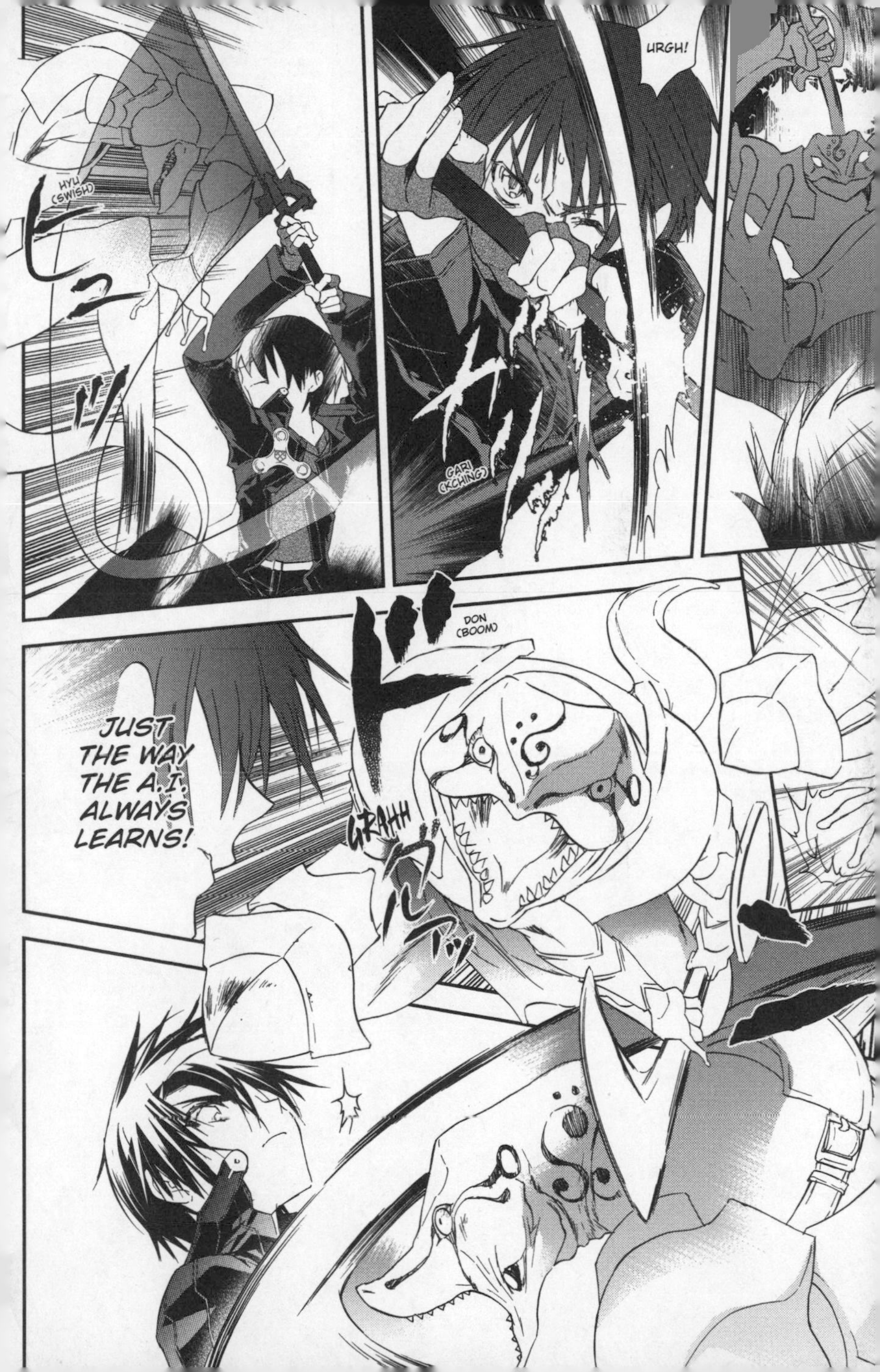
URGH!
GARI (KCHING)
HYU (SWISH)
DON (BOOM)
JUST THE WAY THE A.I. ALWAYS LEARNS!
GRAHH

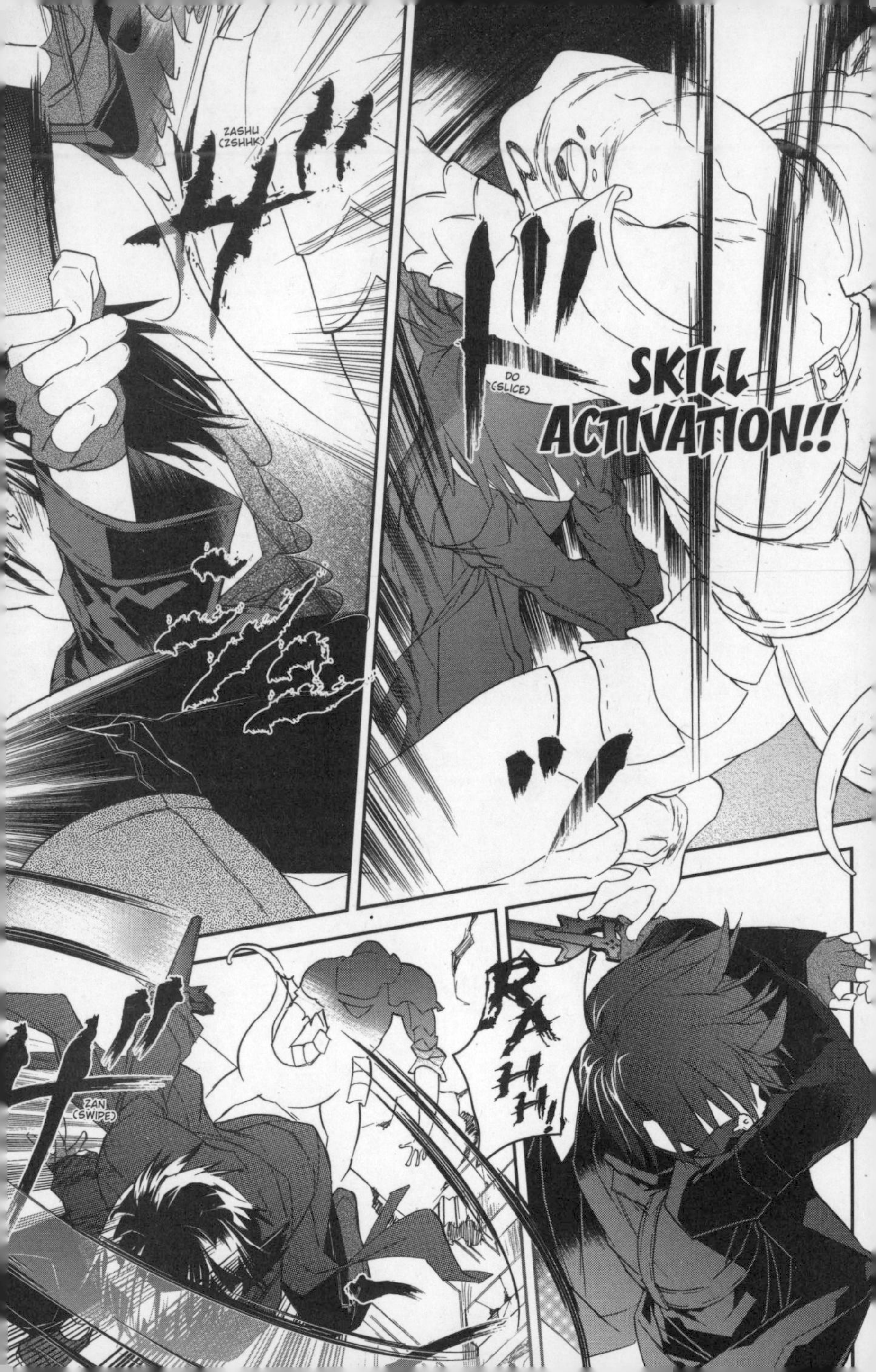
SKILL ACTIVATION!!
DO (SLICE)
ZASHU (ZSHHK)
RAHH!
ZAN (SWIPE)

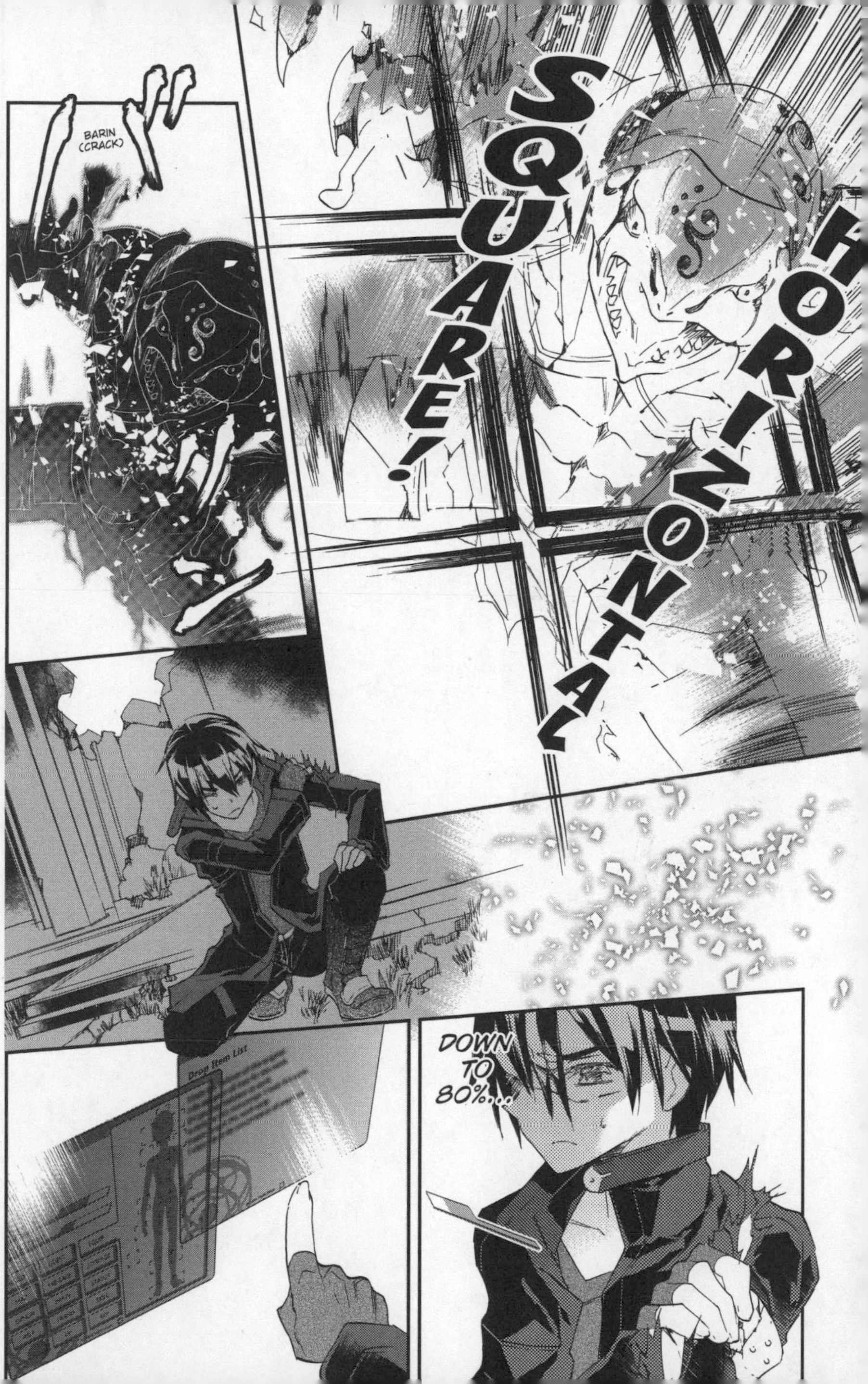
HORIZONTAL SQUARE!
BARIN (CRACK)
DOWN TO 80%...
Drop Item List

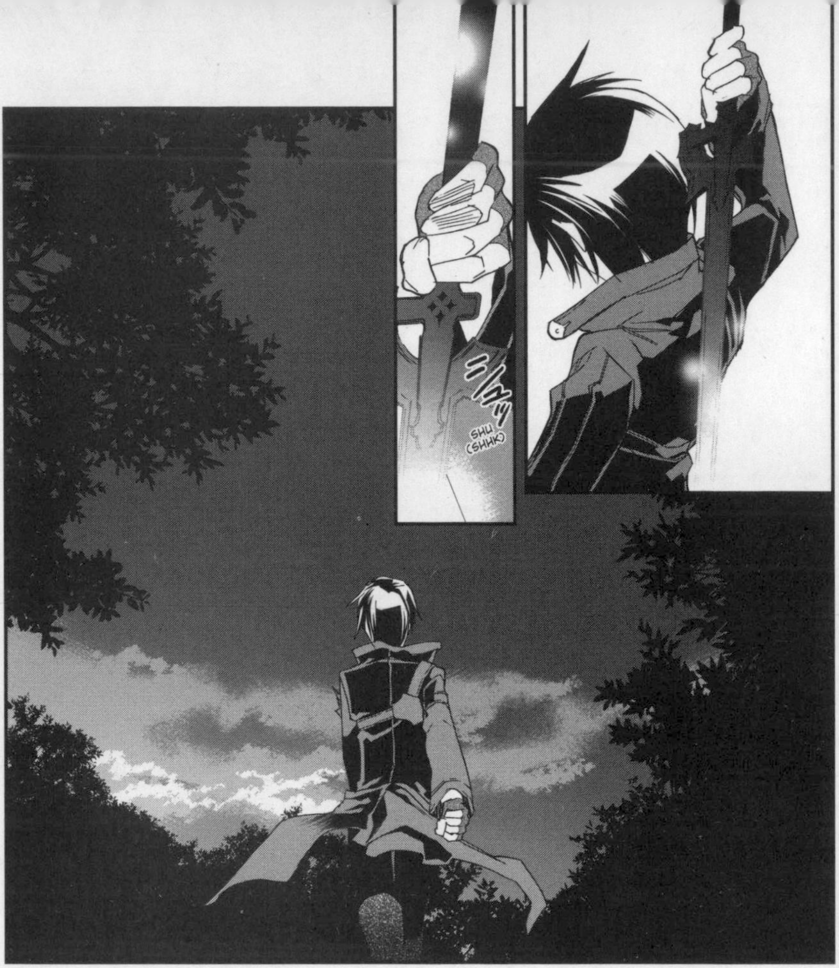
SHU
(SHHK)

IT'S BEEN TWO YEARS. THERE ARE TWENTY-SIX FLOORS LEFT TO CONQUER AND SIX THOUSAND SURVIVORS.

SUCH IS THE PRESENT STATE OF AINCRAD.

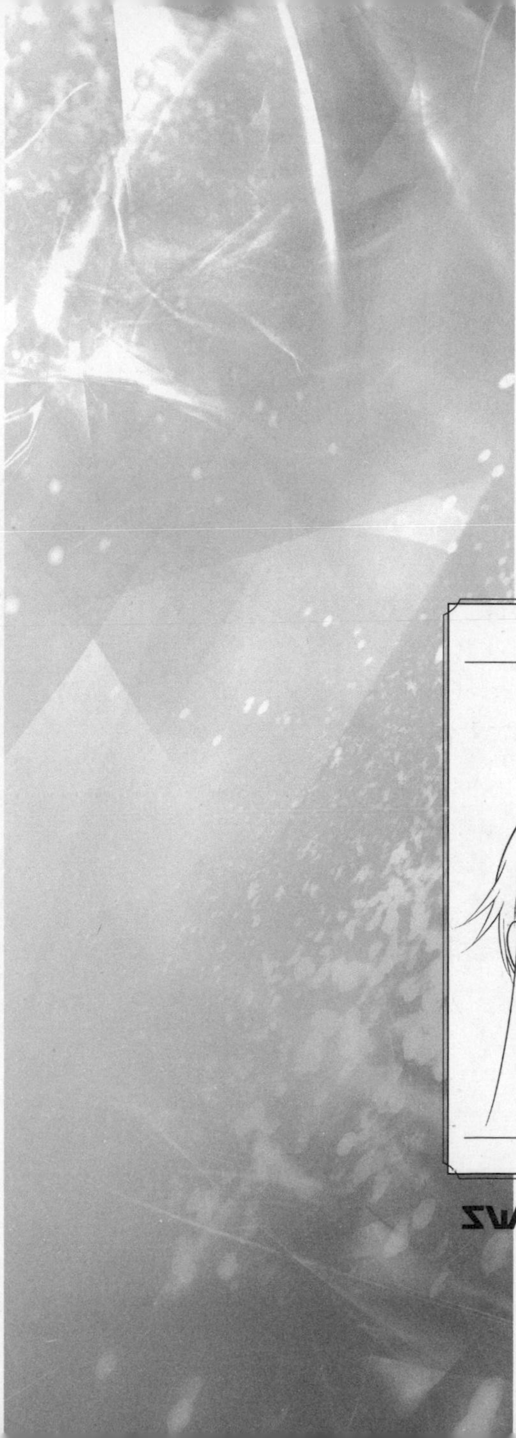

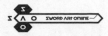

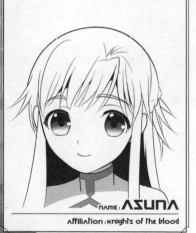

character

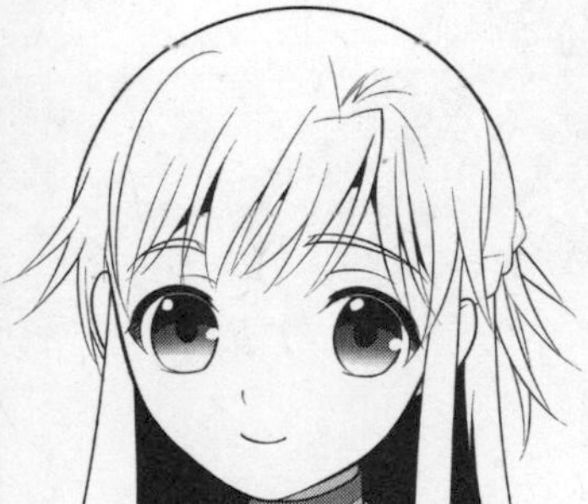

name : ASUNA

Affiliation : knights of the blood

SWORD ART ONLINE
Aincrad

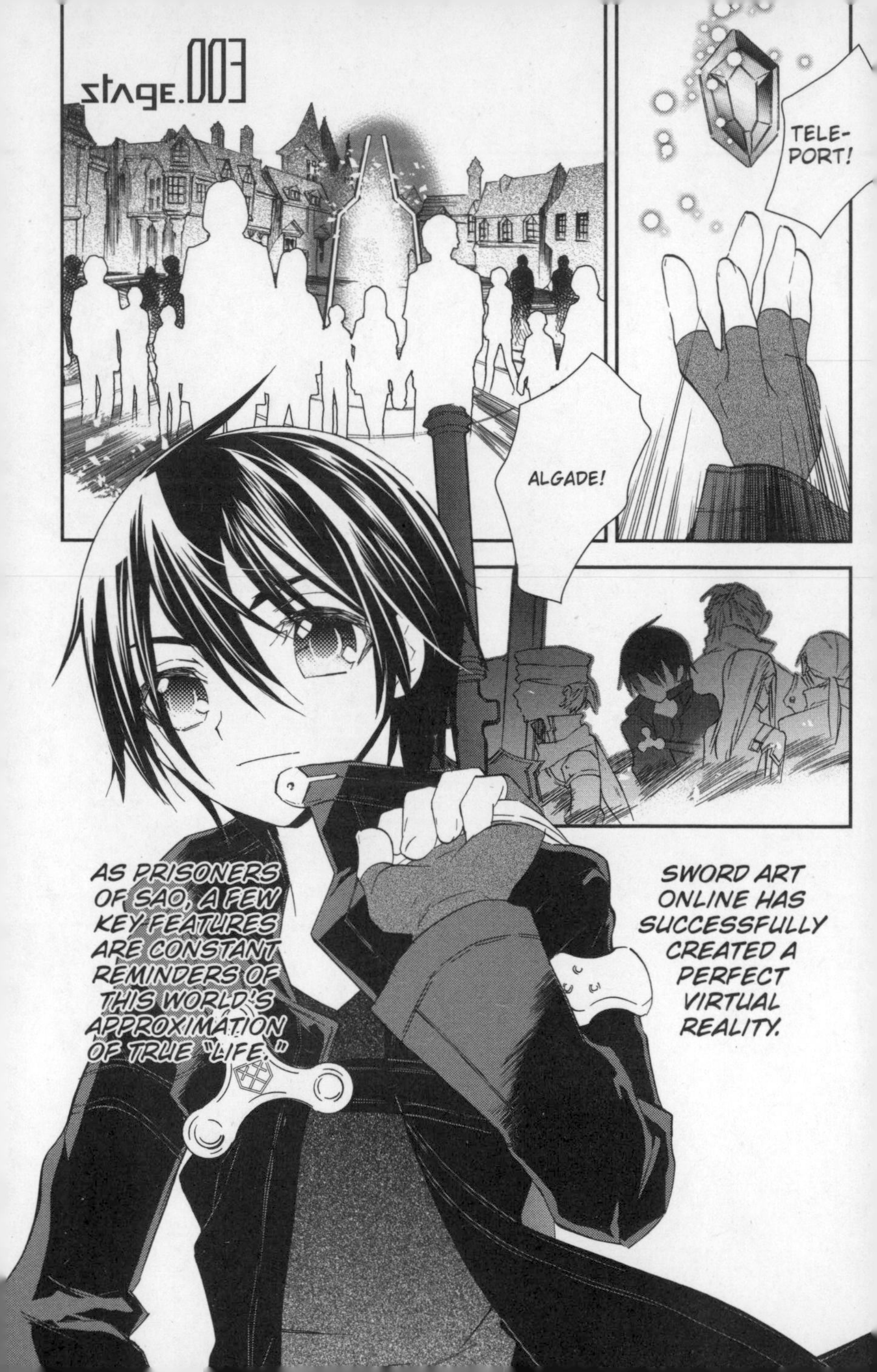
TELE-PORT!
ALGADE!
stage.003
SWORD ART ONLINE HAS SUCCESSFULLY CREATED A PERFECT VIRTUAL REALITY.
AS PRISONERS OF SAO, A FEW KEY FEATURES ARE CONSTANT REMINDERS OF THIS WORLD'S APPROXIMATION OF TRUE "LIFE."

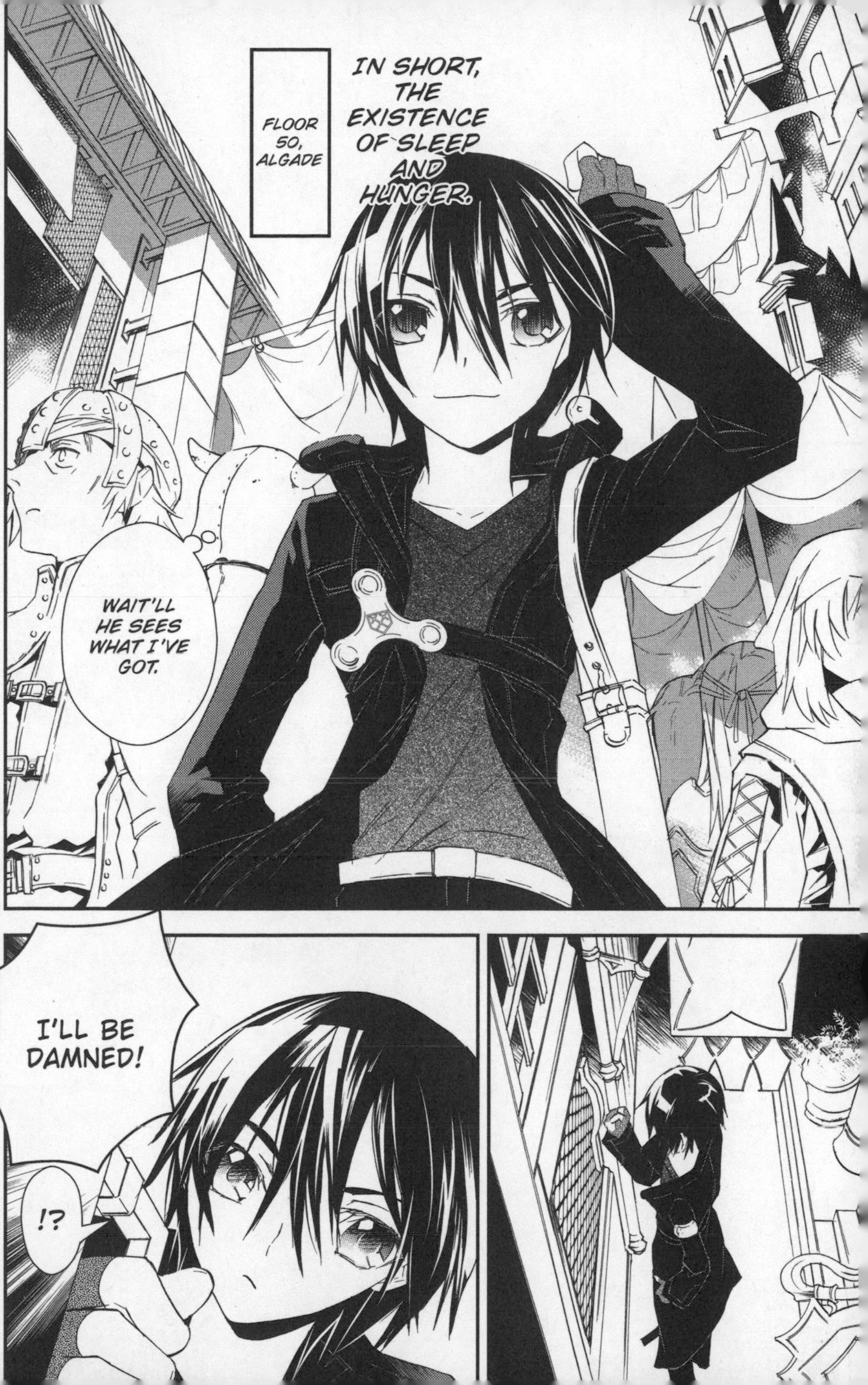
IN SHORT, THE EXISTENCE OF SLEEP AND HUNGER.
FLOOR 50, ALGADE
WAIT'LL HE SEES WHAT I'VE GOT.
I'LL BE DAMNED!
!?

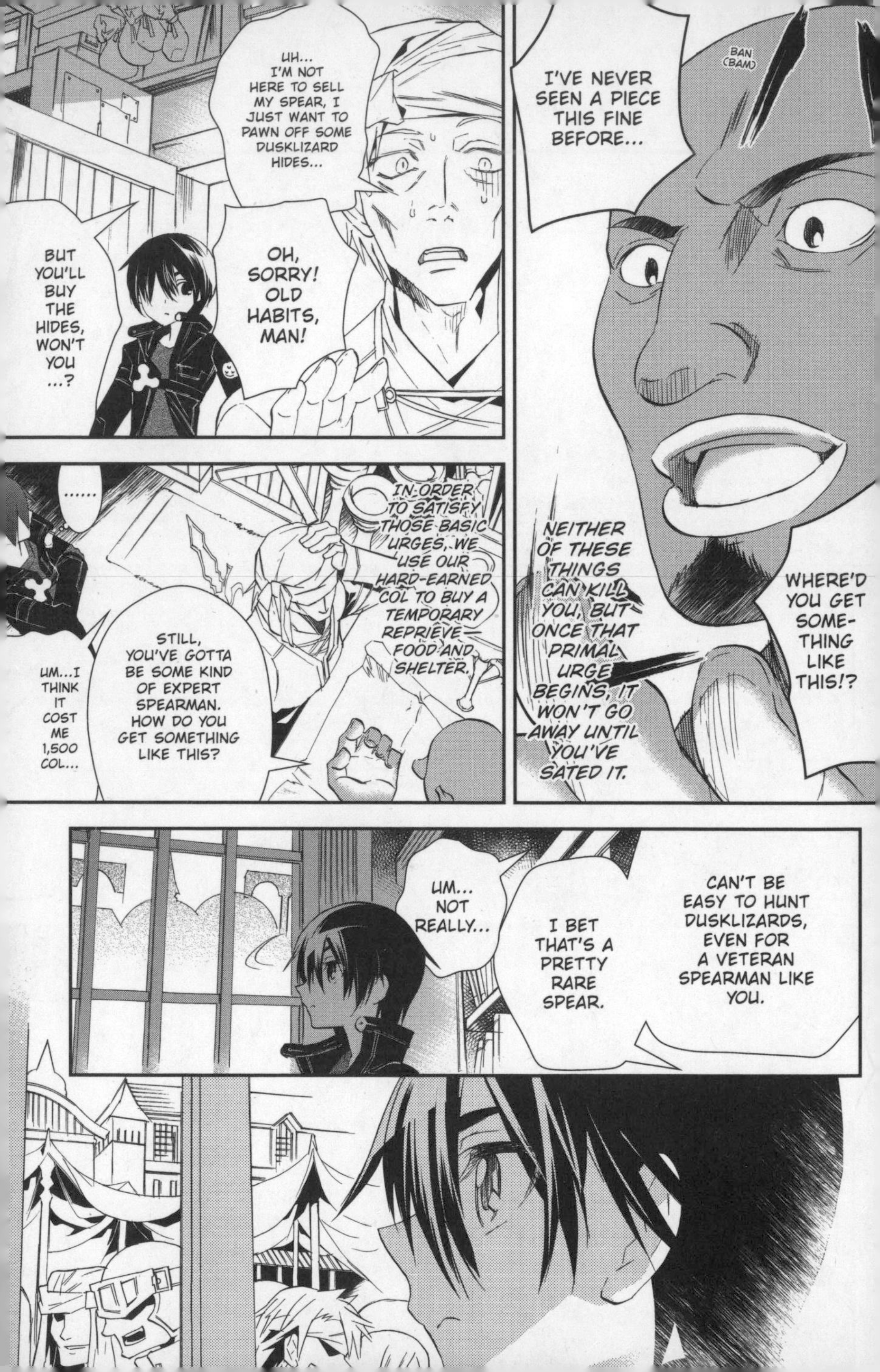
BAN (BAM)
I'VE NEVER SEEN A PIECE THIS FINE BEFORE...
WHERE'D YOU GET SOME-THING LIKE THIS!?
NEITHER OF THESE THINGS CAN KILL YOU, BUT ONCE THAT PRIMAL URGE BEGINS, IT WON'T GO AWAY UNTIL YOU'VE SATED IT.
UH... I'M NOT HERE TO SELL MY SPEAR, I JUST WANT TO PAWN OFF SOME DUSKLIZARD HIDES...
OH, SORRY! OLD HABITS, MAN!
BUT YOU'LL BUY THE HIDES, WON'T YOU ...?
IN ORDER TO SATISFY THOSE BASIC URGES, WE USE OUR HARD-EARNED COL TO BUY A TEMPORARY REPRIEVE—FOOD AND SHELTER.
......
STILL, YOU'VE GOTTA BE SOME KIND OF EXPERT SPEARMAN. HOW DO YOU GET SOMETHING LIKE THIS?
UM...I THINK IT COST ME 1,500 COL...
CAN'T BE EASY TO HUNT DUSKLIZARDS, EVEN FOR A VETERAN SPEARMAN LIKE YOU.
I BET THAT'S A PRETTY RARE SPEAR.
UM... NOT REALLY...

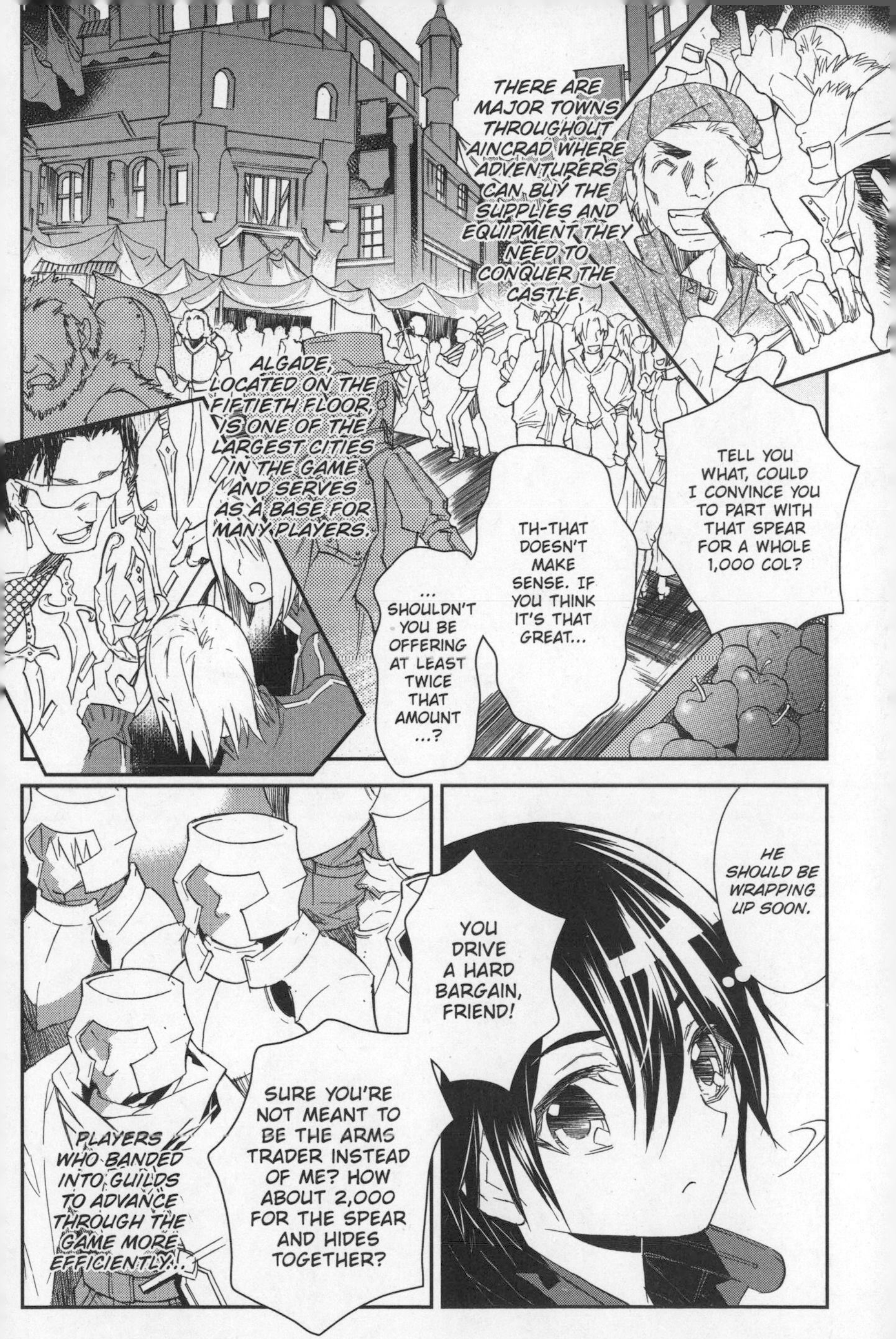
THERE ARE MAJOR TOWNS THROUGHOUT AINCRAD WHERE ADVENTURERS CAN BUY THE SUPPLIES AND EQUIPMENT THEY NEED TO CONQUER THE CASTLE.
ALGADE, LOCATED ON THE FIFTIETH FLOOR, IS ONE OF THE LARGEST CITIES IN THE GAME AND SERVES AS A BASE FOR MANY PLAYERS.
TELL YOU WHAT, COULD I CONVINCE YOU TO PART WITH THAT SPEAR FOR A WHOLE 1,000 COL?
TH-THAT DOESN'T MAKE SENSE. IF YOU THINK IT'S THAT GREAT...
... SHOULDN'T YOU BE OFFERING AT LEAST TWICE THAT AMOUNT ...?
HE SHOULD BE WRAPPING UP SOON.
YOU DRIVE A HARD BARGAIN, FRIEND!
SURE YOU'RE NOT MEANT TO BE THE ARMS TRADER INSTEAD OF ME? HOW ABOUT 2,000 FOR THE SPEAR AND HIDES TOGETHER?
PLAYERS WHO BANDED INTO GUILDS TO ADVANCE THROUGH THE GAME MORE EFFICIENTLY...

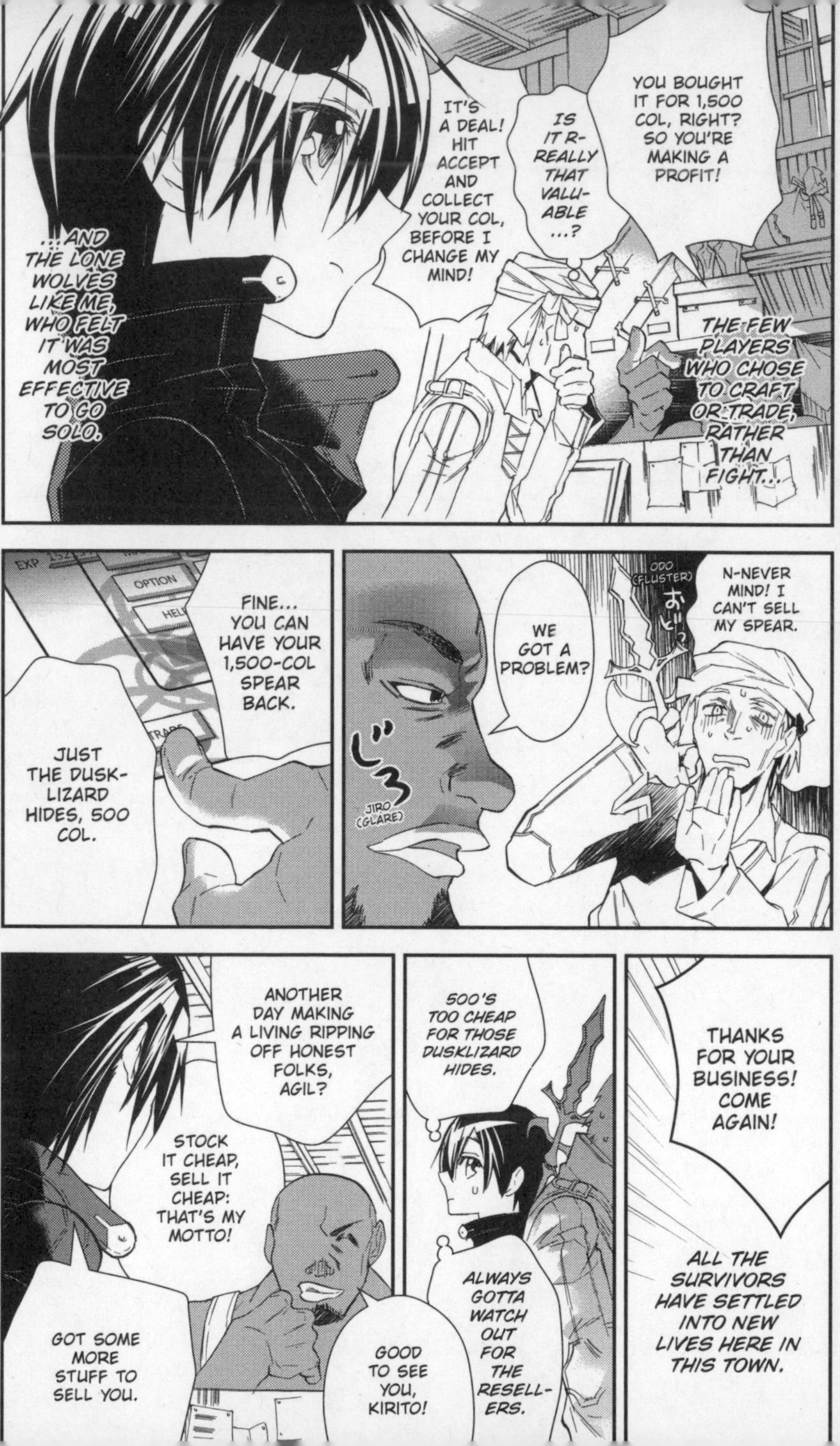
YOU BOUGHT IT FOR 1,500 COL, RIGHT? SO YOU'RE MAKING A PROFIT!
IS IT R-REALLY THAT VALUABLE ...?
IT'S A DEAL! HIT ACCEPT AND COLLECT YOUR COL, BEFORE I CHANGE MY MIND!
THE FEW PLAYERS WHO CHOSE TO CRAFT OR TRADE, RATHER THAN FIGHT...
...AND THE LONE WOLVES LIKE ME, WHO FELT IT WAS MOST EFFECTIVE TO GO SOLO.
N-NEVER MIND! I CAN'T SELL MY SPEAR.
ODO (FLUSTER)
WE GOT A PROBLEM?
JIRO (GLARE)
FINE... YOU CAN HAVE YOUR 1,500-COL SPEAR BACK.
JUST THE DUSK-LIZARD HIDES, 500 COL.
THANKS FOR YOUR BUSINESS! COME AGAIN!
ALL THE SURVIVORS HAVE SETTLED INTO NEW LIVES HERE IN THIS TOWN.
500'S TOO CHEAP FOR THOSE DUSKLIZARD HIDES.
ALWAYS GOTTA WATCH OUT FOR THE RESELLERS.
ANOTHER DAY MAKING A LIVING RIPPING OFF HONEST FOLKS, AGIL?
STOCK IT CHEAP, SELL IT CHEAP: THAT'S MY MOTTO!
GOOD TO SEE YOU, KIRITO!
GOT SOME MORE STUFF TO SELL YOU.

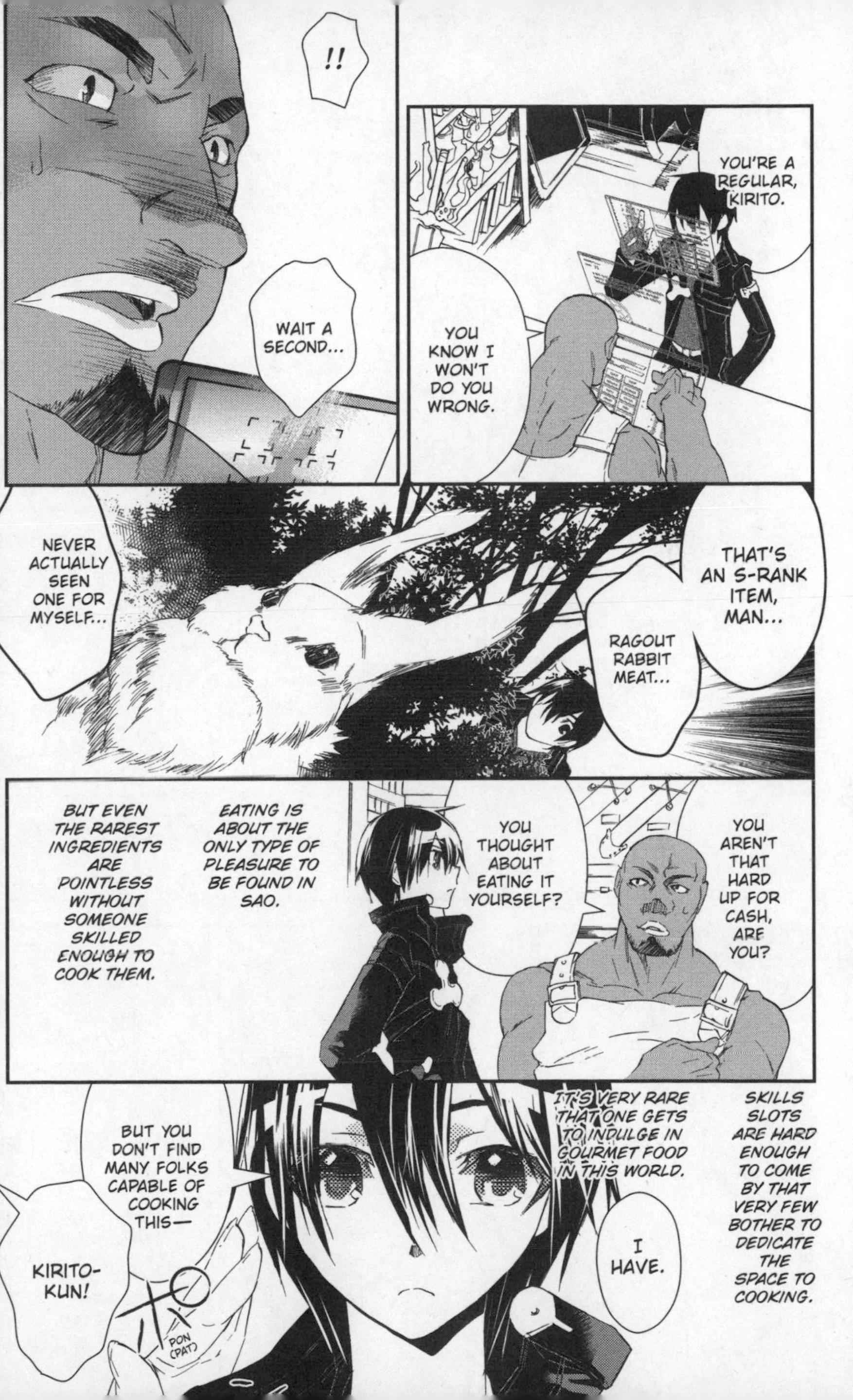
YOU'RE A REGULAR, KIRITO.
YOU KNOW I WON'T DO YOU WRONG.
!!
WAIT A SECOND...
THAT'S AN S-RANK ITEM, MAN...
RAGOUT RABBIT MEAT...
NEVER ACTUALLY SEEN ONE FOR MYSELF...
YOU AREN'T THAT HARD UP FOR CASH, ARE YOU?
YOU THOUGHT ABOUT EATING IT YOURSELF?
EATING IS ABOUT THE ONLY TYPE OF PLEASURE TO BE FOUND IN SAO.
BUT EVEN THE RAREST INGREDIENTS ARE POINTLESS WITHOUT SOMEONE SKILLED ENOUGH TO COOK THEM.
SKILLS SLOTS ARE HARD ENOUGH TO COME BY THAT VERY FEW BOTHER TO DEDICATE THE SPACE TO COOKING.
IT'S VERY RARE THAT ONE GETS TO INDULGE IN GOURMET FOOD IN THIS WORLD.
I HAVE.
BUT YOU DON'T FIND MANY FOLKS CAPABLE OF COOKING THIS—
KIRITO-KUN!
PON (PAT)

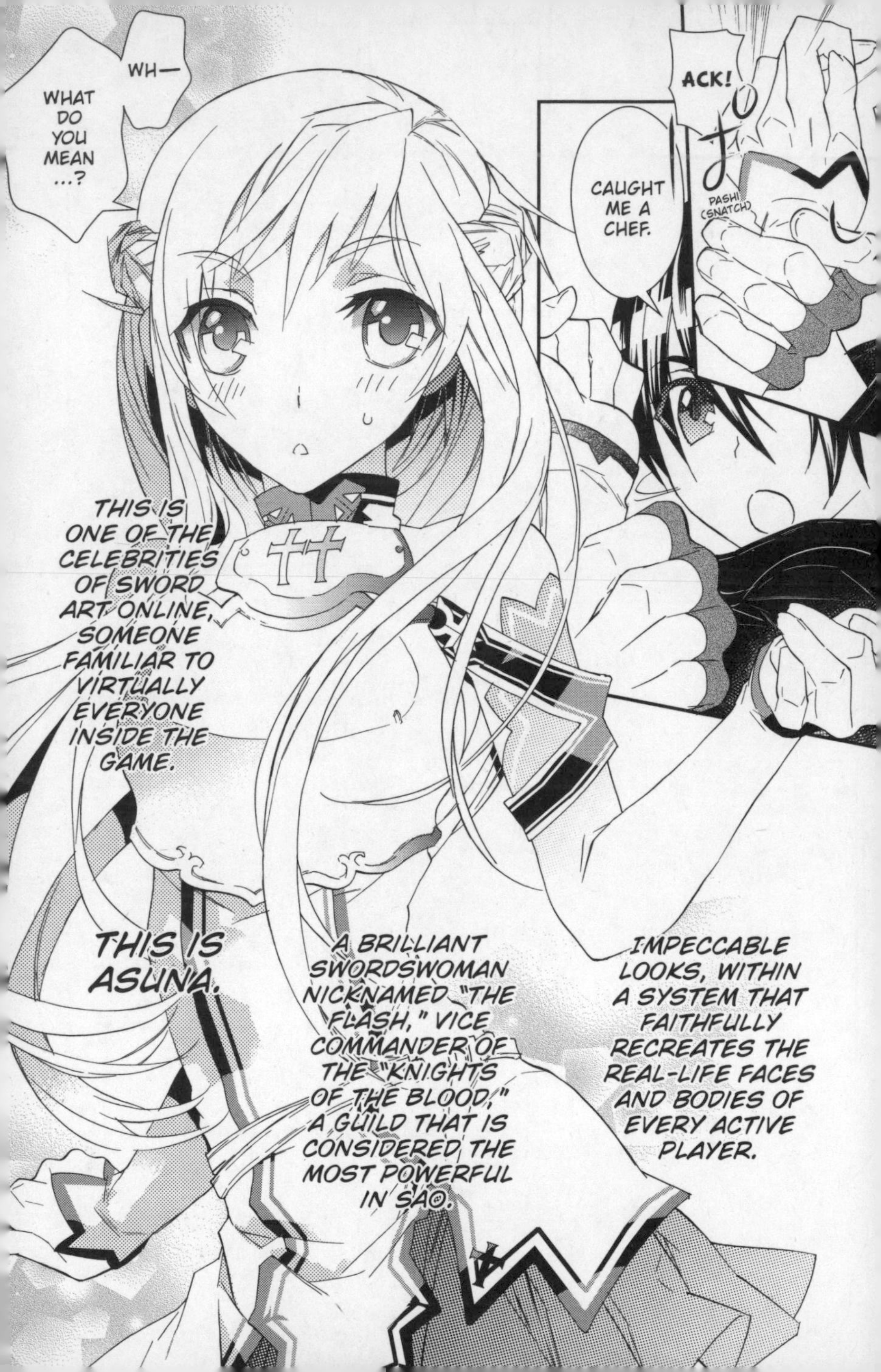
ACK!
PASHI (SNATCH)
CAUGHT ME A CHEF.
WH—
WHAT DO YOU MEAN ...?
THIS IS ONE OF THE CELEBRITIES OF SWORD ART ONLINE, SOMEONE FAMILIAR TO VIRTUALLY EVERYONE INSIDE THE GAME.
IMPECCABLE LOOKS, WITHIN A SYSTEM THAT FAITHFULLY RECREATES THE REAL-LIFE FACES AND BODIES OF EVERY ACTIVE PLAYER.
A BRILLIANT SWORDSWOMAN NICKNAMED "THE FLASH," VICE COMMANDER OF THE "KNIGHTS OF THE BLOOD," A GUILD THAT IS CONSIDERED THE MOST POWERFUL IN SAO.
THIS IS ASUNA.

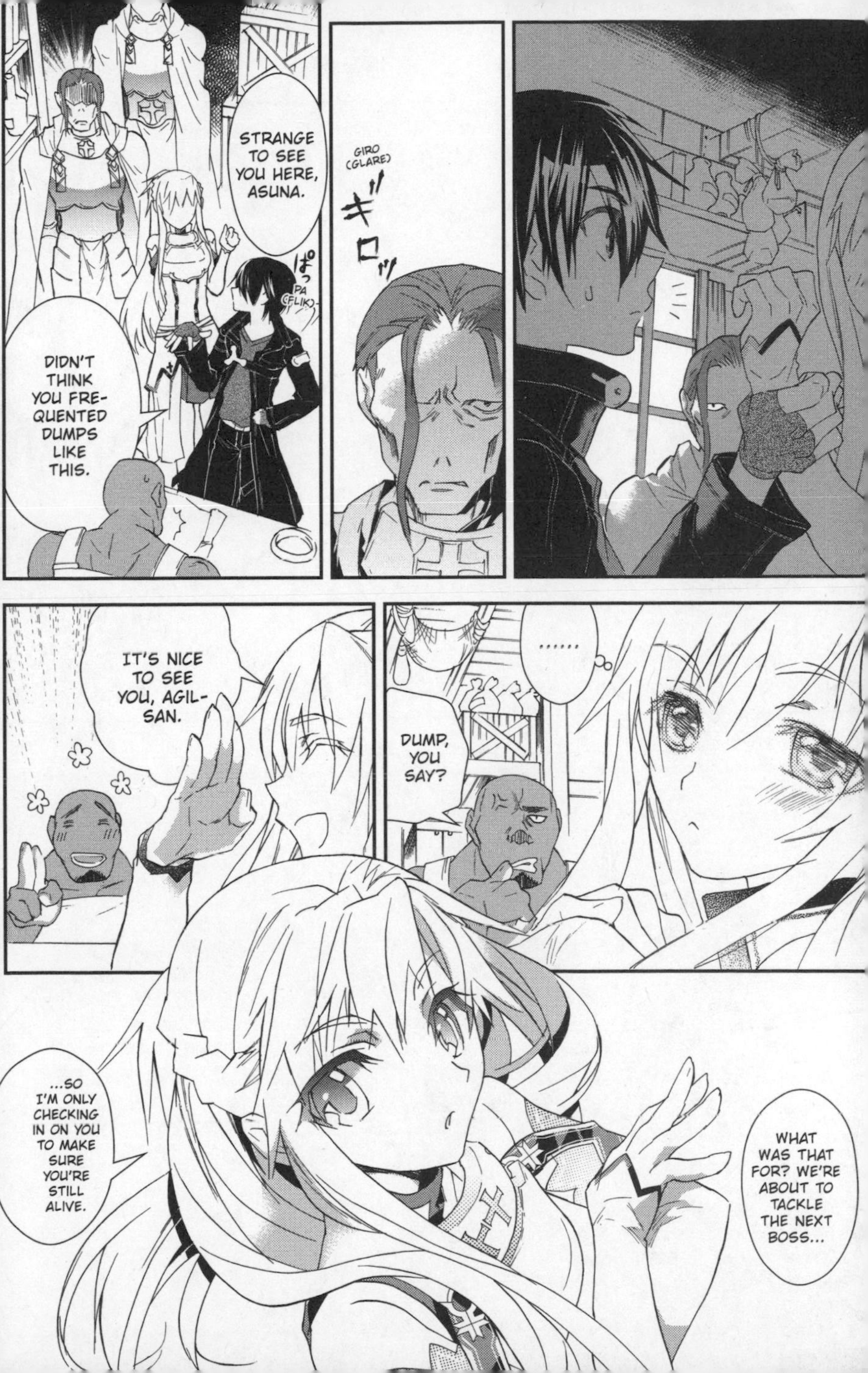
ギロッ
GIRO (GLARE)
STRANGE TO SEE YOU HERE, ASUNA.
ぱっ
PA (FLIK)
DIDN'T THINK YOU FRE-QUENTED DUMPS LIKE THIS.
......
DUMP, YOU SAY?
IT'S NICE TO SEE YOU, AGIL-SAN.
WHAT WAS THAT FOR? WE'RE ABOUT TO TACKLE THE NEXT BOSS...
...SO I'M ONLY CHECKING IN ON YOU TO MAKE SURE YOU'RE STILL ALIVE.

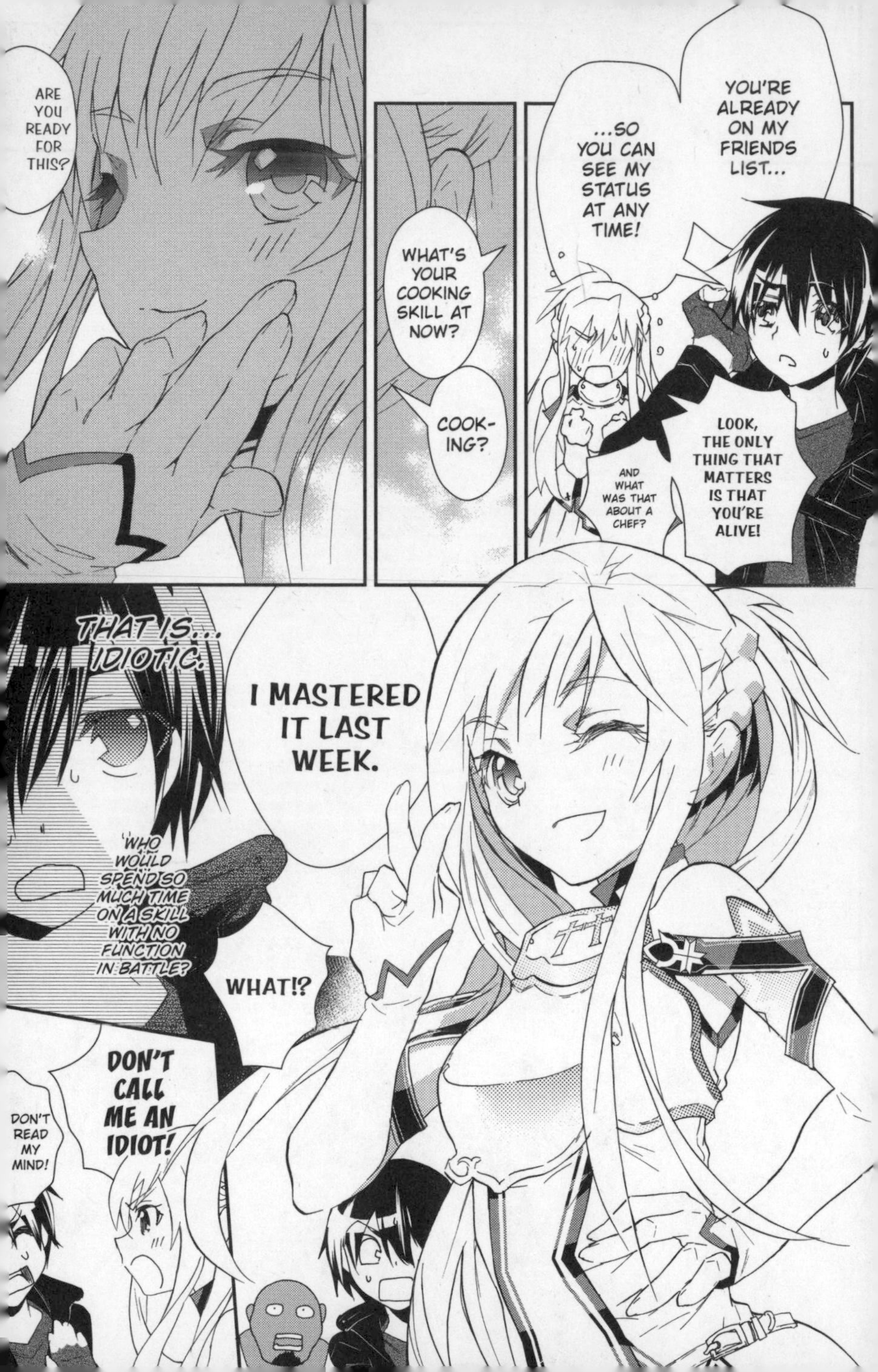
YOU'RE ALREADY ON MY FRIENDS LIST...
...SO YOU CAN SEE MY STATUS AT ANY TIME!
LOOK, THE ONLY THING THAT MATTERS IS THAT YOU'RE ALIVE!
AND WHAT WAS THAT ABOUT A CHEF?
WHAT'S YOUR COOKING SKILL AT NOW?
COOK-ING?
ARE YOU READY FOR THIS?
I MASTERED IT LAST WEEK.
THAT IS... IDIOTIC.
'WHO WOULD SPEND SO MUCH TIME ON A SKILL WITH NO FUNCTION IN BATTLE?
WHAT!?
DON'T CALL ME AN IDIOT!
DON'T READ MY MIND!

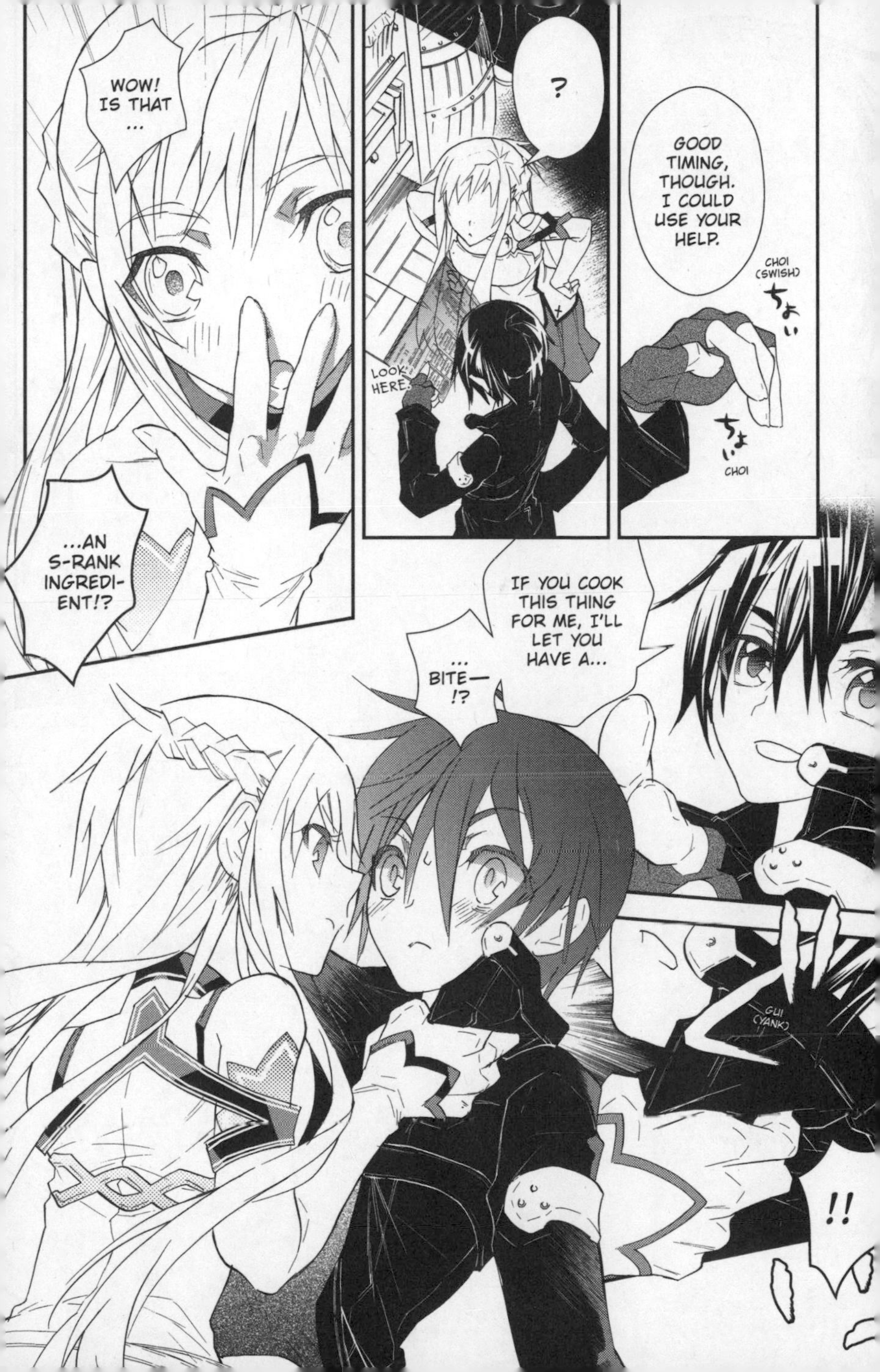
GOOD TIMING, THOUGH. I COULD USE YOUR HELP.
CHOI (SWISH)
ちょい
ちょい
CHOI
?
LOOK HERE.
WOW! IS THAT ...
...AN S-RANK INGREDIENT!?
IF YOU COOK THIS THING FOR ME, I'LL LET YOU HAVE A...
... BITE— !?
GUI (YANK)
!!

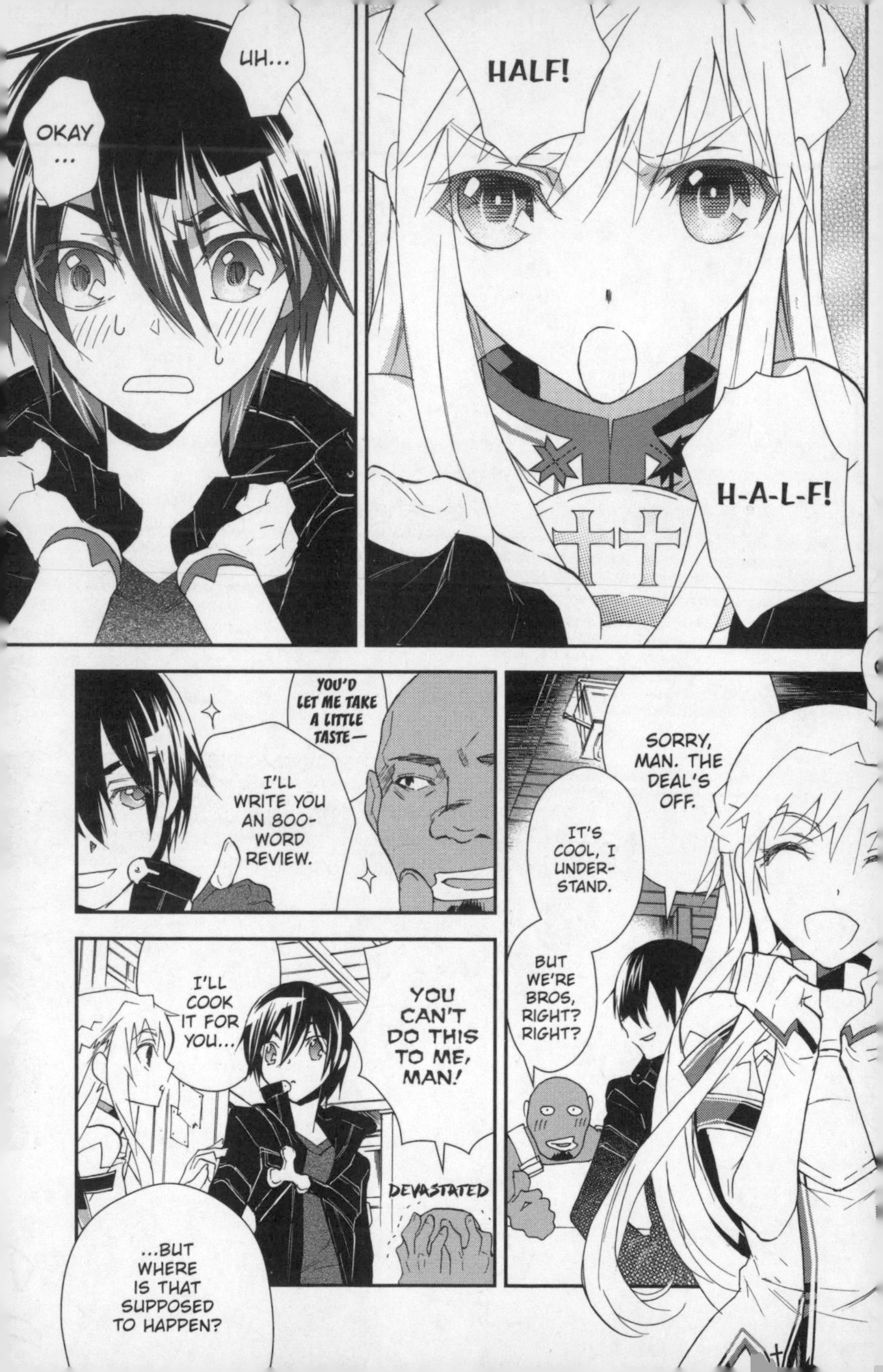
HALF!
H-A-L-F!
UH...
OKAY...
SORRY, MAN. THE DEAL'S OFF.
IT'S COOL, I UNDERSTAND.
BUT WE'RE BROS, RIGHT? RIGHT?
YOU'D LET ME TAKE A LITTLE TASTE—
I'LL WRITE YOU AN 800-WORD REVIEW.
YOU CAN'T DO THIS TO ME, MAN!
DEVASTATED
I'LL COOK IT FOR YOU...
...BUT WHERE IS THAT SUPPOSED TO HAPPEN?

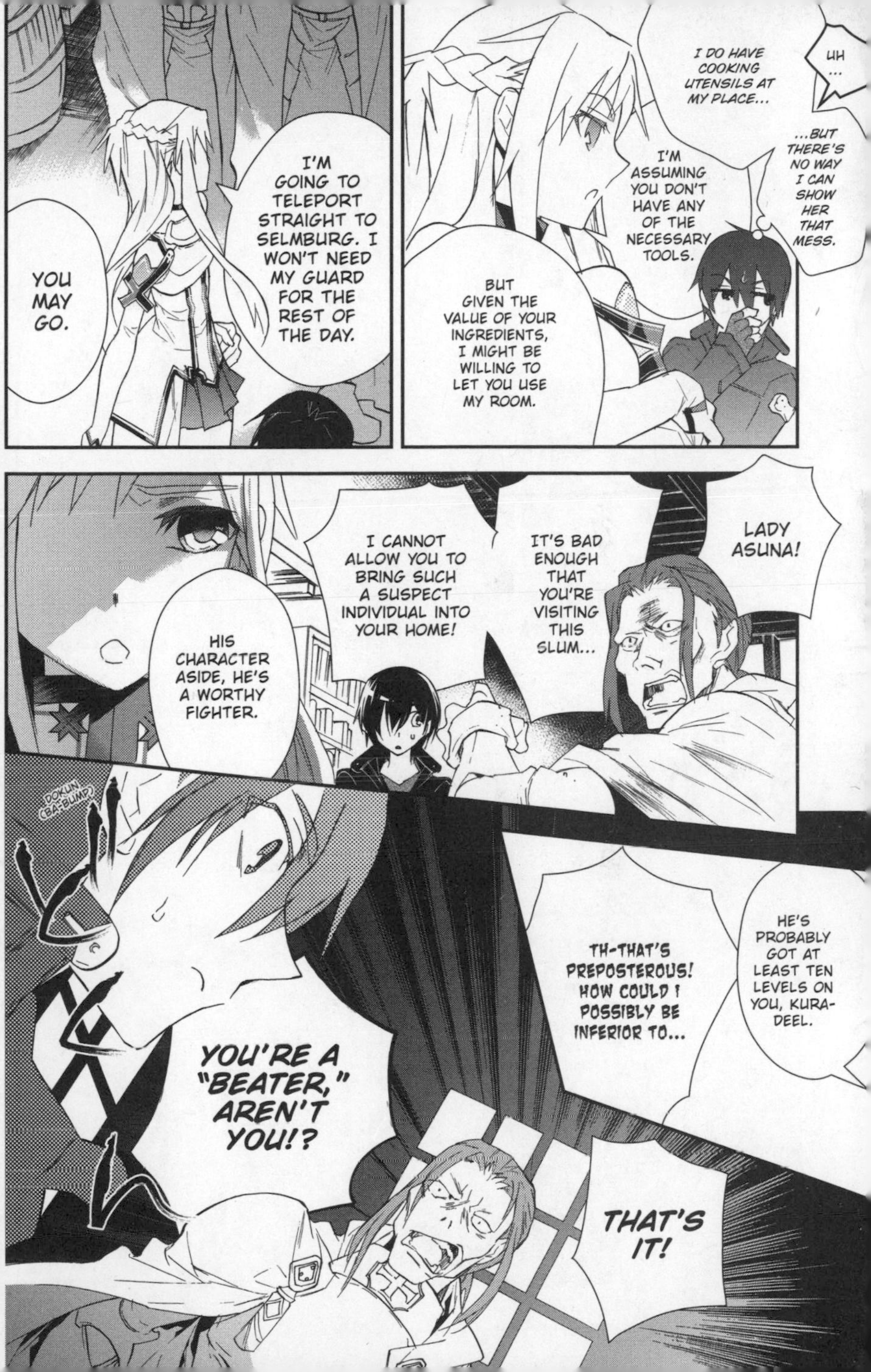
UH ...
I DO HAVE COOKING UTENSILS AT MY PLACE...
...BUT THERE'S NO WAY I CAN SHOW HER THAT MESS.
I'M ASSUMING YOU DON'T HAVE ANY OF THE NECESSARY TOOLS.
BUT GIVEN THE VALUE OF YOUR INGREDIENTS, I MIGHT BE WILLING TO LET YOU USE MY ROOM.
I'M GOING TO TELEPORT STRAIGHT TO SELMBURG. I WON'T NEED MY GUARD FOR THE REST OF THE DAY.
YOU MAY GO.
LADY ASUNA!
IT'S BAD ENOUGH THAT YOU'RE VISITING THIS SLUM...
I CANNOT ALLOW YOU TO BRING SUCH A SUSPECT INDIVIDUAL INTO YOUR HOME!
HIS CHARACTER ASIDE, HE'S A WORTHY FIGHTER.
HE'S PROBABLY GOT AT LEAST TEN LEVELS ON YOU, KURA-DEEL.
TH-THAT'S PREPOSTEROUS! HOW COULD I POSSIBLY BE INFERIOR TO...
DOKUN (BA-BUMP)
THAT'S IT!
YOU'RE A "BEATER," AREN'T YOU!?

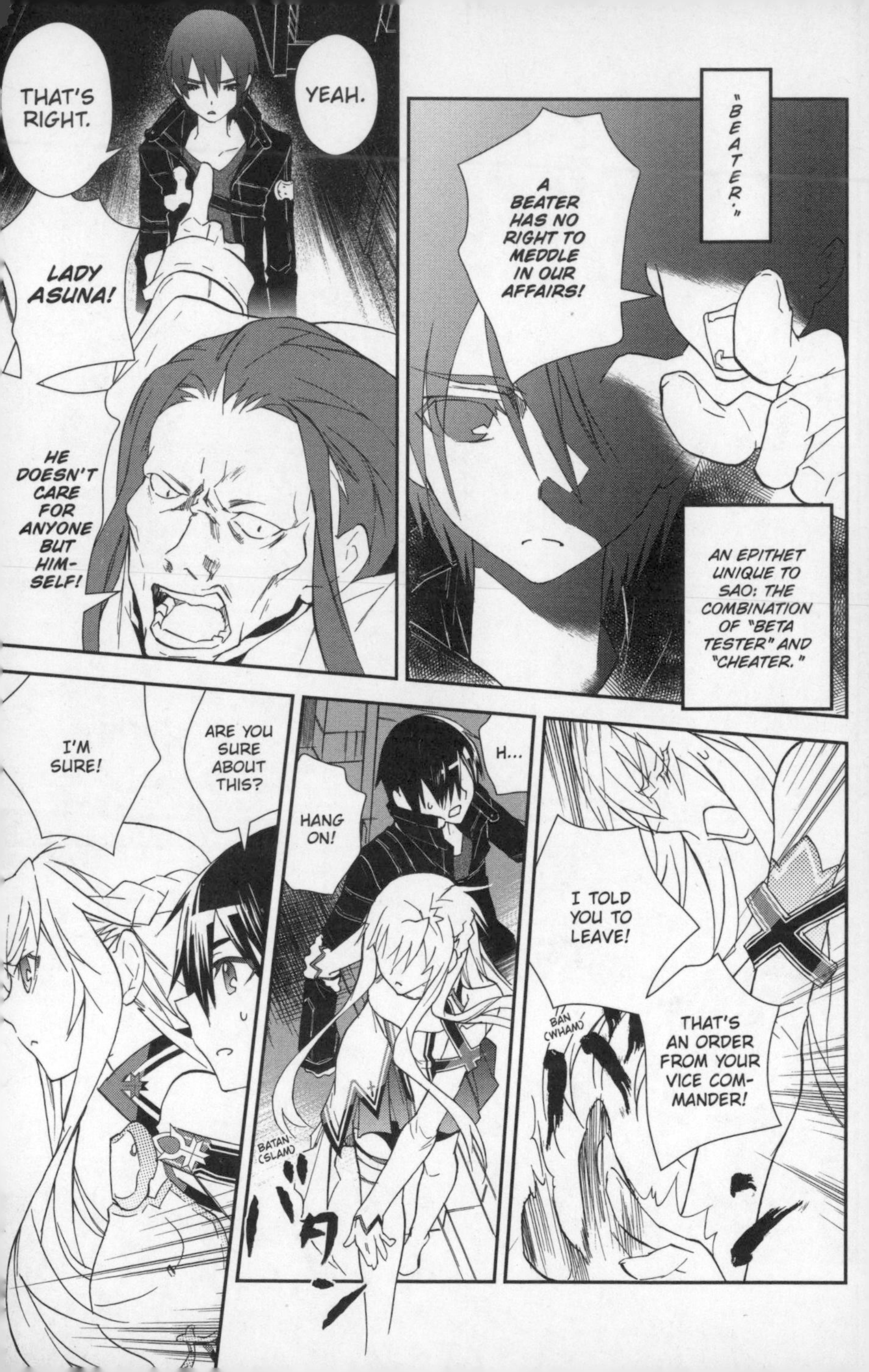
"BEATER."
A BEATER HAS NO RIGHT TO MEDDLE IN OUR AFFAIRS!
AN EPITHET UNIQUE TO SAO: THE COMBINATION OF "BETA TESTER" AND "CHEATER."
YEAH.
THAT'S RIGHT.
LADY ASUNA!
HE DOESN'T CARE FOR ANYONE BUT HIM-SELF!
I TOLD YOU TO LEAVE!
THAT'S AN ORDER FROM YOUR VICE COM-MANDER!
BAN (WHAM)
H...
HANG ON!
BATAN (SLAM)
ARE YOU SURE ABOUT THIS?
I'M SURE!

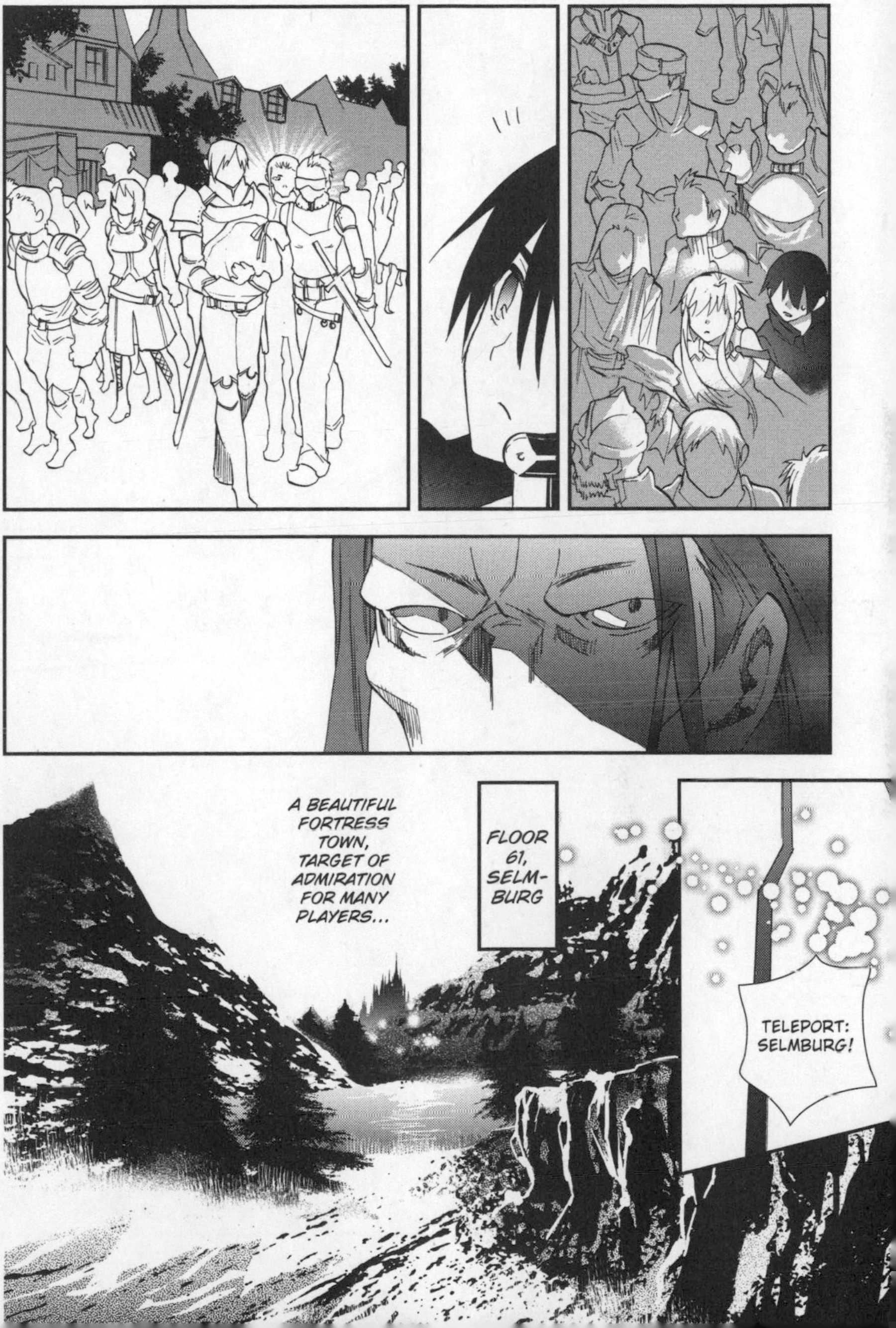
TELEPORT: SELMBURG!
FLOOR 61, SELMBURG
A BEAUTIFUL FORTRESS TOWN, TARGET OF ADMIRATION FOR MANY PLAYERS...

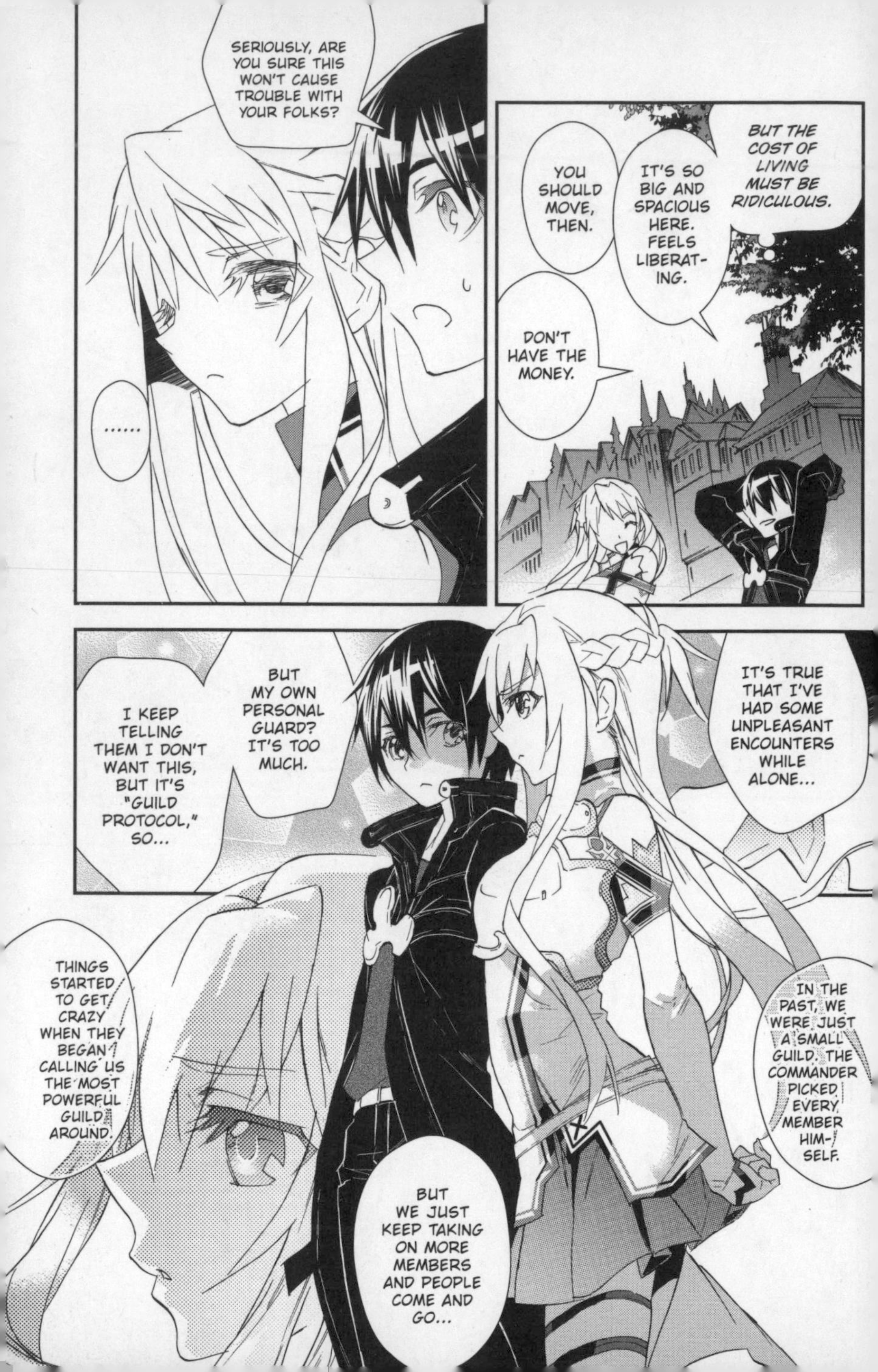
BUT THE COST OF LIVING MUST BE RIDICULOUS.
IT'S SO BIG AND SPACIOUS HERE. FEELS LIBERAT-ING.
YOU SHOULD MOVE, THEN.
DON'T HAVE THE MONEY.
SERIOUSLY, ARE YOU SURE THIS WON'T CAUSE TROUBLE WITH YOUR FOLKS?
......
IT'S TRUE THAT I'VE HAD SOME UNPLEASANT ENCOUNTERS WHILE ALONE...
BUT MY OWN PERSONAL GUARD? IT'S TOO MUCH.
I KEEP TELLING THEM I DON'T WANT THIS, BUT IT'S "GUILD PROTOCOL," SO...
IN THE PAST, WE WERE JUST A SMALL GUILD. THE COMMANDER PICKED EVERY MEMBER HIM-SELF.
THINGS STARTED TO GET CRAZY WHEN THEY BEGAN CALLING US THE MOST POWERFUL GUILD AROUND.
BUT WE JUST KEEP TAKING ON MORE MEMBERS AND PEOPLE COME AND GO...

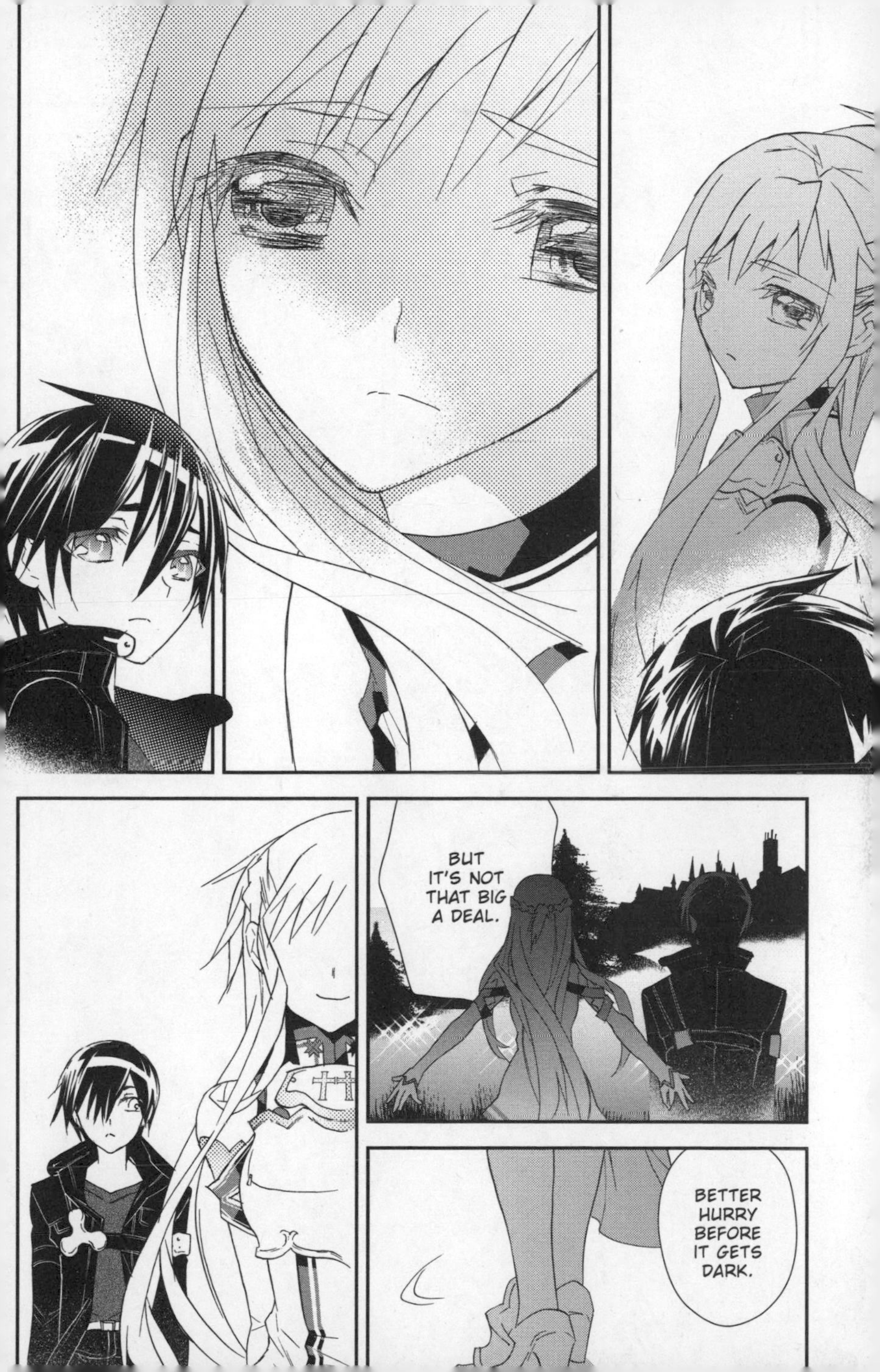
BUT IT'S NOT THAT BIG A DEAL.
BETTER HURRY BEFORE IT GETS DARK.

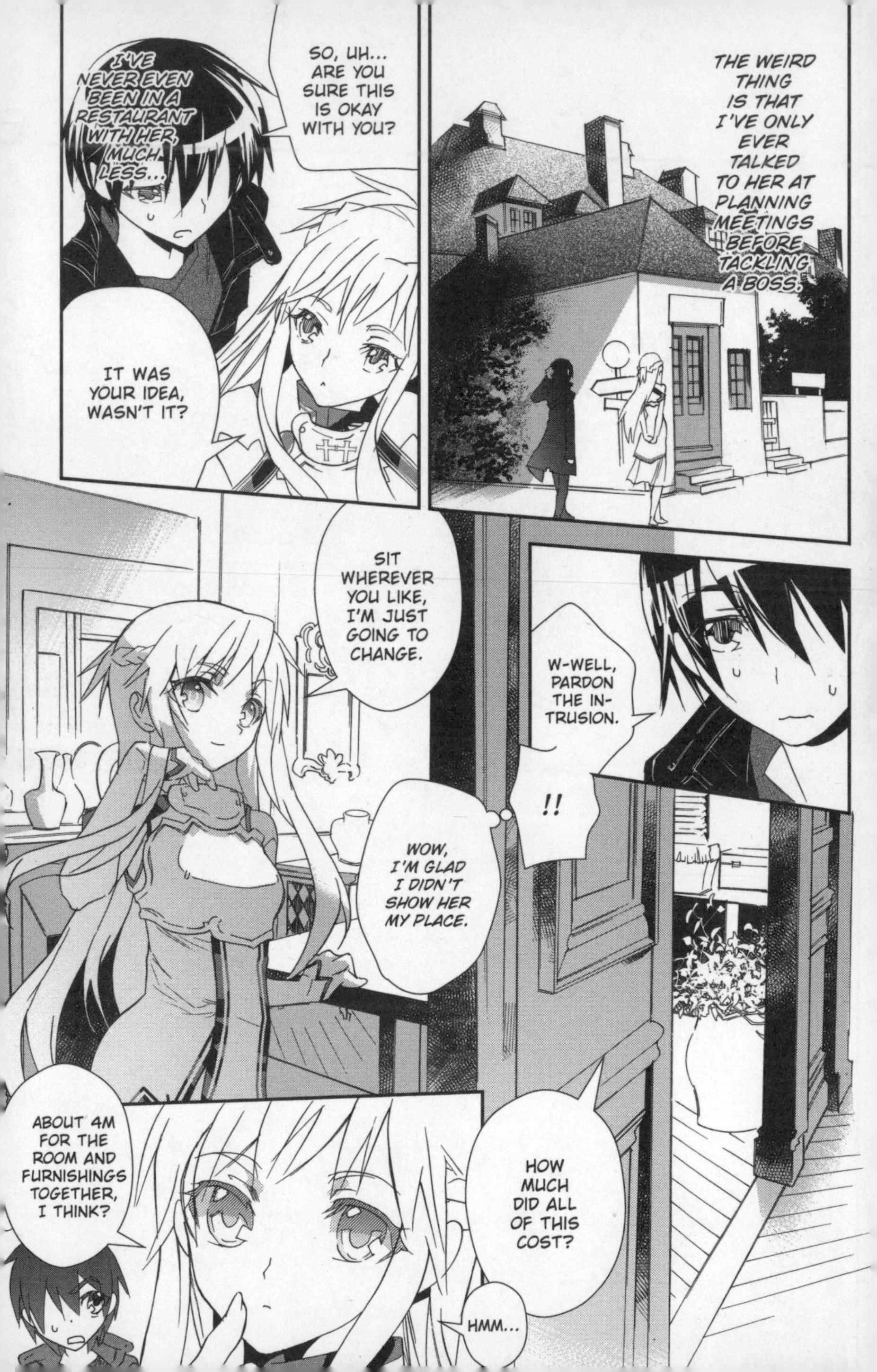
THE WEIRD THING IS THAT I'VE ONLY EVER TALKED TO HER AT PLANNING MEETINGS BEFORE TACKLING A BOSS.
SO, UH... ARE YOU SURE THIS IS OKAY WITH YOU?
I'VE NEVER EVEN BEEN IN A RESTAURANT WITH HER, MUCH LESS...
IT WAS YOUR IDEA, WASN'T IT?
W-WELL, PARDON THE IN-TRUSION.
!!
SIT WHEREVER YOU LIKE, I'M JUST GOING TO CHANGE.
WOW, I'M GLAD I DIDN'T SHOW HER MY PLACE.
HOW MUCH DID ALL OF THIS COST?
HMM...
ABOUT 4M FOR THE ROOM AND FURNISHINGS TOGETHER, I THINK?

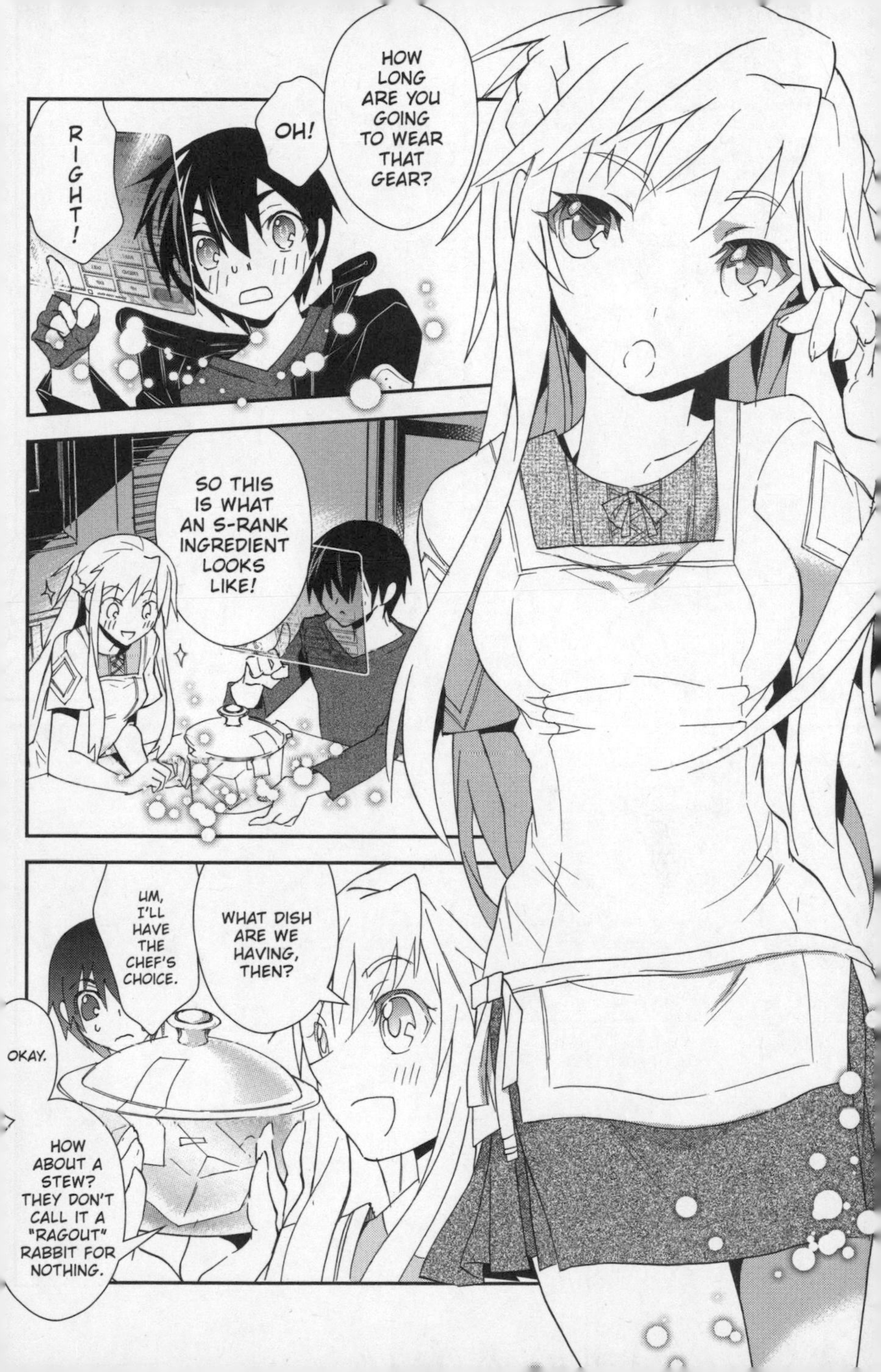
HOW LONG ARE YOU GOING TO WEAR THAT GEAR?
OH!
RIGHT!
SO THIS IS WHAT AN S-RANK INGREDIENT LOOKS LIKE!
WHAT DISH ARE WE HAVING, THEN?
UM, I'LL HAVE THE CHEF'S CHOICE.
OKAY.
HOW ABOUT A STEW? THEY DON'T CALL IT A "RAGOUT" RABBIT FOR NOTHING.

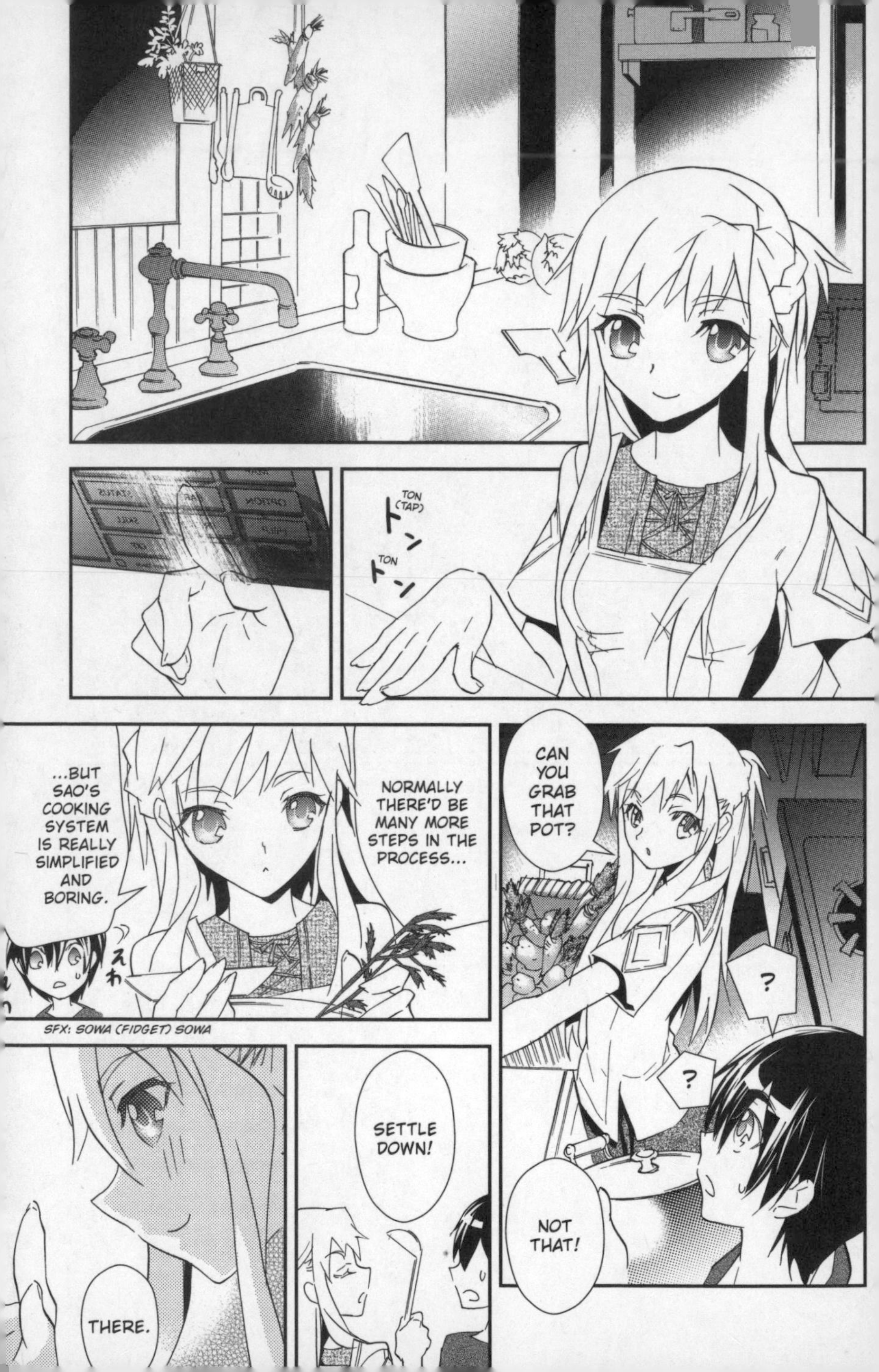
TON (TAP)
TON
CAN YOU GRAB THAT POT?
?
?
NOT THAT!
NORMALLY THERE'D BE MANY MORE STEPS IN THE PROCESS...
...BUT SAO'S COOKING SYSTEM IS REALLY SIMPLIFIED AND BORING.
SFX: SOWA (FIDGET) SOWA
SETTLE DOWN!
THERE.

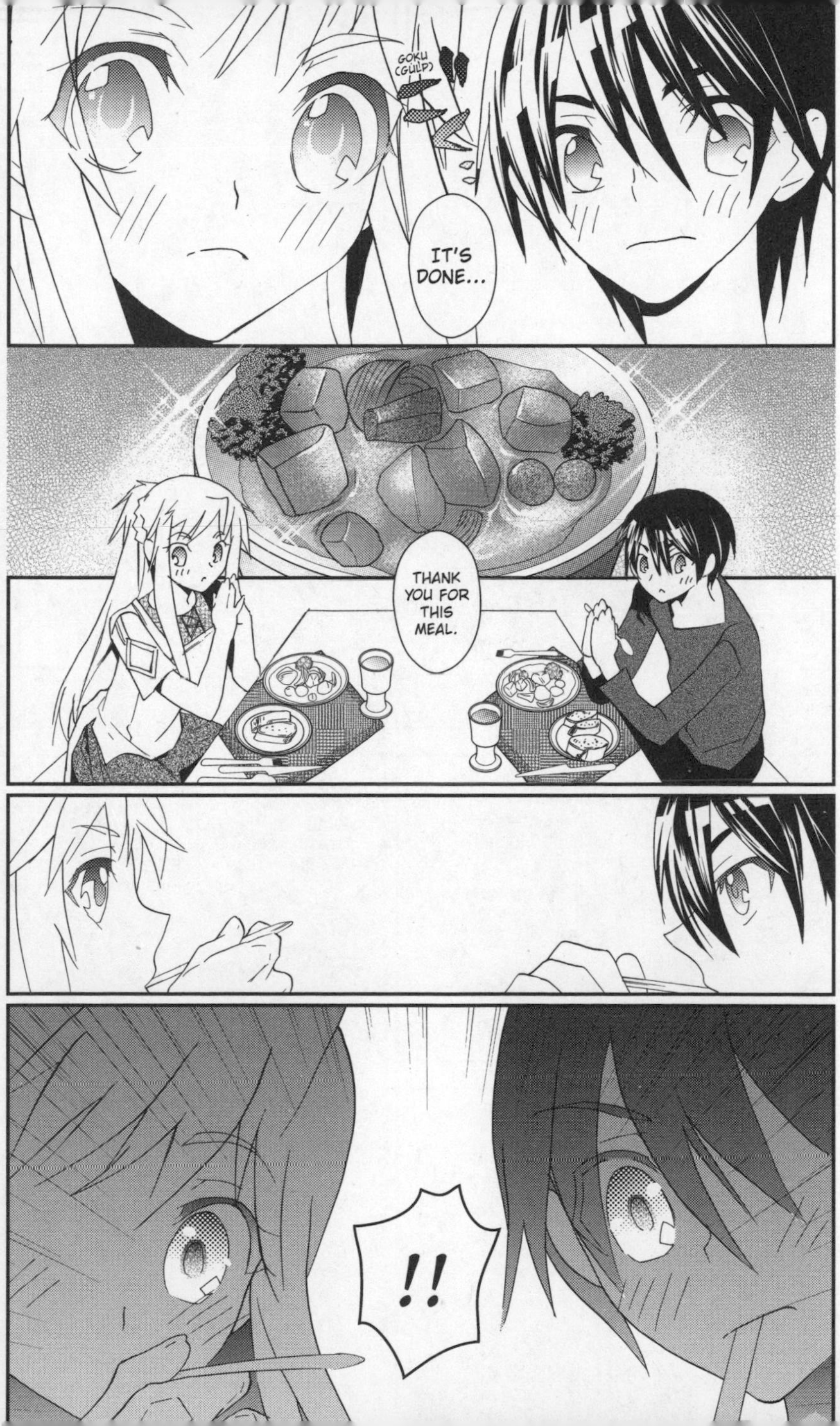
GOKU (GULP)
IT'S DONE...
THANK YOU FOR THIS MEAL.
!!

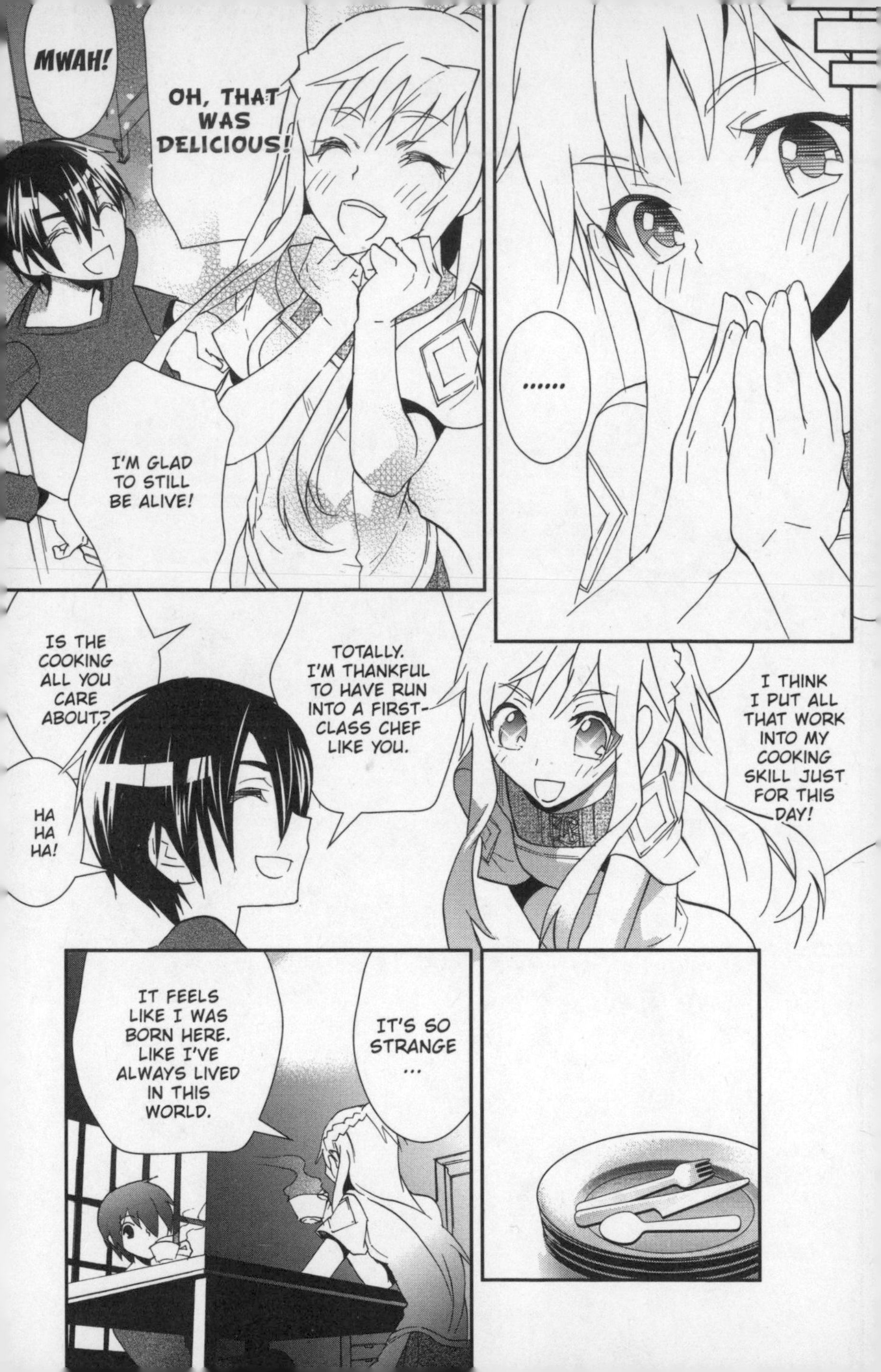
......
MWAH!
OH, THAT WAS DELICIOUS!
I'M GLAD TO STILL BE ALIVE!
I THINK I PUT ALL THAT WORK INTO MY COOKING SKILL JUST FOR THIS DAY!
TOTALLY. I'M THANKFUL TO HAVE RUN INTO A FIRST-CLASS CHEF LIKE YOU.
IS THE COOKING ALL YOU CARE ABOUT?
HA HA HA!
IT'S SO STRANGE ...
IT FEELS LIKE I WAS BORN HERE. LIKE I'VE ALWAYS LIVED IN THIS WORLD.

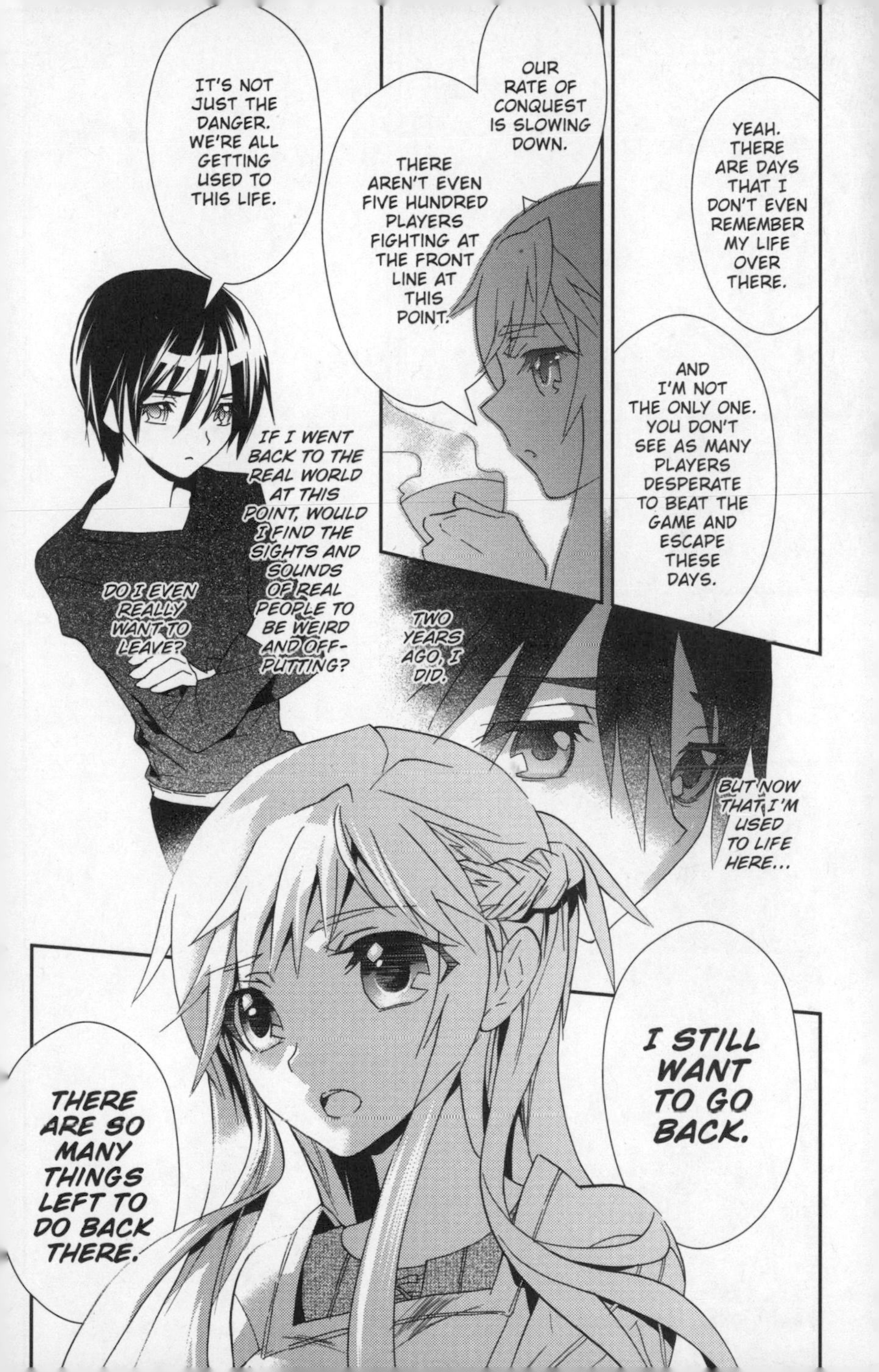
YEAH. THERE ARE DAYS THAT I DON'T EVEN REMEMBER MY LIFE OVER THERE.
AND I'M NOT THE ONLY ONE. YOU DON'T SEE AS MANY PLAYERS DESPERATE TO BEAT THE GAME AND ESCAPE THESE DAYS.
OUR RATE OF CONQUEST IS SLOWING DOWN.
THERE AREN'T EVEN FIVE HUNDRED PLAYERS FIGHTING AT THE FRONT LINE AT THIS POINT.
IT'S NOT JUST THE DANGER. WE'RE ALL GETTING USED TO THIS LIFE.
IF I WENT BACK TO THE REAL WORLD AT THIS POINT, WOULD I FIND THE SIGHTS AND SOUNDS OF REAL PEOPLE TO BE WEIRD AND OFF-PUTTING?
DO I EVEN REALLY WANT TO LEAVE?
TWO YEARS AGO, I DID.
BUT NOW THAT I'M USED TO LIFE HERE...
I STILL WANT TO GO BACK.
THERE ARE SO MANY THINGS LEFT TO DO BACK THERE.

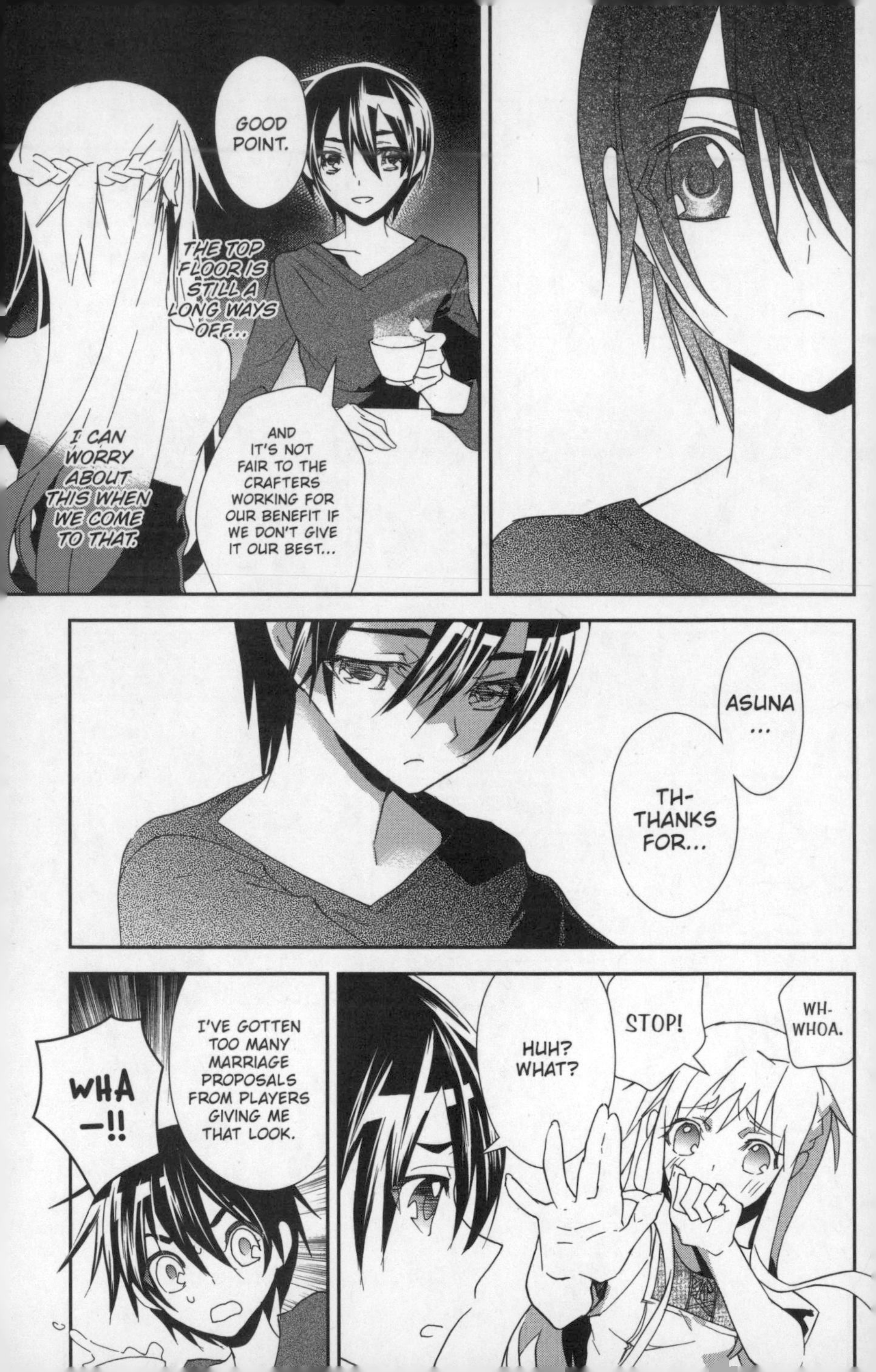
GOOD POINT.
THE TOP FLOOR IS STILL A LONG WAYS OFF...
AND IT'S NOT FAIR TO THE CRAFTERS WORKING FOR OUR BENEFIT IF WE DON'T GIVE IT OUR BEST...
I CAN WORRY ABOUT THIS WHEN WE COME TO THAT.
ASUNA ...
TH-THANKS FOR...
WH-WHOA.
STOP!
HUH? WHAT?
I'VE GOTTEN TOO MANY MARRIAGE PROPOSALS FROM PLAYERS GIVING ME THAT LOOK.
WHA—!!

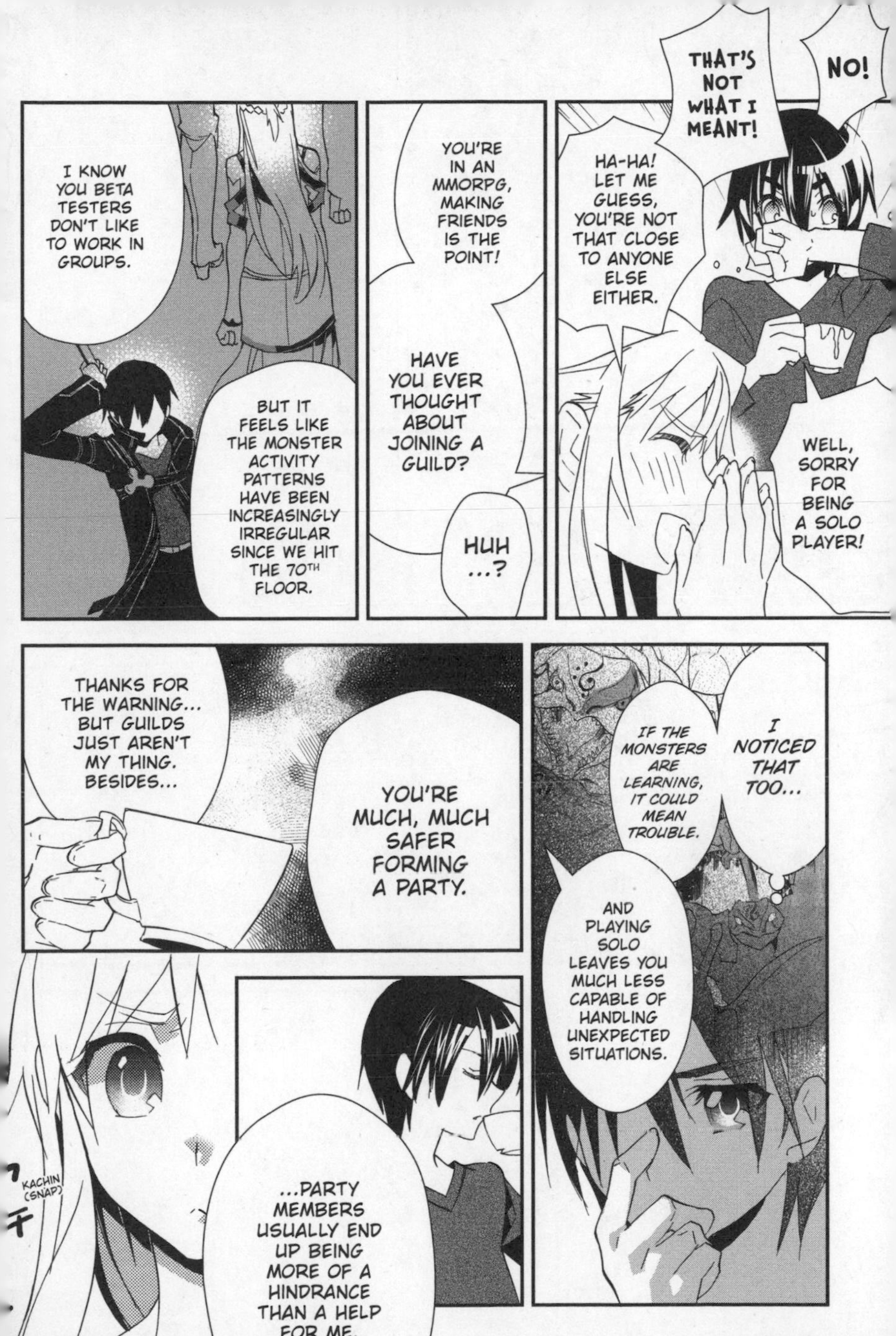
NO!
THAT'S NOT WHAT I MEANT!
HA-HA! LET ME GUESS, YOU'RE NOT THAT CLOSE TO ANYONE ELSE EITHER.
WELL, SORRY FOR BEING A SOLO PLAYER!
YOU'RE IN AN MMORPG, MAKING FRIENDS IS THE POINT!
HAVE YOU EVER THOUGHT ABOUT JOINING A GUILD?
HUH ...?
I KNOW YOU BETA TESTERS DON'T LIKE TO WORK IN GROUPS.
BUT IT FEELS LIKE THE MONSTER ACTIVITY PATTERNS HAVE BEEN INCREASINGLY IRREGULAR SINCE WE HIT THE 70TH FLOOR.
I NOTICED THAT TOO...
IF THE MONSTERS ARE LEARNING, IT COULD MEAN TROUBLE.
AND PLAYING SOLO LEAVES YOU MUCH LESS CAPABLE OF HANDLING UNEXPECTED SITUATIONS.
YOU'RE MUCH, MUCH SAFER FORMING A PARTY.
THANKS FOR THE WARNING... BUT GUILDS JUST AREN'T MY THING. BESIDES...
...PARTY MEMBERS USUALLY END UP BEING MORE OF A HINDRANCE THAN A HELP FOR ME.
KACHIN (SNAP)

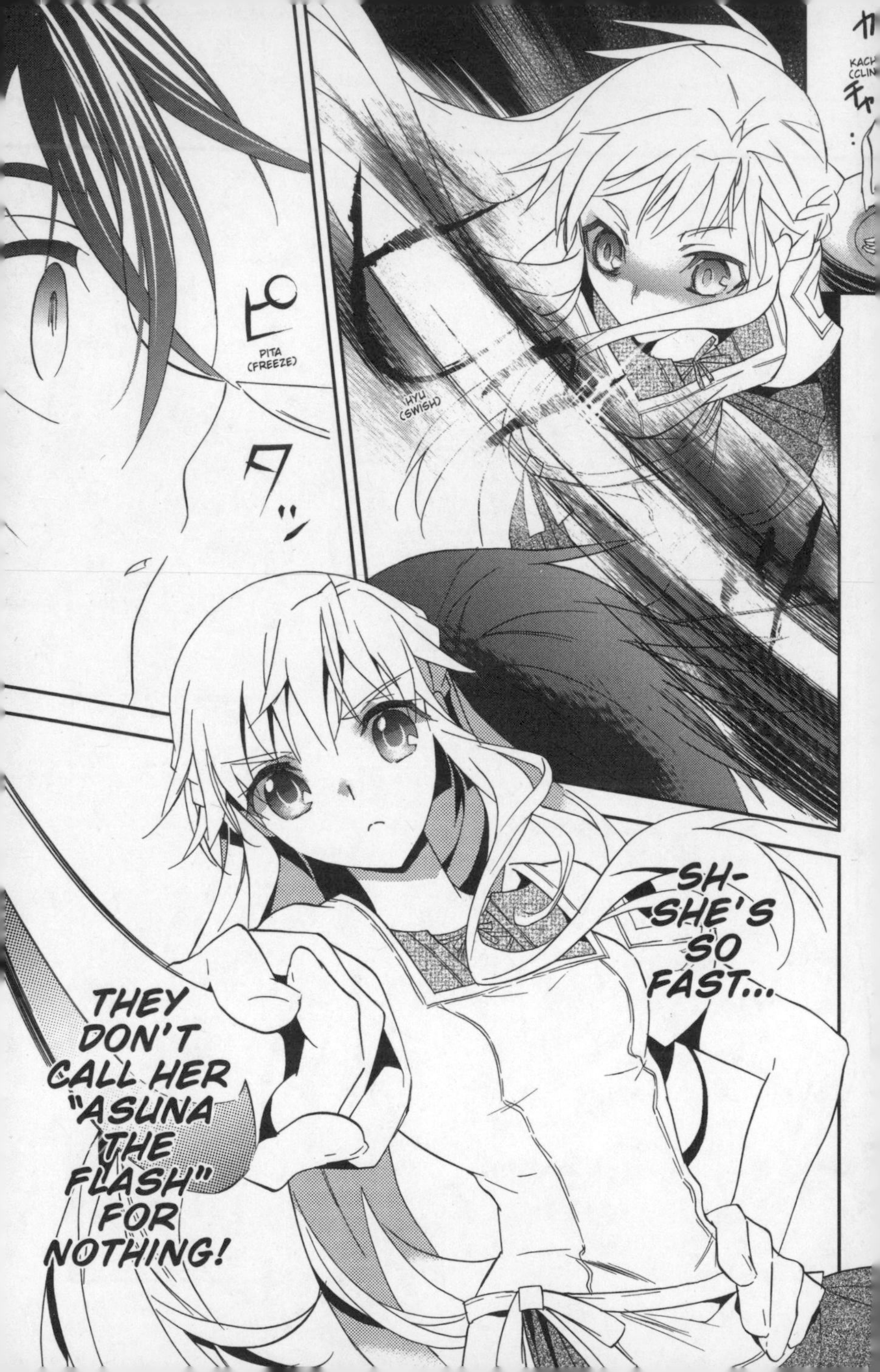
KACH
(CLIN
HYU
(SWISH)
PITA
(FREEZE)
SH-SHE'S SO FAST...
THEY DON'T CALL HER "ASUNA THE FLASH" FOR NOTHING!

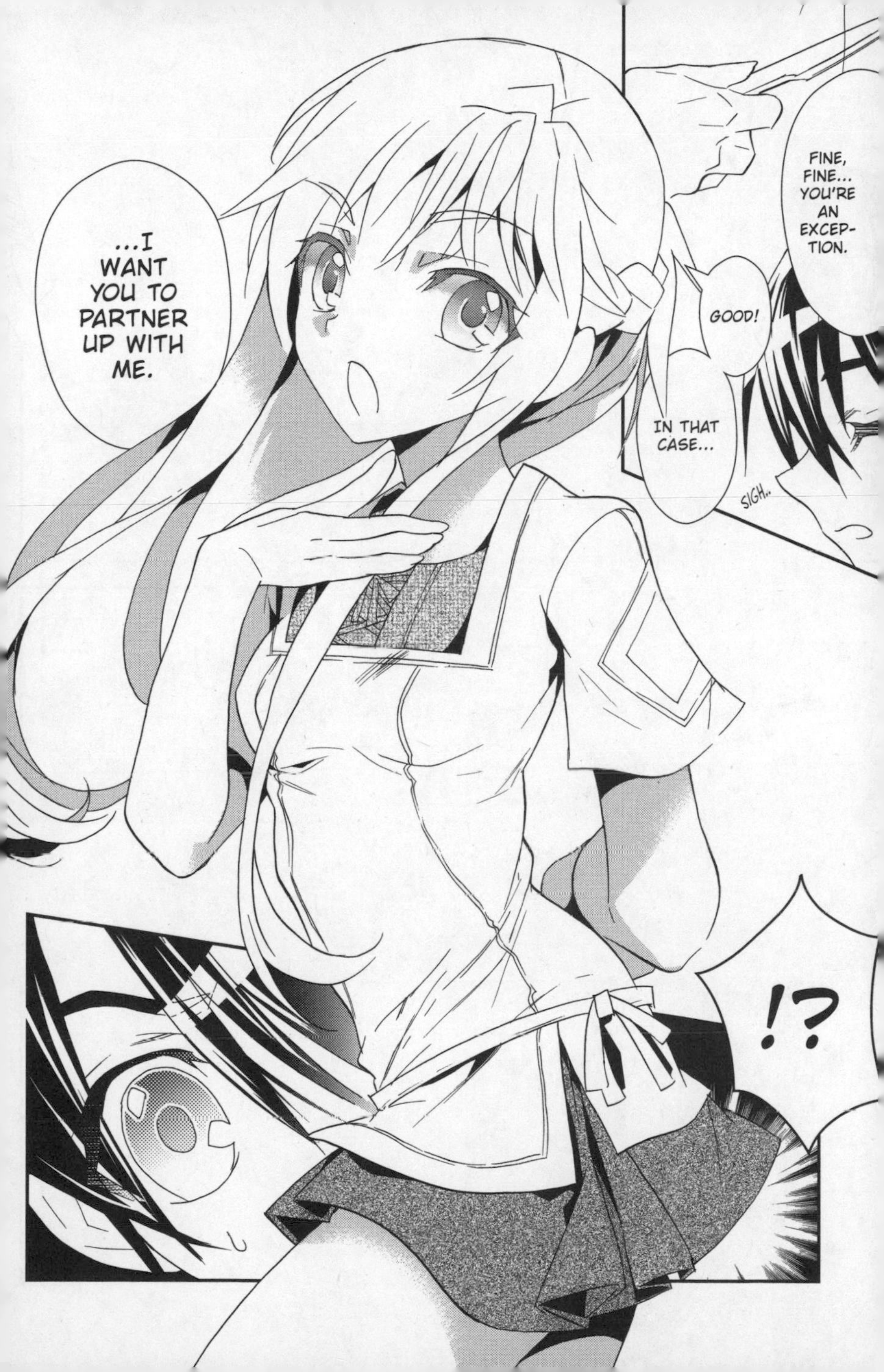
FINE, FINE... YOU'RE AN EXCEPTION.
SIGH..
GOOD!
IN THAT CASE...
...I WANT YOU TO PARTNER UP WITH ME.
!?

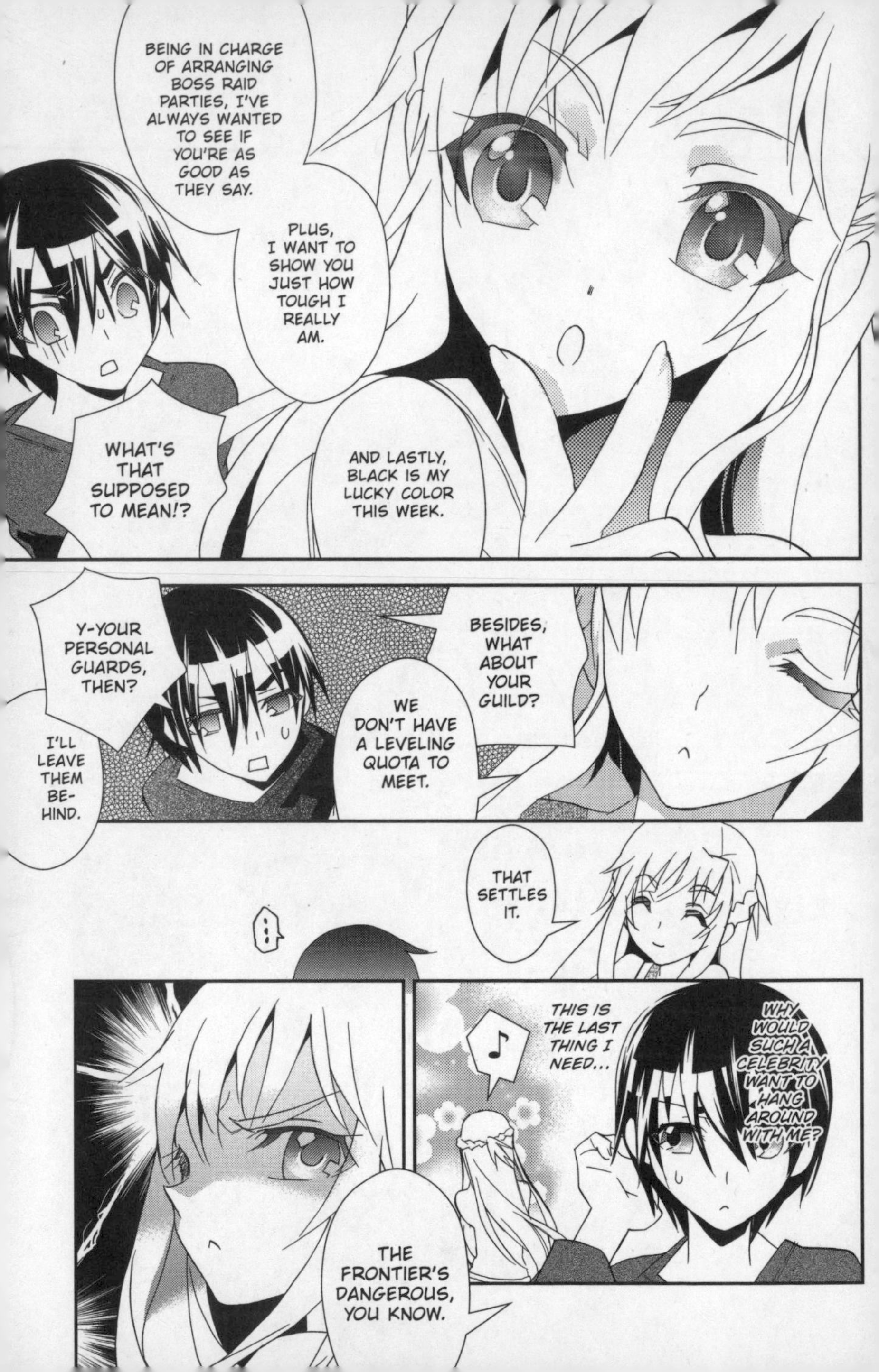
BEING IN CHARGE OF ARRANGING BOSS RAID PARTIES, I'VE ALWAYS WANTED TO SEE IF YOU'RE AS GOOD AS THEY SAY.
PLUS, I WANT TO SHOW YOU JUST HOW TOUGH I REALLY AM.
AND LASTLY, BLACK IS MY LUCKY COLOR THIS WEEK.
WHAT'S THAT SUPPOSED TO MEAN!?
BESIDES, WHAT ABOUT YOUR GUILD?
WE DON'T HAVE A LEVELING QUOTA TO MEET.
Y-YOUR PERSONAL GUARDS, THEN?
I'LL LEAVE THEM BE-HIND.
THAT SETTLES IT.
...
WHY WOULD SUCH A CELEBRITY WANT TO HANG AROUND WITH ME?
THIS IS THE LAST THING I NEED...
♪
THE FRONTIER'S DANGEROUS, YOU KNOW.

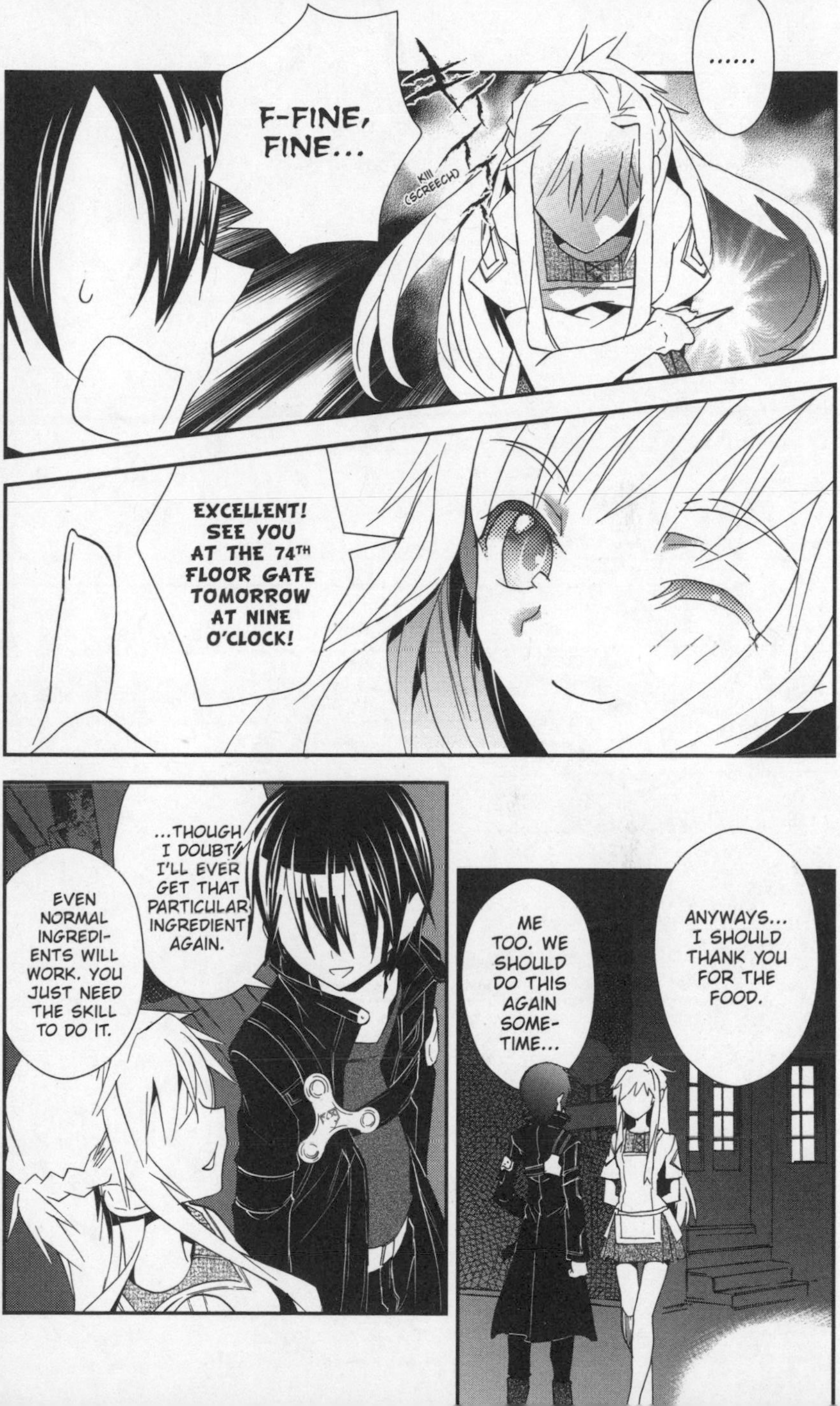
......
KIII (SCREECH)
F-FINE, FINE...
EXCELLENT! SEE YOU AT THE 74TH FLOOR GATE TOMORROW AT NINE O'CLOCK!
ANYWAYS... I SHOULD THANK YOU FOR THE FOOD.
ME TOO. WE SHOULD DO THIS AGAIN SOMETIME...
...THOUGH I DOUBT I'LL EVER GET THAT PARTICULAR INGREDIENT AGAIN.
EVEN NORMAL INGREDIENTS WILL WORK. YOU JUST NEED THE SKILL TO DO IT.

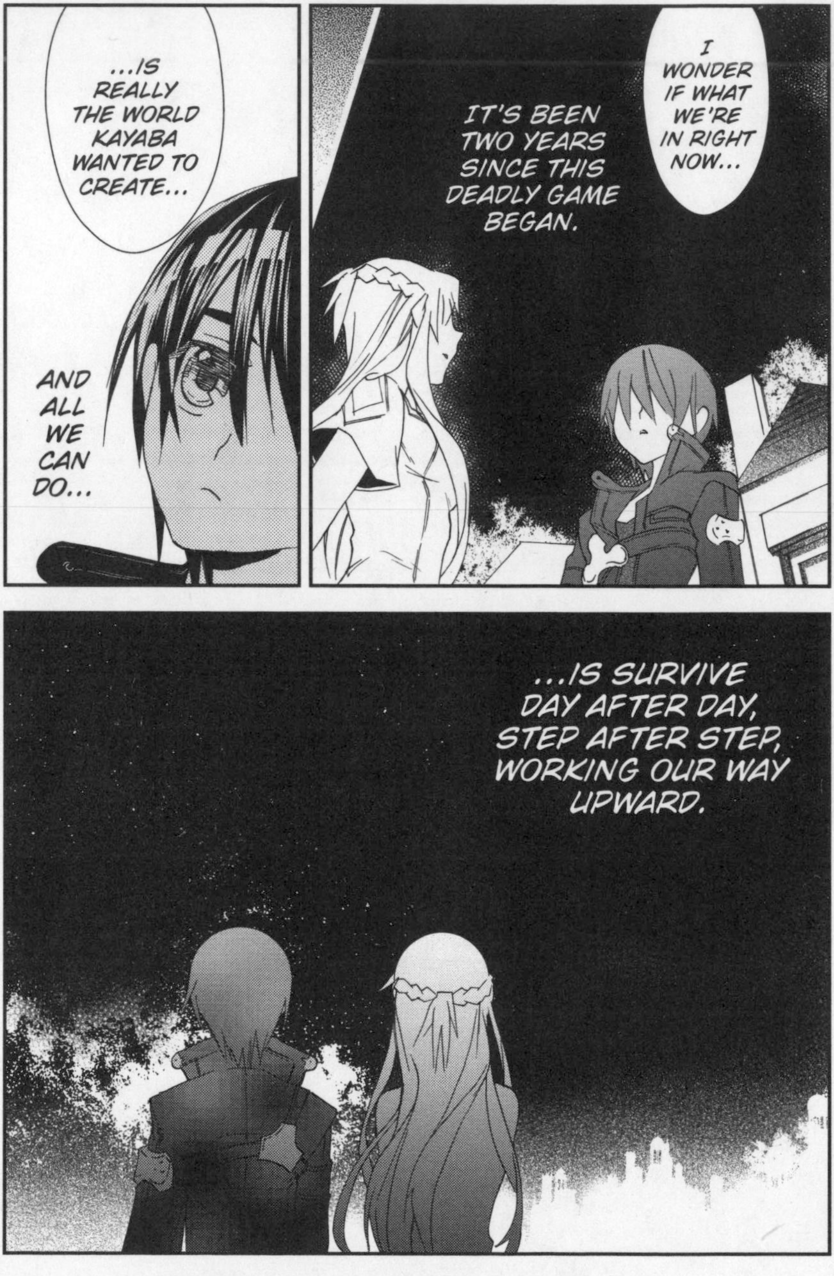
I WONDER IF WHAT WE'RE IN RIGHT NOW...
IT'S BEEN TWO YEARS SINCE THIS DEADLY GAME BEGAN.
...IS REALLY THE WORLD KAYABA WANTED TO CREATE...
AND ALL WE CAN DO...
...IS SURVIVE DAY AFTER DAY, STEP AFTER STEP, WORKING OUR WAY UPWARD.

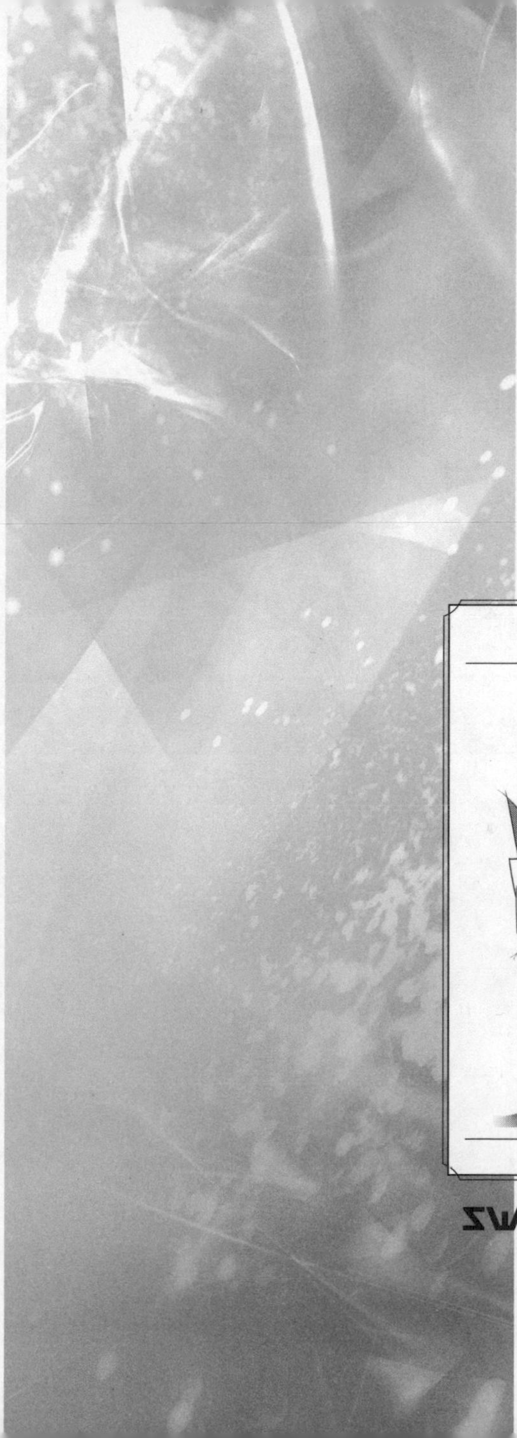

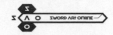

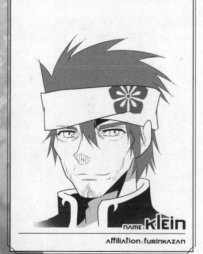

character

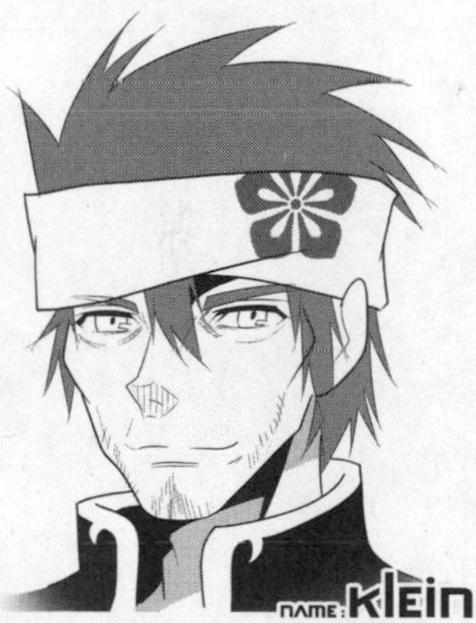

NAME: Klein

Affiliation: Furinkazan

SWORD ART ONLINE
AINCRAD

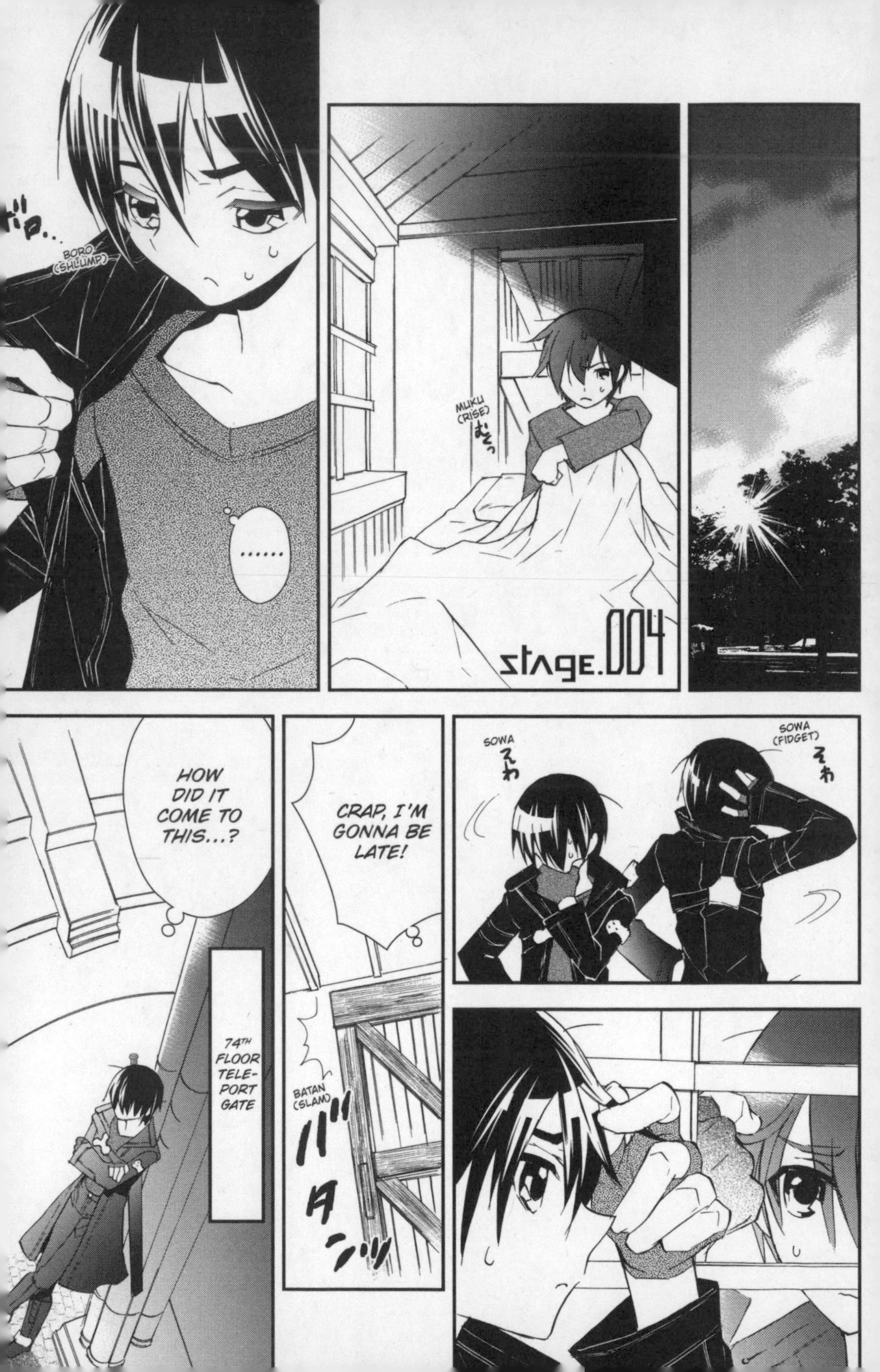
MUKU (RISE)
むくっ
stage.004
BORO (SHLUMP)
......
SOWA (FIDGET)
そわ
SOWA
そわ
CRAP, I'M GONNA BE LATE!
BATAN (SLAM)
HOW DID IT COME TO THIS...?
74TH FLOOR TELEPORT GATE

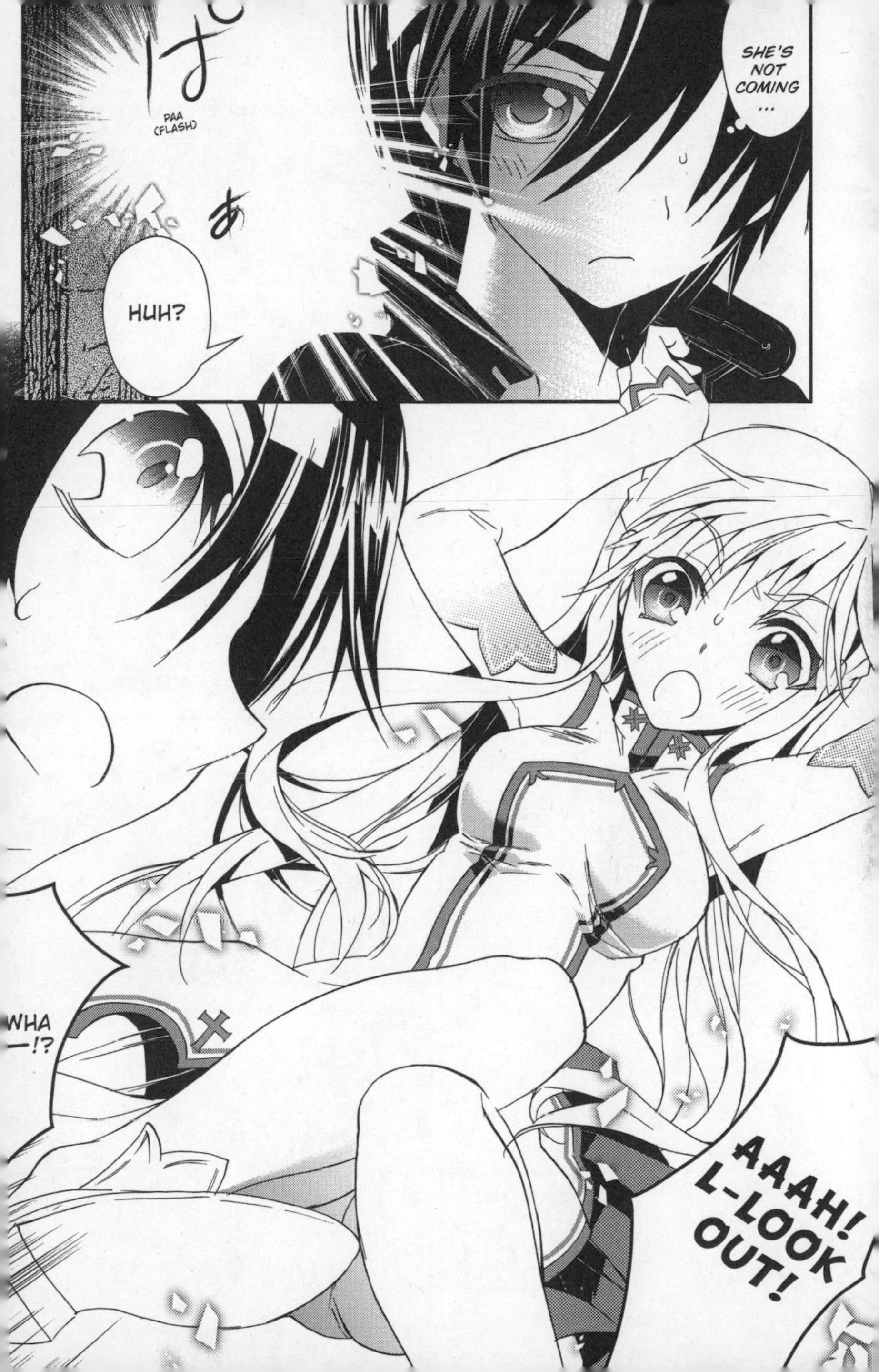
SHE'S NOT COMING ...
ぱ
PAA (FLASH)
あ
HUH?
AAAH! L-LOOK OUT!
WHA—!?

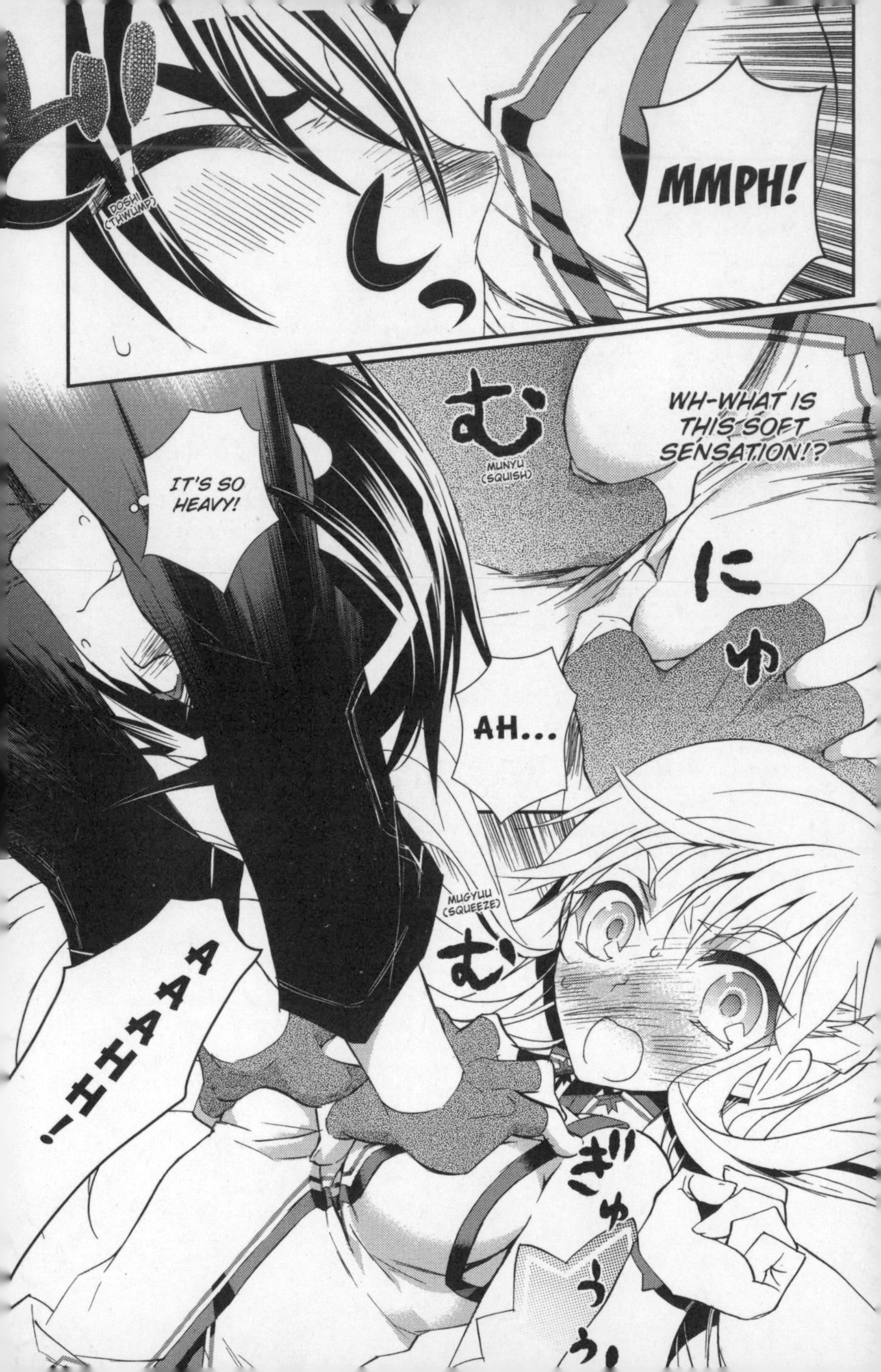
MMPH!
DOSHI (THWUMP)
WH-WHAT IS THIS SOFT SENSATION!?
MUNYU (SQUISH)
IT'S SO HEAVY!
AH...
MUGYUU (SQUEEZE)
AAAAEE-!

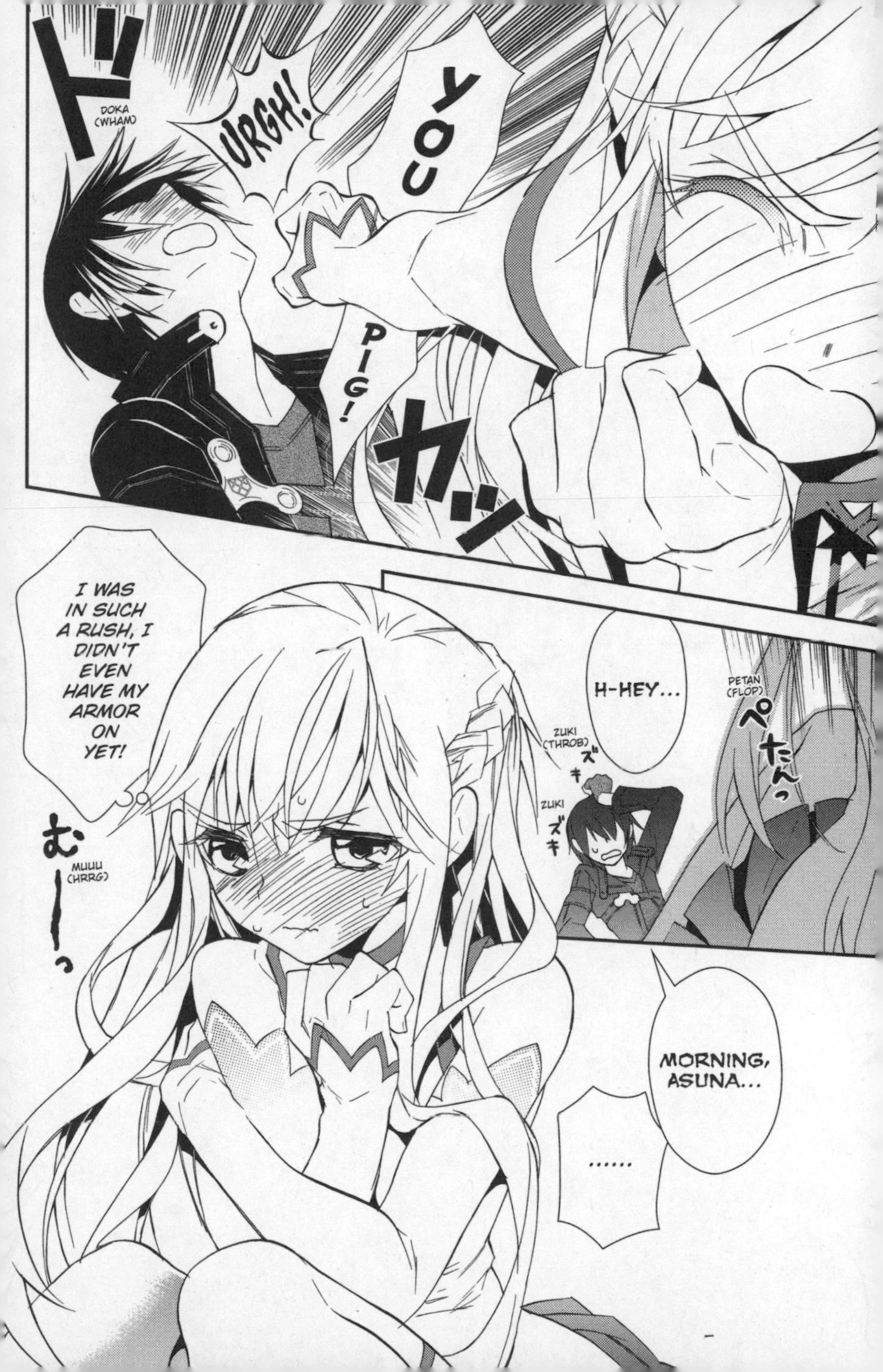
YOU PIG!
URGH!
DOKA (WHAM)
PETAN (FLOP)
H-HEY...
ZUKI (THROB)
ZUKI
MORNING, ASUNA...
......
I WAS IN SUCH A RUSH, I DIDN'T EVEN HAVE MY ARMOR ON YET!
MUUU (HRRG)

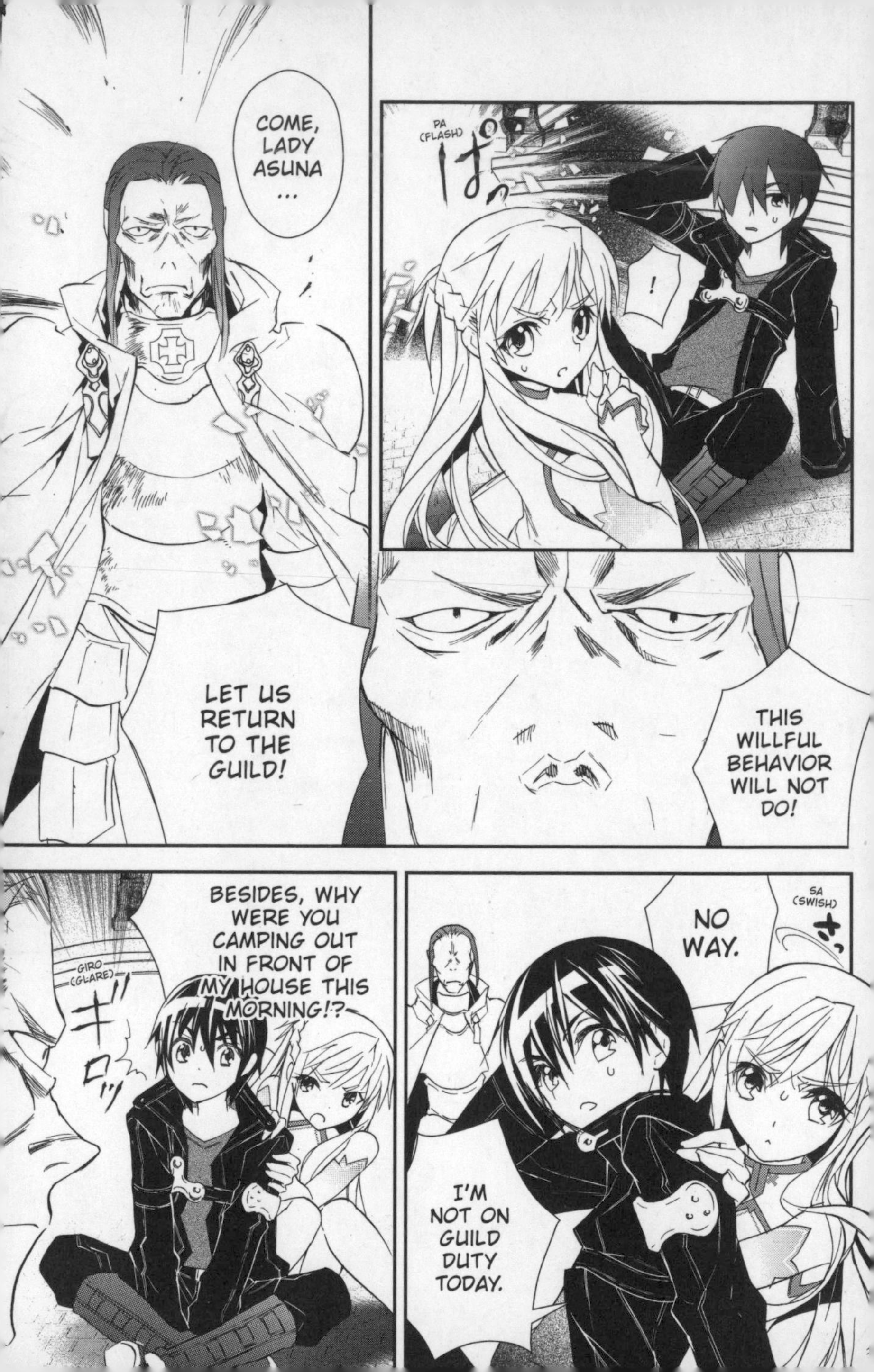
PA (FLASH)
!
THIS WILLFUL BEHAVIOR WILL NOT DO!
LET US RETURN TO THE GUILD!
COME, LADY ASUNA...
SA (SWISH)
NO WAY.
I'M NOT ON GUILD DUTY TODAY.
BESIDES, WHY WERE YOU CAMPING OUT IN FRONT OF MY HOUSE THIS MORNING!?
GIRO (GLARE)

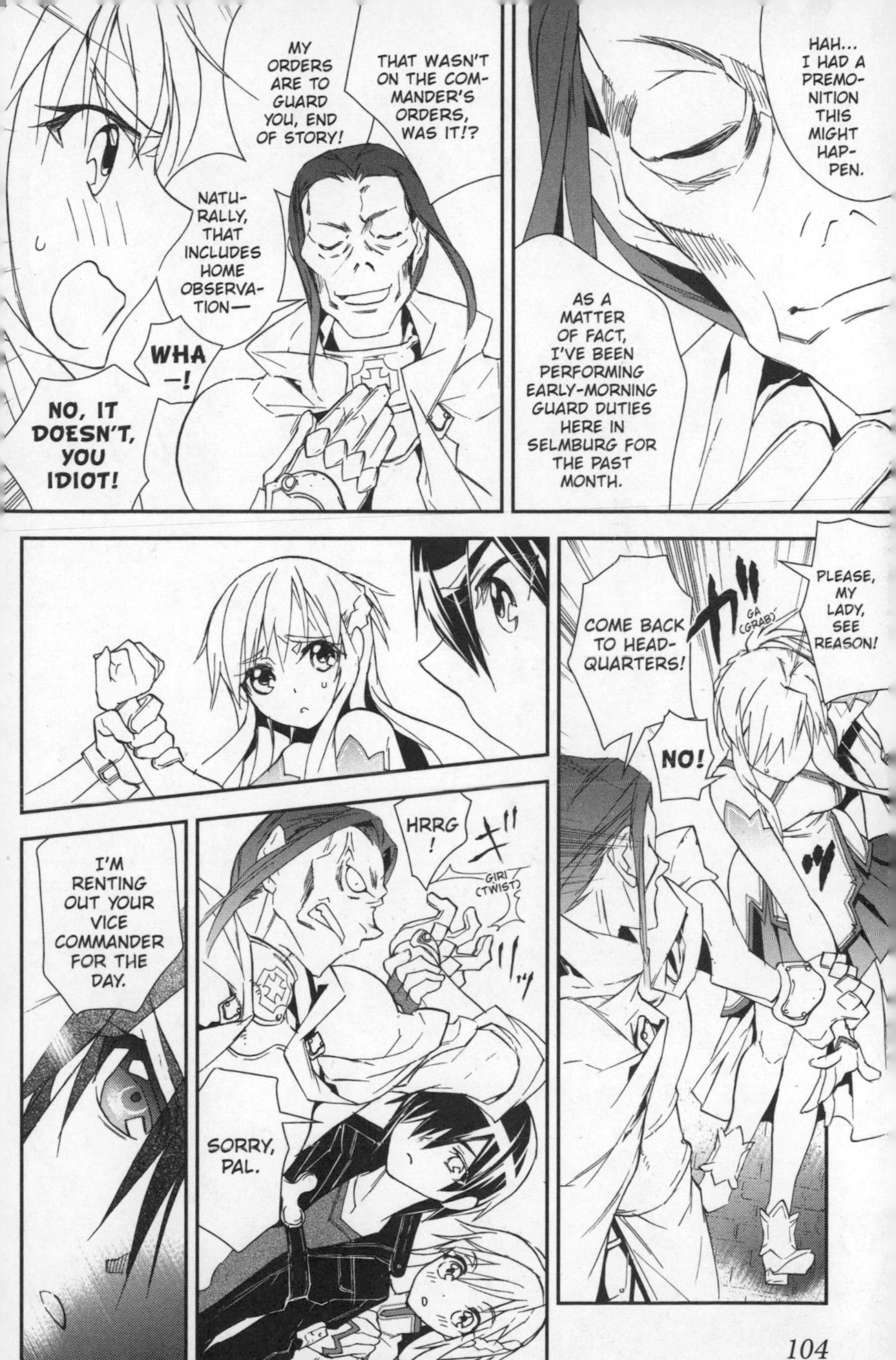
HAH... I HAD A PREMONITION THIS MIGHT HAPPEN.
AS A MATTER OF FACT, I'VE BEEN PERFORMING EARLY-MORNING GUARD DUTIES HERE IN SELMBURG FOR THE PAST MONTH.
THAT WASN'T ON THE COMMANDER'S ORDERS, WAS IT!?
MY ORDERS ARE TO GUARD YOU, END OF STORY!
NATURALLY, THAT INCLUDES HOME OBSERVATION—
WHA—!
NO, IT DOESN'T, YOU IDIOT!
PLEASE, MY LADY, SEE REASON!
GA (GRAB)
COME BACK TO HEADQUARTERS!
NO!
HRRG!
GIRI (TWIST)
SORRY, PAL.
I'M RENTING OUT YOUR VICE COMMANDER FOR THE DAY.

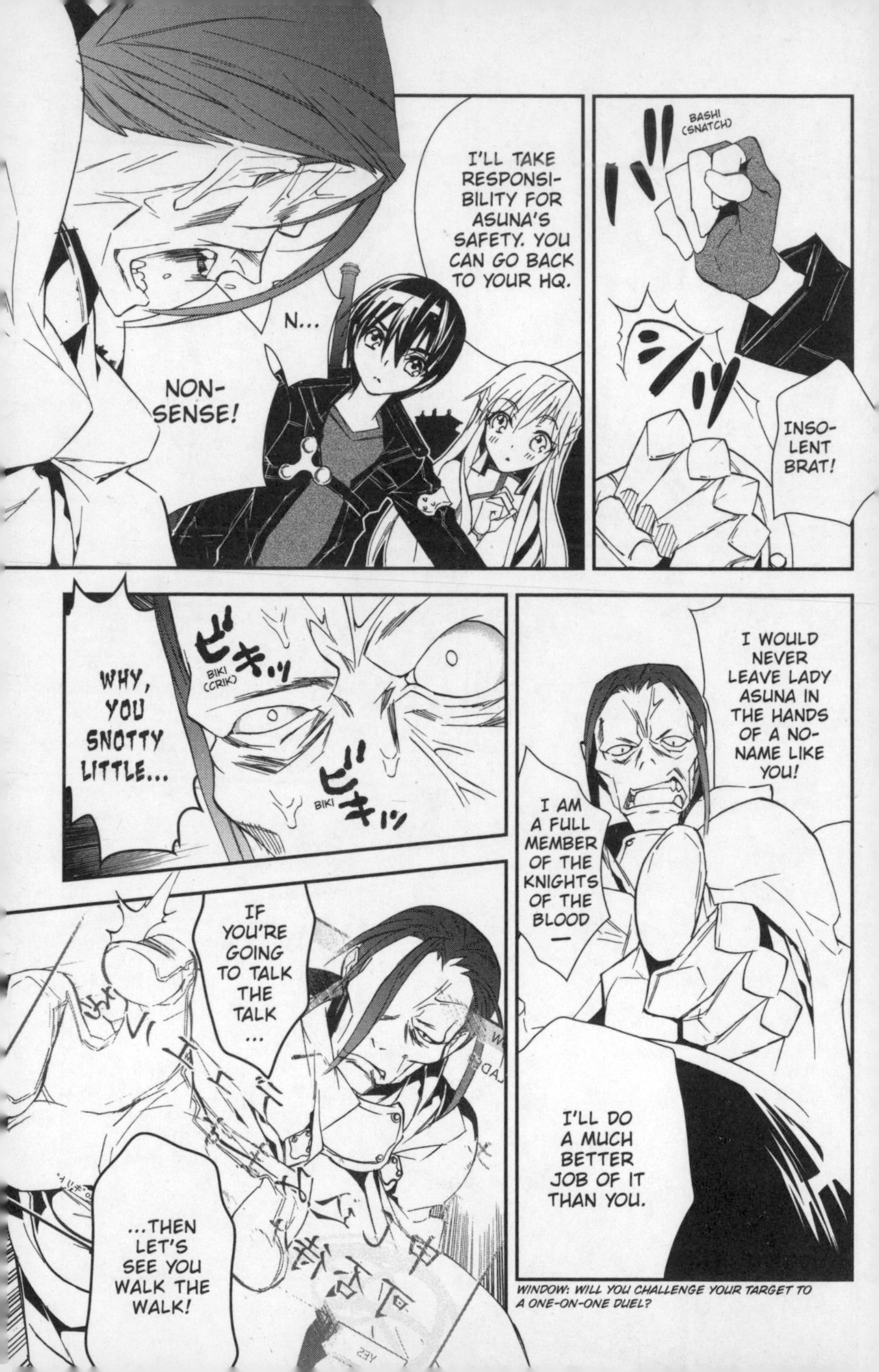
BASHI (SNATCH)
INSO-LENT BRAT!
I'LL TAKE RESPONSI-BILITY FOR ASUNA'S SAFETY. YOU CAN GO BACK TO YOUR HQ.
N...
NON-SENSE!
I WOULD NEVER LEAVE LADY ASUNA IN THE HANDS OF A NO-NAME LIKE YOU!
I AM A FULL MEMBER OF THE KNIGHTS OF THE BLOOD—
I'LL DO A MUCH BETTER JOB OF IT THAN YOU.
WINDOW: WILL YOU CHALLENGE YOUR TARGET TO A ONE-ON-ONE DUEL?
BIKI (CRIK)
BIKI
WHY, YOU SNOTTY LITTLE...
IF YOU'RE GOING TO TALK THE TALK...
...THEN LET'S SEE YOU WALK THE WALK!

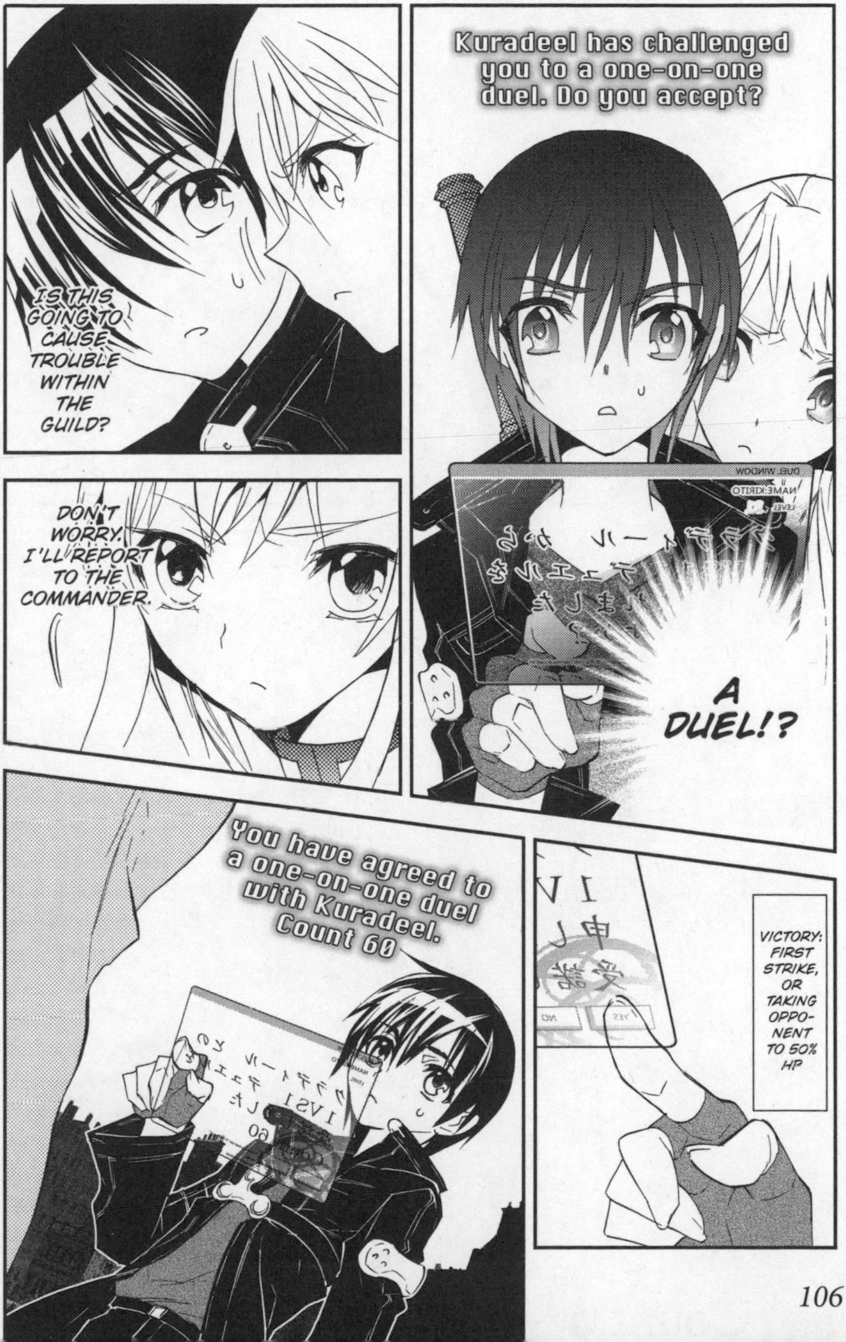

Kuradeel has challenged you to a one-on-one duel. Do you accept?
A DUEL!?
IS THIS GOING TO CAUSE TROUBLE WITHIN THE GUILD?
DON'T WORRY. I'LL REPORT TO THE COMMANDER.
VICTORY: FIRST STRIKE, OR TAKING OPPONENT TO 50% HP
You have agreed to a one-on-one duel with Kuradeel. Count 60

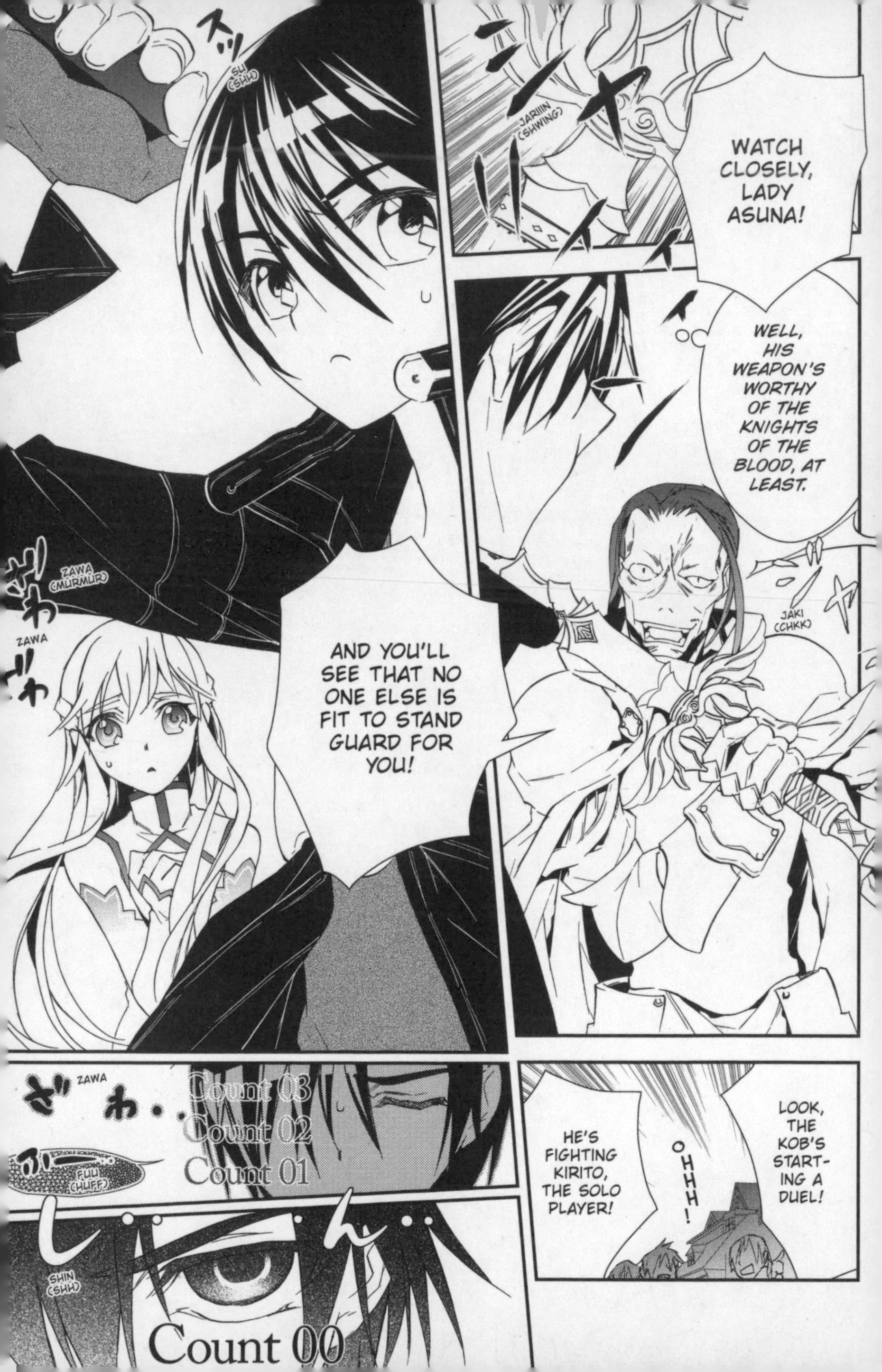
JARIIN (SHWING)
WATCH CLOSELY, LADY ASUNA!
WELL, HIS WEAPON'S WORTHY OF THE KNIGHTS OF THE BLOOD, AT LEAST.
JAKI (CHKK)
SU (SHH)
ZAWA (MURMUR)
ZAWA
AND YOU'LL SEE THAT NO ONE ELSE IS FIT TO STAND GUARD FOR YOU!
LOOK, THE KOB'S START-ING A DUEL!
OHHH!
HE'S FIGHTING KIRITO, THE SOLO PLAYER!
ZAWA
Count 03
Count 02
Count 01
FUU (CHUFF)
SHIN (SHH)
Count 00

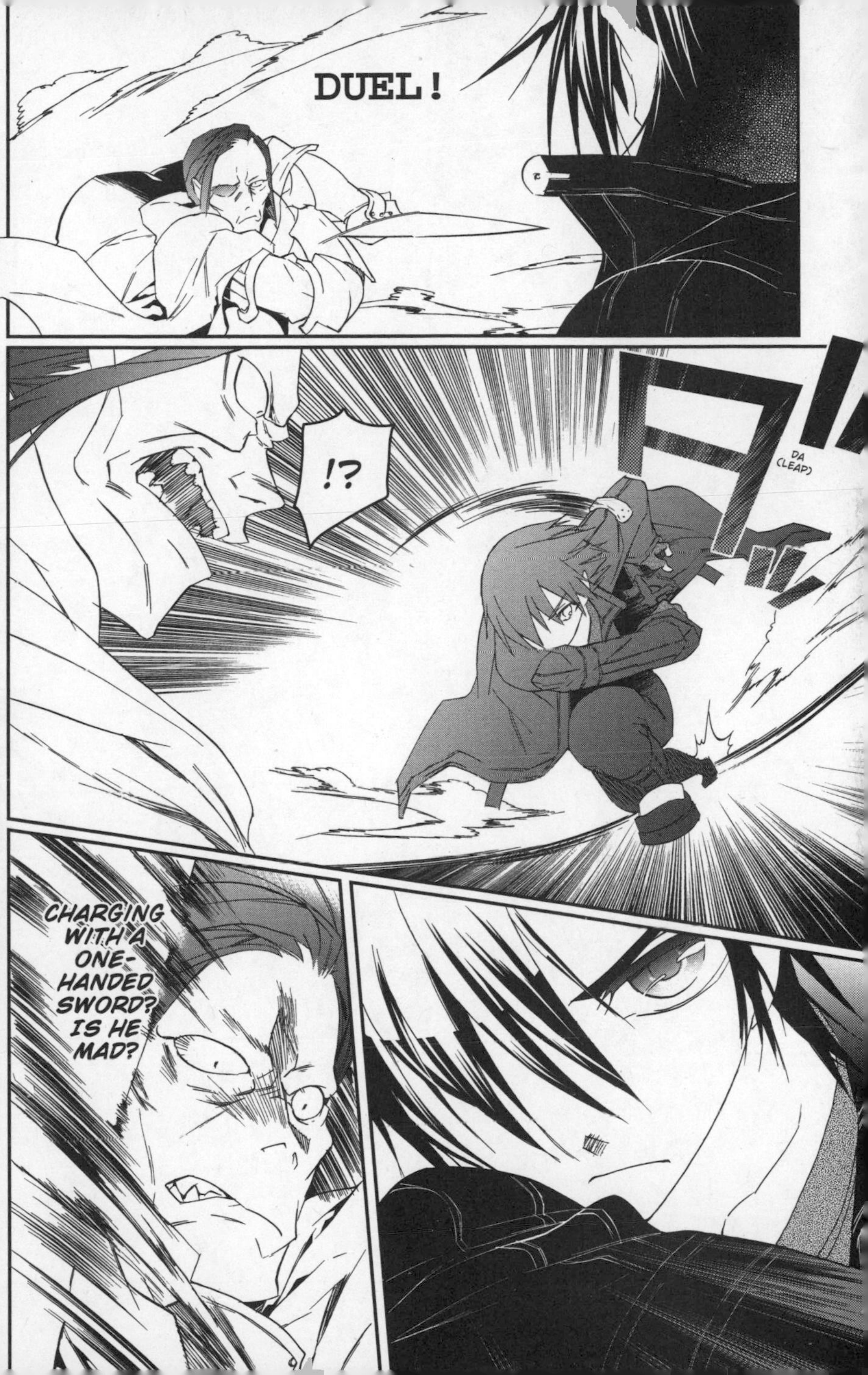
DUEL!
DA (LEAP)
!?
CHARGING WITH A ONE-HANDED SWORD? IS HE MAD?

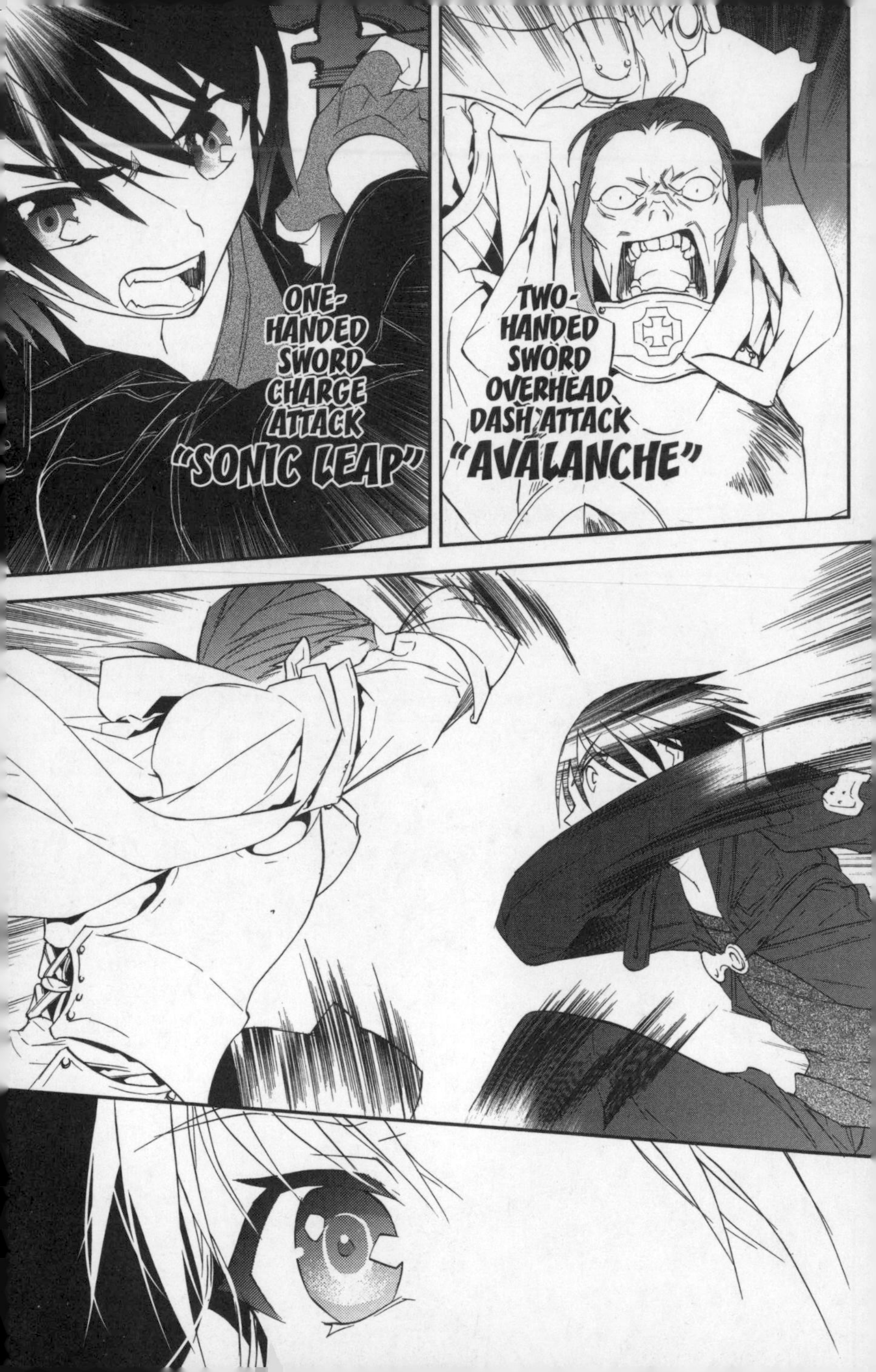
TWO-HANDED SWORD OVERHEAD DASH ATTACK
"AVALANCHE"
ONE-HANDED SWORD CHARGE ATTACK
"SONIC LEAP"

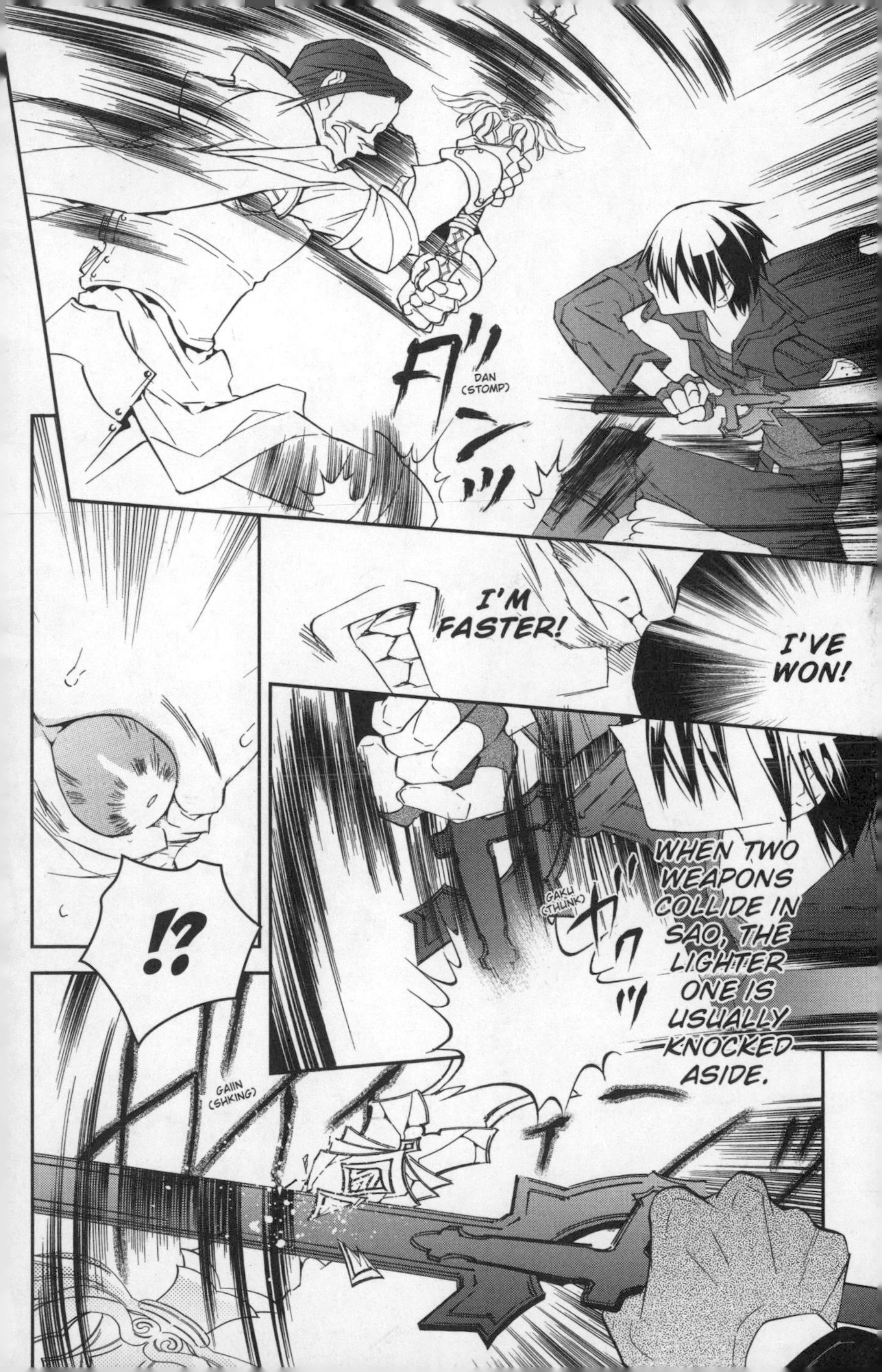
DAN
(STOMP)
I'M FASTER!
I'VE WON!
GAKU
(THUNK)
WHEN TWO WEAPONS COLLIDE IN SAO, THE LIGHTER ONE IS USUALLY KNOCKED ASIDE.
!?
GAIIN
(SHKING)

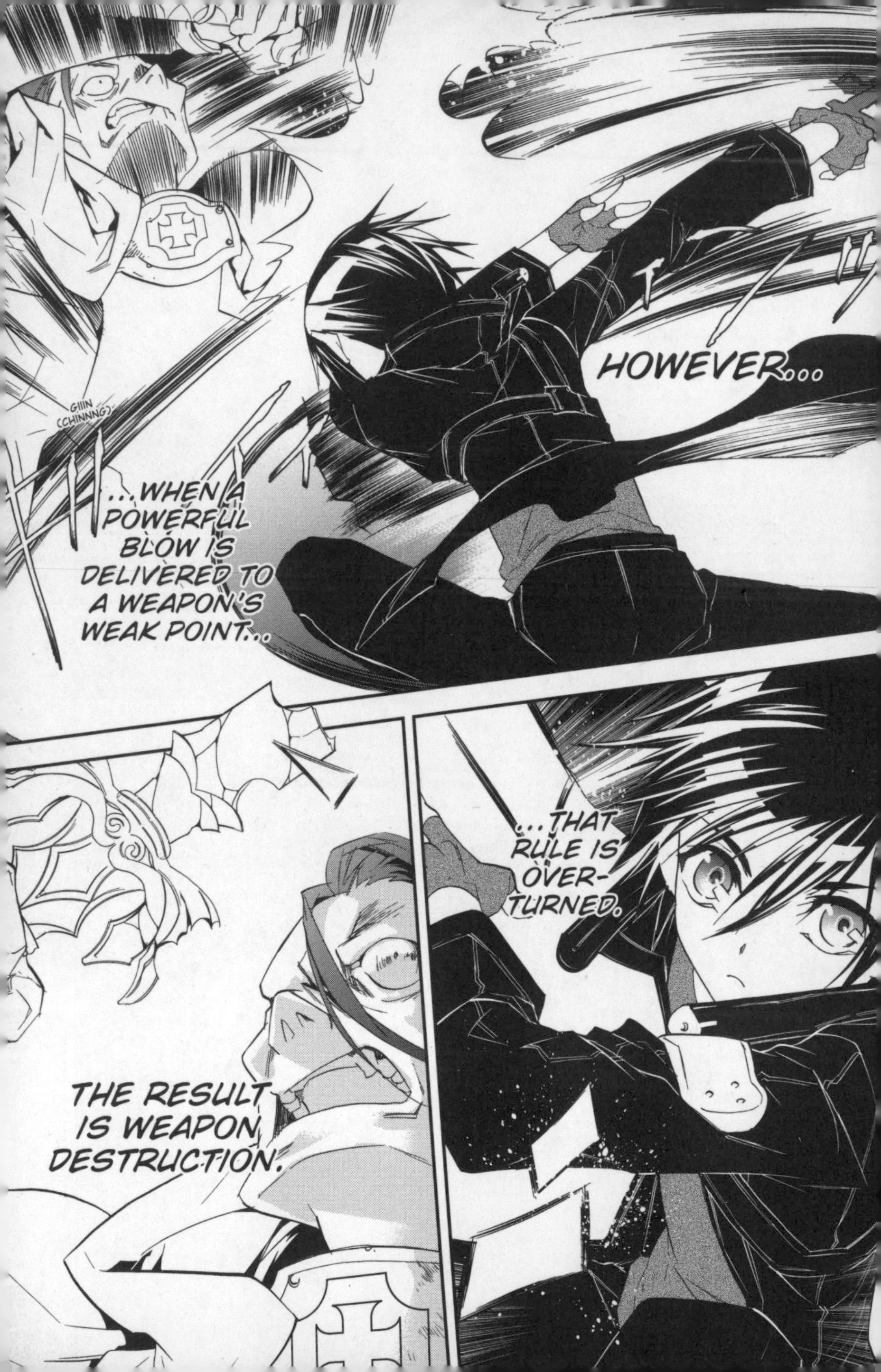
HOWEVER...
GIIN (CHINNNG)
...WHEN A POWERFUL BLOW IS DELIVERED TO A WEAPON'S WEAK POINT...
...THAT RULE IS OVER-TURNED.
THE RESULT IS WEAPON DESTRUCTION.

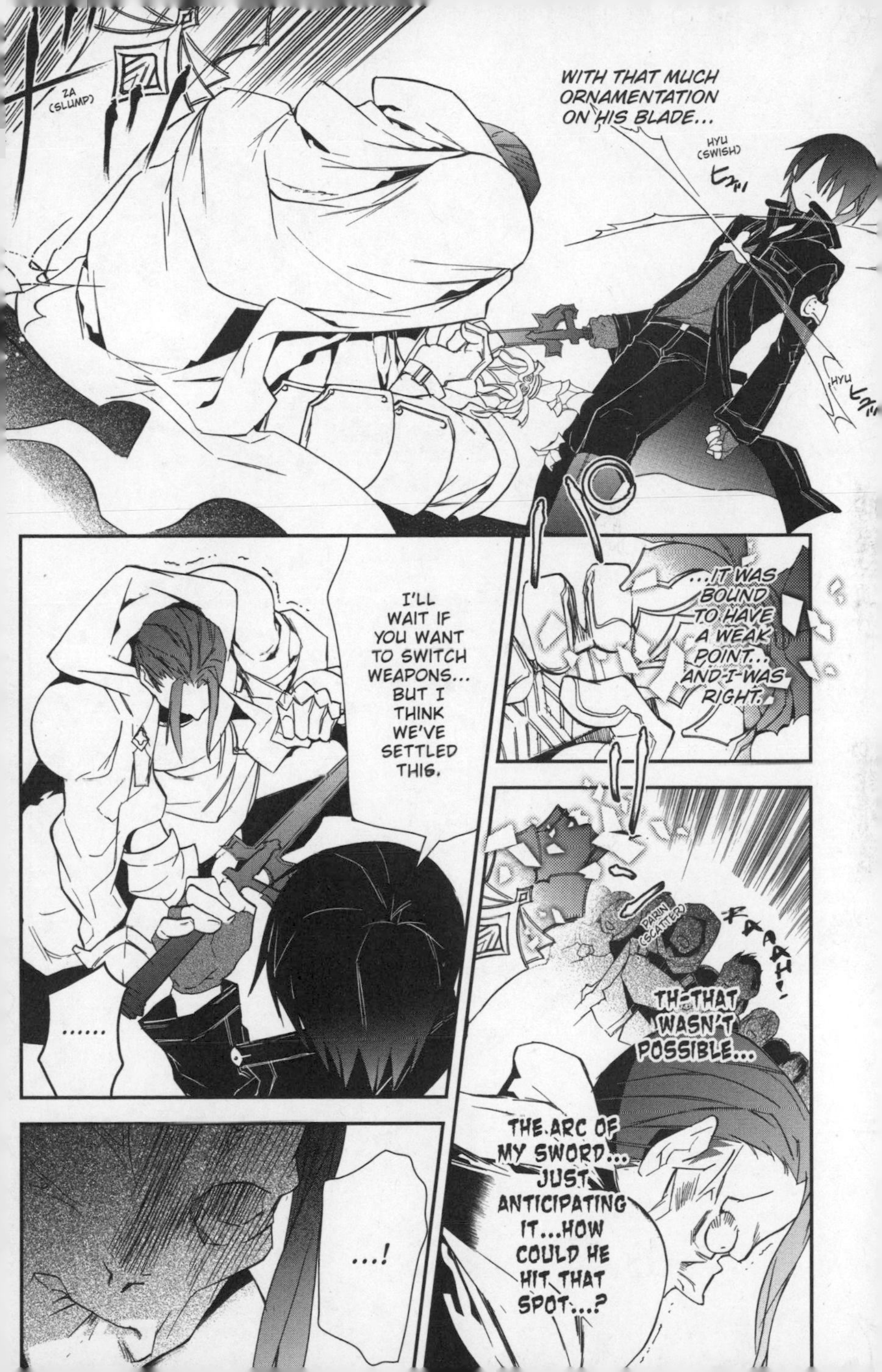

WITH THAT MUCH ORNAMENTATION ON HIS BLADE…
HYU (SWISH)
HYU
ZA (SLUMP)
…IT WAS BOUND TO HAVE A WEAK POINT… AND I WAS RIGHT.
I'LL WAIT IF YOU WANT TO SWITCH WEAPONS… BUT I THINK WE'VE SETTLED THIS.
……
FAAAH!
PARIN (SCATTER)
TH-THAT WASN'T POSSIBLE…
THE ARC OF MY SWORD… JUST ANTICIPATING IT…HOW COULD HE HIT THAT SPOT…?
…!

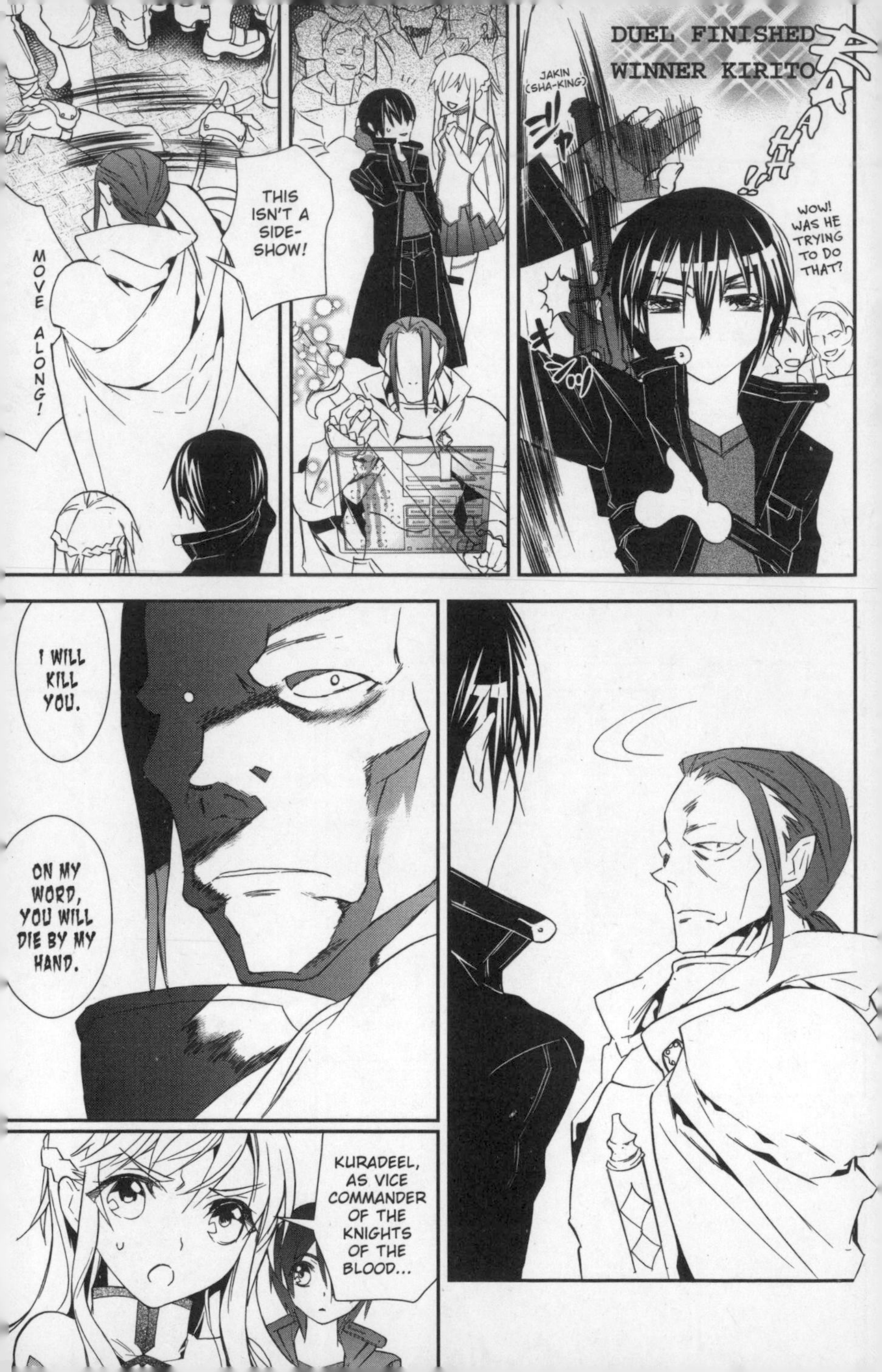
DUEL FINISHED
WINNER KIRITO
JAKIN (SHA-KING)
WOW! WAS HE TRYING TO DO THAT?
THIS ISN'T A SIDE-SHOW!
MOVE ALONG!
I WILL KILL YOU.
ON MY WORD, YOU WILL DIE BY MY HAND.
KURADEEL, AS VICE COMMANDER OF THE KNIGHTS OF THE BLOOD...

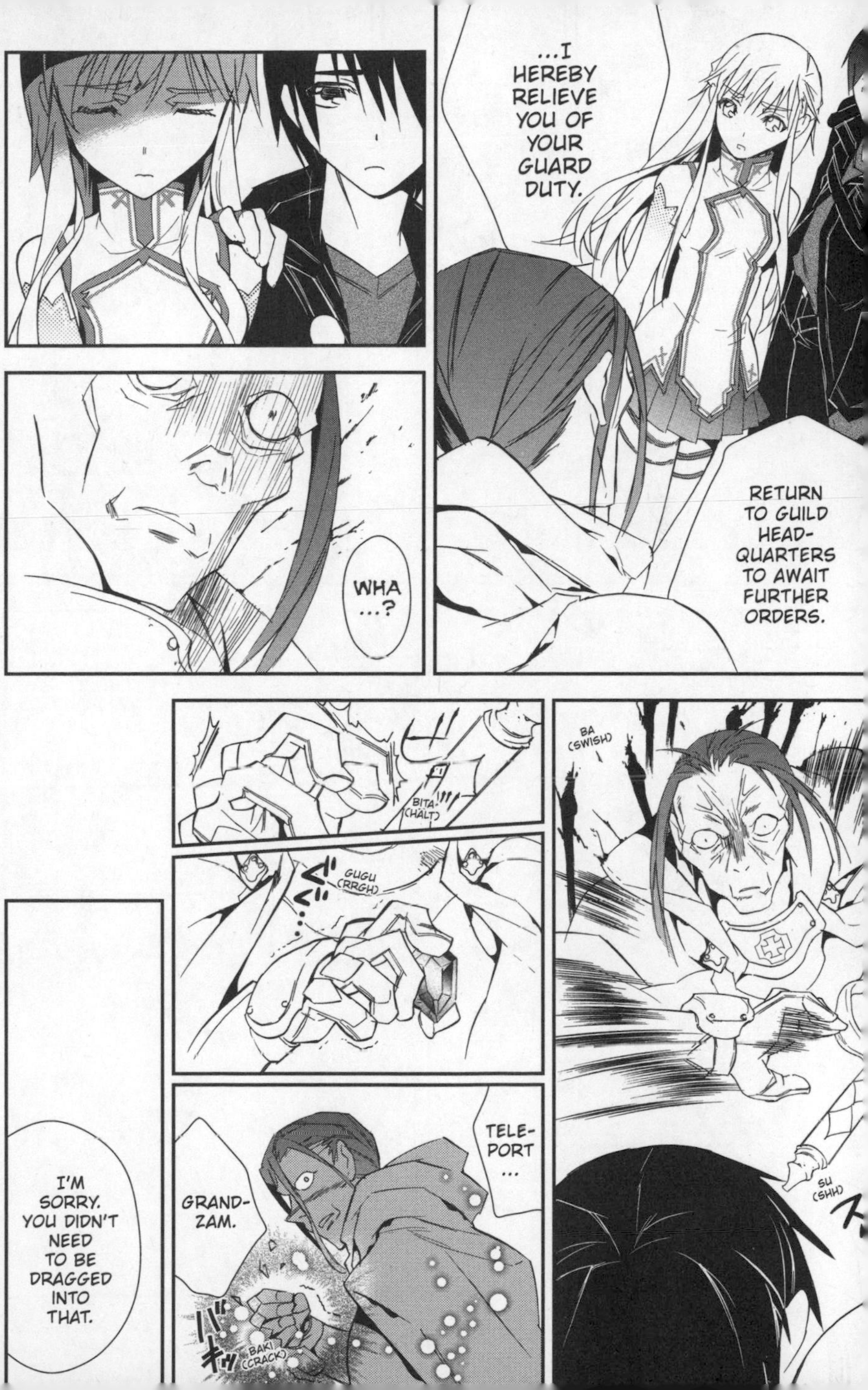
...I HEREBY RELIEVE YOU OF YOUR GUARD DUTY.
RETURN TO GUILD HEAD-QUARTERS TO AWAIT FURTHER ORDERS.
WHA ...?
BA (SWISH)
SU (SHH)
BITA (HALT)
GUGU (RRGH)
TELE-PORT ...
GRAND-ZAM.
BAKI (CRACK)
I'M SORRY. YOU DIDN'T NEED TO BE DRAGGED INTO THAT.

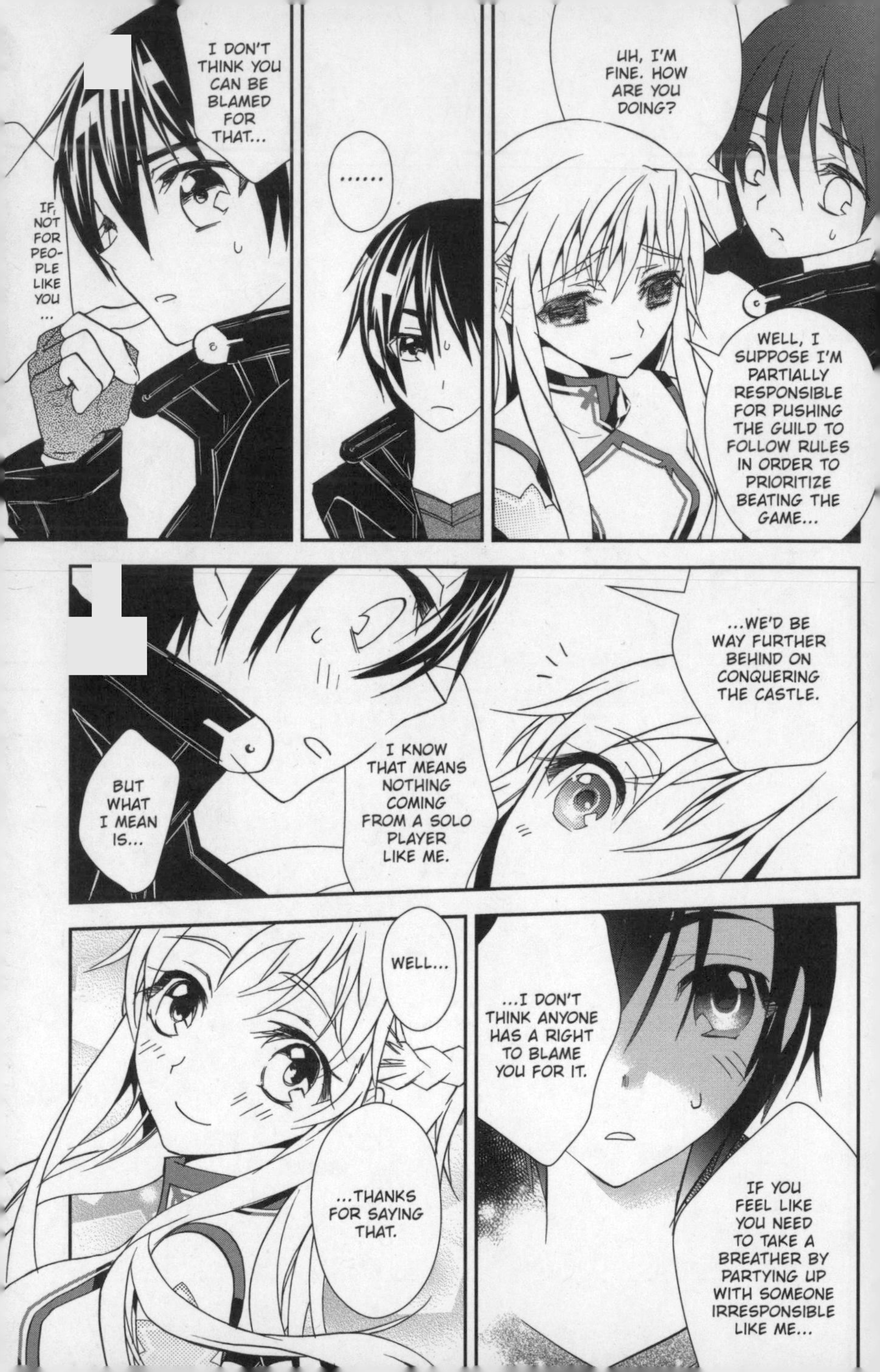
UH, I'M FINE. HOW ARE YOU DOING?
WELL, I SUPPOSE I'M PARTIALLY RESPONSIBLE FOR PUSHING THE GUILD TO FOLLOW RULES IN ORDER TO PRIORITIZE BEATING THE GAME...
......
I DON'T THINK YOU CAN BE BLAMED FOR THAT...
IF, NOT FOR PEO-PLE LIKE YOU...
...WE'D BE WAY FURTHER BEHIND ON CONQUERING THE CASTLE.
I KNOW THAT MEANS NOTHING COMING FROM A SOLO PLAYER LIKE ME.
BUT WHAT I MEAN IS...
...I DON'T THINK ANYONE HAS A RIGHT TO BLAME YOU FOR IT.
IF YOU FEEL LIKE YOU NEED TO TAKE A BREATHER BY PARTYING UP WITH SOMEONE IRRESPONSIBLE LIKE ME...
WELL...
...THANKS FOR SAYING THAT.

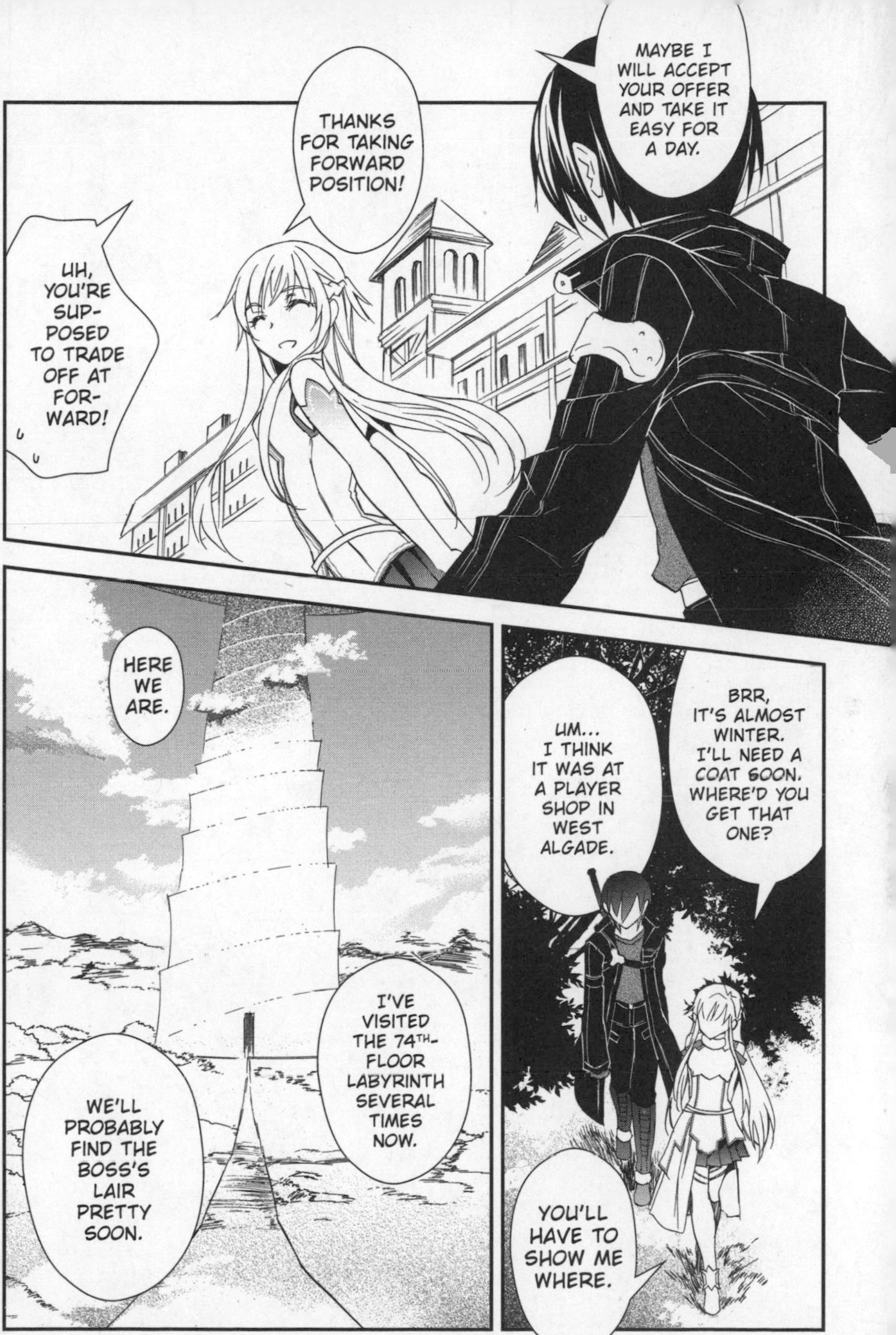
MAYBE I WILL ACCEPT YOUR OFFER AND TAKE IT EASY FOR A DAY.
THANKS FOR TAKING FORWARD POSITION!
UH, YOU'RE SUP-POSED TO TRADE OFF AT FOR-WARD!
BRR, IT'S ALMOST WINTER. I'LL NEED A COAT SOON. WHERE'D YOU GET THAT ONE?
UM... I THINK IT WAS AT A PLAYER SHOP IN WEST ALGADE.
YOU'LL HAVE TO SHOW ME WHERE.
HERE WE ARE.
I'VE VISITED THE 74TH-FLOOR LABYRINTH SEVERAL TIMES NOW.
WE'LL PROBABLY FIND THE BOSS'S LAIR PRETTY SOON.

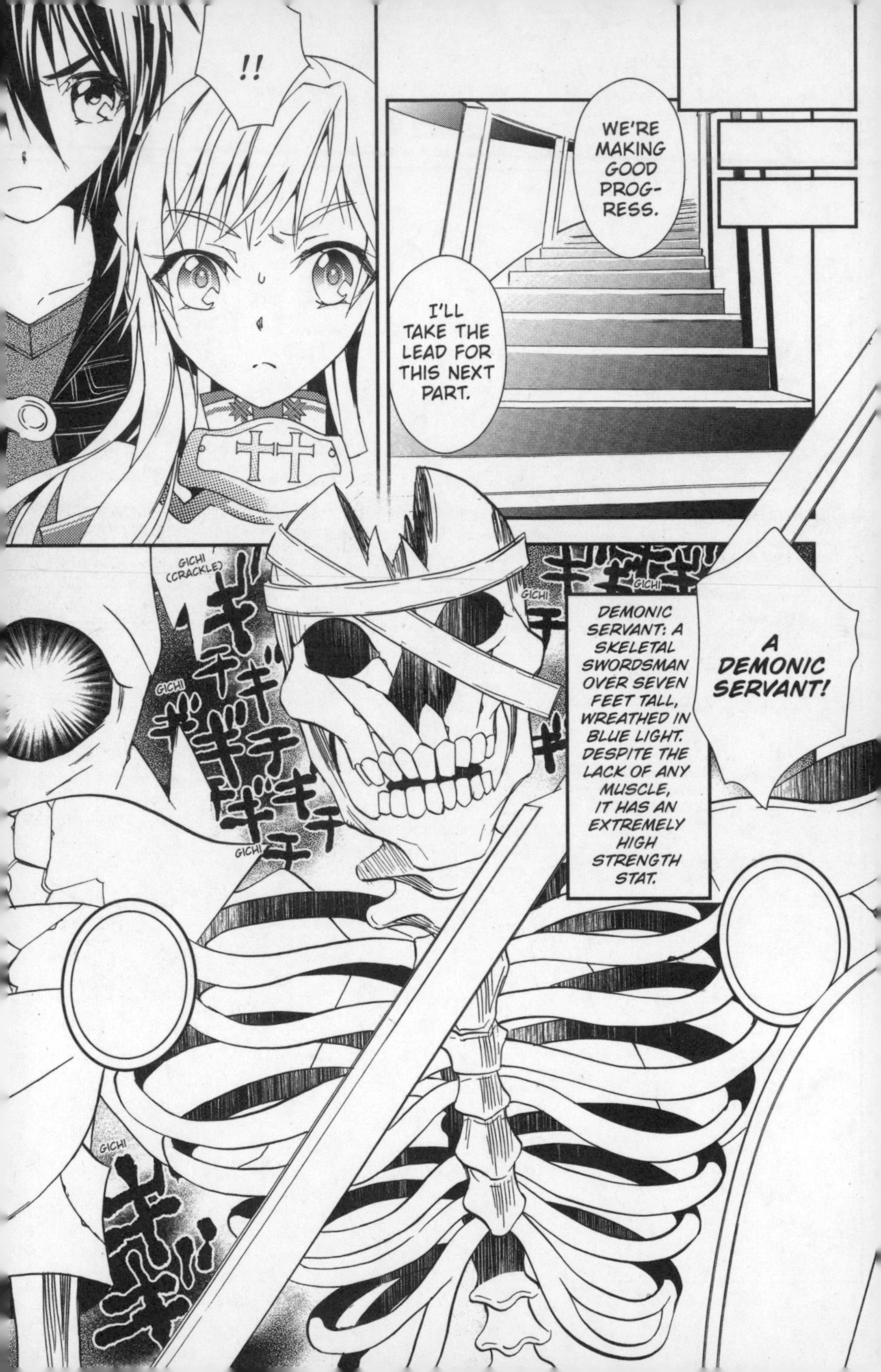
WE'RE MAKING GOOD PROG-RESS.
I'LL TAKE THE LEAD FOR THIS NEXT PART.
!!
A DEMONIC SERVANT!
DEMONIC SERVANT: A SKELETAL SWORDSMAN OVER SEVEN FEET TALL, WREATHED IN BLUE LIGHT. DESPITE THE LACK OF ANY MUSCLE, IT HAS AN EXTREMELY HIGH STRENGTH STAT.
GICHI
GICHI
GICHI (CRACKLE)
GICHI
GICHI
GICHI

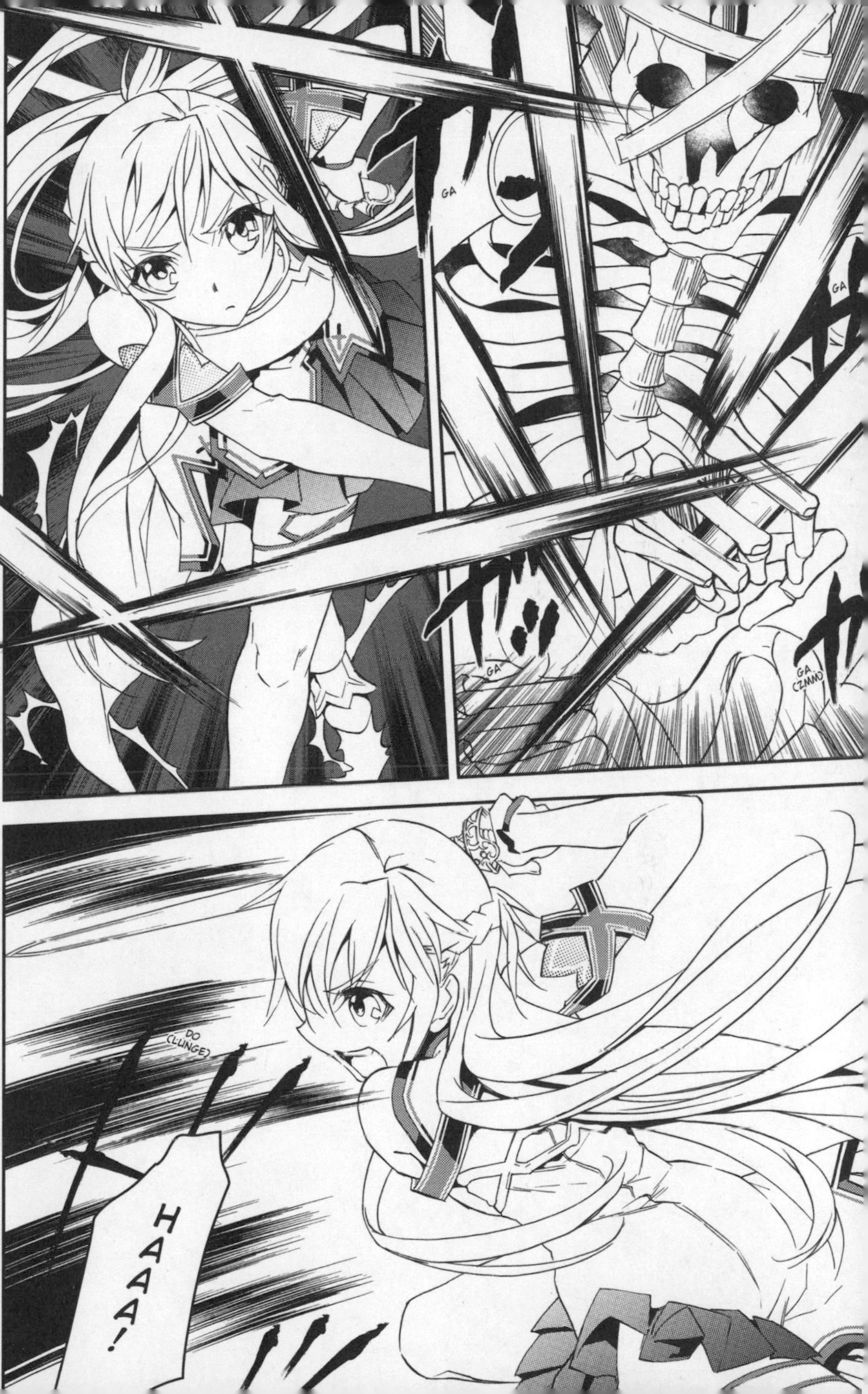
GA
GA
GA
GA
(ZMM)
DO
(LUNGE)
HAAAA!

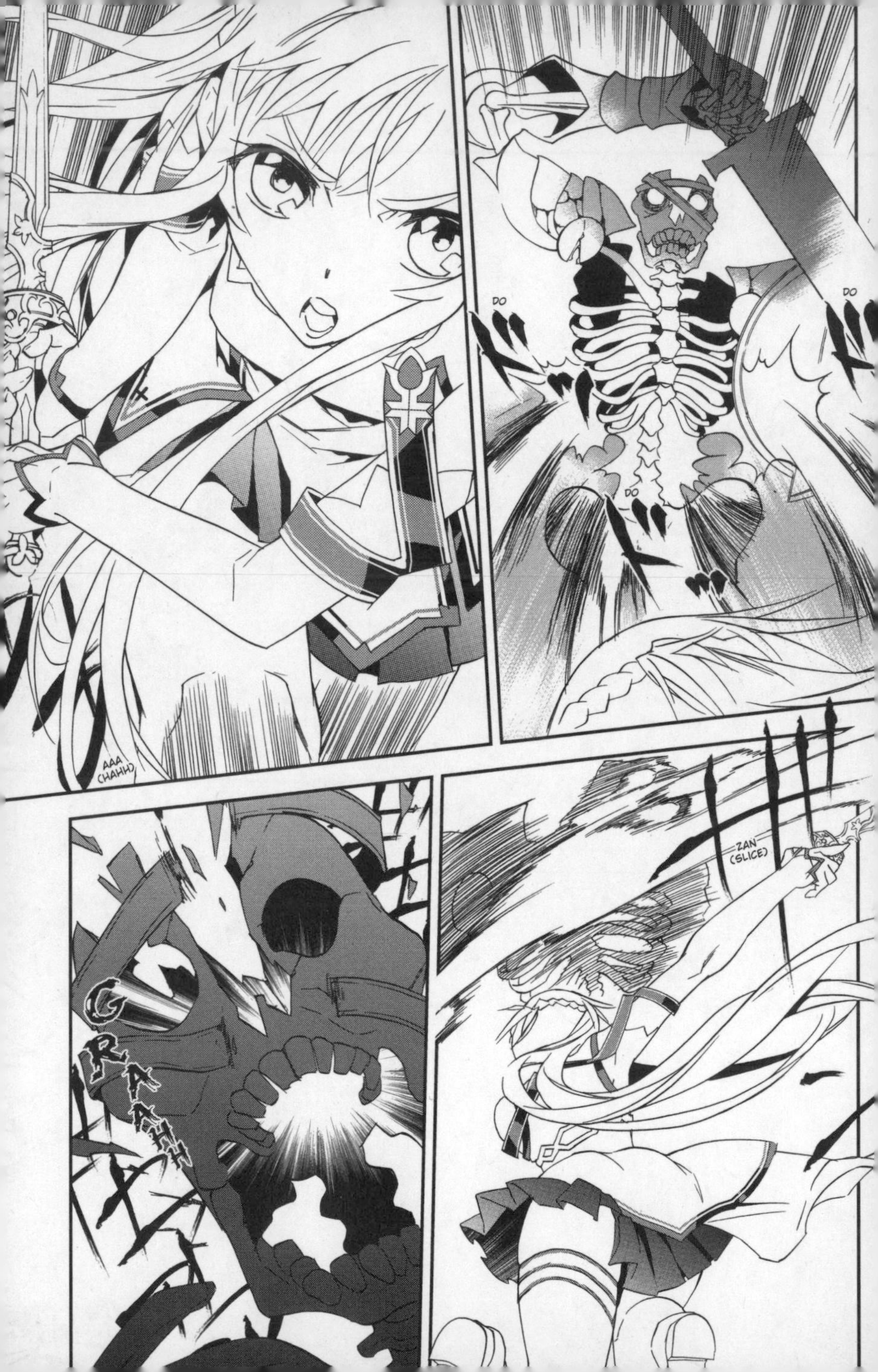
DO
DO
DO
AAA
(HAHH)
ZAN
(SLICE)
GRAAHH

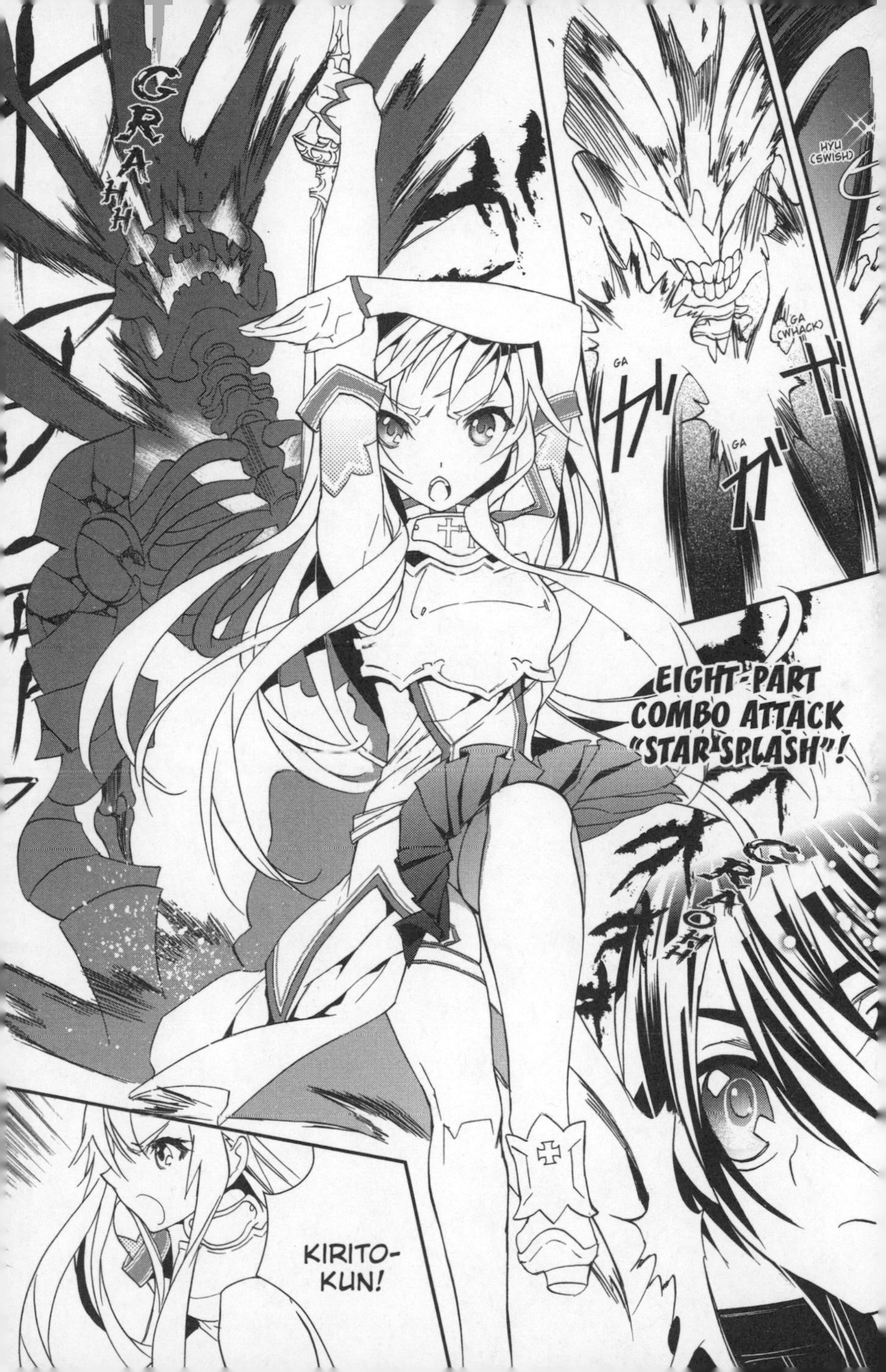
HYU (SWISH)
GA (WHACK)
GA
GA
GRAHH
EIGHT-PART COMBO ATTACK "STAR SPLASH"!
KIRITO-KUN!

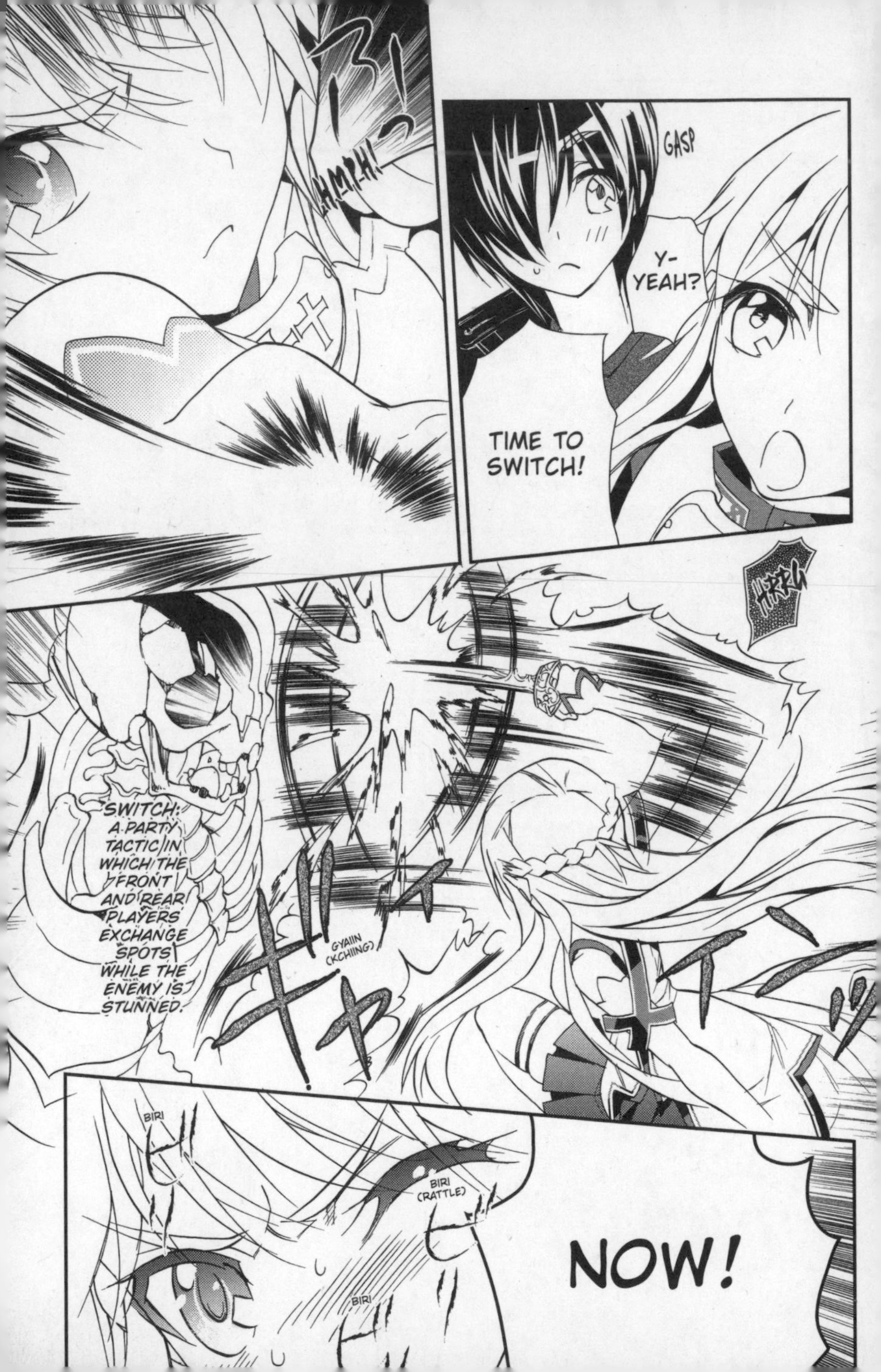
GASP
Y-YEAH?
TIME TO SWITCH!
HMPH!
HRRG
SWITCH: A PARTY TACTIC IN WHICH THE FRONT AND REAR PLAYERS EXCHANGE SPOTS WHILE THE ENEMY IS STUNNED.
GYAIIN (KCHIING)
NOW!
BIRI (RATTLE)
BIRI
BIRI

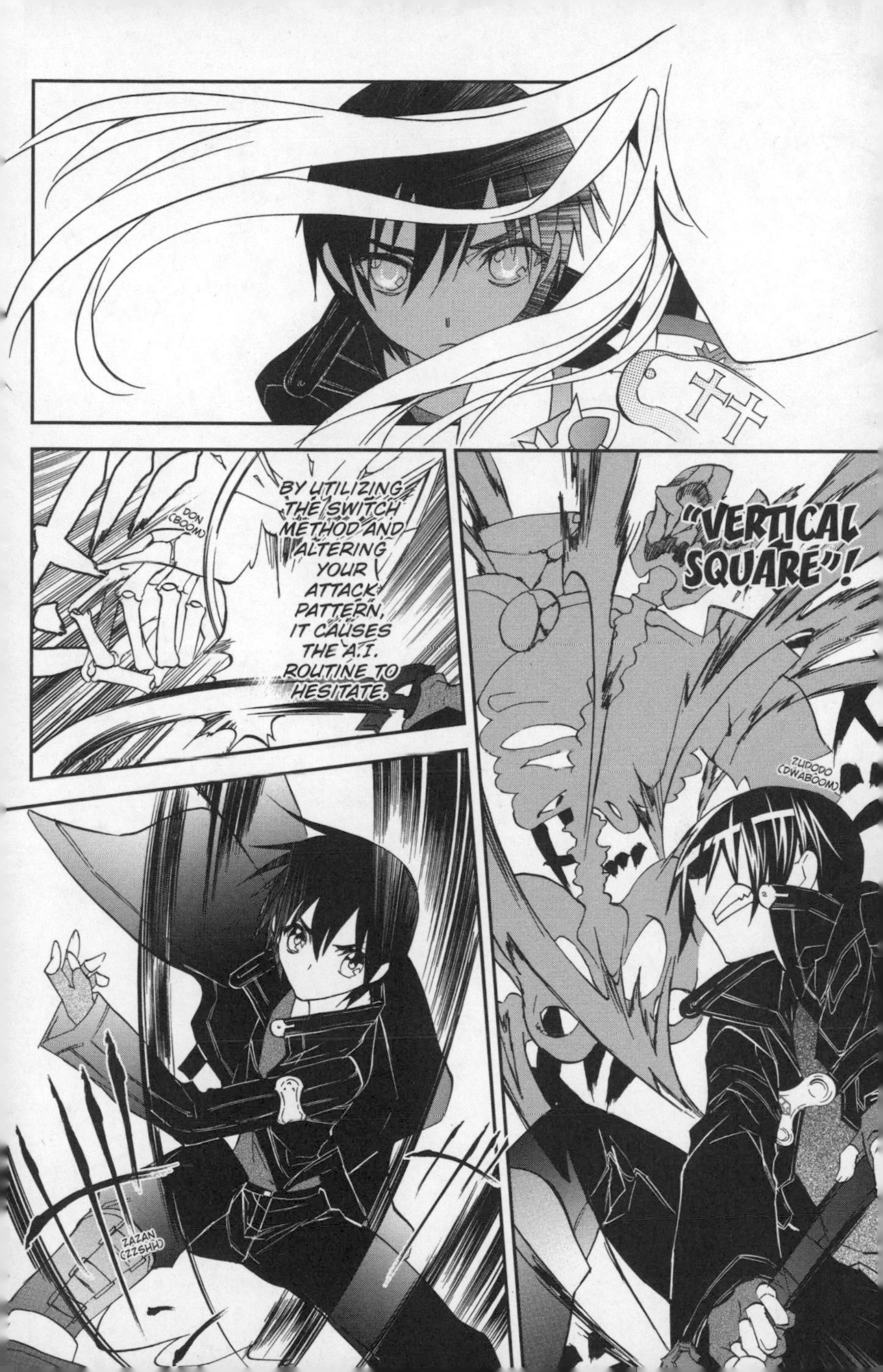
"VERTICAL SQUARE"!
ZUDODO (DWABOOM)
BY UTILIZING THE SWITCH METHOD AND ALTERING YOUR ATTACK PATTERN, IT CAUSES THE A.I. ROUTINE TO HESITATE.
DON (BOOM)
ZAZAN (ZZSHH)

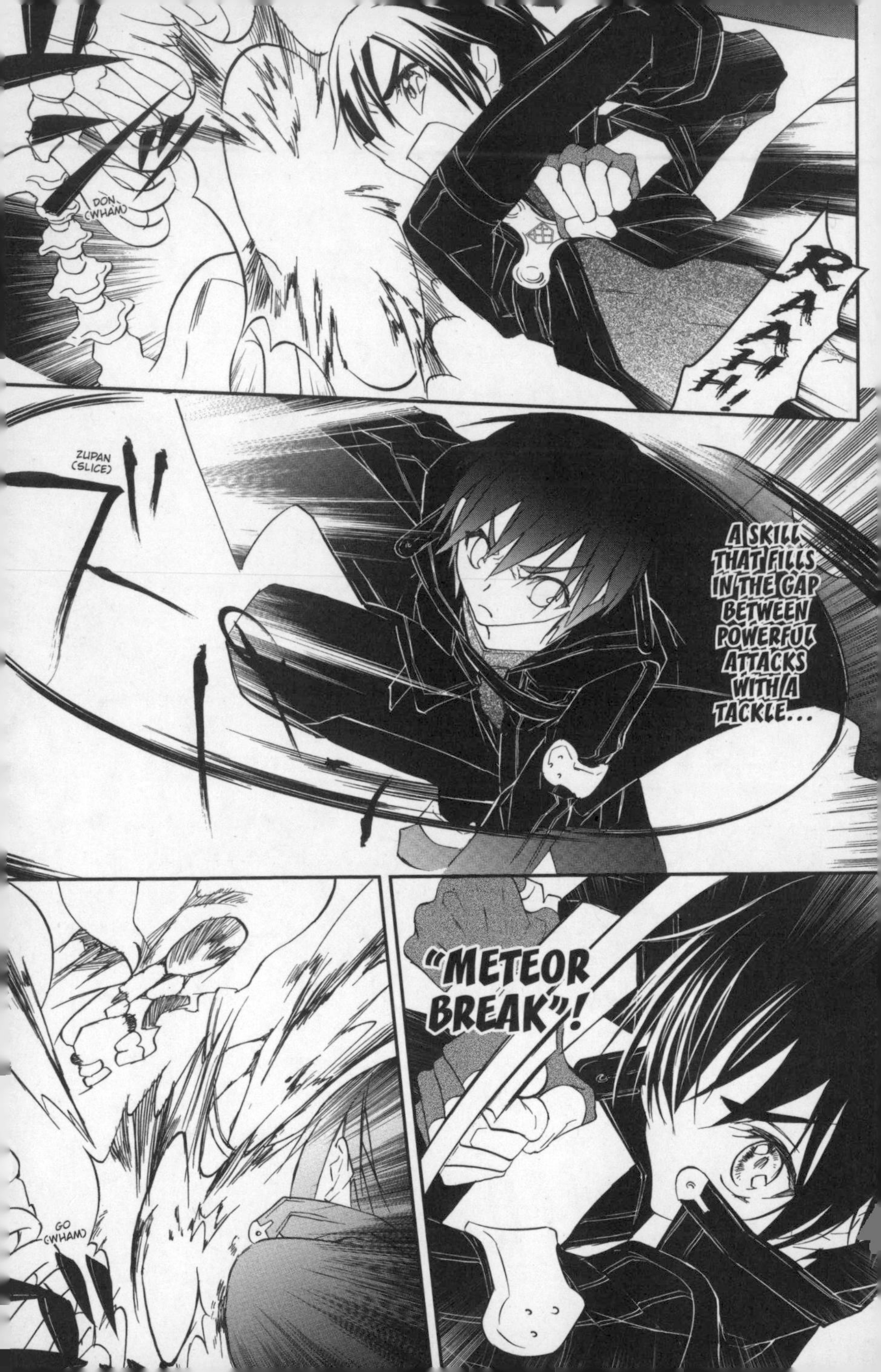
RAAH!
DON (WHAM)
A SKILL THAT FILLS IN THE GAP BETWEEN POWERFUL ATTACKS WITH A TACKLE...
ZUPAN (SLICE)
"METEOR BREAK"!
GO (WHAM)

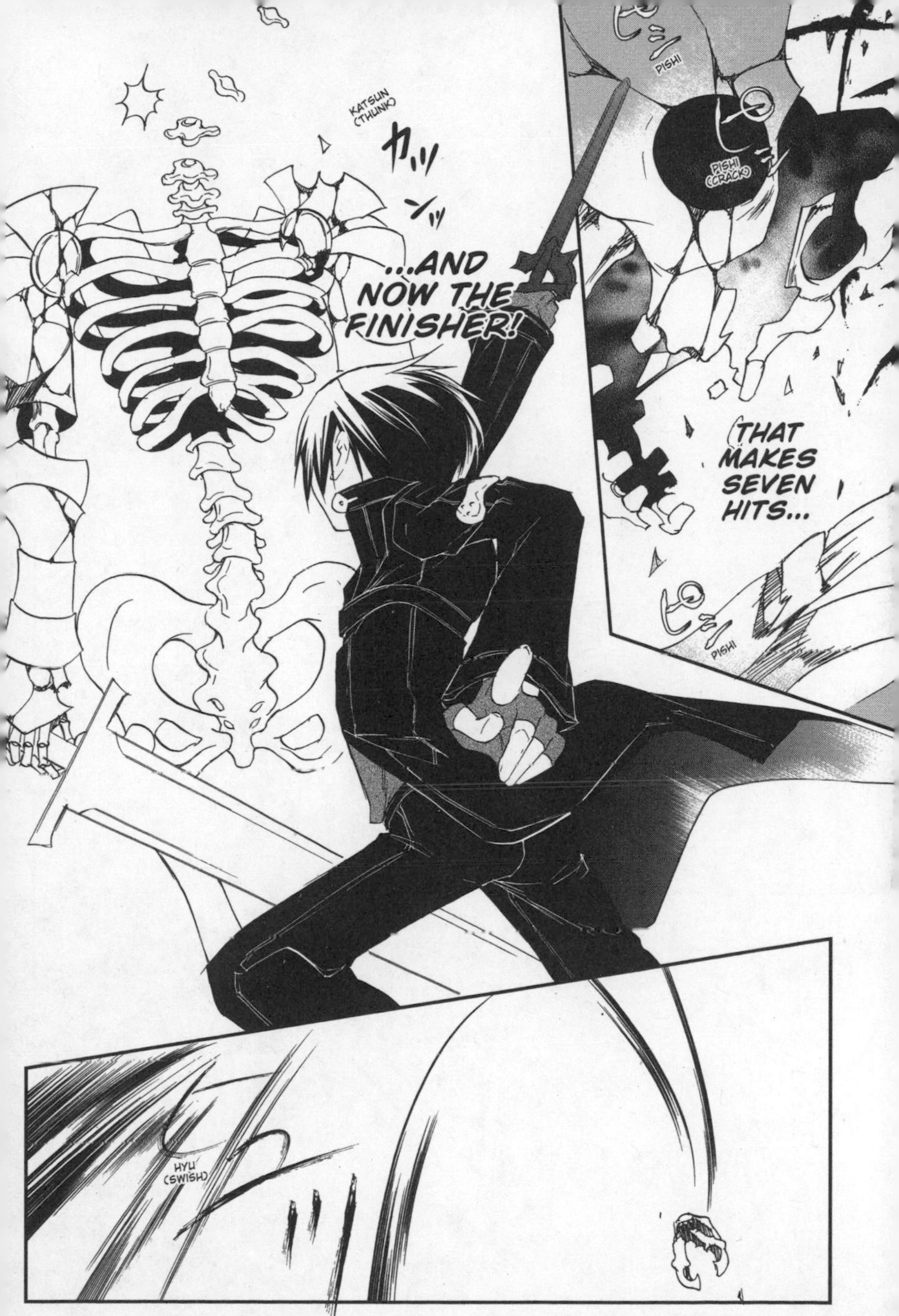
PISHI
PISHI (CRACK)
THAT MAKES SEVEN HITS...
PISHI
KATSUN (THUNK)
...AND NOW THE FINISHER!
HYU (SWISH)

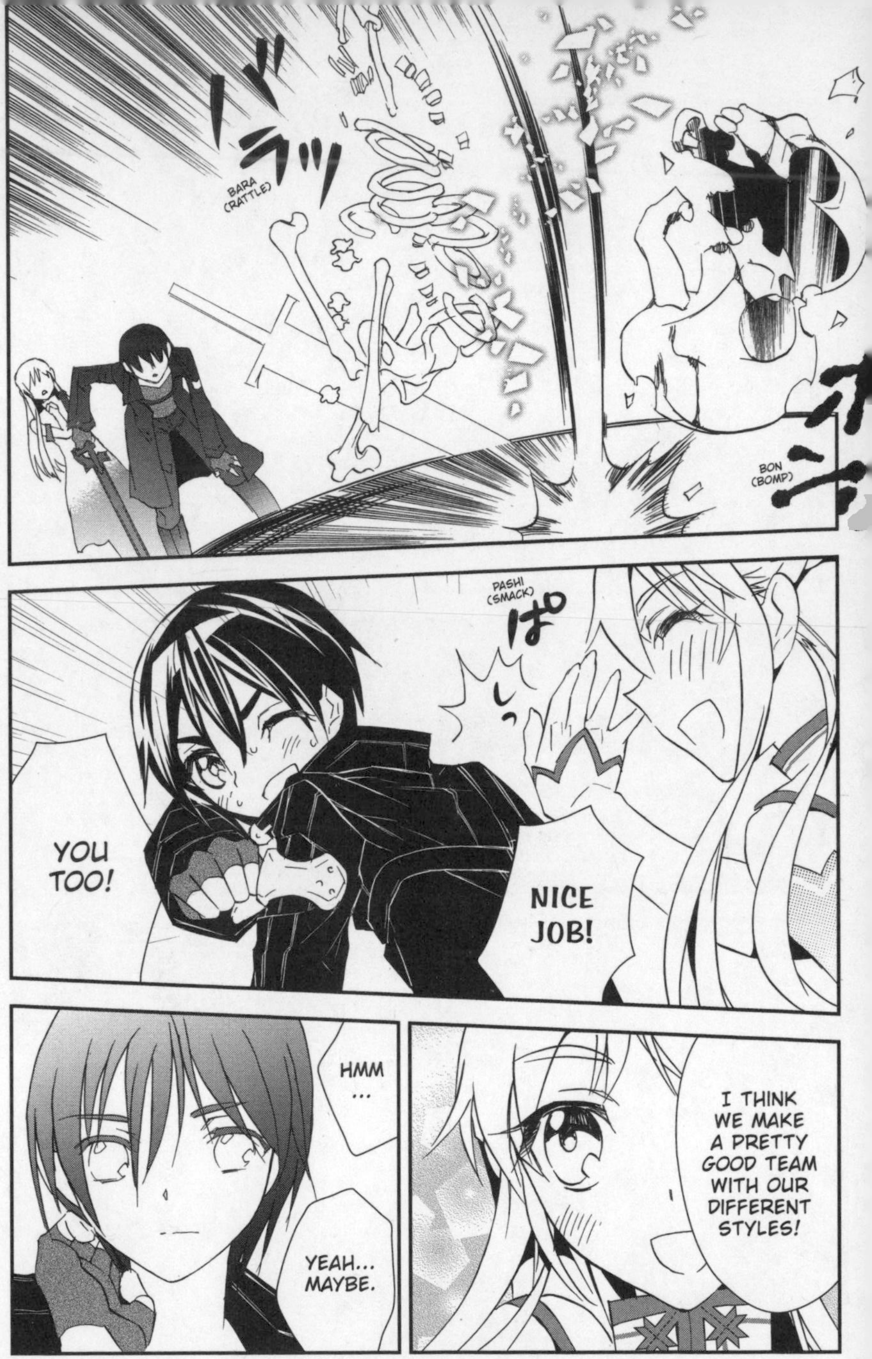
BON
(BOMP)
バラッ
BARA
(RATTLE)
PASHI
(SMACK)
ぱしっ
NICE JOB!
YOU TOO!
I THINK WE MAKE A PRETTY GOOD TEAM WITH OUR DIFFERENT STYLES!
HMM...
YEAH... MAYBE.

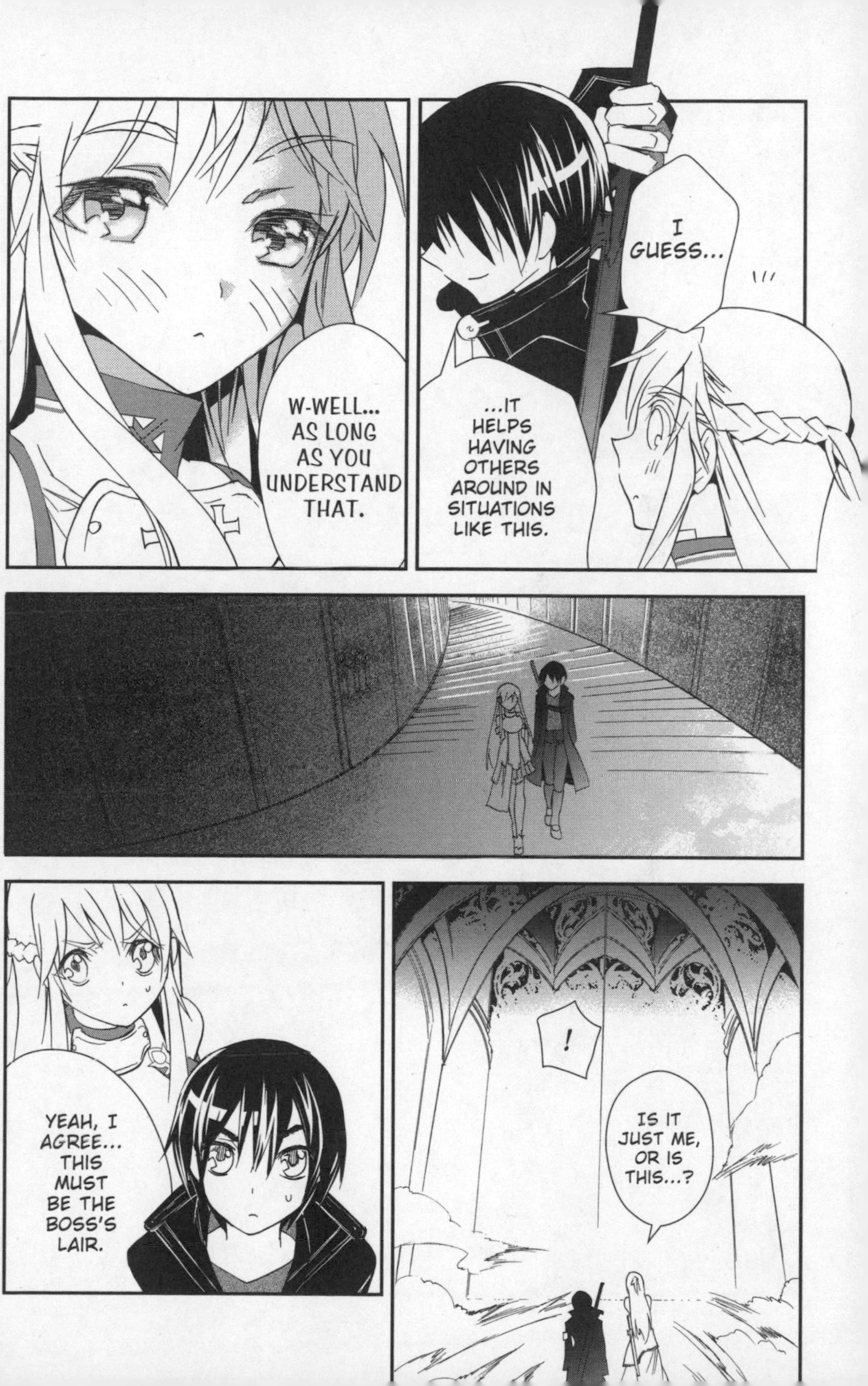
I GUESS...
...IT HELPS HAVING OTHERS AROUND IN SITUATIONS LIKE THIS.
W-WELL... AS LONG AS YOU UNDERSTAND THAT.
!
IS IT JUST ME, OR IS THIS...?
YEAH, I AGREE... THIS MUST BE THE BOSS'S LAIR.

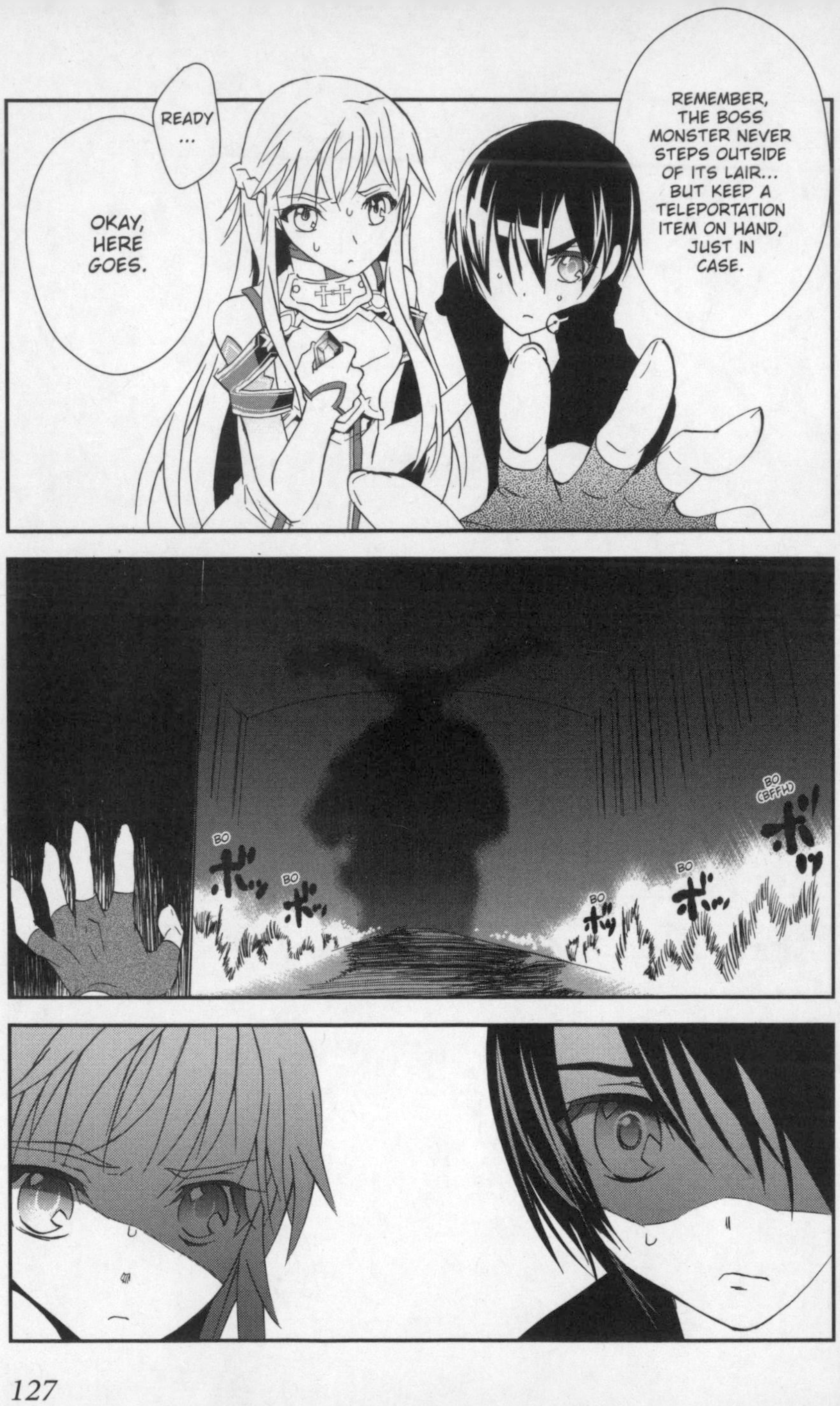
REMEMBER, THE BOSS MONSTER NEVER STEPS OUTSIDE OF ITS LAIR... BUT KEEP A TELEPORTATION ITEM ON HAND, JUST IN CASE.
READY ...
OKAY, HERE GOES.
BO (BFFH)
BO
BO
BO
BO

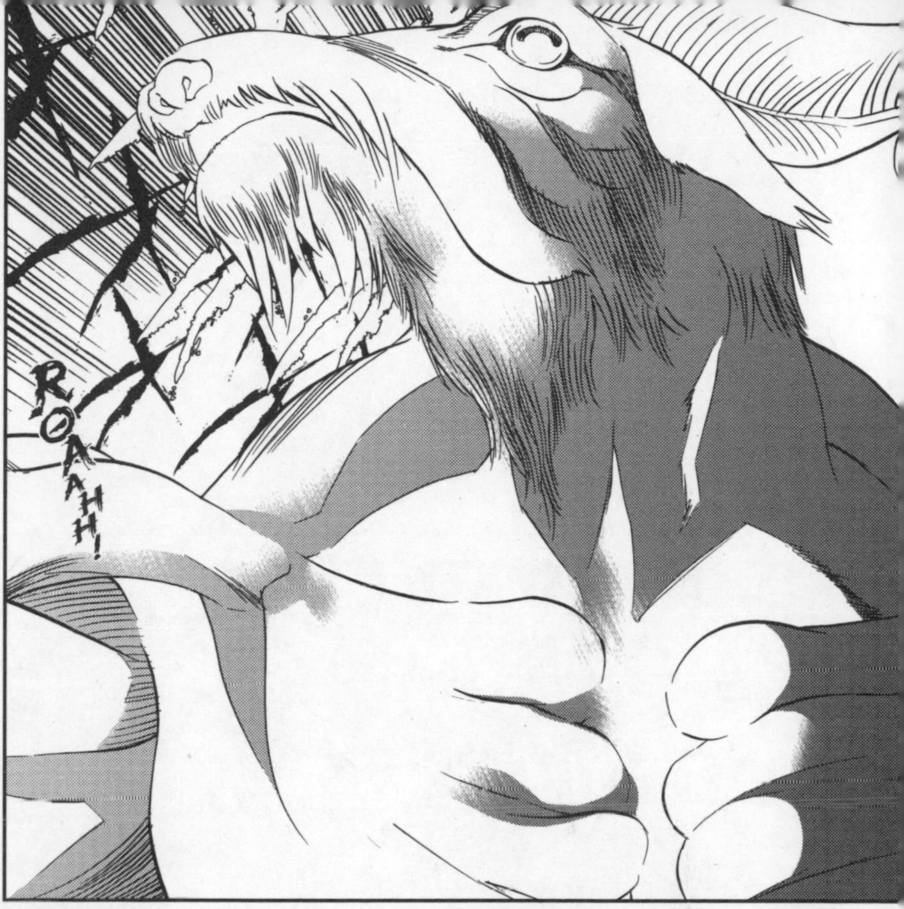
ROAAHH!

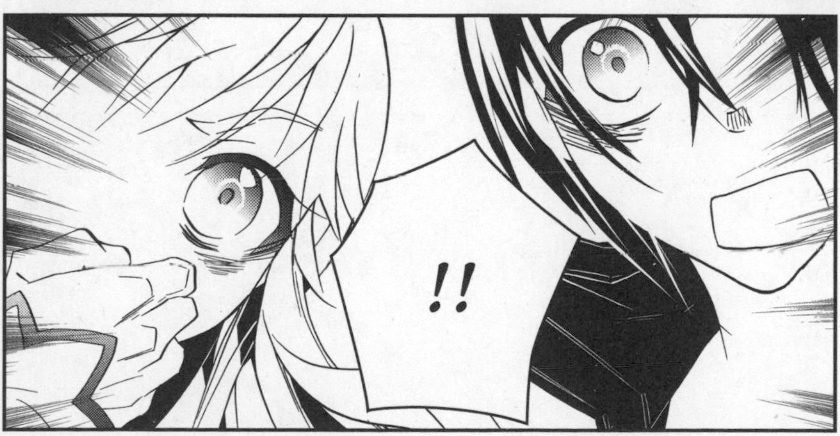
!!

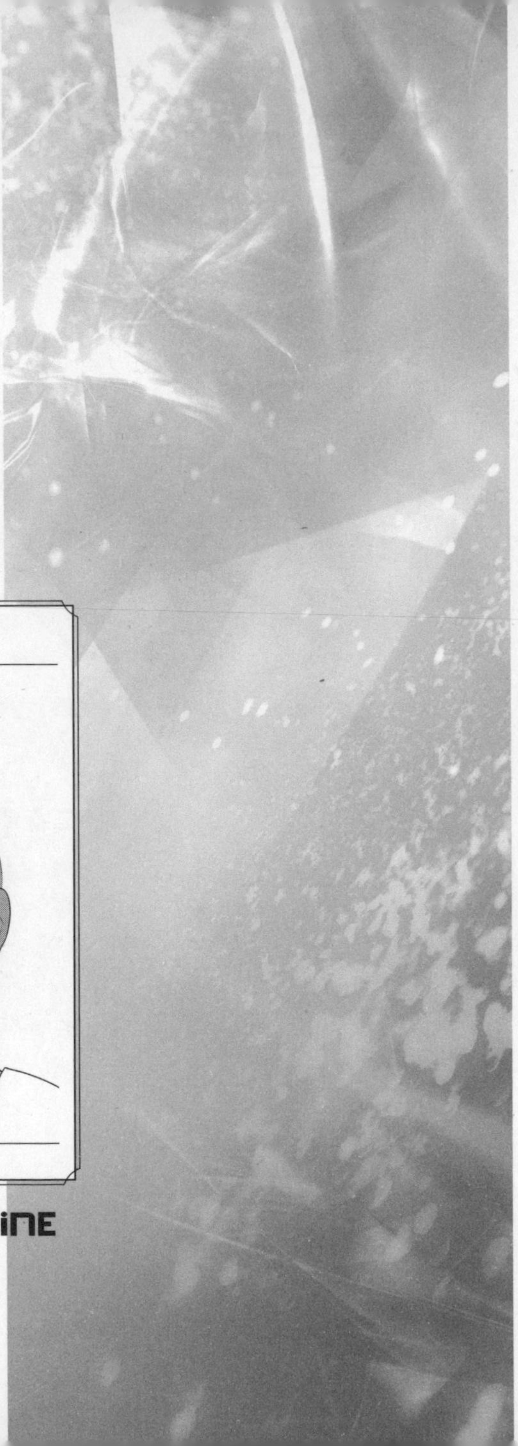

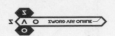

character

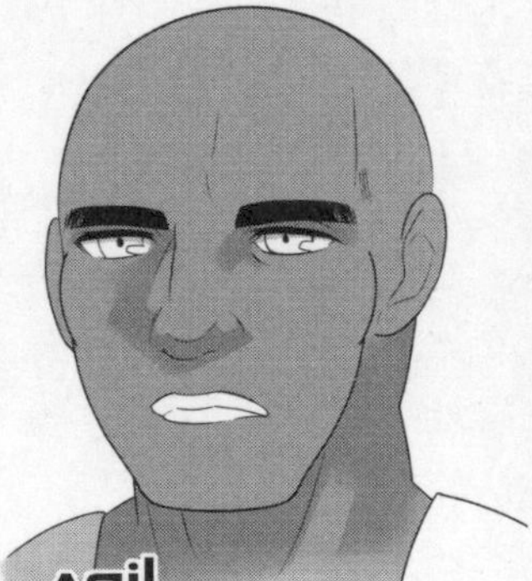

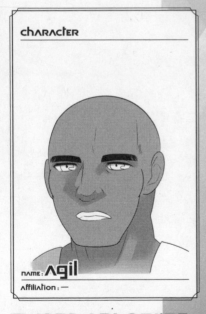

NAME: Agil

Affiliation: —

SWORD ART ONLINE
Aincrad

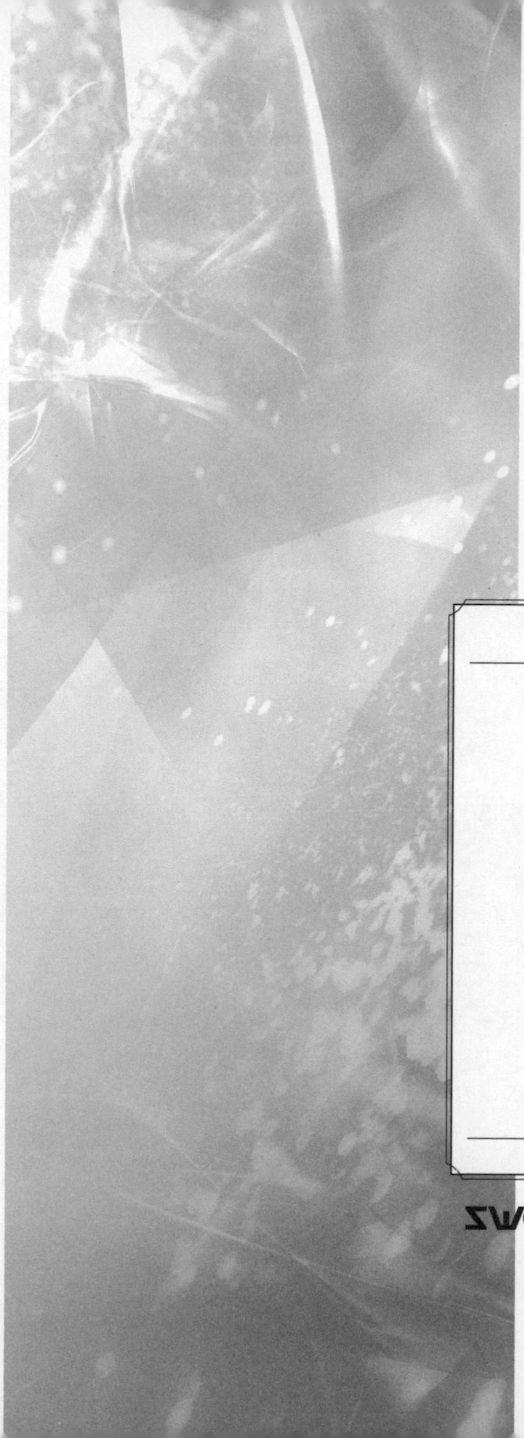

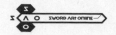

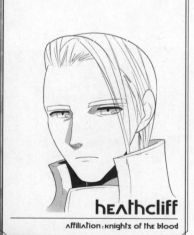

character

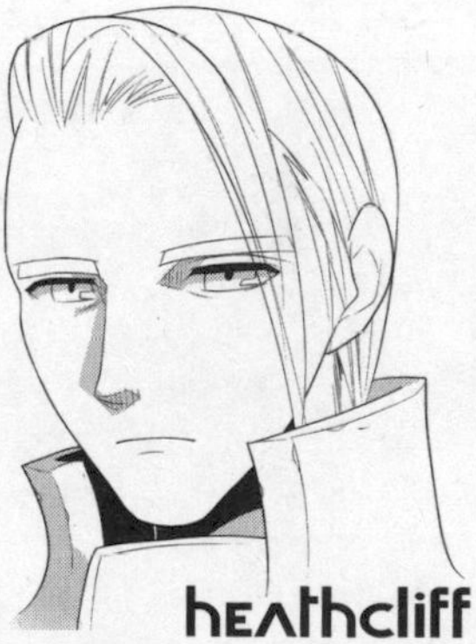

heathcliff

affiliation : knights of the blood

SWORD ART ONLINE

aincrad

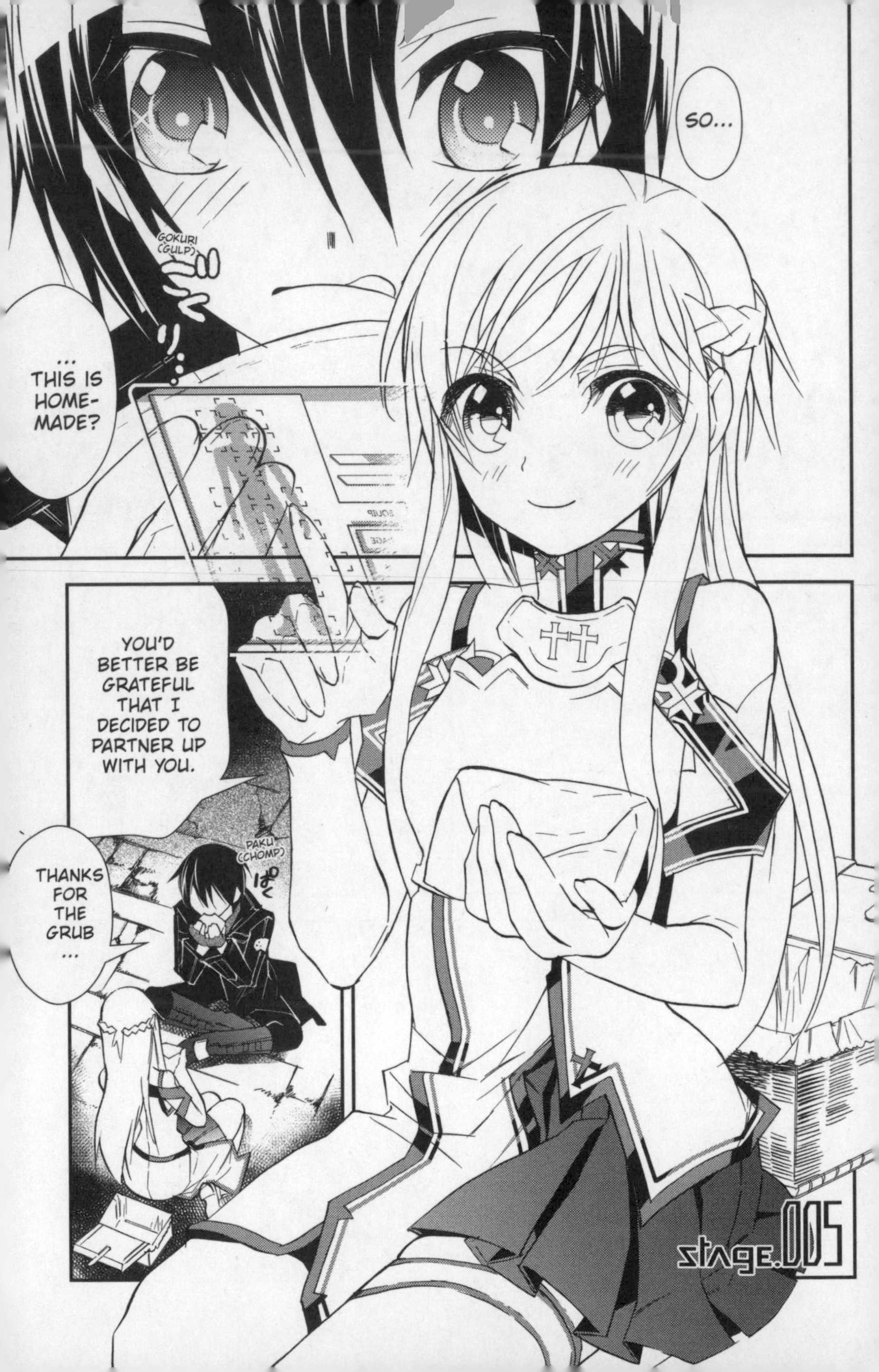
SO...
GOKURI (GULP)
... THIS IS HOME-MADE?
YOU'D BETTER BE GRATEFUL THAT I DECIDED TO PARTNER UP WITH YOU.
PAKU (CHOMP)
THANKS FOR THE GRUB ...
stage.005

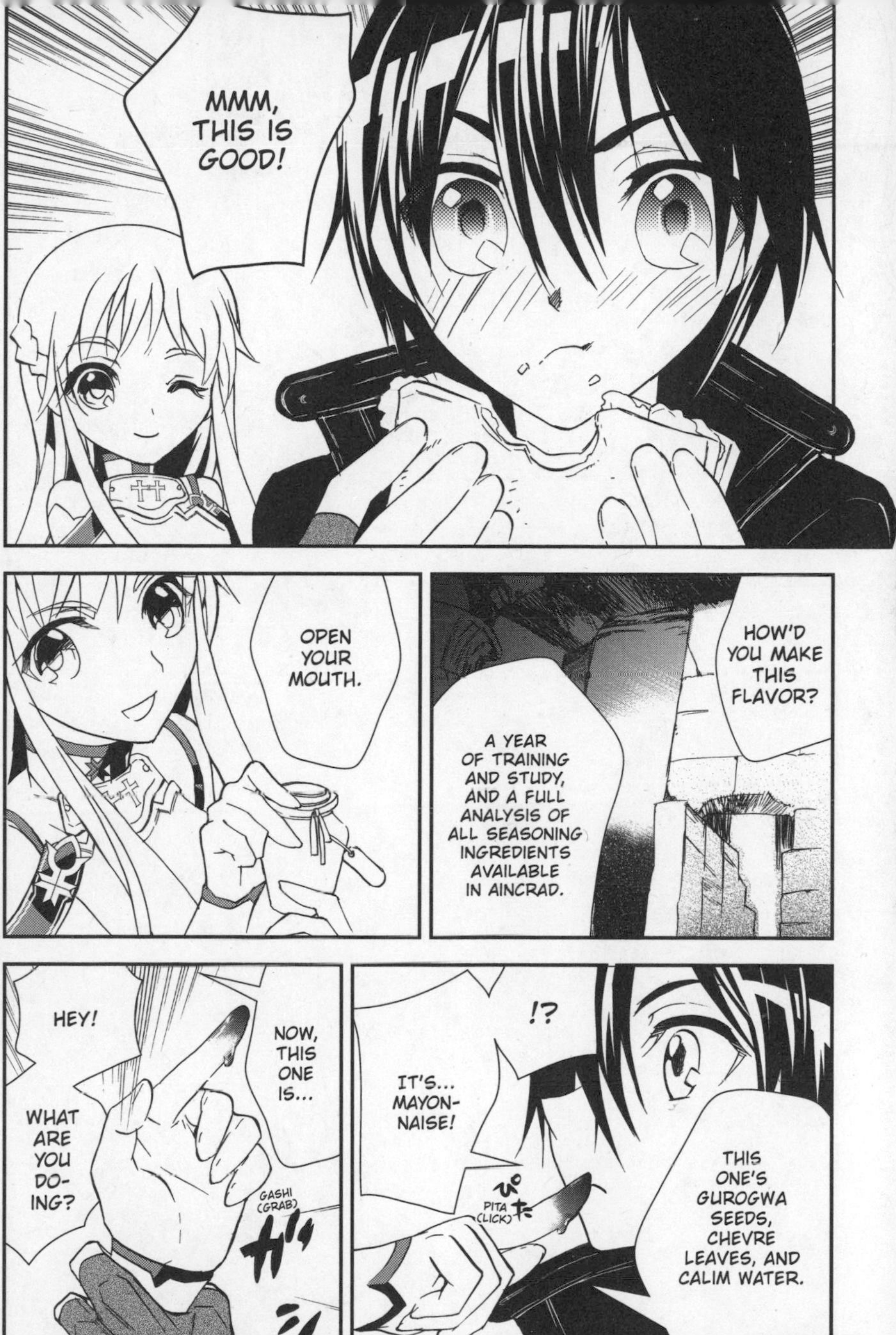
MMM, THIS IS GOOD!
HOW'D YOU MAKE THIS FLAVOR?
A YEAR OF TRAINING AND STUDY, AND A FULL ANALYSIS OF ALL SEASONING INGREDIENTS AVAILABLE IN AINCRAD.
OPEN YOUR MOUTH.
!?
IT'S... MAYON-NAISE!
THIS ONE'S GUROGWA SEEDS, CHEVRE LEAVES, AND CALIM WATER.
PITA (CLICK)
NOW, THIS ONE IS...
HEY!
WHAT ARE YOU DO-ING?
GASHI (GRAB)

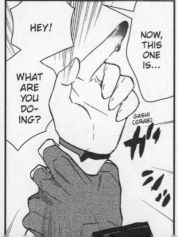

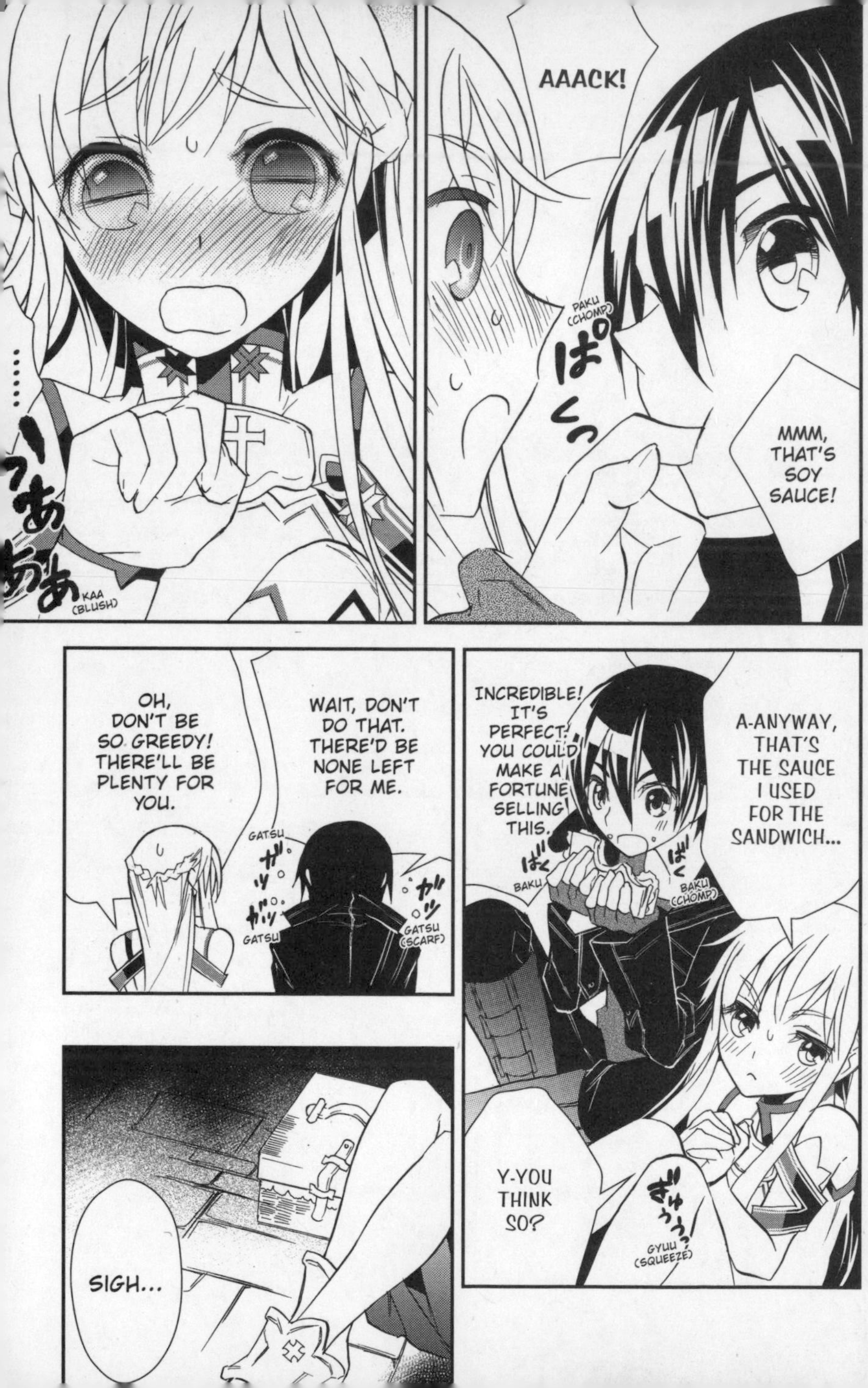
AAACK!
ぱくっ
PAKU (CHOMP)
MMM, THAT'S SOY SAUCE!
......
かあああ
KAA (BLUSH)
A-ANYWAY, THAT'S THE SAUCE I USED FOR THE SANDWICH...
INCREDIBLE! IT'S PERFECT! YOU COULD MAKE A FORTUNE SELLING THIS.
ばく
BAKU (CHOMP)
ばく
BAKU
ぎゅううっ
GYUU (SQUEEZE)
Y-YOU THINK SO?
WAIT, DON'T DO THAT. THERE'D BE NONE LEFT FOR ME.
OH, DON'T BE SO GREEDY! THERE'LL BE PLENTY FOR YOU.
ガツ
GATSU (SCARF)
ガツ
GATSU
ガツ
GATSU
SIGH...

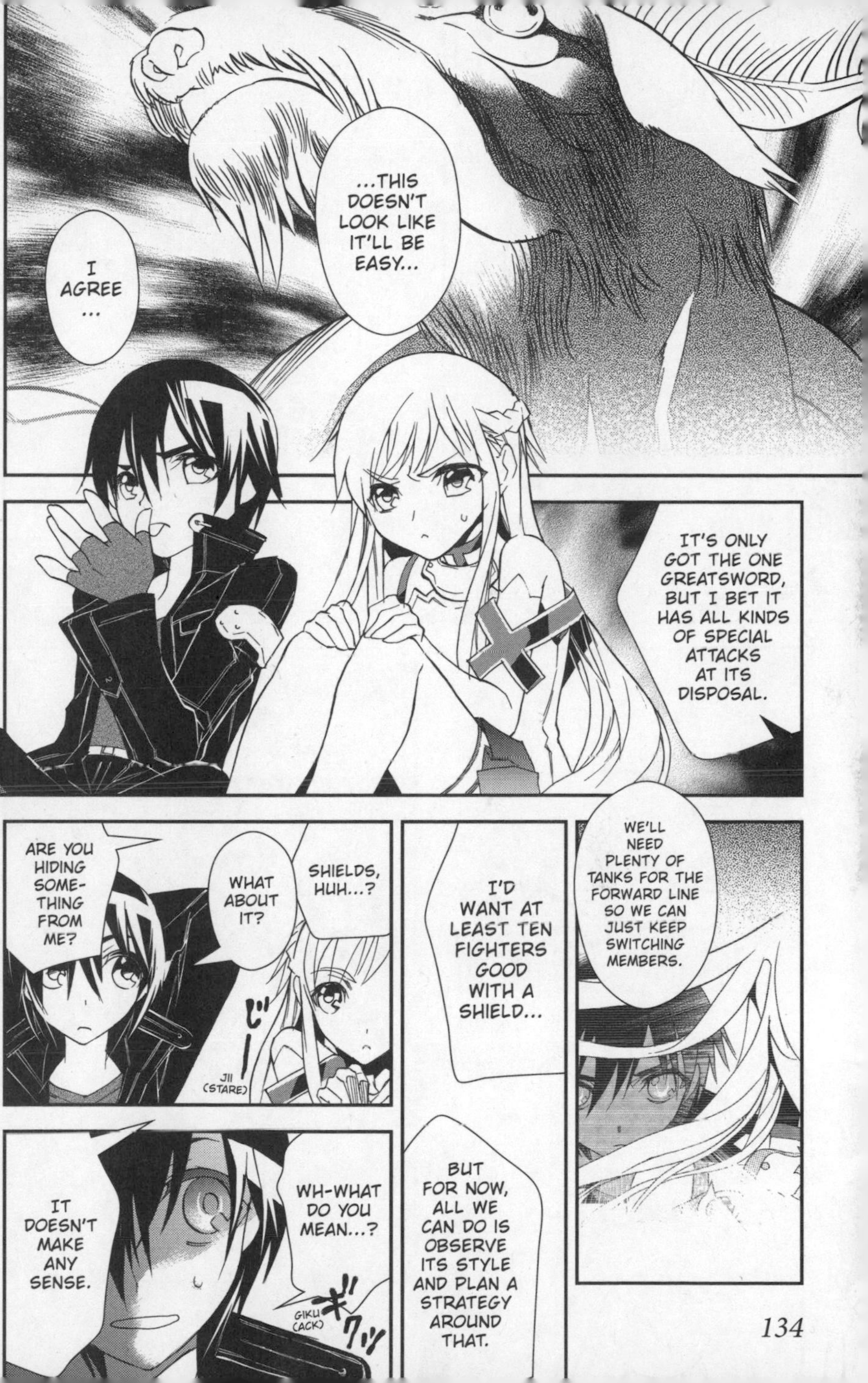
...THIS DOESN'T LOOK LIKE IT'LL BE EASY...
I AGREE...
IT'S ONLY GOT THE ONE GREATSWORD, BUT I BET IT HAS ALL KINDS OF SPECIAL ATTACKS AT ITS DISPOSAL.
WE'LL NEED PLENTY OF TANKS FOR THE FORWARD LINE SO WE CAN JUST KEEP SWITCHING MEMBERS.
I'D WANT AT LEAST TEN FIGHTERS GOOD WITH A SHIELD...
BUT FOR NOW, ALL WE CAN DO IS OBSERVE ITS STYLE AND PLAN A STRATEGY AROUND THAT.
SHIELDS, HUH...?
WHAT ABOUT IT?
ARE YOU HIDING SOMETHING FROM ME?
JII (STARE)
WH-WHAT DO YOU MEAN...?
GIKU (ACK)
IT DOESN'T MAKE ANY SENSE.

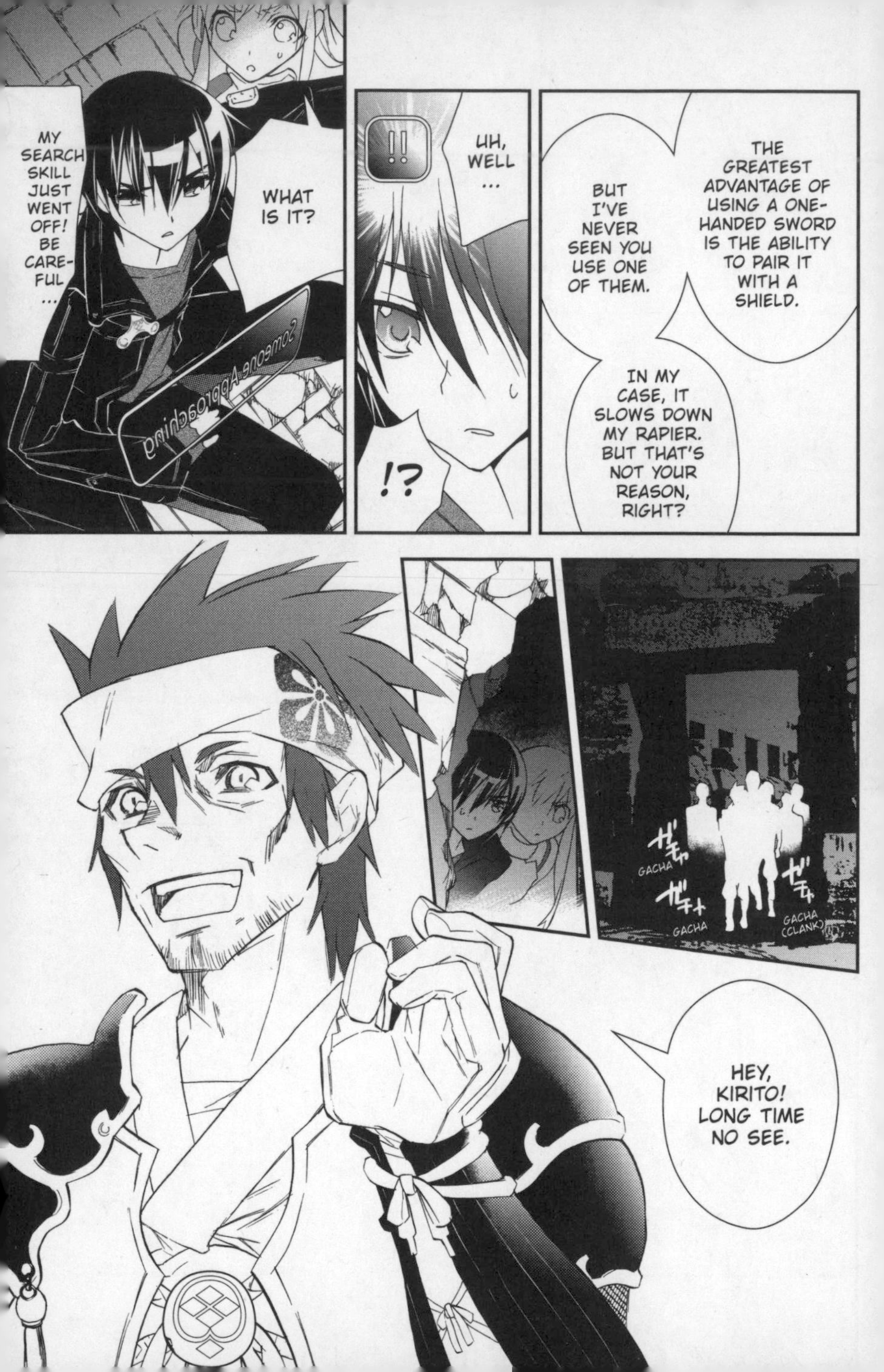
THE GREATEST ADVANTAGE OF USING A ONE-HANDED SWORD IS THE ABILITY TO PAIR IT WITH A SHIELD.
BUT I'VE NEVER SEEN YOU USE ONE OF THEM.
IN MY CASE, IT SLOWS DOWN MY RAPIER. BUT THAT'S NOT YOUR REASON, RIGHT?
!!
UH, WELL ...
!?
WHAT IS IT?
MY SEARCH SKILL JUST WENT OFF! BE CARE-FUL ...
Someone Approaching
ガチャ
GACHA (CLANK)
ガチャ
GACHA
ガチャ
GACHA
HEY, KIRITO! LONG TIME NO SEE.

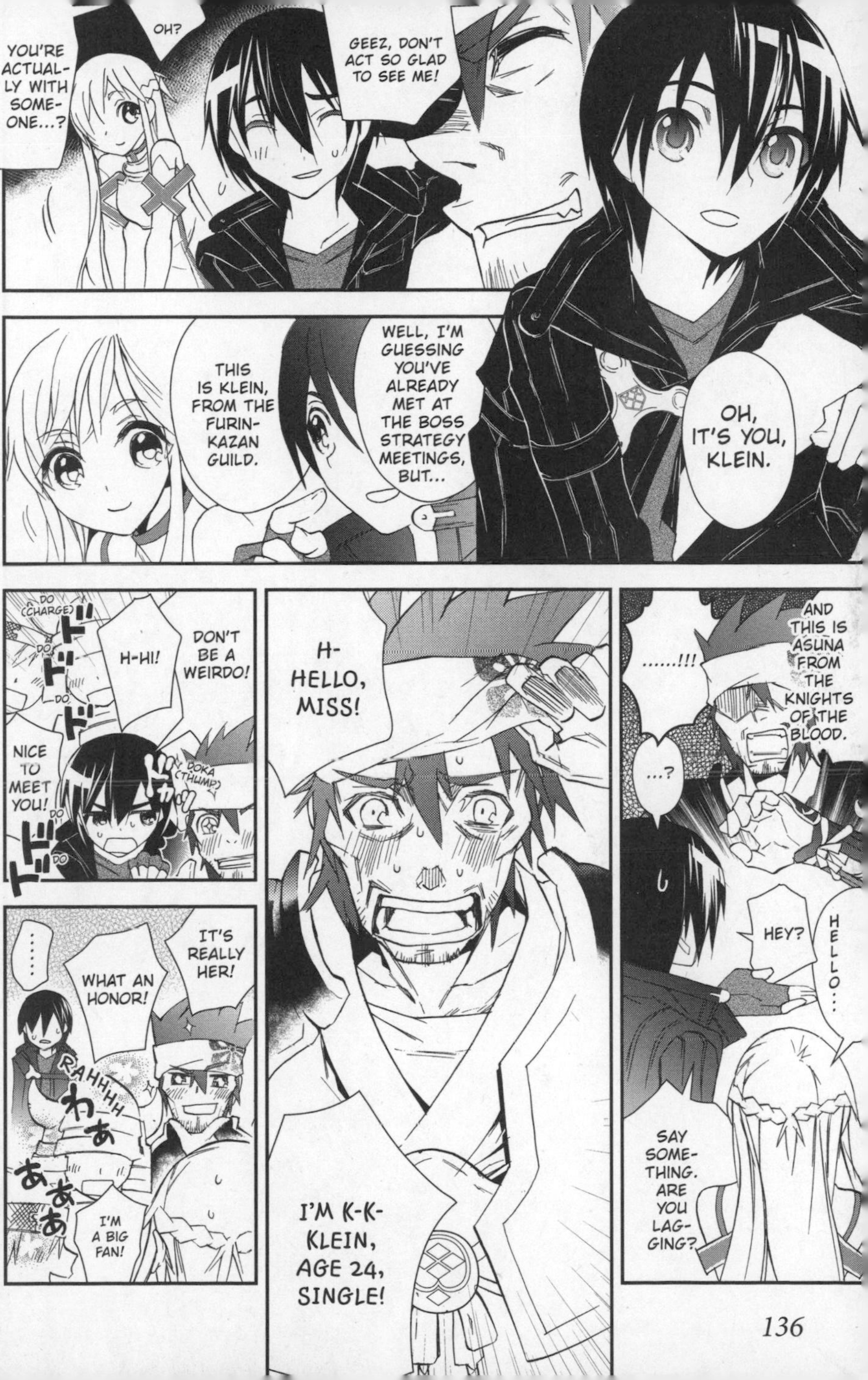
OH, IT'S YOU, KLEIN.
GEEZ, DON'T ACT SO GLAD TO SEE ME!
OH?
YOU'RE ACTUAL-LY WITH SOME-ONE...?
WELL, I'M GUESSING YOU'VE ALREADY MET AT THE BOSS STRATEGY MEETINGS, BUT...
THIS IS KLEIN, FROM THE FURIN-KAZAN GUILD.
AND THIS IS ASUNA FROM THE KNIGHTS OF THE BLOOD.
......!!!
...?
HEY?
HELLO...
SAY SOME-THING. ARE YOU LAG-GING?
H-HELLO, MISS!
I'M K-K-KLEIN, AGE 24, SINGLE!
DO (CHARGE)
DO
DO
DON'T BE A WEIRDO!
H-HI!
DOKA (THUMP)
NICE TO MEET YOU!
DO
DO
IT'S REALLY HER!
WHAT AN HONOR!
......
RAHHHH
I'M A BIG FAN!

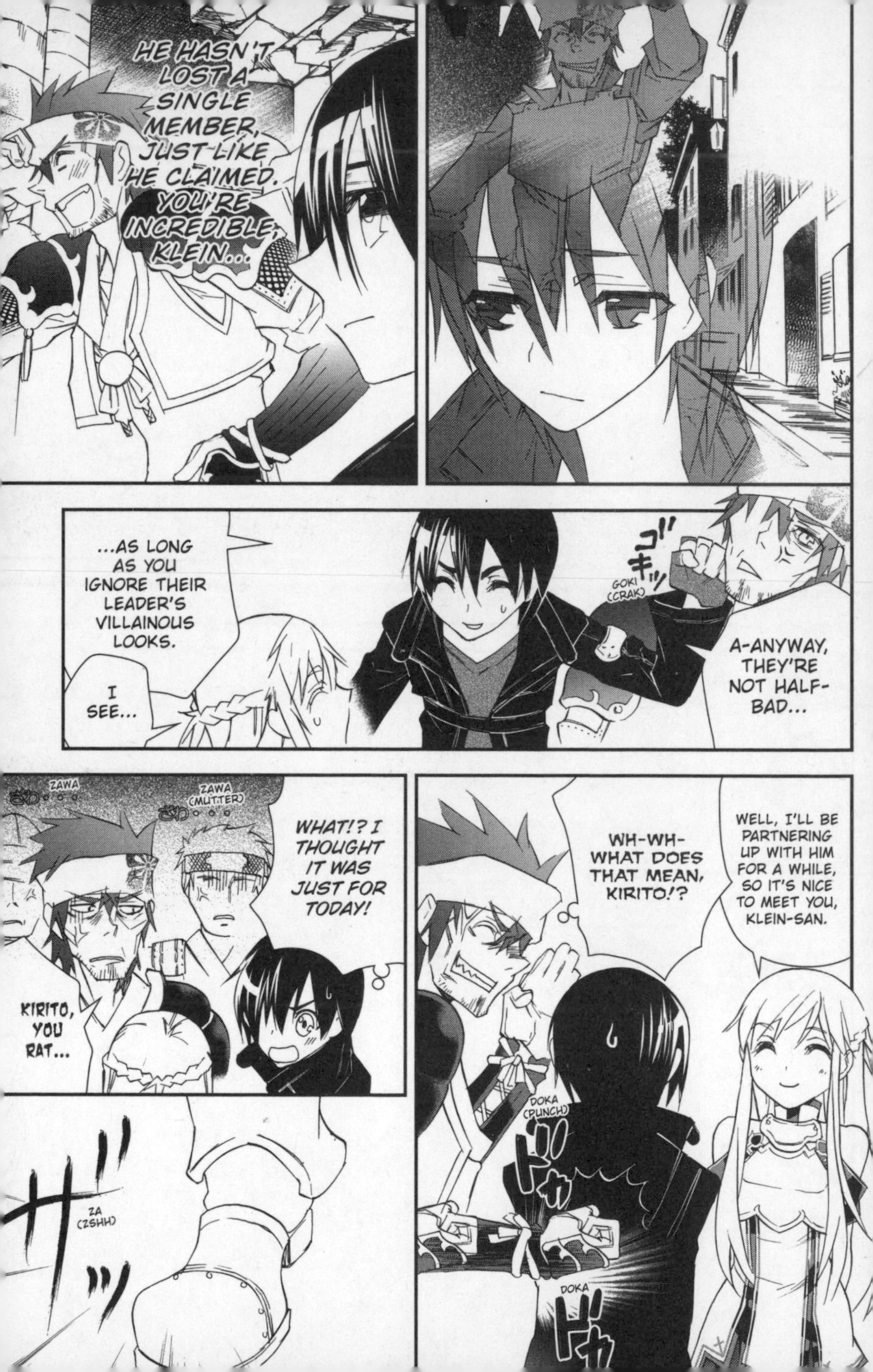
HE HASN'T LOST A SINGLE MEMBER, JUST LIKE HE CLAIMED. YOU'RE INCREDIBLE, KLEIN...
GOKI (CRAK)
A-ANYWAY, THEY'RE NOT HALF-BAD...
...AS LONG AS YOU IGNORE THEIR LEADER'S VILLAINOUS LOOKS.
I SEE...
WELL, I'LL BE PARTNERING UP WITH HIM FOR A WHILE, SO IT'S NICE TO MEET YOU, KLEIN-SAN.
WH-WH-WHAT DOES THAT MEAN, KIRITO!?
DOKA (PUNCH)
DOKA
ZAWA (MUTTER)
ZAWA
WHAT!? I THOUGHT IT WAS JUST FOR TODAY!
KIRITO, YOU RAT...
ZA (ZSHH)

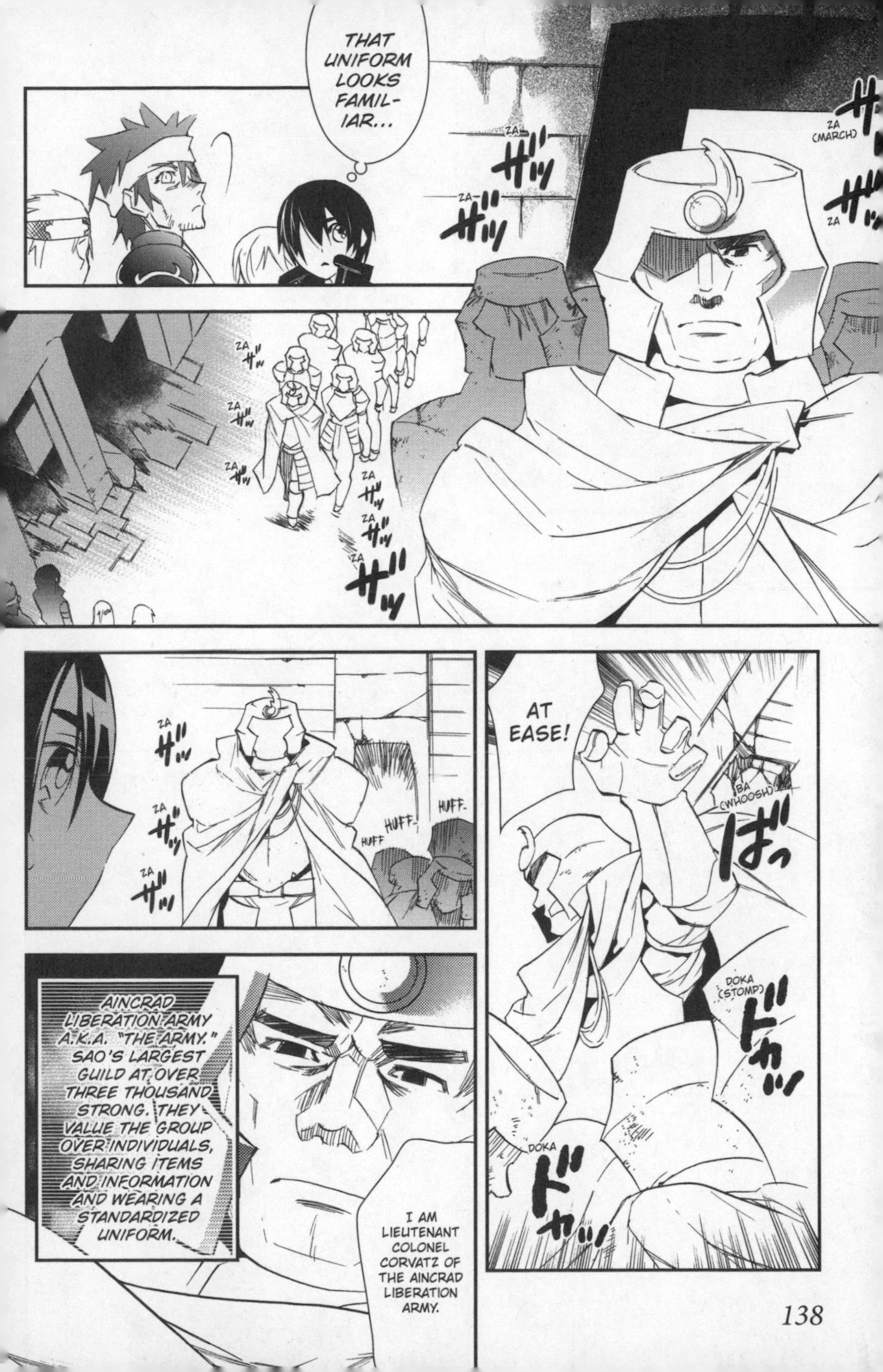
ZA (MARCH)
ZA
THAT UNIFORM LOOKS FAMIL-IAR...
ZA
ZA
ZA
ZA
ZA
ZA
ZA
ZA
AT EASE!
BA (WHOOSH)
DOKA (STOMP)
DOKA
ZA
ZA
ZA
HUFF
HUFF
HUFF
AINCRAD LIBERATION ARMY A.K.A. "THE ARMY." SAO'S LARGEST GUILD AT OVER THREE THOUSAND STRONG. THEY VALUE THE GROUP OVER INDIVIDUALS, SHARING ITEMS AND INFORMATION AND WEARING A STANDARDIZED UNIFORM.
I AM LIEUTENANT COLONEL CORVATZ OF THE AINCRAD LIBERATION ARMY.

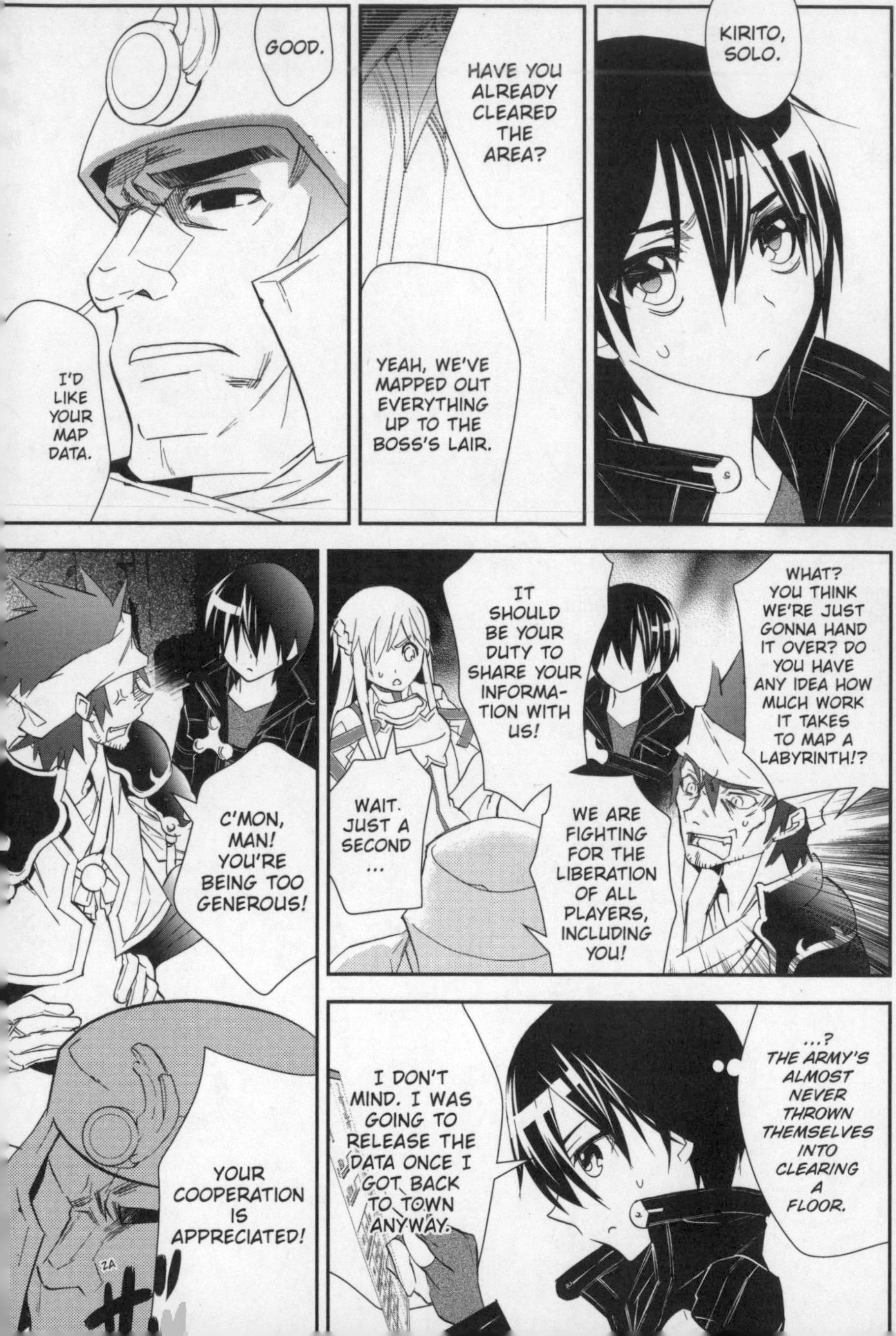
KIRITO, SOLO.
HAVE YOU ALREADY CLEARED THE AREA?
YEAH, WE'VE MAPPED OUT EVERYTHING UP TO THE BOSS'S LAIR.
GOOD.
I'D LIKE YOUR MAP DATA.
WHAT? YOU THINK WE'RE JUST GONNA HAND IT OVER? DO YOU HAVE ANY IDEA HOW MUCH WORK IT TAKES TO MAP A LABYRINTH!?
IT SHOULD BE YOUR DUTY TO SHARE YOUR INFORMATION WITH US!
WE ARE FIGHTING FOR THE LIBERATION OF ALL PLAYERS, INCLUDING YOU!
WAIT. JUST A SECOND ...
...? THE ARMY'S ALMOST NEVER THROWN THEMSELVES INTO CLEARING A FLOOR.
I DON'T MIND. I WAS GOING TO RELEASE THE DATA ONCE I GOT BACK TO TOWN ANYWAY.
C'MON, MAN! YOU'RE BEING TOO GENEROUS!
YOUR COOPERATION IS APPRECIATED!
ZA

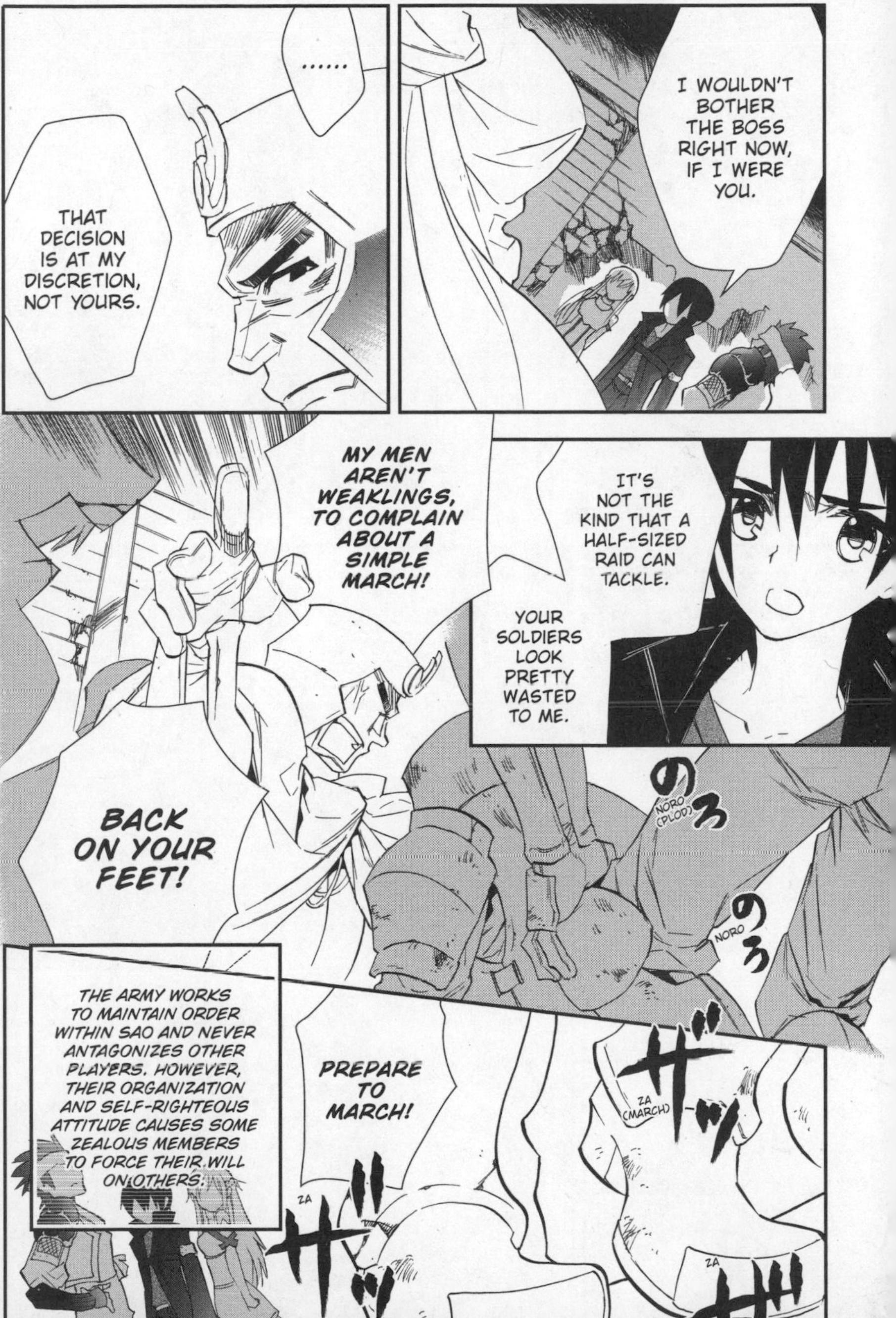

I WOULDN'T BOTHER THE BOSS RIGHT NOW, IF I WERE YOU.
......
THAT DECISION IS AT MY DISCRETION, NOT YOURS.
IT'S NOT THE KIND THAT A HALF-SIZED RAID CAN TACKLE.
YOUR SOLDIERS LOOK PRETTY WASTED TO ME.
MY MEN AREN'T WEAKLINGS, TO COMPLAIN ABOUT A SIMPLE MARCH!
NORO (PLOD)
NORO
BACK ON YOUR FEET!
ZA (MARCH)
PREPARE TO MARCH!
ZA
ZA
THE ARMY WORKS TO MAINTAIN ORDER WITHIN SAO AND NEVER ANTAGONIZES OTHER PLAYERS. HOWEVER, THEIR ORGANIZATION AND SELF-RIGHTEOUS ATTITUDE CAUSES SOME ZEALOUS MEMBERS TO FORCE THEIR WILL ON OTHERS.

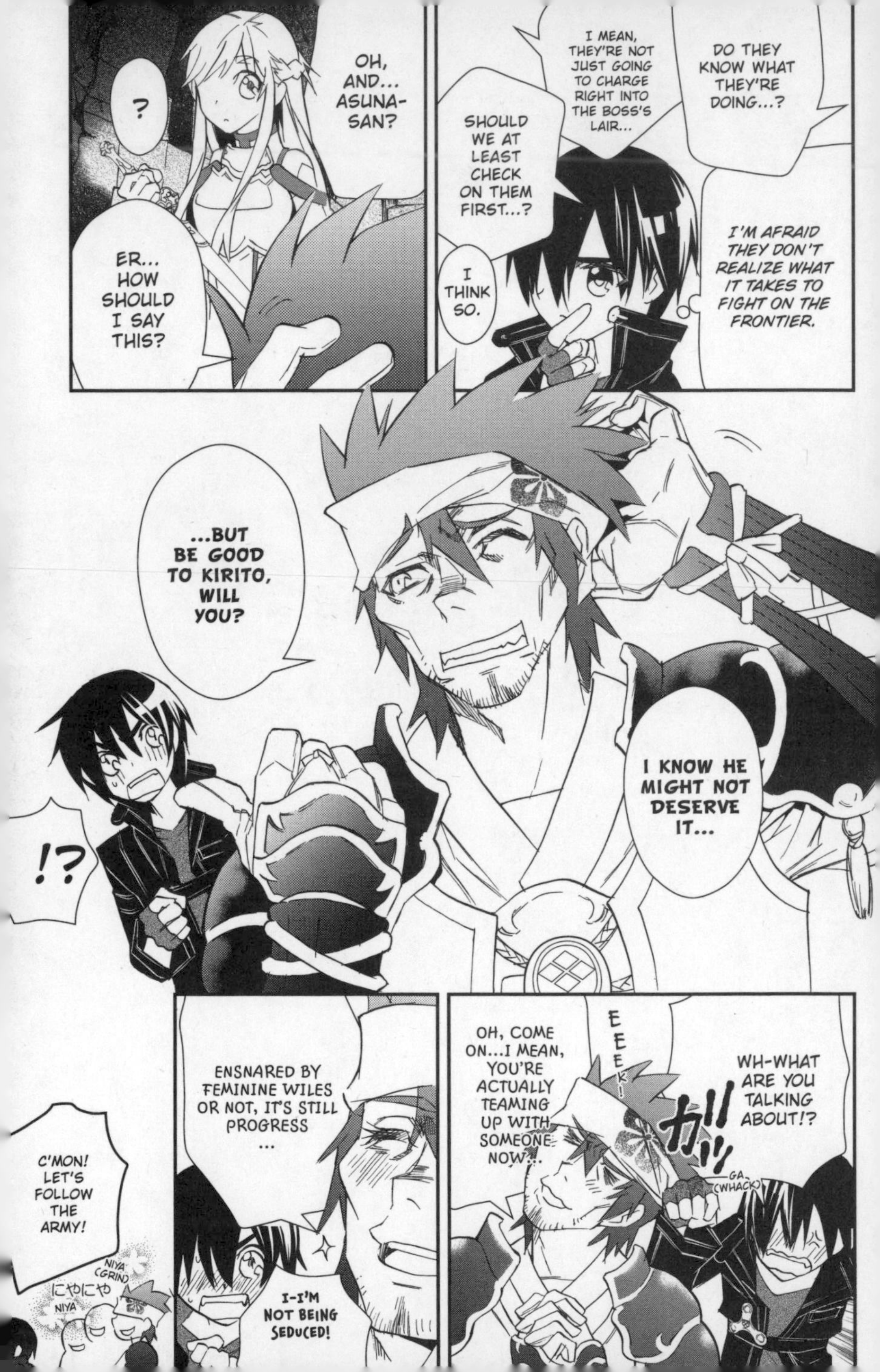
DO THEY KNOW WHAT THEY'RE DOING...?
I MEAN, THEY'RE NOT JUST GOING TO CHARGE RIGHT INTO THE BOSS'S LAIR...
SHOULD WE AT LEAST CHECK ON THEM FIRST...?
I'M AFRAID THEY DON'T REALIZE WHAT IT TAKES TO FIGHT ON THE FRONTIER.
I THINK SO.
OH, AND... ASUNA-SAN?
?
ER... HOW SHOULD I SAY THIS?
I KNOW HE MIGHT NOT DESERVE IT...
...BUT BE GOOD TO KIRITO, WILL YOU?
!?
WH-WHAT ARE YOU TALKING ABOUT!?
ガッ
GA (WHACK)
EEEK!
OH, COME ON...I MEAN, YOU'RE ACTUALLY TEAMING UP WITH SOMEONE NOW...
ENSNARED BY FEMININE WILES OR NOT, IT'S STILL PROGRESS...
C'MON! LET'S FOLLOW THE ARMY!
I-I'M NOT BEING SEDUCED!
NIYA (GRIN)
にやにや
NIYA

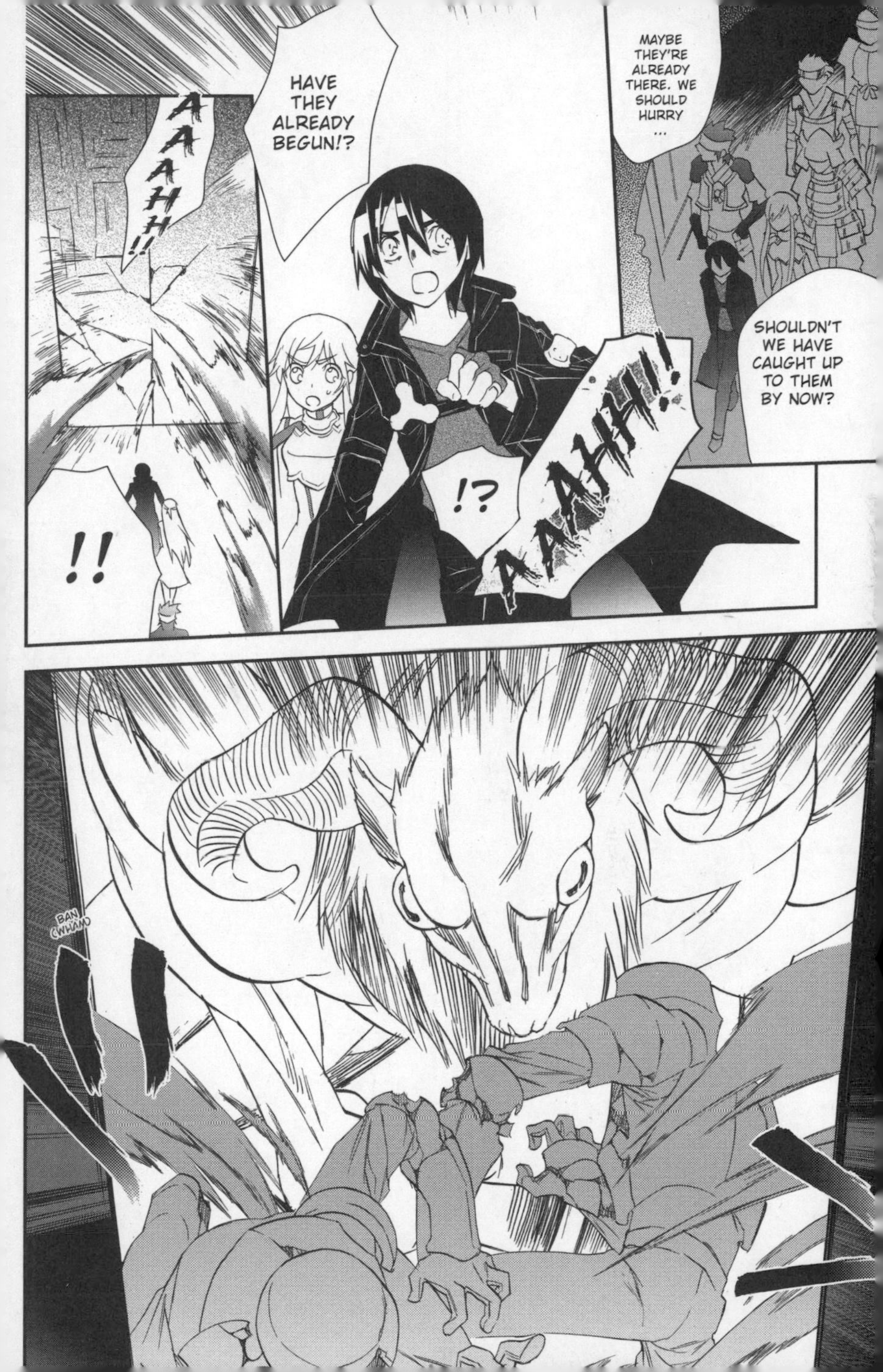
MAYBE THEY'RE ALREADY THERE. WE SHOULD HURRY ...
SHOULDN'T WE HAVE CAUGHT UP TO THEM BY NOW?
AAAHH!!
!?
HAVE THEY ALREADY BEGUN!?
AAAHH!!
!!
BAN (WHAM)

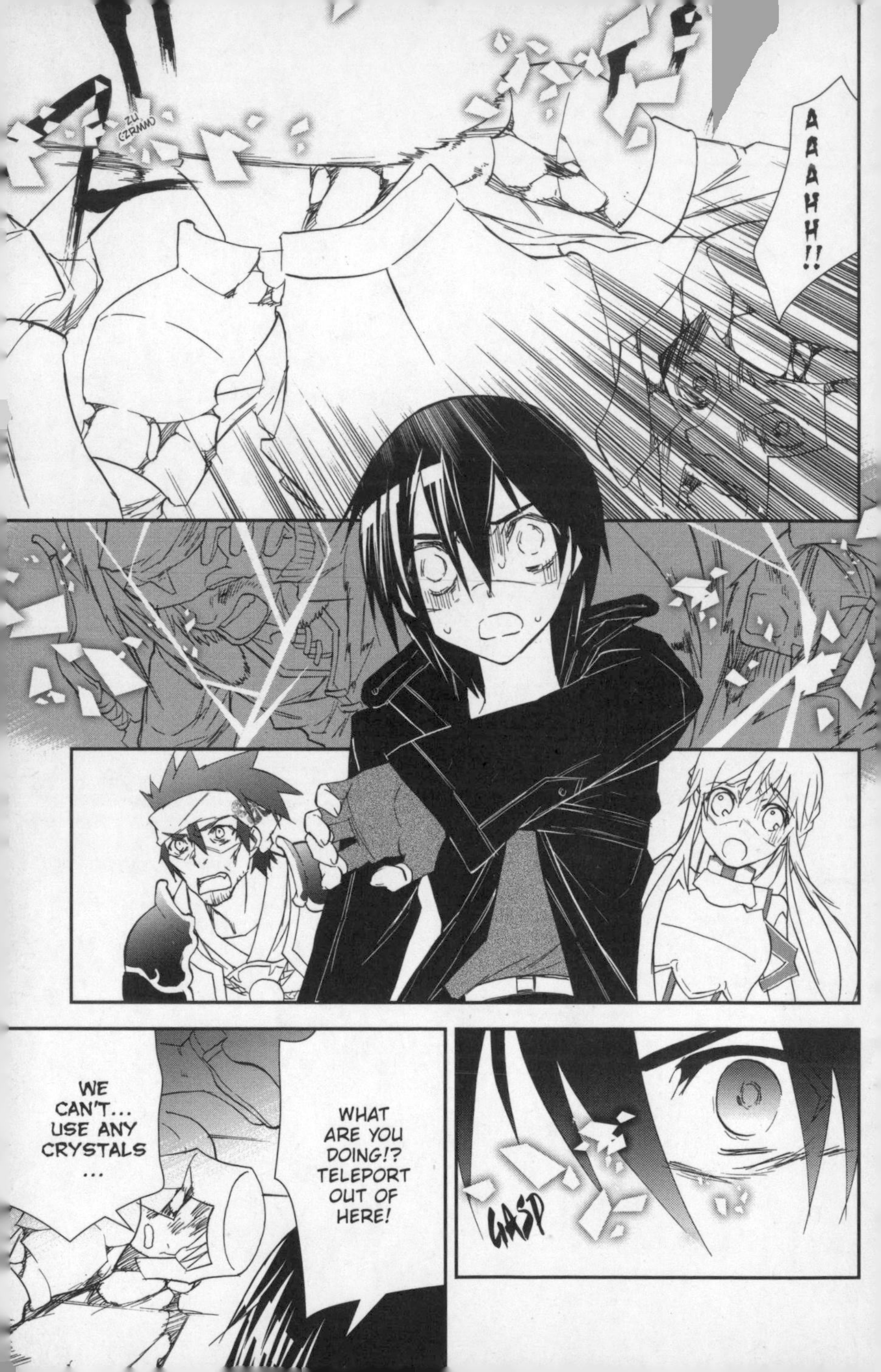
AAAAHH!!
ZU (ZRMM)
GASP
WHAT ARE YOU DOING!? TELEPORT OUT OF HERE!
WE CAN'T... USE ANY CRYSTALS ...

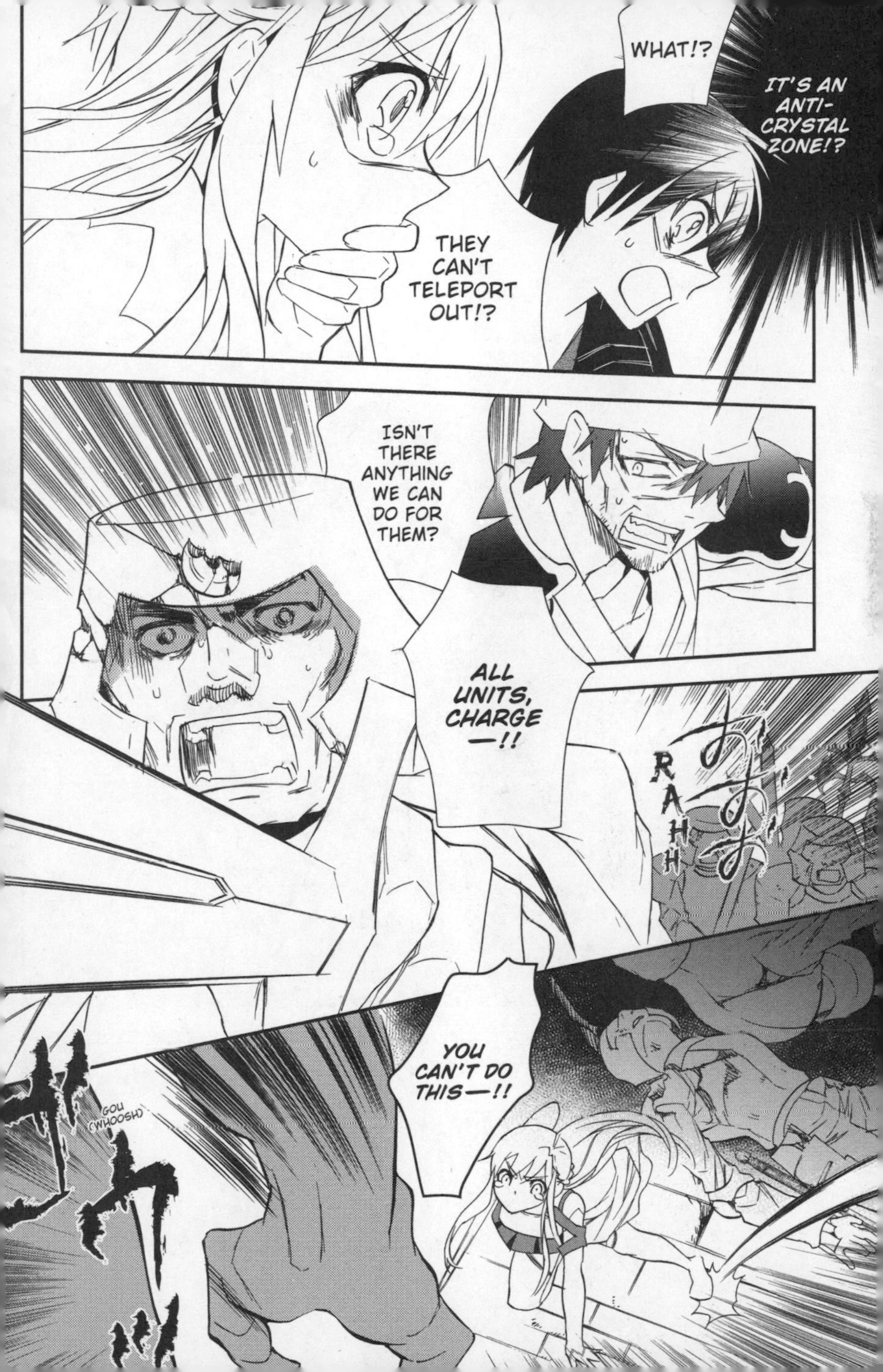
WHAT!?
IT'S AN ANTI-CRYSTAL ZONE!?
THEY CAN'T TELEPORT OUT!?
ISN'T THERE ANYTHING WE CAN DO FOR THEM?
ALL UNITS, CHARGE—!!
RAHH
YOU CAN'T DO THIS—!!
GOU (WHOOSH)

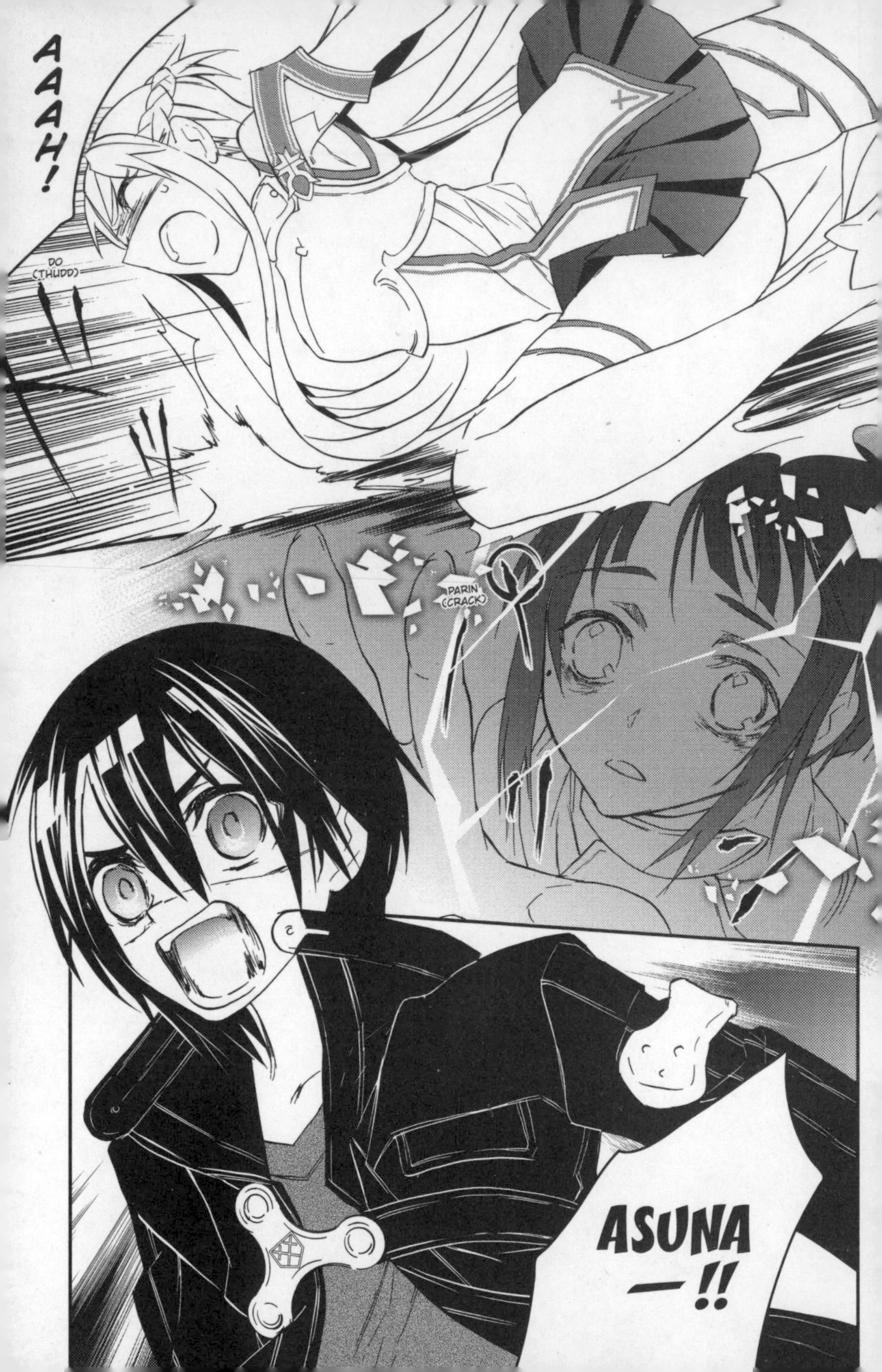
AAAAH!
DO
(THUDD)
PARIN
(CRACK)
ASUNA
—!!

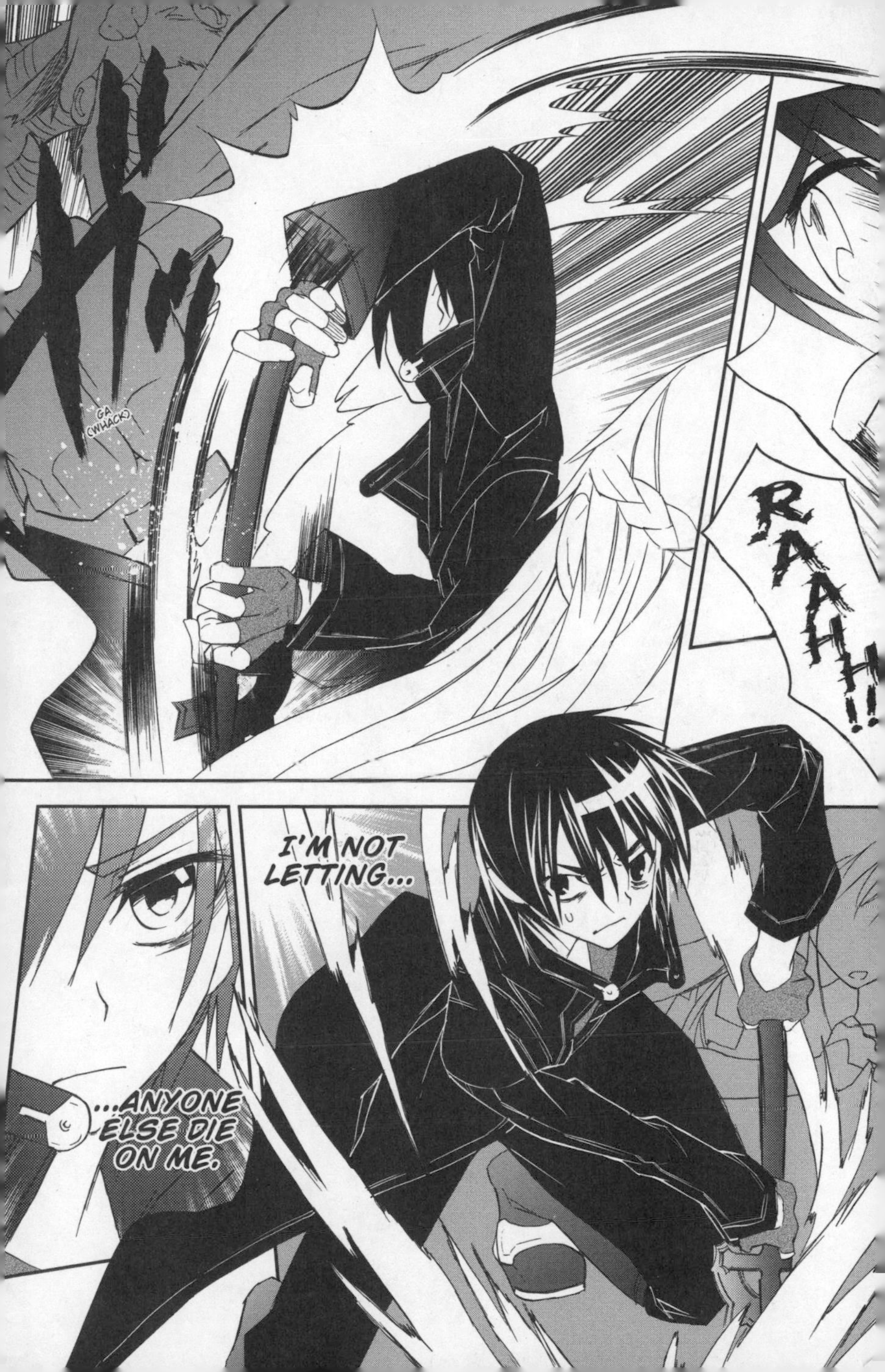
RAAHH!!
GA (WHACK)
I'M NOT LETTING...
...ANYONE ELSE DIE ON ME.

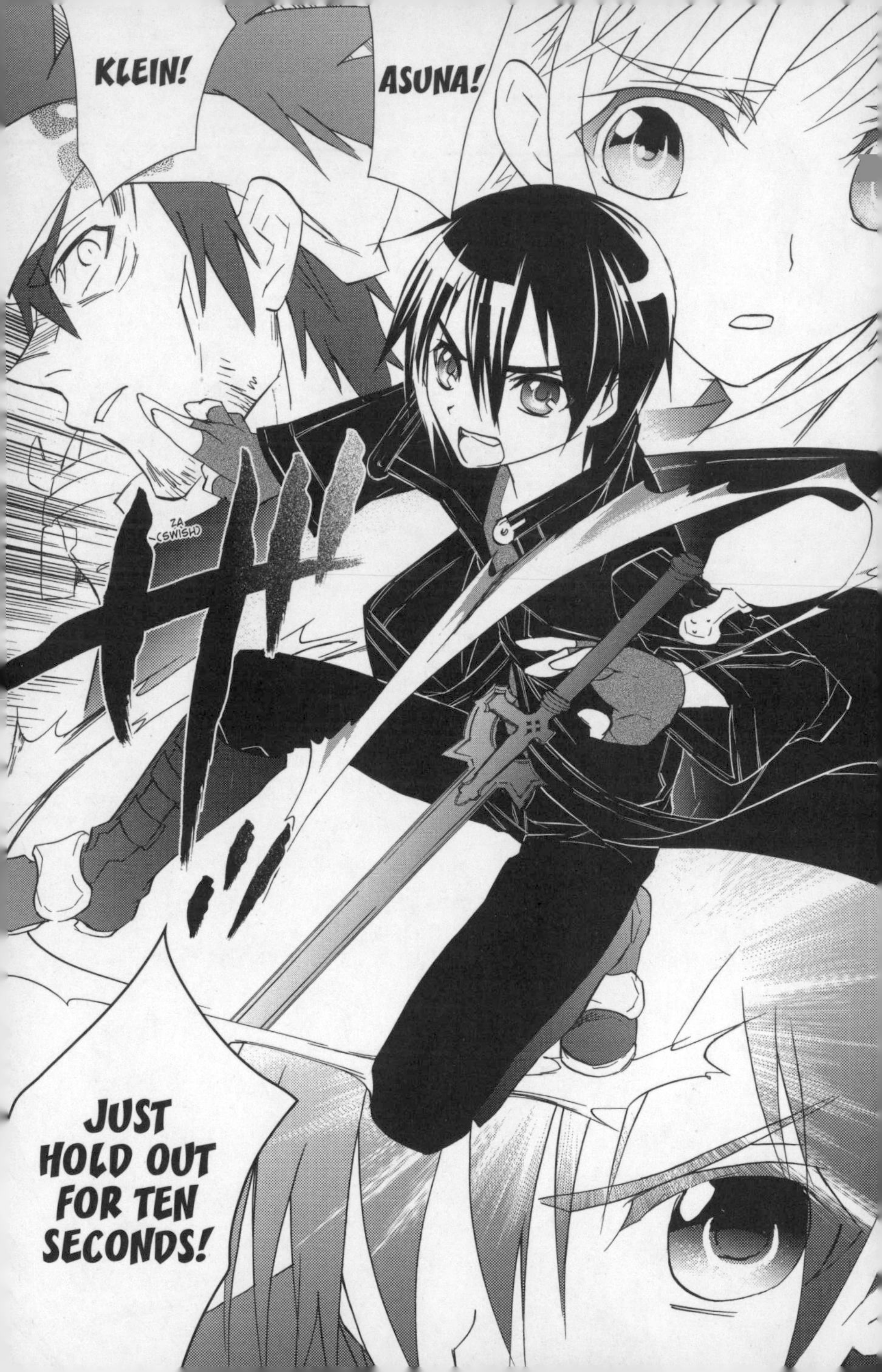
ASUNA!
KLEIN!
ZA (SWISH)
JUST HOLD OUT FOR TEN SECONDS!

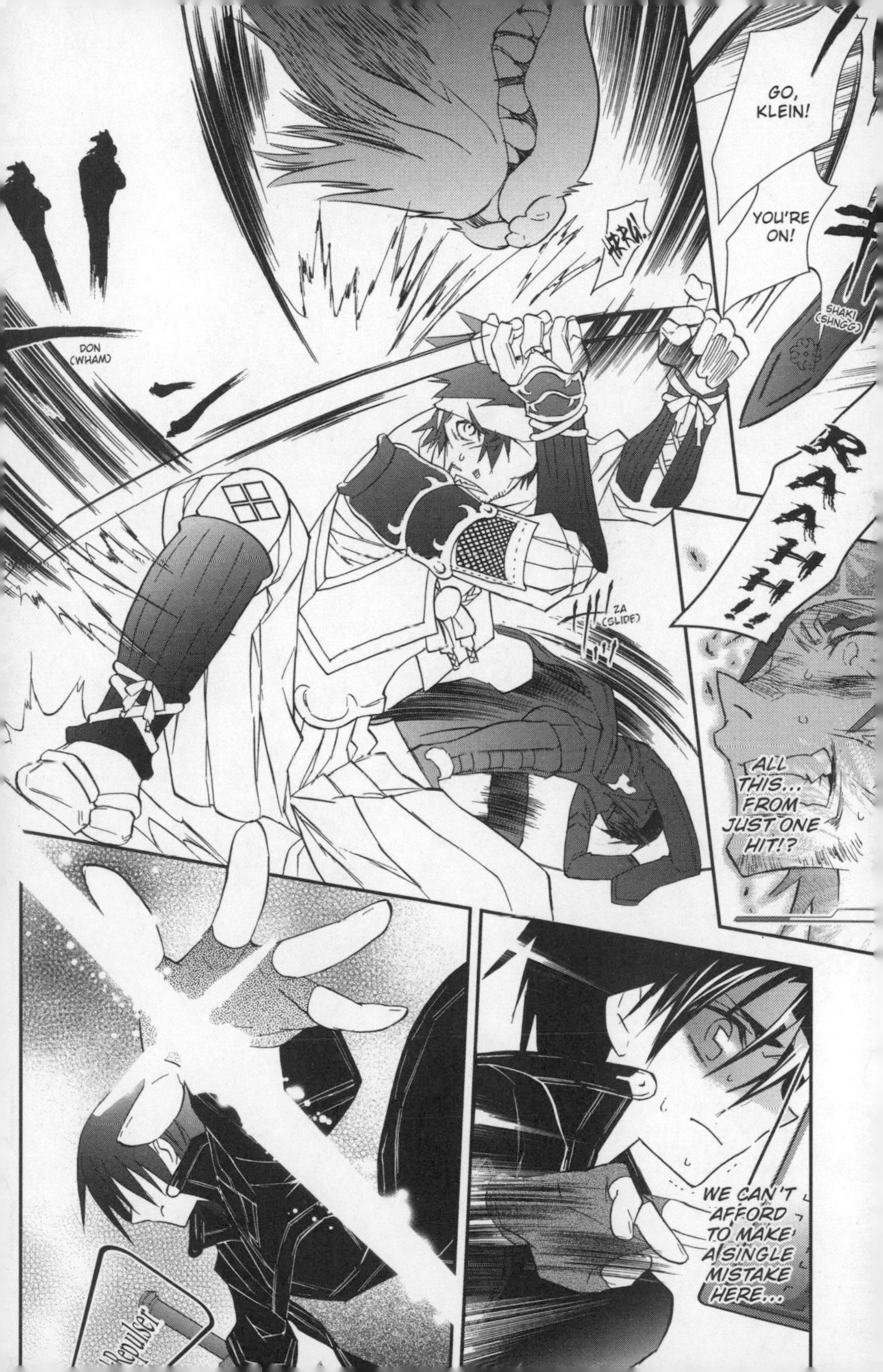
GO, KLEIN!
YOU'RE ON!
SHAKI (SHNGG)
HRRG!
DON (WHAM)
RAAHH!!
ZA (SLIDE)
ALL THIS... FROM JUST ONE HIT!?
WE CAN'T AFFORD TO MAKE A SINGLE MISTAKE HERE...
Repulser

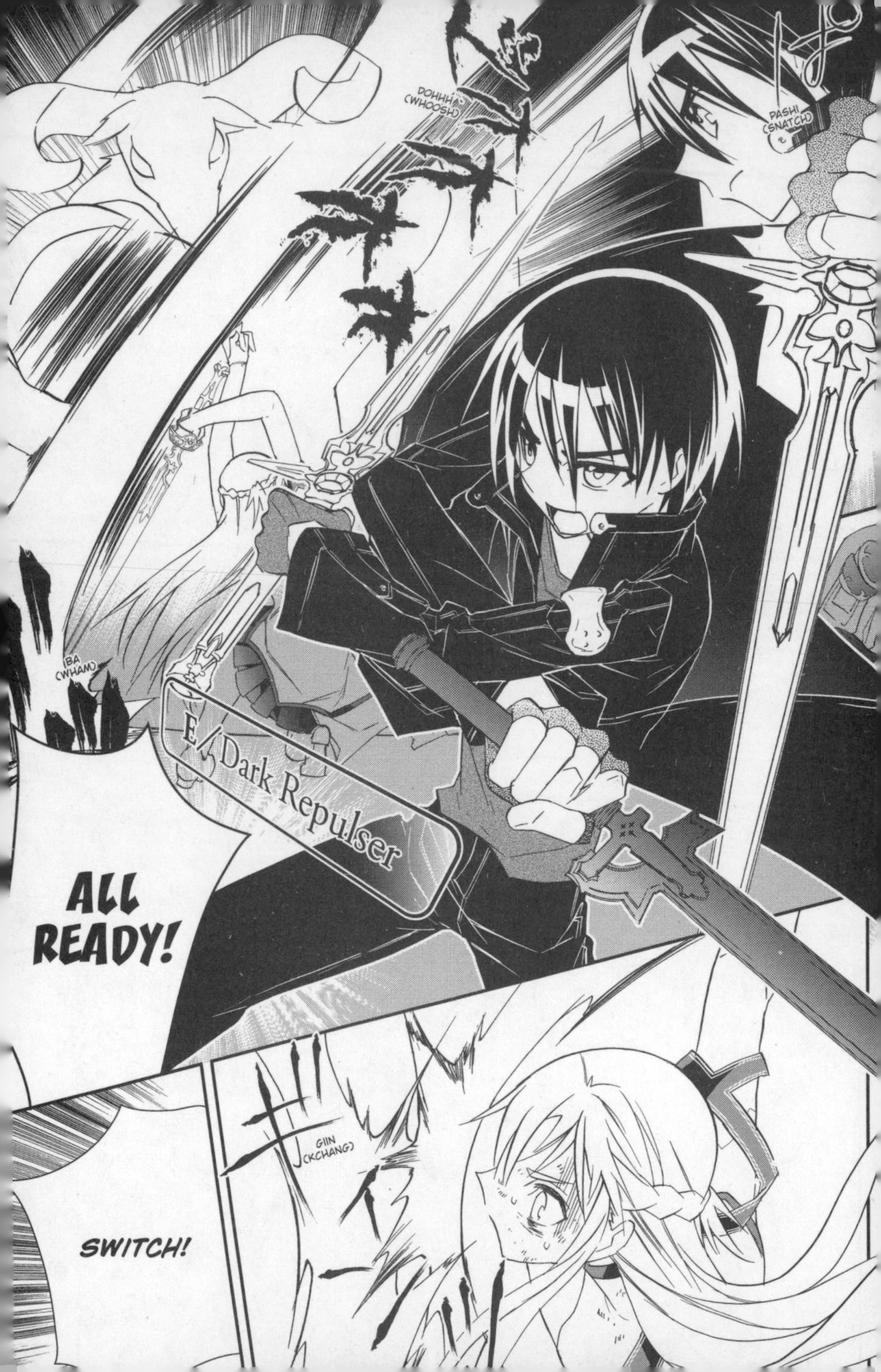
PASHI (SNATCH)
DOHHHA (WHOOSH)
E/ Dark Repulser
BA (WHAM)
ALL READY!
GIIN (KCHANG)
SWITCH!

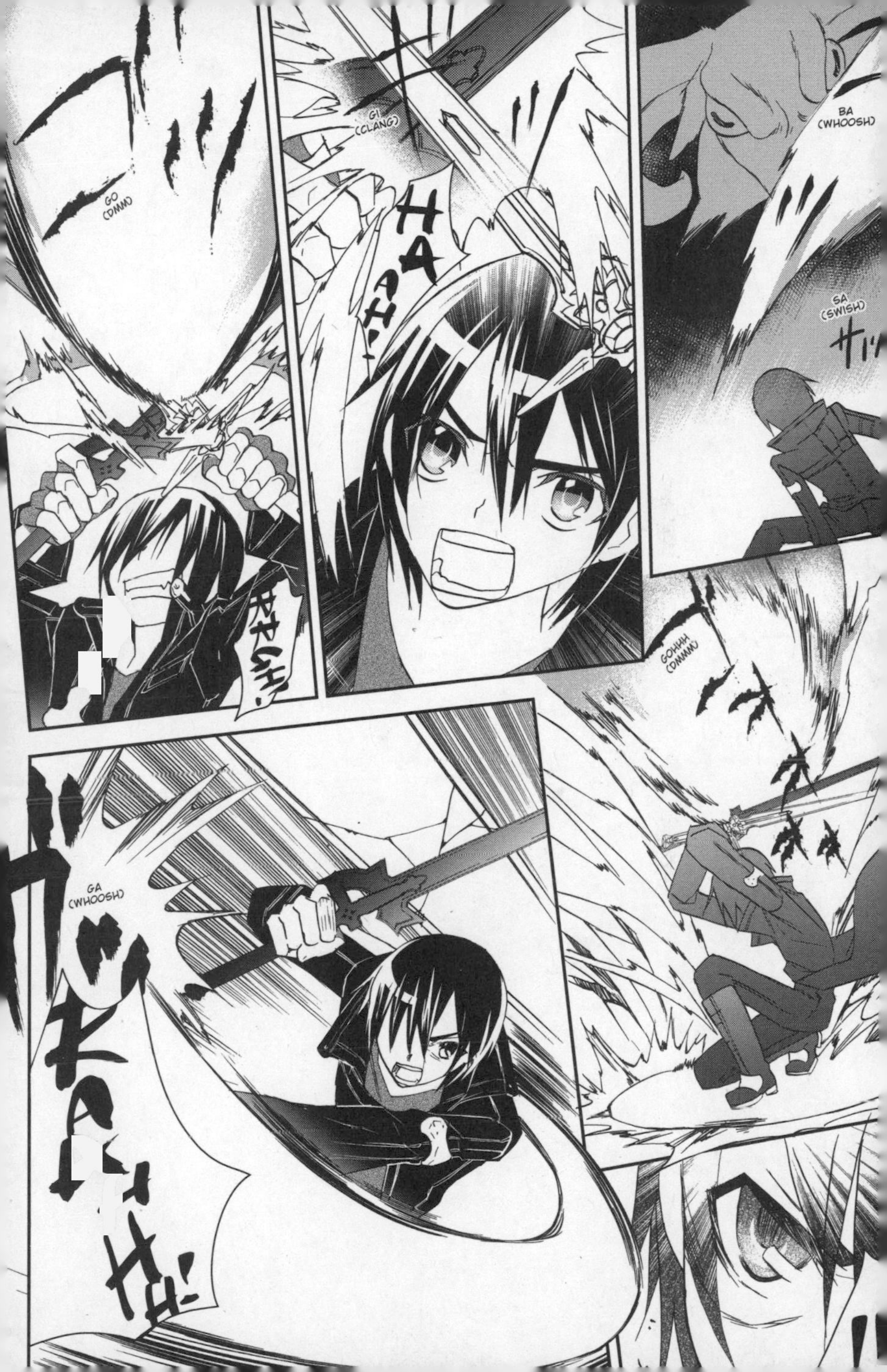
BA (WHOOSH)
SA (SWISH)
GI (CLANG)
HAAH!
GO (DMM)
RRGH!
GOHHH (DMMM)
GA (WHOOSH)

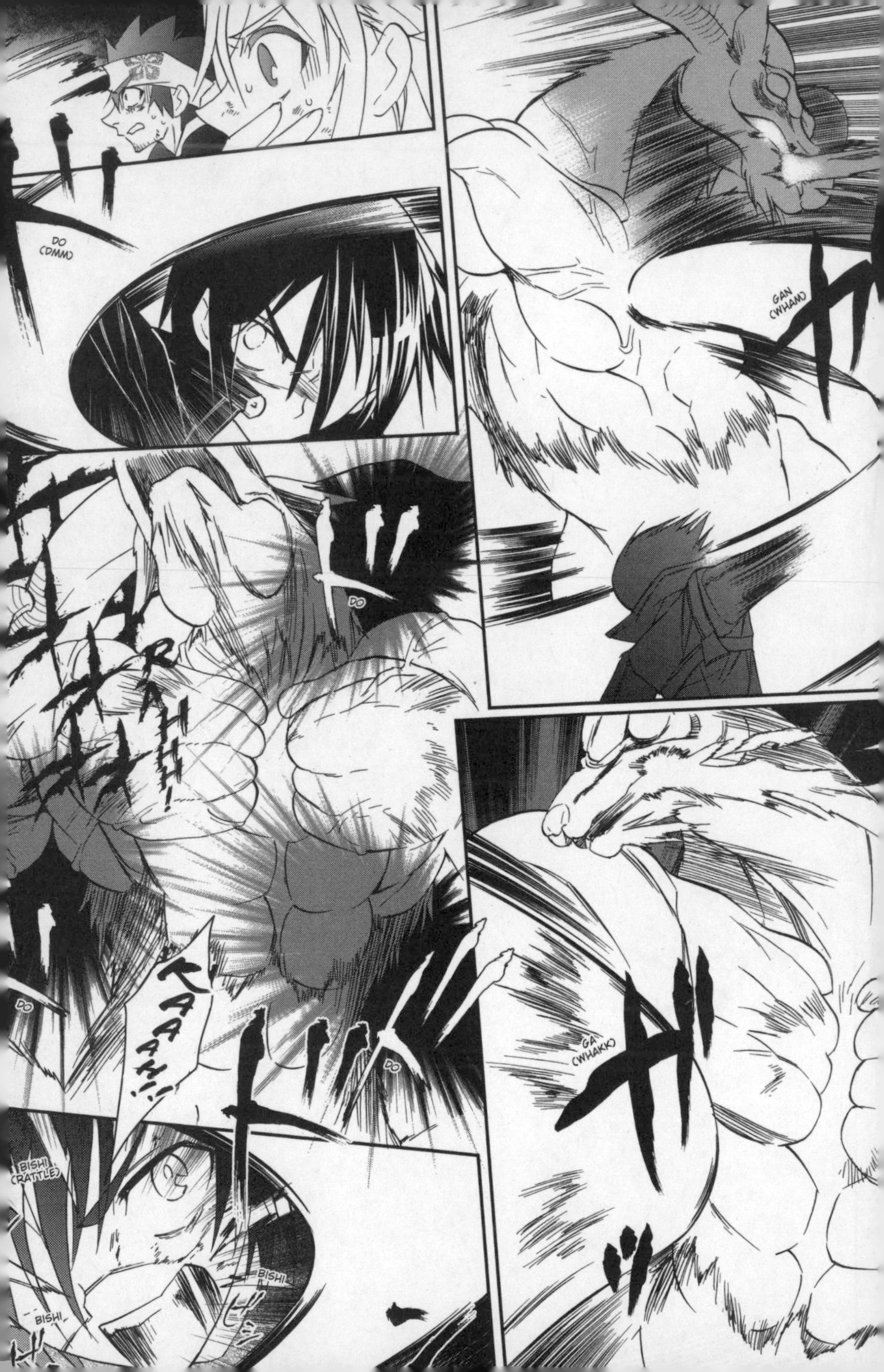
GAN (WHAM)
DO (DMM)
DO
RAHHH!
DO
KAAAAH!!
DO
GA (WHAKK)
BISHI (RATTLE)
BISHI
BISHI

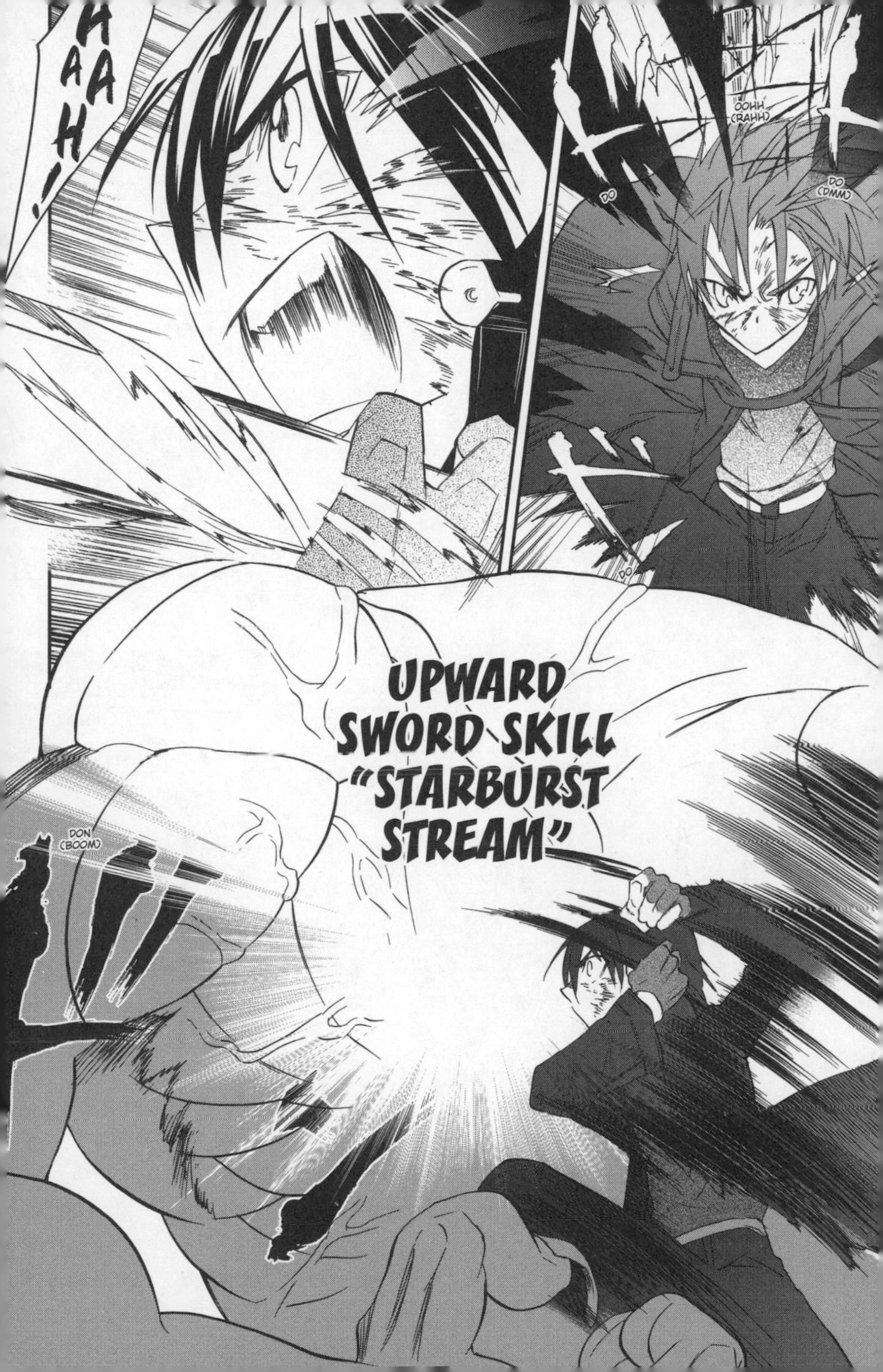

OOHH (RAHH)
DO (DMM)
DO
DO
HAAAH!!
UPWARD SWORD SKILL "STARBURST STREAM"
DON (BOOM)

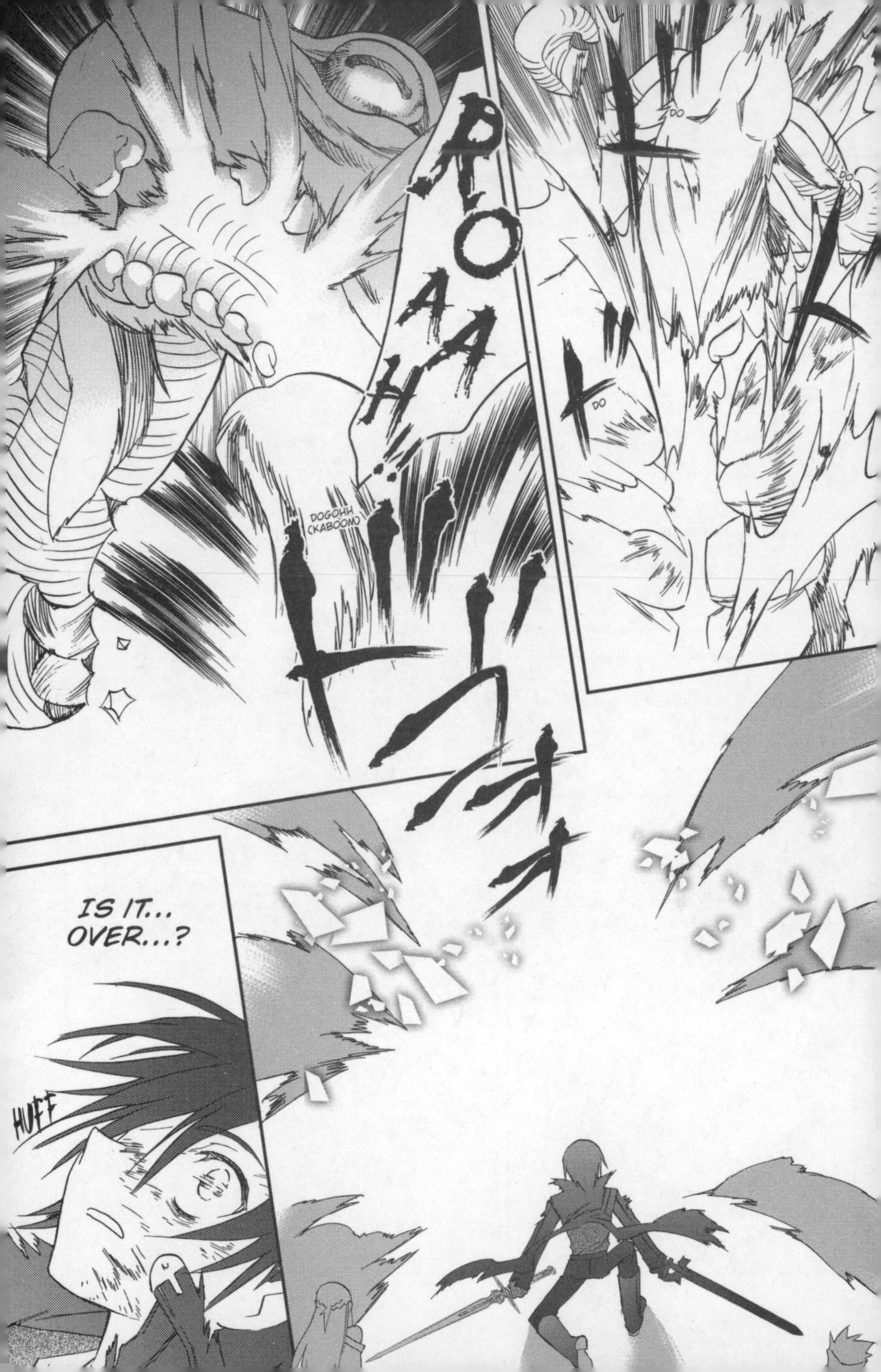
DO
DO
DO
ROAAH...!!
DOGOHH (KABOOM)
IS IT... OVER...?
HUFF

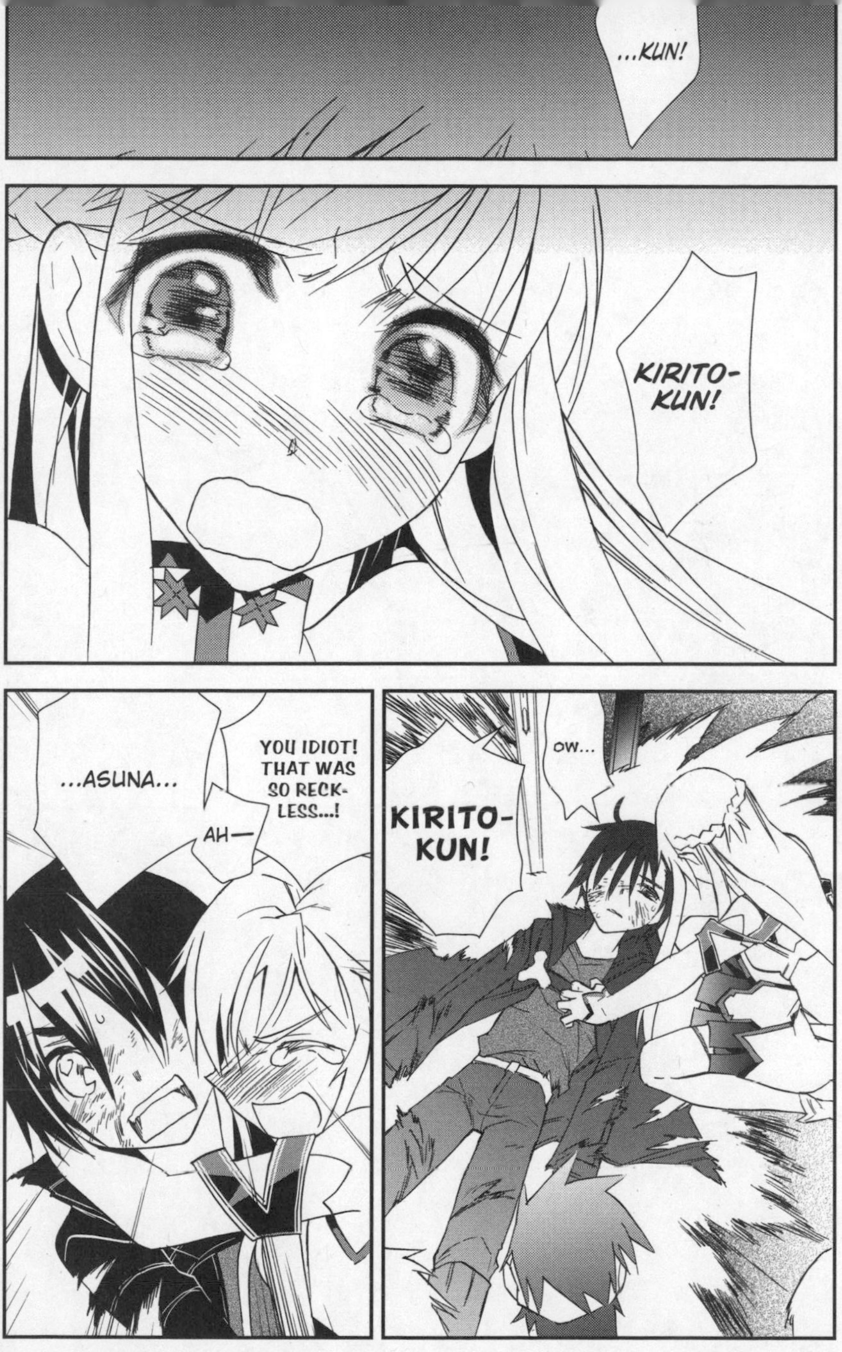
...KUN!
KIRITO-KUN!
OW...
KIRITO-KUN!
YOU IDIOT! THAT WAS SO RECK-LESS...!
...ASUNA...
AH—

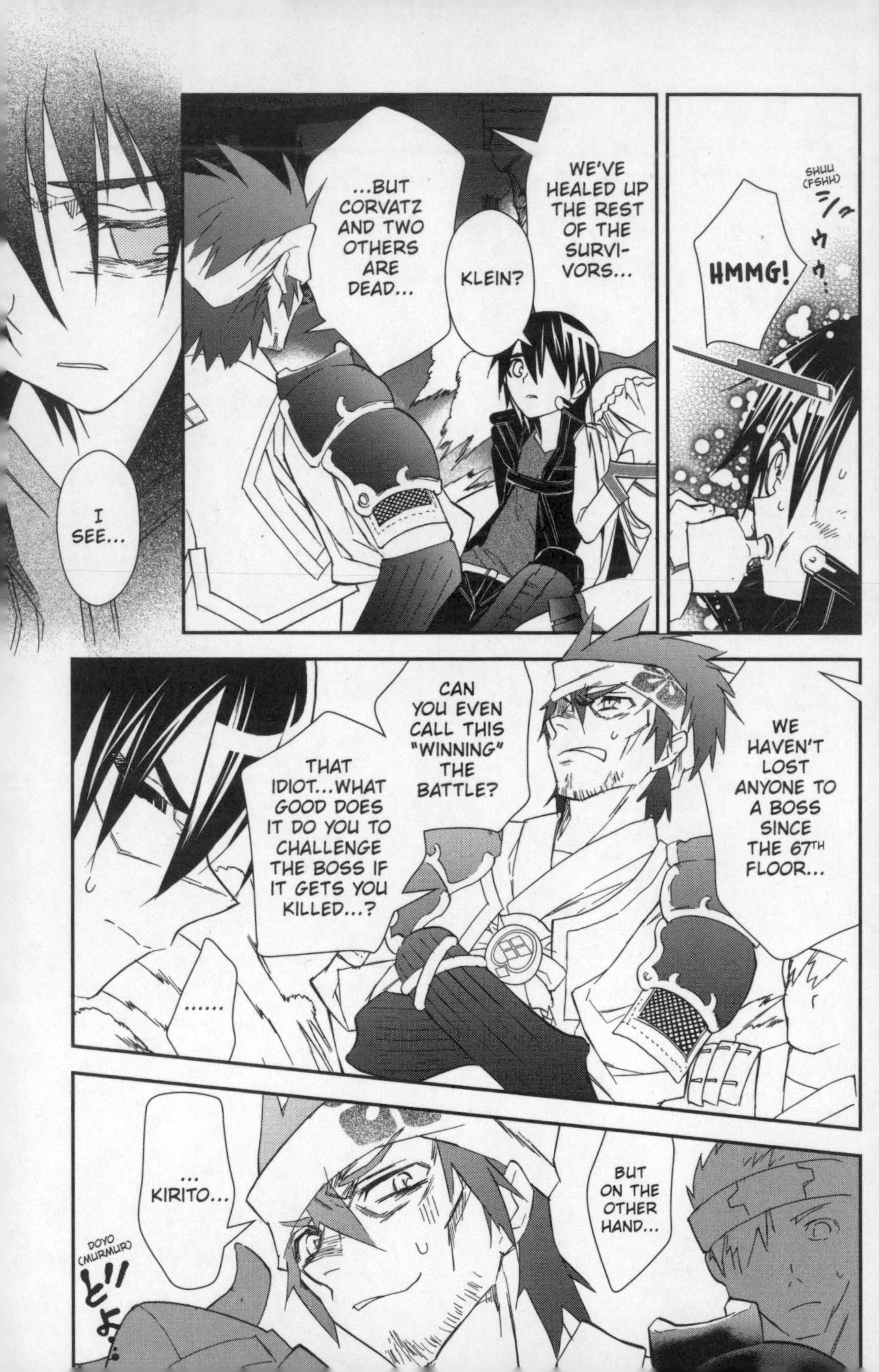
SHUU (FSHH)
HMMG!
WE'VE HEALED UP THE REST OF THE SURVI-VORS...
KLEIN?
...BUT CORVATZ AND TWO OTHERS ARE DEAD...
I SEE...
WE HAVEN'T LOST ANYONE TO A BOSS SINCE THE 67TH FLOOR...
CAN YOU EVEN CALL THIS "WINNING" THE BATTLE?
THAT IDIOT...WHAT GOOD DOES IT DO YOU TO CHALLENGE THE BOSS IF IT GETS YOU KILLED...?
......
BUT ON THE OTHER HAND...
... KIRITO...
DOYO (MURMUR)

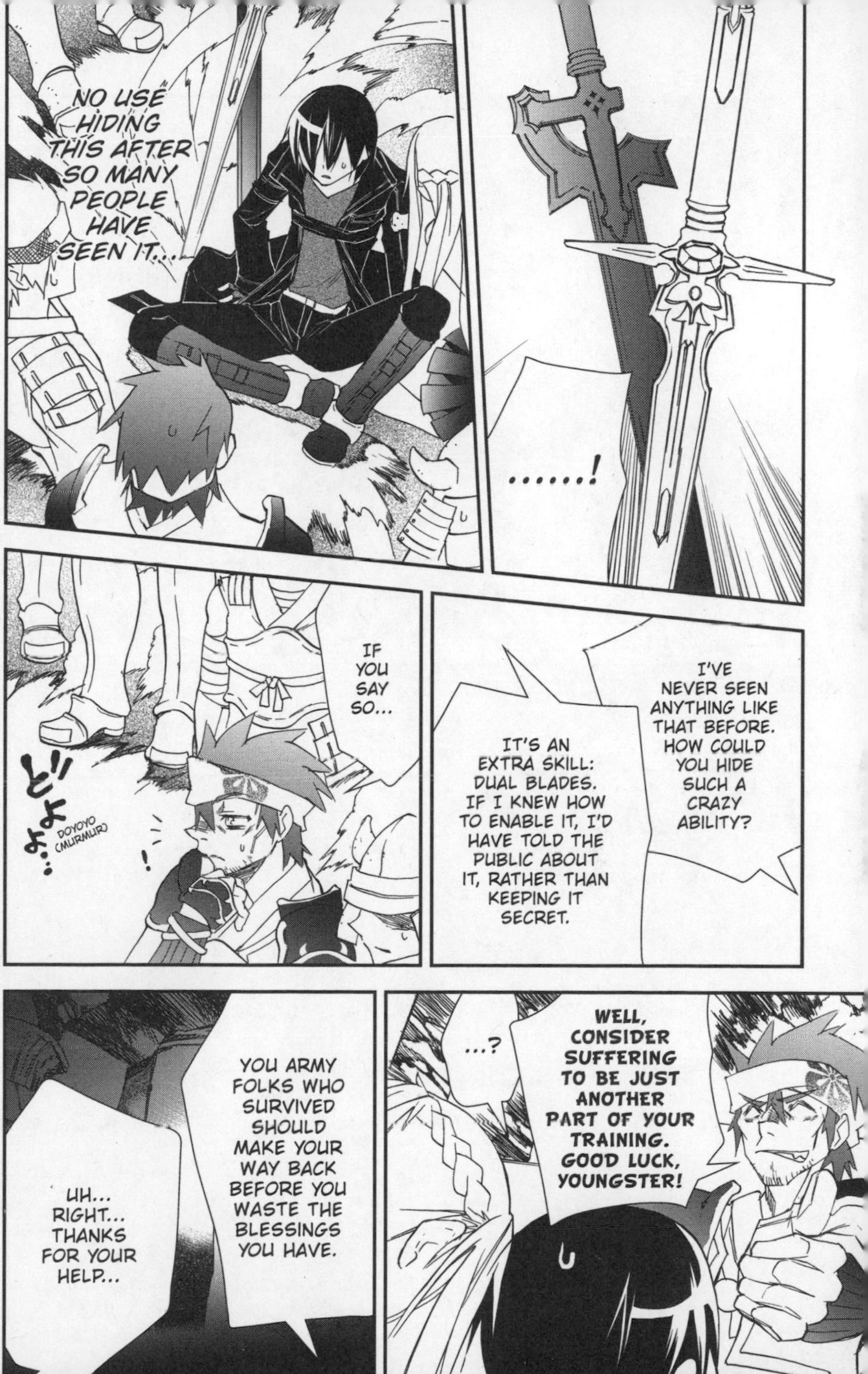
......!
NO USE HIDING THIS AFTER SO MANY PEOPLE HAVE SEEN IT...
I'VE NEVER SEEN ANYTHING LIKE THAT BEFORE. HOW COULD YOU HIDE SUCH A CRAZY ABILITY?
IT'S AN EXTRA SKILL: DUAL BLADES. IF I KNEW HOW TO ENABLE IT, I'D HAVE TOLD THE PUBLIC ABOUT IT, RATHER THAN KEEPING IT SECRET.
IF YOU SAY SO...
どよよ...
DOYOYO (MURMUR)
!
WELL, CONSIDER SUFFERING TO BE JUST ANOTHER PART OF YOUR TRAINING. GOOD LUCK, YOUNGSTER!
...?
YOU ARMY FOLKS WHO SURVIVED SHOULD MAKE YOUR WAY BACK BEFORE YOU WASTE THE BLESSINGS YOU HAVE.
UH... RIGHT... THANKS FOR YOUR HELP...

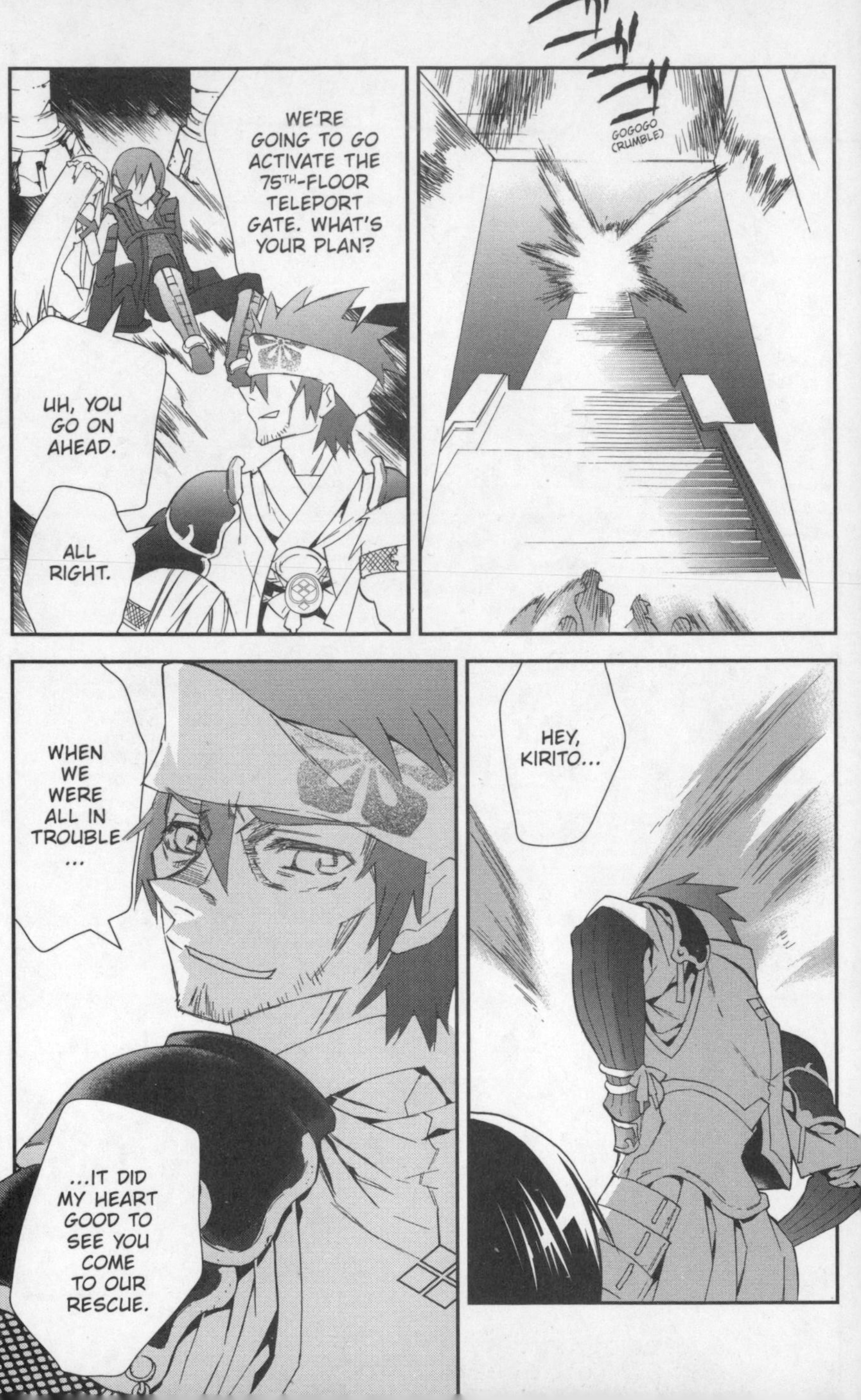
GOGOGO (RUMBLE)
WE'RE GOING TO GO ACTIVATE THE 75TH-FLOOR TELEPORT GATE. WHAT'S YOUR PLAN?
UH, YOU GO ON AHEAD.
ALL RIGHT.
HEY, KIRITO...
WHEN WE WERE ALL IN TROUBLE...
...IT DID MY HEART GOOD TO SEE YOU COME TO OUR RESCUE.

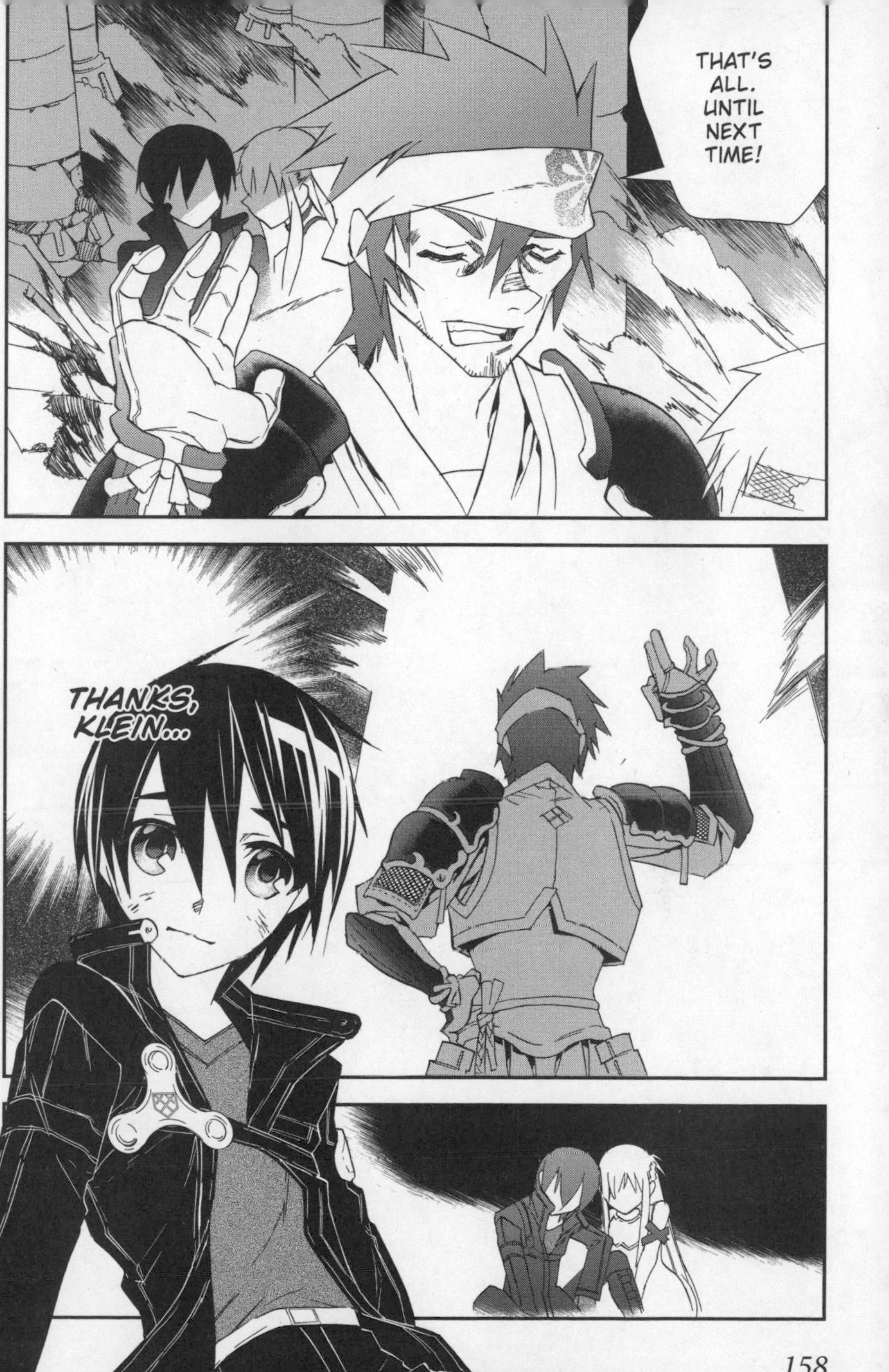
THAT'S ALL. UNTIL NEXT TIME!
THANKS, KLEIN...

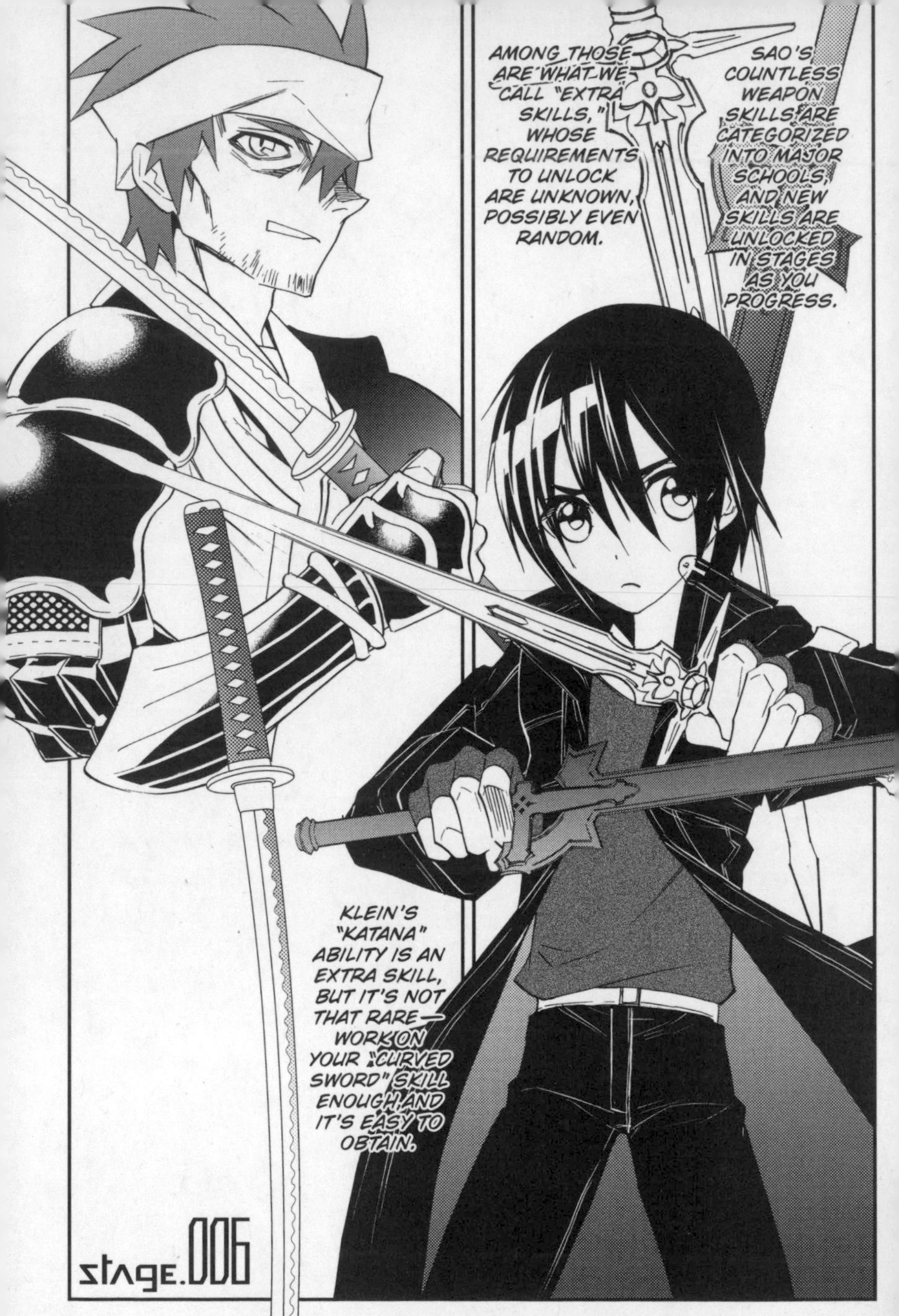
SAO'S COUNTLESS WEAPON SKILLS ARE CATEGORIZED INTO MAJOR SCHOOLS, AND NEW SKILLS ARE UNLOCKED IN STAGES AS YOU PROGRESS.
AMONG THOSE ARE WHAT WE CALL "EXTRA SKILLS," WHOSE REQUIREMENTS TO UNLOCK ARE UNKNOWN, POSSIBLY EVEN RANDOM.
KLEIN'S "KATANA" ABILITY IS AN EXTRA SKILL, BUT IT'S NOT THAT RARE— WORK ON YOUR "CURVED SWORD" SKILL ENOUGH AND IT'S EASY TO OBTAIN.
stage.006

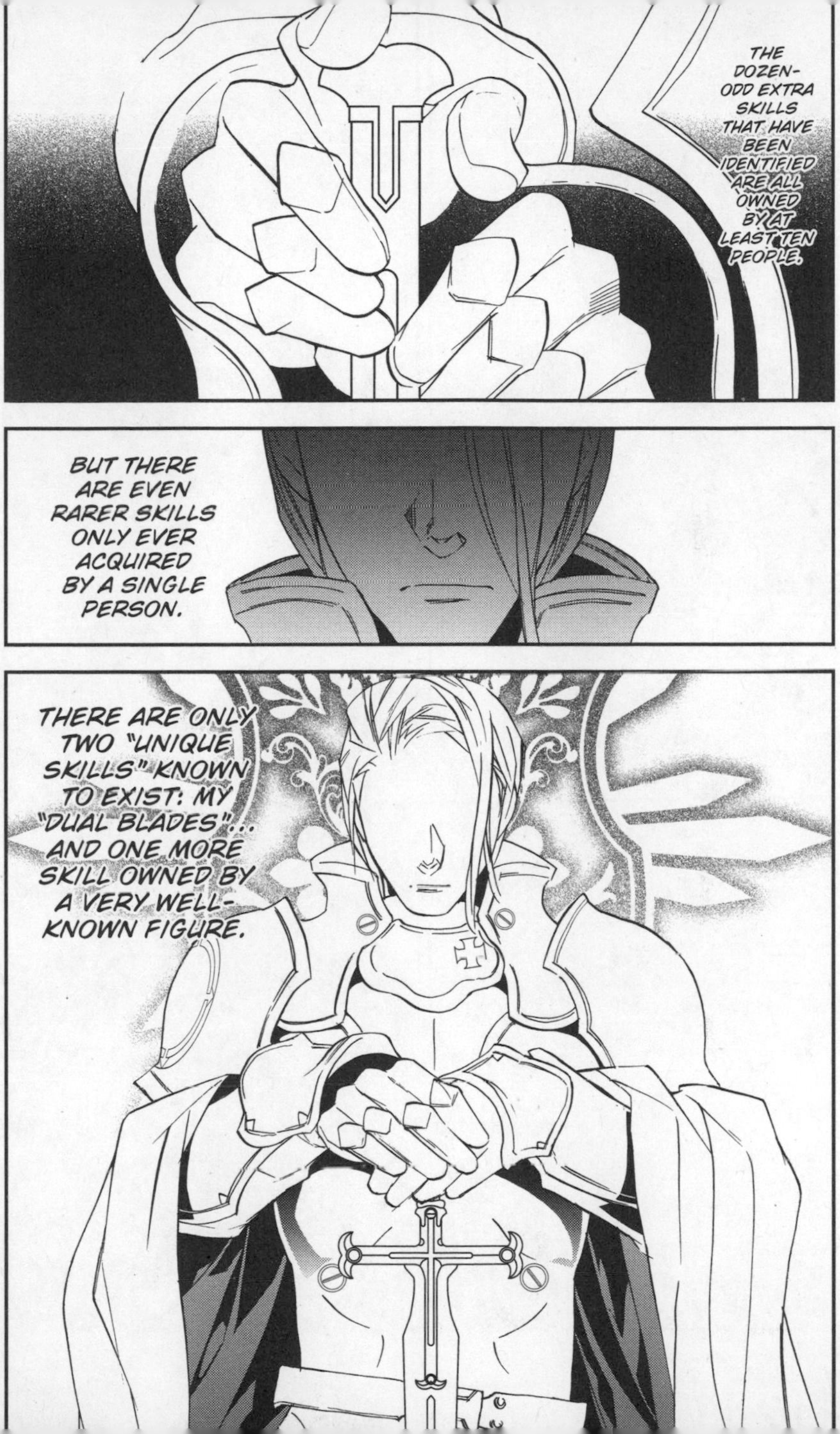
THE DOZEN-ODD EXTRA SKILLS THAT HAVE BEEN IDENTIFIED ARE ALL OWNED BY AT LEAST TEN PEOPLE.
BUT THERE ARE EVEN RARER SKILLS ONLY EVER ACQUIRED BY A SINGLE PERSON.
THERE ARE ONLY TWO "UNIQUE SKILLS" KNOWN TO EXIST: MY "DUAL BLADES"... AND ONE MORE SKILL OWNED BY A VERY WELL-KNOWN FIGURE.

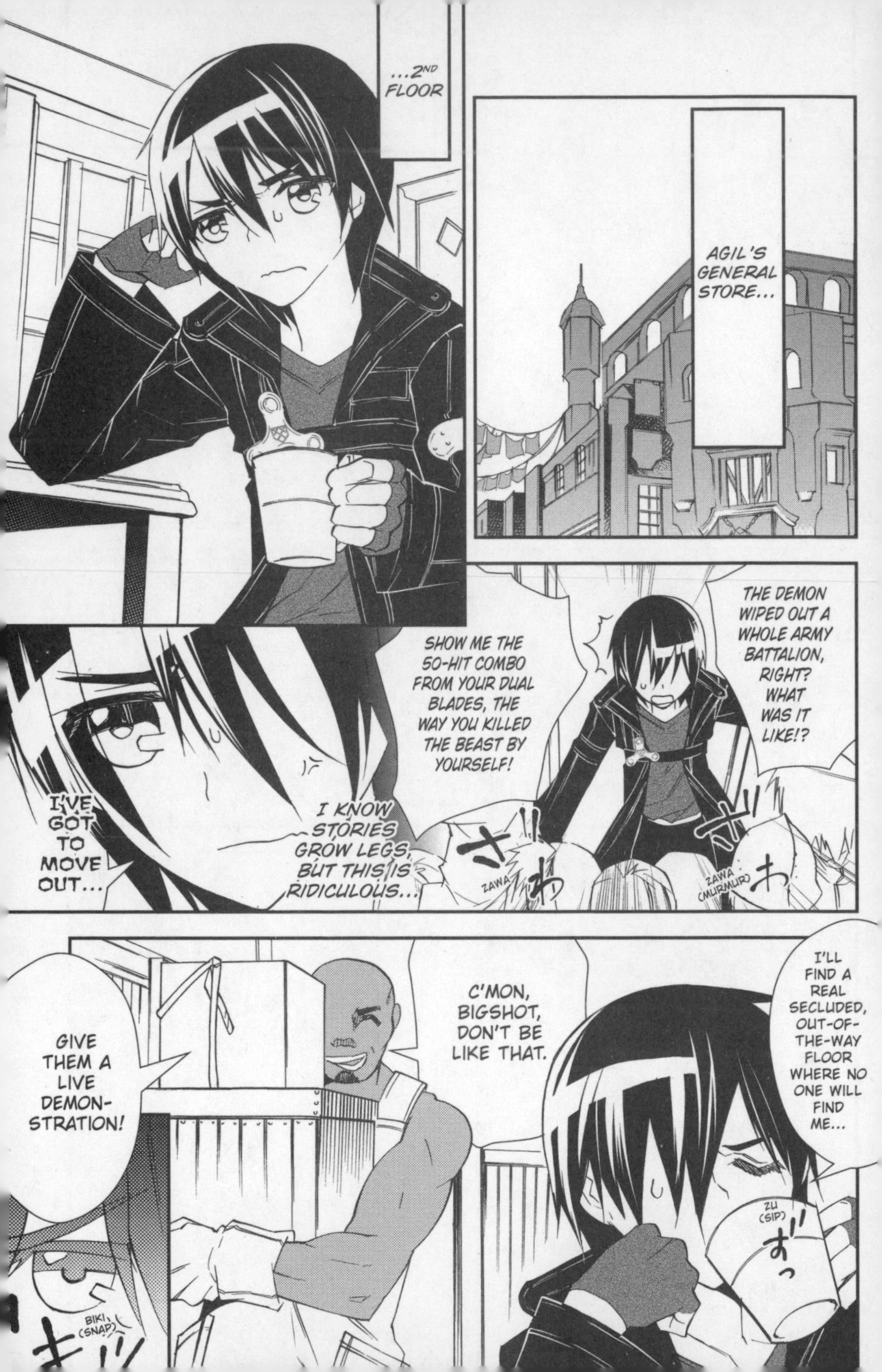
AGIL'S GENERAL STORE...
...2ND FLOOR
THE DEMON WIPED OUT A WHOLE ARMY BATTALION, RIGHT? WHAT WAS IT LIKE!?
SHOW ME THE 50-HIT COMBO FROM YOUR DUAL BLADES, THE WAY YOU KILLED THE BEAST BY YOURSELF!
ZAWA (MURMUR)
ZAWA
I KNOW STORIES GROW LEGS, BUT THIS IS RIDICULOUS...
I'VE GOT TO MOVE OUT...
I'LL FIND A REAL SECLUDED, OUT-OF-THE-WAY FLOOR WHERE NO ONE WILL FIND ME...
ZU (SIP)
C'MON, BIGSHOT, DON'T BE LIKE THAT.
GIVE THEM A LIVE DEMONSTRATION!
BIKI (SNAP)

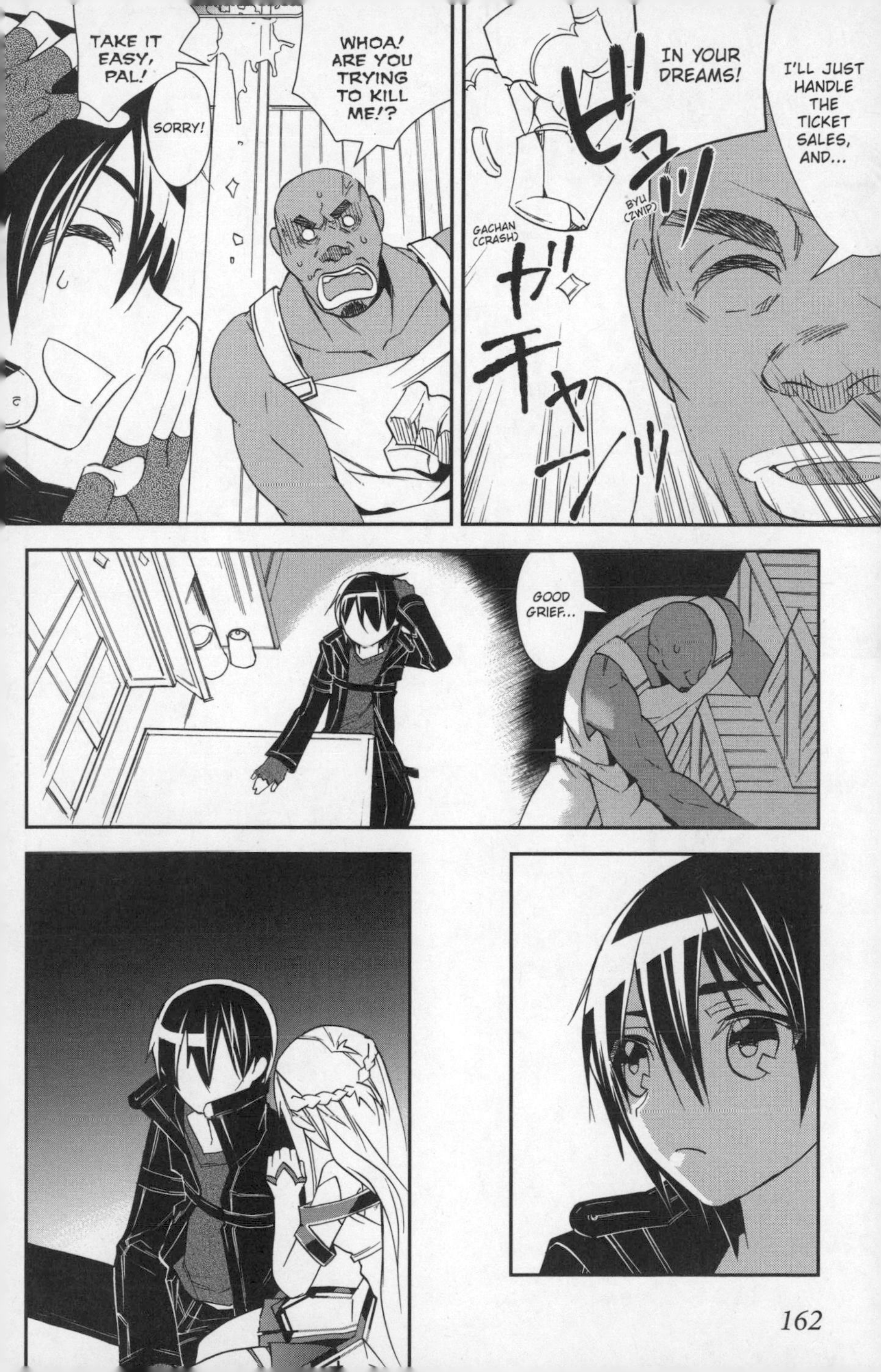
I'LL JUST HANDLE THE TICKET SALES, AND...
IN YOUR DREAMS!
BYU (ZWIP)
GACHAN (CRASH)
WHOA! ARE YOU TRYING TO KILL ME!?
TAKE IT EASY, PAL!
SORRY!
GOOD GRIEF...

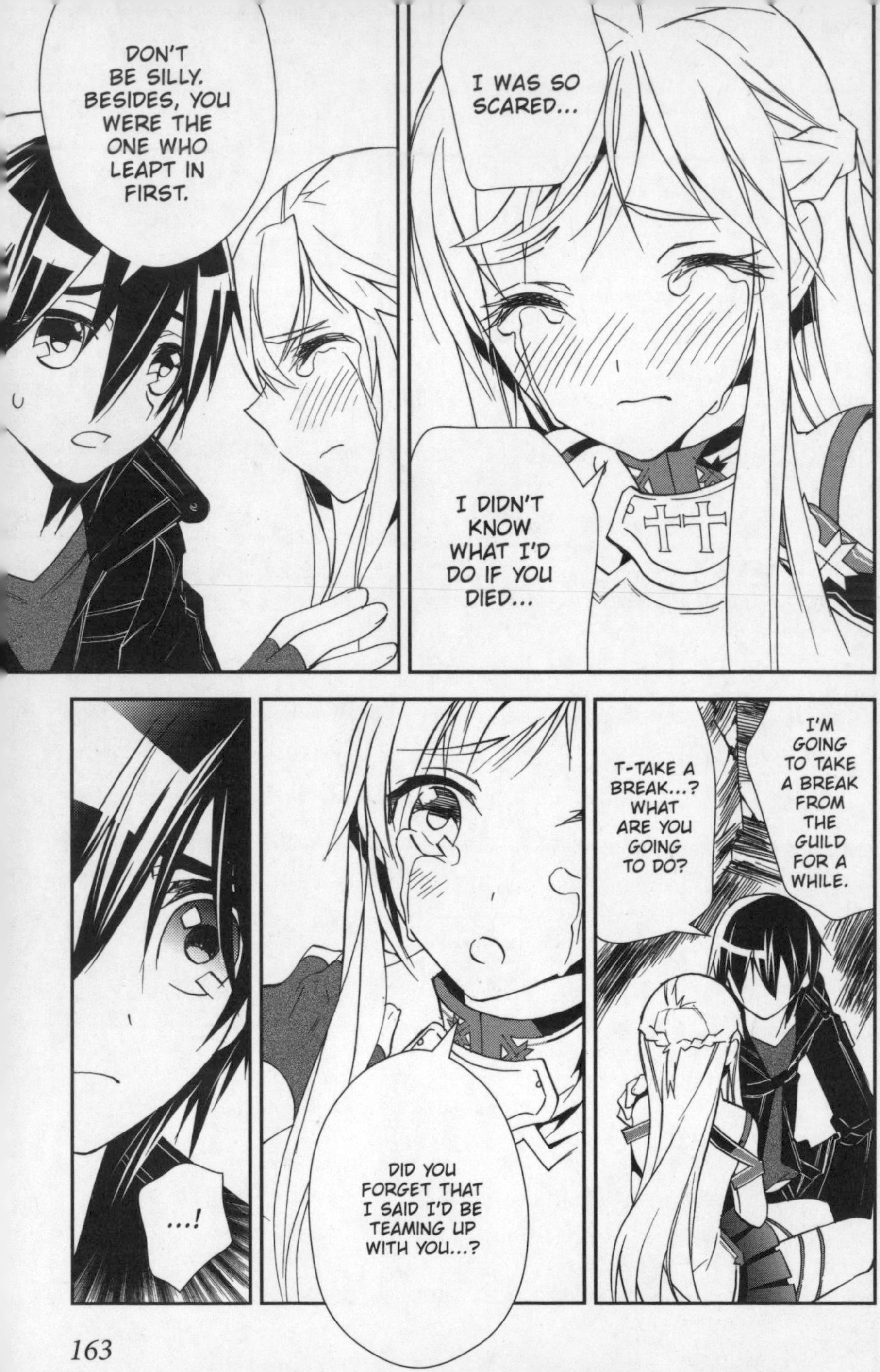
I WAS SO SCARED...
I DIDN'T KNOW WHAT I'D DO IF YOU DIED...
DON'T BE SILLY. BESIDES, YOU WERE THE ONE WHO LEAPT IN FIRST.
I'M GOING TO TAKE A BREAK FROM THE GUILD FOR A WHILE.
T-TAKE A BREAK...? WHAT ARE YOU GOING TO DO?
DID YOU FORGET THAT I SAID I'D BE TEAMING UP WITH YOU...?
...!

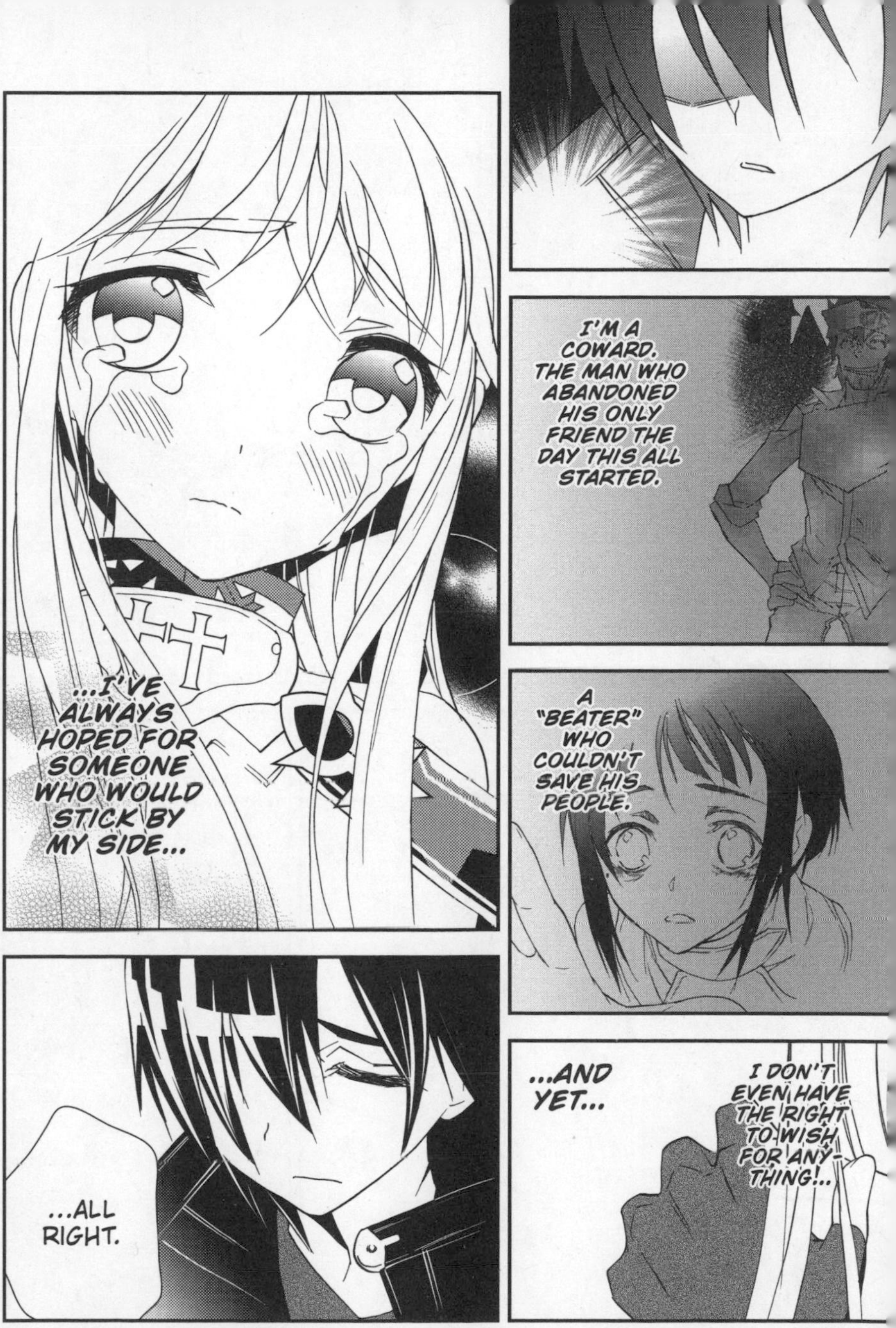
I'M A COWARD. THE MAN WHO ABANDONED HIS ONLY FRIEND THE DAY THIS ALL STARTED.
A "BEATER" WHO COULDN'T SAVE HIS PEOPLE.
...I'VE ALWAYS HOPED FOR SOMEONE WHO WOULD STICK BY MY SIDE...
I DON'T EVEN HAVE THE RIGHT TO WISH FOR ANY-THING!..
...AND YET...
...ALL RIGHT.

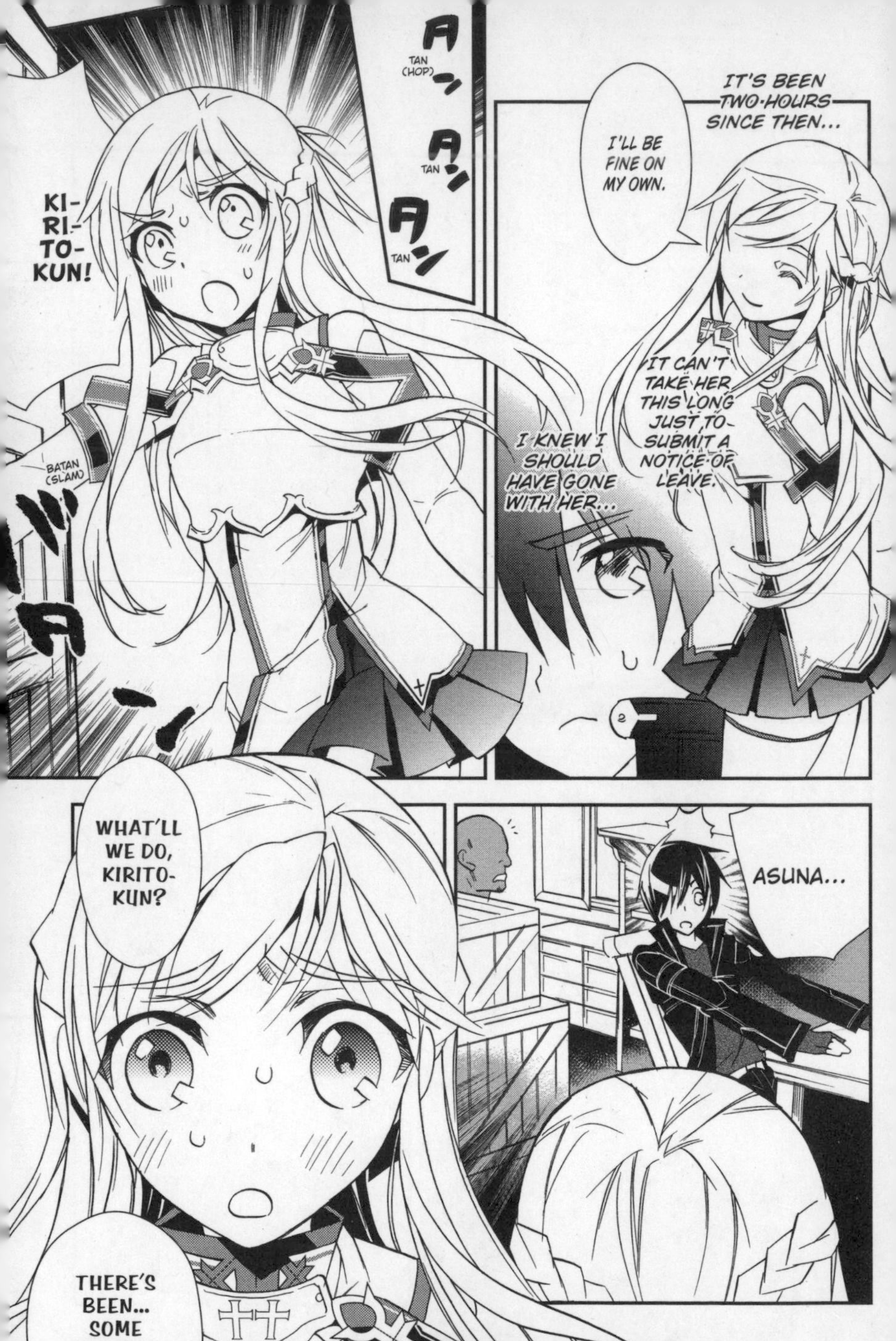
IT'S BEEN TWO HOURS SINCE THEN...
I'LL BE FINE ON MY OWN.
IT CAN'T TAKE HER THIS LONG JUST TO SUBMIT A NOTICE OF LEAVE.
I KNEW I SHOULD HAVE GONE WITH HER...
TAN (HOP)
TAN
TAN
KI-RI-TO-KUN!
BATAN (SLAM)
ASUNA...
WHAT'LL WE DO, KIRITO-KUN?
THERE'S BEEN... SOME TROUBLE.

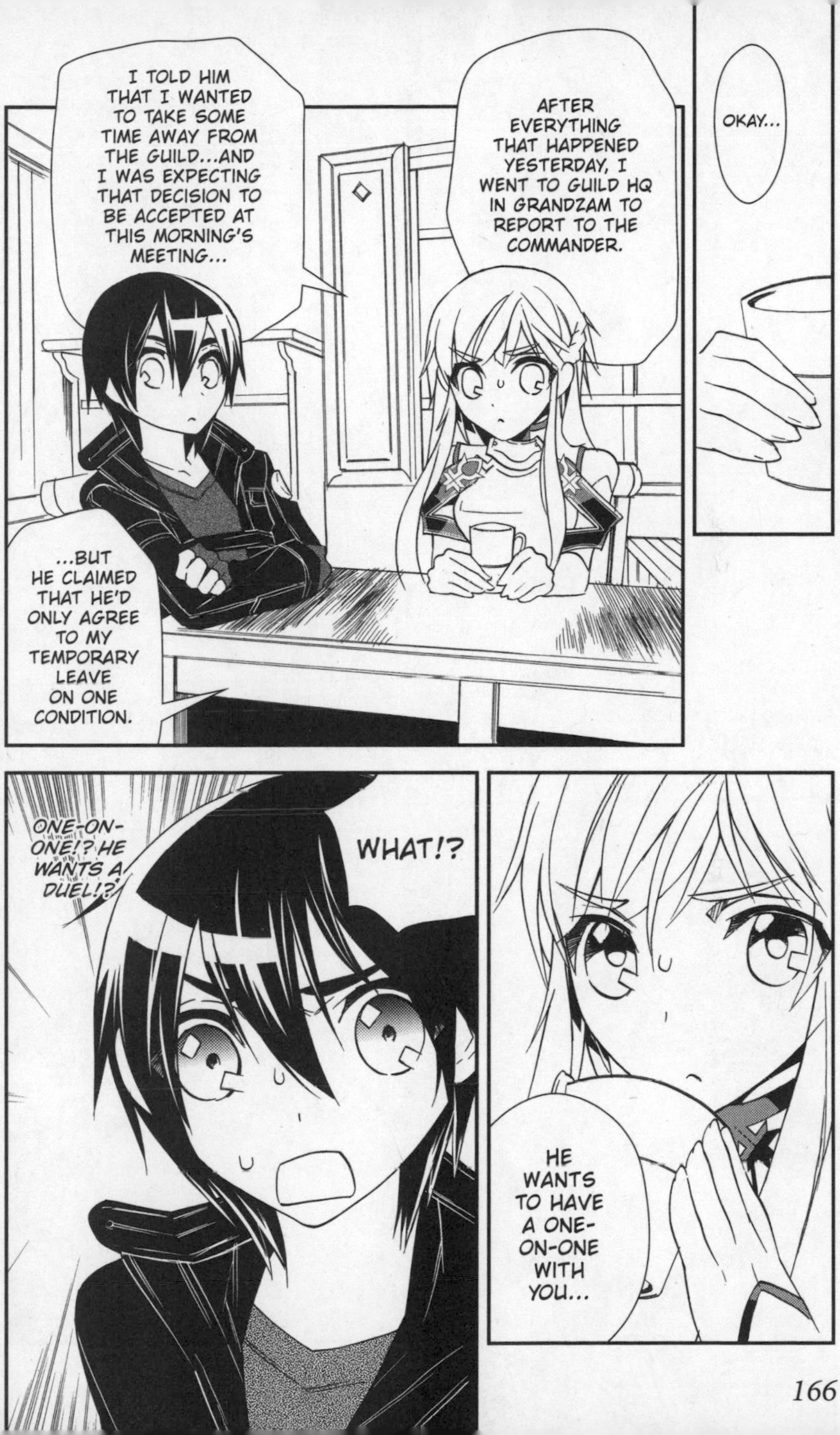
OKAY...
AFTER EVERYTHING THAT HAPPENED YESTERDAY, I WENT TO GUILD HQ IN GRANDZAM TO REPORT TO THE COMMANDER.
I TOLD HIM THAT I WANTED TO TAKE SOME TIME AWAY FROM THE GUILD...AND I WAS EXPECTING THAT DECISION TO BE ACCEPTED AT THIS MORNING'S MEETING...
...BUT HE CLAIMED THAT HE'D ONLY AGREE TO MY TEMPORARY LEAVE ON ONE CONDITION.
HE WANTS TO HAVE A ONE-ON-ONE WITH YOU...
WHAT!?
ONE-ON-ONE!? HE WANTS A DUEL!?

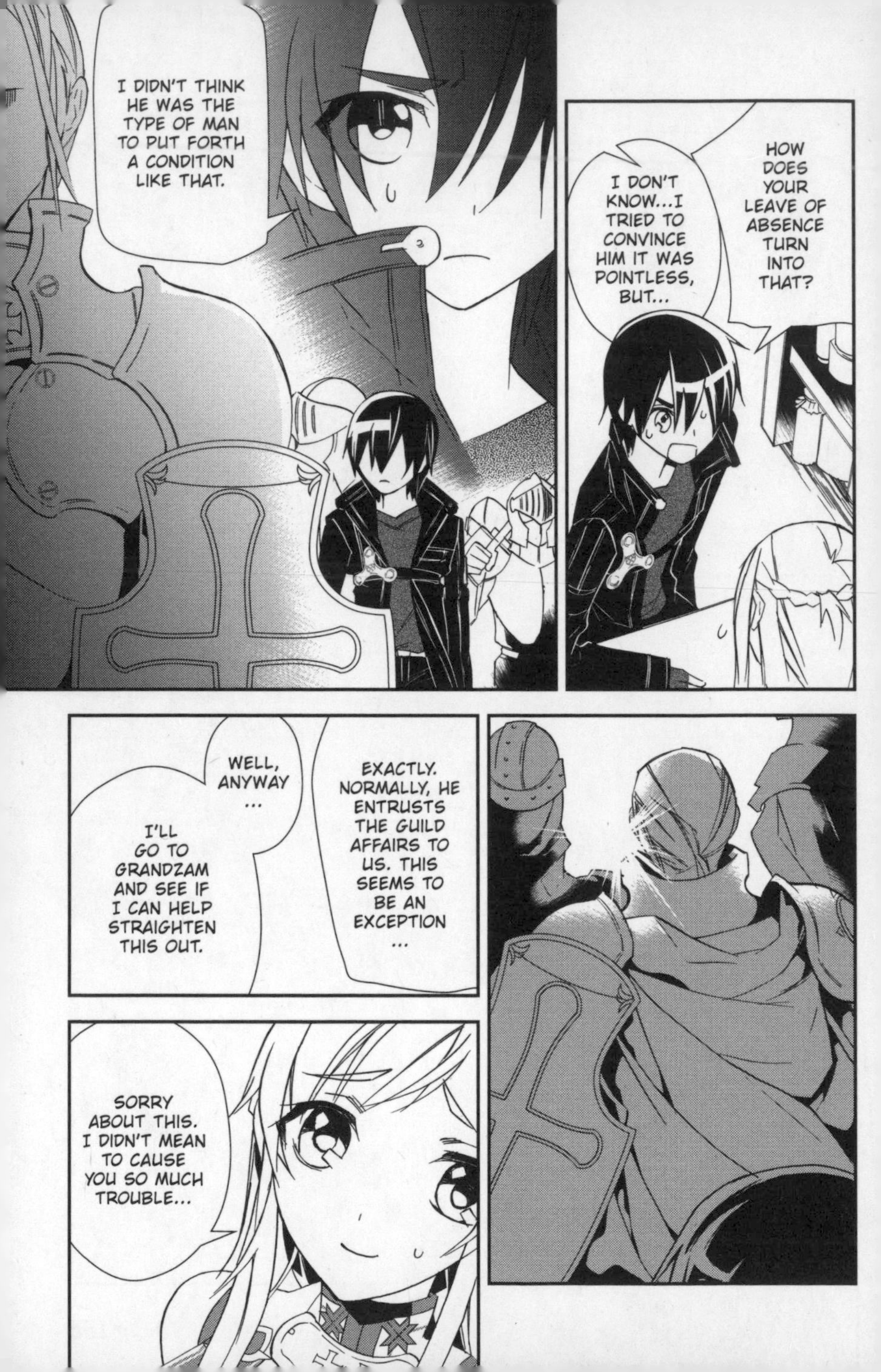
HOW DOES YOUR LEAVE OF ABSENCE TURN INTO THAT?
I DON'T KNOW...I TRIED TO CONVINCE HIM IT WAS POINTLESS, BUT...
I DIDN'T THINK HE WAS THE TYPE OF MAN TO PUT FORTH A CONDITION LIKE THAT.
EXACTLY. NORMALLY, HE ENTRUSTS THE GUILD AFFAIRS TO US. THIS SEEMS TO BE AN EXCEPTION...
WELL, ANYWAY...
I'LL GO TO GRANDZAM AND SEE IF I CAN HELP STRAIGHTEN THIS OUT.
SORRY ABOUT THIS. I DIDN'T MEAN TO CAUSE YOU SO MUCH TROUBLE...

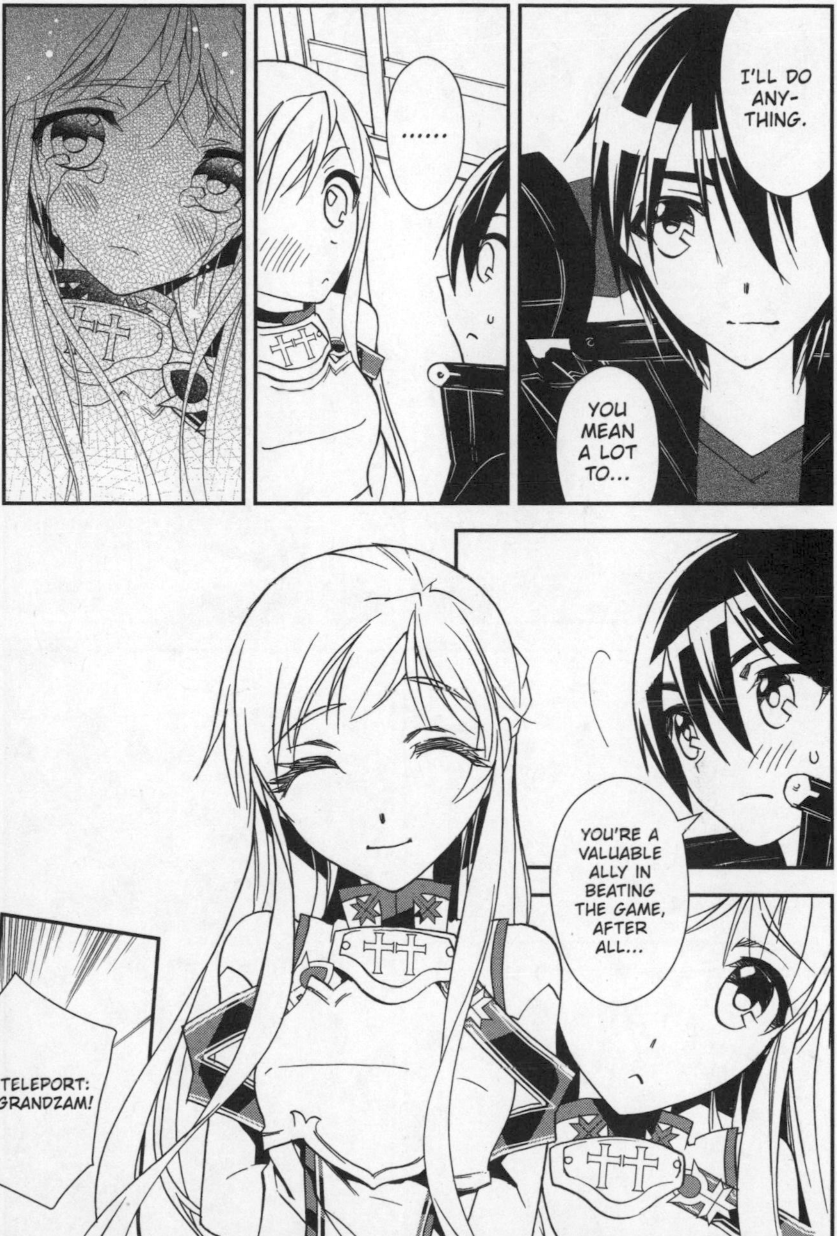
I'LL DO ANY-THING.
YOU MEAN A LOT TO...
......
YOU'RE A VALUABLE ALLY IN BEATING THE GAME, AFTER ALL...
TELEPORT: GRANDZAM!

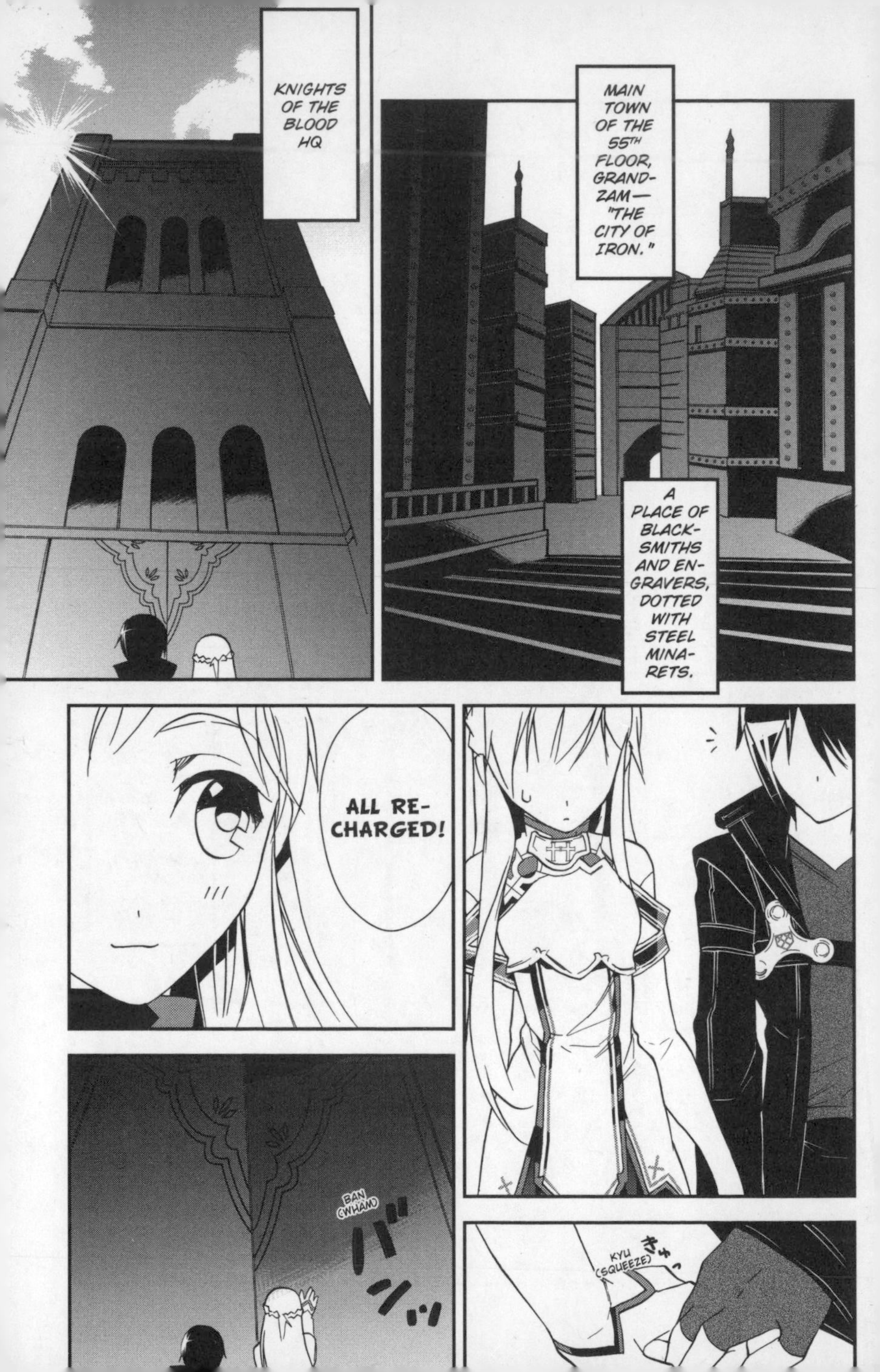
MAIN TOWN OF THE 55TH FLOOR, GRAND-ZAM—"THE CITY OF IRON."
A PLACE OF BLACK-SMITHS AND EN-GRAVERS, DOTTED WITH STEEL MINA-RETS.
KNIGHTS OF THE BLOOD HQ
ALL RE-CHARGED!
KYU (SQUEEZE)
BAN (WHAM)

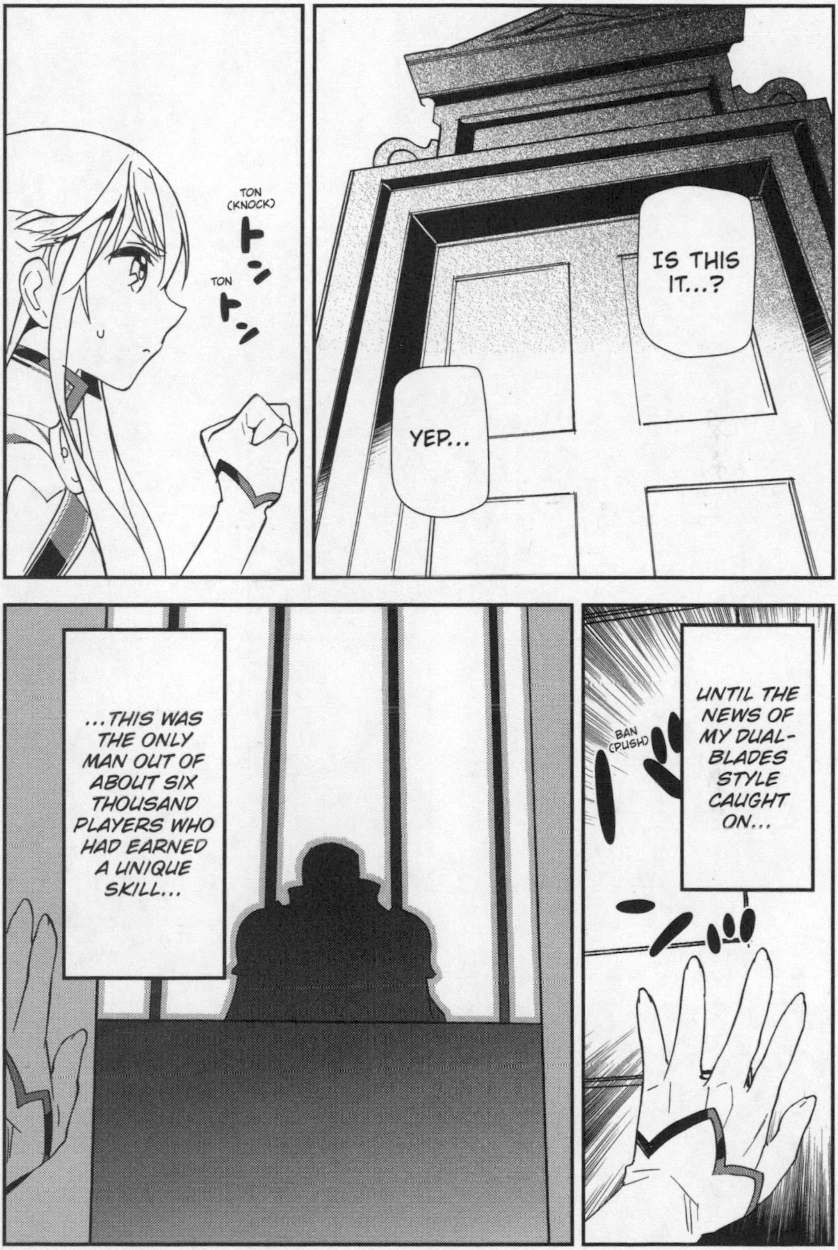
IS THIS IT...?
YEP...
TON (KNOCK)
トン
TON
トン
UNTIL THE NEWS OF MY DUAL-BLADES STYLE CAUGHT ON...
BAN (PUSH)
...THIS WAS THE ONLY MAN OUT OF ABOUT SIX THOUSAND PLAYERS WHO HAD EARNED A UNIQUE SKILL...

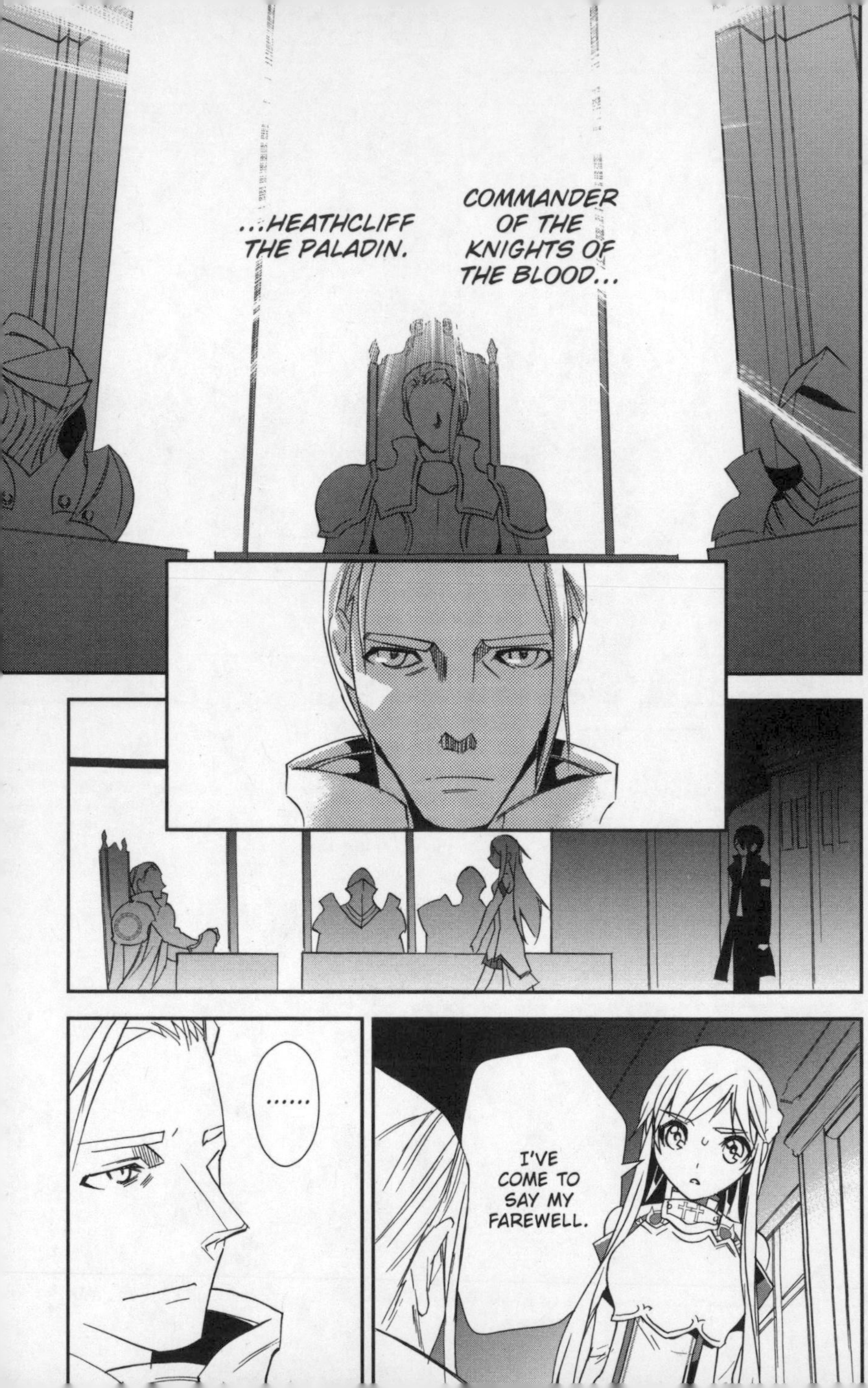
COMMANDER OF THE KNIGHTS OF THE BLOOD...
...HEATHCLIFF THE PALADIN.
I'VE COME TO SAY MY FAREWELL.
......

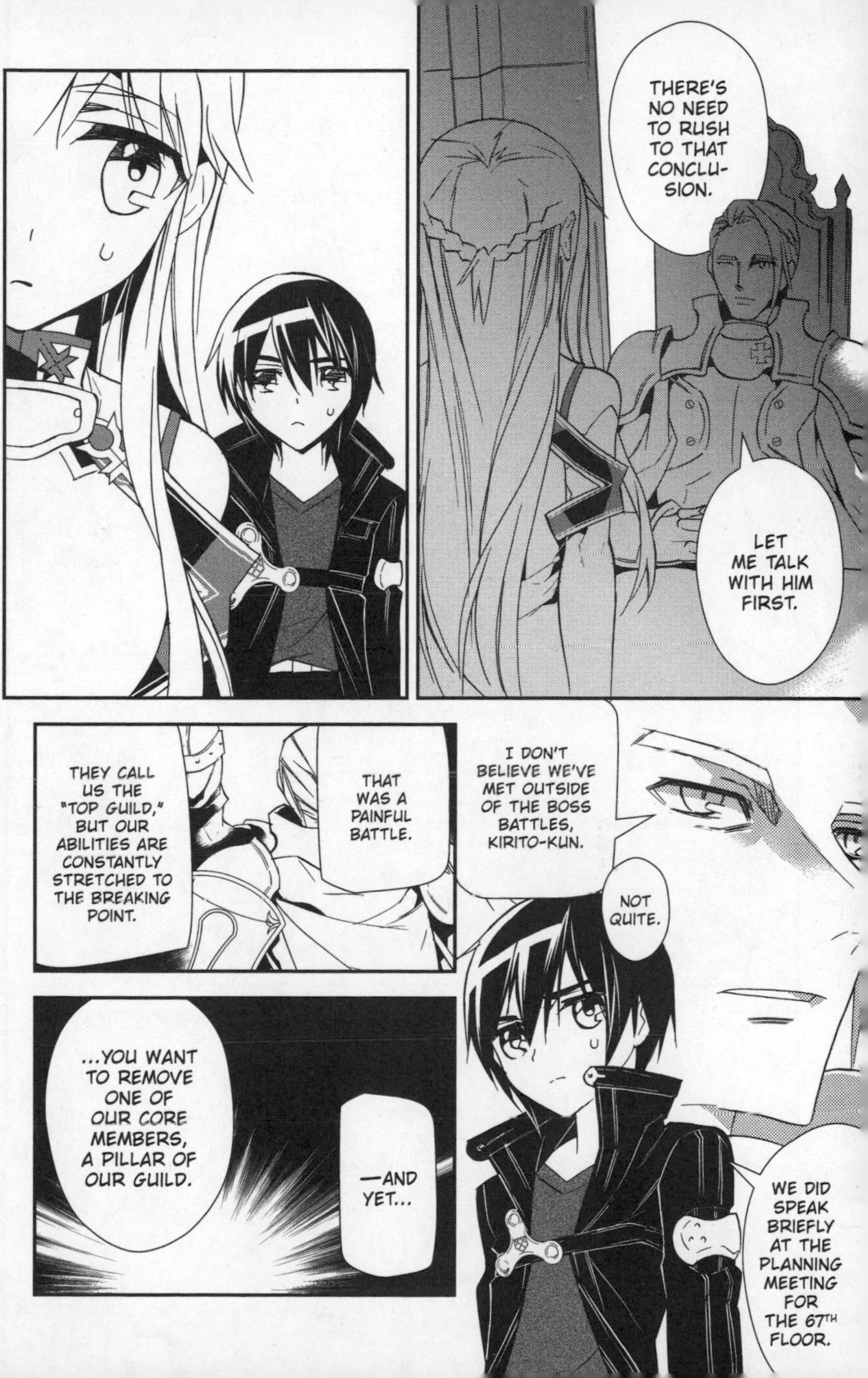
THERE'S NO NEED TO RUSH TO THAT CONCLUSION.
LET ME TALK WITH HIM FIRST.
I DON'T BELIEVE WE'VE MET OUTSIDE OF THE BOSS BATTLES, KIRITO-KUN.
NOT QUITE.
WE DID SPEAK BRIEFLY AT THE PLANNING MEETING FOR THE 67TH FLOOR.
THAT WAS A PAINFUL BATTLE.
THEY CALL US THE "TOP GUILD," BUT OUR ABILITIES ARE CONSTANTLY STRETCHED TO THE BREAKING POINT.
—AND YET...
...YOU WANT TO REMOVE ONE OF OUR CORE MEMBERS, A PILLAR OF OUR GUILD.

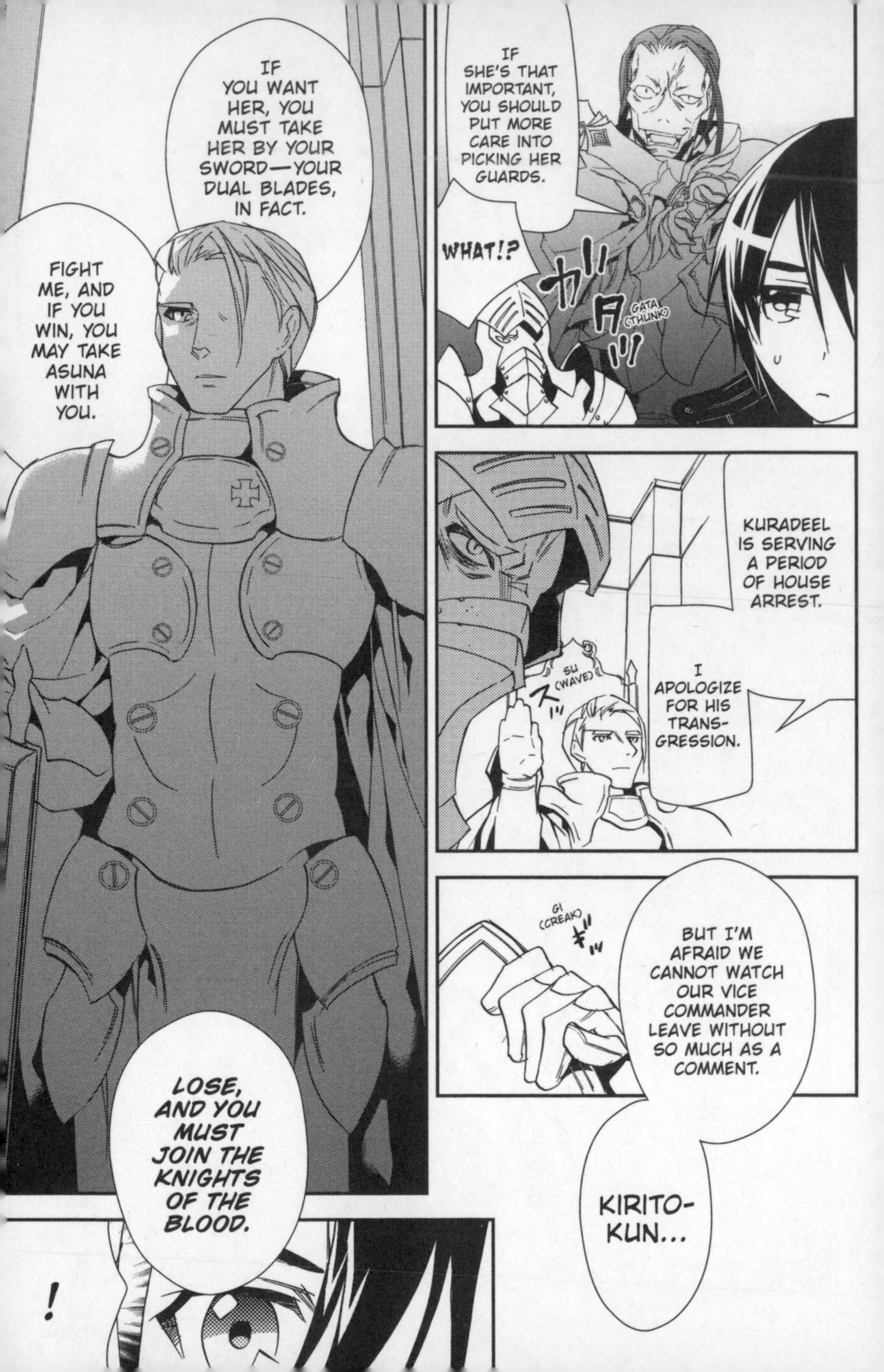
IF SHE'S THAT IMPORTANT, YOU SHOULD PUT MORE CARE INTO PICKING HER GUARDS.
WHAT!?
GATA (THUNK)
KURADEEL IS SERVING A PERIOD OF HOUSE ARREST.
I APOLOGIZE FOR HIS TRANS-GRESSION.
SU (WAVE)
GI (CREAK)
BUT I'M AFRAID WE CANNOT WATCH OUR VICE COMMANDER LEAVE WITHOUT SO MUCH AS A COMMENT.
KIRITO-KUN...
IF YOU WANT HER, YOU MUST TAKE HER BY YOUR SWORD—YOUR DUAL BLADES, IN FACT.
FIGHT ME, AND IF YOU WIN, YOU MAY TAKE ASUNA WITH YOU.
LOSE, AND YOU MUST JOIN THE KNIGHTS OF THE BLOOD.
!

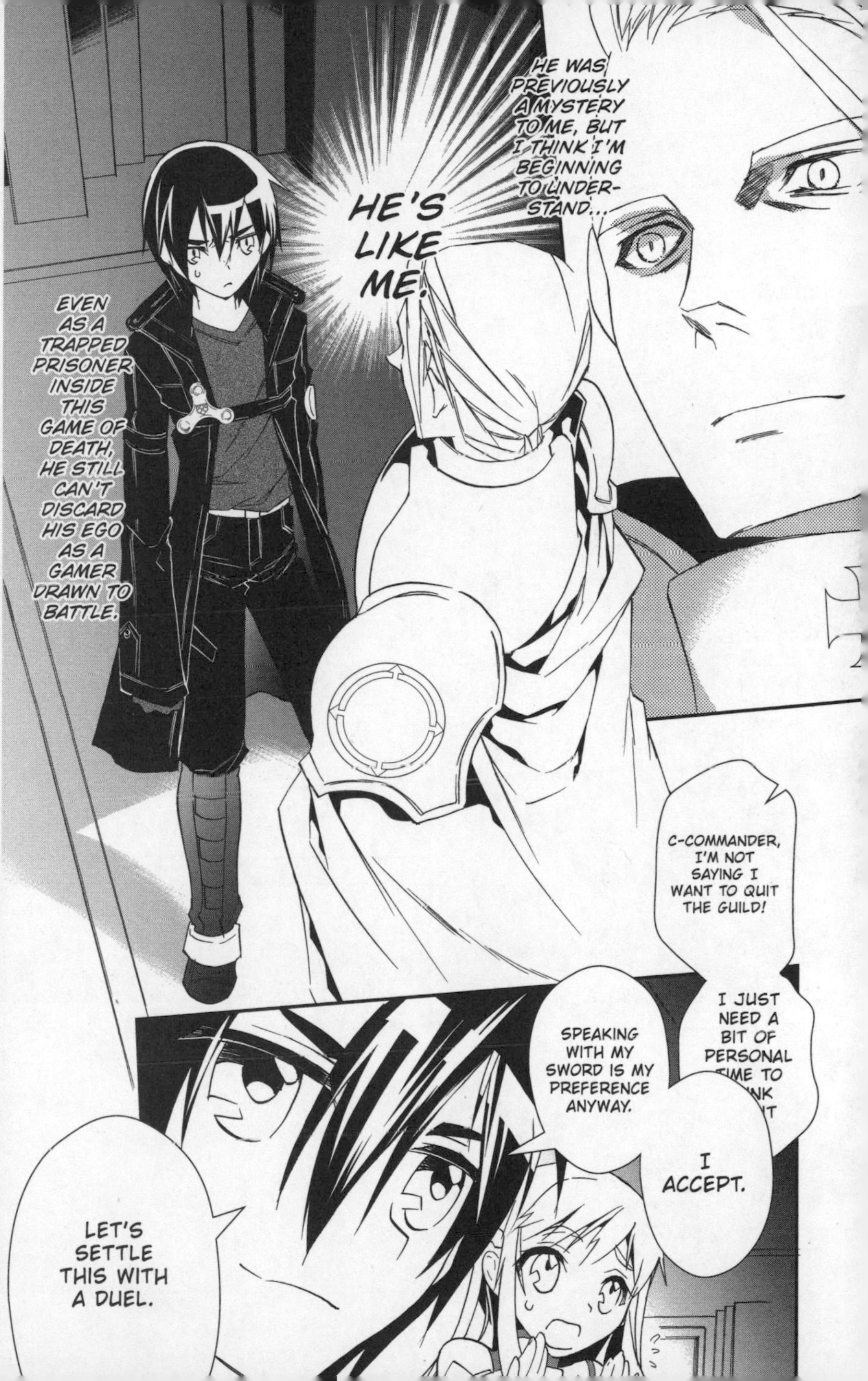
HE WAS PREVIOUSLY A MYSTERY TO ME, BUT I THINK I'M BEGINNING TO UNDER-STAND...
HE'S LIKE ME.
EVEN AS A TRAPPED PRISONER INSIDE THIS GAME OF DEATH, HE STILL CAN'T DISCARD HIS EGO AS A GAMER DRAWN TO BATTLE.
C-COMMANDER, I'M NOT SAYING I WANT TO QUIT THE GUILD!
I JUST NEED A BIT OF PERSONAL TIME TO
SPEAKING WITH MY SWORD IS MY PREFERENCE ANYWAY.
I ACCEPT.
LET'S SETTLE THIS WITH A DUEL.

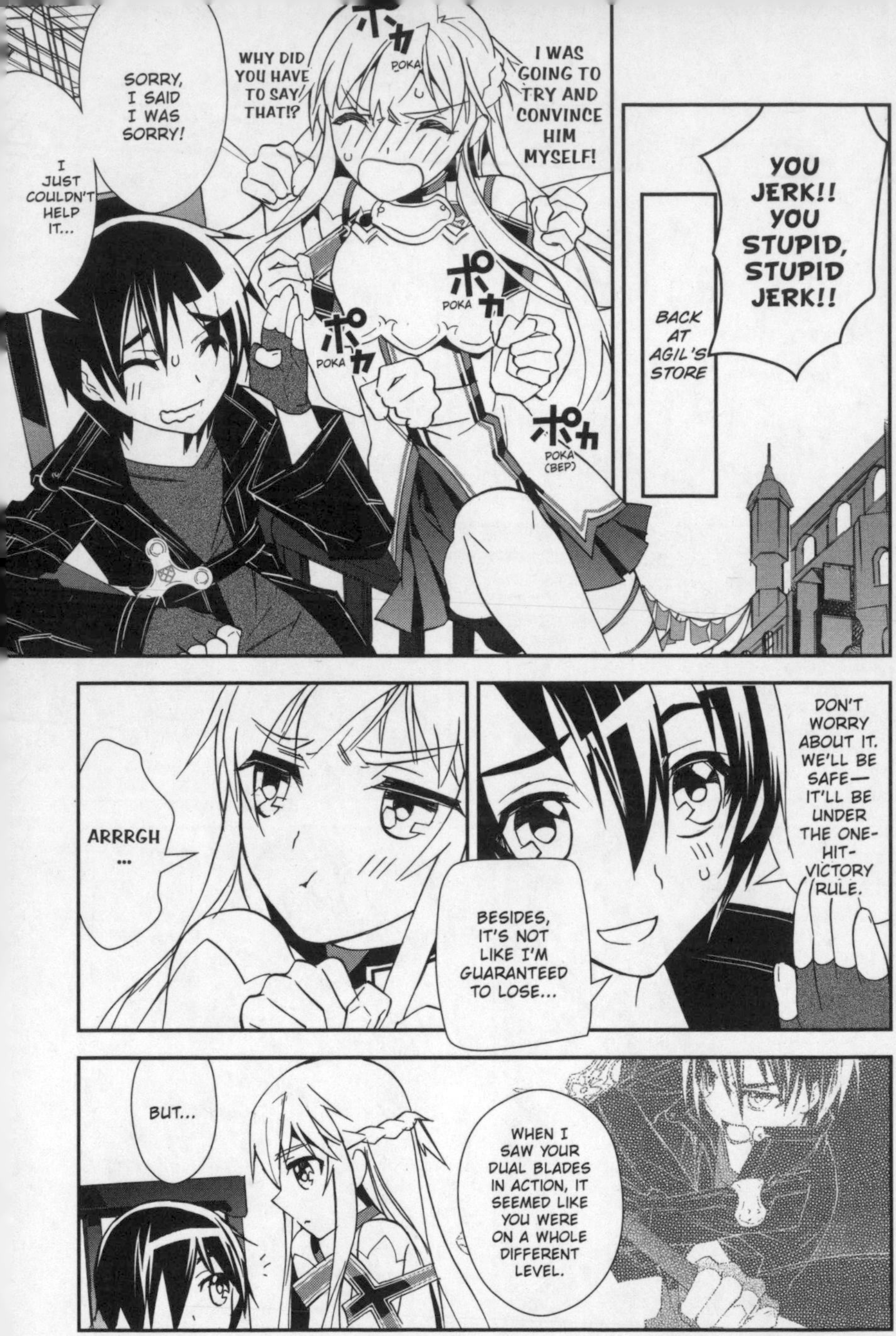
YOU JERK!! YOU STUPID, STUPID JERK!!
BACK AT AGIL'S STORE
I WAS GOING TO TRY AND CONVINCE HIM MYSELF!
ポカ
POKA
WHY DID YOU HAVE TO SAY THAT!?
SORRY, I SAID I WAS SORRY!
I JUST COULDN'T HELP IT...
ポカ
POKA
ポカ
POKA
ポカ
POKA (BEP)
DON'T WORRY ABOUT IT. WE'LL BE SAFE— IT'LL BE UNDER THE ONE-HIT-VICTORY RULE.
BESIDES, IT'S NOT LIKE I'M GUARANTEED TO LOSE...
ARRRGH ...
WHEN I SAW YOUR DUAL BLADES IN ACTION, IT SEEMED LIKE YOU WERE ON A WHOLE DIFFERENT LEVEL.
BUT...

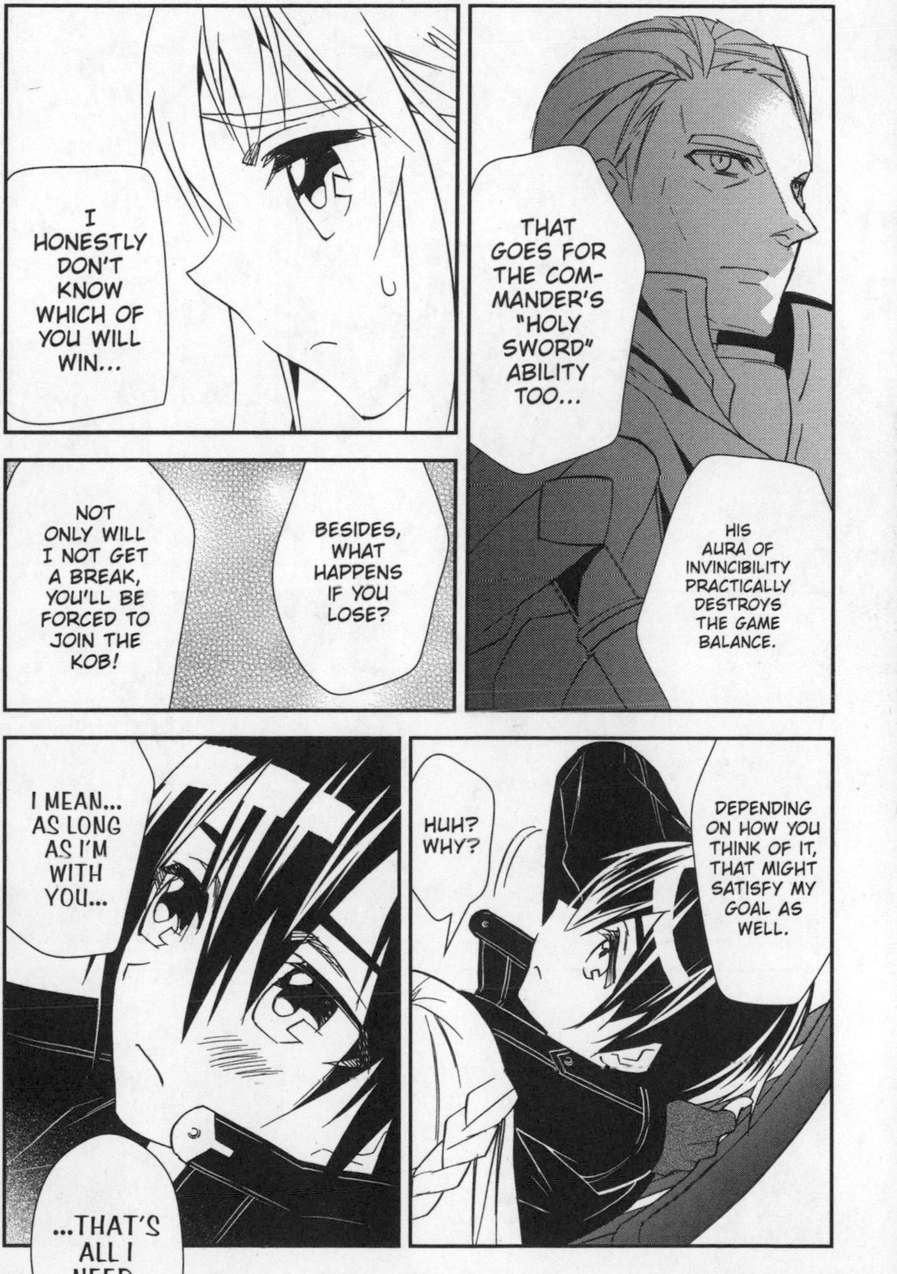
THAT GOES FOR THE COMMANDER'S "HOLY SWORD" ABILITY TOO...
HIS AURA OF INVINCIBILITY PRACTICALLY DESTROYS THE GAME BALANCE.
I HONESTLY DON'T KNOW WHICH OF YOU WILL WIN...
BESIDES, WHAT HAPPENS IF YOU LOSE?
NOT ONLY WILL I NOT GET A BREAK, YOU'LL BE FORCED TO JOIN THE KOB!
DEPENDING ON HOW YOU THINK OF IT, THAT MIGHT SATISFY MY GOAL AS WELL.
HUH? WHY?
I MEAN... AS LONG AS I'M WITH YOU...
...THAT'S ALL I NEED.

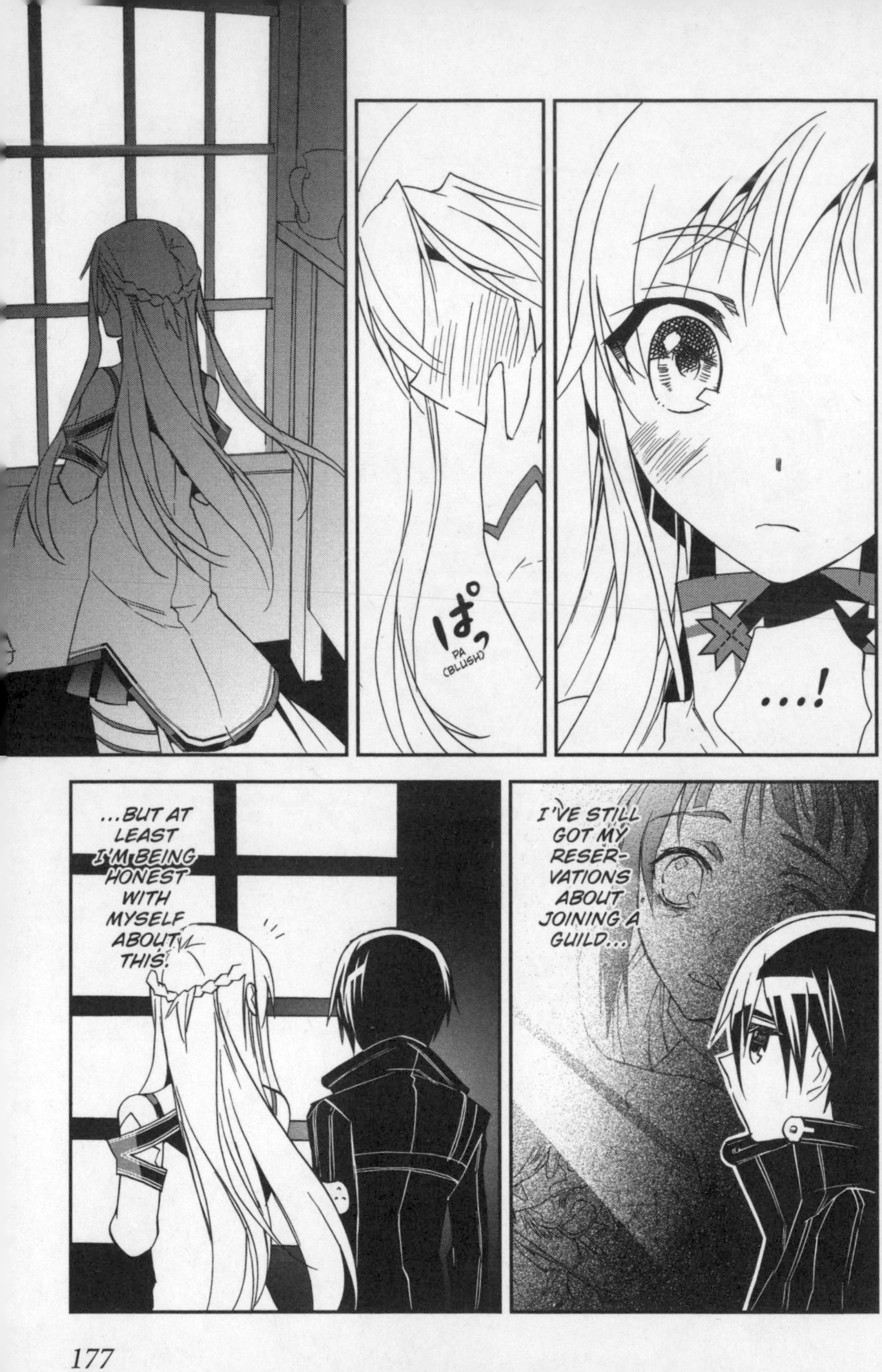
...!
ぱっ
PA (BLUSH)
I'VE STILL GOT MY RESERVATIONS ABOUT JOINING A GUILD...
...BUT AT LEAST I'M BEING HONEST WITH MYSELF ABOUT THIS!

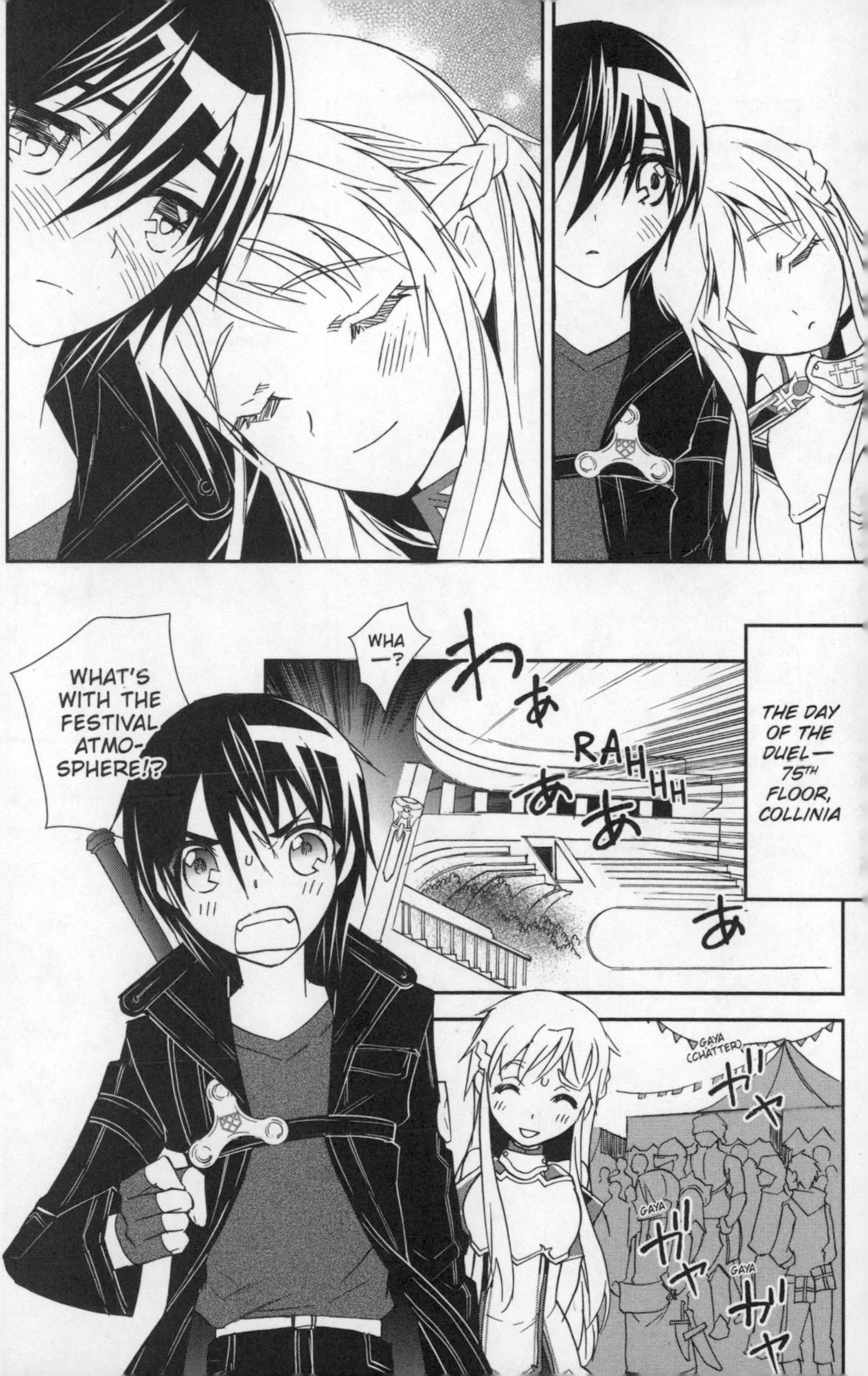
THE DAY OF THE DUEL— 75TH FLOOR, COLLINIA
RAHHHH
WHA—?
WHAT'S WITH THE FESTIVAL ATMOSPHERE!?
GAYA (CHATTER)
GAYA
GAYA

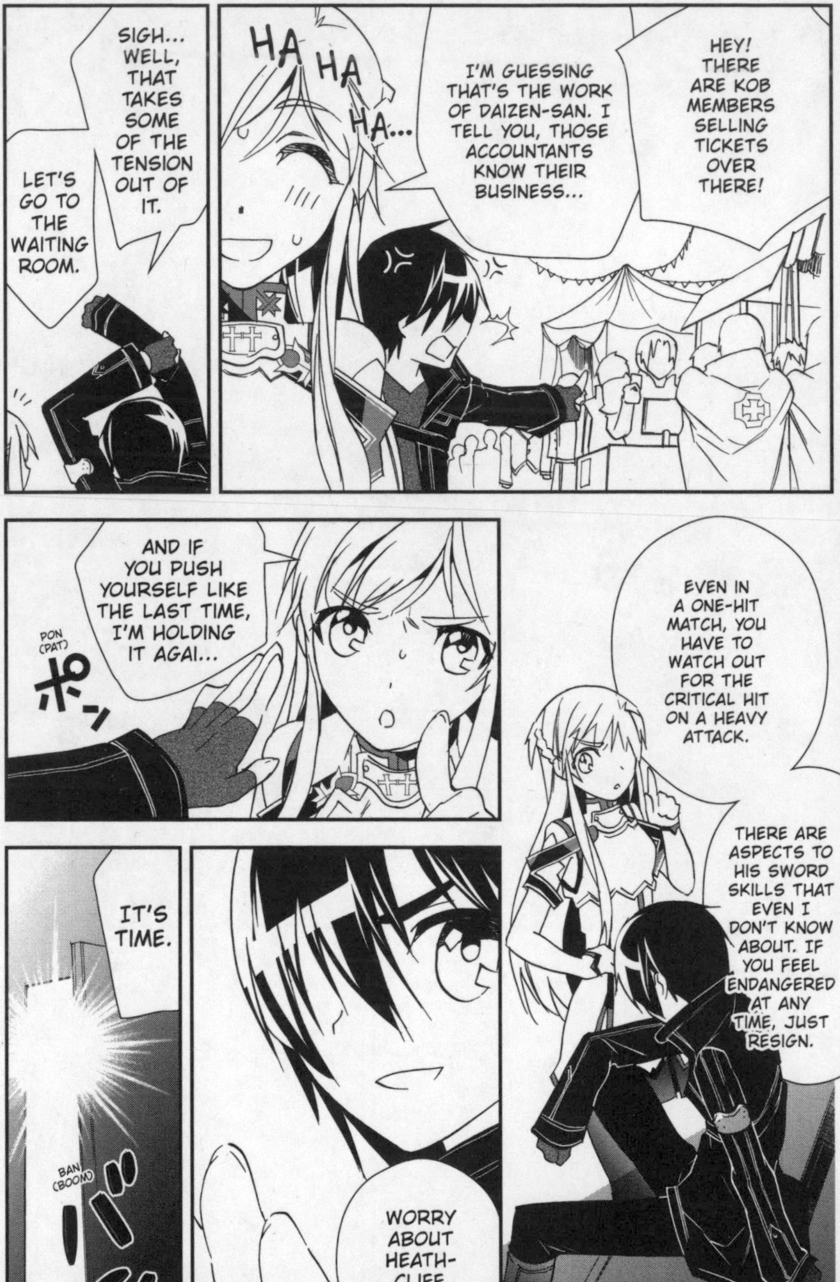
HEY! THERE ARE KOB MEMBERS SELLING TICKETS OVER THERE!
I'M GUESSING THAT'S THE WORK OF DAIZEN-SAN. I TELL YOU, THOSE ACCOUNTANTS KNOW THEIR BUSINESS...
HA HA HA...
SIGH... WELL, THAT TAKES SOME OF THE TENSION OUT OF IT.
LET'S GO TO THE WAITING ROOM.
EVEN IN A ONE-HIT MATCH, YOU HAVE TO WATCH OUT FOR THE CRITICAL HIT ON A HEAVY ATTACK.
THERE ARE ASPECTS TO HIS SWORD SKILLS THAT EVEN I DON'T KNOW ABOUT. IF YOU FEEL ENDANGERED AT ANY TIME, JUST RESIGN.
AND IF YOU PUSH YOURSELF LIKE THE LAST TIME, I'M HOLDING IT AGAI...
PON (PAT)
WORRY ABOUT HEATH-CLIFF, NOT ME.
IT'S TIME.
BAN (BOOM)

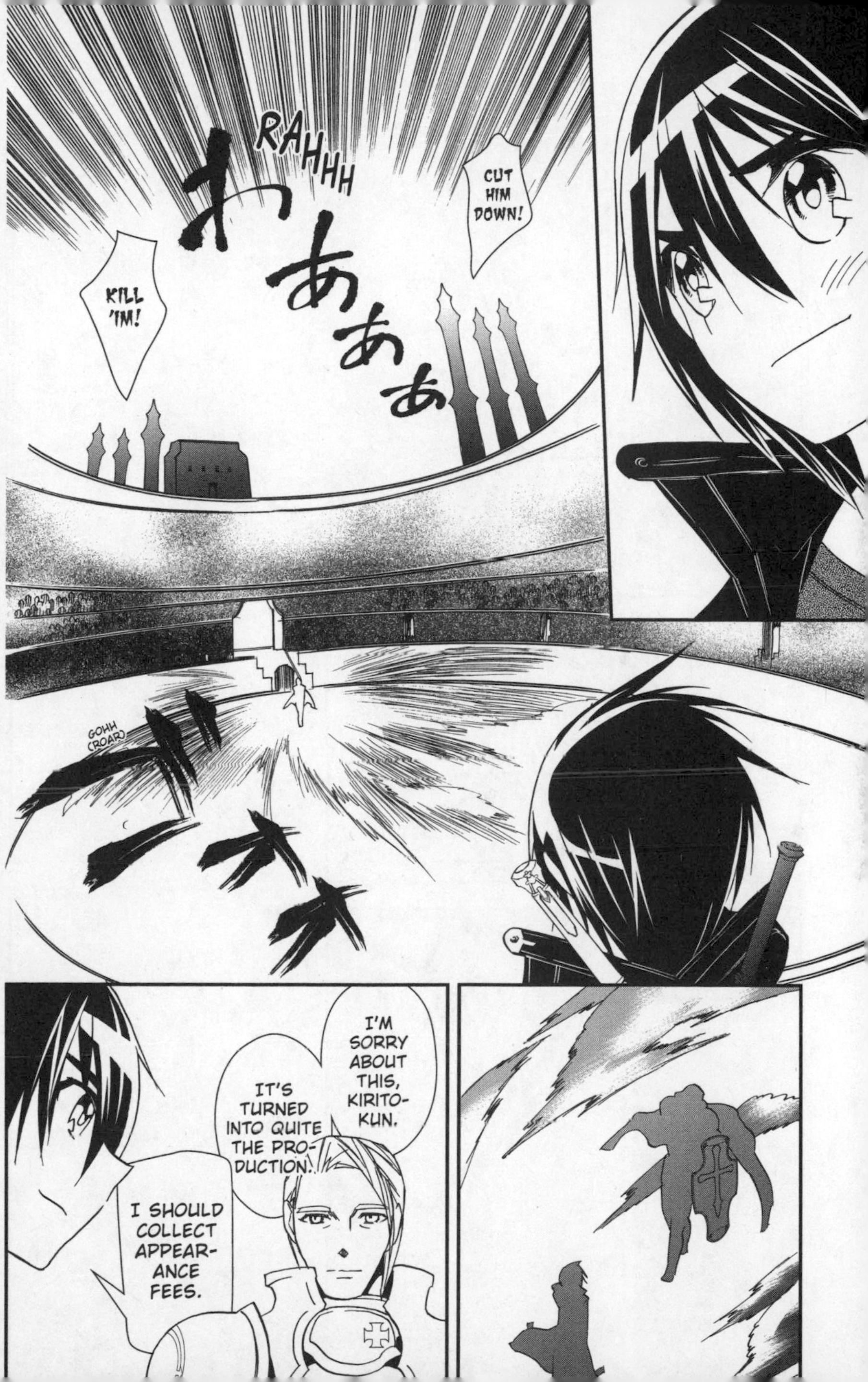
CUT HIM DOWN!
RAHHHH
KILL 'IM!
GOHH (ROAR)
I'M SORRY ABOUT THIS, KIRITO-KUN.
IT'S TURNED INTO QUITE THE PRODUCTION.
I SHOULD COLLECT APPEARANCE FEES.

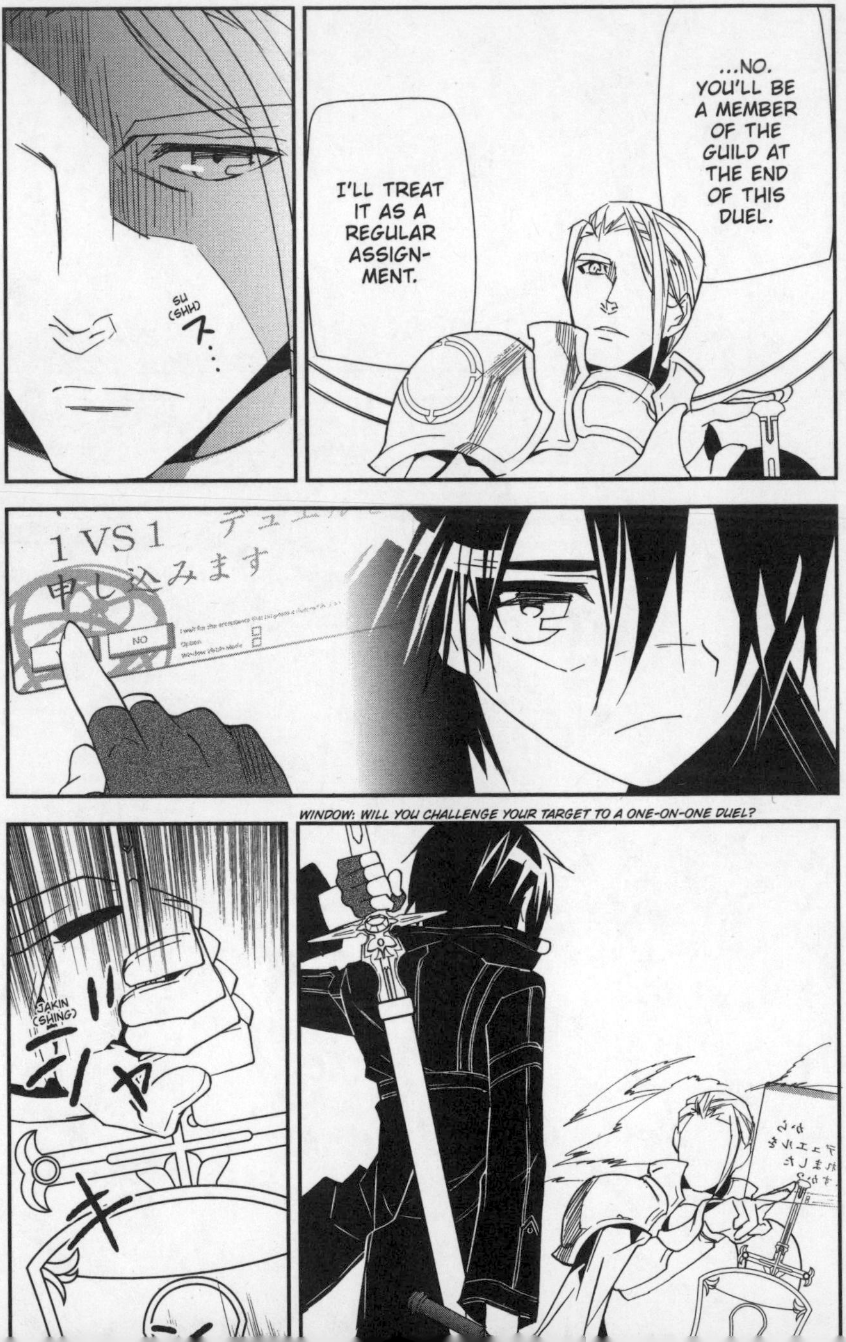
...NO. YOU'LL BE A MEMBER OF THE GUILD AT THE END OF THIS DUEL.
I'LL TREAT IT AS A REGULAR ASSIGNMENT.
SU (SHH)
1 VS 1
申し込みます
NO
WINDOW: WILL YOU CHALLENGE YOUR TARGET TO A ONE-ON-ONE DUEL?
JAKIN (SHING)

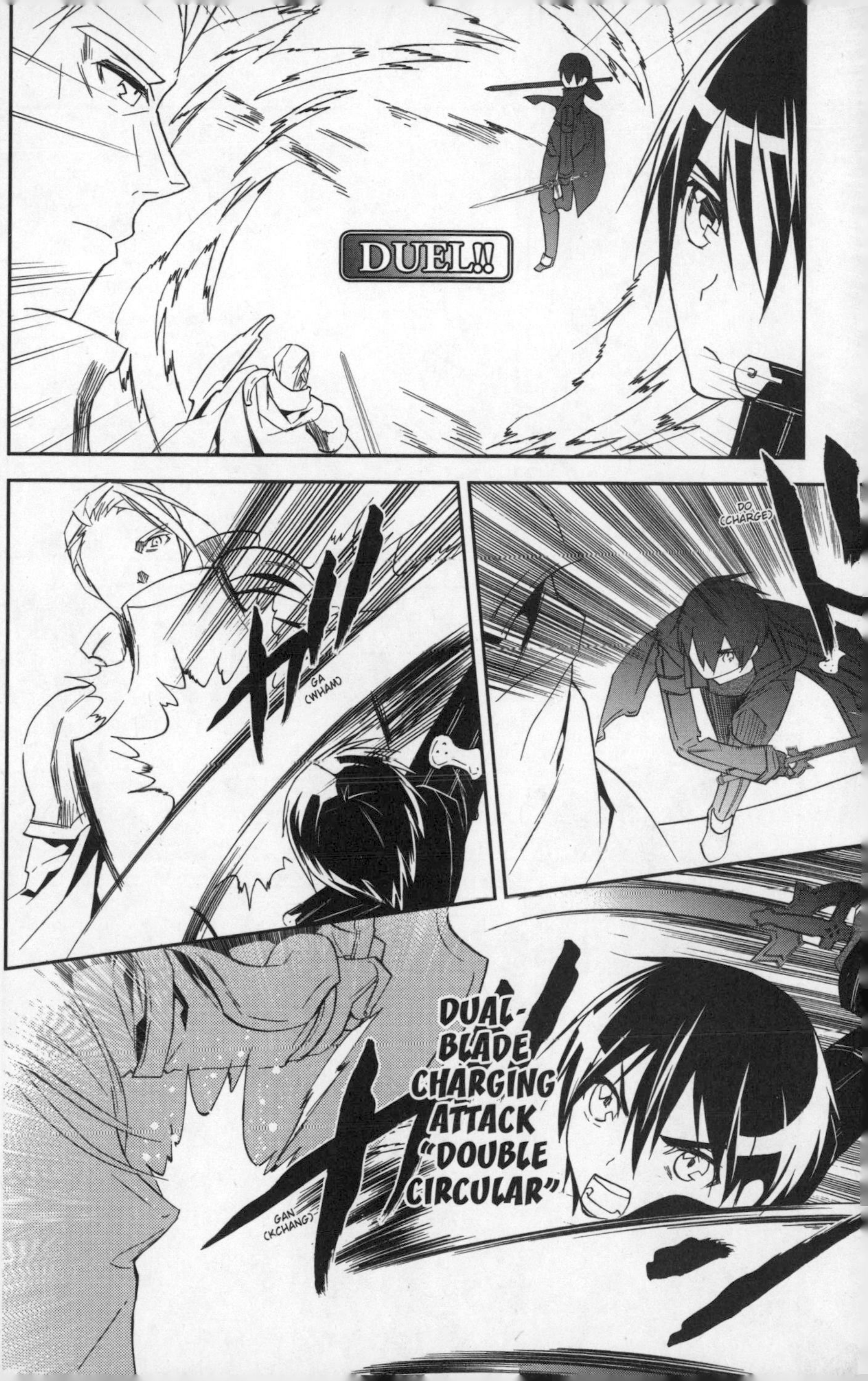
DUEL!!
DO (CHARGE)
GA (WHAM)
DUAL-BLADE CHARGING ATTACK "DOUBLE CIRCULAR"
GAN (KCHANG)

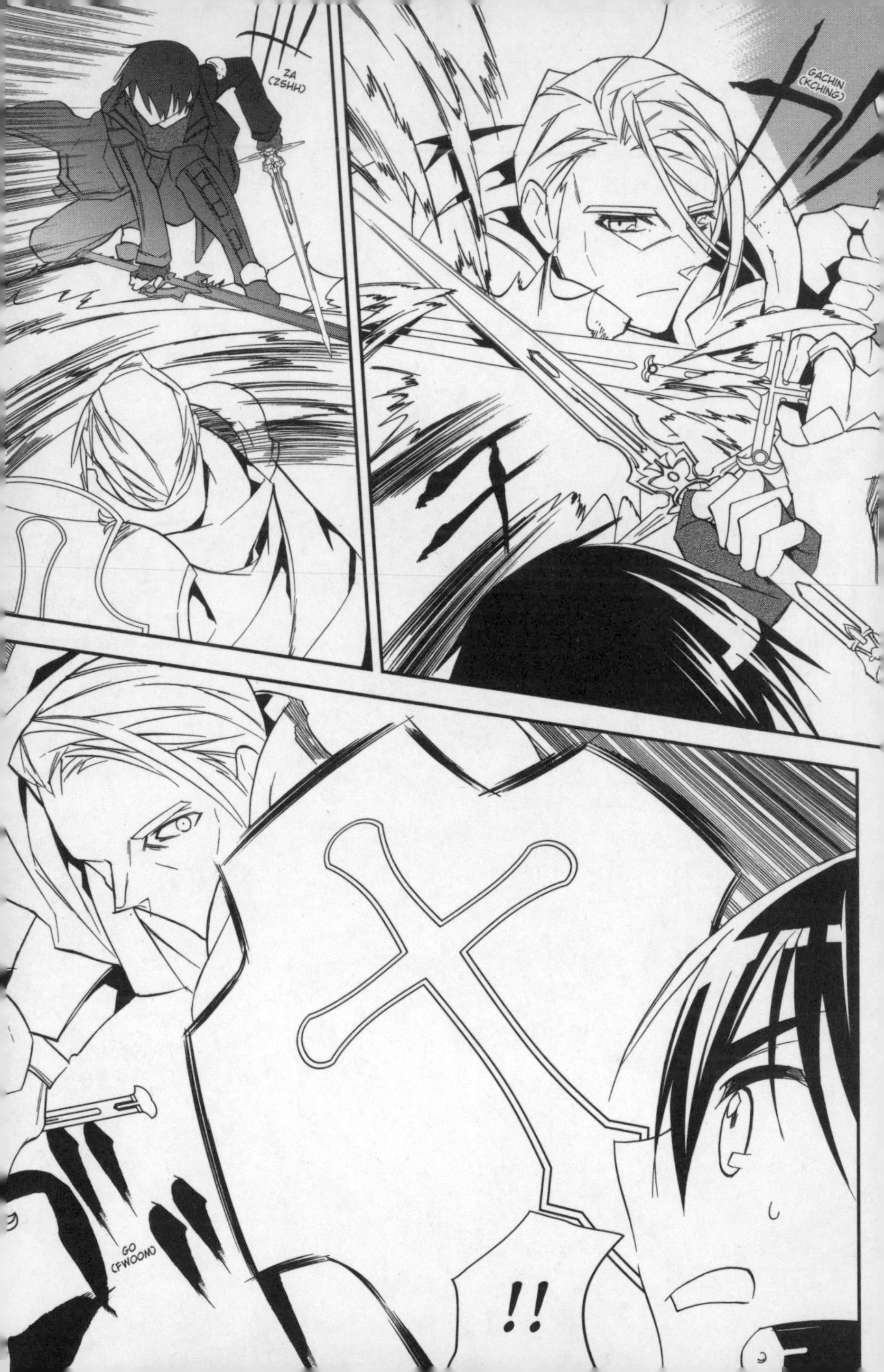
GACHIN
(KCHING)
ZA
(ZSHH)
!!
GO
(FWOOM)

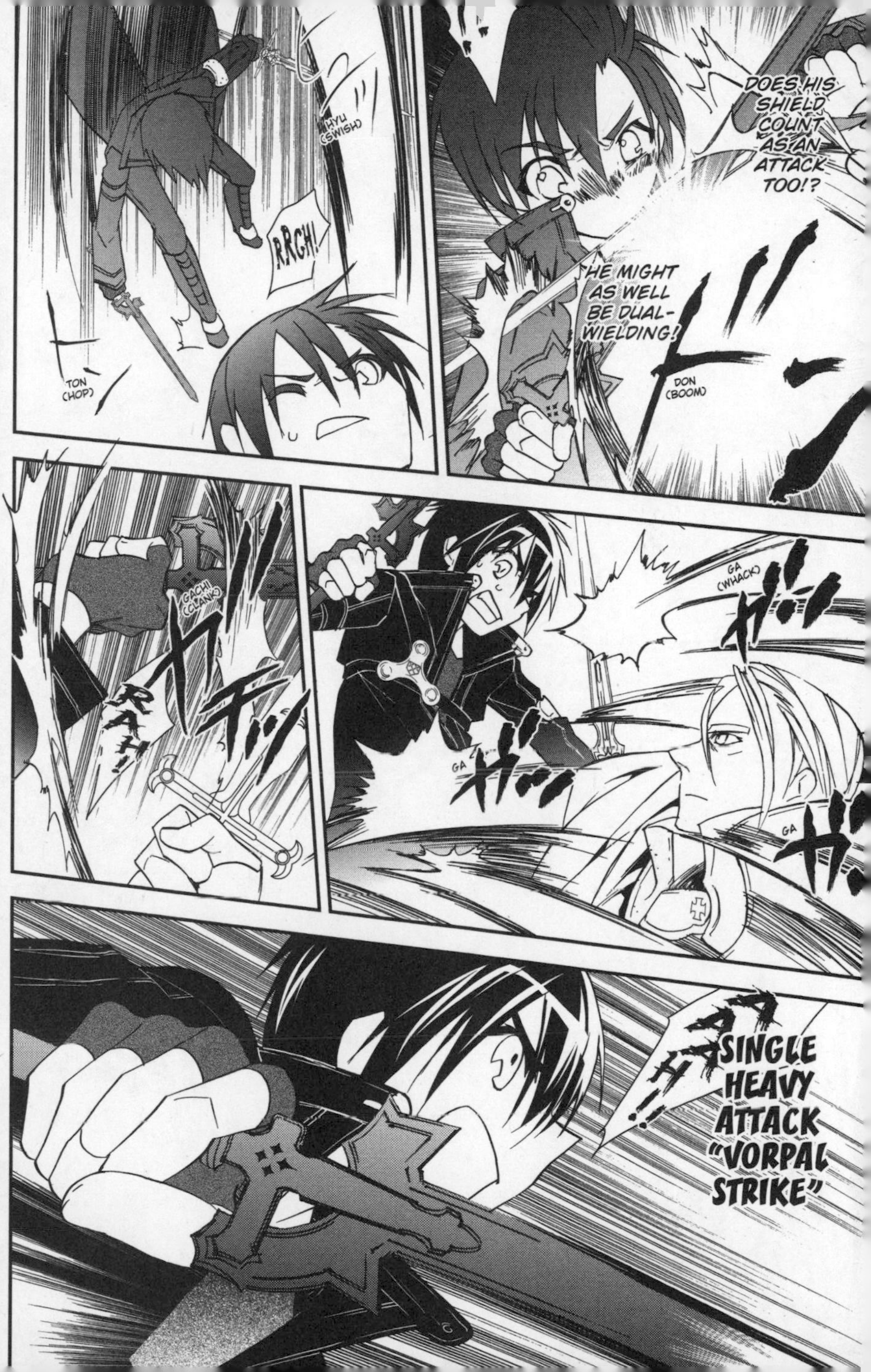
DOES HIS SHIELD COUNT AS AN ATTACK TOO!?
HE MIGHT AS WELL BE DUAL-WIELDING!
DON (BOOM)
HYU (SWISH)
RRCH!
TON (HOP)
GA (WHACK)
GA
GA
GACHI (CLANK)
RAH!
AAH!!
SINGLE HEAVY ATTACK "VORPAL STRIKE"

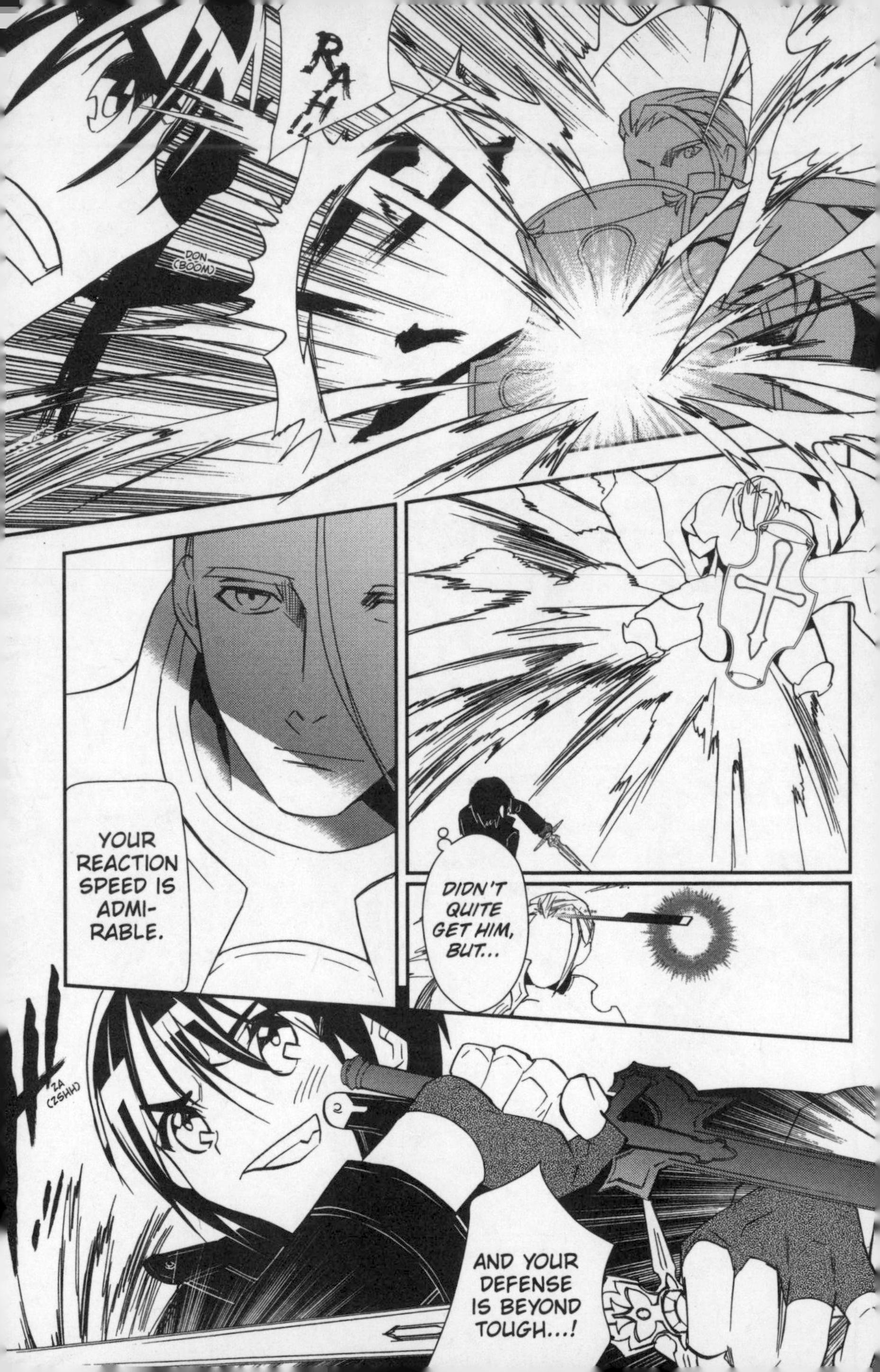
RAH!!
DON (BOOM)
DIDN'T QUITE GET HIM, BUT...
YOUR REACTION SPEED IS ADMI-RABLE.
ZA (ZSHH)
AND YOUR DEFENSE IS BEYOND TOUGH...!

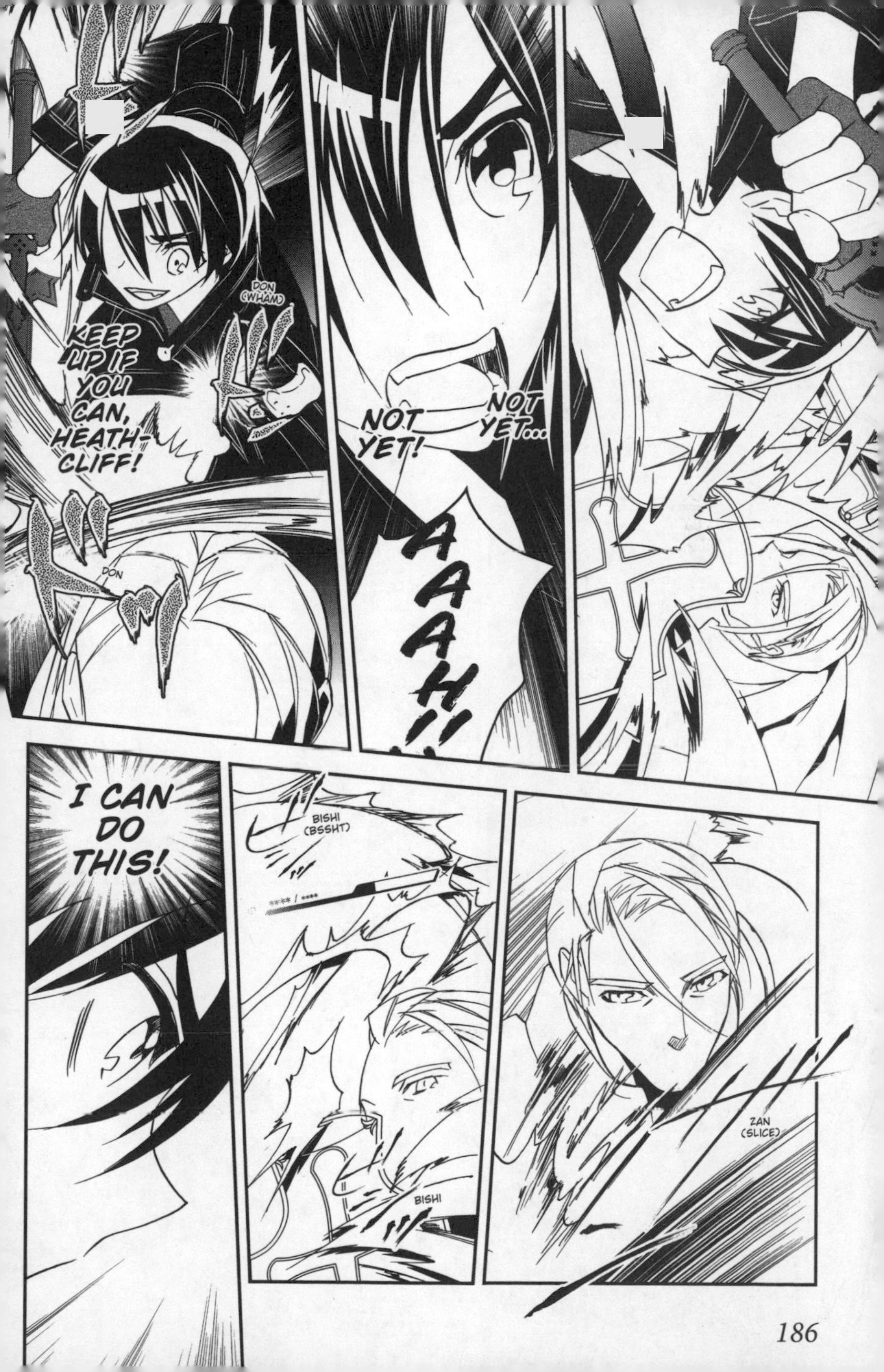
NOT YET...
NOT YET!
AAAAH!!
DON (WHAM)
KEEP UP IF YOU CAN, HEATH-CLIFF!
DON
ZAN (SLICE)
BISHI (BSSHT)
BISHI
I CAN DO THIS!

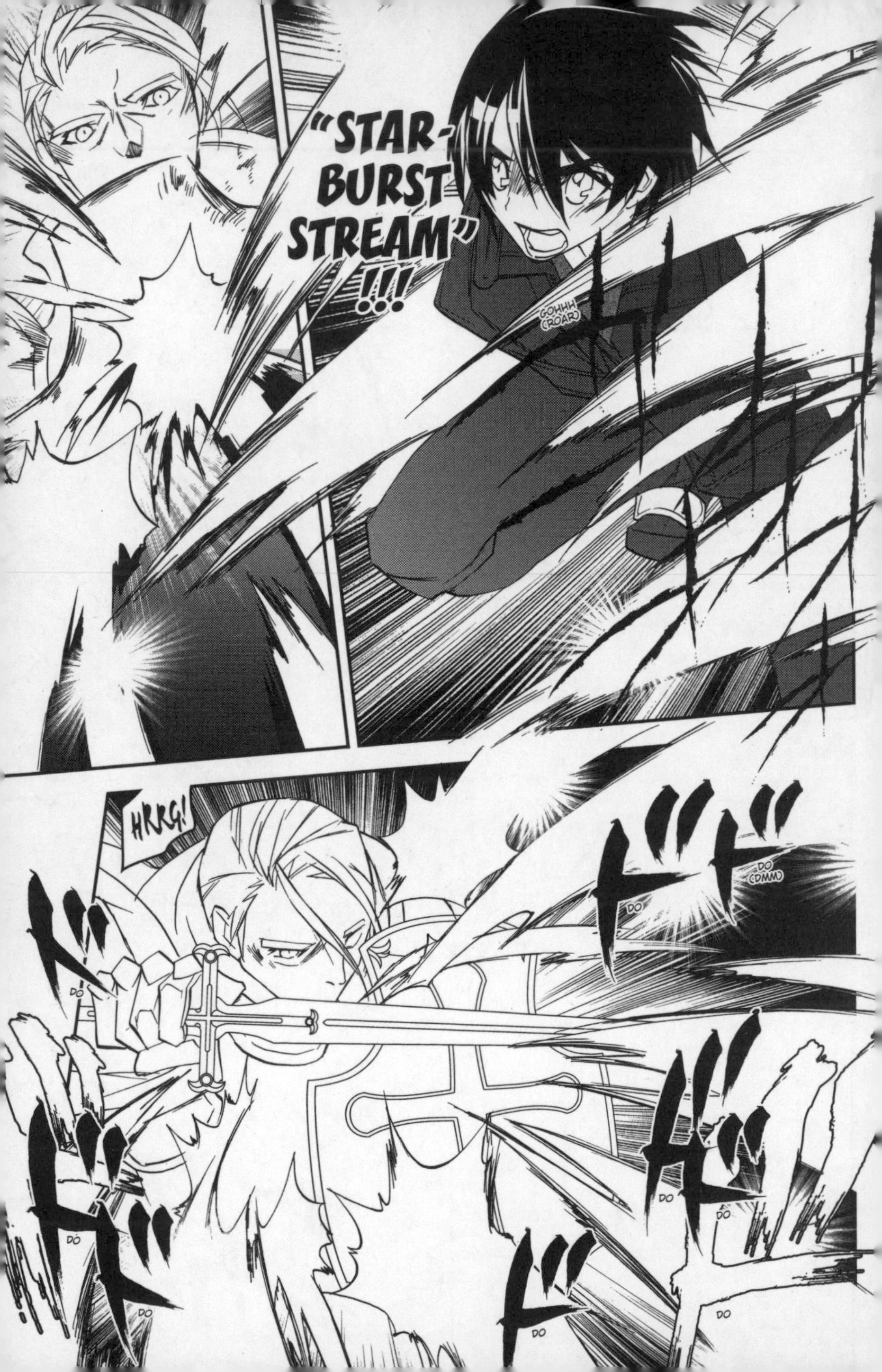
"STAR-BURST STREAM"!!!
GOHHH (ROAR)
DO (DMM)
DO
HRRG!
DO
DO
DO
DO
DO
DO
DO

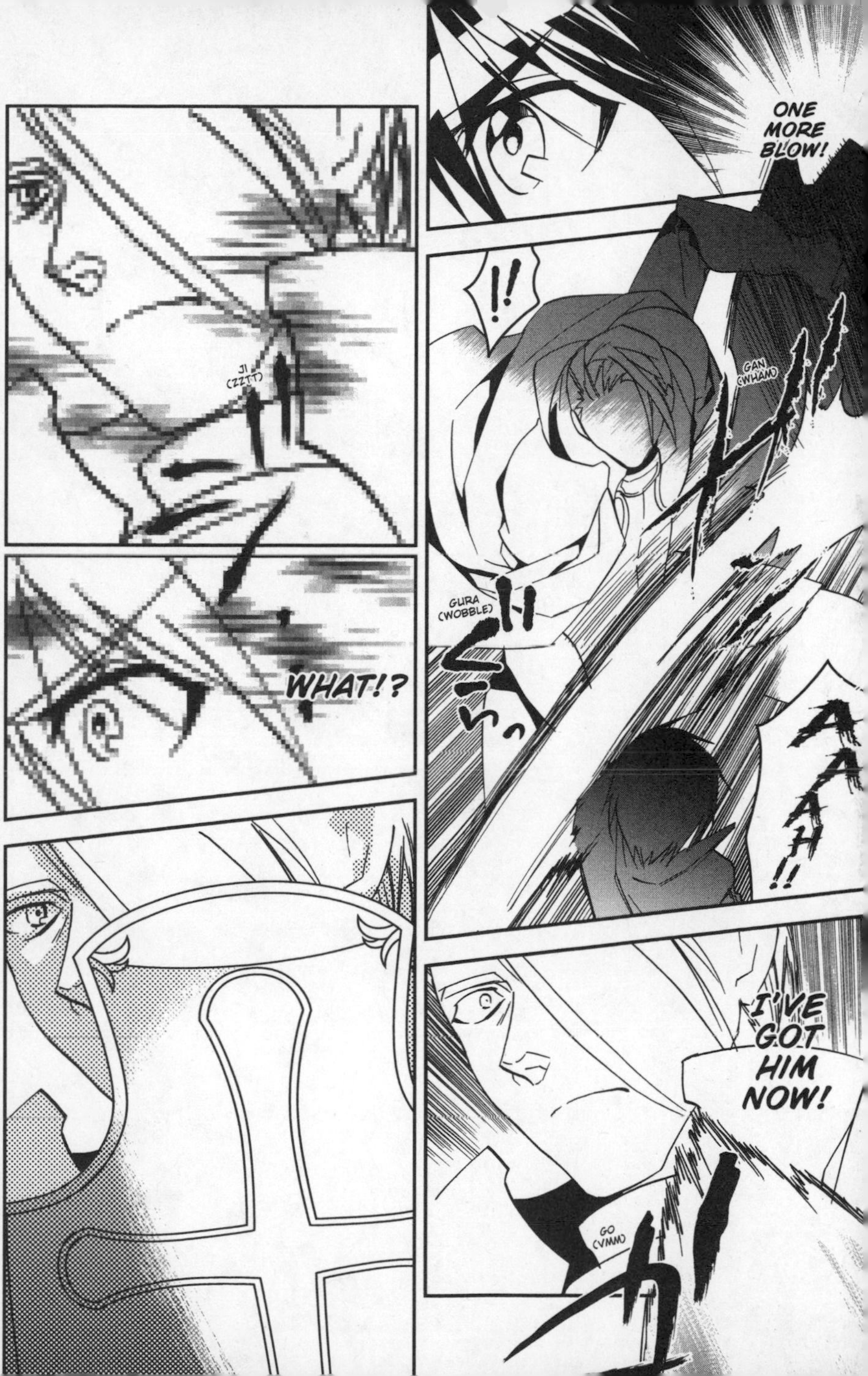
ONE MORE BLOW!
!!
GAN (WHAM)
GURA (WOBBLE)
AAAH!!
I'VE GOT HIM NOW!
GO (VMM)
JI (ZZTT)
WHAT!?

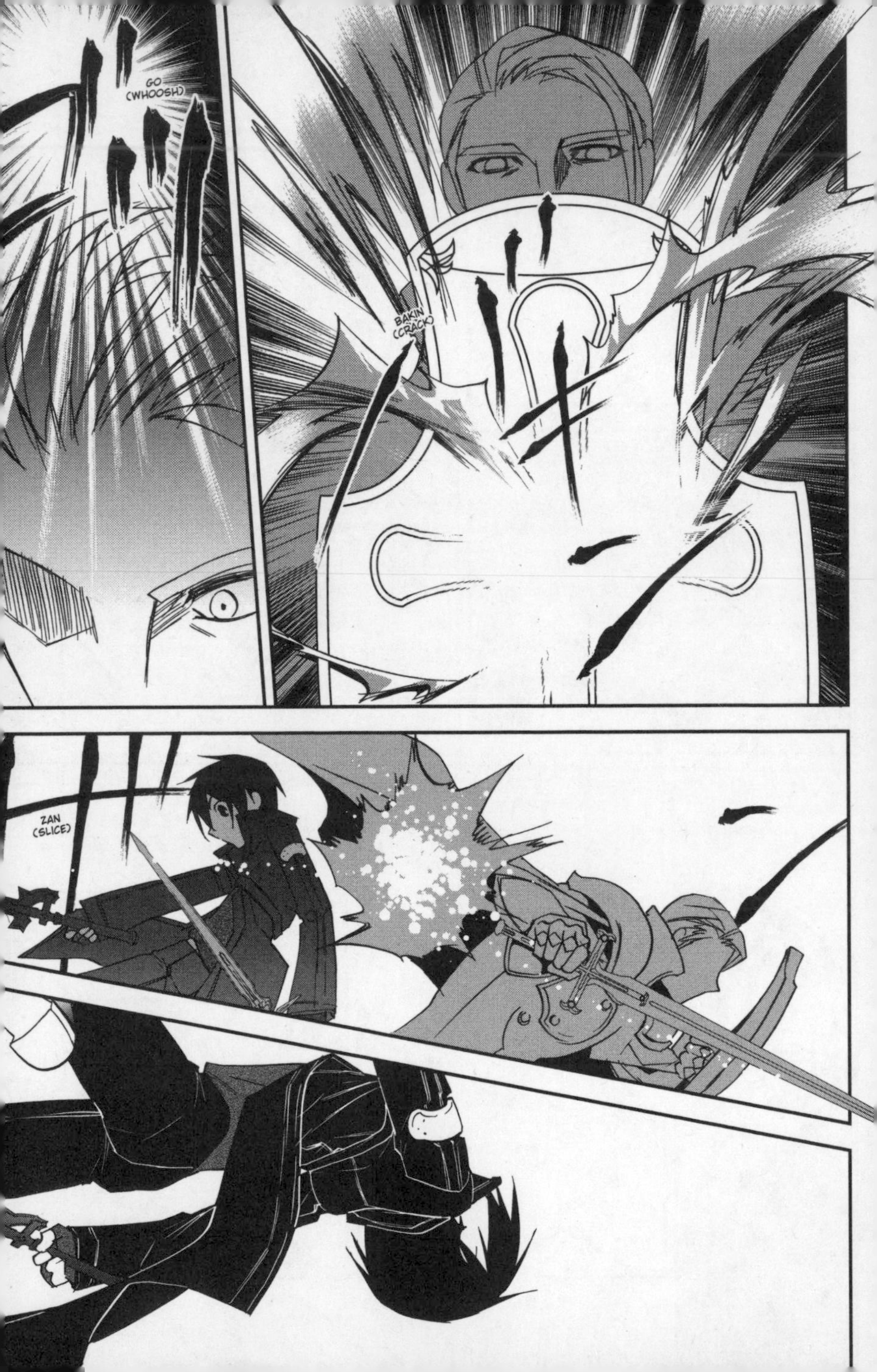
BAKIN (CRACK)
GO (WHOOSH)
ZAN (SLICE)

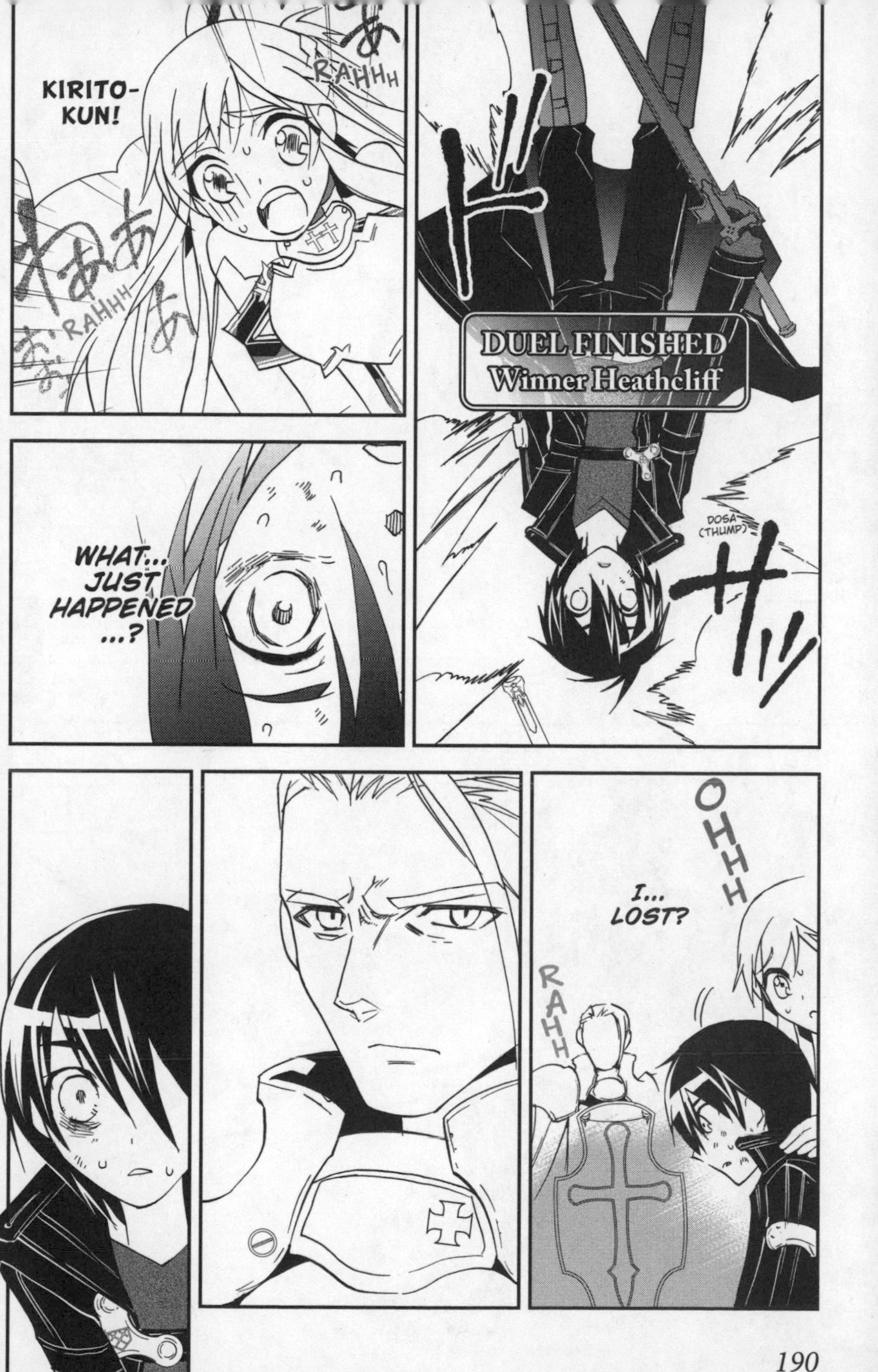
DUEL FINISHED
Winner Heathcliff
DOSA (THUMP)
RAHHH
KIRITO-KUN!
RAHHH
WHAT... JUST HAPPENED ...?
OHHH
I... LOST?
RAHH

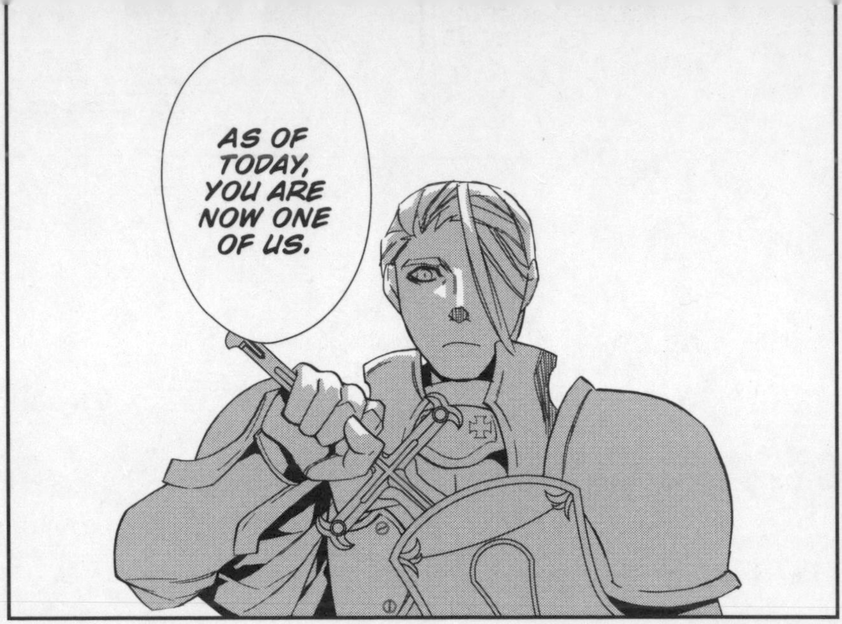
AS OF TODAY, YOU ARE NOW ONE OF US.
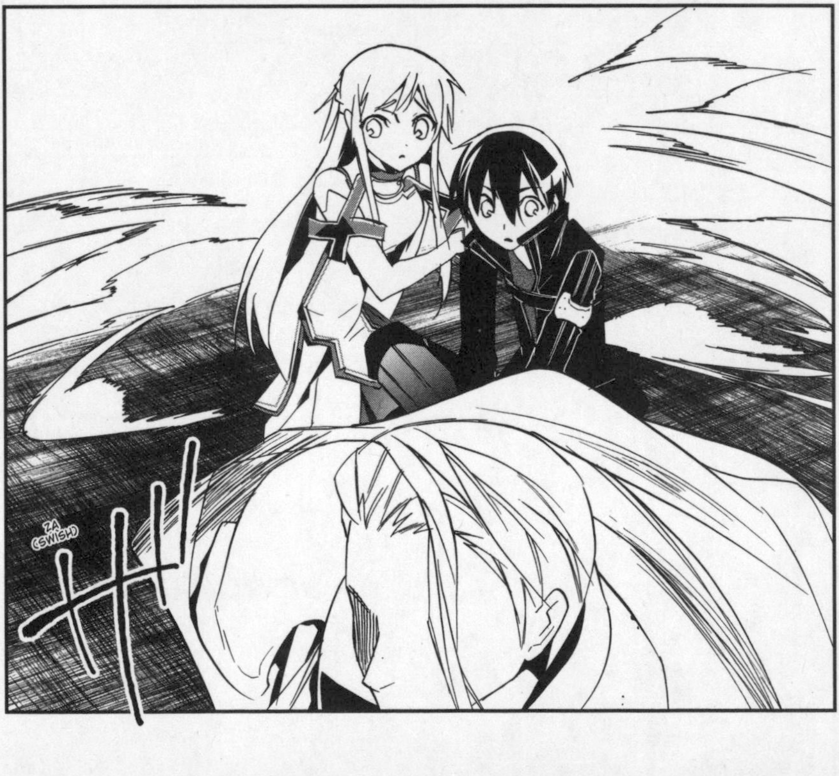
ZA (SWISH)

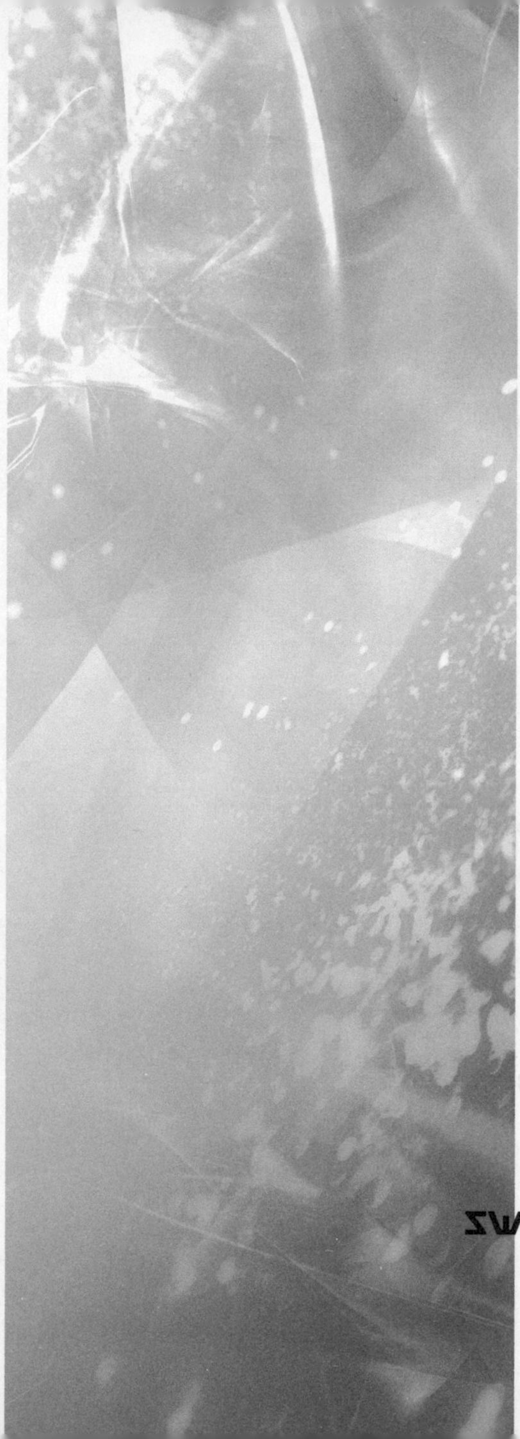

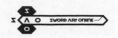

SWORD ART ONLINE
AINCRAD

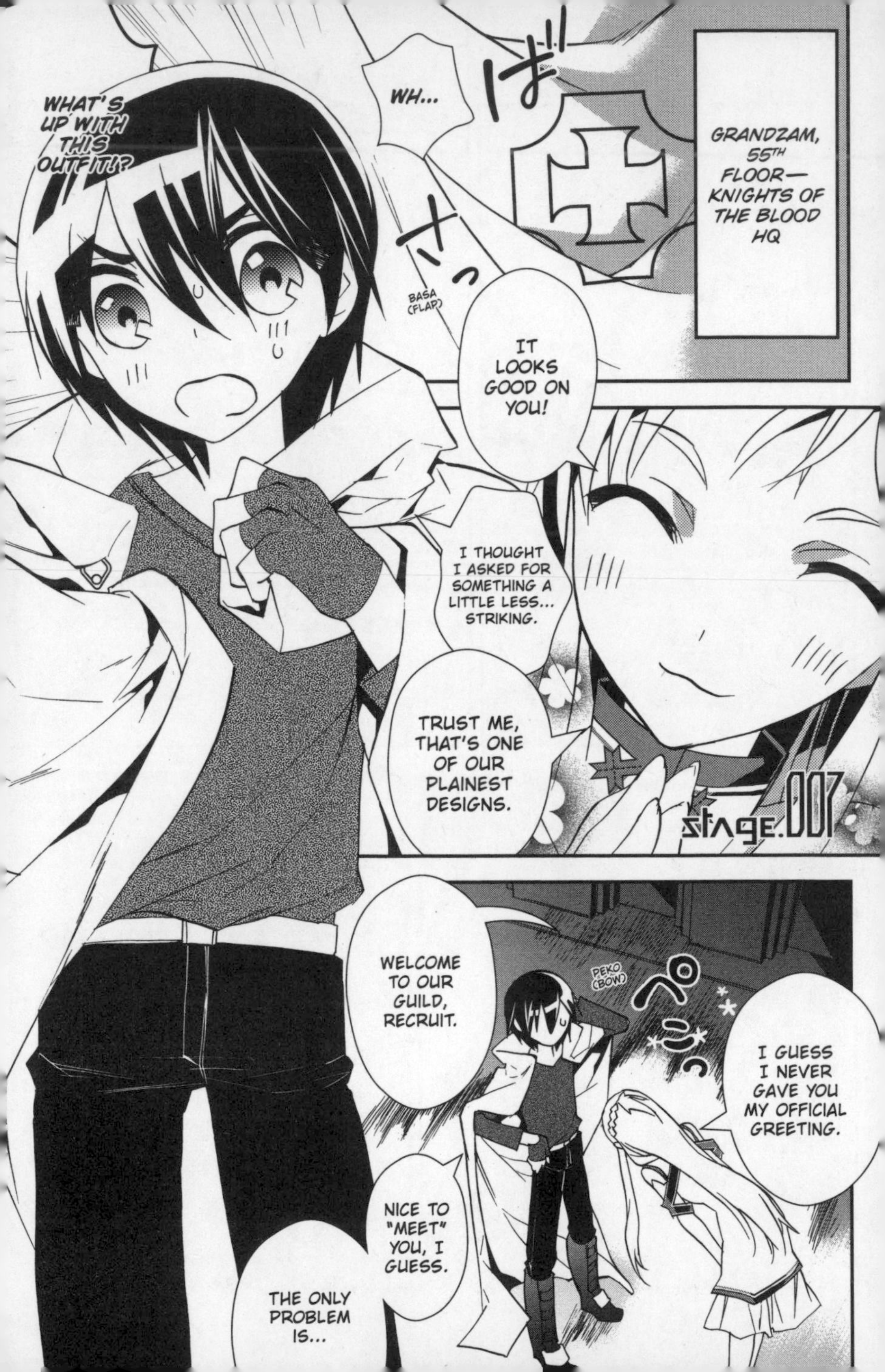
GRANDZAM, 55TH FLOOR—KNIGHTS OF THE BLOOD HQ
WH...
BASA (FLAP)
WHAT'S UP WITH THIS OUTFIT!?
IT LOOKS GOOD ON YOU!
I THOUGHT I ASKED FOR SOMETHING A LITTLE LESS... STRIKING.
TRUST ME, THAT'S ONE OF OUR PLAINEST DESIGNS.
stage.007
I GUESS I NEVER GAVE YOU MY OFFICIAL GREETING.
PEKO (BOW)
WELCOME TO OUR GUILD, RECRUIT.
NICE TO "MEET" YOU, I GUESS.
THE ONLY PROBLEM IS...

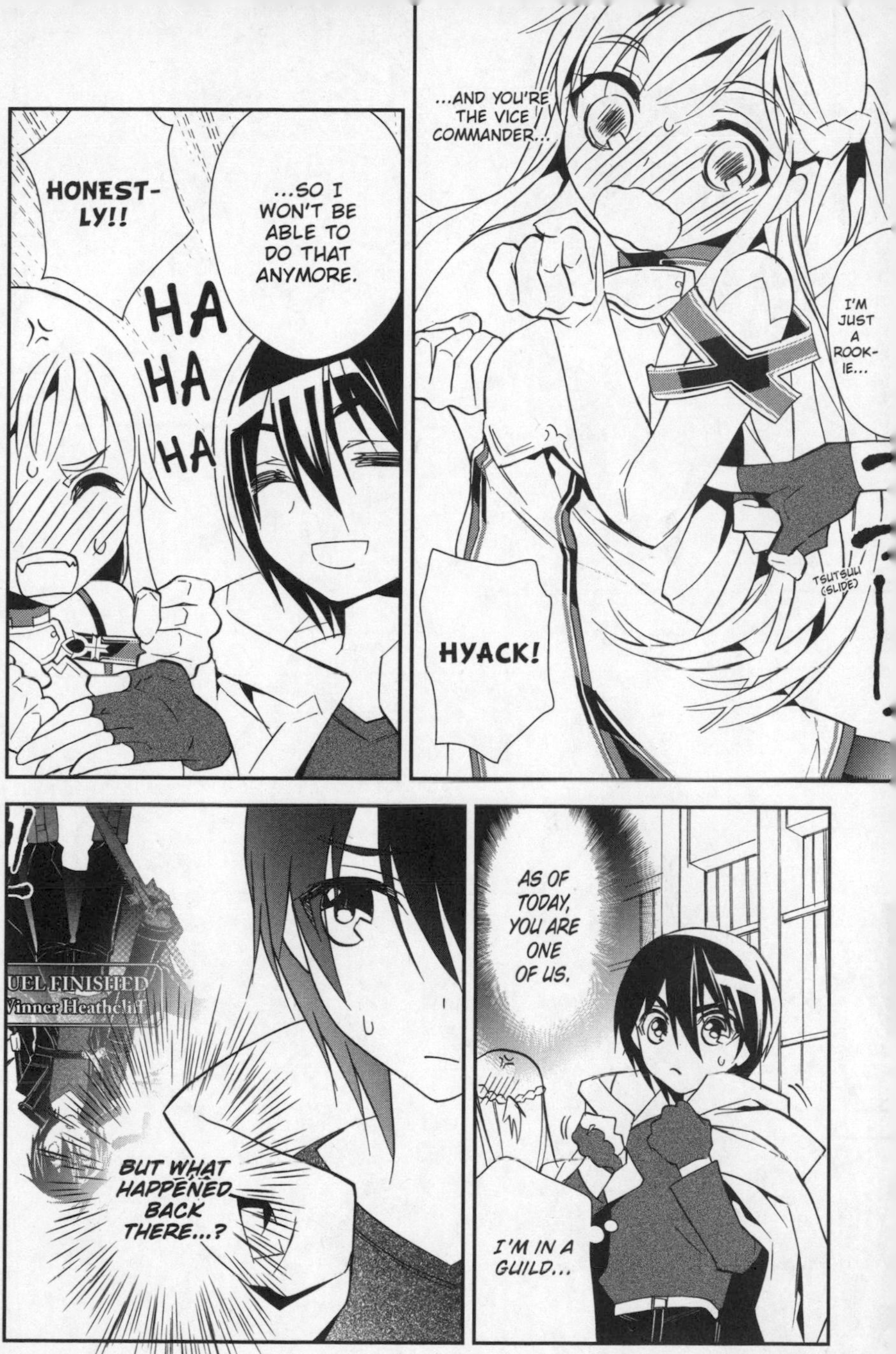
...AND YOU'RE THE VICE COMMANDER...
I'M JUST A ROOK-IE...
TSUTSULI (SLIDE)
HYACK!
...SO I WON'T BE ABLE TO DO THAT ANYMORE.
HONEST-LY!!
HA HA HA
AS OF TODAY, YOU ARE ONE OF US.
I'M IN A GUILD...
UEL FINISHED
Winner Heathcliff
BUT WHAT HAPPENED BACK THERE...?

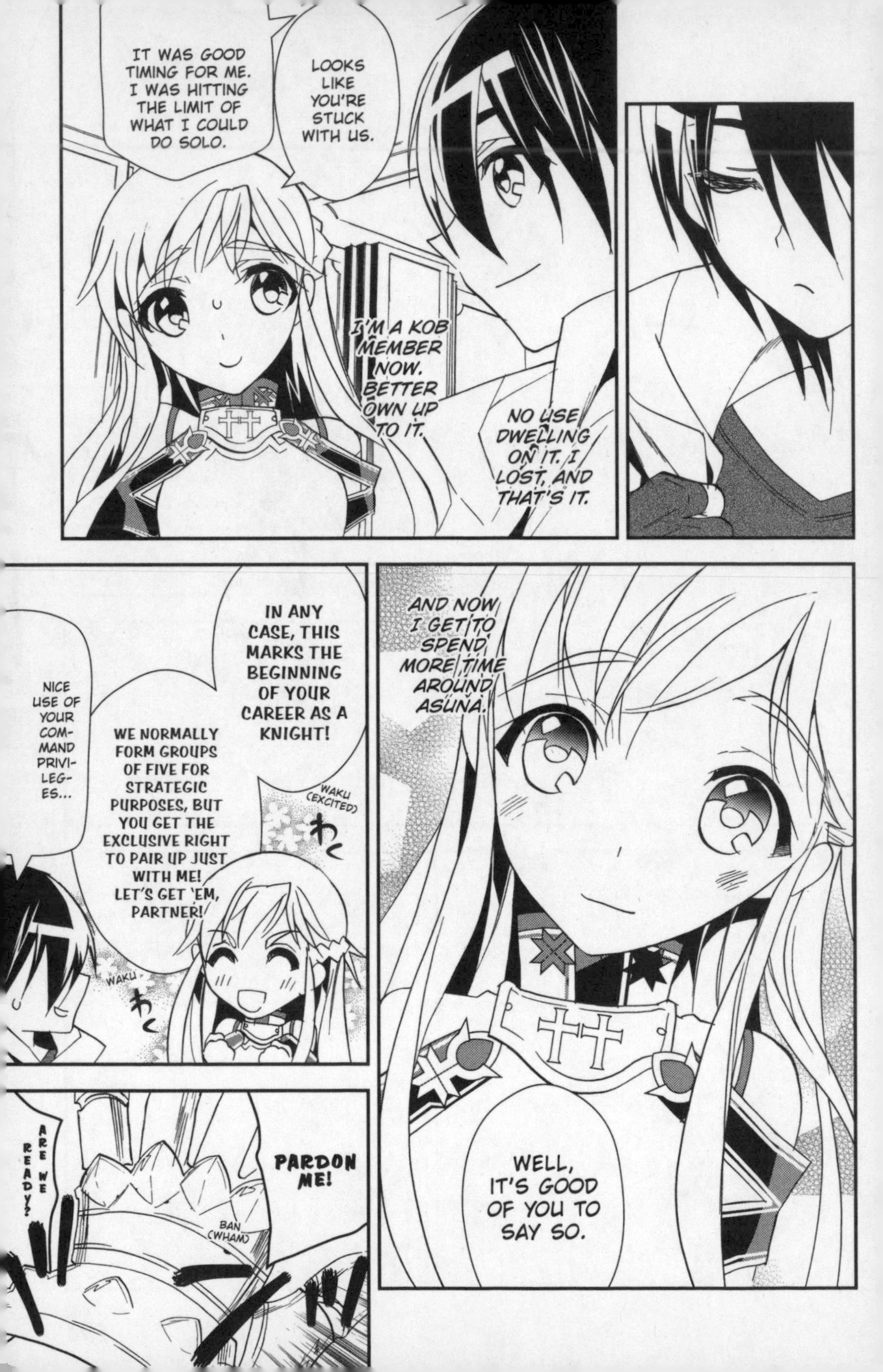

LOOKS LIKE YOU'RE STUCK WITH US.
IT WAS GOOD TIMING FOR ME. I WAS HITTING THE LIMIT OF WHAT I COULD DO SOLO.
NO USE DWELLING ON IT. I LOST, AND THAT'S IT.
I'M A KOB MEMBER NOW. BETTER OWN UP TO IT.
AND NOW I GET TO SPEND MORE TIME AROUND ASUNA.
WELL, IT'S GOOD OF YOU TO SAY SO.
IN ANY CASE, THIS MARKS THE BEGINNING OF YOUR CAREER AS A KNIGHT!
WE NORMALLY FORM GROUPS OF FIVE FOR STRATEGIC PURPOSES, BUT YOU GET THE EXCLUSIVE RIGHT TO PAIR UP JUST WITH ME! LET'S GET 'EM, PARTNER!
WAKU (EXCITED)
わく
NICE USE OF YOUR COMMAND PRIVILEGES...
WAKU
わく
PARDON ME!
BAN (WHAM)
ARE WE READY?

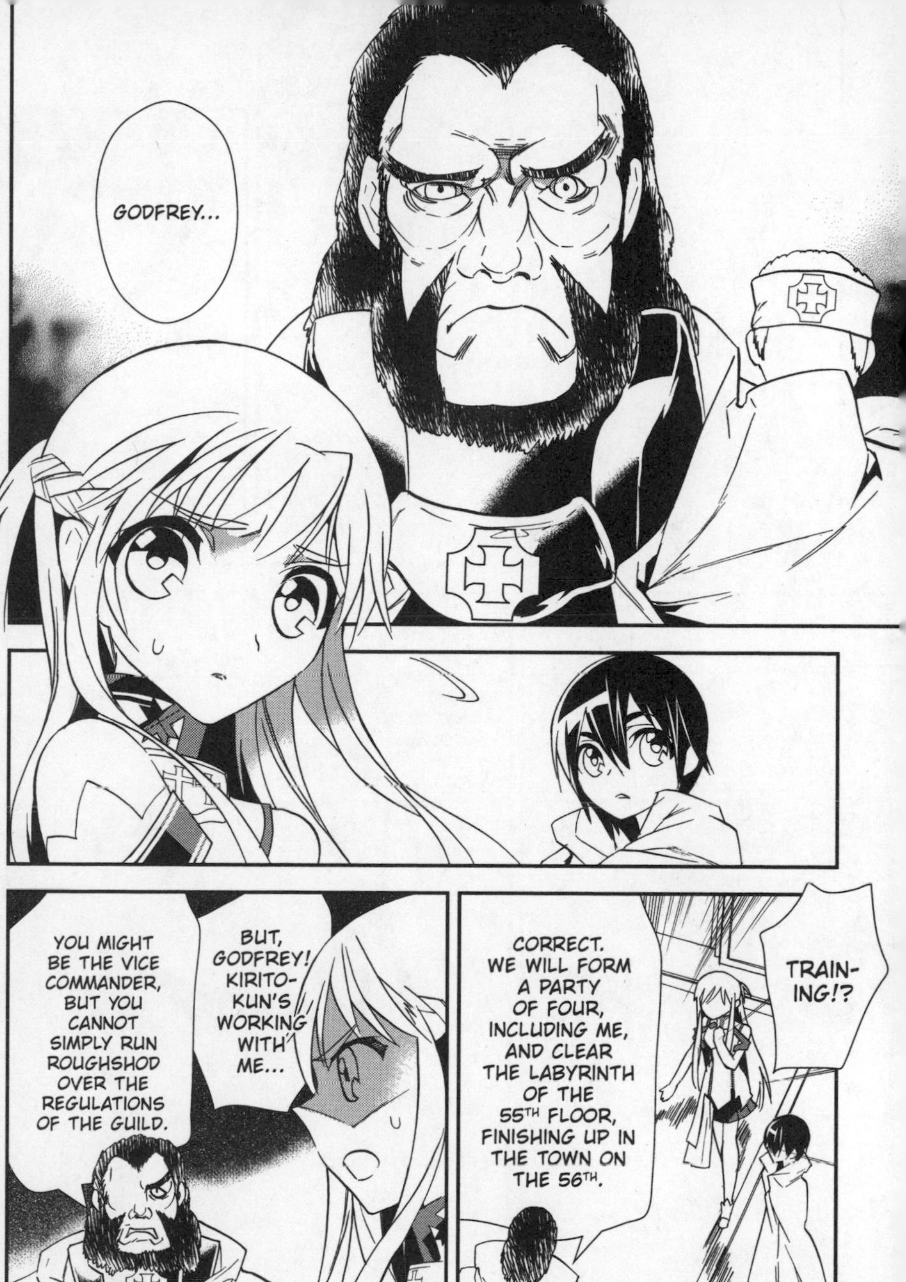
GODFREY...
TRAIN-ING!?
CORRECT. WE WILL FORM A PARTY OF FOUR, INCLUDING ME, AND CLEAR THE LABYRINTH OF THE 55TH FLOOR, FINISHING UP IN THE TOWN ON THE 56TH.
BUT, GODFREY! KIRITO-KUN'S WORKING WITH ME...
YOU MIGHT BE THE VICE COMMANDER, BUT YOU CANNOT SIMPLY RUN ROUGHSHOD OVER THE REGULATIONS OF THE GUILD.

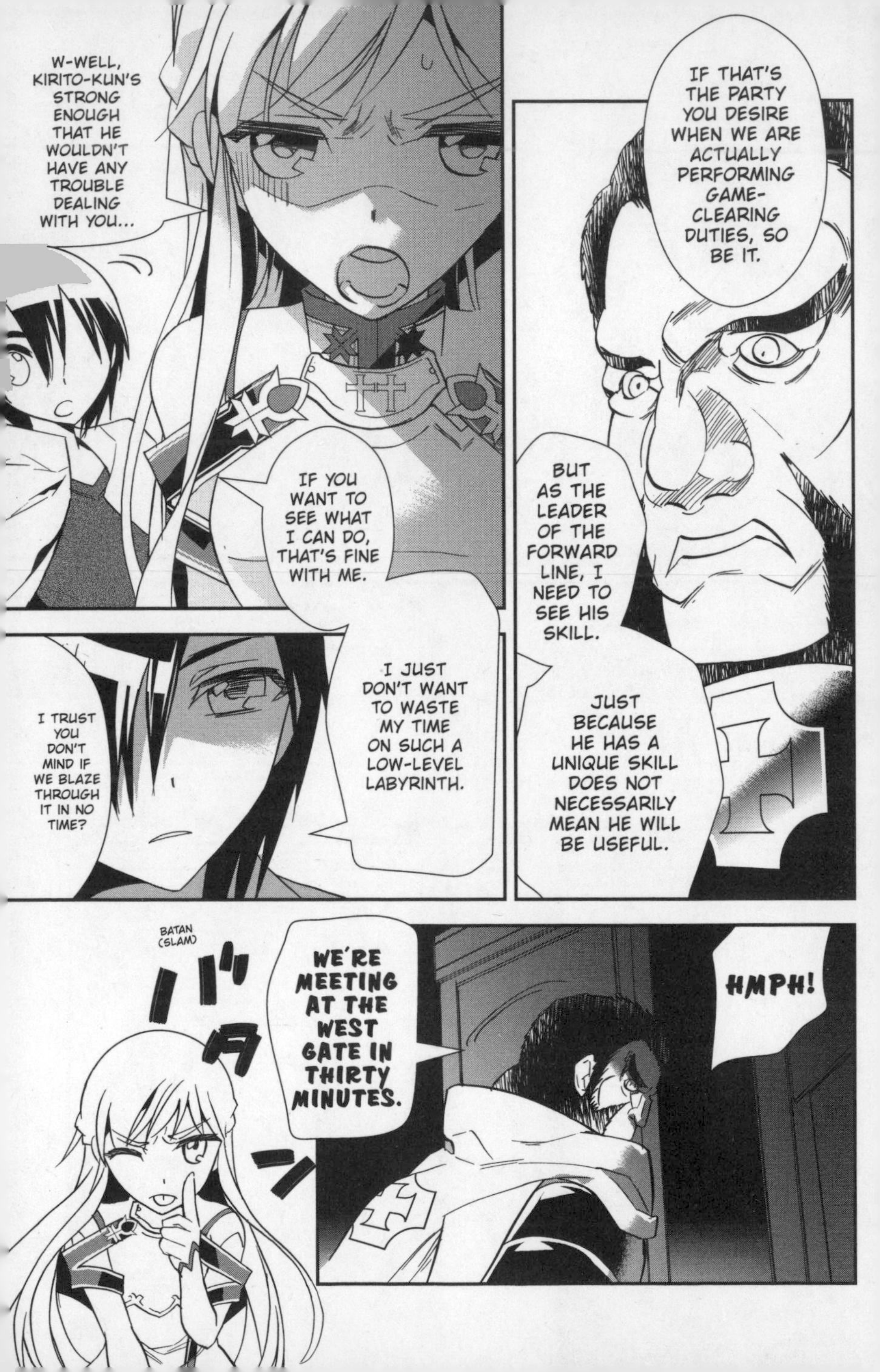
IF THAT'S THE PARTY YOU DESIRE WHEN WE ARE ACTUALLY PERFORMING GAME-CLEARING DUTIES, SO BE IT.
BUT AS THE LEADER OF THE FORWARD LINE, I NEED TO SEE HIS SKILL.
JUST BECAUSE HE HAS A UNIQUE SKILL DOES NOT NECESSARILY MEAN HE WILL BE USEFUL.
W-WELL, KIRITO-KUN'S STRONG ENOUGH THAT HE WOULDN'T HAVE ANY TROUBLE DEALING WITH YOU...
IF YOU WANT TO SEE WHAT I CAN DO, THAT'S FINE WITH ME.
I JUST DON'T WANT TO WASTE MY TIME ON SUCH A LOW-LEVEL LABYRINTH.
I TRUST YOU DON'T MIND IF WE BLAZE THROUGH IT IN NO TIME?
HMPH!
WE'RE MEETING AT THE WEST GATE IN THIRTY MINUTES.
BATAN (SLAM)

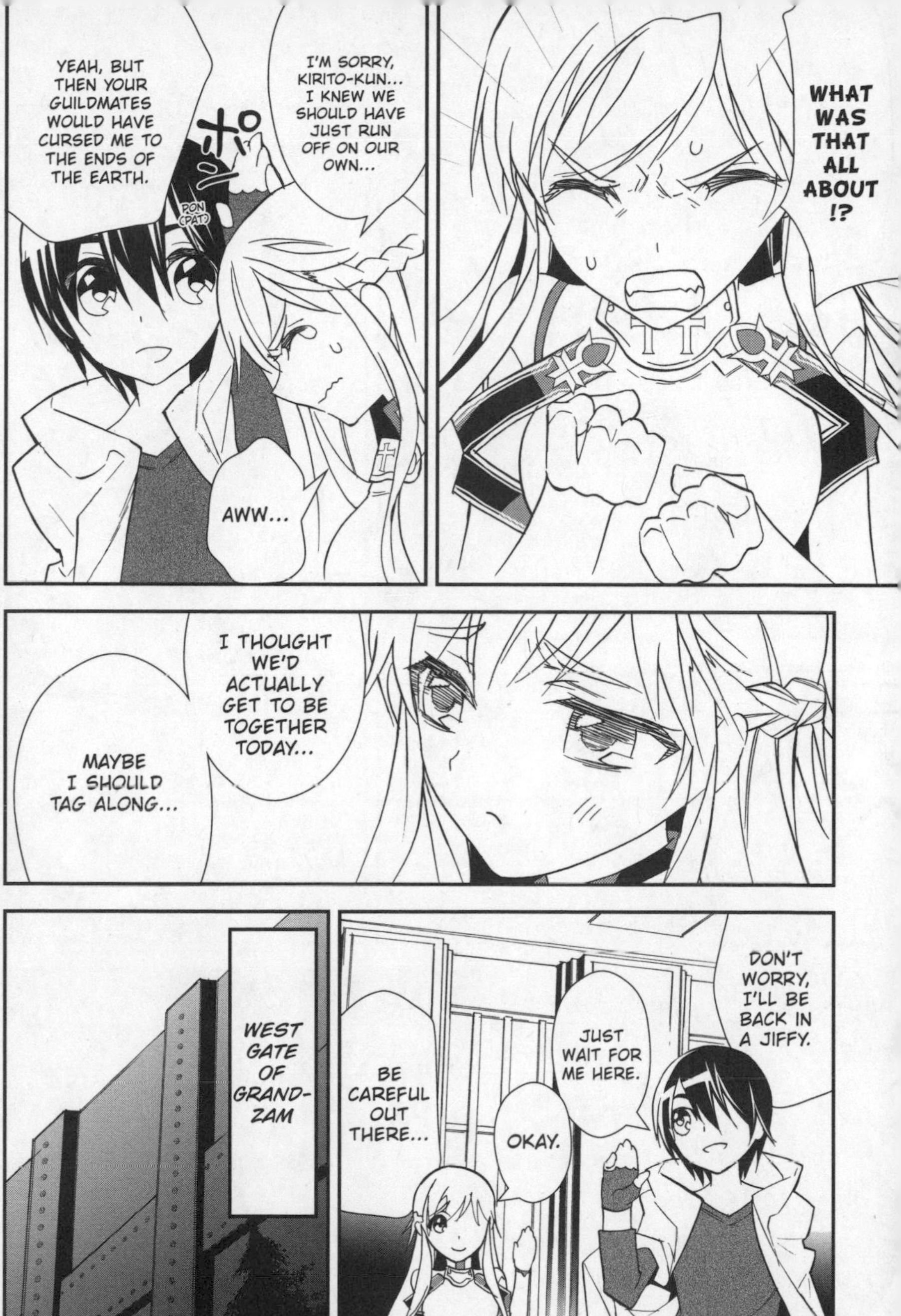
WHAT WAS THAT ALL ABOUT !?
I'M SORRY, KIRITO-KUN... I KNEW WE SHOULD HAVE JUST RUN OFF ON OUR OWN...
YEAH, BUT THEN YOUR GUILDMATES WOULD HAVE CURSED ME TO THE ENDS OF THE EARTH.
PON (PAT)
AWW...
I THOUGHT WE'D ACTUALLY GET TO BE TOGETHER TODAY...
MAYBE I SHOULD TAG ALONG...
DON'T WORRY, I'LL BE BACK IN A JIFFY.
JUST WAIT FOR ME HERE.
OKAY.
BE CAREFUL OUT THERE...
WEST GATE OF GRAND-ZAM

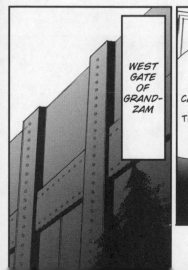

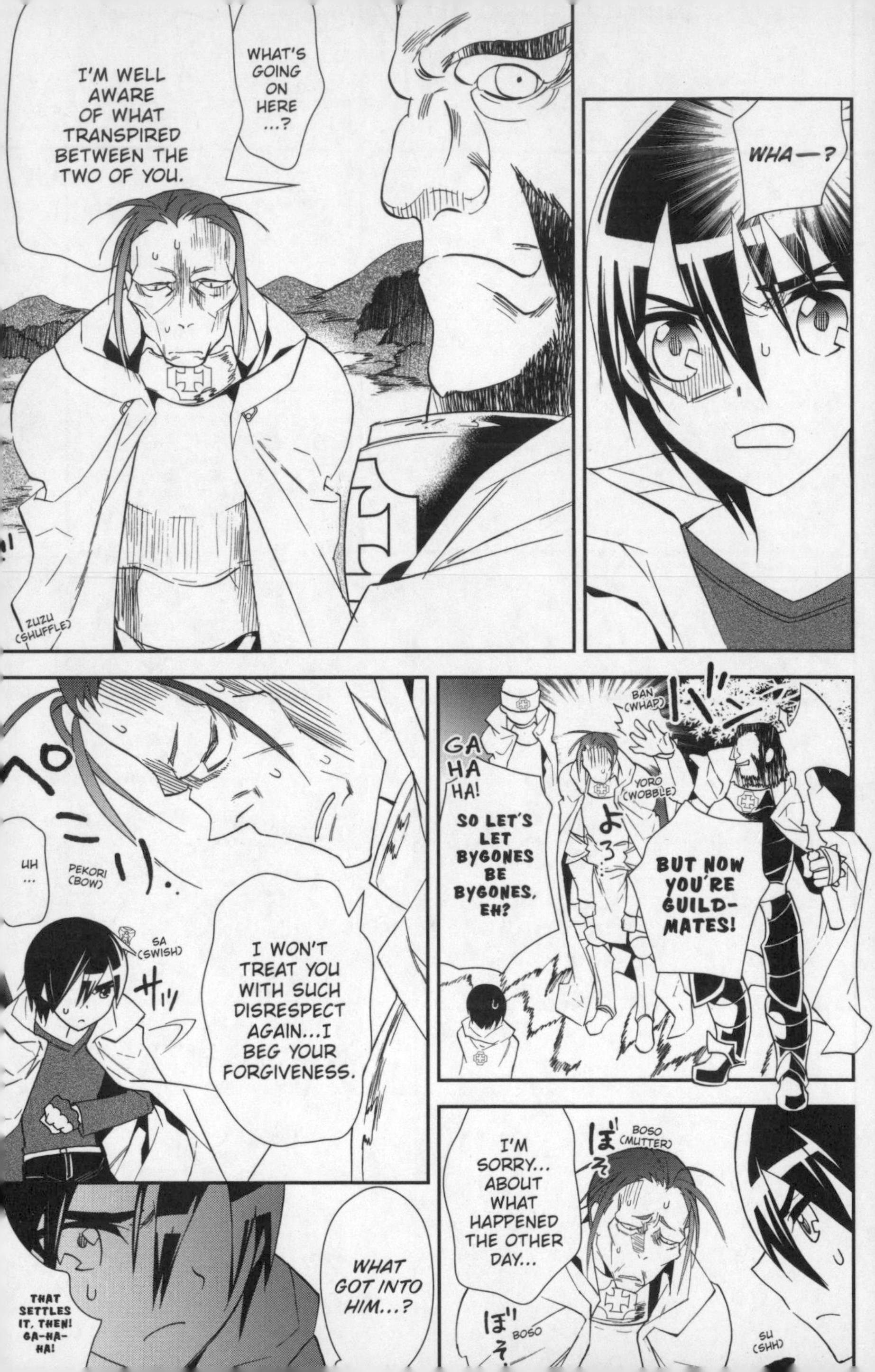
WHA—?
WHAT'S GOING ON HERE...?
I'M WELL AWARE OF WHAT TRANSPIRED BETWEEN THE TWO OF YOU.
ZUZU (SHUFFLE)
BAN (WHAP)
BUT NOW YOU'RE GUILD-MATES!
YORO (WOBBLE)
SO LET'S LET BYGONES BE BYGONES, EH?
GA HA HA!
I WON'T TREAT YOU WITH SUCH DISRESPECT AGAIN...I BEG YOUR FORGIVENESS.
PEKORI (BOW)
UH...
SA (SWISH)
SU (SHH)
BOSO (MUTTER)
I'M SORRY... ABOUT WHAT HAPPENED THE OTHER DAY...
BOSO
WHAT GOT INTO HIM...?
THAT SETTLES IT, THEN! GA-HA-HA!

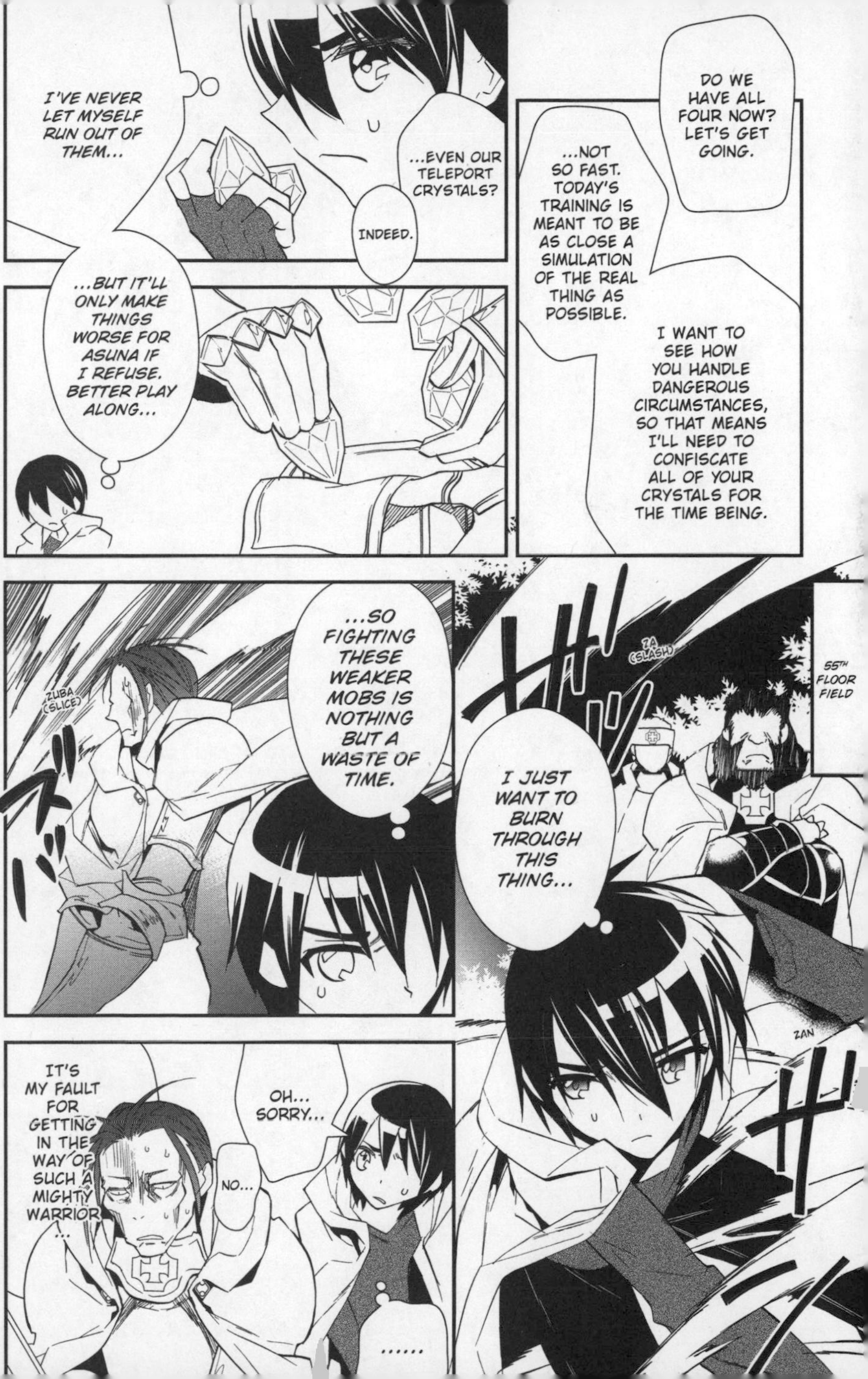
DO WE HAVE ALL FOUR NOW? LET'S GET GOING.
...NOT SO FAST. TODAY'S TRAINING IS MEANT TO BE AS CLOSE A SIMULATION OF THE REAL THING AS POSSIBLE.
I WANT TO SEE HOW YOU HANDLE DANGEROUS CIRCUMSTANCES, SO THAT MEANS I'LL NEED TO CONFISCATE ALL OF YOUR CRYSTALS FOR THE TIME BEING.
...EVEN OUR TELEPORT CRYSTALS?
INDEED.
I'VE NEVER LET MYSELF RUN OUT OF THEM...
...BUT IT'LL ONLY MAKE THINGS WORSE FOR ASUNA IF I REFUSE. BETTER PLAY ALONG...
55TH FLOOR FIELD
ZA (SLASH)
I JUST WANT TO BURN THROUGH THIS THING...
ZAN
...SO FIGHTING THESE WEAKER MOBS IS NOTHING BUT A WASTE OF TIME.
ZUBA (SLICE)
OH... SORRY...
IT'S MY FAULT FOR GETTING IN THE WAY OF SUCH A MIGHTY WARRIOR...
NO...
......

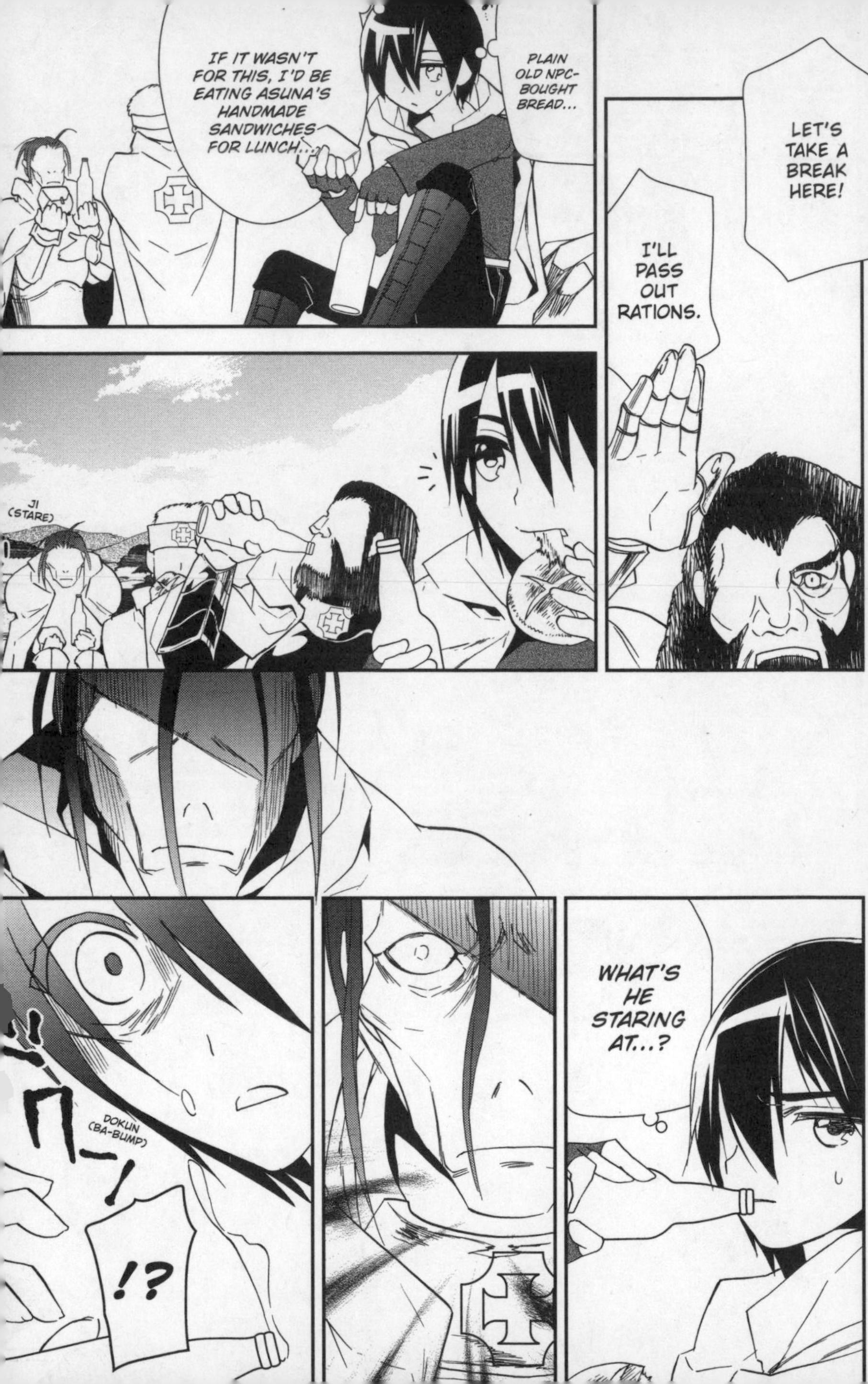
LET'S TAKE A BREAK HERE!
I'LL PASS OUT RATIONS.
PLAIN OLD NPC-BOUGHT BREAD...
IF IT WASN'T FOR THIS, I'D BE EATING ASUNA'S HANDMADE SANDWICHES FOR LUNCH...
JI (STARE)
WHAT'S HE STARING AT...?
DOKUN (BA-BUMP)
!?

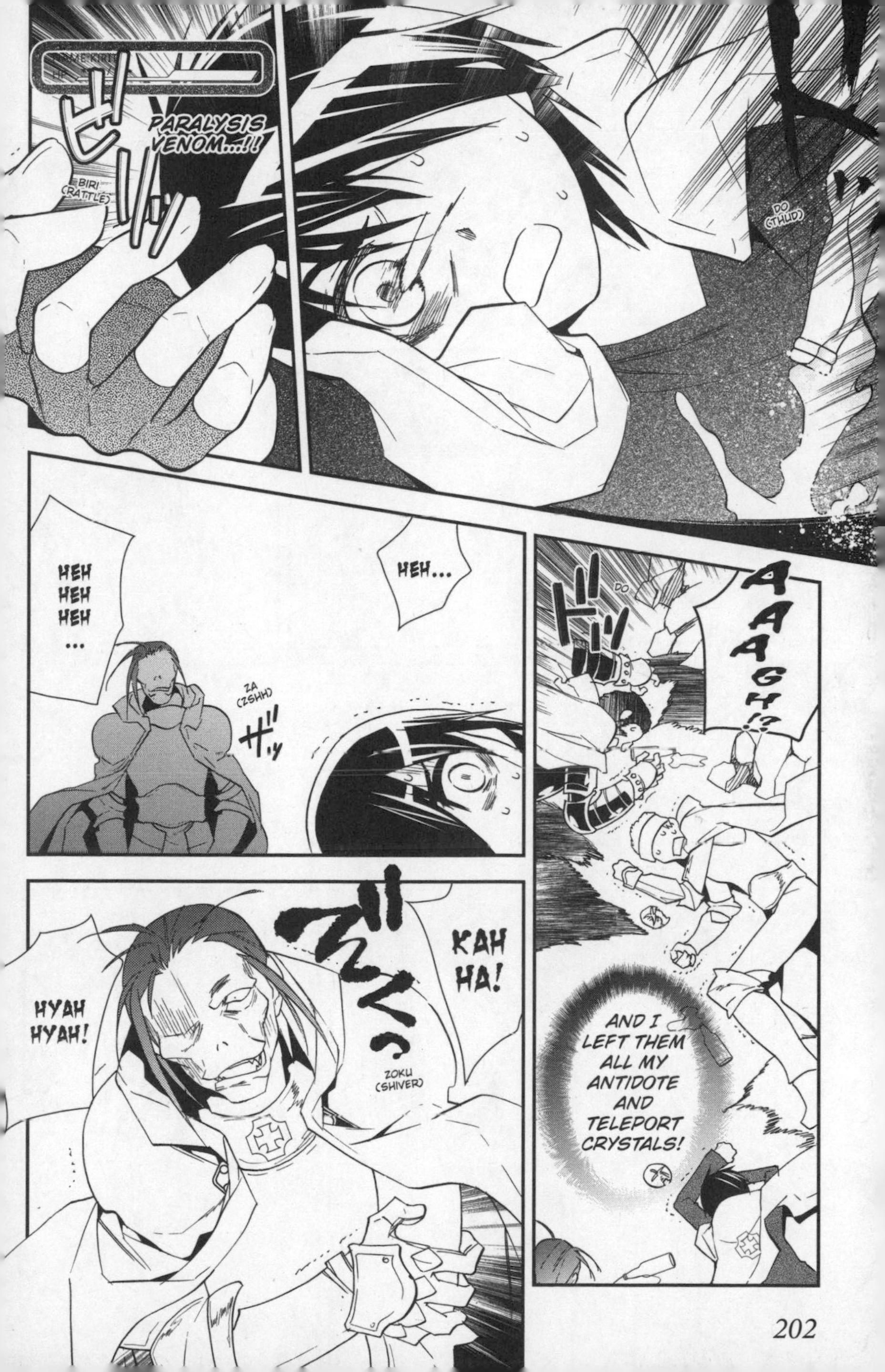
DO
(THUD)
PARALYSIS VENOM...!!
BIRI
(RATTLE)
AAAGH!?
DO
AND I LEFT THEM ALL MY ANTIDOTE AND TELEPORT CRYSTALS!
HEH...
ZA
(ZSHH)
HEH HEH HEH ...
KAH HA!
ZOKU
(SHIVER)
HYAH HYAH!

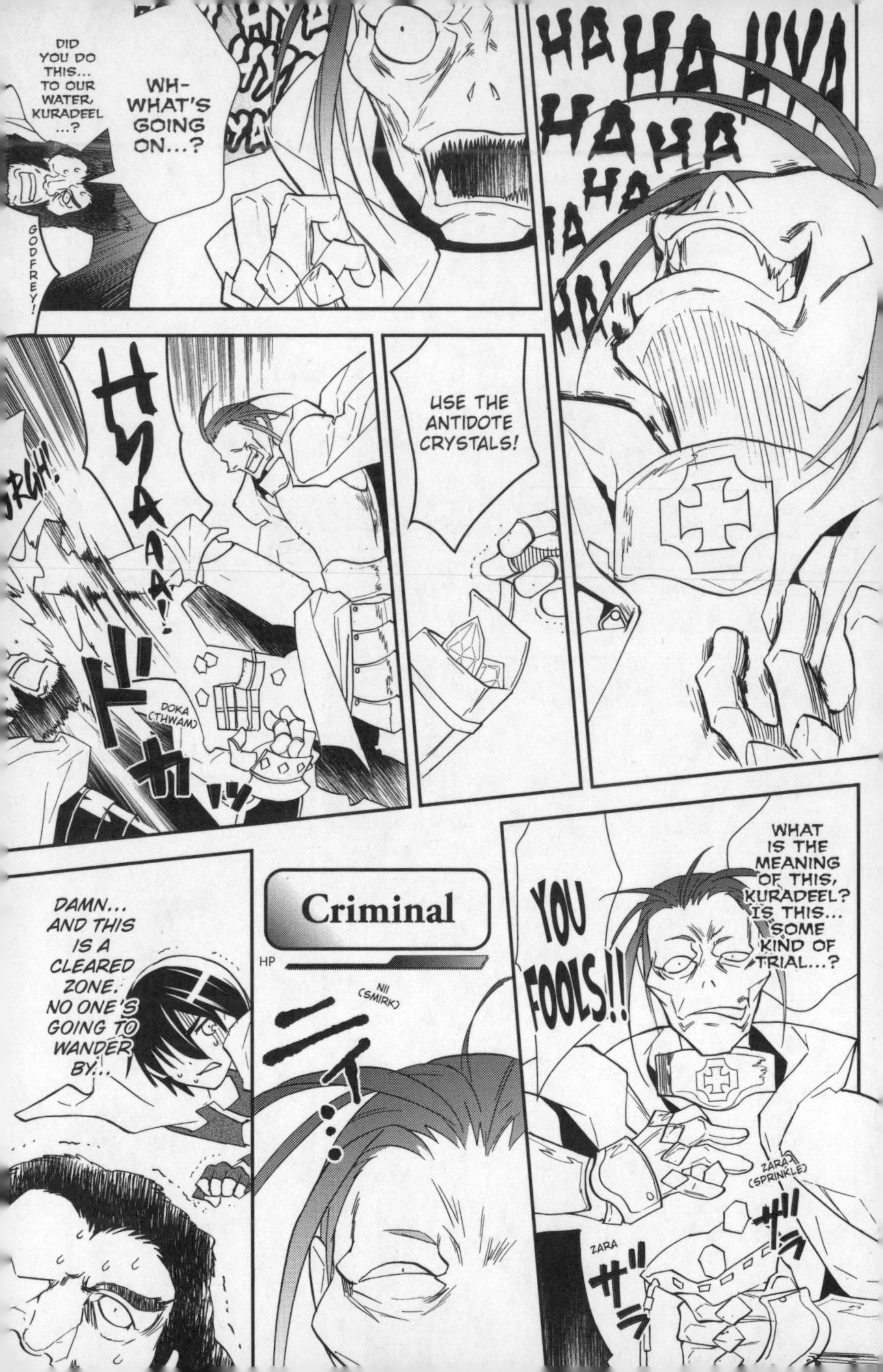
HA HA HYA
HA HA
HA
HA
HA!
WH-WHAT'S GOING ON...?
DID YOU DO THIS... TO OUR WATER, KURADEEL ...?
GODFREY!
USE THE ANTIDOTE CRYSTALS!
RGH!
DOKA (THWAM)
WHAT IS THE MEANING OF THIS, KURADEEL? IS THIS... SOME KIND OF TRIAL...?
YOU FOOLS!!
ZARA (SPRINKLE)
ZARA
Criminal
HP
NII (SMIRK)
DAMN... AND THIS IS A CLEARED ZONE. NO ONE'S GOING TO WANDER BY...

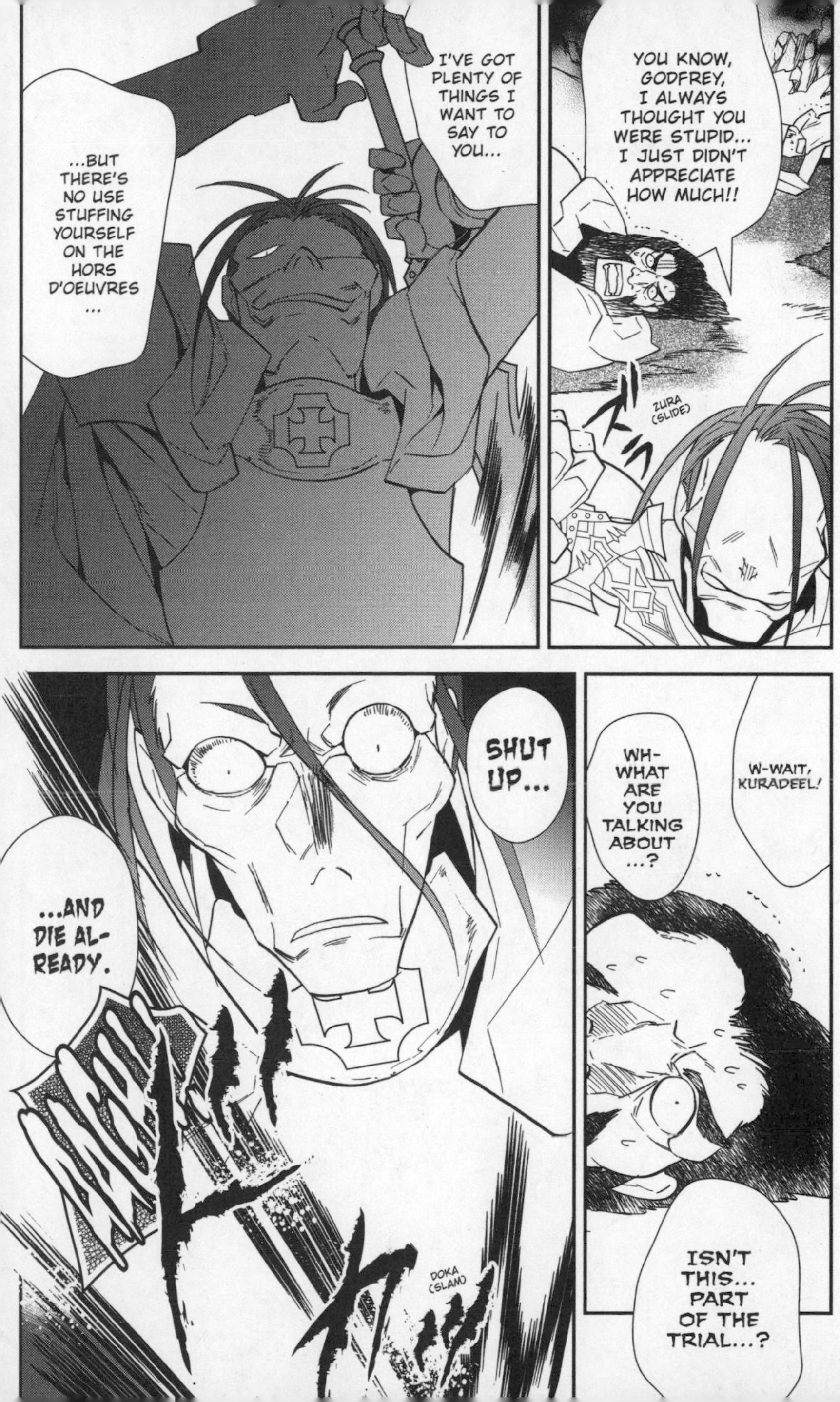
YOU KNOW, GODFREY, I ALWAYS THOUGHT YOU WERE STUPID... I JUST DIDN'T APPRECIATE HOW MUCH!!
ZURA (SLIDE)
I'VE GOT PLENTY OF THINGS I WANT TO SAY TO YOU...
...BUT THERE'S NO USE STUFFING YOURSELF ON THE HORS D'OEUVRES ...
W-WAIT, KURADEEL!
WH-WHAT ARE YOU TALKING ABOUT ...?
ISN'T THIS... PART OF THE TRIAL...?
SHUT UP...
...AND DIE AL-READY.
DOKA (SLAM)

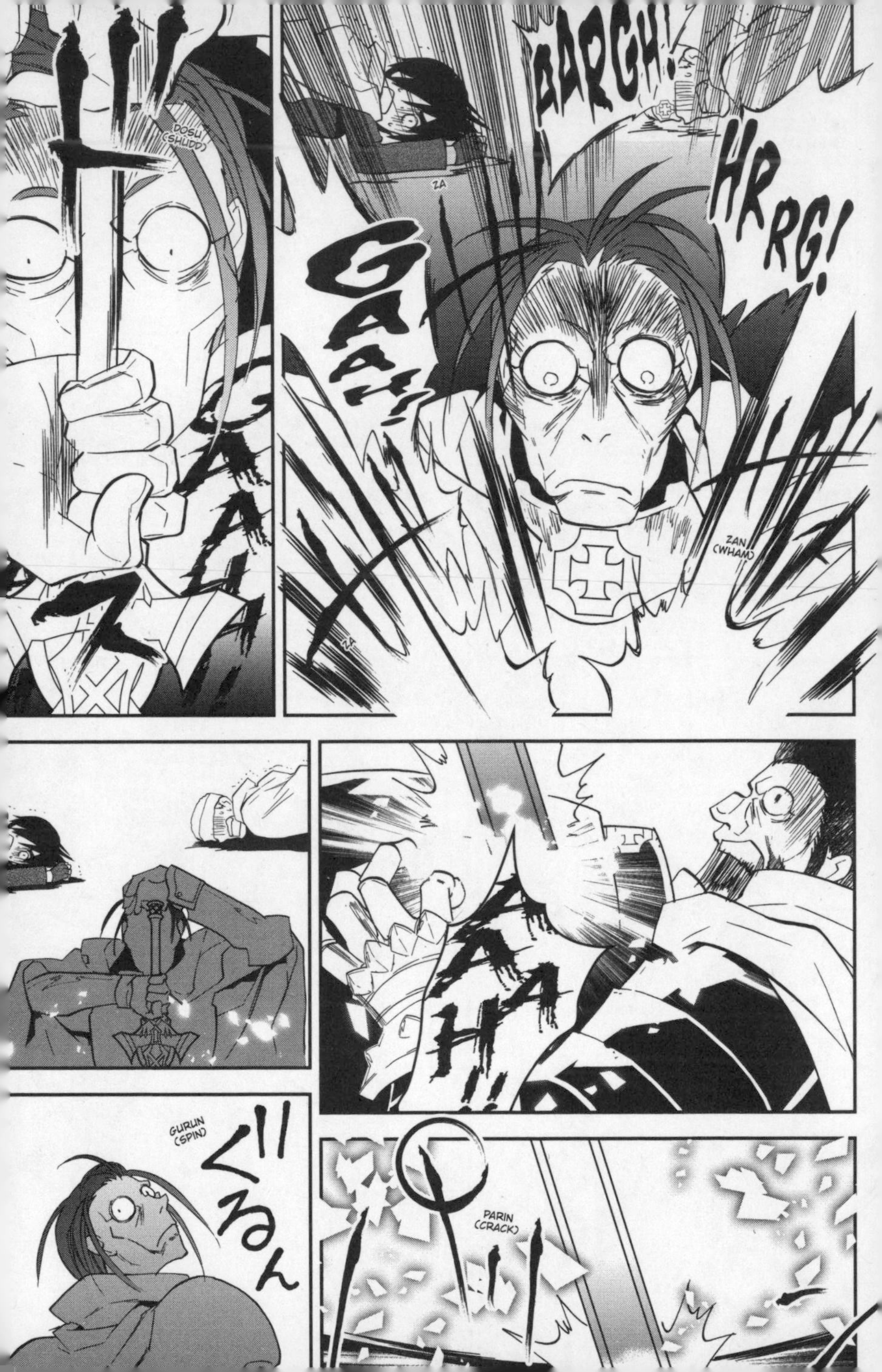
AARGH!
HRRG!
ZA
GAAAH!
ZAN (WHAM)
ZA
DOSU (SHUDD)
GAAAH
AAAH!!
PARIN (CRACK)
GURUN (SPIN)
ぐるん

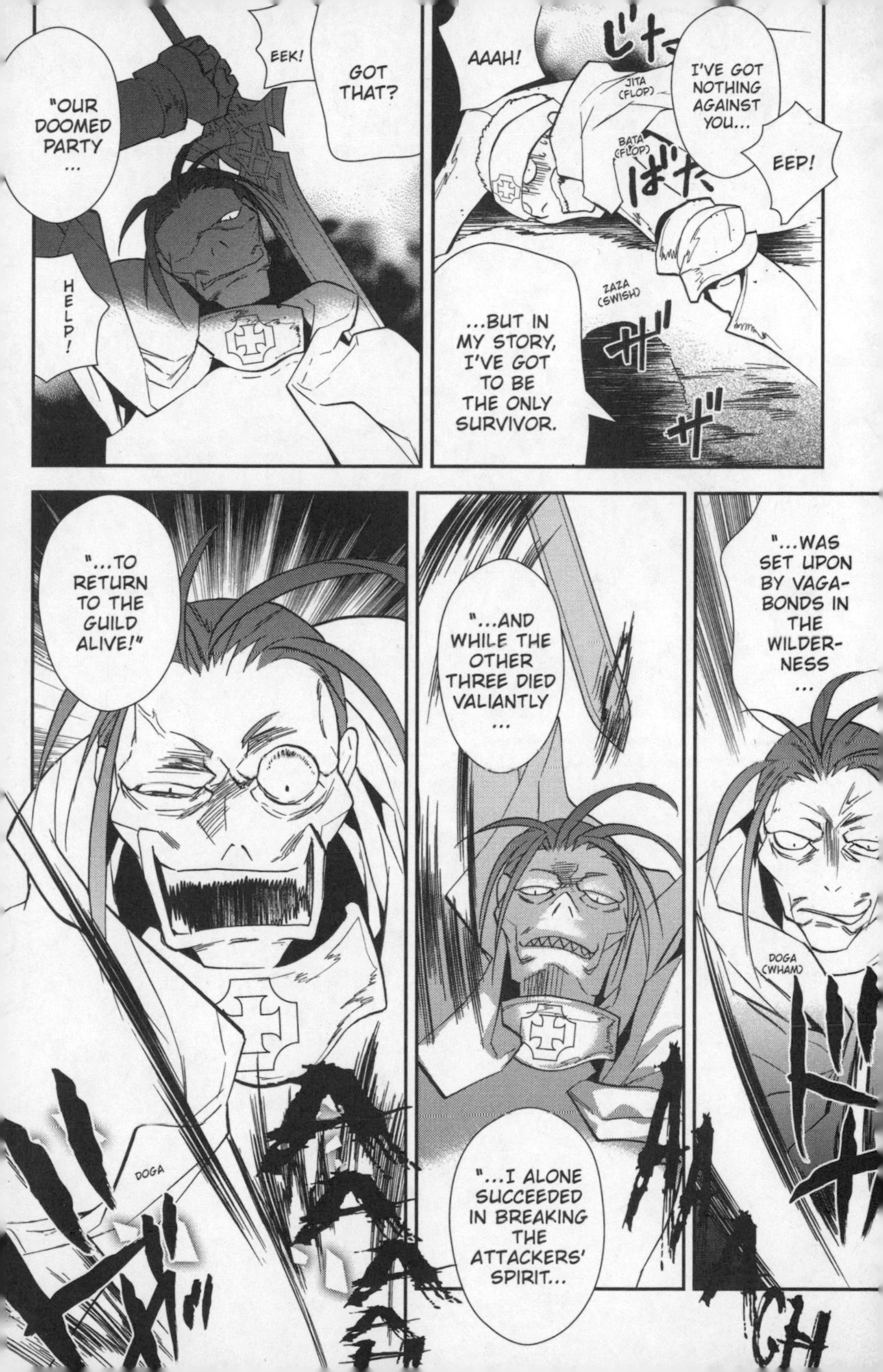
I'VE GOT NOTHING AGAINST YOU...
EEP!
JITA (FLOP)
BATA (FLOP)
AAAH!
ZAZA (SWISH)
...BUT IN MY STORY, I'VE GOT TO BE THE ONLY SURVIVOR.
GOT THAT?
EEK!
"OUR DOOMED PARTY ...
HELP!
"...WAS SET UPON BY VAGA-BONDS IN THE WILDER-NESS ...
DOGA (WHAM)
"...AND WHILE THE OTHER THREE DIED VALIANTLY ...
"...I ALONE SUCCEEDED IN BREAKING THE ATTACKERS' SPIRIT...
"...TO RETURN TO THE GUILD ALIVE!"
DOGA

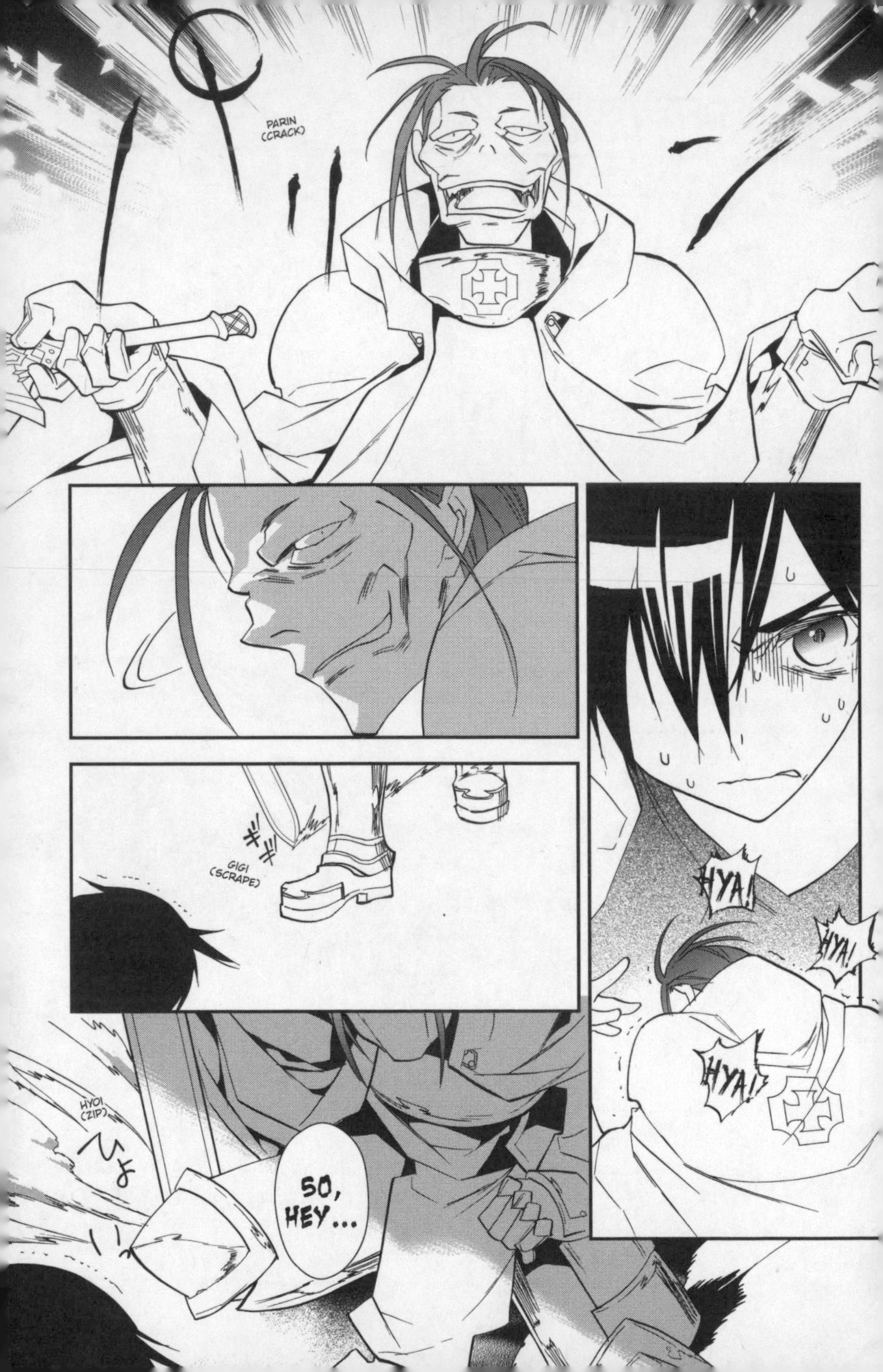
PARIN (CRACK)
HYA!
HYA!
HYA!
ギギ
GIGI (SCRAPE)
ひょ
HYOI (ZIP)
SO, HEY...

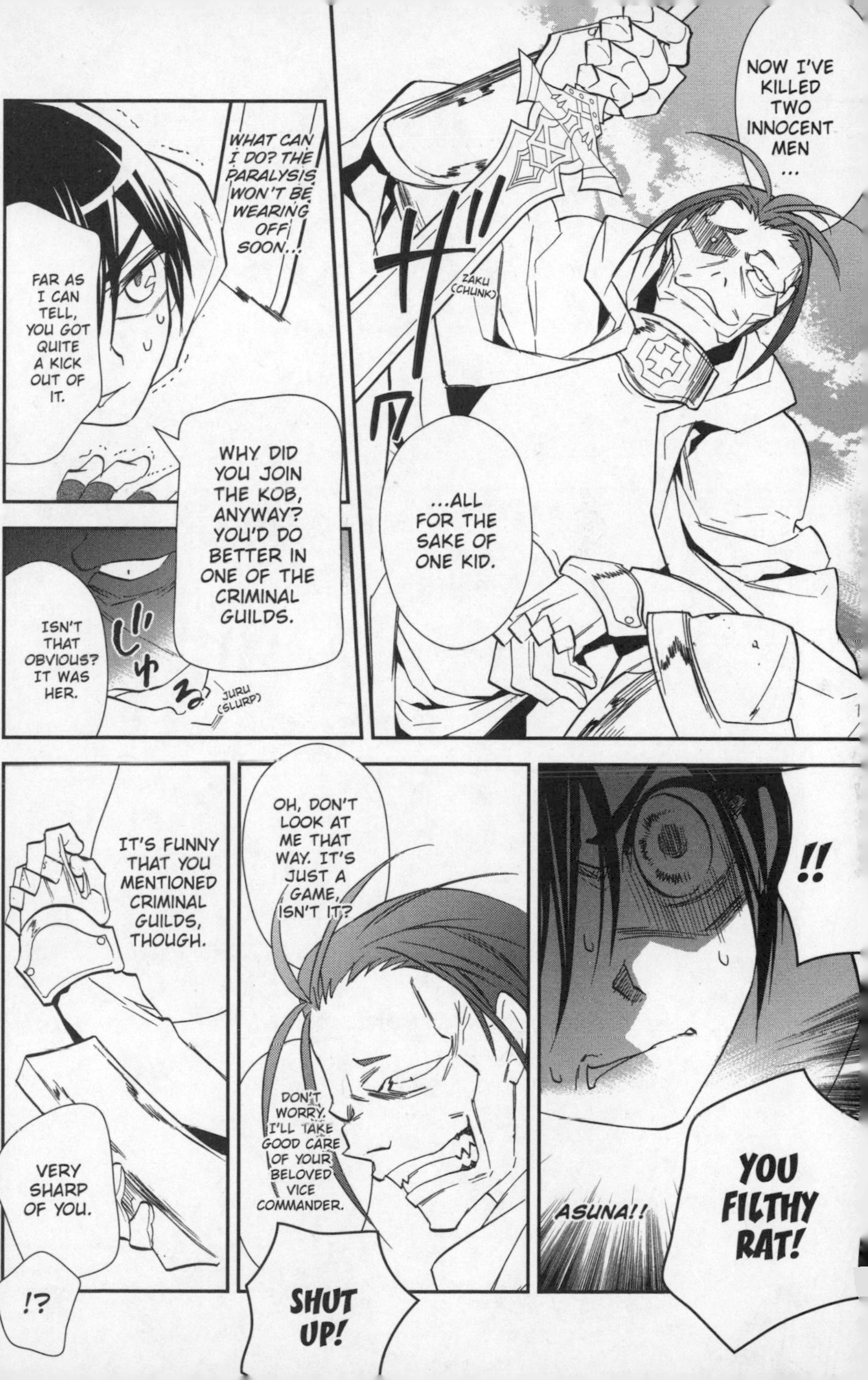
NOW I'VE KILLED TWO INNOCENT MEN ...
ZAKU (CHUNK)
...ALL FOR THE SAKE OF ONE KID.
WHAT CAN I DO? THE PARALYSIS WON'T BE WEARING OFF SOON...
FAR AS I CAN TELL, YOU GOT QUITE A KICK OUT OF IT.
WHY DID YOU JOIN THE KOB, ANYWAY? YOU'D DO BETTER IN ONE OF THE CRIMINAL GUILDS.
ISN'T THAT OBVIOUS? IT WAS HER.
JURU (SLURP)
!!
YOU FILTHY RAT!
ASUNA!!
OH, DON'T LOOK AT ME THAT WAY. IT'S JUST A GAME, ISN'T IT?
DON'T WORRY. I'LL TAKE GOOD CARE OF YOUR BELOVED VICE COMMANDER.
SHUT UP!
IT'S FUNNY THAT YOU MENTIONED CRIMINAL GUILDS, THOUGH.
VERY SHARP OF YOU.
!?

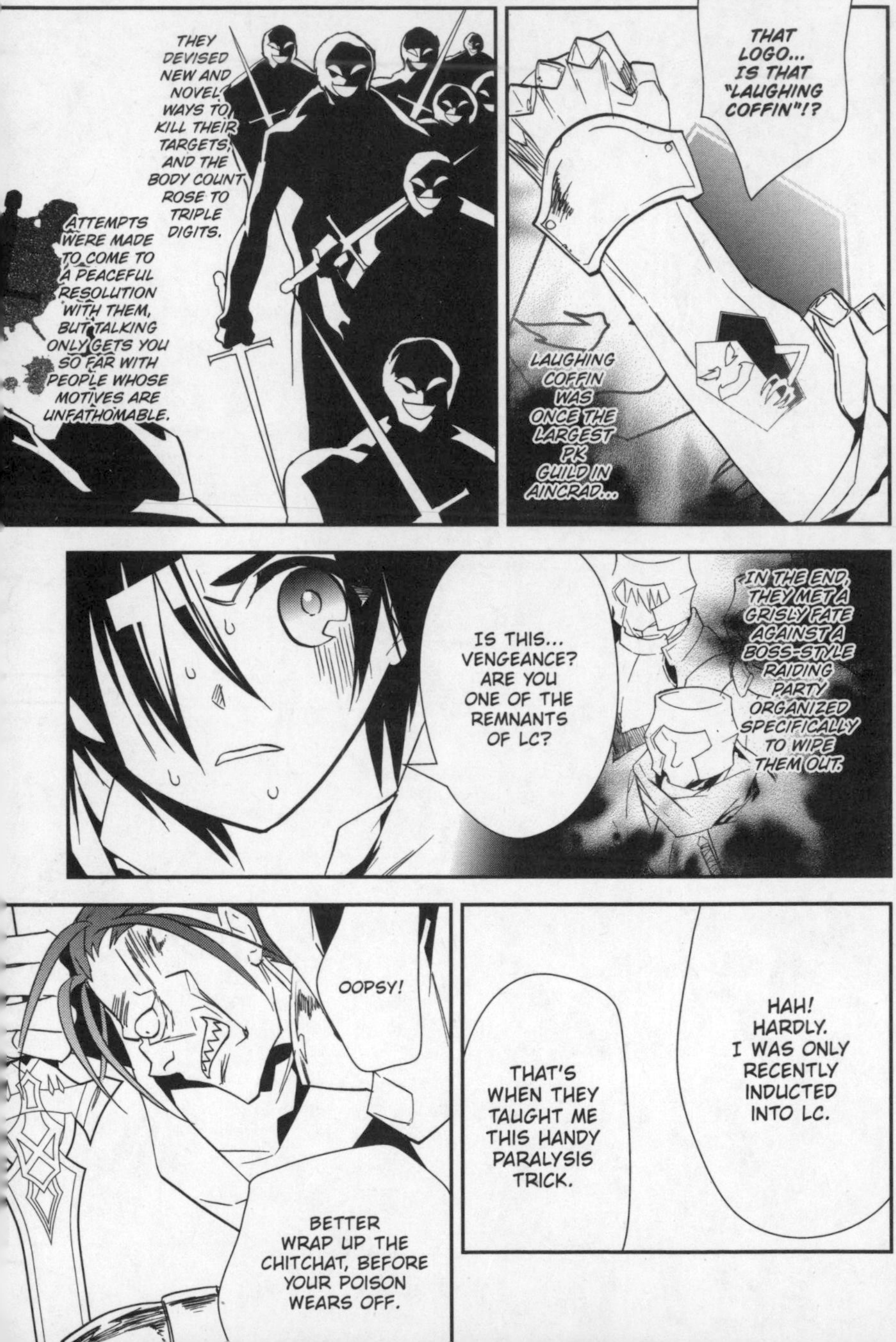
THAT LOGO... IS THAT "LAUGHING COFFIN"!?
LAUGHING COFFIN WAS ONCE THE LARGEST PK GUILD IN AINCRAD...
THEY DEVISED NEW AND NOVEL WAYS TO KILL THEIR TARGETS, AND THE BODY COUNT ROSE TO TRIPLE DIGITS.
ATTEMPTS WERE MADE TO COME TO A PEACEFUL RESOLUTION WITH THEM, BUT TALKING ONLY GETS YOU SO FAR WITH PEOPLE WHOSE MOTIVES ARE UNFATHOMABLE.
IN THE END, THEY MET A GRISLY FATE AGAINST A BOSS-STYLE RAIDING PARTY ORGANIZED SPECIFICALLY TO WIPE THEM OUT.
IS THIS... VENGEANCE? ARE YOU ONE OF THE REMNANTS OF LC?
HAH! HARDLY. I WAS ONLY RECENTLY INDUCTED INTO LC.
THAT'S WHEN THEY TAUGHT ME THIS HANDY PARALYSIS TRICK.
OOPSY!
BETTER WRAP UP THE CHITCHAT, BEFORE YOUR POISON WEARS OFF.

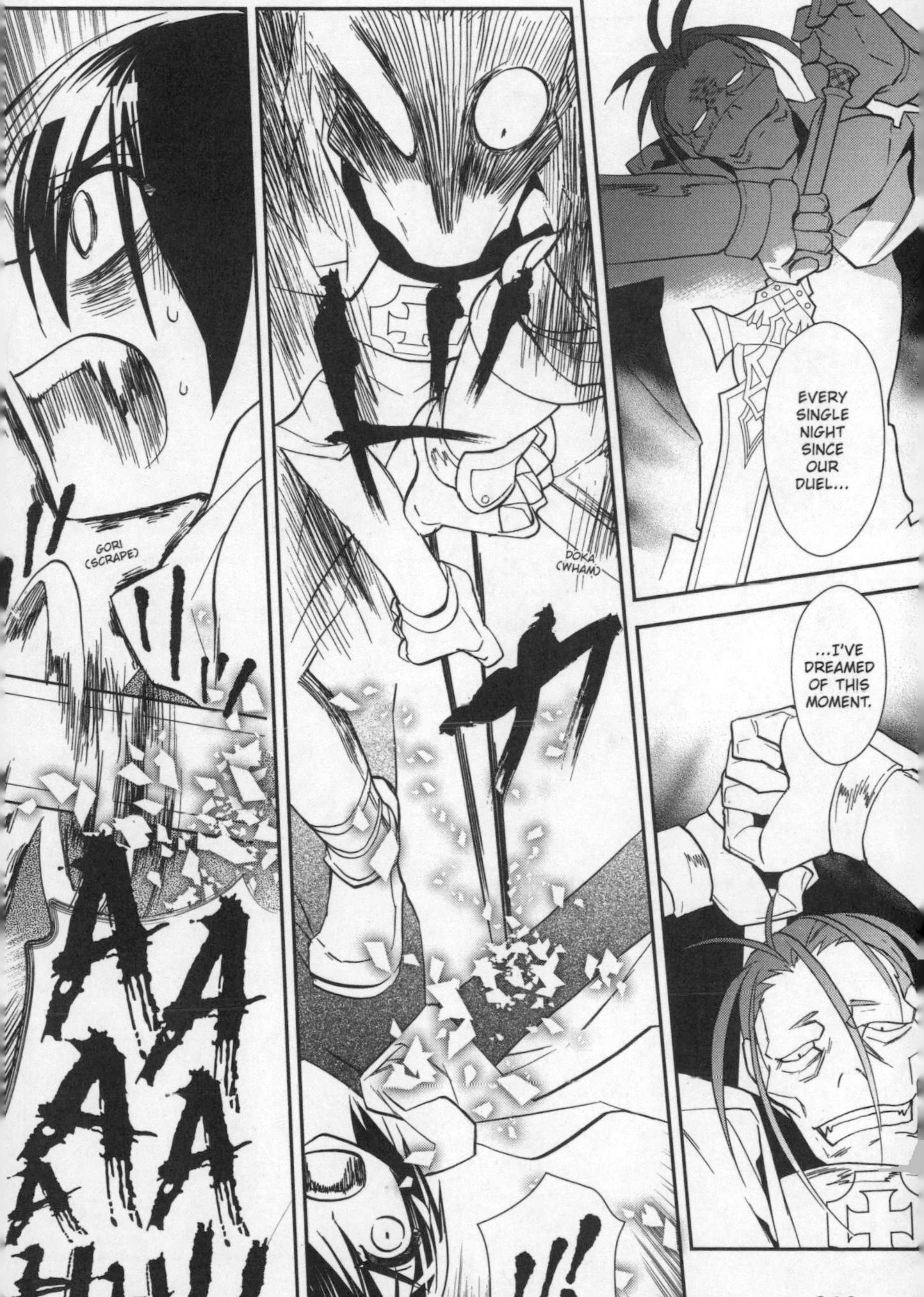
EVERY SINGLE NIGHT SINCE OUR DUEL...
...I'VE DREAMED OF THIS MOMENT.
DOKA (WHAM)
!!!
GORI (SCRAPE)
AAAAAAAHH!!

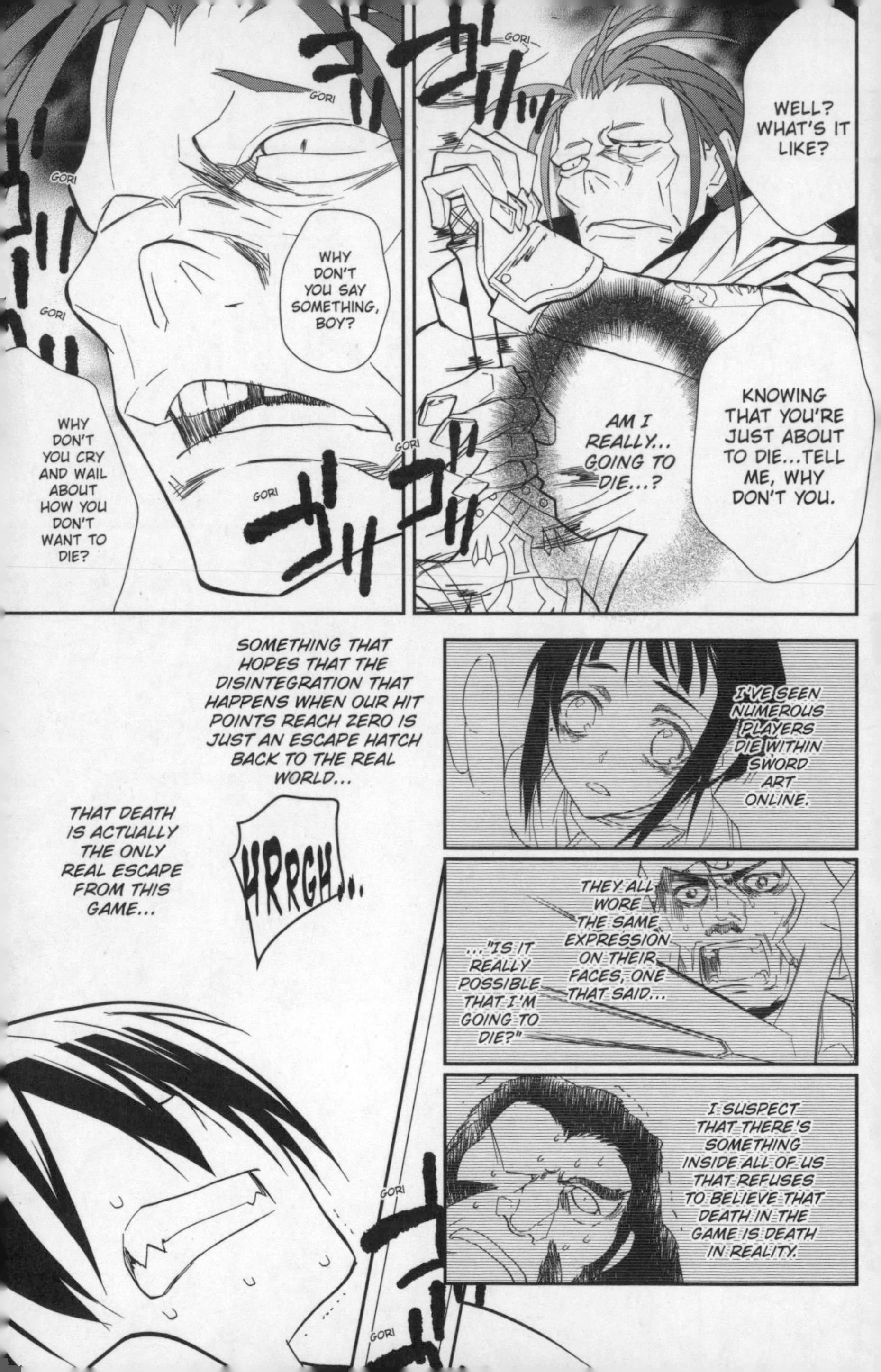
GORI
WELL? WHAT'S IT LIKE?
KNOWING THAT YOU'RE JUST ABOUT TO DIE...TELL ME, WHY DON'T YOU.
AM I REALLY... GOING TO DIE...?
GORI
GORI
WHY DON'T YOU SAY SOMETHING, BOY?
GORI
GORI
WHY DON'T YOU CRY AND WAIL ABOUT HOW YOU DON'T WANT TO DIE?
GORI
I'VE SEEN NUMEROUS PLAYERS DIE WITHIN SWORD ART ONLINE.
THEY ALL WORE THE SAME EXPRESSION ON THEIR FACES, ONE THAT SAID...
..."IS IT REALLY POSSIBLE THAT I'M GOING TO DIE?"
I SUSPECT THAT THERE'S SOMETHING INSIDE ALL OF US THAT REFUSES TO BELIEVE THAT DEATH IN THE GAME IS DEATH IN REALITY.
SOMETHING THAT HOPES THAT THE DISINTEGRATION THAT HAPPENS WHEN OUR HIT POINTS REACH ZERO IS JUST AN ESCAPE HATCH BACK TO THE REAL WORLD...
THAT DEATH IS ACTUALLY THE ONLY REAL ESCAPE FROM THIS GAME...
HRRGH...
GORI
GORI

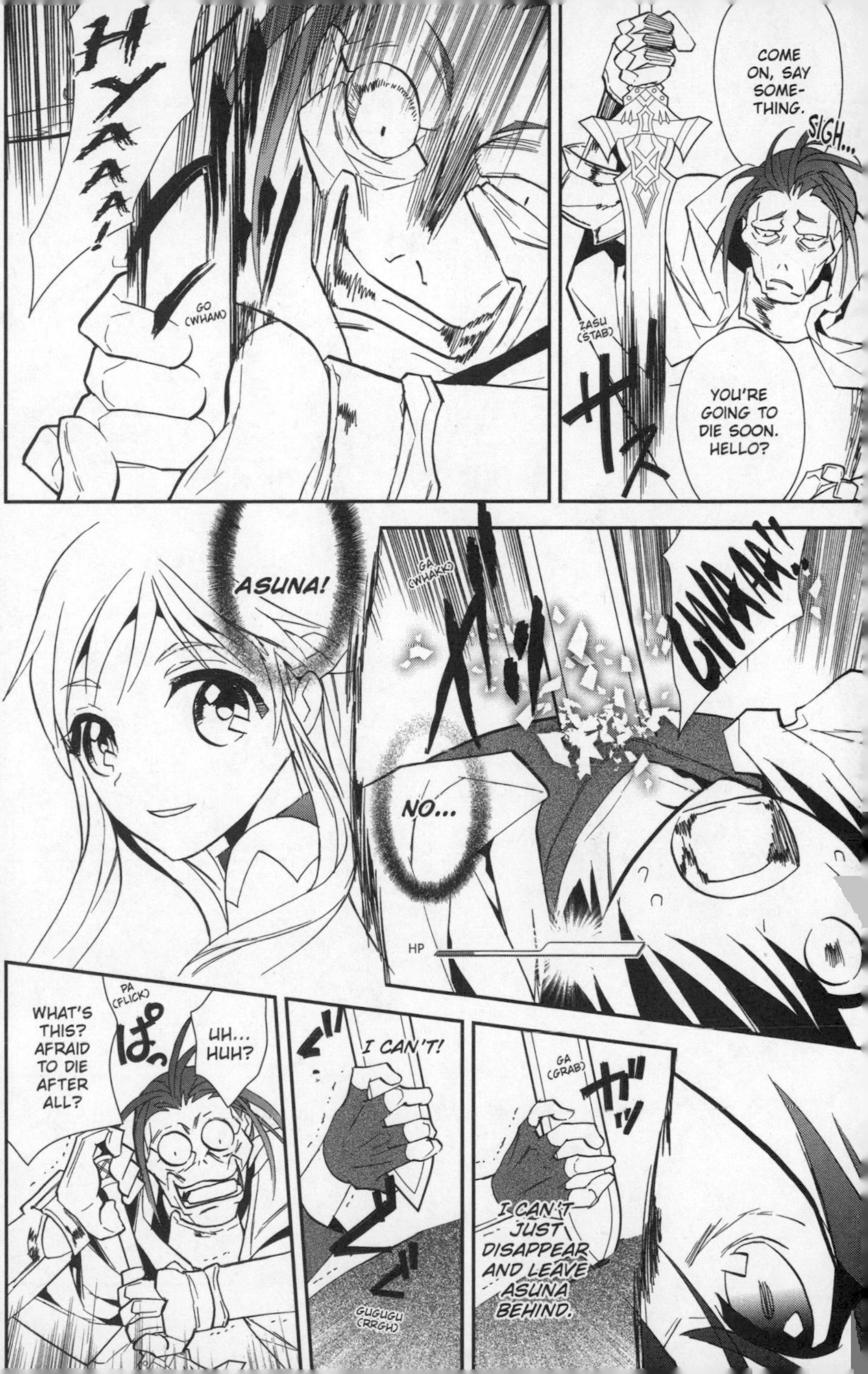

COME ON, SAY SOME-THING.
SIGH...
ZASU (STAB)
YOU'RE GOING TO DIE SOON. HELLO?
HYAAA!
GO (WHAM)
GA (WHAKK)
GWAAA!!..
HP
ASUNA!
NO...
GA (GRAB)
I CAN'T JUST DISAPPEAR AND LEAVE ASUNA BEHIND.
I CAN'T!
GUGUGU (RRGH)
UH... HUH?
PA (FLICK)
ぱっ
WHAT'S THIS? AFRAID TO DIE AFTER ALL?

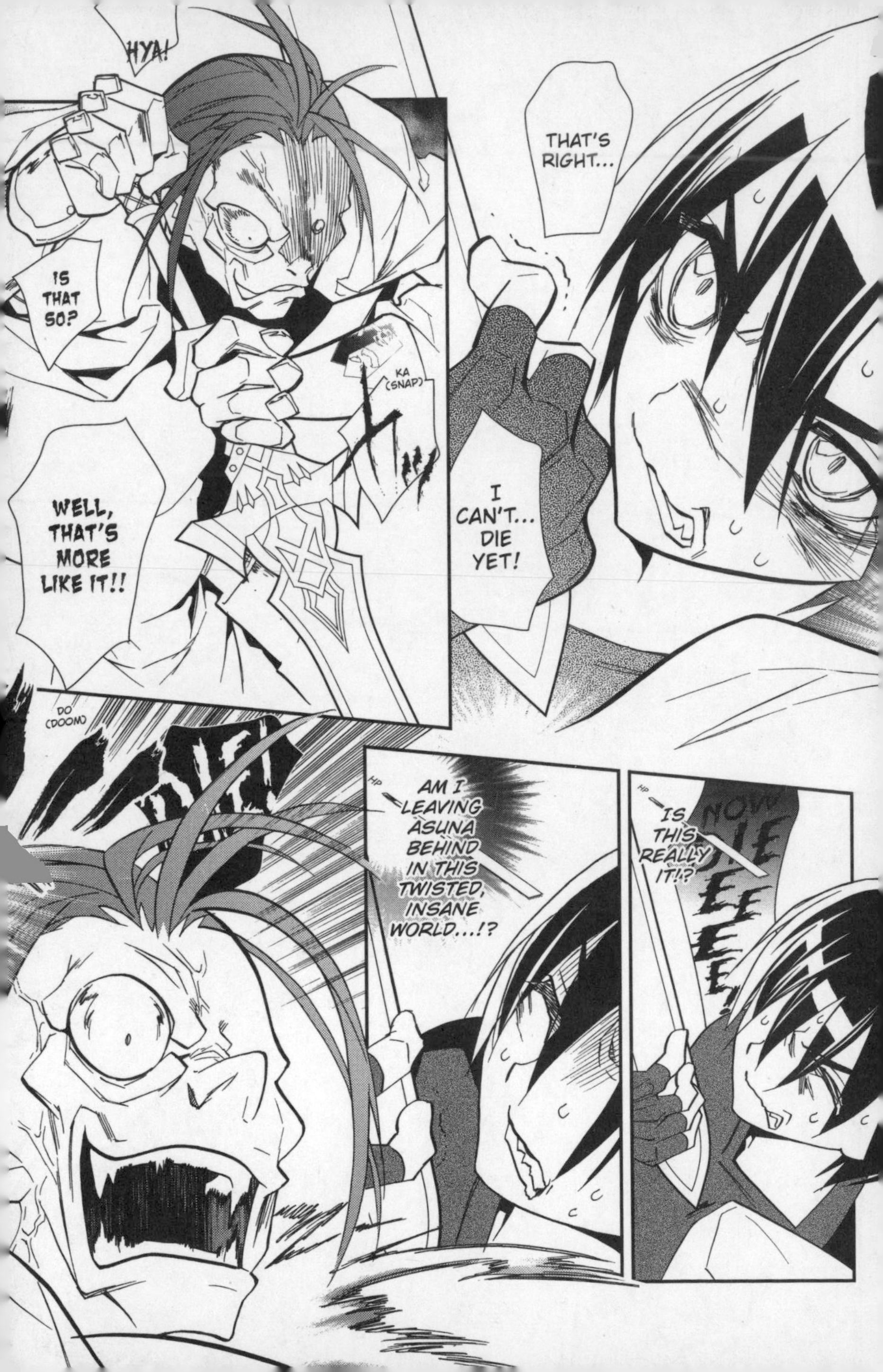
THAT'S RIGHT...
I CAN'T... DIE YET!
HYA!
IS THAT SO?
KA (SNAP)
WELL, THAT'S MORE LIKE IT!!
HP
IS THIS REALLY IT!?
NOW DIEEEEE!
HP
AM I LEAVING ASUNA BEHIND IN THIS TWISTED, INSANE WORLD...!?
DO (DOOM)

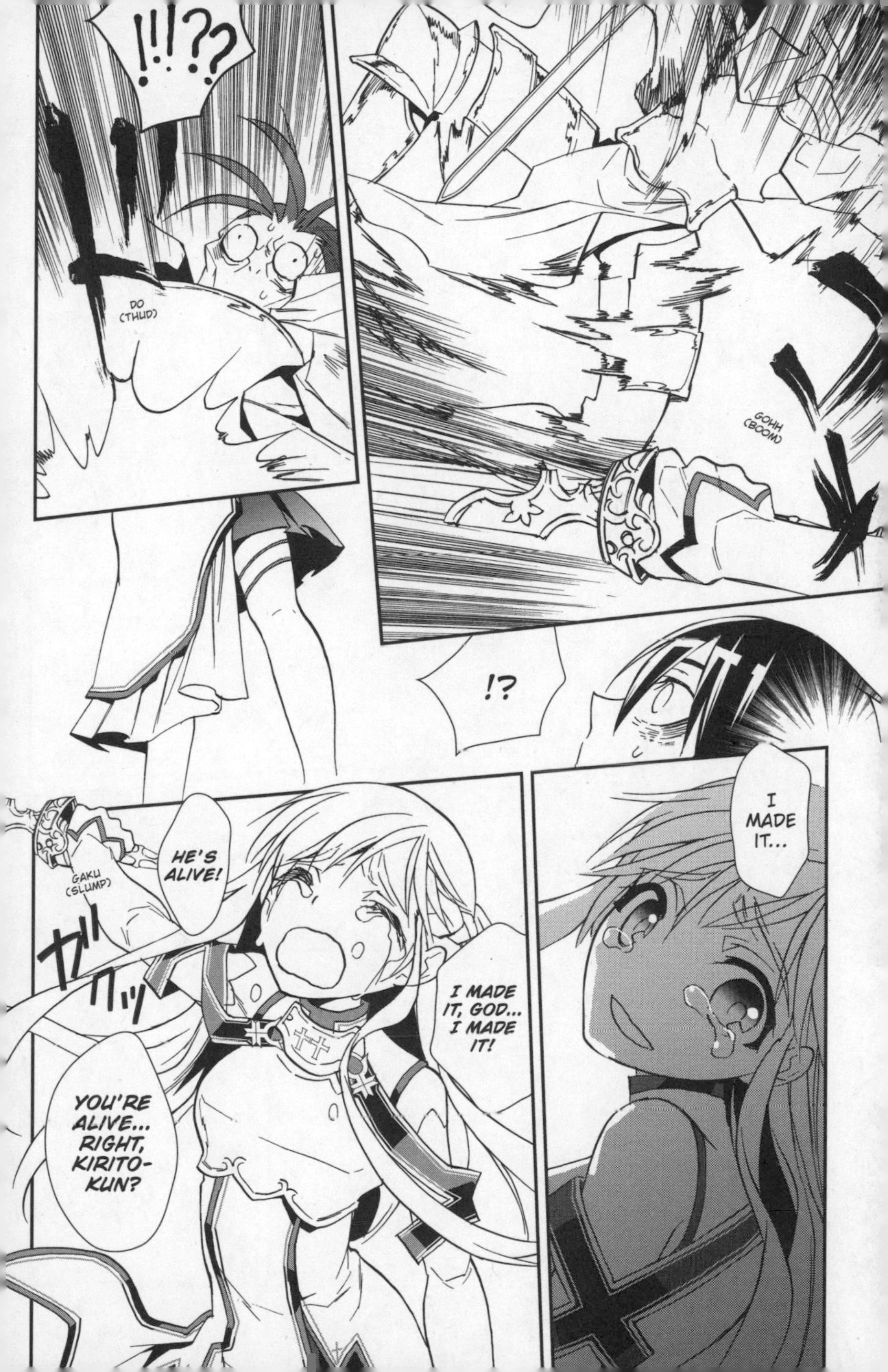
GOHH
(BOOM)
!!??
DO
(THUD)
!?
I MADE IT...
HE'S ALIVE!
GAKU
(SLUMP)
ガクッ
I MADE IT, GOD... I MADE IT!
YOU'RE ALIVE... RIGHT, KIRITO-KUN?

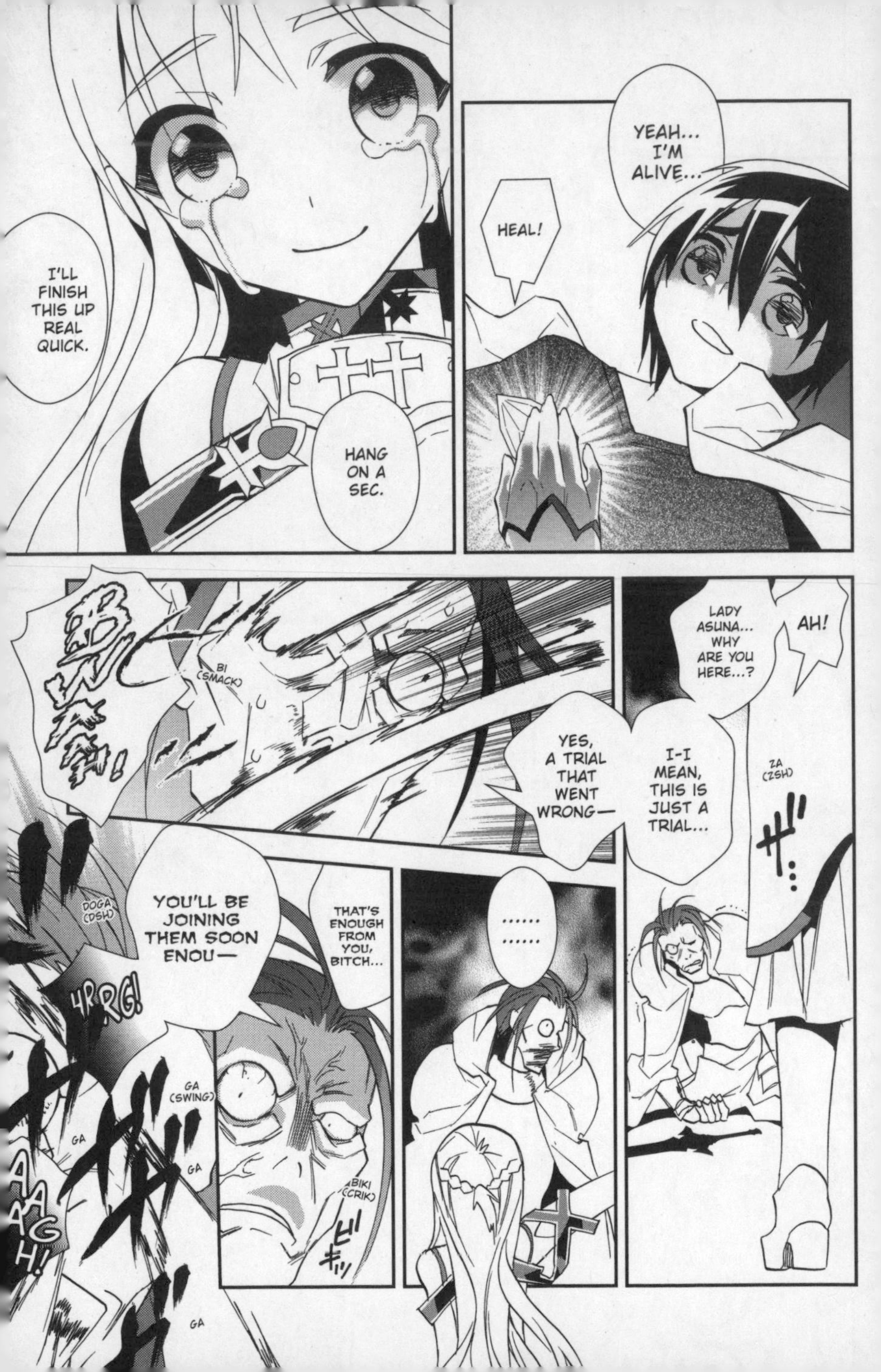
YEAH... I'M ALIVE...
HEAL!
HANG ON A SEC.
I'LL FINISH THIS UP REAL QUICK.
AH!
LADY ASUNA... WHY ARE YOU HERE...?
ZA (ZSH)
I-I MEAN, THIS IS JUST A TRIAL...
YES, A TRIAL THAT WENT WRONG—
BI (SMACK)
......
......
THAT'S ENOUGH FROM YOU, BITCH...
YOU'LL BE JOINING THEM SOON ENOU—
BIKI (CRIK)
GA (SWING)
URRG!
DOGA (DSH)
GA
GA
AAAGH!
GA

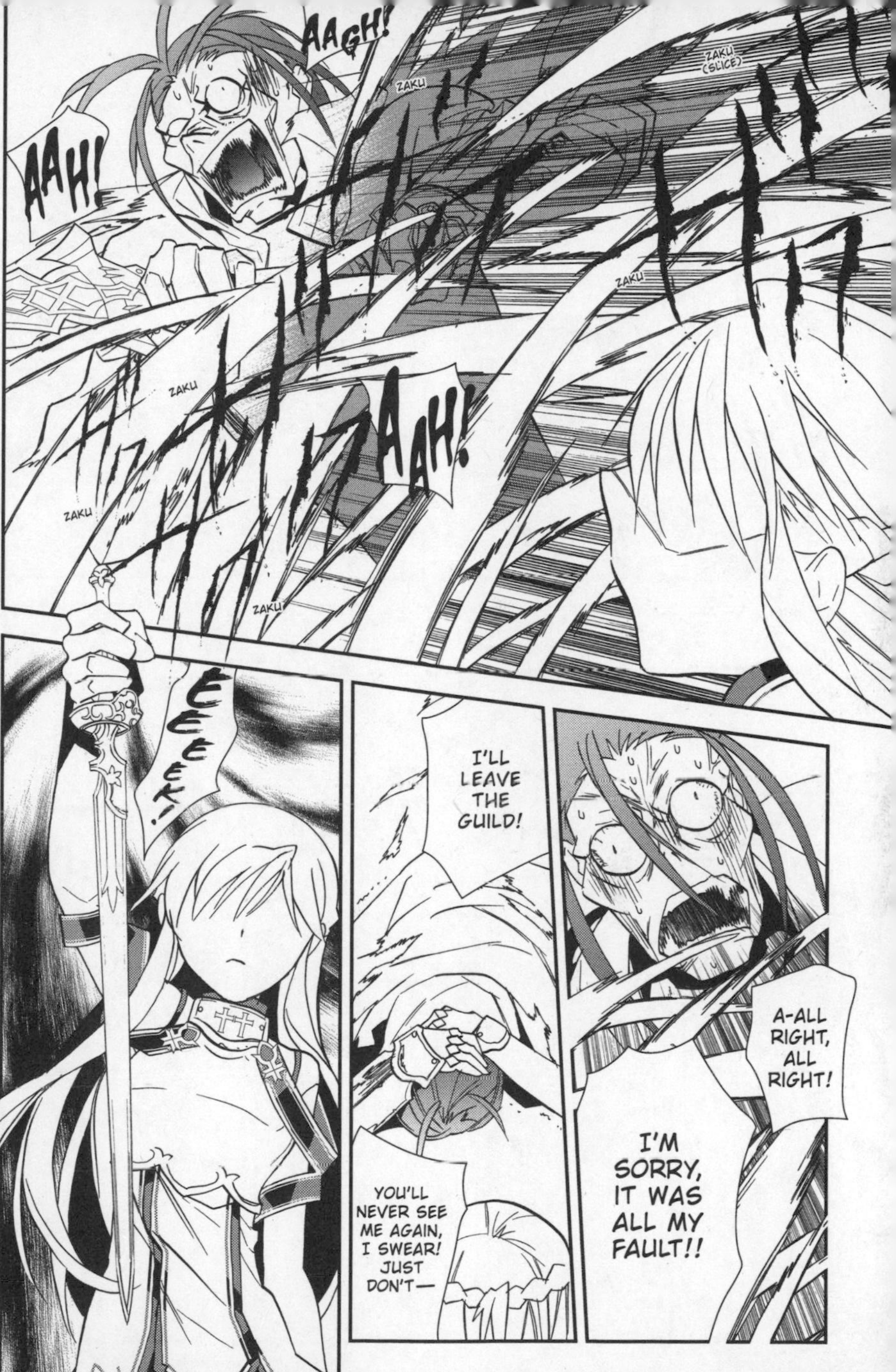
ZAKU (SLICE)
AAGH!
ZAKU
ZAKU
AAH!
AAH!
ZAKU
ZAKU
ZAKU
A-ALL RIGHT, ALL RIGHT!
I'M SORRY, IT WAS ALL MY FAULT!!
I'LL LEAVE THE GUILD!
YOU'LL NEVER SEE ME AGAIN, I SWEAR! JUST DON'T—
EEEEEK!!

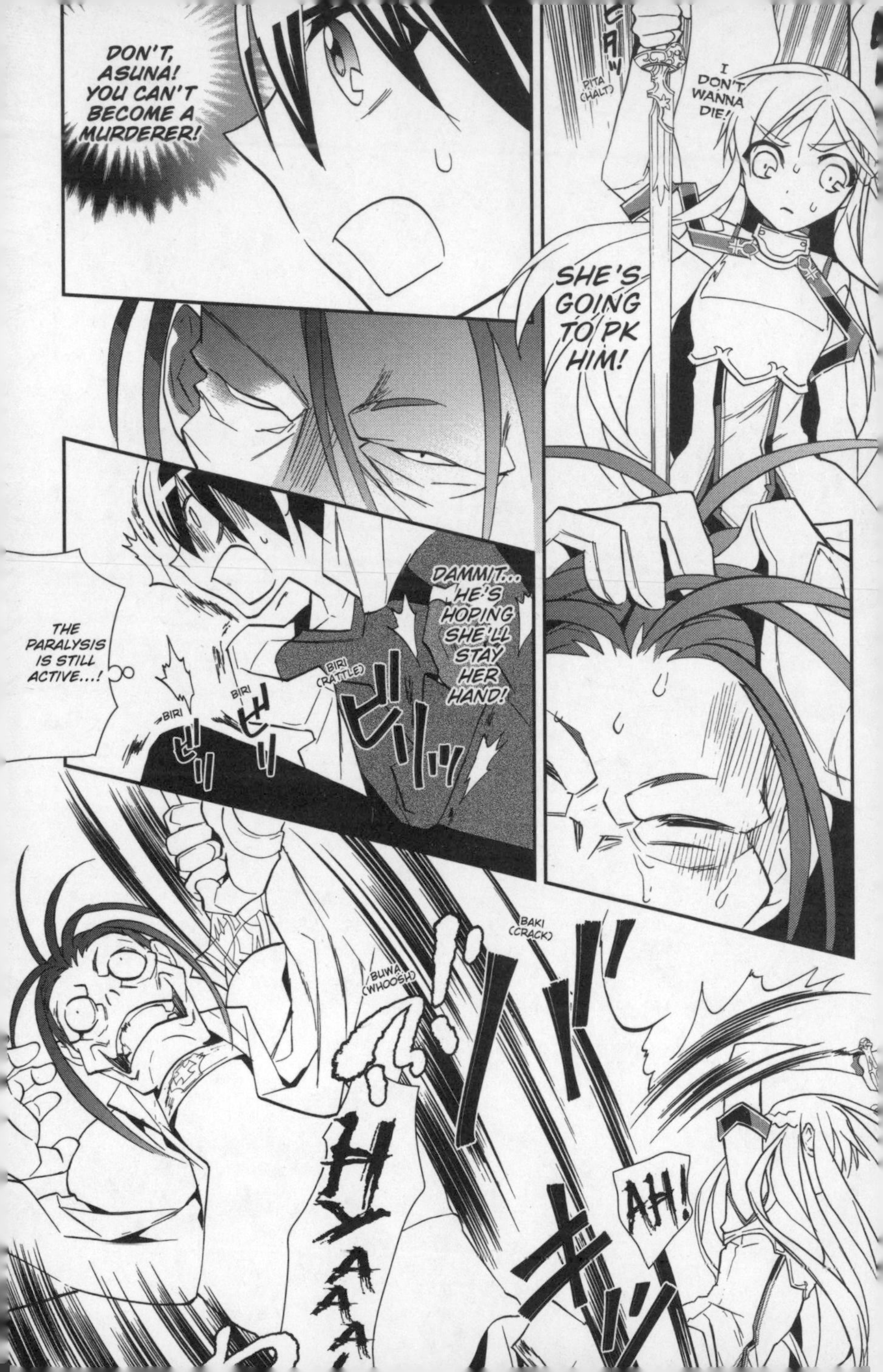

PITA (HALT)
I DON'T WANNA DIE!
SHE'S GOING TO PK HIM!
DON'T, ASUNA! YOU CAN'T BECOME A MURDERER!
DAMMIT... HE'S HOPING SHE'LL STAY HER HAND!
BIRI (RATTLE)
BIRI
BIRI
THE PARALYSIS IS STILL ACTIVE...!
BAKI (CRACK)
AH!
BUWA (WHOOSH)
HYAAAA

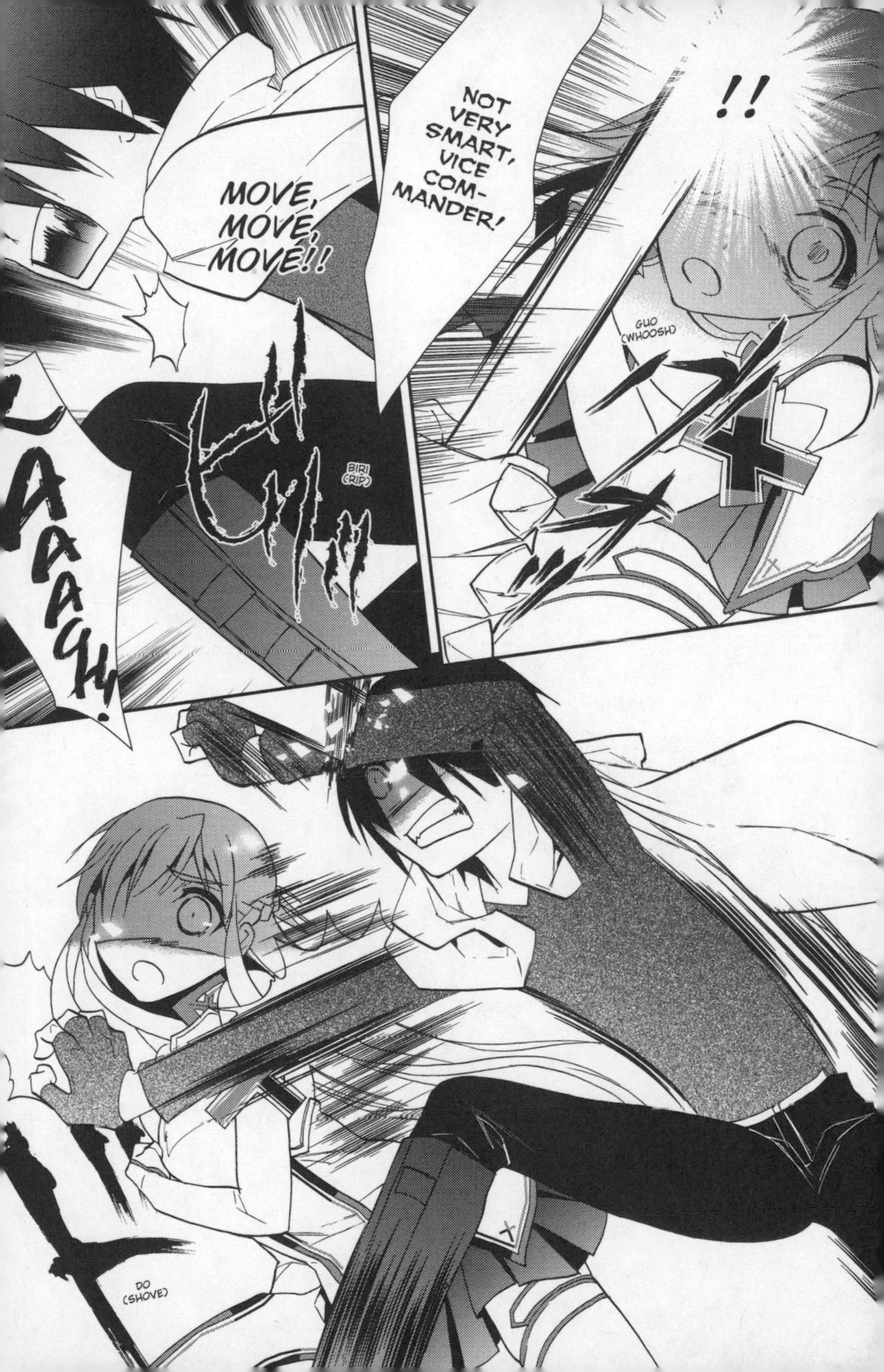
NOT VERY SMART, VICE COMMANDER!
!!
GUO (WHOOSH)
MOVE, MOVE, MOVE!!
BIRI (RIP)
AAAAGH!
DO (SHOVE)

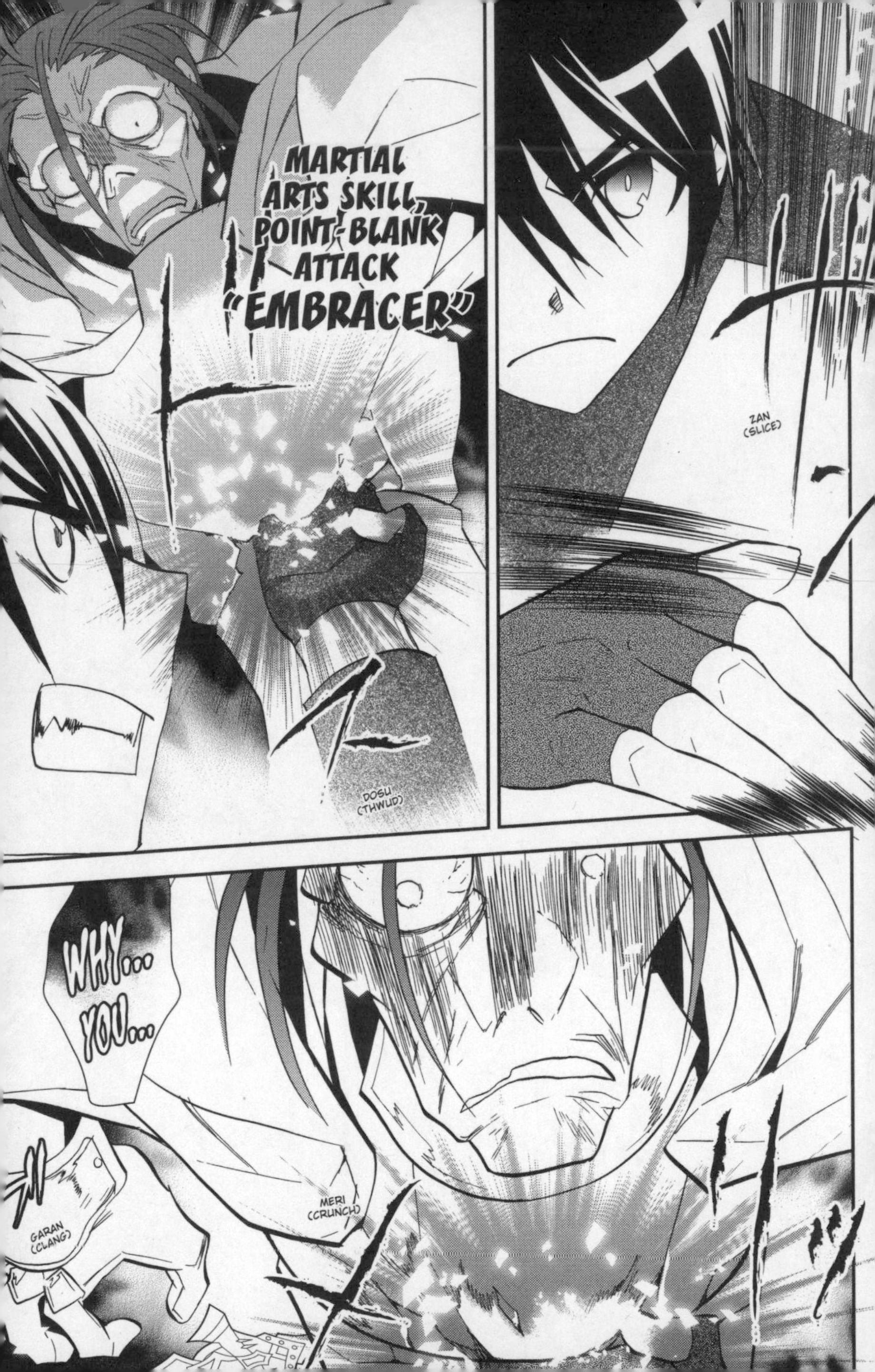
ZAN (SLICE)
MARTIAL ARTS SKILL, POINT-BLANK ATTACK "EMBRACER"
DOSU (THWUD)
WHY... YOU...
MERI (CRUNCH)
GARAN (CLANG)

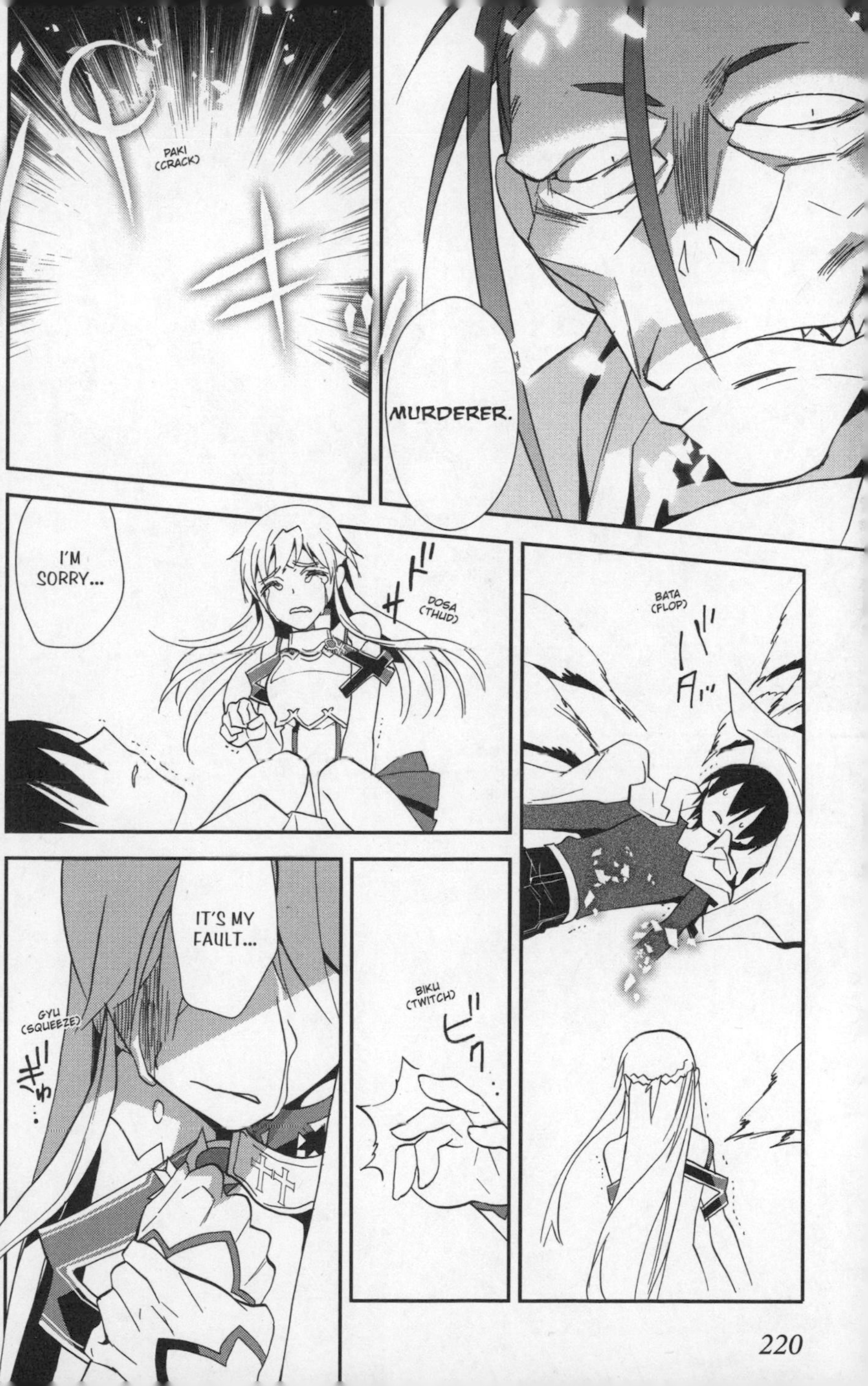
MURDERER.
PAKI (CRACK)
BATA (FLOP)
DOSA (THUD)
I'M SORRY...
BIKU (TWITCH)
IT'S MY FAULT...
GYU (SQUEEZE)

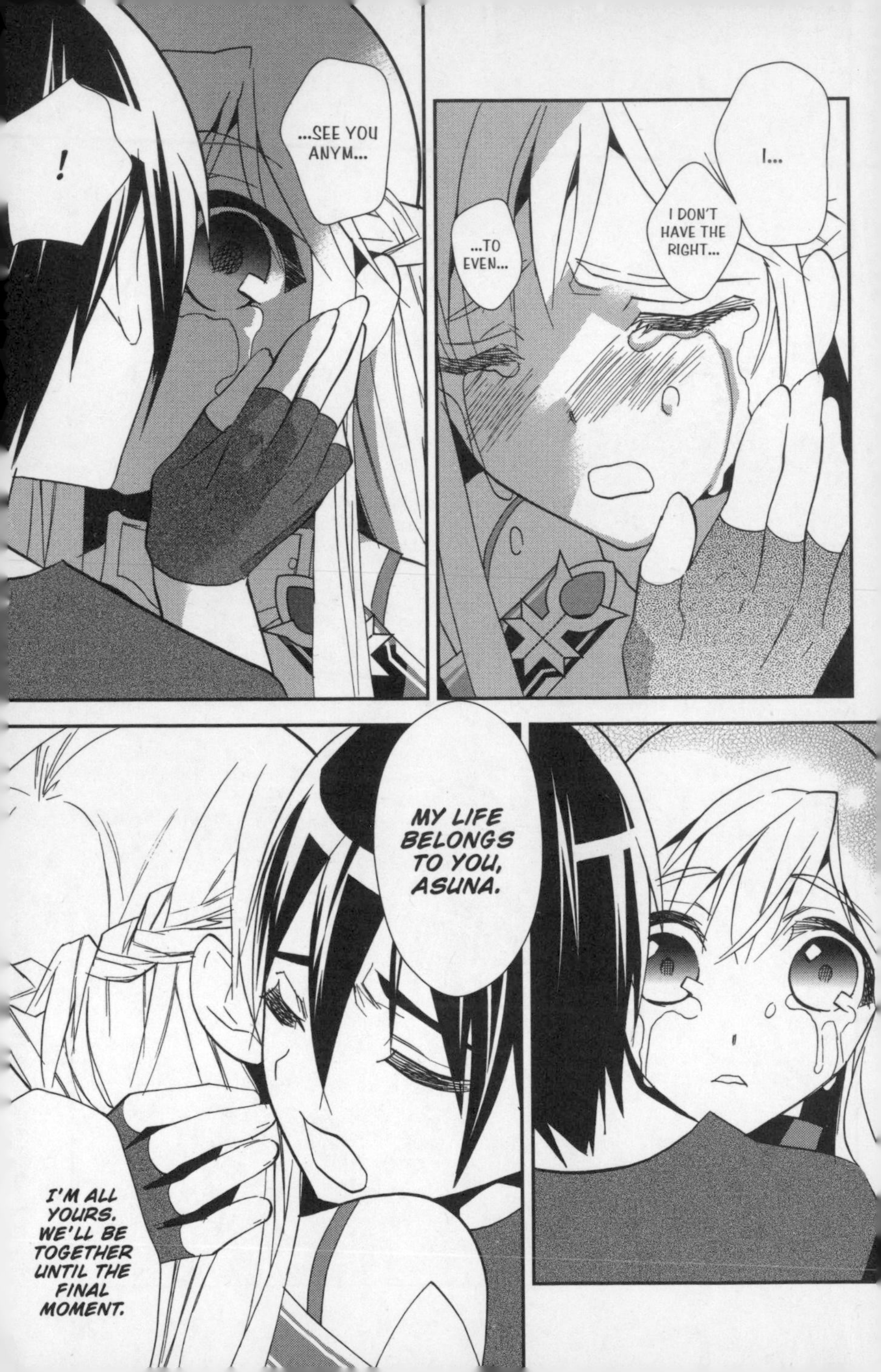
I...
I DON'T HAVE THE RIGHT...
...TO EVEN...
...SEE YOU ANYM...
!
MY LIFE BELONGS TO YOU, ASUNA.
I'M ALL YOURS. WE'LL BE TOGETHER UNTIL THE FINAL MOMENT.

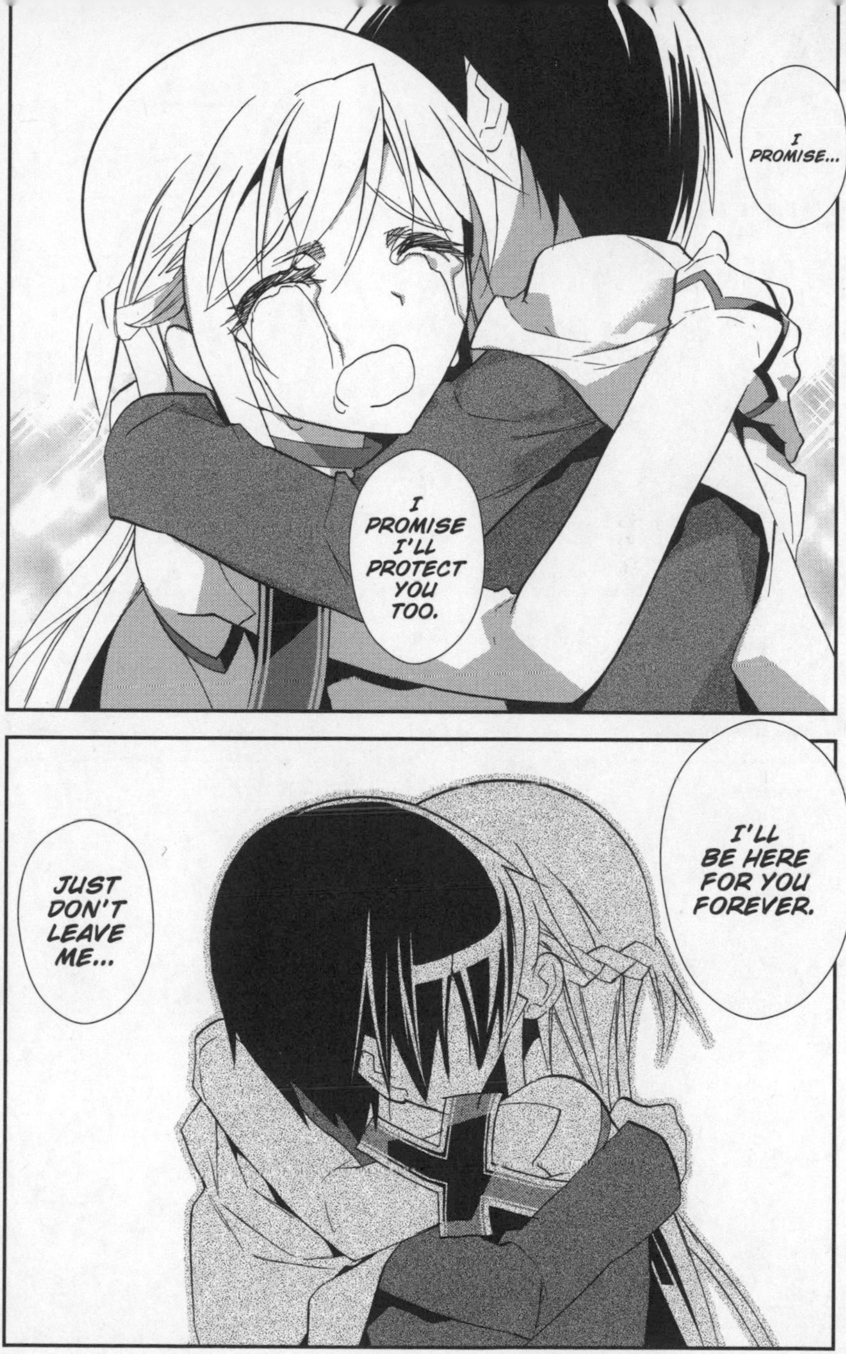
I PROMISE...
I PROMISE I'LL PROTECT YOU TOO.
I'LL BE HERE FOR YOU FOREVER.
JUST DON'T LEAVE ME...

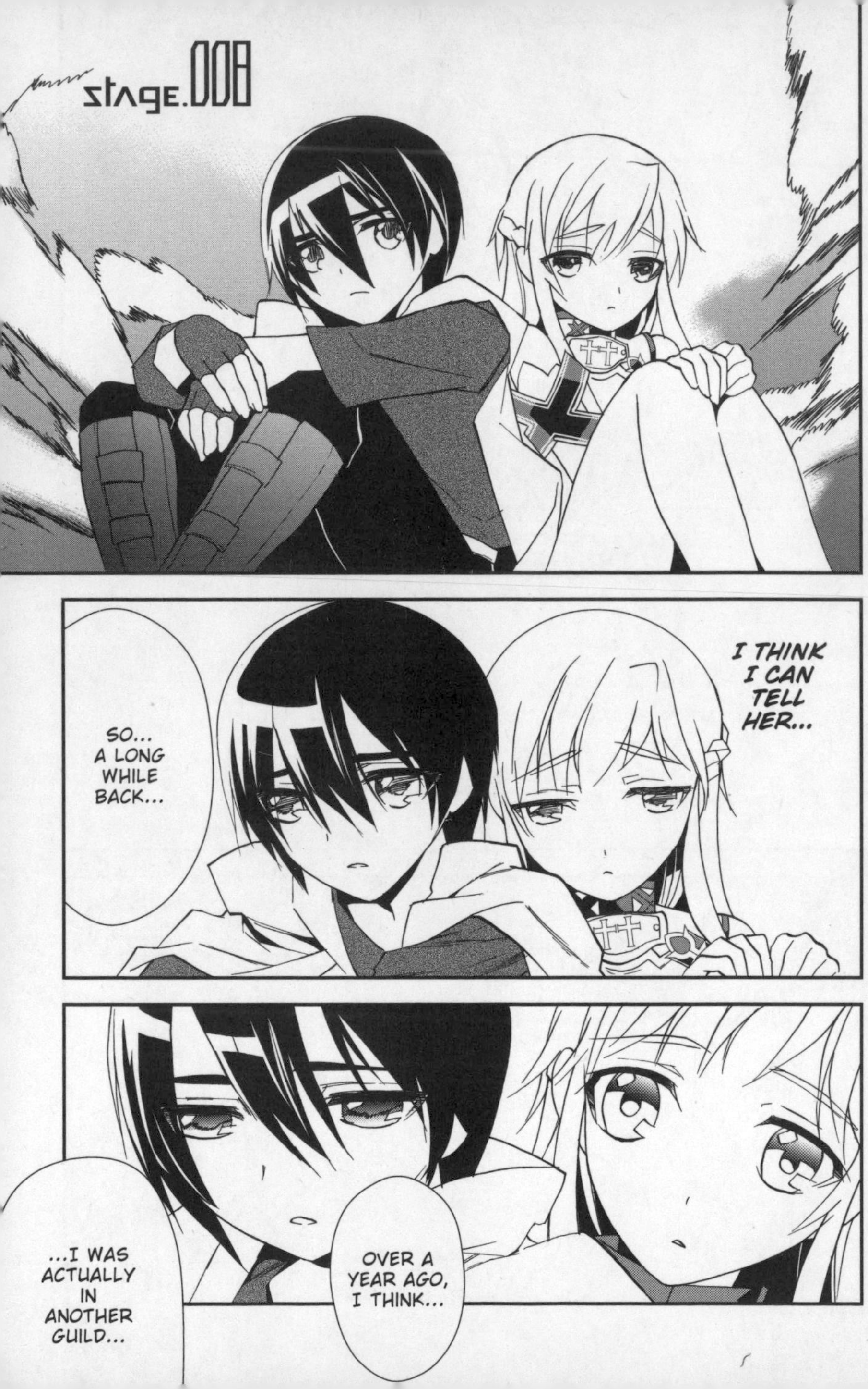
stage.008
I THINK I CAN TELL HER...
SO... A LONG WHILE BACK...
OVER A YEAR AGO, I THINK...
...I WAS ACTUALLY IN ANOTHER GUILD...

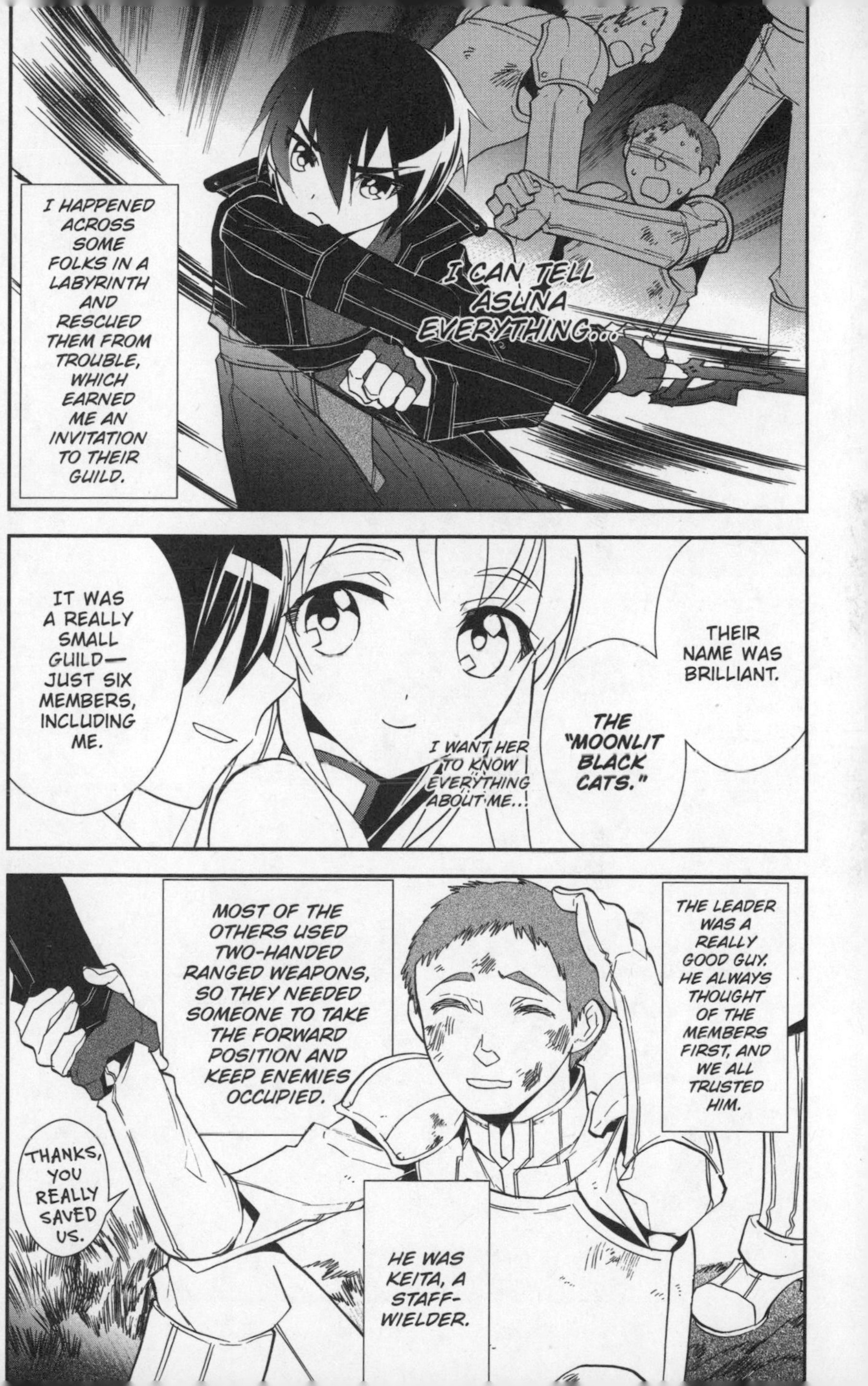
I CAN TELL ASUNA EVERYTHING...
I HAPPENED ACROSS SOME FOLKS IN A LABYRINTH AND RESCUED THEM FROM TROUBLE, WHICH EARNED ME AN INVITATION TO THEIR GUILD.
THEIR NAME WAS BRILLIANT.
THE "MOONLIT BLACK CATS."
I WANT HER TO KNOW EVERYTHING ABOUT ME...
IT WAS A REALLY SMALL GUILD—JUST SIX MEMBERS, INCLUDING ME.
THE LEADER WAS A REALLY GOOD GUY. HE ALWAYS THOUGHT OF THE MEMBERS FIRST, AND WE ALL TRUSTED HIM.
MOST OF THE OTHERS USED TWO-HANDED RANGED WEAPONS, SO THEY NEEDED SOMEONE TO TAKE THE FORWARD POSITION AND KEEP ENEMIES OCCUPIED.
HE WAS KEITA, A STAFF-WIELDER.
THANKS, YOU REALLY SAVED US.

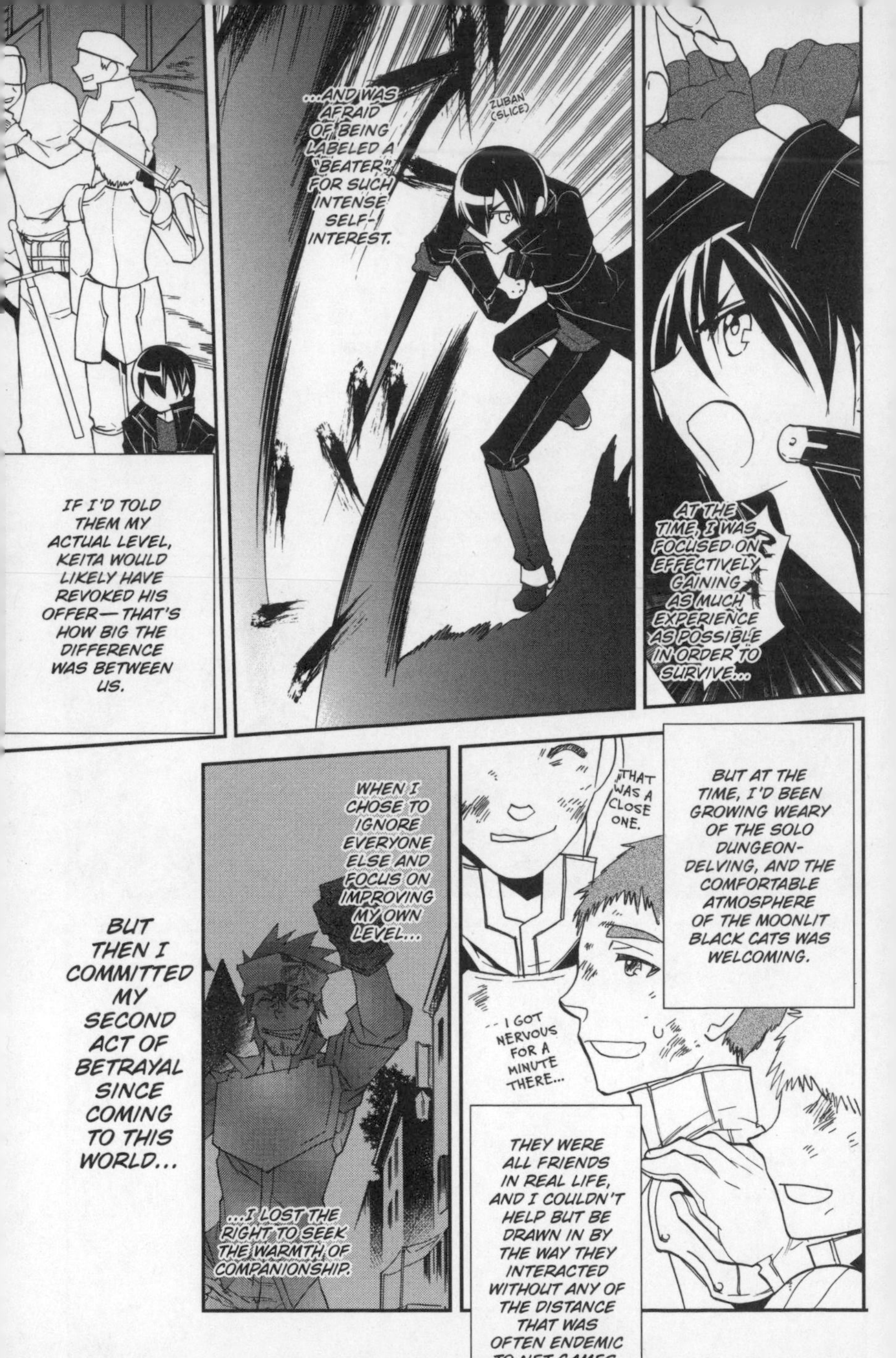
AT THE TIME, I WAS FOCUSED ON EFFECTIVELY GAINING AS MUCH EXPERIENCE AS POSSIBLE IN ORDER TO SURVIVE...
ZUBAN (SLICE)
...AND WAS AFRAID OF BEING LABELED A "BEATER" FOR SUCH INTENSE SELF-INTEREST.
IF I'D TOLD THEM MY ACTUAL LEVEL, KEITA WOULD LIKELY HAVE REVOKED HIS OFFER—THAT'S HOW BIG THE DIFFERENCE WAS BETWEEN US.
BUT AT THE TIME, I'D BEEN GROWING WEARY OF THE SOLO DUNGEON-DELVING, AND THE COMFORTABLE ATMOSPHERE OF THE MOONLIT BLACK CATS WAS WELCOMING.
THAT WAS A CLOSE ONE.
--I GOT NERVOUS FOR A MINUTE THERE...
THEY WERE ALL FRIENDS IN REAL LIFE, AND I COULDN'T HELP BUT BE DRAWN IN BY THE WAY THEY INTERACTED WITHOUT ANY OF THE DISTANCE THAT WAS OFTEN ENDEMIC TO NET GAMES.
WHEN I CHOSE TO IGNORE EVERYONE ELSE AND FOCUS ON IMPROVING MY OWN LEVEL...
...I LOST THE RIGHT TO SEEK THE WARMTH OF COMPANIONSHIP.
BUT THEN I COMMITTED MY SECOND ACT OF BETRAYAL SINCE COMING TO THIS WORLD...

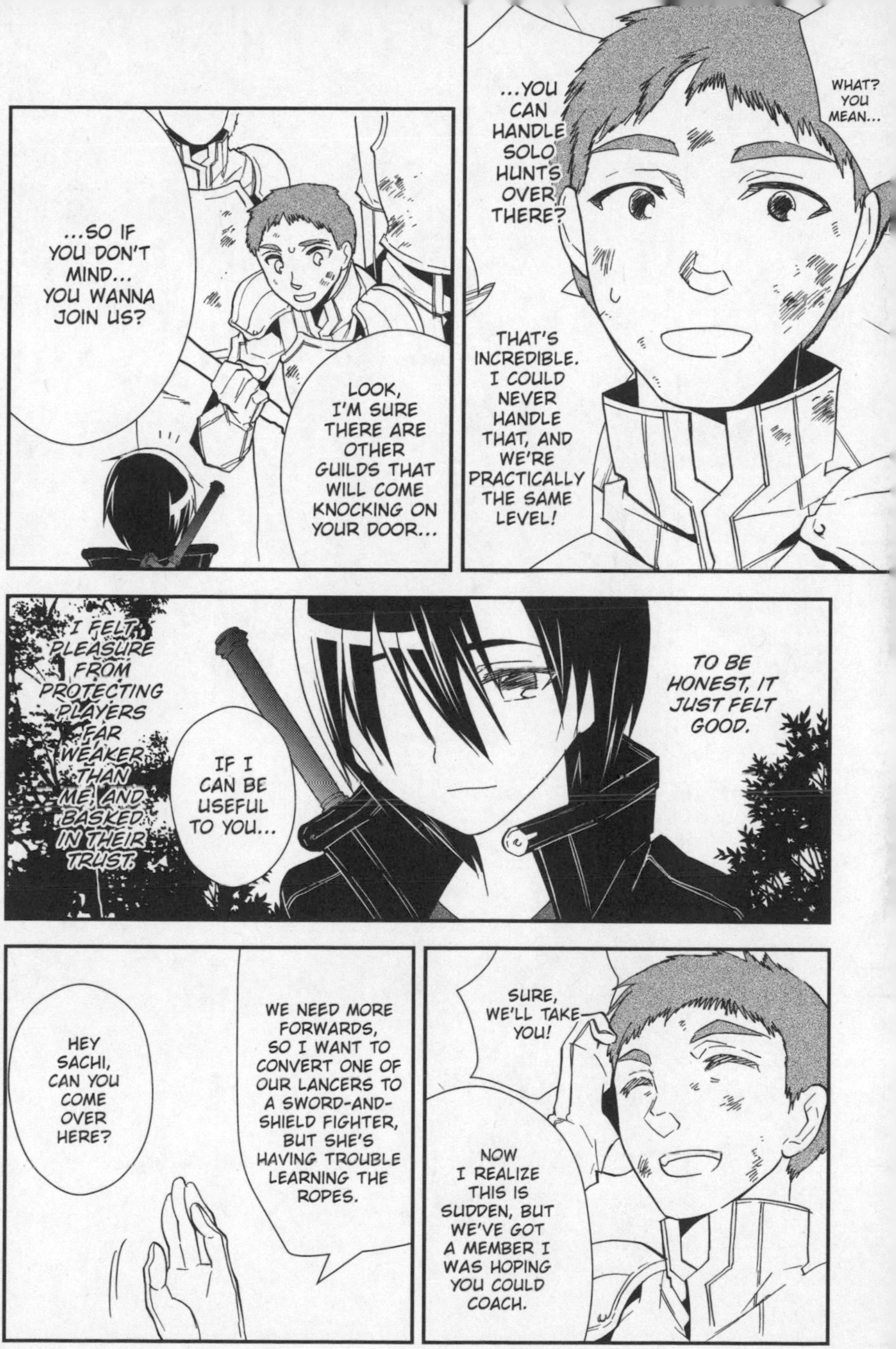
WHAT? YOU MEAN...
...YOU CAN HANDLE SOLO HUNTS OVER THERE?
THAT'S INCREDIBLE. I COULD NEVER HANDLE THAT, AND WE'RE PRACTICALLY THE SAME LEVEL!
LOOK, I'M SURE THERE ARE OTHER GUILDS THAT WILL COME KNOCKING ON YOUR DOOR...
...SO IF YOU DON'T MIND... YOU WANNA JOIN US?
TO BE HONEST, IT JUST FELT GOOD.
IF I CAN BE USEFUL TO YOU...
I FELT PLEASURE FROM PROTECTING PLAYERS FAR WEAKER THAN ME, AND BASKED IN THEIR TRUST.
SURE, WE'LL TAKE YOU!
NOW I REALIZE THIS IS SUDDEN, BUT WE'VE GOT A MEMBER I WAS HOPING YOU COULD COACH.
WE NEED MORE FORWARDS, SO I WANT TO CONVERT ONE OF OUR LANCERS TO A SWORD-AND-SHIELD FIGHTER, BUT SHE'S HAVING TROUBLE LEARNING THE ROPES.
HEY SACHI, CAN YOU COME OVER HERE?

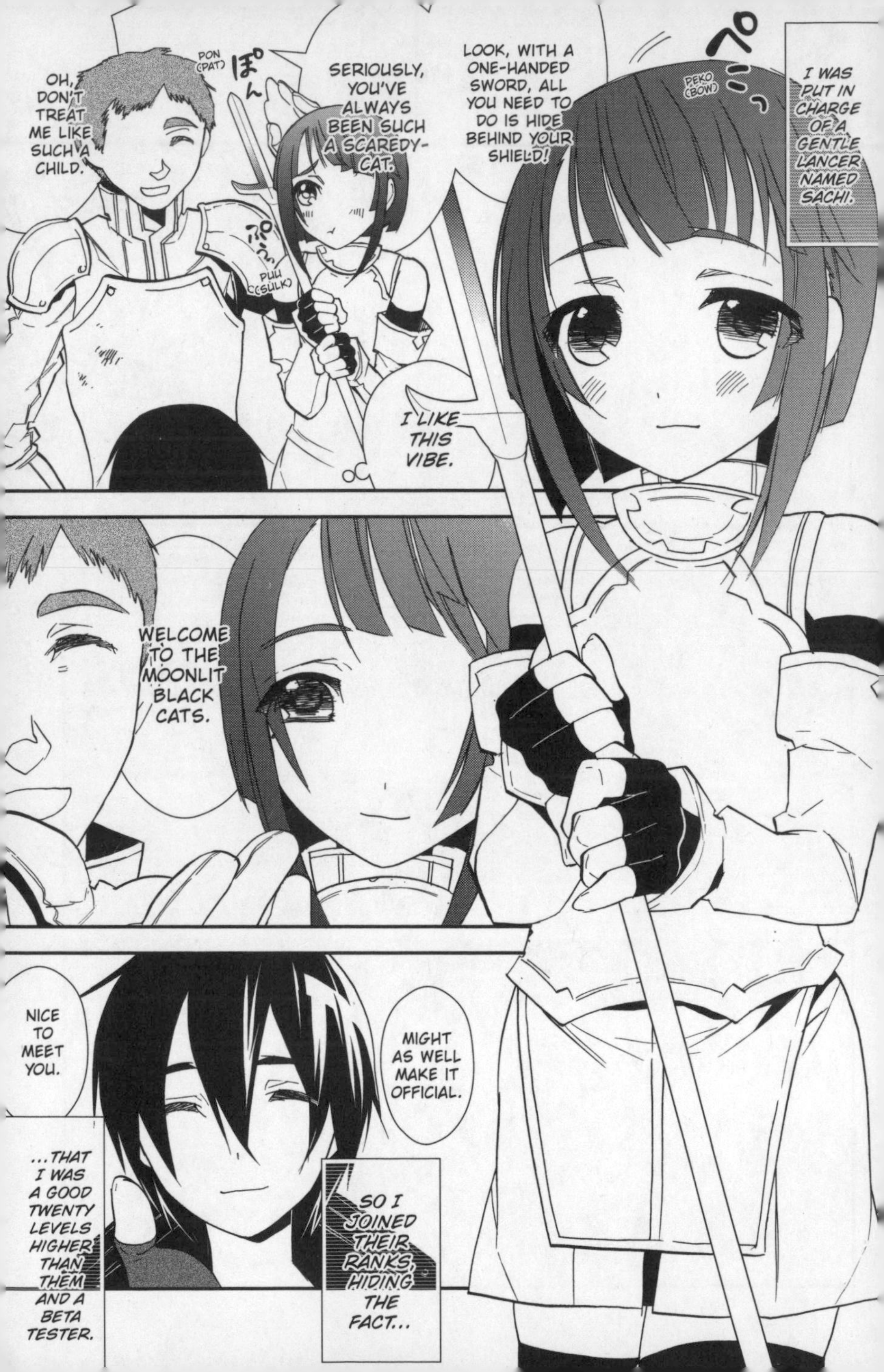
I WAS PUT IN CHARGE OF A GENTLE LANCER NAMED SACHI.
PEKO (BOW)
LOOK, WITH A ONE-HANDED SWORD, ALL YOU NEED TO DO IS HIDE BEHIND YOUR SHIELD!
SERIOUSLY, YOU'VE ALWAYS BEEN SUCH A SCAREDY-CAT.
PON (PAT)
OH, DON'T TREAT ME LIKE SUCH A CHILD.
PUU (SULK)
I LIKE THIS VIBE.
WELCOME TO THE MOONLIT BLACK CATS.
MIGHT AS WELL MAKE IT OFFICIAL.
NICE TO MEET YOU.
SO I JOINED THEIR RANKS, HIDING THE FACT...
...THAT I WAS A GOOD TWENTY LEVELS HIGHER THAN THEM AND A BETA TESTER.

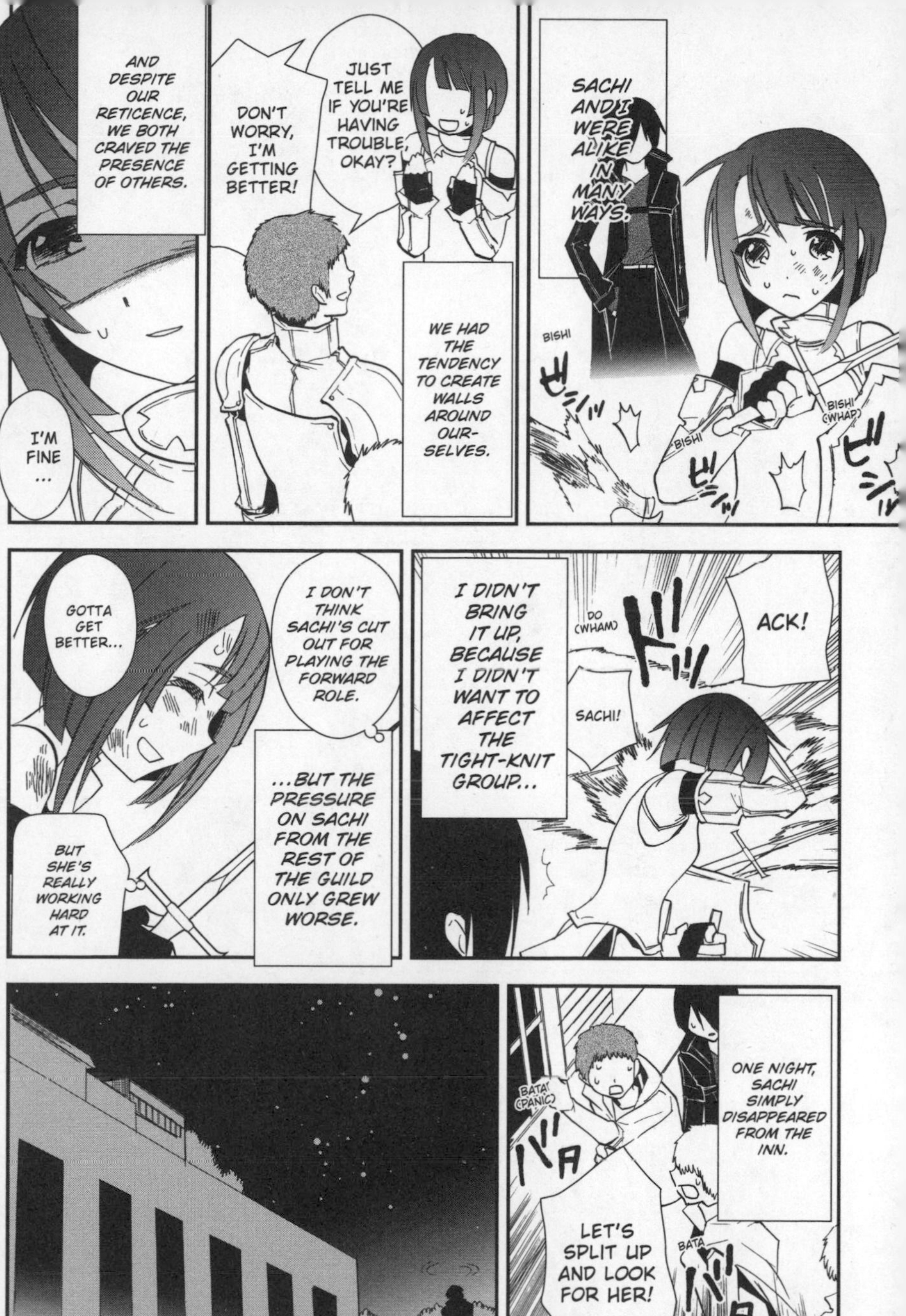
SACHI AND I WERE ALIKE IN MANY WAYS.
BISHI
BISHI (WHAP)
BISHI
JUST TELL ME IF YOU'RE HAVING TROUBLE, OKAY?
DON'T WORRY, I'M GETTING BETTER!
WE HAD THE TENDENCY TO CREATE WALLS AROUND OURSELVES.
AND DESPITE OUR RETICENCE, WE BOTH CRAVED THE PRESENCE OF OTHERS.
I'M FINE ...
ACK!
I DIDN'T BRING IT UP, BECAUSE I DIDN'T WANT TO AFFECT THE TIGHT-KNIT GROUP...
DO (WHAM)
SACHI!
I DON'T THINK SACHI'S CUT OUT FOR PLAYING THE FORWARD ROLE.
GOTTA GET BETTER...
...BUT THE PRESSURE ON SACHI FROM THE REST OF THE GUILD ONLY GREW WORSE.
BUT SHE'S REALLY WORKING HARD AT IT.
ONE NIGHT, SACHI SIMPLY DISAPPEARED FROM THE INN.
BATA (PANIC)
LET'S SPLIT UP AND LOOK FOR HER!
BATA

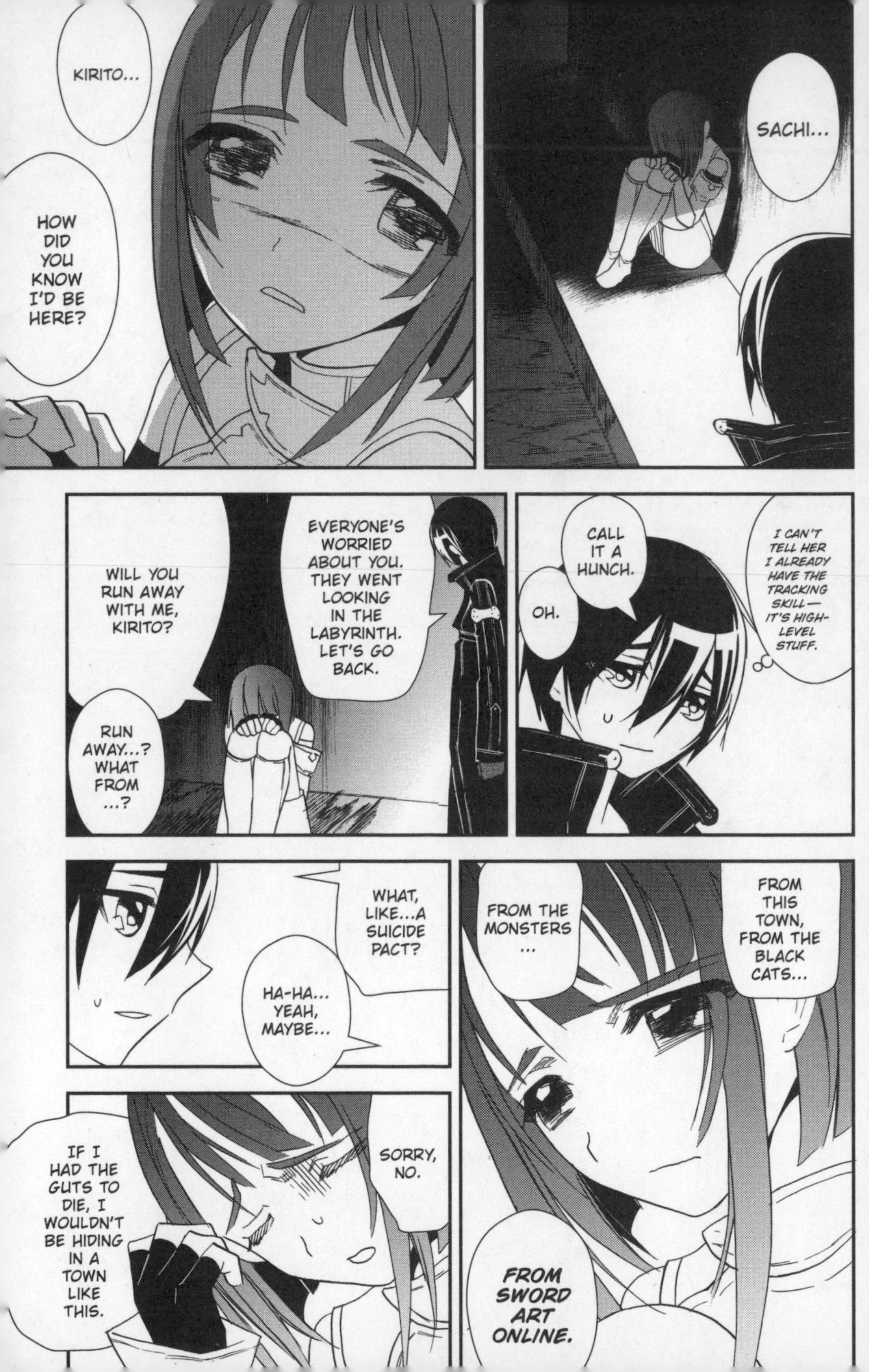
SACHI...
KIRITO...
HOW DID YOU KNOW I'D BE HERE?
CALL IT A HUNCH.
I CAN'T TELL HER I ALREADY HAVE THE TRACKING SKILL—IT'S HIGH-LEVEL STUFF.
OH.
EVERYONE'S WORRIED ABOUT YOU. THEY WENT LOOKING IN THE LABYRINTH. LET'S GO BACK.
WILL YOU RUN AWAY WITH ME, KIRITO?
RUN AWAY...? WHAT FROM...?
FROM THIS TOWN, FROM THE BLACK CATS...
FROM THE MONSTERS...
FROM SWORD ART ONLINE.
WHAT, LIKE...A SUICIDE PACT?
HA-HA... YEAH, MAYBE...
SORRY, NO.
IF I HAD THE GUTS TO DIE, I WOULDN'T BE HIDING IN A TOWN LIKE THIS.

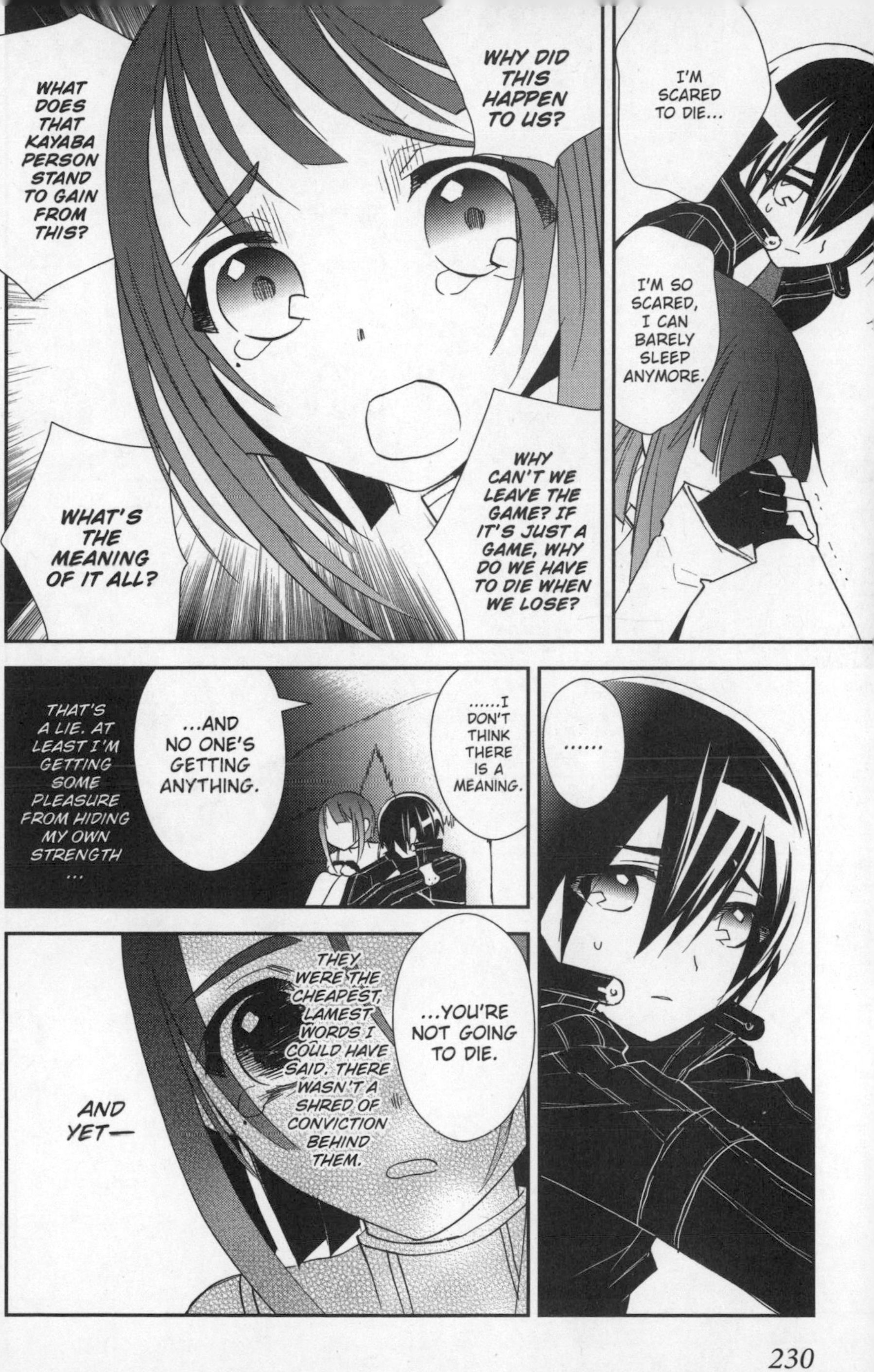
I'M SCARED TO DIE...
I'M SO SCARED, I CAN BARELY SLEEP ANYMORE.
WHY DID THIS HAPPEN TO US?
WHAT DOES THAT KAYABA PERSON STAND TO GAIN FROM THIS?
WHY CAN'T WE LEAVE THE GAME? IF IT'S JUST A GAME, WHY DO WE HAVE TO DIE WHEN WE LOSE?
WHAT'S THE MEANING OF IT ALL?
......
......I DON'T THINK THERE IS A MEANING.
...AND NO ONE'S GETTING ANYTHING.
THAT'S A LIE. AT LEAST I'M GETTING SOME PLEASURE FROM HIDING MY OWN STRENGTH ...
...YOU'RE NOT GOING TO DIE.
THEY WERE THE CHEAPEST, LAMEST WORDS I COULD HAVE SAID. THERE WASN'T A SHRED OF CONVICTION BEHIND THEM.
AND YET—

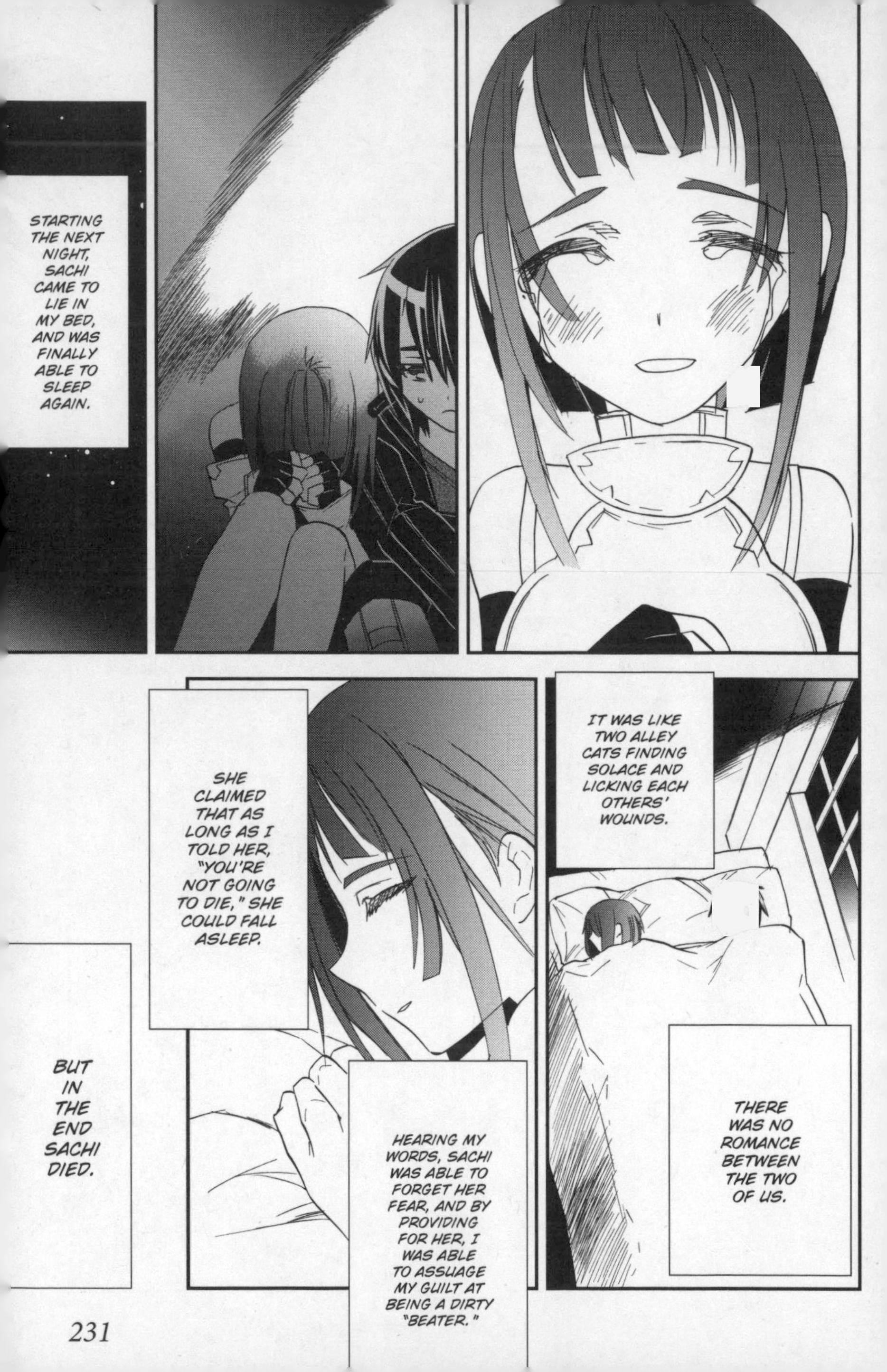
STARTING THE NEXT NIGHT, SACHI CAME TO LIE IN MY BED, AND WAS FINALLY ABLE TO SLEEP AGAIN.
IT WAS LIKE TWO ALLEY CATS FINDING SOLACE AND LICKING EACH OTHERS' WOUNDS.
THERE WAS NO ROMANCE BETWEEN THE TWO OF US.
SHE CLAIMED THAT AS LONG AS I TOLD HER, "YOU'RE NOT GOING TO DIE," SHE COULD FALL ASLEEP.
HEARING MY WORDS, SACHI WAS ABLE TO FORGET HER FEAR, AND BY PROVIDING FOR HER, I WAS ABLE TO ASSUAGE MY GUILT AT BEING A DIRTY "BEATER."
BUT IN THE END SACHI DIED.

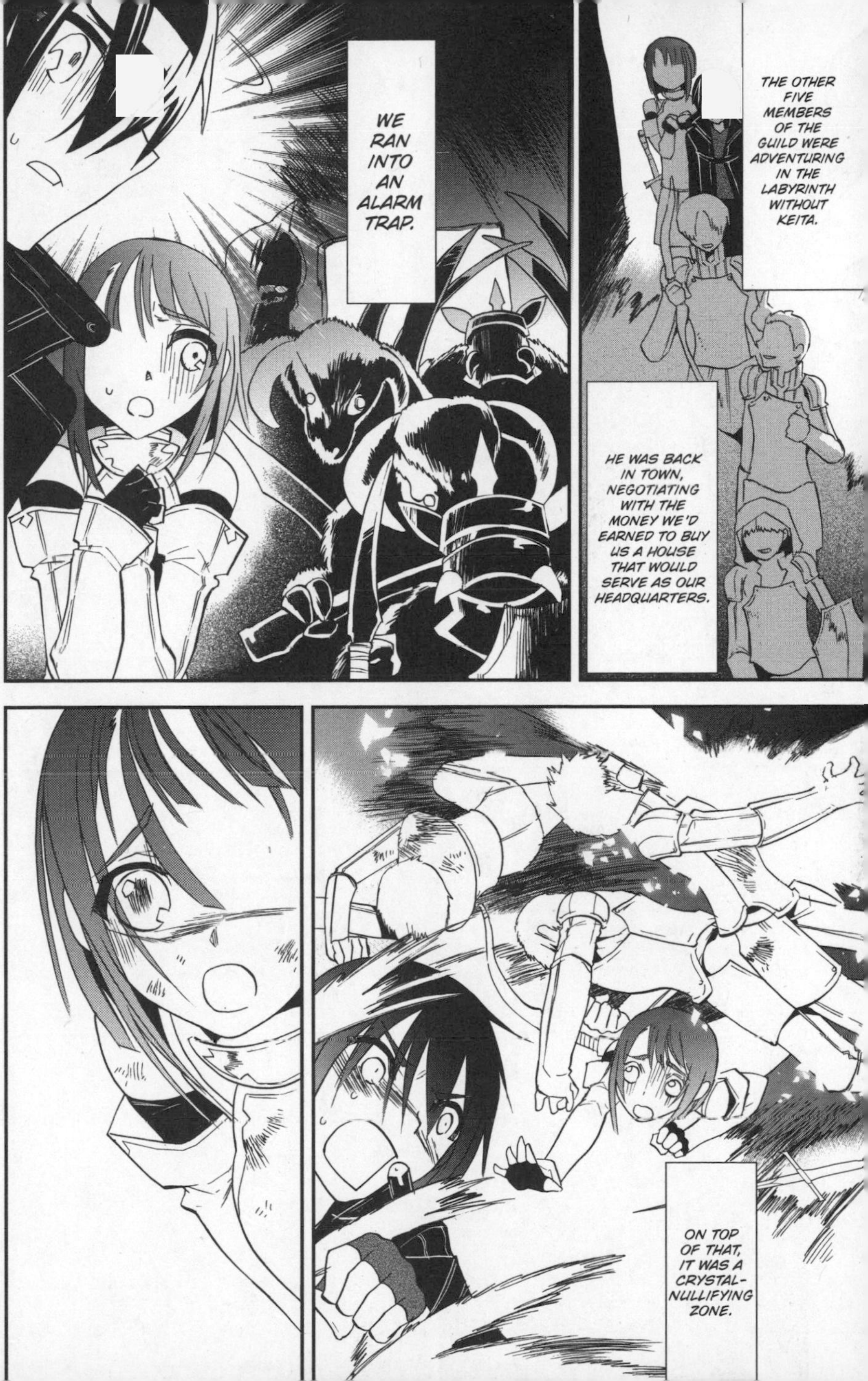
THE OTHER FIVE MEMBERS OF THE GUILD WERE ADVENTURING IN THE LABYRINTH WITHOUT KEITA.
HE WAS BACK IN TOWN, NEGOTIATING WITH THE MONEY WE'D EARNED TO BUY US A HOUSE THAT WOULD SERVE AS OUR HEADQUARTERS.
WE RAN INTO AN ALARM TRAP.
ON TOP OF THAT, IT WAS A CRYSTAL-NULLIFYING ZONE.

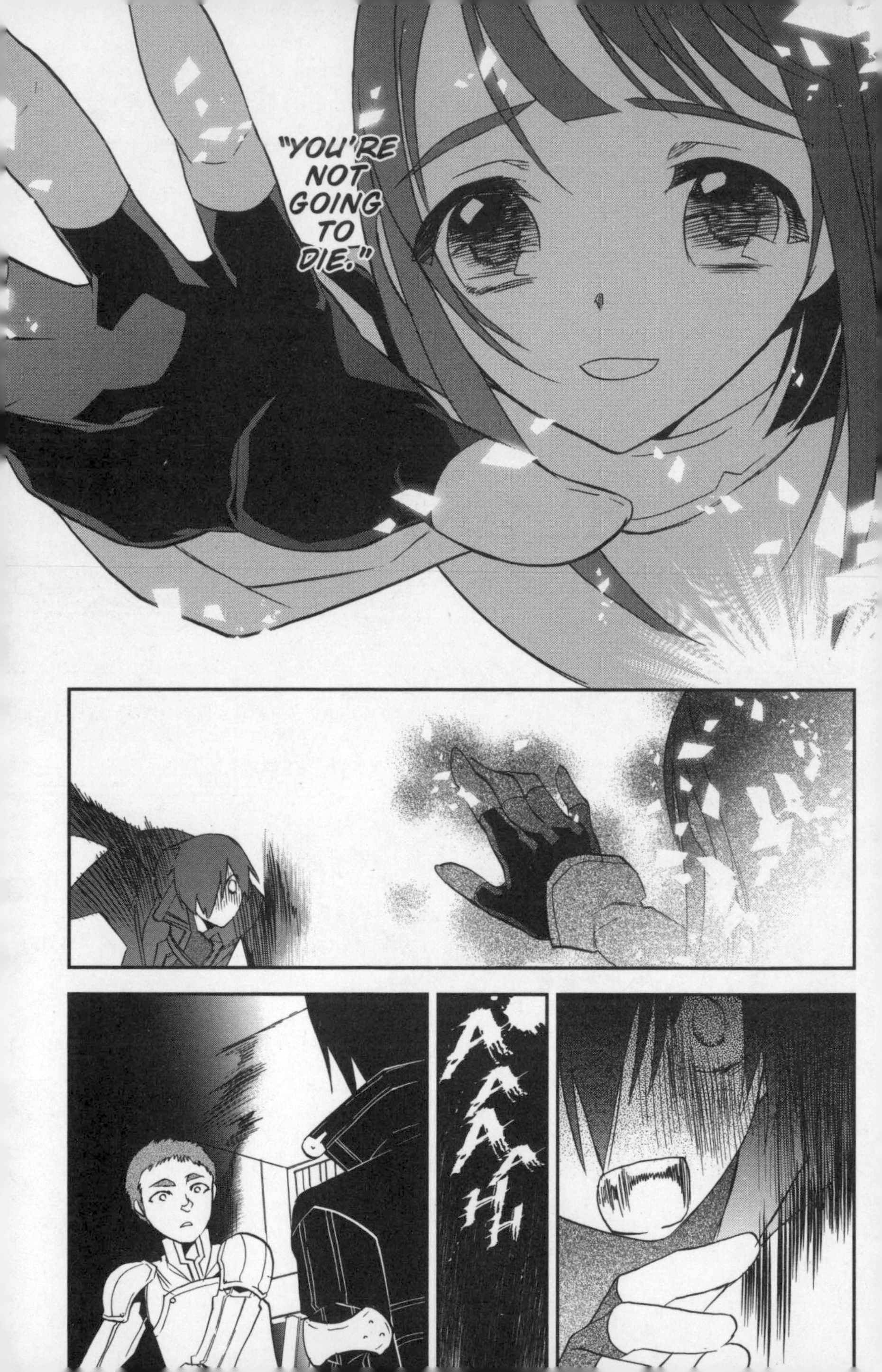
"YOU'RE NOT GOING TO DIE."
AAAAHH

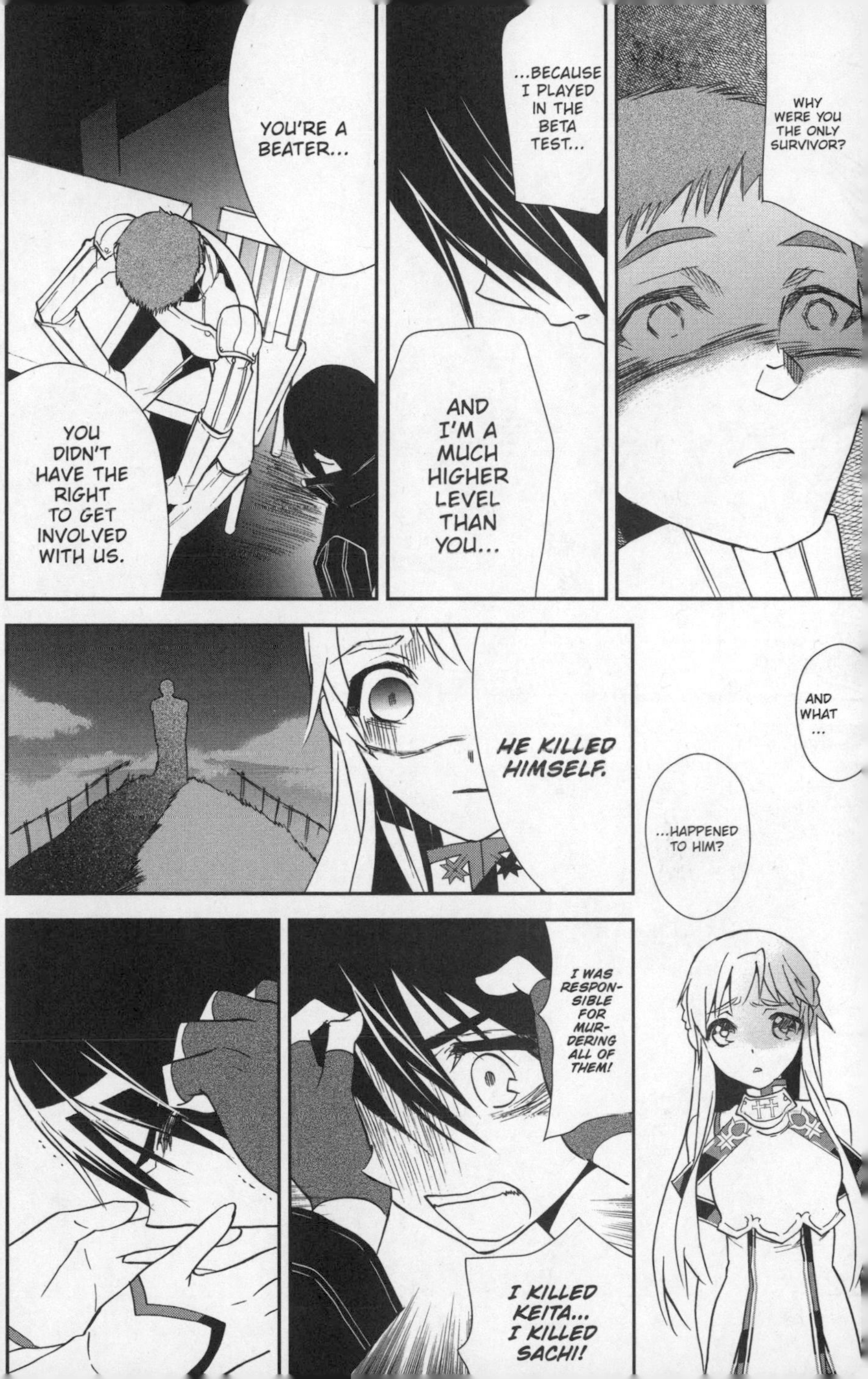
WHY WERE YOU THE ONLY SURVIVOR?
...BECAUSE I PLAYED IN THE BETA TEST...
AND I'M A MUCH HIGHER LEVEL THAN YOU...
YOU'RE A BEATER...
YOU DIDN'T HAVE THE RIGHT TO GET INVOLVED WITH US.
AND WHAT...
...HAPPENED TO HIM?
HE KILLED HIMSELF.
I WAS RESPONSIBLE FOR MURDERING ALL OF THEM!
I KILLED KEITA... I KILLED SACHI!

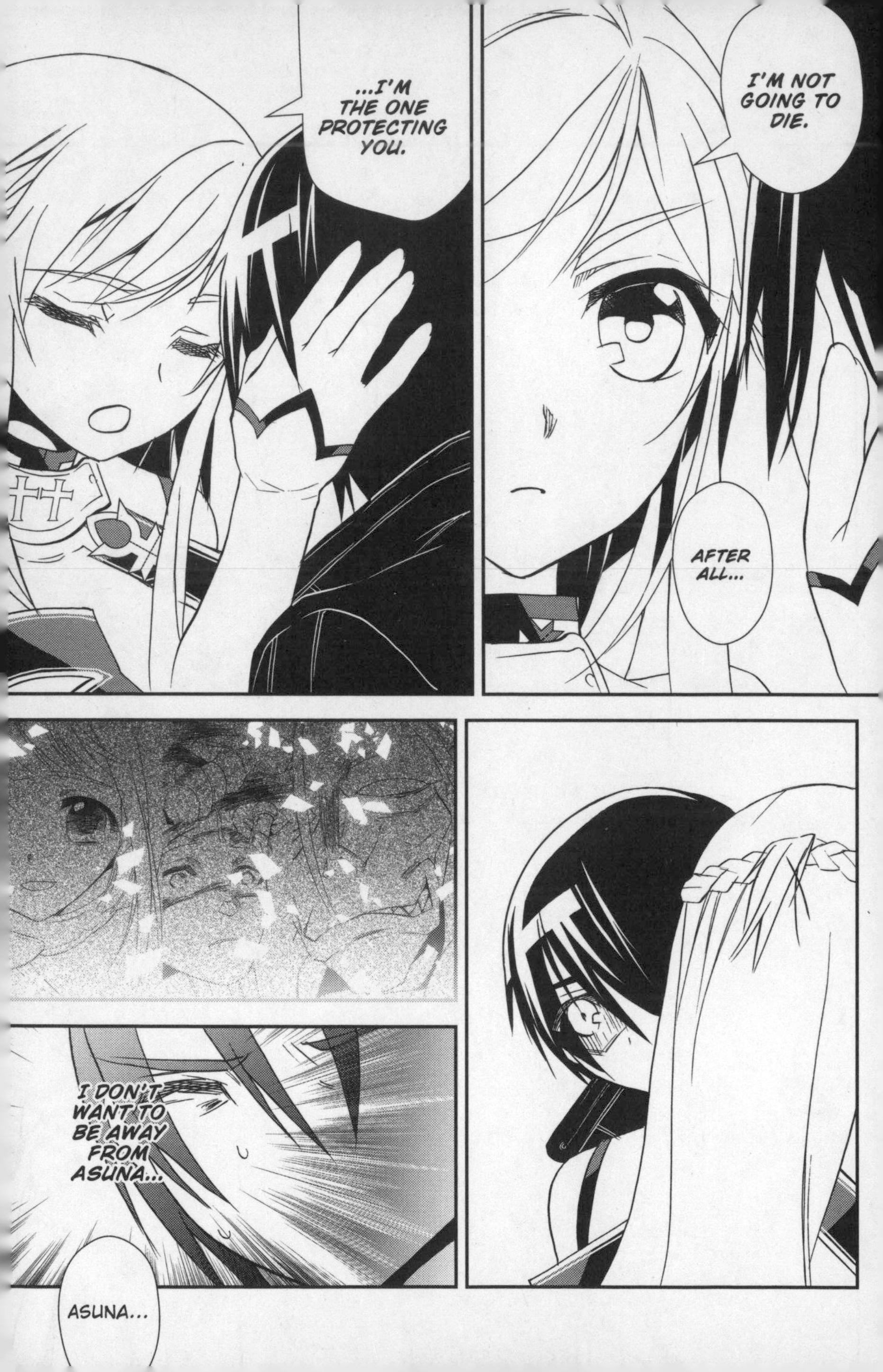
I'M NOT GOING TO DIE.
AFTER ALL...
...I'M THE ONE PROTECTING YOU.
I DON'T WANT TO BE AWAY FROM ASUNA...
ASUNA...

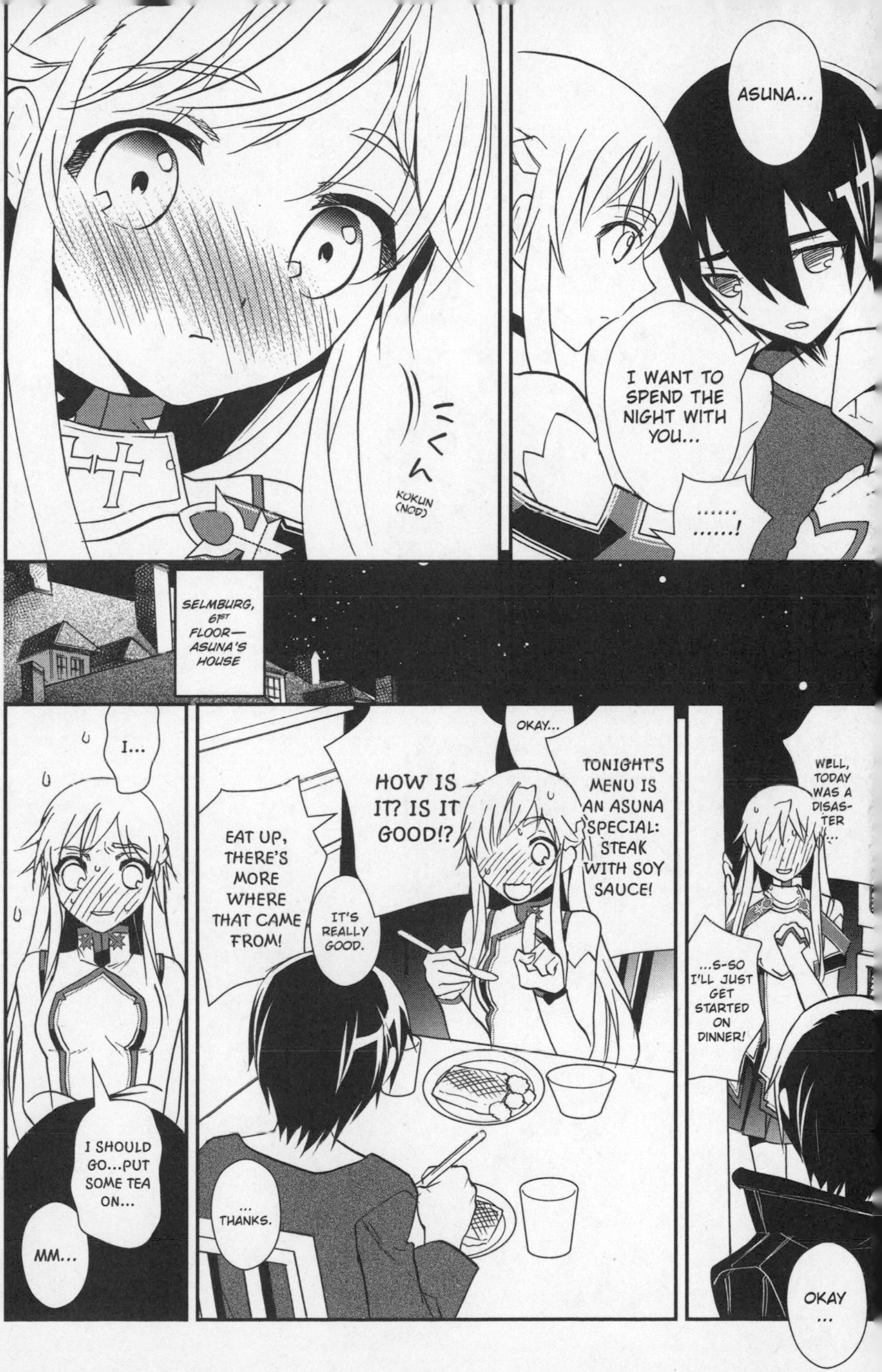
ASUNA...
I WANT TO SPEND THE NIGHT WITH YOU...
......
......!
こくん
KOKUN (NOD)
SELMBURG, 61ST FLOOR—ASUNA'S HOUSE
WELL, TODAY WAS A DISASTER...
...S-SO I'LL JUST GET STARTED ON DINNER!
OKAY...
OKAY...
TONIGHT'S MENU IS AN ASUNA SPECIAL: STEAK WITH SOY SAUCE!
HOW IS IT? IS IT GOOD!?
IT'S REALLY GOOD.
EAT UP, THERE'S MORE WHERE THAT CAME FROM!
...THANKS.
I...
I SHOULD GO...PUT SOME TEA ON...
MM...

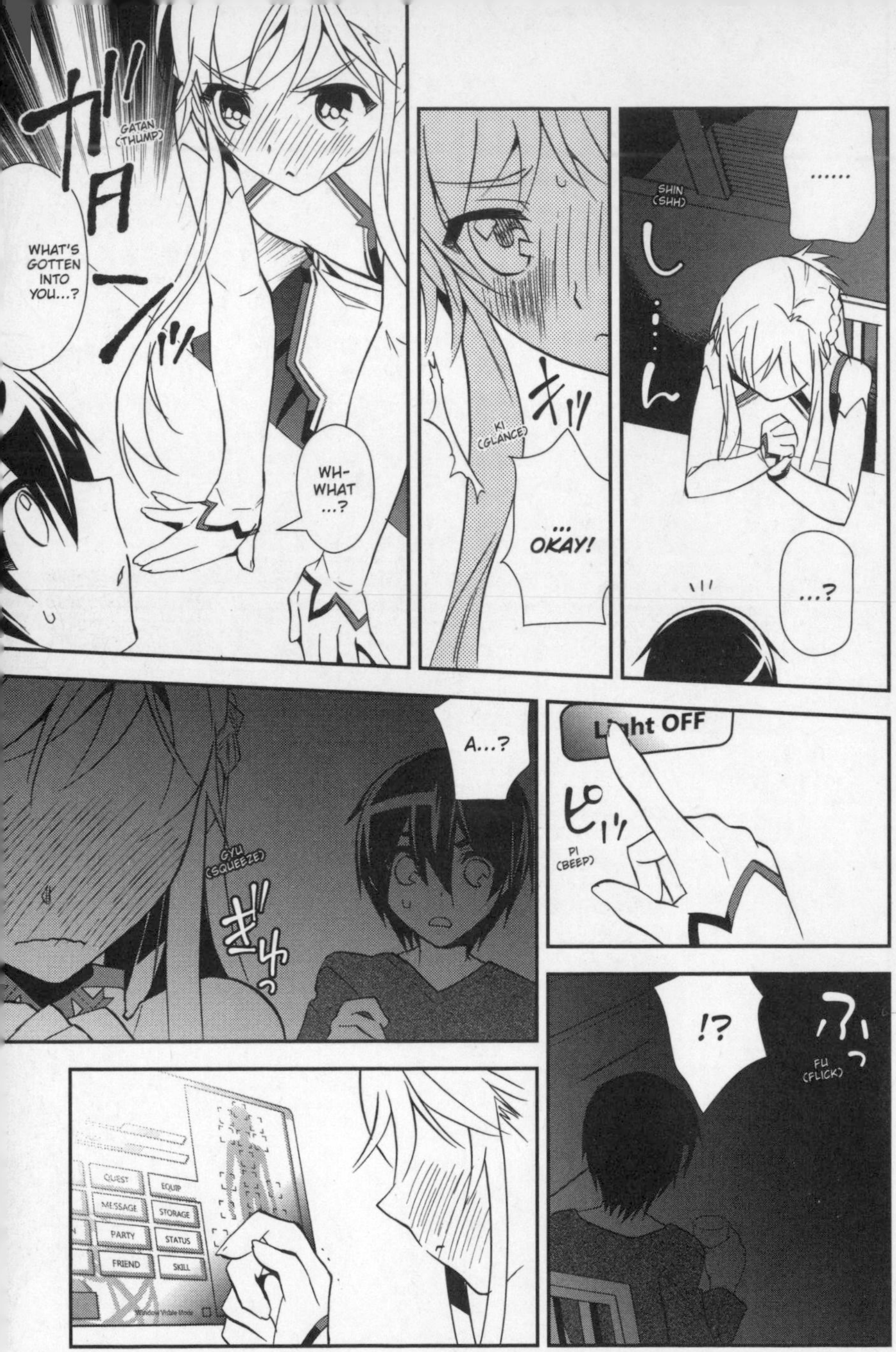

......
SHIN (SHH)
...?
KI (GLANCE)
...OKAY!
GATAN (THUMP)
WH-WHAT ...?
WHAT'S GOTTEN INTO YOU...?
Light OFF
PI (BEEP)
A...?
GYU (SQUEEZE)
FU (FLICK)
!?
QUEST
EQUIP
MESSAGE
STORAGE
PARTY
STATUS
FRIEND
SKILL

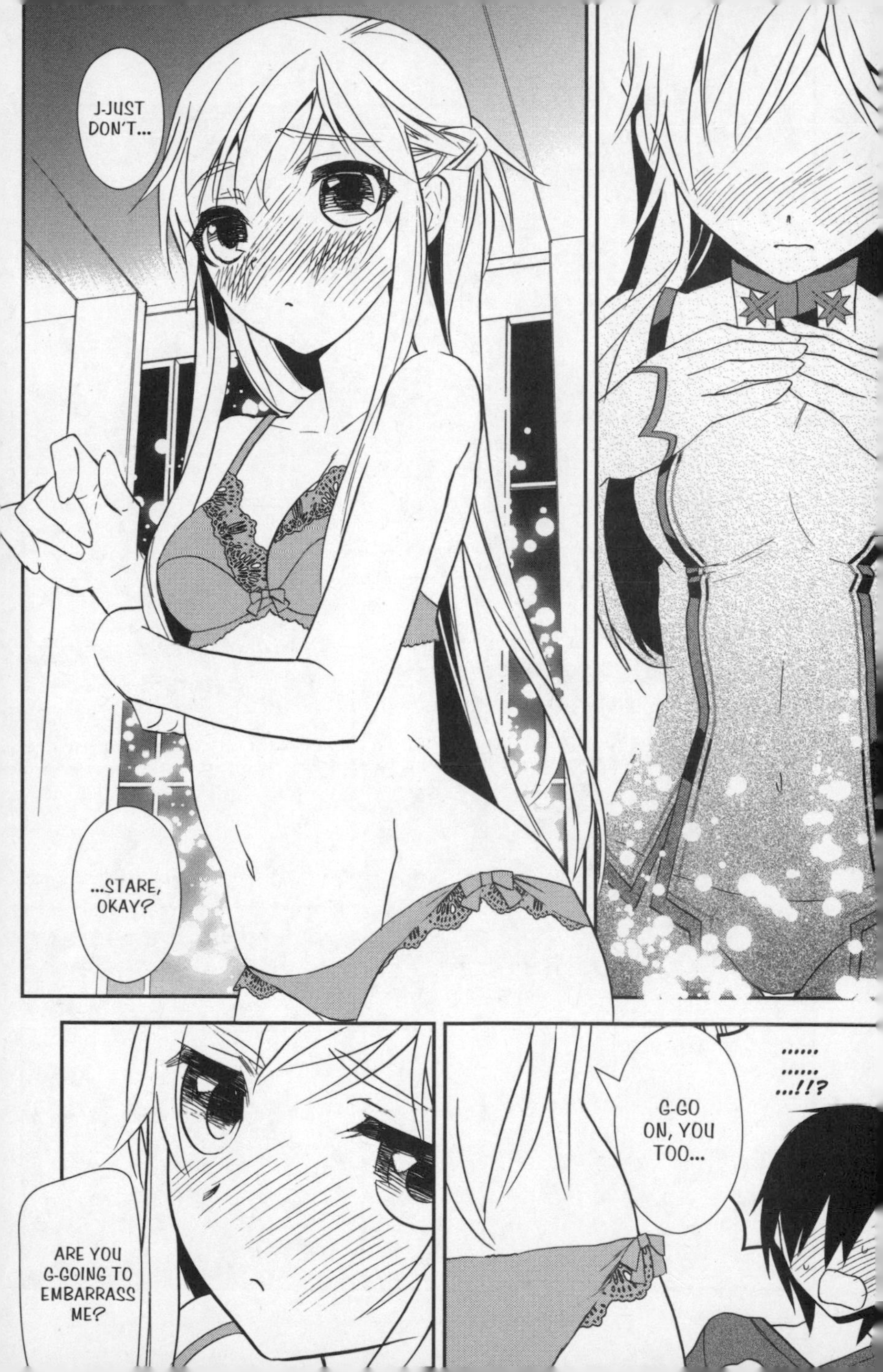
J-JUST DON'T...
...STARE, OKAY?
......
......
...!!?
G-GO ON, YOU TOO...
ARE YOU G-GOING TO EMBARRASS ME?

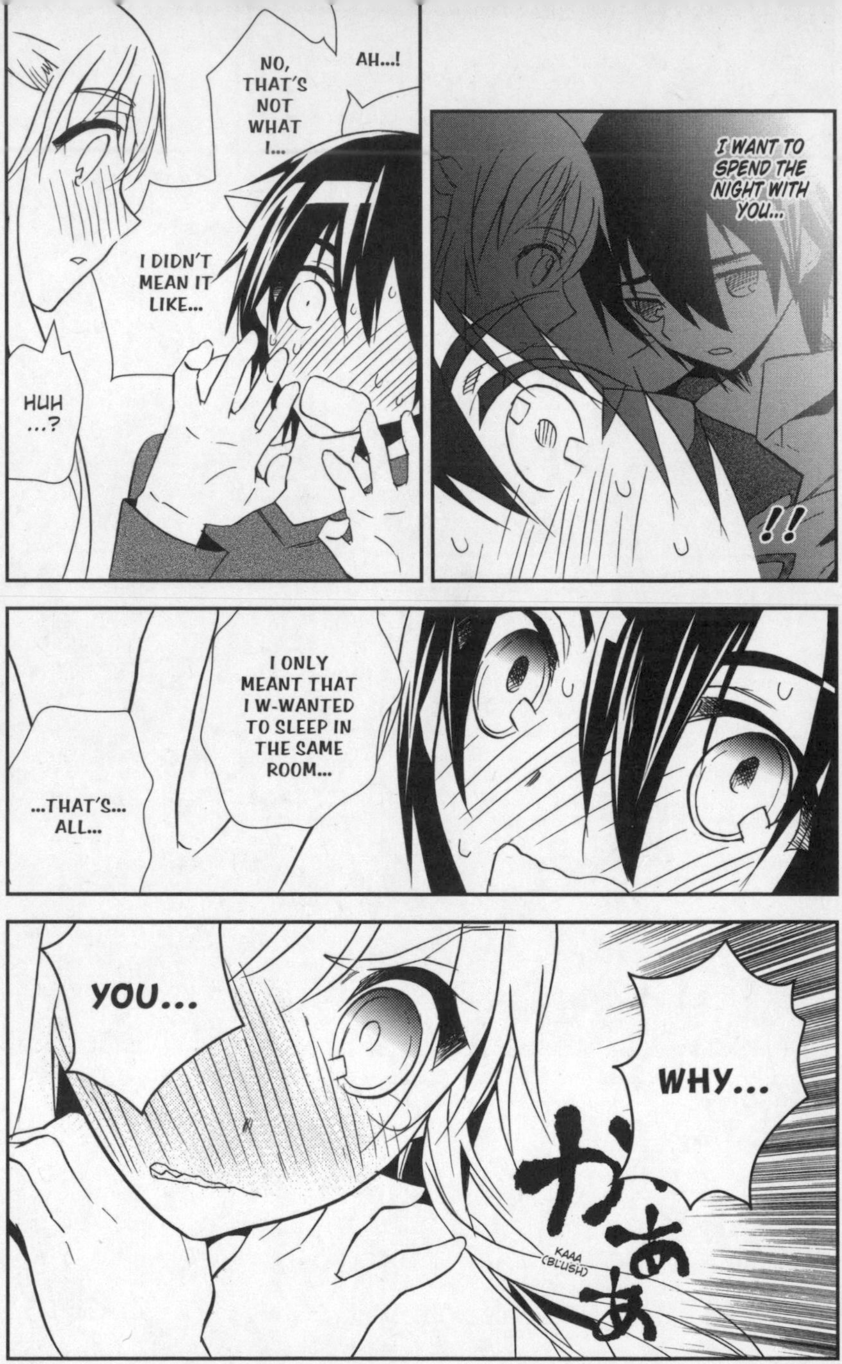
I WANT TO SPEND THE NIGHT WITH YOU...
!!
AH...!
NO, THAT'S NOT WHAT I...
I DIDN'T MEAN IT LIKE...
HUH ...?
I ONLY MEANT THAT I W-WANTED TO SLEEP IN THE SAME ROOM...
...THAT'S... ALL...
WHY...
YOU...
かぁぁ
KAAA (BLUSH)

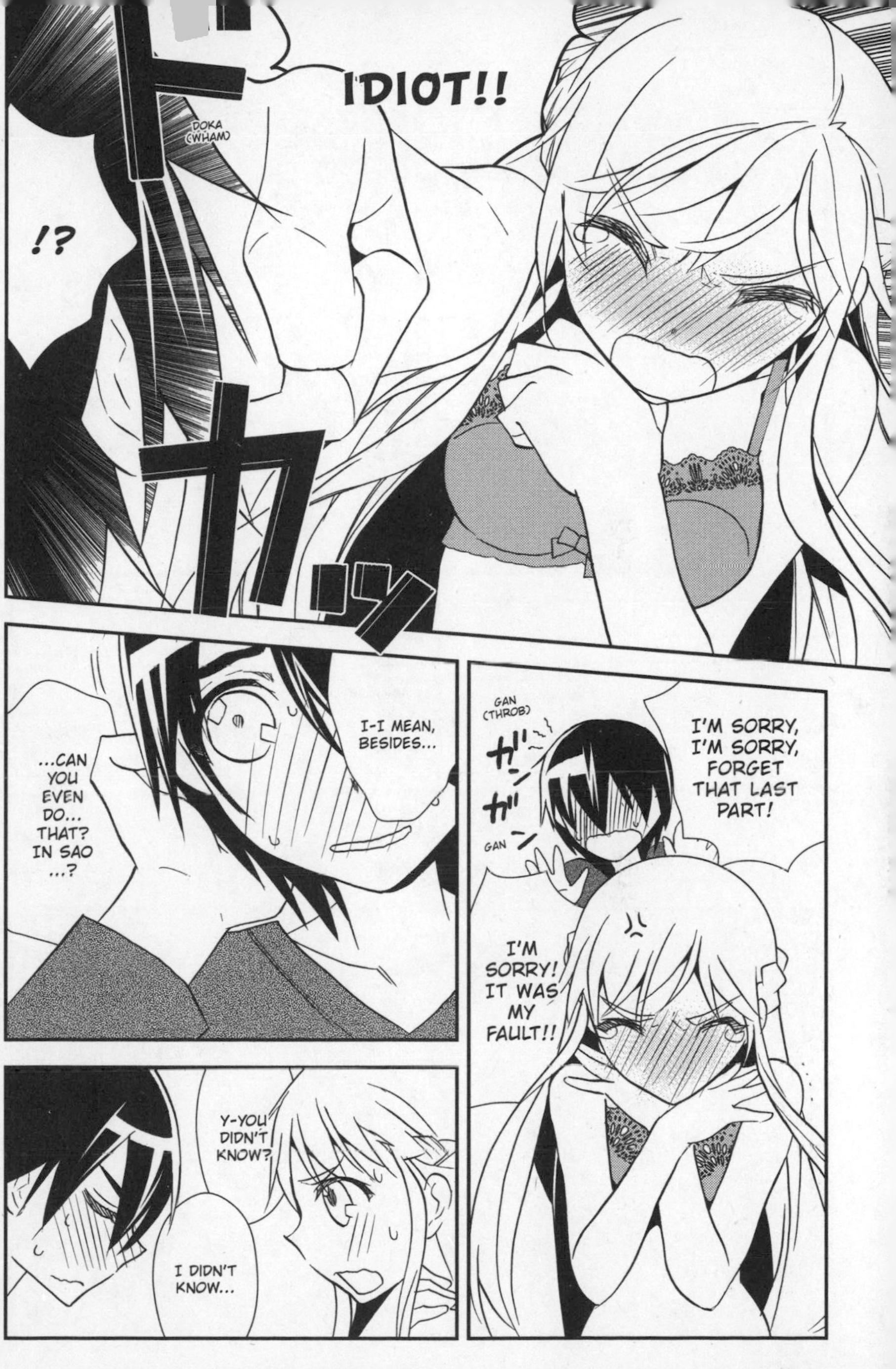

IDIOT!!
DOKA (WHAM)
!?
GAN (THROB)
I'M SORRY, I'M SORRY, FORGET THAT LAST PART!
GAN
I'M SORRY! IT WAS MY FAULT!!
I-I MEAN, BESIDES...
...CAN YOU EVEN DO... THAT? IN SAO ...?
Y-YOU DIDN'T KNOW?
I DIDN'T KNOW...

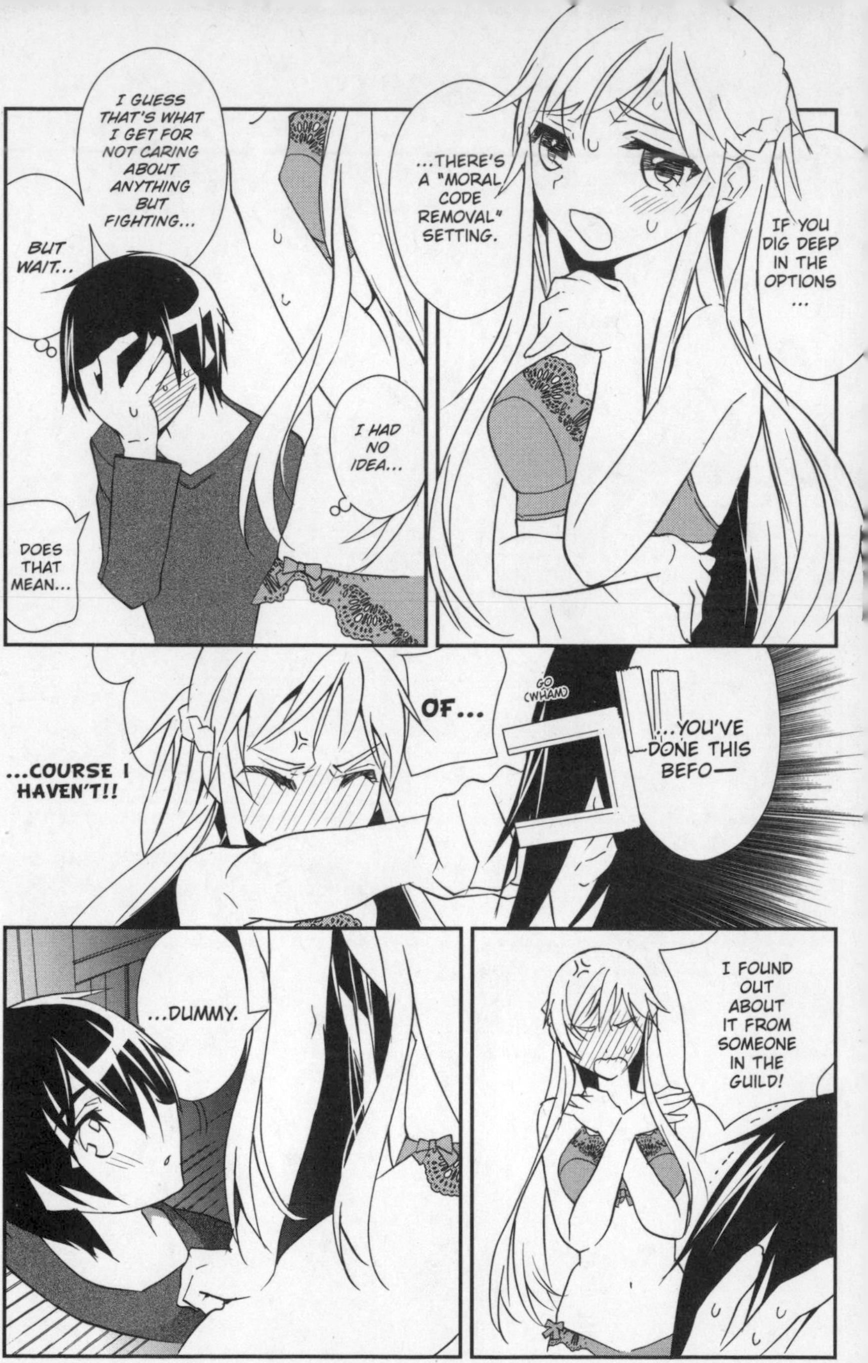
IF YOU DIG DEEP IN THE OPTIONS ...
...THERE'S A "MORAL CODE REMOVAL" SETTING.
I HAD NO IDEA...
I GUESS THAT'S WHAT I GET FOR NOT CARING ABOUT ANYTHING BUT FIGHTING...
BUT WAIT...
DOES THAT MEAN...
GO (WHAM)
...YOU'VE DONE THIS BEFO—
OF...
...COURSE I HAVEN'T!!
I FOUND OUT ABOUT IT FROM SOMEONE IN THE GUILD!
...DUMMY.

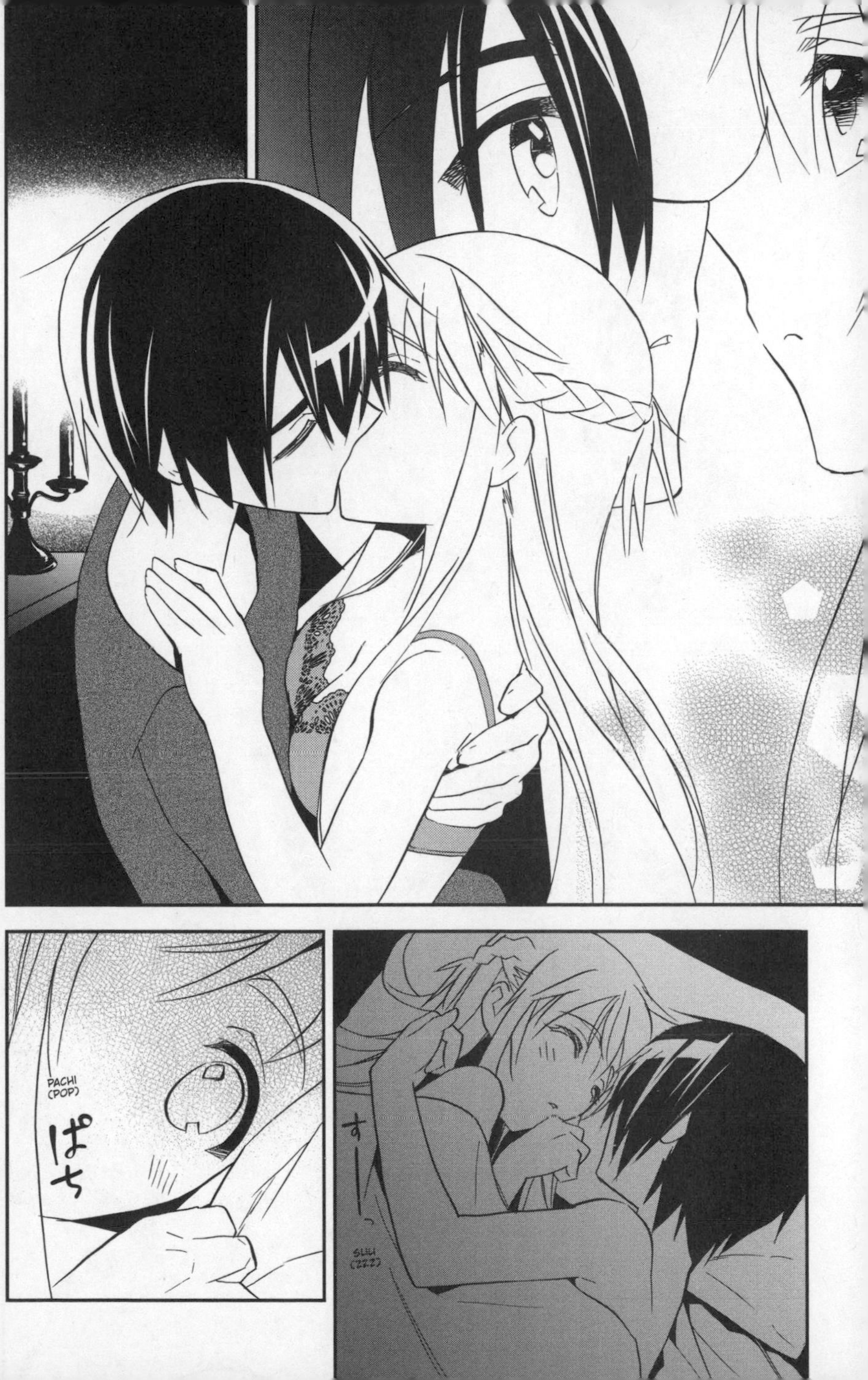
すー
SUU
(ZZZ)
PACHI
(POP)
ぱち

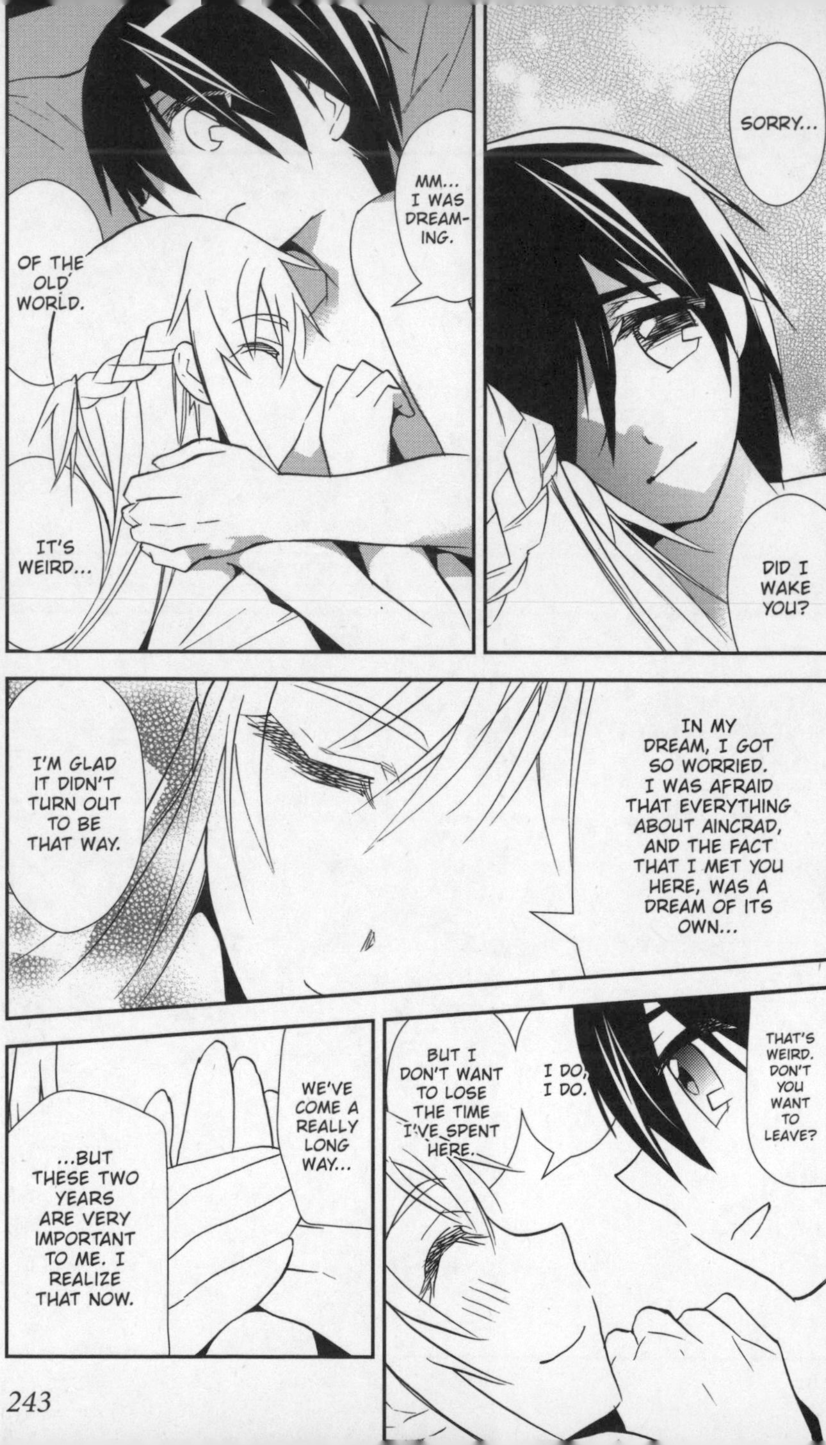
SORRY...
DID I WAKE YOU?
MM... I WAS DREAMING.
OF THE OLD WORLD.
IT'S WEIRD...
IN MY DREAM, I GOT SO WORRIED. I WAS AFRAID THAT EVERYTHING ABOUT AINCRAD, AND THE FACT THAT I MET YOU HERE, WAS A DREAM OF ITS OWN...
I'M GLAD IT DIDN'T TURN OUT TO BE THAT WAY.
THAT'S WEIRD. DON'T YOU WANT TO LEAVE?
I DO, I DO.
BUT I DON'T WANT TO LOSE THE TIME I'VE SPENT HERE.
WE'VE COME A REALLY LONG WAY...
...BUT THESE TWO YEARS ARE VERY IMPORTANT TO ME. I REALIZE THAT NOW.

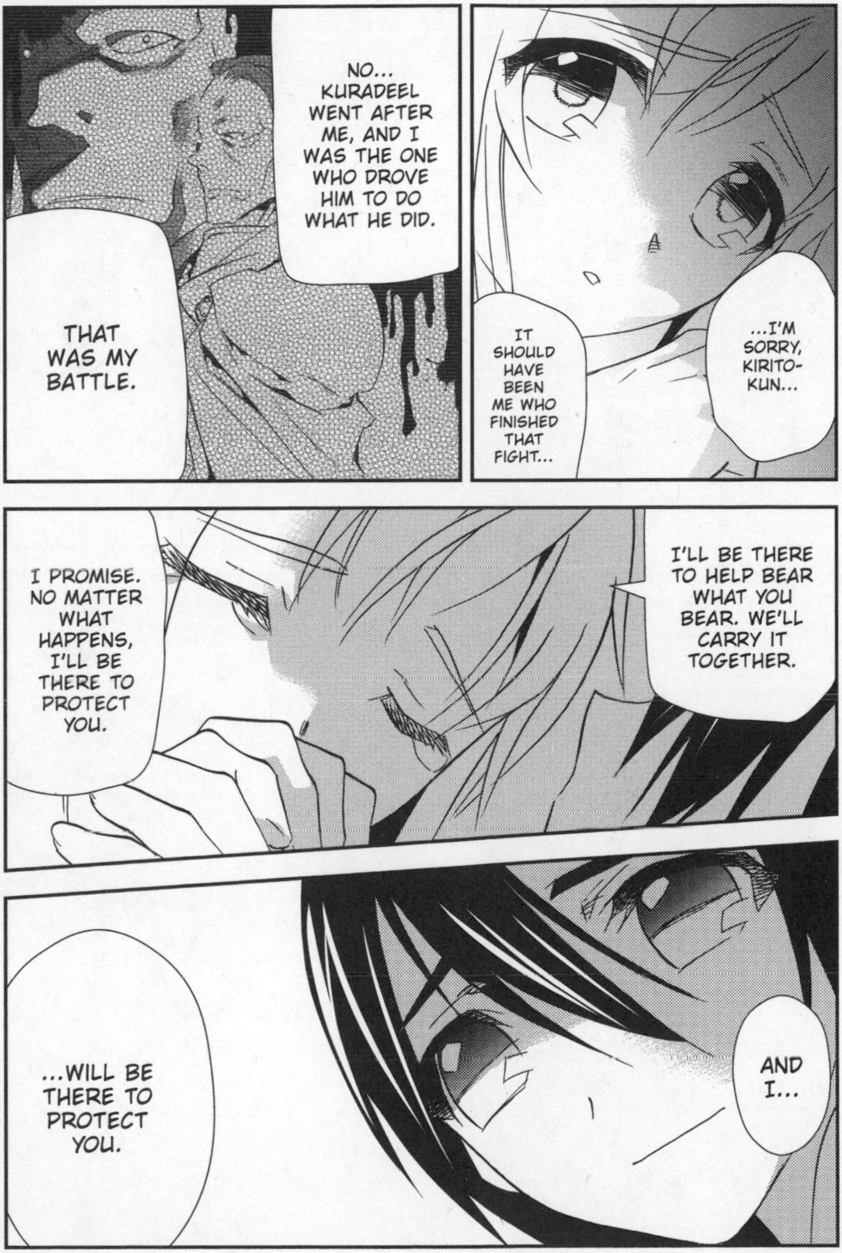
...I'M SORRY, KIRITO-KUN...
IT SHOULD HAVE BEEN ME WHO FINISHED THAT FIGHT...
NO... KURADEEL WENT AFTER ME, AND I WAS THE ONE WHO DROVE HIM TO DO WHAT HE DID.
THAT WAS MY BATTLE.
I'LL BE THERE TO HELP BEAR WHAT YOU BEAR. WE'LL CARRY IT TOGETHER.
I PROMISE. NO MATTER WHAT HAPPENS, I'LL BE THERE TO PROTECT YOU.
AND I...
...WILL BE THERE TO PROTECT YOU.

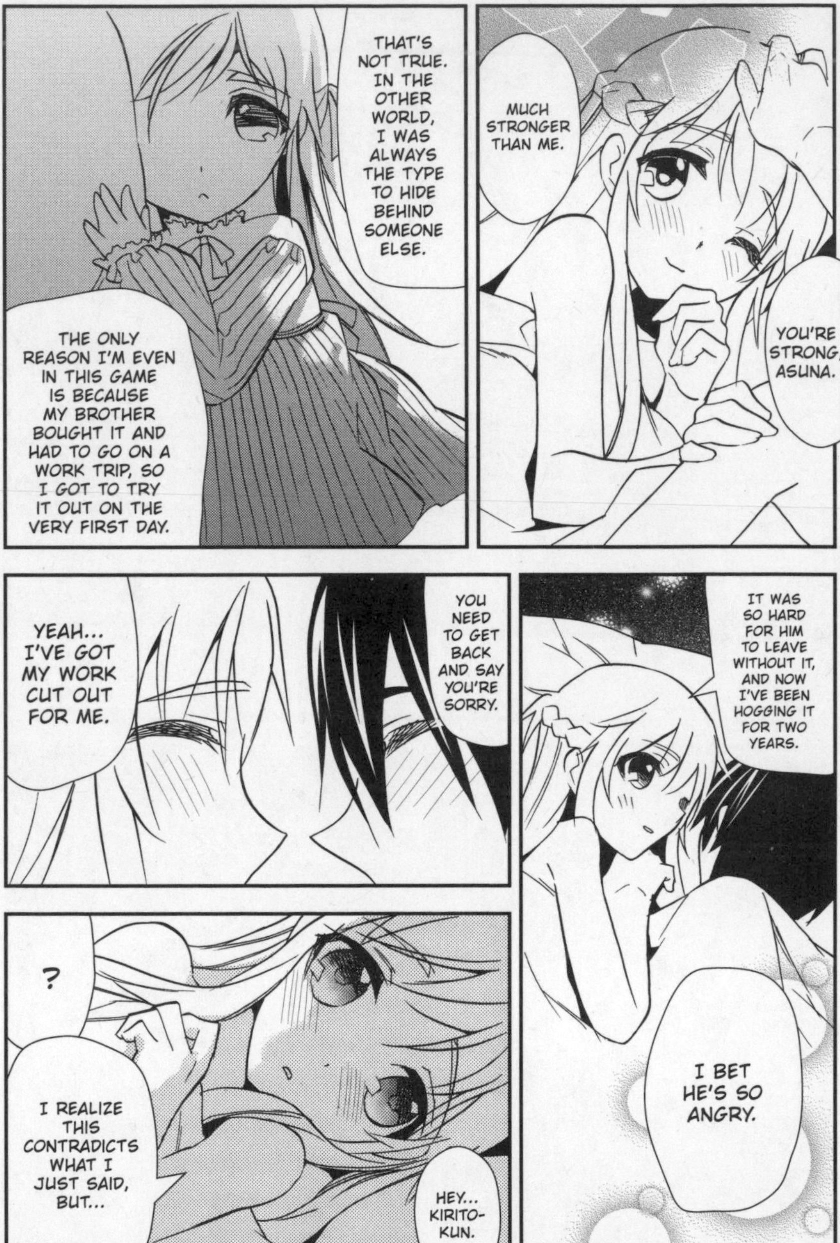
YOU'RE STRONG, ASUNA.
MUCH STRONGER THAN ME.
THAT'S NOT TRUE. IN THE OTHER WORLD, I WAS ALWAYS THE TYPE TO HIDE BEHIND SOMEONE ELSE.
THE ONLY REASON I'M EVEN IN THIS GAME IS BECAUSE MY BROTHER BOUGHT IT AND HAD TO GO ON A WORK TRIP, SO I GOT TO TRY IT OUT ON THE VERY FIRST DAY.
IT WAS SO HARD FOR HIM TO LEAVE WITHOUT IT, AND NOW I'VE BEEN HOGGING IT FOR TWO YEARS.
I BET HE'S SO ANGRY.
YOU NEED TO GET BACK AND SAY YOU'RE SORRY.
YEAH... I'VE GOT MY WORK CUT OUT FOR ME.
HEY... KIRITO-KUN.
?
I REALIZE THIS CONTRADICTS WHAT I JUST SAID, BUT...

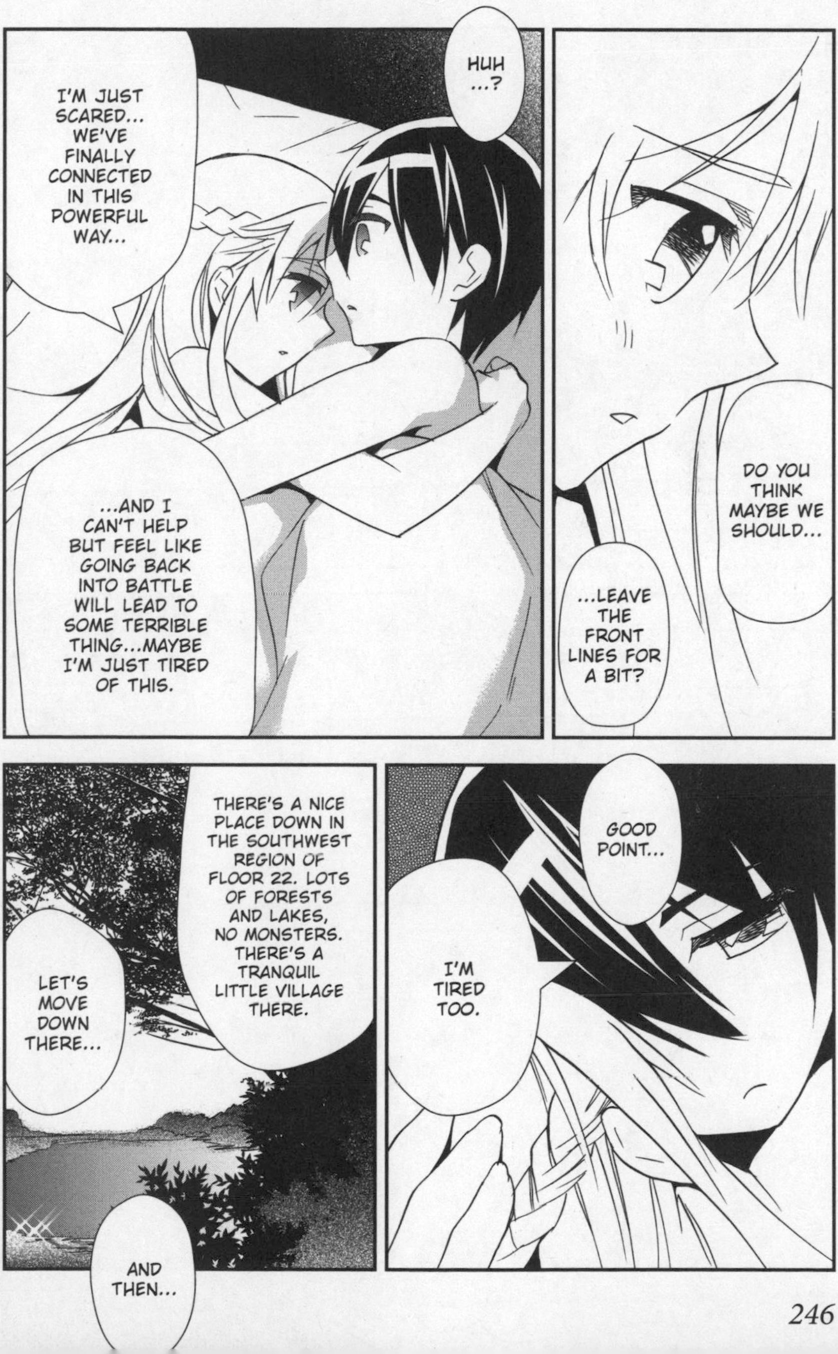
DO YOU THINK MAYBE WE SHOULD...
...LEAVE THE FRONT LINES FOR A BIT?
HUH ...?
I'M JUST SCARED... WE'VE FINALLY CONNECTED IN THIS POWERFUL WAY...
...AND I CAN'T HELP BUT FEEL LIKE GOING BACK INTO BATTLE WILL LEAD TO SOME TERRIBLE THING...MAYBE I'M JUST TIRED OF THIS.
GOOD POINT...
I'M TIRED TOO.
THERE'S A NICE PLACE DOWN IN THE SOUTHWEST REGION OF FLOOR 22. LOTS OF FORESTS AND LAKES, NO MONSTERS. THERE'S A TRANQUIL LITTLE VILLAGE THERE.
LET'S MOVE DOWN THERE...
AND THEN...

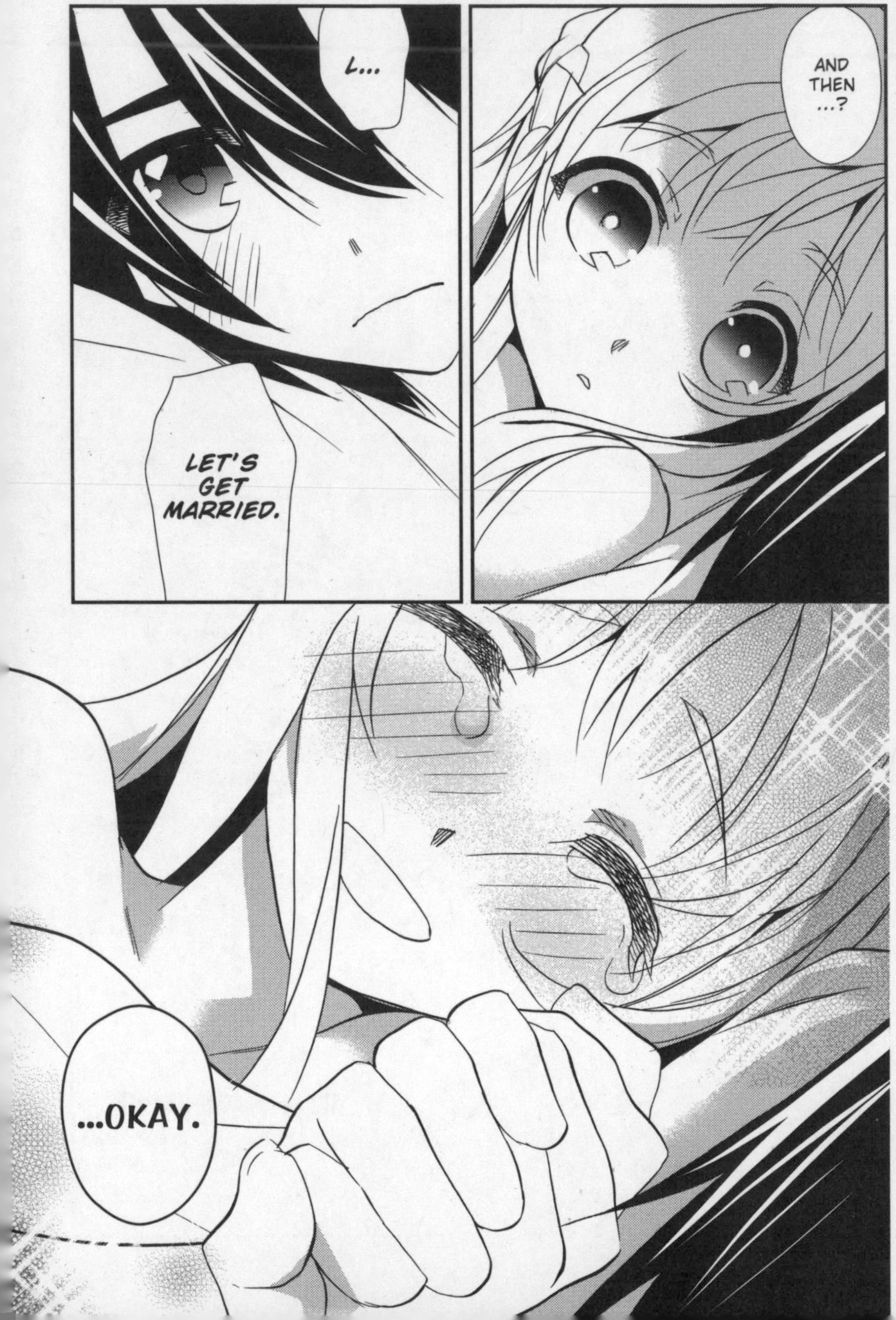
AND THEN ...?
I...
LET'S GET MARRIED.
...OKAY.

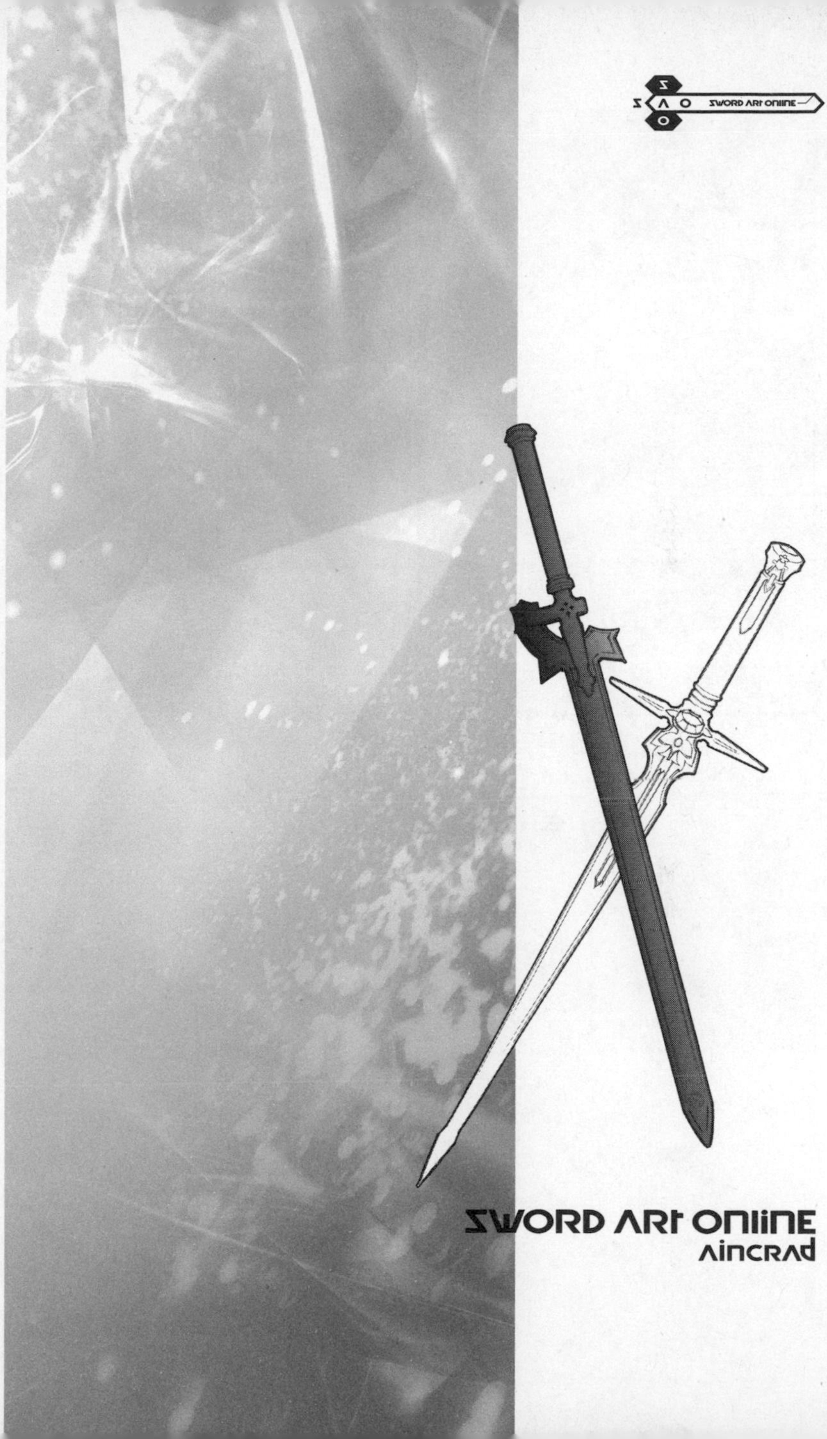

SWORD ART ONLINE

AINCRAD

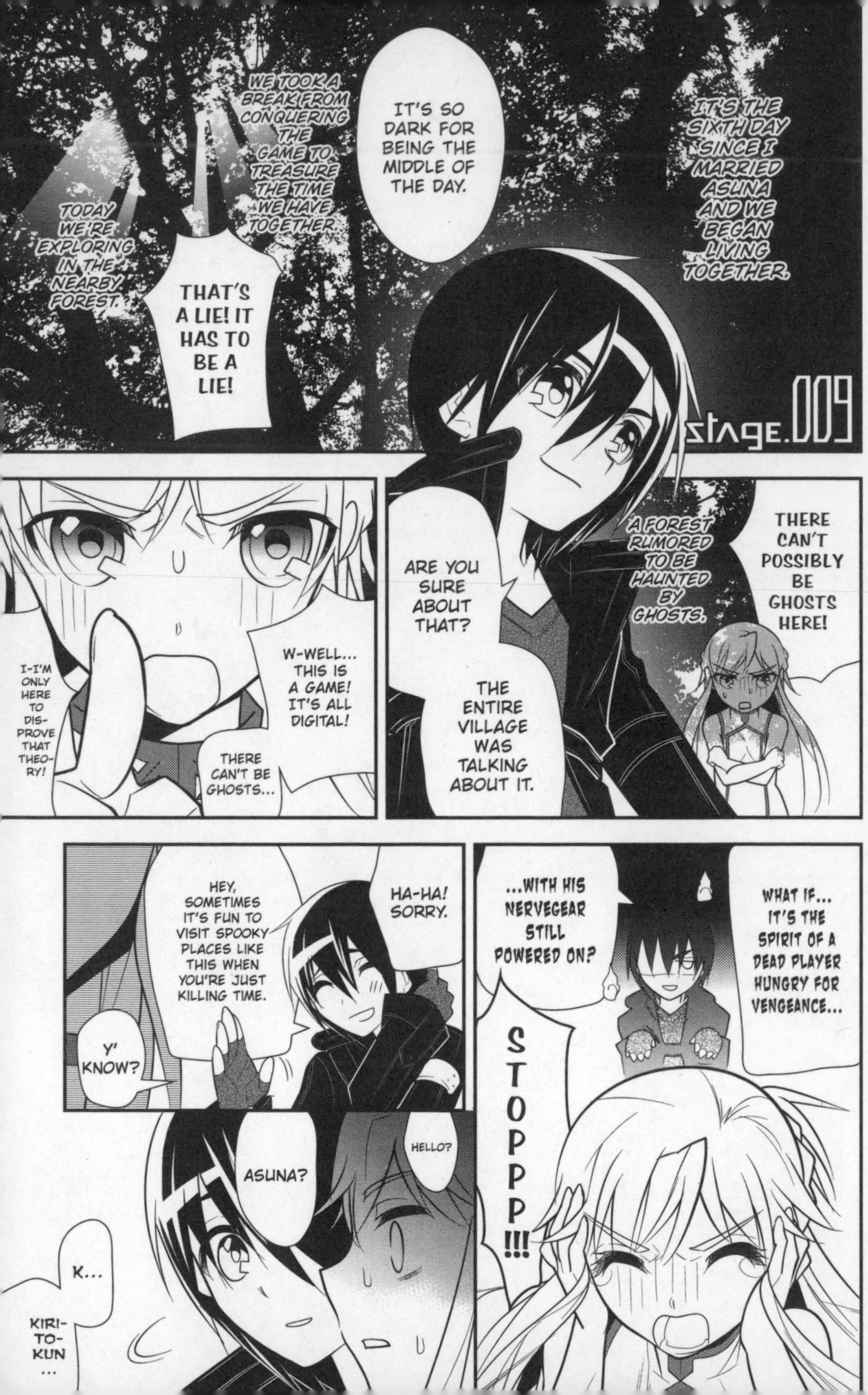
IT'S THE SIXTH DAY SINCE I MARRIED ASUNA AND WE BEGAN LIVING TOGETHER.
stage.009
IT'S SO DARK FOR BEING THE MIDDLE OF THE DAY.
WE TOOK A BREAK FROM CONQUERING THE GAME TO TREASURE THE TIME WE HAVE TOGETHER.
TODAY WE'RE EXPLORING IN THE NEARBY FOREST.
THAT'S A LIE! IT HAS TO BE A LIE!
THERE CAN'T POSSIBLY BE GHOSTS HERE!
A FOREST RUMORED TO BE HAUNTED BY GHOSTS.
ARE YOU SURE ABOUT THAT?
THE ENTIRE VILLAGE WAS TALKING ABOUT IT.
W-WELL... THIS IS A GAME! IT'S ALL DIGITAL!
THERE CAN'T BE GHOSTS...
I-I'M ONLY HERE TO DIS-PROVE THAT THEORY!
WHAT IF... IT'S THE SPIRIT OF A DEAD PLAYER HUNGRY FOR VENGEANCE...
...WITH HIS NERVEGEAR STILL POWERED ON?
HA-HA! SORRY.
HEY, SOMETIMES IT'S FUN TO VISIT SPOOKY PLACES LIKE THIS WHEN YOU'RE JUST KILLING TIME.
Y' KNOW?
STOPPP!!!
HELLO?
ASUNA?
K...
KIRI-TO-KUN...

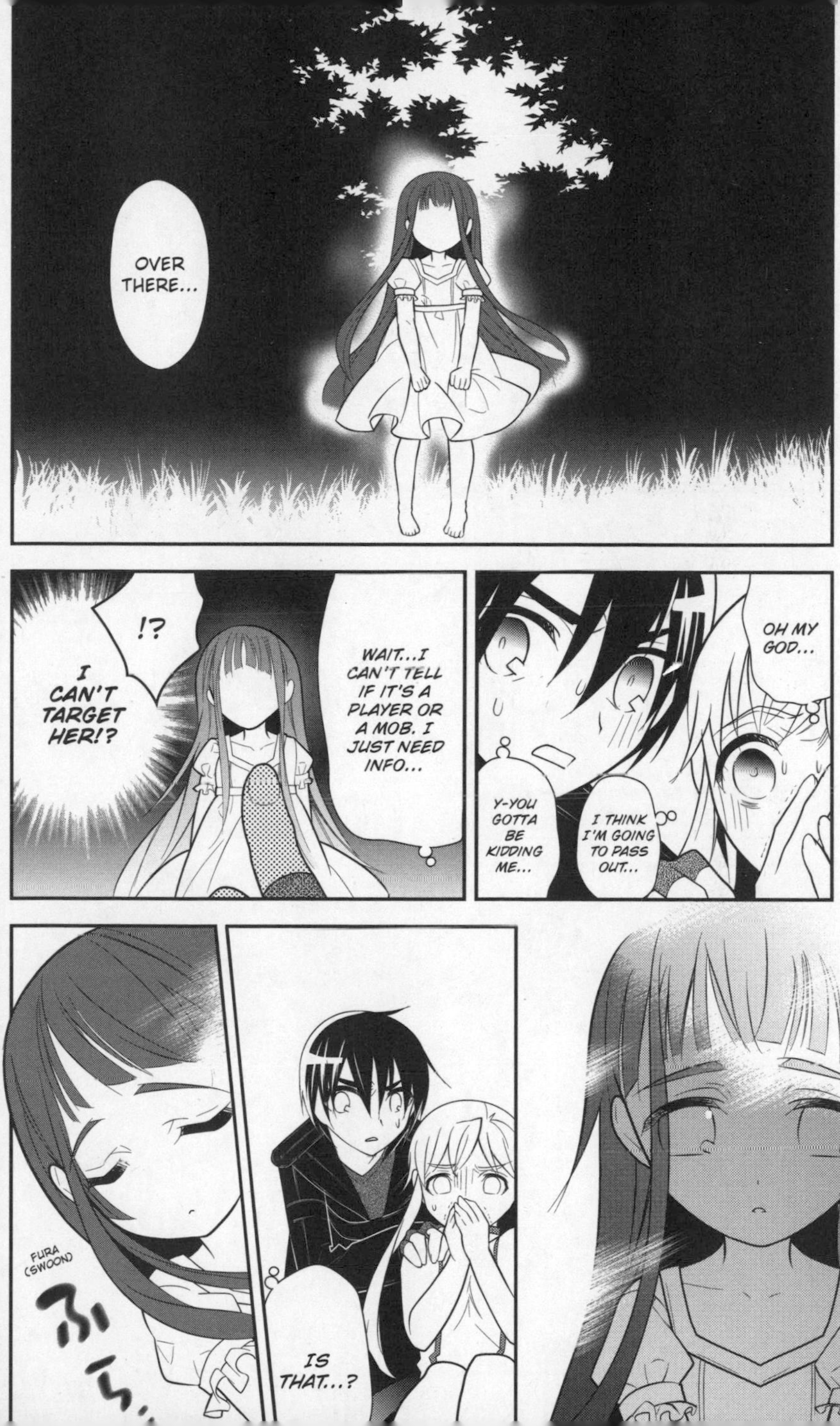
OVER THERE...
OH MY GOD...
I THINK I'M GOING TO PASS OUT...
Y-YOU GOTTA BE KIDDING ME...
WAIT...I CAN'T TELL IF IT'S A PLAYER OR A MOB. I JUST NEED INFO...
!?
I CAN'T TARGET HER!?
IS THAT...?
FURA (SWOON)
ふら

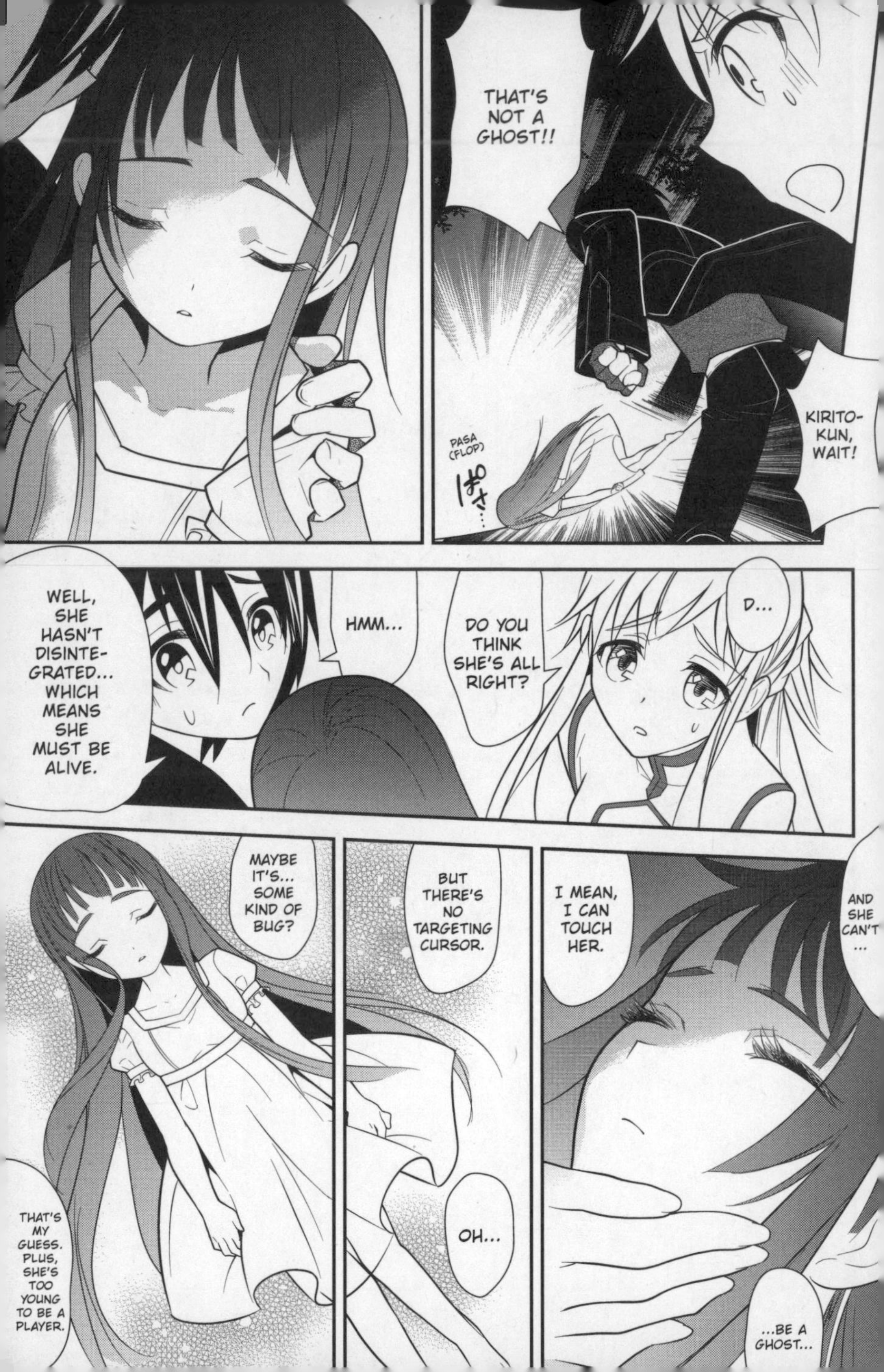
THAT'S NOT A GHOST!!
KIRITO-KUN, WAIT!
PASA (FLOP)
ぱさ…
D...
DO YOU THINK SHE'S ALL RIGHT?
HMM...
WELL, SHE HASN'T DISINTEGRATED... WHICH MEANS SHE MUST BE ALIVE.
AND SHE CAN'T ...
I MEAN, I CAN TOUCH HER.
...BE A GHOST...
BUT THERE'S NO TARGETING CURSOR.
OH...
MAYBE IT'S... SOME KIND OF BUG?
THAT'S MY GUESS. PLUS, SHE'S TOO YOUNG TO BE A PLAYER.

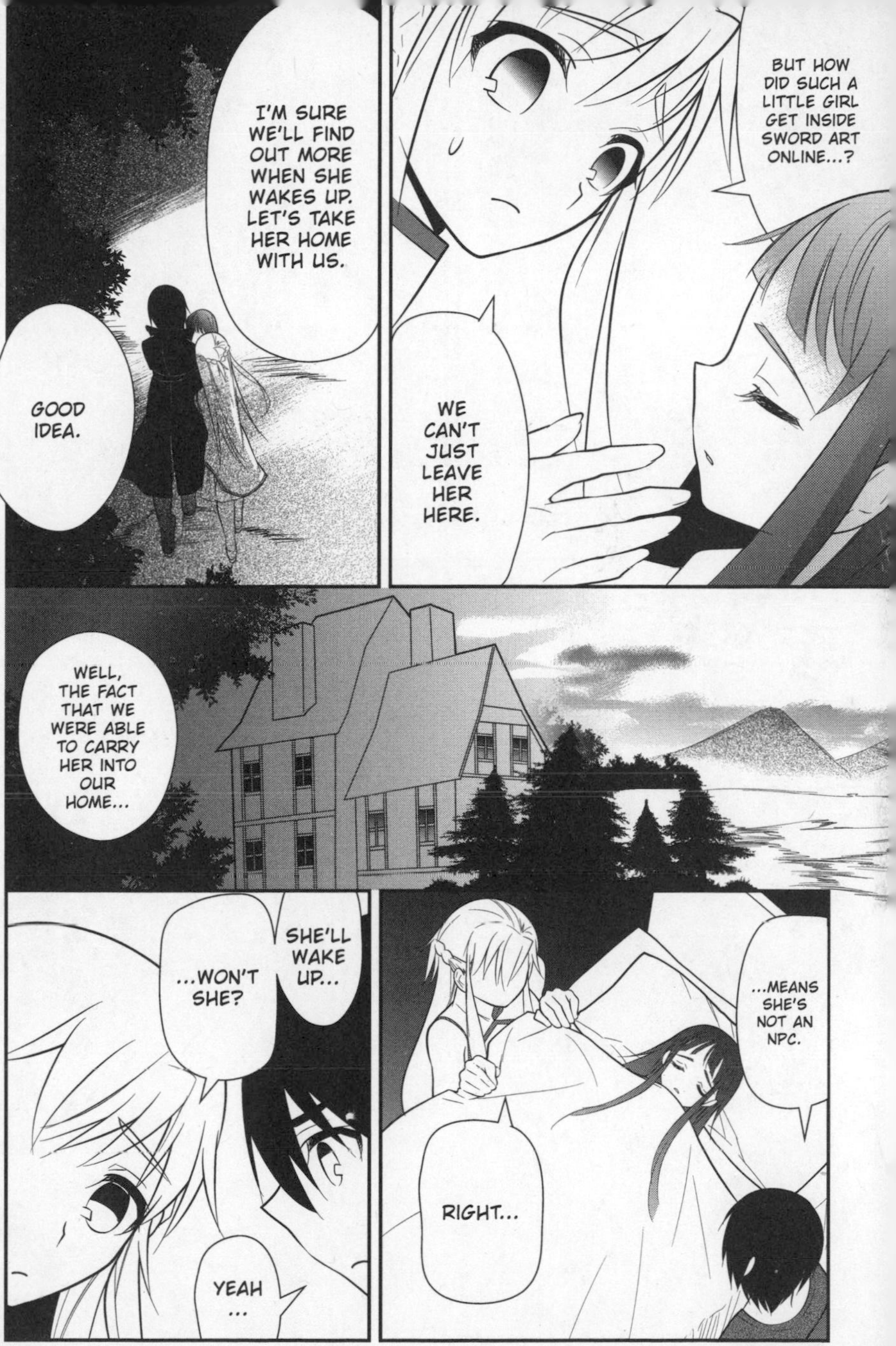
BUT HOW DID SUCH A LITTLE GIRL GET INSIDE SWORD ART ONLINE...?
WE CAN'T JUST LEAVE HER HERE.
I'M SURE WE'LL FIND OUT MORE WHEN SHE WAKES UP. LET'S TAKE HER HOME WITH US.
GOOD IDEA.
WELL, THE FACT THAT WE WERE ABLE TO CARRY HER INTO OUR HOME...
...MEANS SHE'S NOT AN NPC.
RIGHT...
SHE'LL WAKE UP...
...WON'T SHE?
YEAH ...

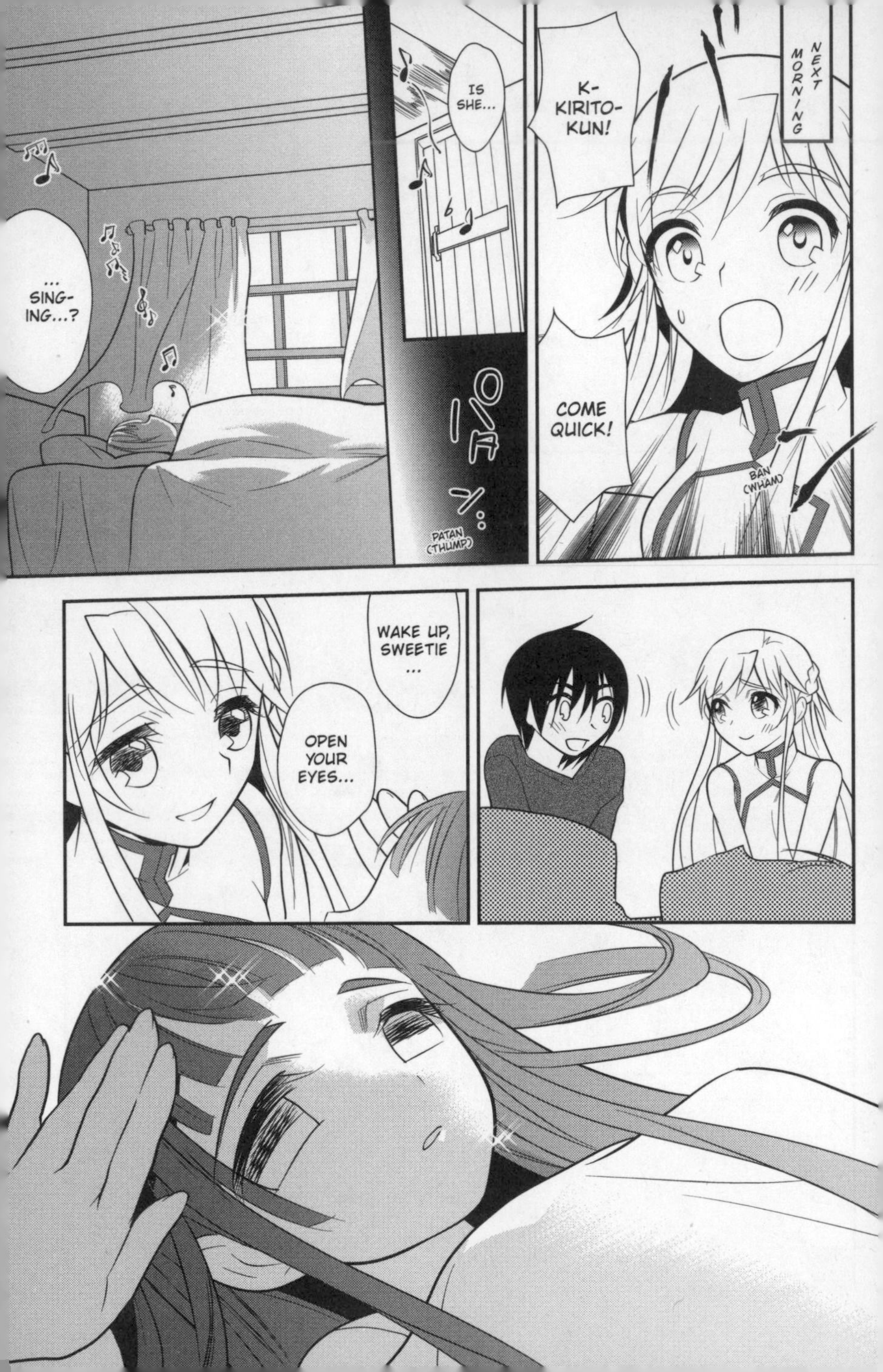
NEXT MORNING
K-KIRITO-KUN!
COME QUICK!
BAN (WHAM)
IS SHE...
PATAN (THUMP)
...SINGING...?
WAKE UP, SWEETIE...
OPEN YOUR EYES...

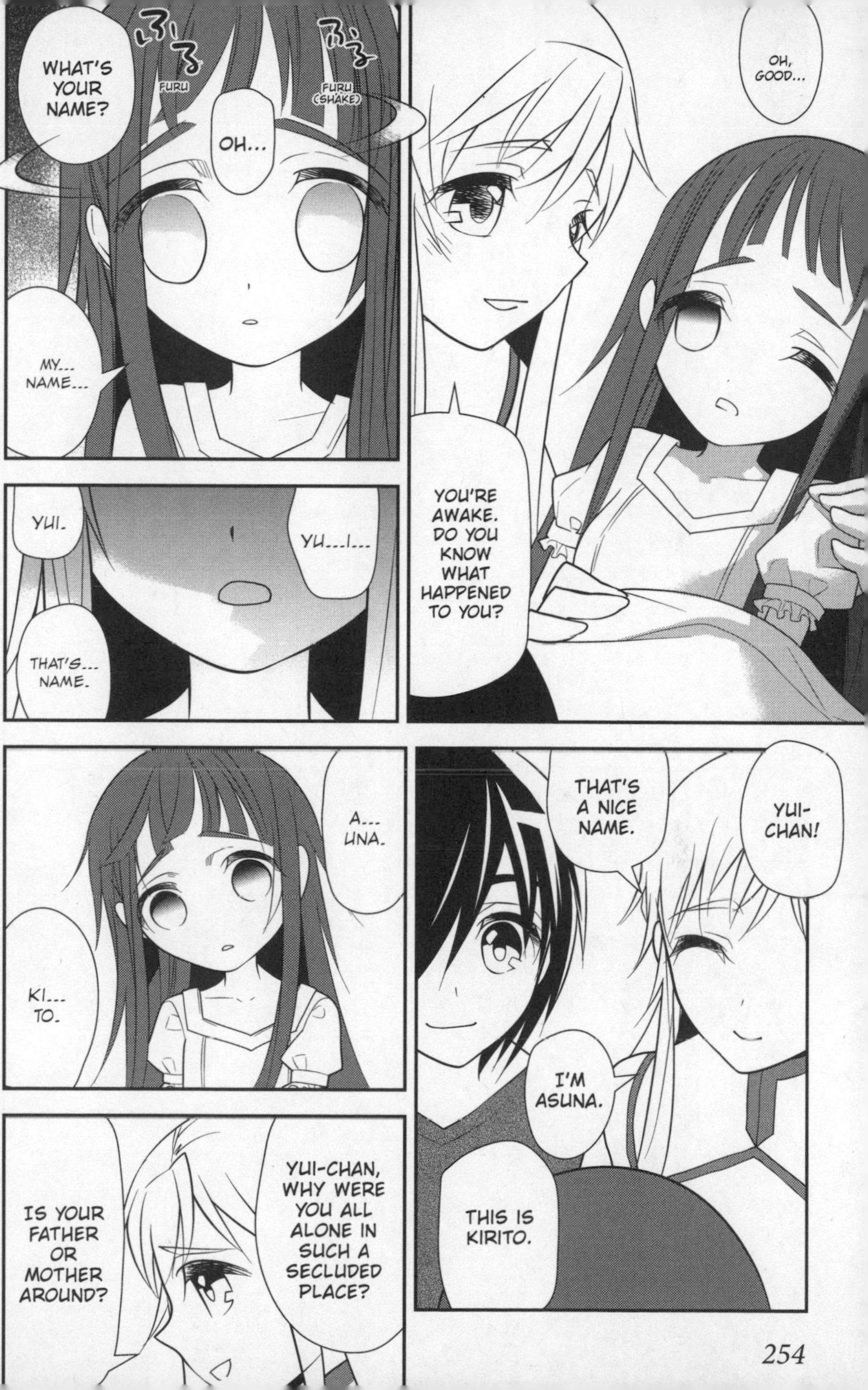
OH, GOOD...
YOU'RE AWAKE. DO YOU KNOW WHAT HAPPENED TO YOU?
ふる FURU (SHAKE)
ふる FURU
WHAT'S YOUR NAME?
OH...
MY... NAME...
YU...I...
YUI.
THAT'S... NAME.
YUI-CHAN!
THAT'S A NICE NAME.
I'M ASUNA.
THIS IS KIRITO.
A... UNA.
KI... TO.
YUI-CHAN, WHY WERE YOU ALL ALONE IN SUCH A SECLUDED PLACE?
IS YOUR FATHER OR MOTHER AROUND?

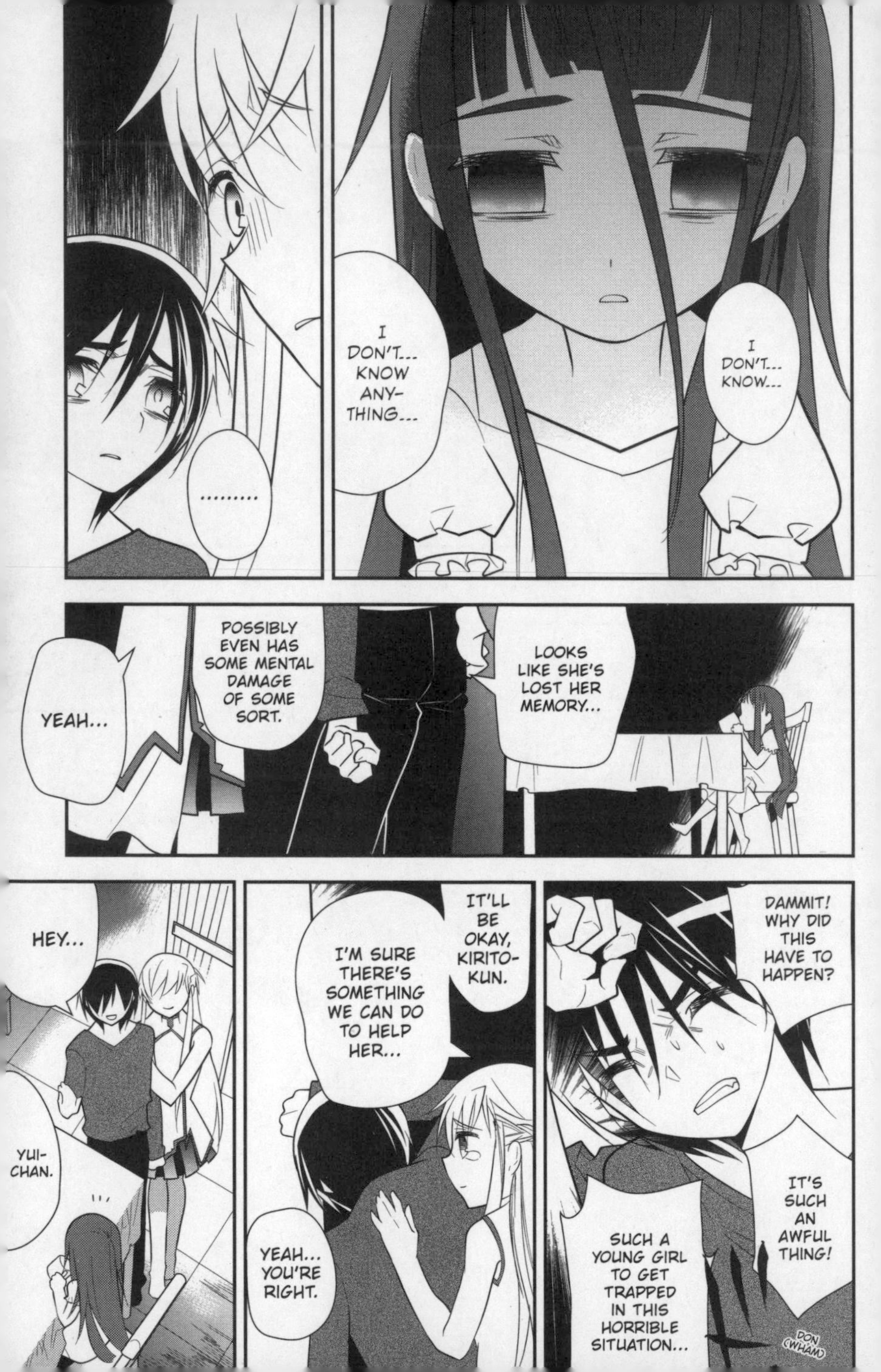
I DON'T... KNOW...
I DON'T... KNOW ANY-THING...
....
LOOKS LIKE SHE'S LOST HER MEMORY...
POSSIBLY EVEN HAS SOME MENTAL DAMAGE OF SOME SORT.
YEAH...
DAMMIT! WHY DID THIS HAVE TO HAPPEN?
IT'S SUCH AN AWFUL THING!
SUCH A YOUNG GIRL TO GET TRAPPED IN THIS HORRIBLE SITUATION...
DON (WHAM)
IT'LL BE OKAY, KIRITO-KUN.
I'M SURE THERE'S SOMETHING WE CAN DO TO HELP HER...
YEAH... YOU'RE RIGHT.
HEY...
YUI-CHAN.

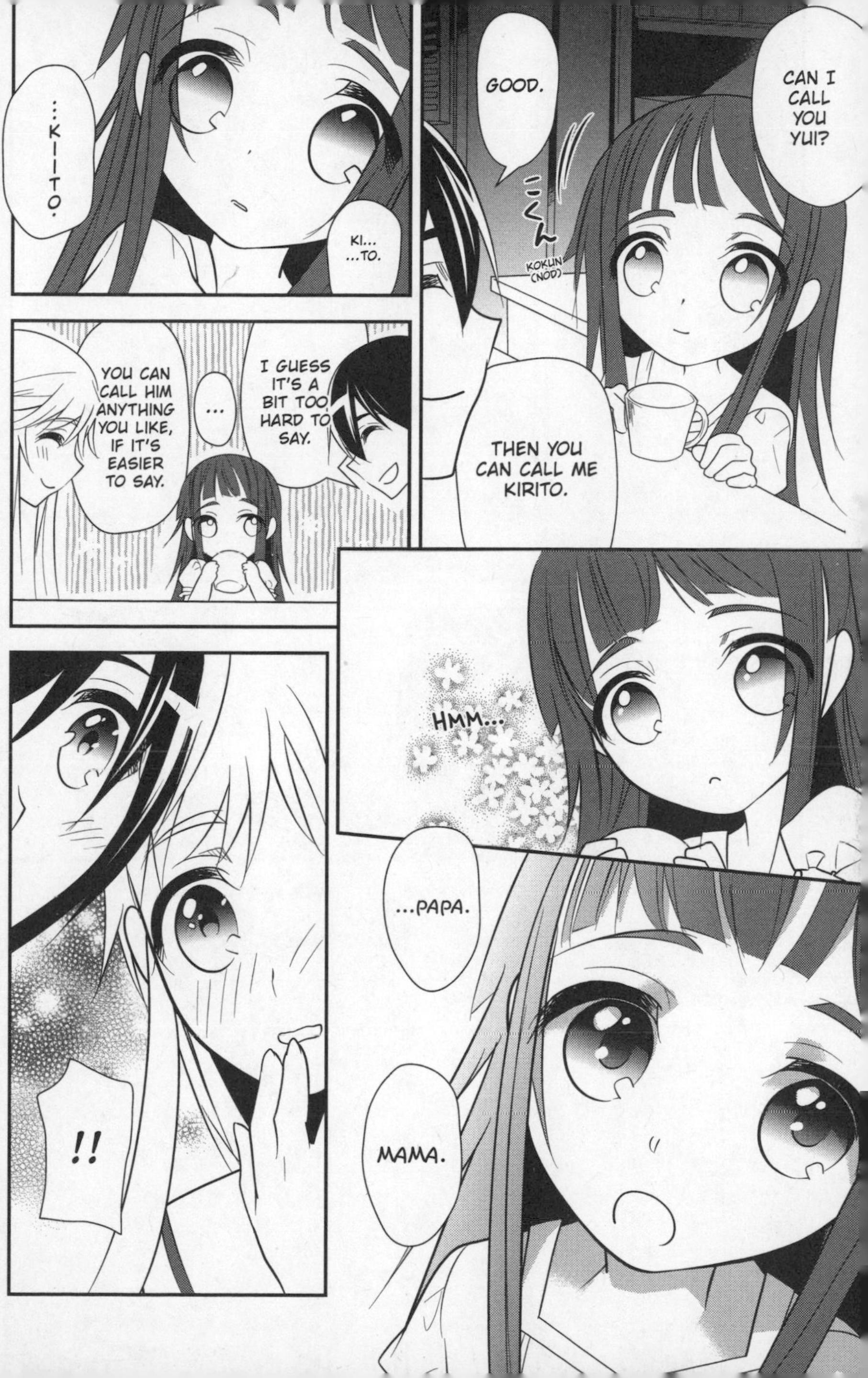

CAN I CALL YOU YUI?
GOOD.
こくん
KOKUN (NOD)
THEN YOU CAN CALL ME KIRITO.
KI... ...TO.
...KIITO.
I GUESS IT'S A BIT TOO HARD TO SAY.
...
YOU CAN CALL HIM ANYTHING YOU LIKE, IF IT'S EASIER TO SAY.
HMM...
...PAPA.
MAMA.
!!

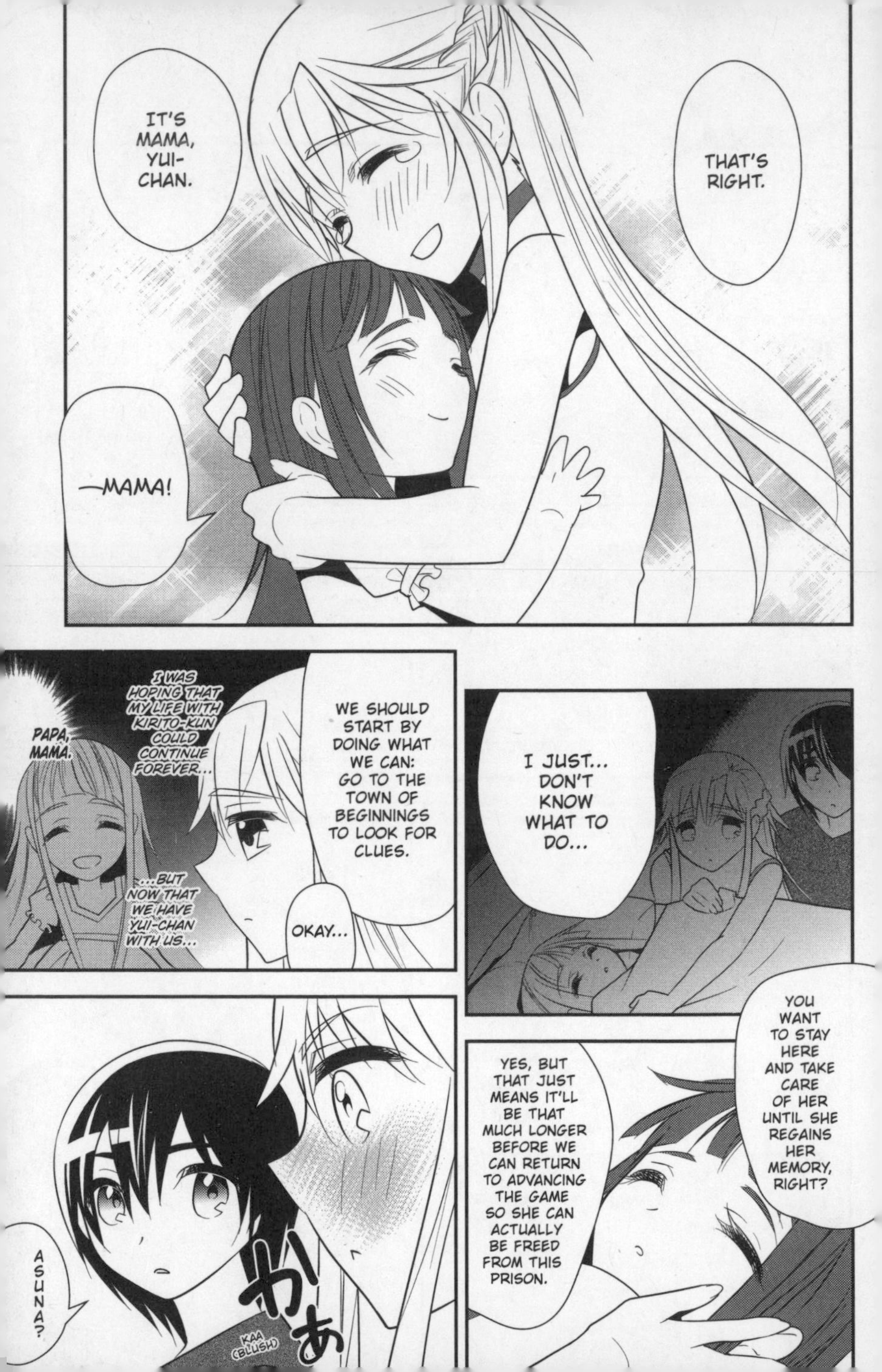
THAT'S RIGHT.
IT'S MAMA, YUI-CHAN.
—MAMA!
I JUST... DON'T KNOW WHAT TO DO...
YOU WANT TO STAY HERE AND TAKE CARE OF HER UNTIL SHE REGAINS HER MEMORY, RIGHT?
YES, BUT THAT JUST MEANS IT'LL BE THAT MUCH LONGER BEFORE WE CAN RETURN TO ADVANCING THE GAME SO SHE CAN ACTUALLY BE FREED FROM THIS PRISON.
WE SHOULD START BY DOING WHAT WE CAN: GO TO THE TOWN OF BEGINNINGS TO LOOK FOR CLUES.
OKAY...
I WAS HOPING THAT MY LIFE WITH KIRITO-KUN COULD CONTINUE FOREVER...
PAPA, MAMA.
...BUT NOW THAT WE HAVE YUI-CHAN WITH US...
KAA (BLUSH)
ASUNA?

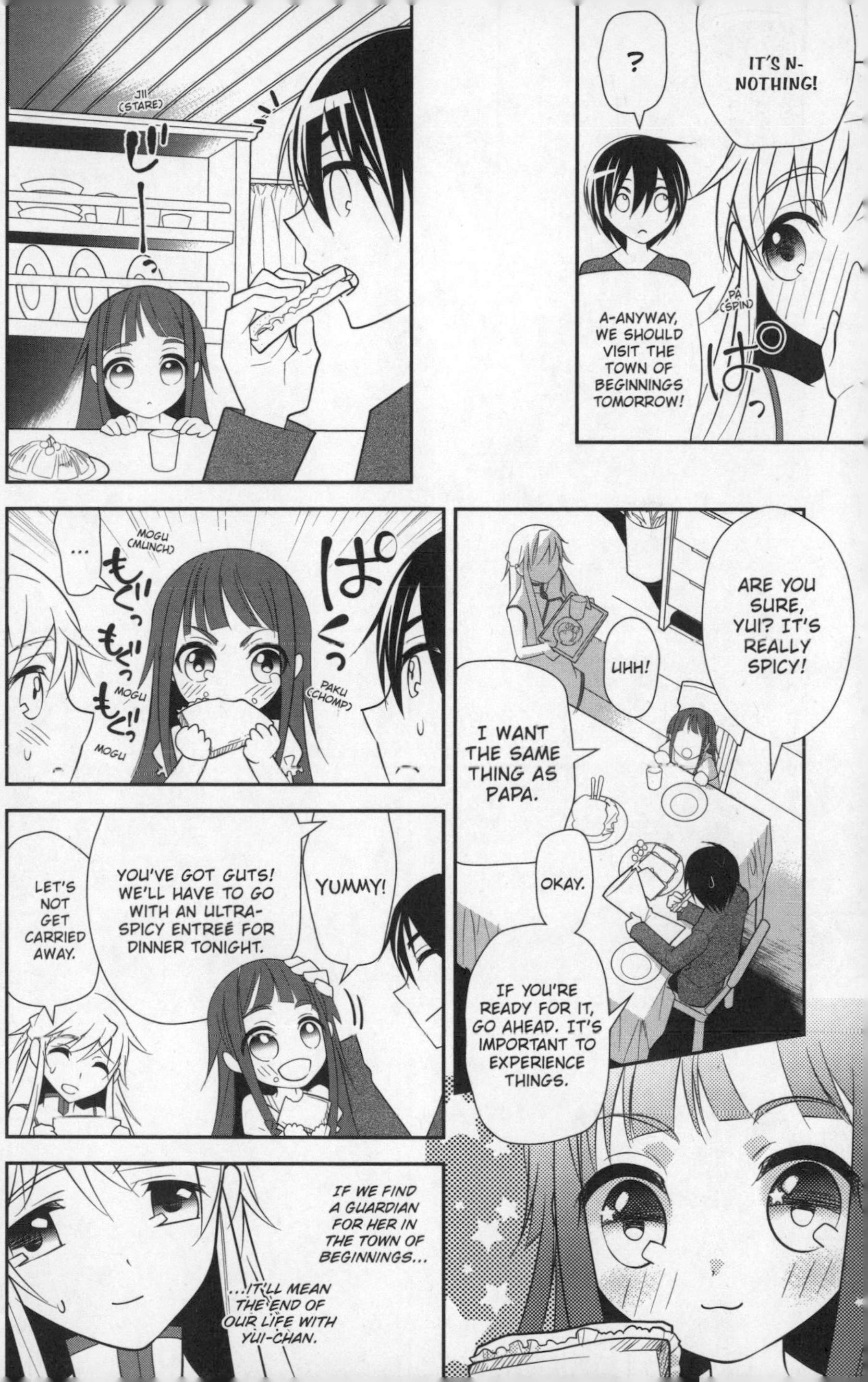
IT'S N-NOTHING!
?
PA (SPIN)
ぱっ
A-ANYWAY, WE SHOULD VISIT THE TOWN OF BEGINNINGS TOMORROW!
JII (STARE)
じー
ARE YOU SURE, YUI? IT'S REALLY SPICY!
UHH!
I WANT THE SAME THING AS PAPA.
OKAY.
IF YOU'RE READY FOR IT, GO AHEAD. IT'S IMPORTANT TO EXPERIENCE THINGS.
ぱくっ
PAKU (CHOMP)
もぐっもぐっもぐっ
MOGU (MUNCH)
MOGU
MOGU
...
YUMMY!
YOU'VE GOT GUTS! WE'LL HAVE TO GO WITH AN ULTRA-SPICY ENTREÉ FOR DINNER TONIGHT.
LET'S NOT GET CARRIED AWAY.
IF WE FIND A GUARDIAN FOR HER IN THE TOWN OF BEGINNINGS...
...IT'LL MEAN THE END OF OUR LIFE WITH YUI-CHAN.

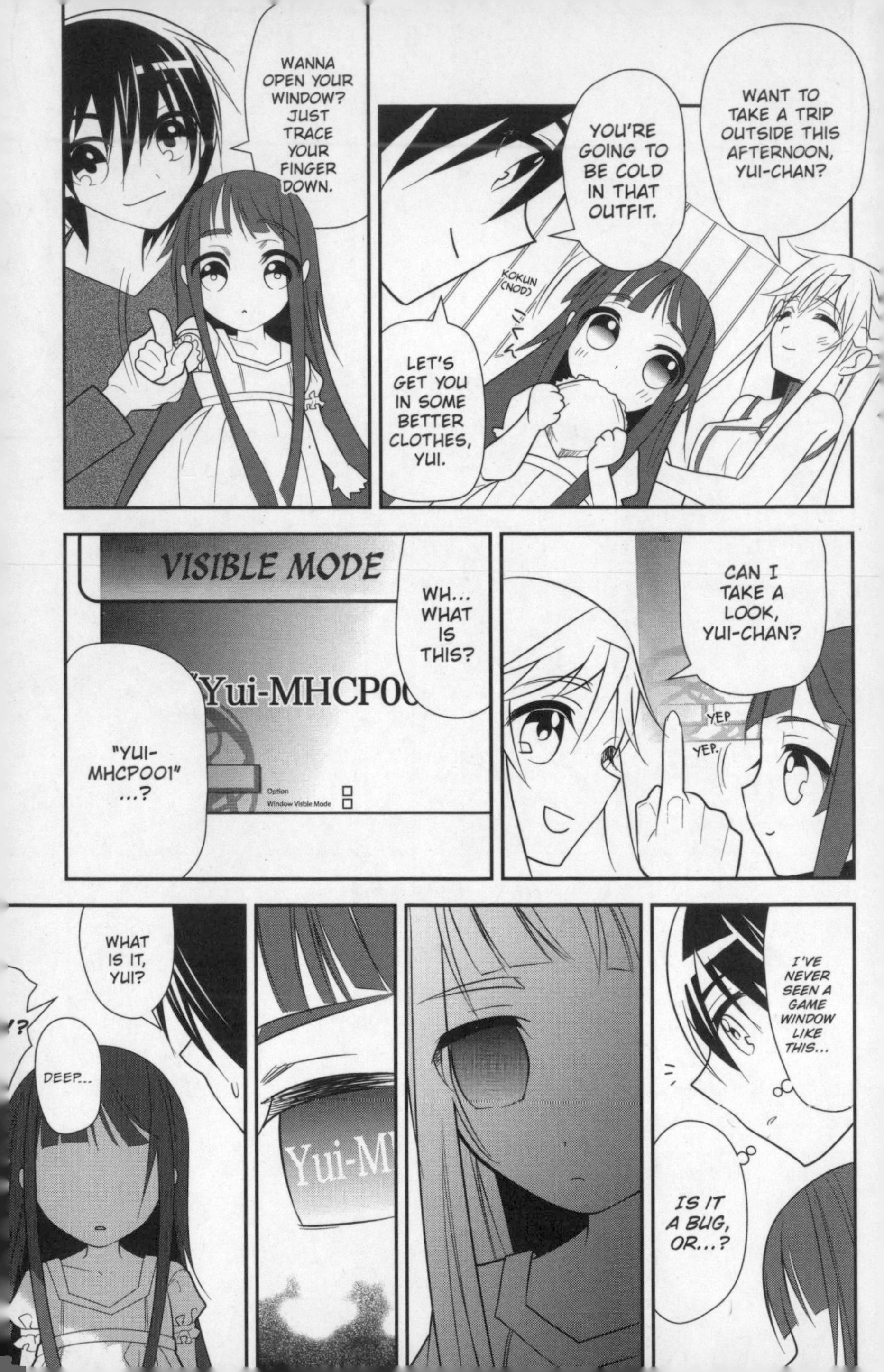
WANT TO TAKE A TRIP OUTSIDE THIS AFTERNOON, YUI-CHAN?
YOU'RE GOING TO BE COLD IN THAT OUTFIT.
KOKUN (NOD)
LET'S GET YOU IN SOME BETTER CLOTHES, YUI.
WANNA OPEN YOUR WINDOW? JUST TRACE YOUR FINGER DOWN.
CAN I TAKE A LOOK, YUI-CHAN?
YEP
YEP.
VISIBLE MODE
WH... WHAT IS THIS?
Yui-MHCP00
"YUI-MHCP001" ...?
Option
Window Visible Mode
I'VE NEVER SEEN A GAME WINDOW LIKE THIS...
IS IT A BUG, OR...?
Yui-M
WHAT IS IT, YUI?
DEEP...

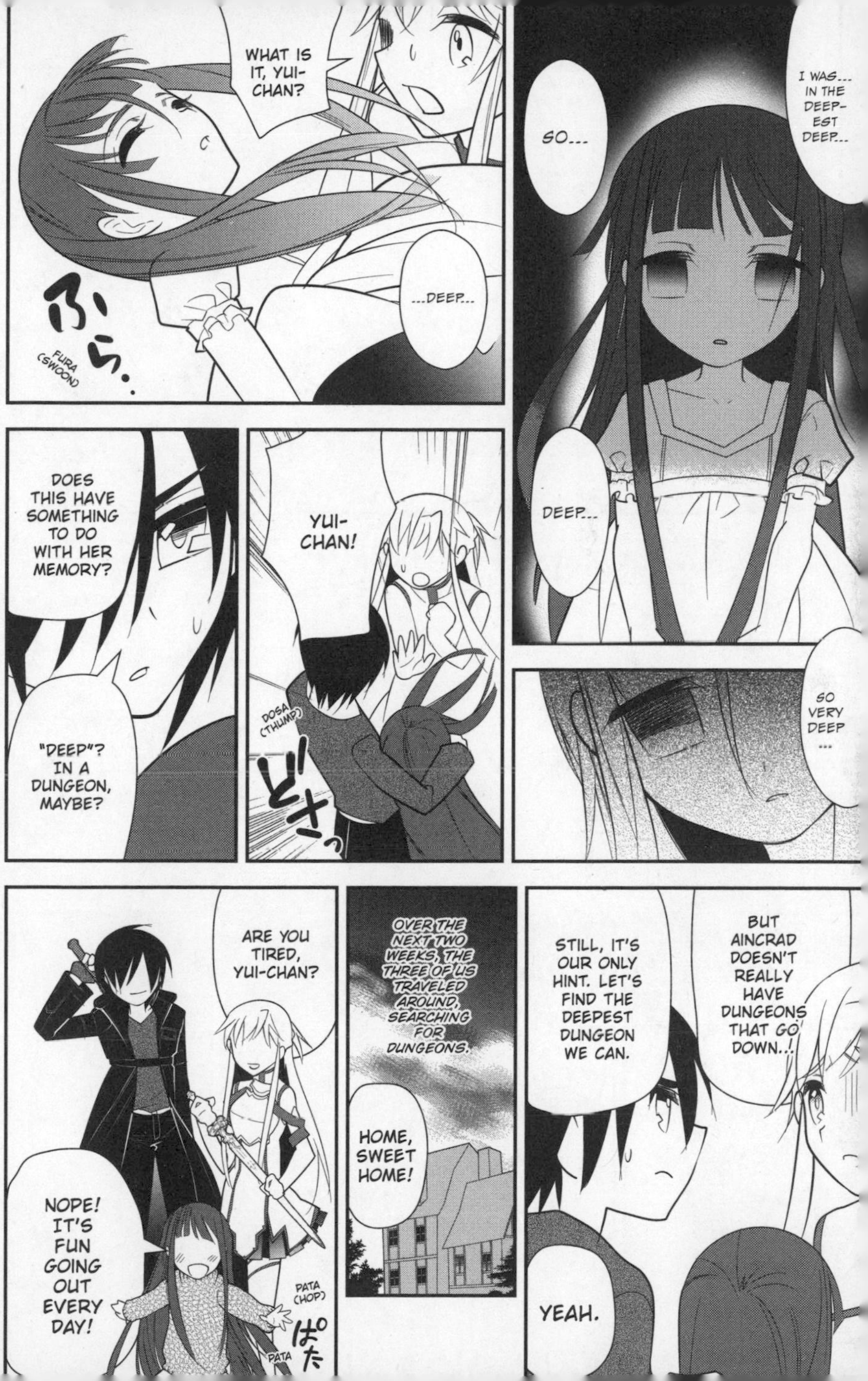
SO...
I WAS... IN THE DEEP-EST DEEP...
DEEP...
WHAT IS IT, YUI-CHAN?
...DEEP...
FURA (SWOON)
SO VERY DEEP ...
YUI-CHAN!
DOSA (THUMP)
DOES THIS HAVE SOMETHING TO DO WITH HER MEMORY?
"DEEP"? IN A DUNGEON, MAYBE?
BUT AINCRAD DOESN'T REALLY HAVE DUNGEONS THAT GO DOWN...!
STILL, IT'S OUR ONLY HINT. LET'S FIND THE DEEPEST DUNGEON WE CAN.
YEAH.
OVER THE NEXT TWO WEEKS, THE THREE OF US TRAVELED AROUND, SEARCHING FOR DUNGEONS.
HOME, SWEET HOME!
ARE YOU TIRED, YUI-CHAN?
NOPE! IT'S FUN GOING OUT EVERY DAY!
PATA (HOP)
PATA

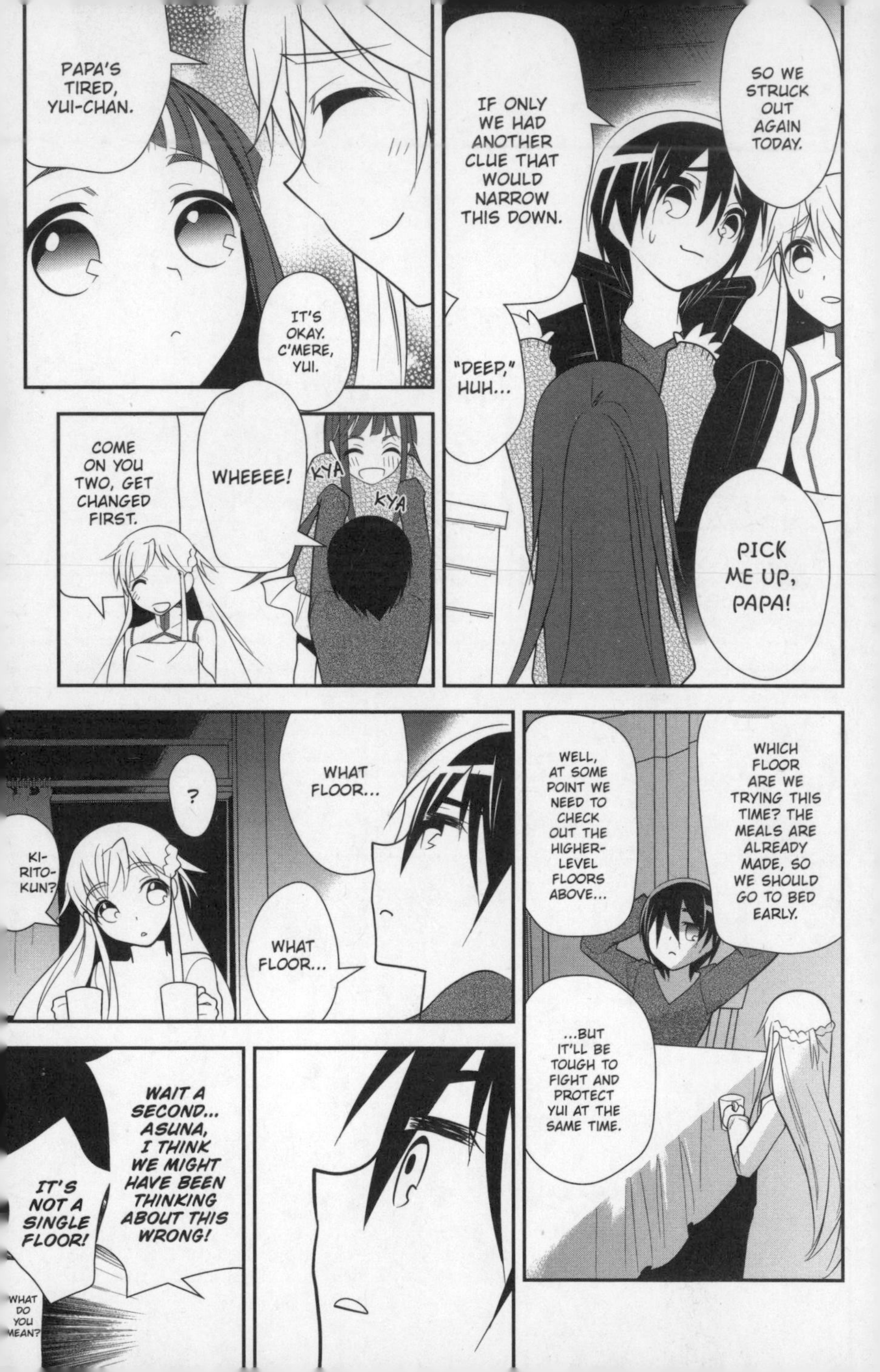
SO WE STRUCK OUT AGAIN TODAY.
IF ONLY WE HAD ANOTHER CLUE THAT WOULD NARROW THIS DOWN.
"DEEP," HUH...
PICK ME UP, PAPA!
PAPA'S TIRED, YUI-CHAN.
IT'S OKAY. C'MERE, YUI.
WHEEEE!
KYA
KYA
COME ON YOU TWO, GET CHANGED FIRST.
WHICH FLOOR ARE WE TRYING THIS TIME? THE MEALS ARE ALREADY MADE, SO WE SHOULD GO TO BED EARLY.
WELL, AT SOME POINT WE NEED TO CHECK OUT THE HIGHER-LEVEL FLOORS ABOVE...
...BUT IT'LL BE TOUGH TO FIGHT AND PROTECT YUI AT THE SAME TIME.
WHAT FLOOR...
?
KI-RITO-KUN?
WHAT FLOOR...
WAIT A SECOND... ASUNA, I THINK WE MIGHT HAVE BEEN THINKING ABOUT THIS WRONG!
IT'S NOT A SINGLE FLOOR!
WHAT DO YOU MEAN?

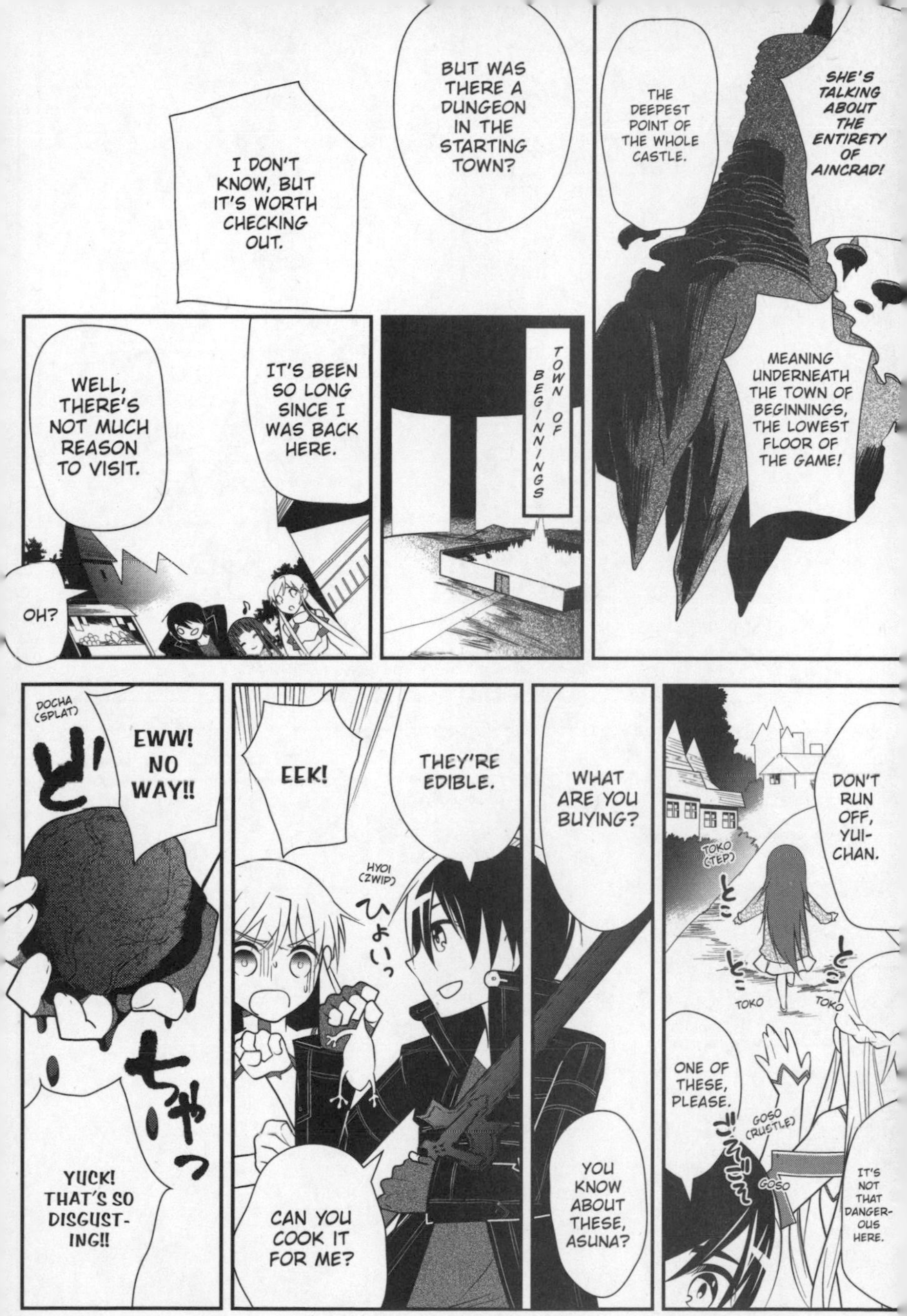
THE DEEPEST POINT OF THE WHOLE CASTLE.
SHE'S TALKING ABOUT THE ENTIRETY OF AINCRAD!
MEANING UNDERNEATH THE TOWN OF BEGINNINGS, THE LOWEST FLOOR OF THE GAME!
BUT WAS THERE A DUNGEON IN THE STARTING TOWN?
I DON'T KNOW, BUT IT'S WORTH CHECKING OUT.
TOWN OF BEGINNINGS
IT'S BEEN SO LONG SINCE I WAS BACK HERE.
WELL, THERE'S NOT MUCH REASON TO VISIT.
OH?
DON'T RUN OFF, YUI-CHAN.
TOKO (TEP)
TOKO
TOKO
ONE OF THESE, PLEASE.
GOSO (RUSTLE)
GOSO
IT'S NOT THAT DANGEROUS HERE.
WHAT ARE YOU BUYING?
YOU KNOW ABOUT THESE, ASUNA?
THEY'RE EDIBLE.
EEK!
HYOI (ZWIP)
ひょいっ
CAN YOU COOK IT FOR ME?
DOCHA (SPLAT)
EWW! NO WAY!!
どちゃっ
YUCK! THAT'S SO DISGUST-ING!!

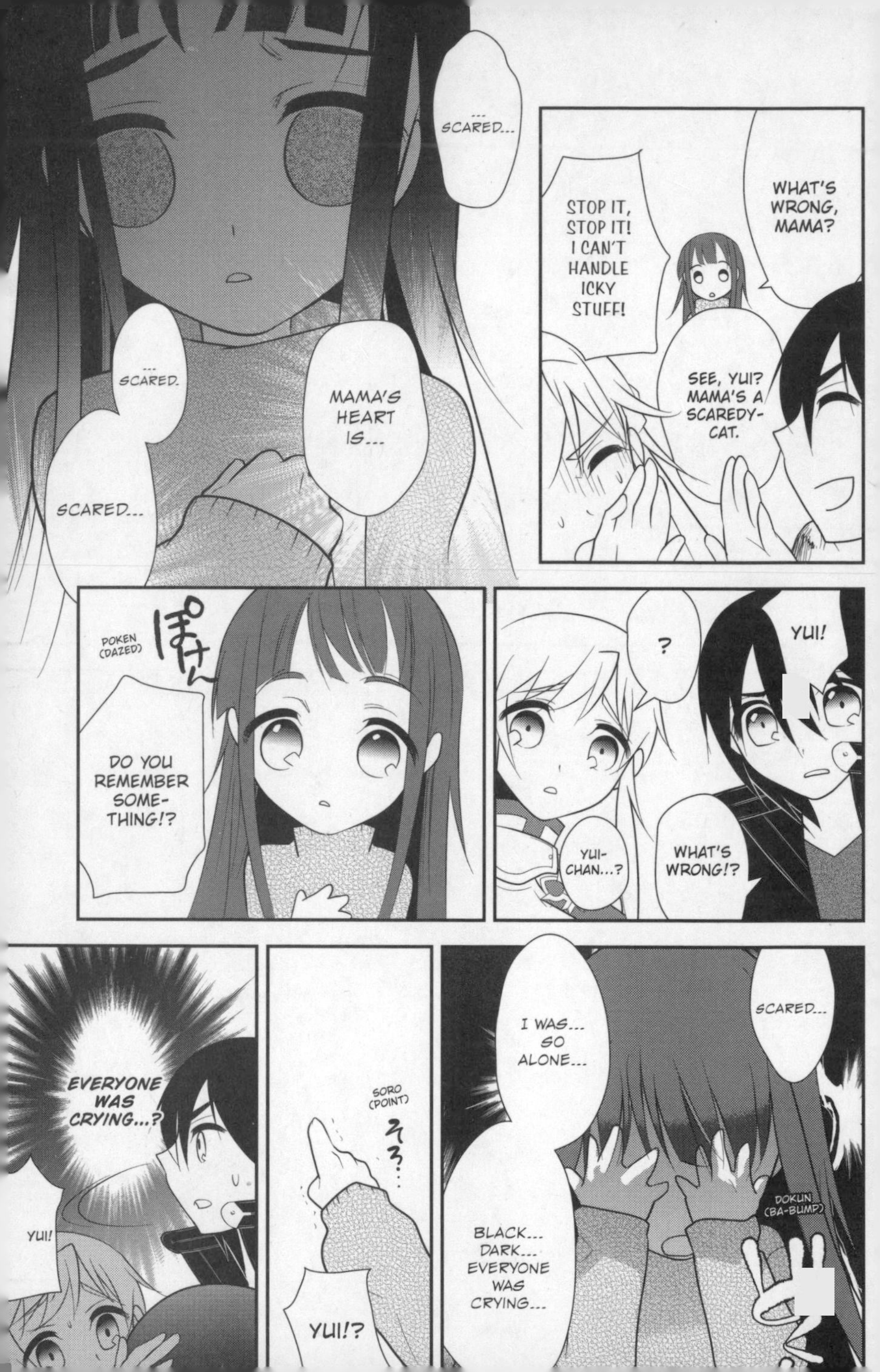
WHAT'S WRONG, MAMA?
STOP IT, STOP IT! I CAN'T HANDLE ICKY STUFF!
SEE, YUI? MAMA'S A SCAREDY-CAT.
...SCARED...
MAMA'S HEART IS...
...SCARED.
SCARED...
YUI!
?
WHAT'S WRONG!?
YUI-CHAN...?
ぽけん
POKEN (DAZED)
DO YOU REMEMBER SOME-THING!?
SCARED...
I WAS... SO ALONE...
DOKUN (BA-BUMP)
BLACK... DARK... EVERYONE WAS CRYING...
そろ...
SORO (POINT)
YUI!?
EVERYONE WAS CRYING...?
YUI!

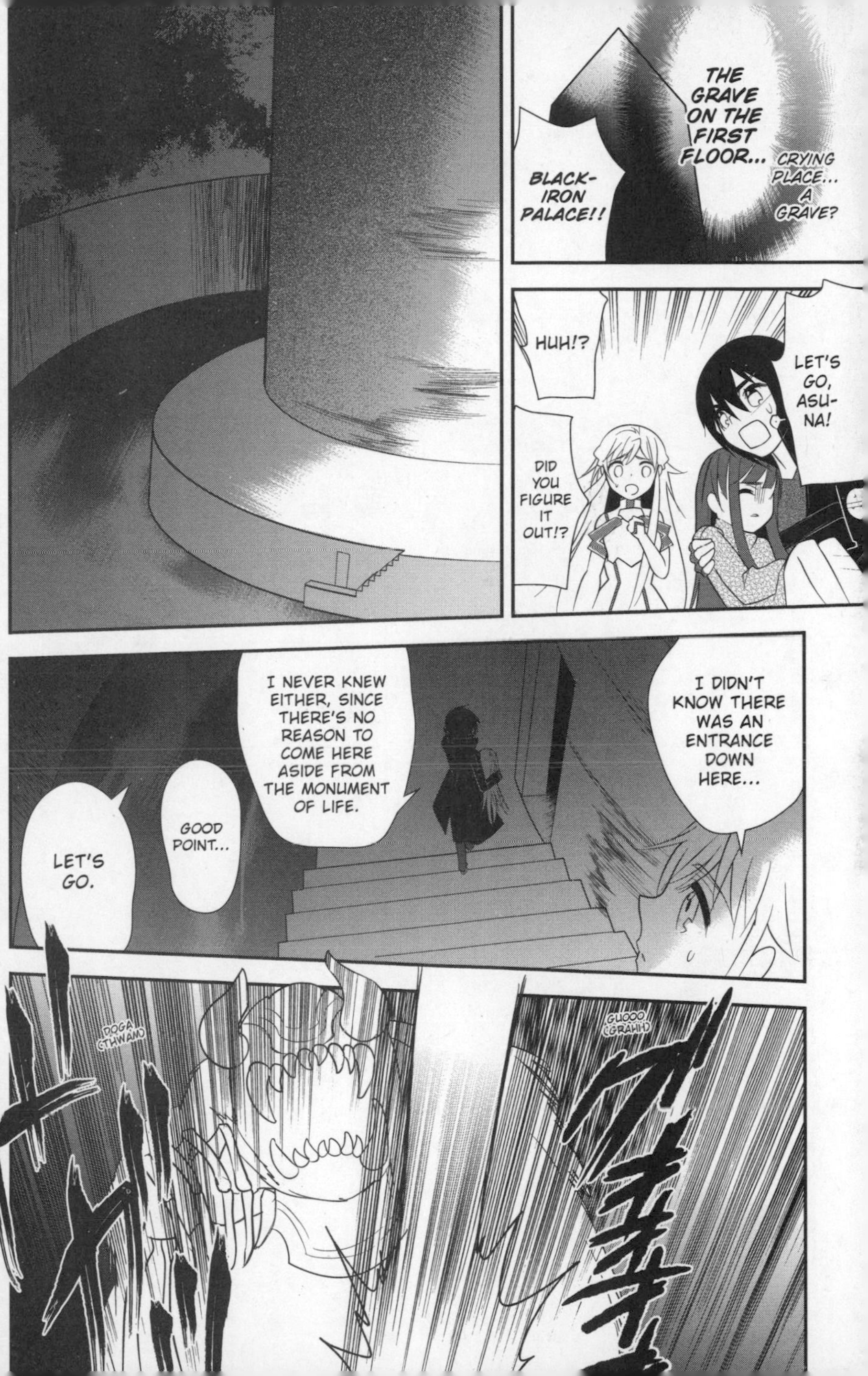
THE GRAVE ON THE FIRST FLOOR...
CRYING PLACE... A GRAVE?
BLACK-IRON PALACE!!
LET'S GO, ASUNA!
HUH!?
DID YOU FIGURE IT OUT!?
I DIDN'T KNOW THERE WAS AN ENTRANCE DOWN HERE...
I NEVER KNEW EITHER, SINCE THERE'S NO REASON TO COME HERE ASIDE FROM THE MONUMENT OF LIFE.
GOOD POINT...
LET'S GO.
GUOOO (GRAHH)
DOGA (THWAM)

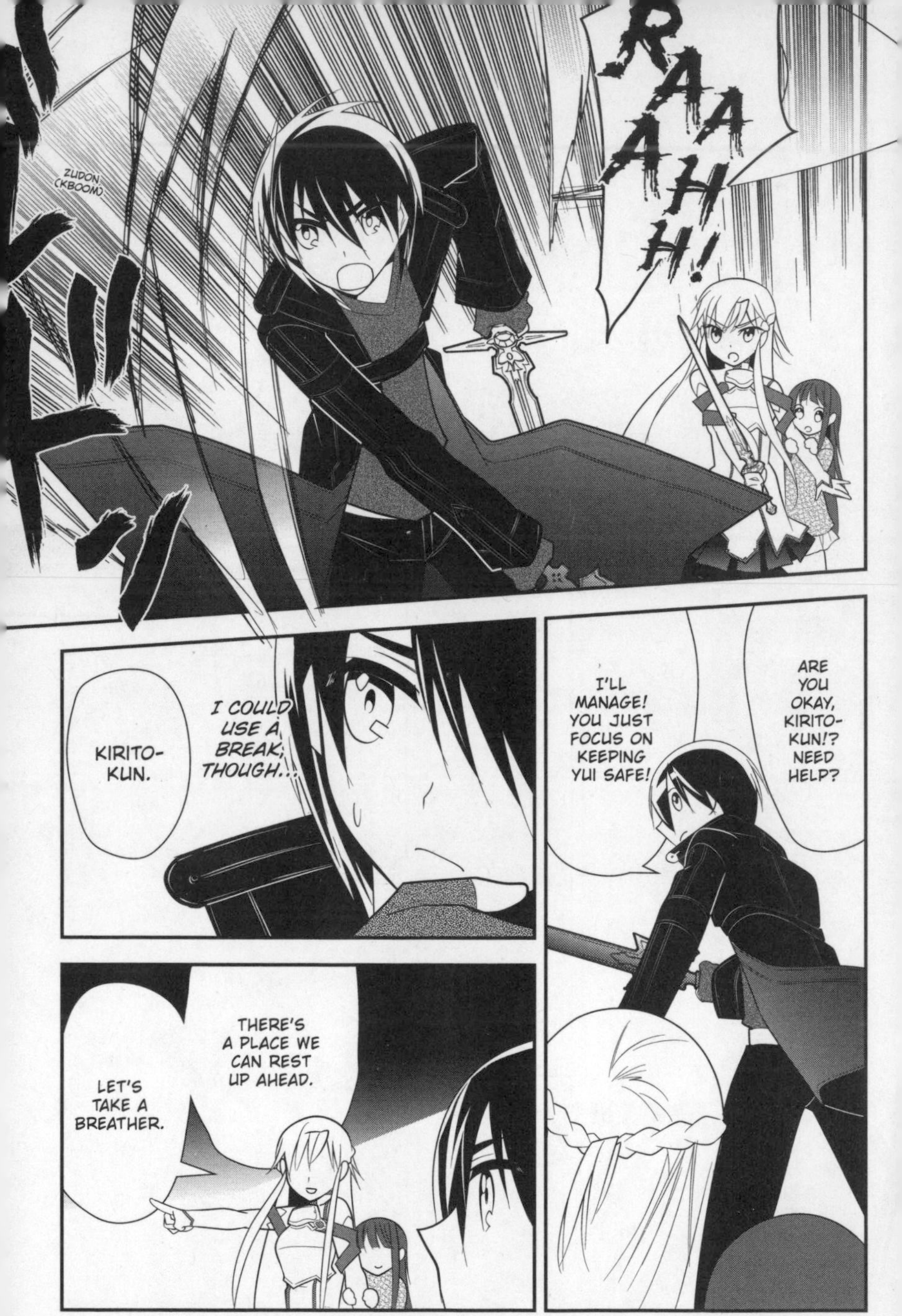
RAAAHH!
ZUDON (KBOOM)
ARE YOU OKAY, KIRITO-KUN!? NEED HELP?
I'LL MANAGE! YOU JUST FOCUS ON KEEPING YUI SAFE!
I COULD USE A BREAK, THOUGH...
KIRITO-KUN.
THERE'S A PLACE WE CAN REST UP AHEAD.
LET'S TAKE A BREATHER.

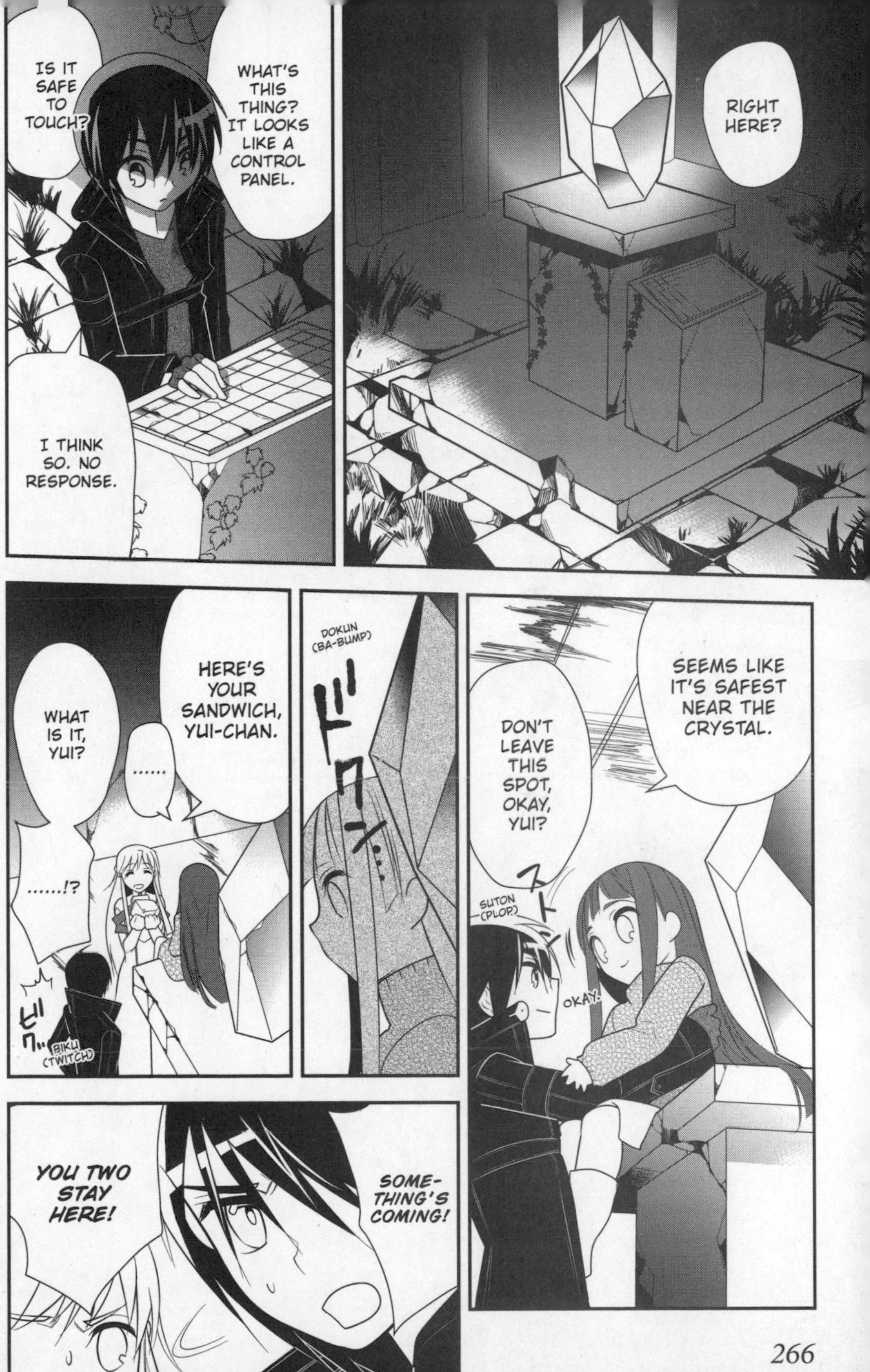
RIGHT HERE?
WHAT'S THIS THING? IT LOOKS LIKE A CONTROL PANEL.
IS IT SAFE TO TOUCH?
I THINK SO. NO RESPONSE.
SEEMS LIKE IT'S SAFEST NEAR THE CRYSTAL.
DON'T LEAVE THIS SPOT, OKAY, YUI?
SUTON (PLOP)
OKAY.
DOKUN (BA-BUMP)
HERE'S YOUR SANDWICH, YUI-CHAN.
WHAT IS IT, YUI?
......
......!?
BIKU (TWITCH)
SOME-THING'S COMING!
YOU TWO STAY HERE!

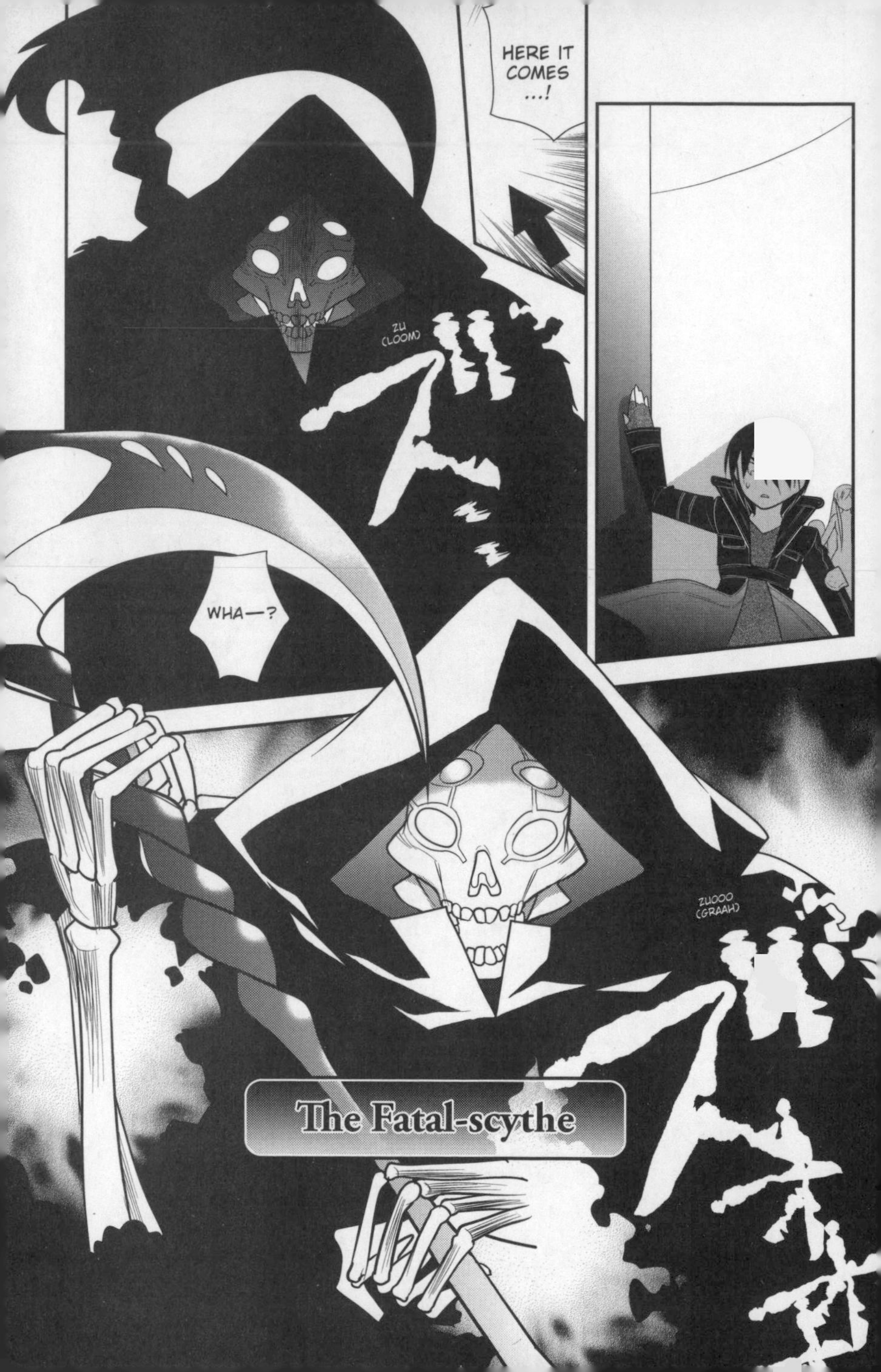
HERE IT COMES ...!
ZU (LOOM)
WHA—?
ZUOOO (GRAAH)
The Fatal-scythe

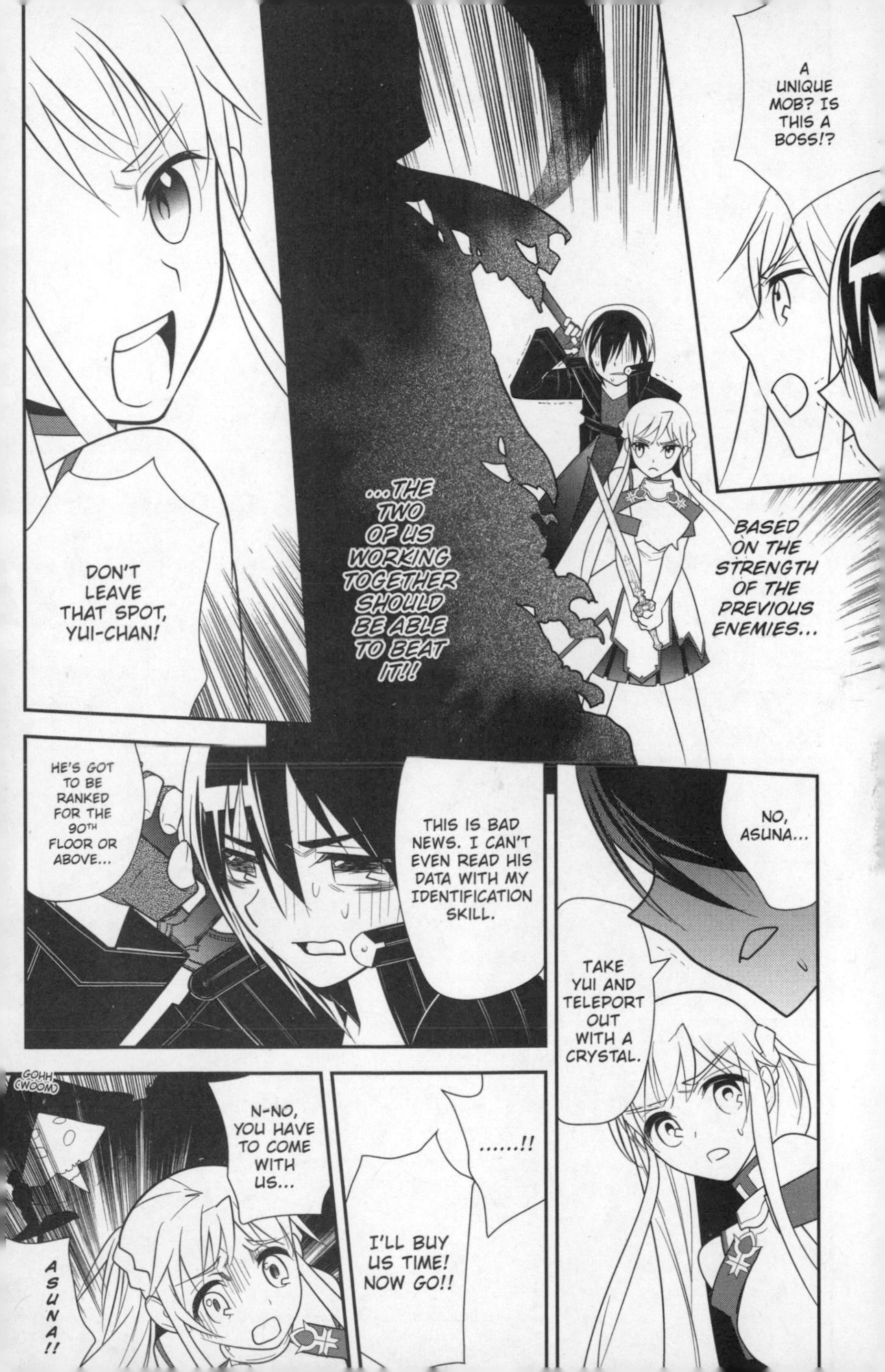
A UNIQUE MOB? IS THIS A BOSS!?
BASED ON THE STRENGTH OF THE PREVIOUS ENEMIES...
...THE TWO OF US WORKING TOGETHER SHOULD BE ABLE TO BEAT IT!!
DON'T LEAVE THAT SPOT, YUI-CHAN!
NO, ASUNA...
TAKE YUI AND TELEPORT OUT WITH A CRYSTAL.
THIS IS BAD NEWS. I CAN'T EVEN READ HIS DATA WITH MY IDENTIFICATION SKILL.
HE'S GOT TO BE RANKED FOR THE 90TH FLOOR OR ABOVE...
......!!
I'LL BUY US TIME! NOW GO!!
N-NO, YOU HAVE TO COME WITH US...
GOHH (WOOM)
ASUNA!!

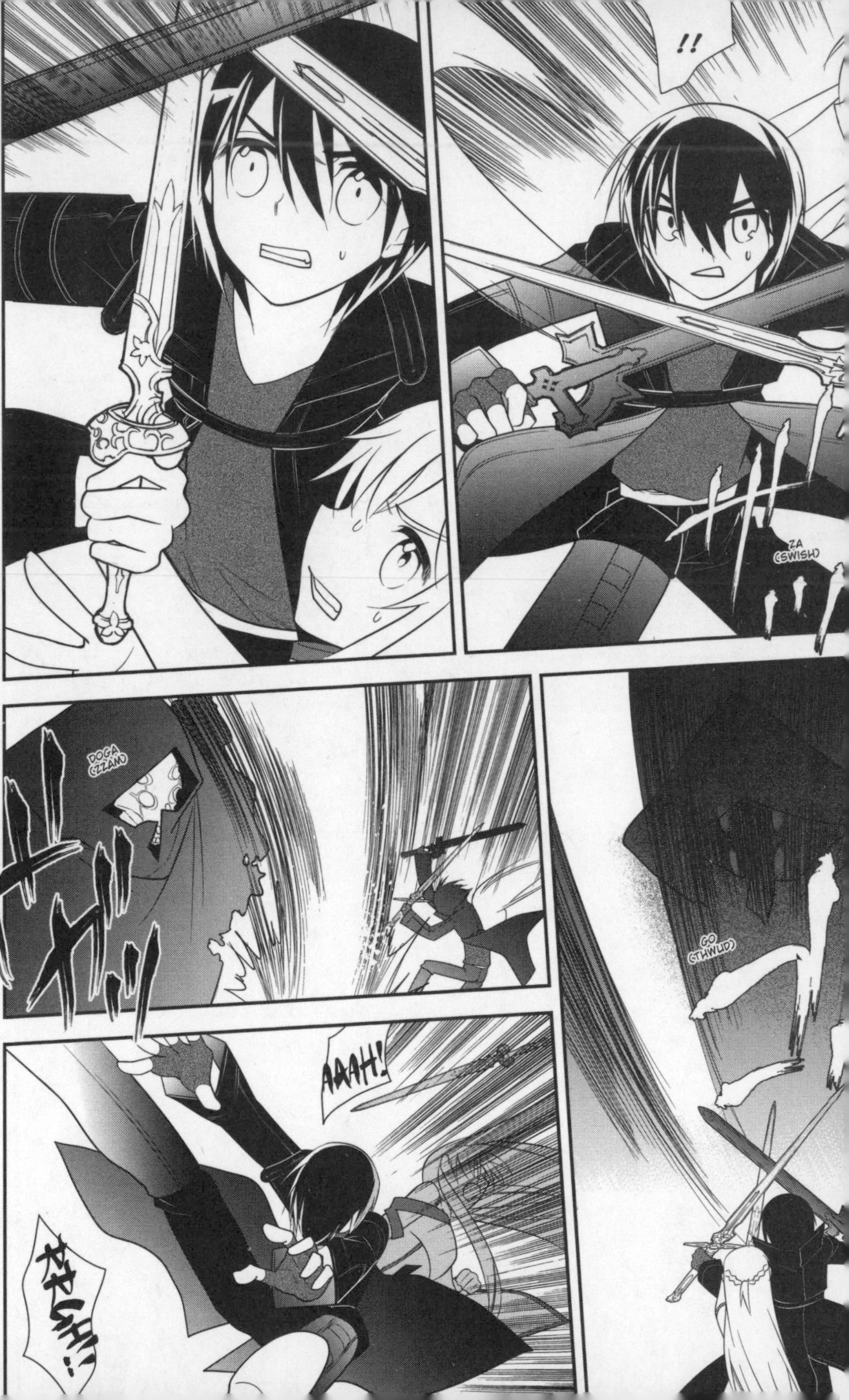
!!
ZA (SWISH)
GO (THWUD)
DOGA (ZZAN)
AAAH!
KRGH!!

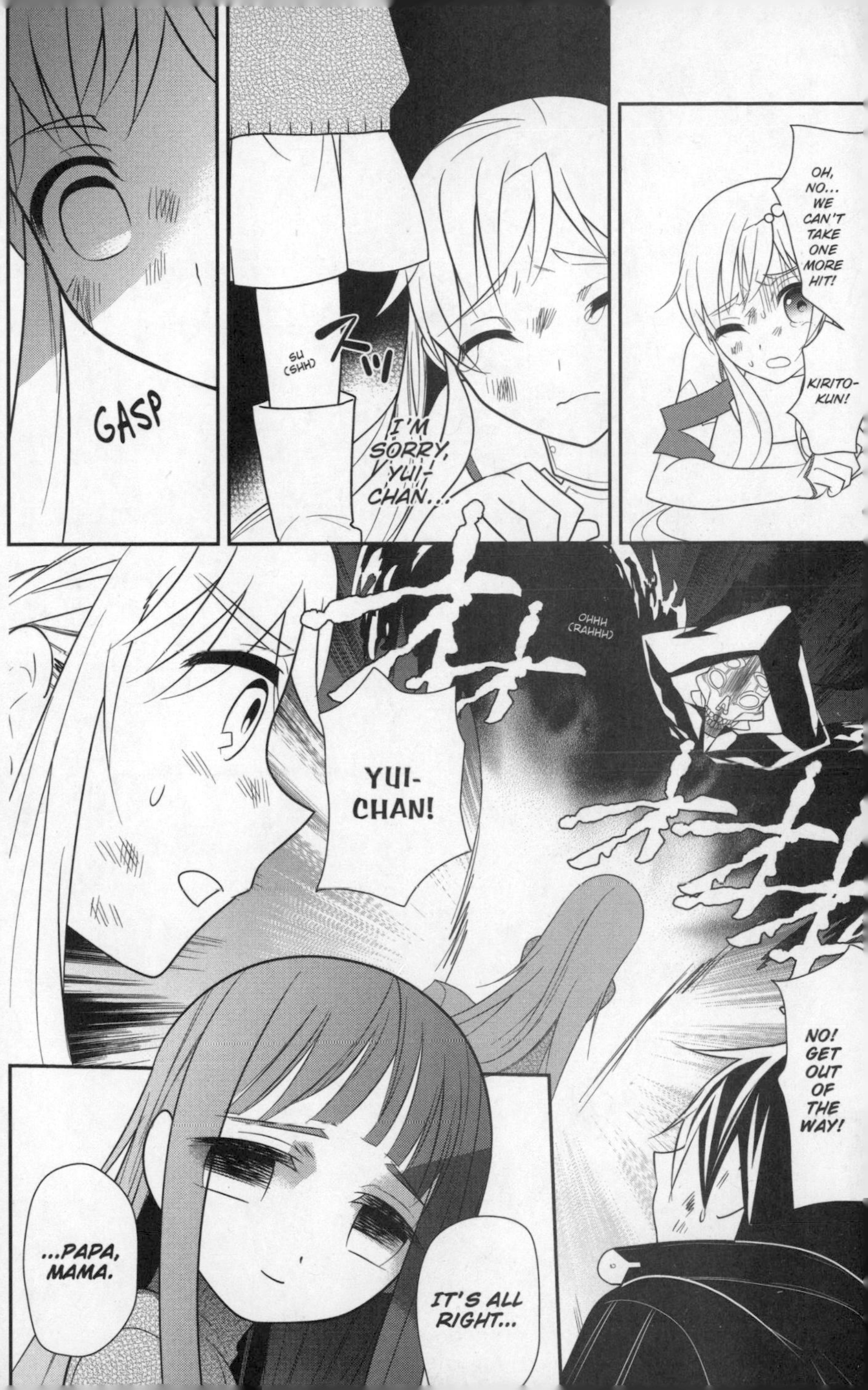
OH, NO... WE CAN'T TAKE ONE MORE HIT!
KIRITO-KUN!
SU (SHH)
I'M SORRY, YUI-CHAN...
GASP
OHHH (RAHHH)
NO! GET OUT OF THE WAY!
YUI-CHAN!
IT'S ALL RIGHT...
...PAPA, MAMA.

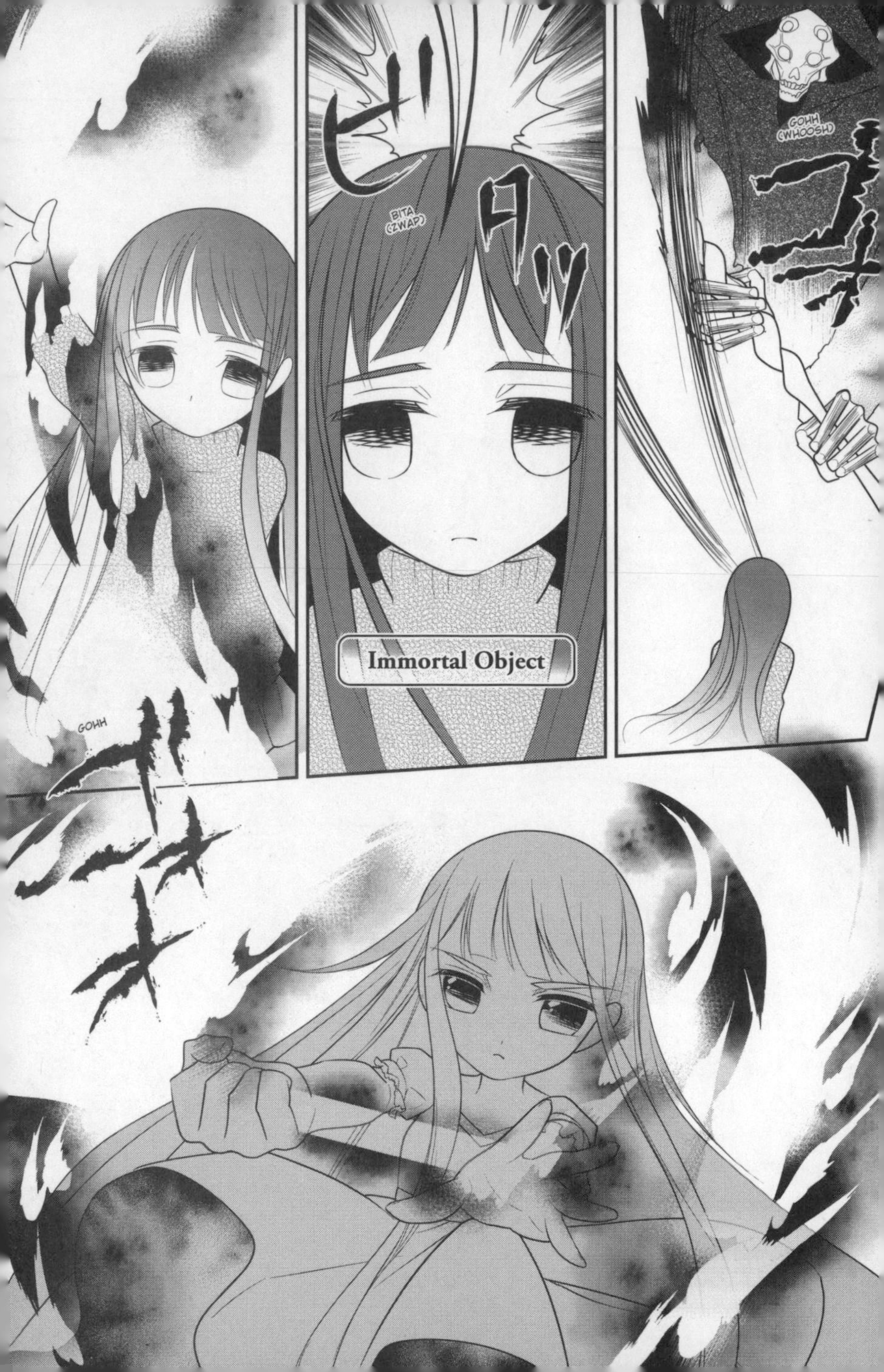
GOHH
(WHOOSH)
BITA
(ZWAP)
Immortal Object
GOHH

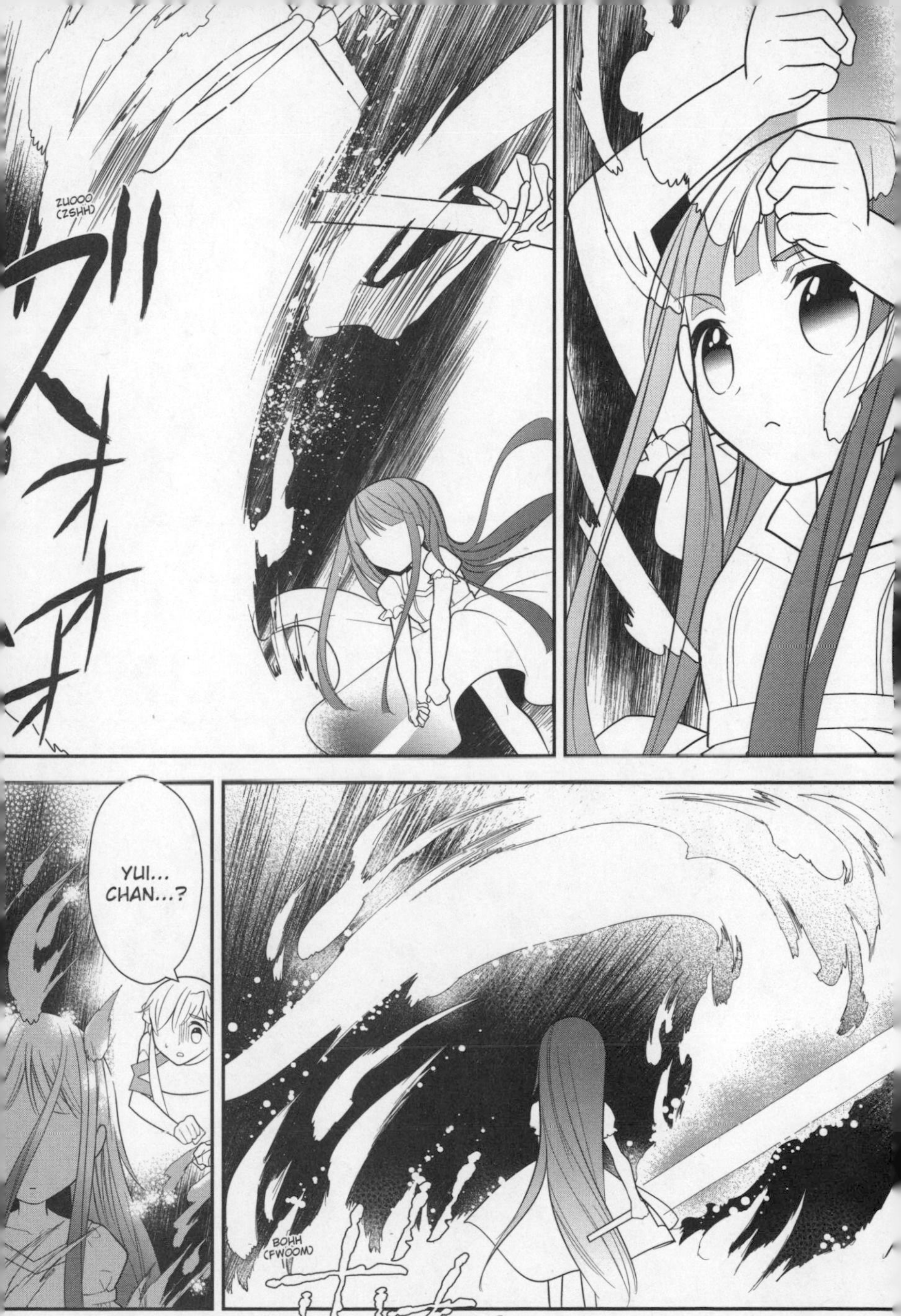
ZUOOO
(ZSHH)
BOHH
(FWOOM)
YUI... CHAN...?

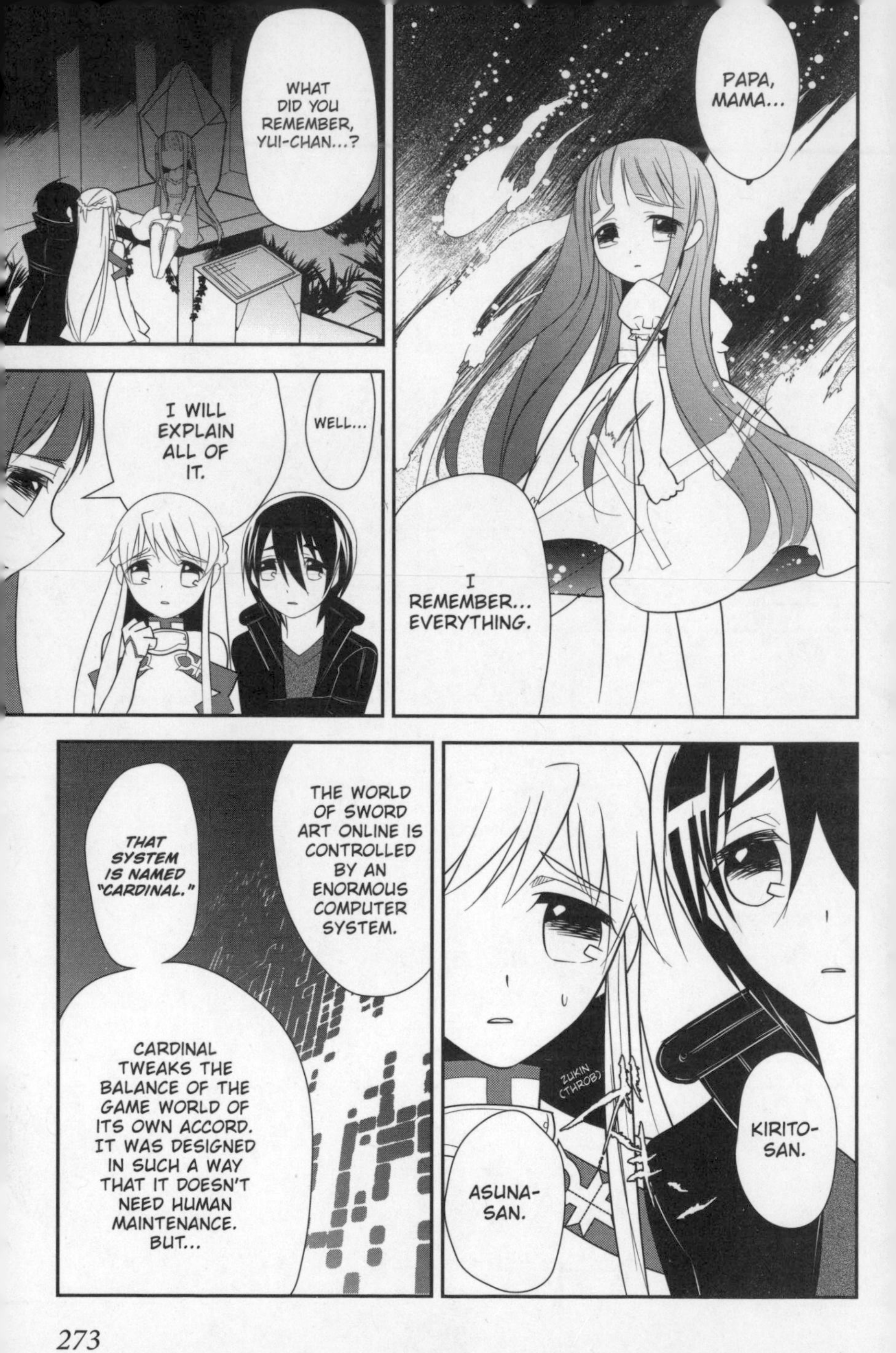
PAPA, MAMA...
I REMEMBER... EVERYTHING.
WHAT DID YOU REMEMBER, YUI-CHAN...?
WELL...
I WILL EXPLAIN ALL OF IT.
KIRITO-SAN.
ZUKIN (THROB)
ASUNA-SAN.
THE WORLD OF SWORD ART ONLINE IS CONTROLLED BY AN ENORMOUS COMPUTER SYSTEM.
THAT SYSTEM IS NAMED "CARDINAL."
CARDINAL TWEAKS THE BALANCE OF THE GAME WORLD OF ITS OWN ACCORD. IT WAS DESIGNED IN SUCH A WAY THAT IT DOESN'T NEED HUMAN MAINTENANCE. BUT...

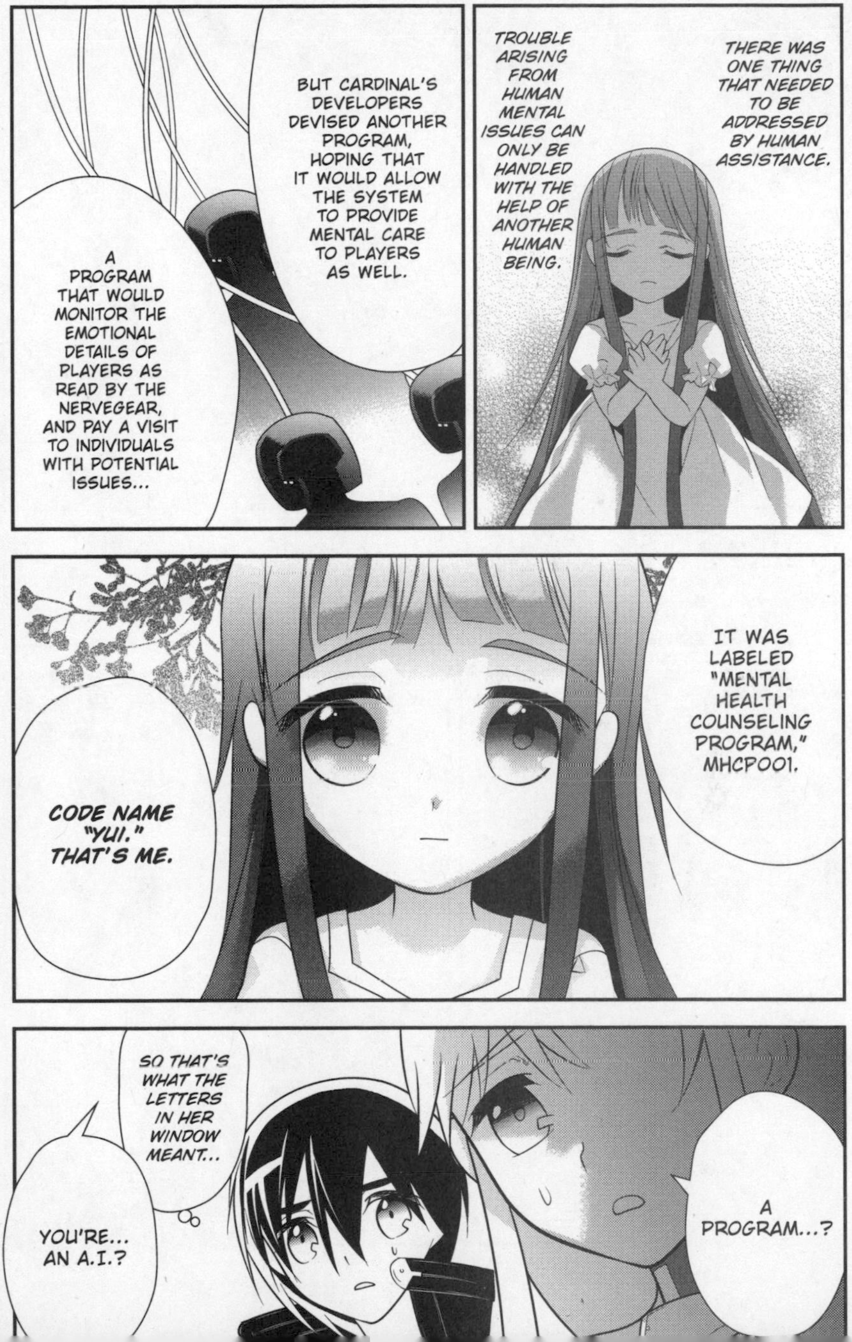
THERE WAS ONE THING THAT NEEDED TO BE ADDRESSED BY HUMAN ASSISTANCE.
TROUBLE ARISING FROM HUMAN MENTAL ISSUES CAN ONLY BE HANDLED WITH THE HELP OF ANOTHER HUMAN BEING.
BUT CARDINAL'S DEVELOPERS DEVISED ANOTHER PROGRAM, HOPING THAT IT WOULD ALLOW THE SYSTEM TO PROVIDE MENTAL CARE TO PLAYERS AS WELL.
A PROGRAM THAT WOULD MONITOR THE EMOTIONAL DETAILS OF PLAYERS AS READ BY THE NERVEGEAR, AND PAY A VISIT TO INDIVIDUALS WITH POTENTIAL ISSUES...
IT WAS LABELED "MENTAL HEALTH COUNSELING PROGRAM," MHCP001.
CODE NAME "YUI." THAT'S ME.
A PROGRAM...?
SO THAT'S WHAT THE LETTERS IN HER WINDOW MEANT...
YOU'RE... AN A.I.?

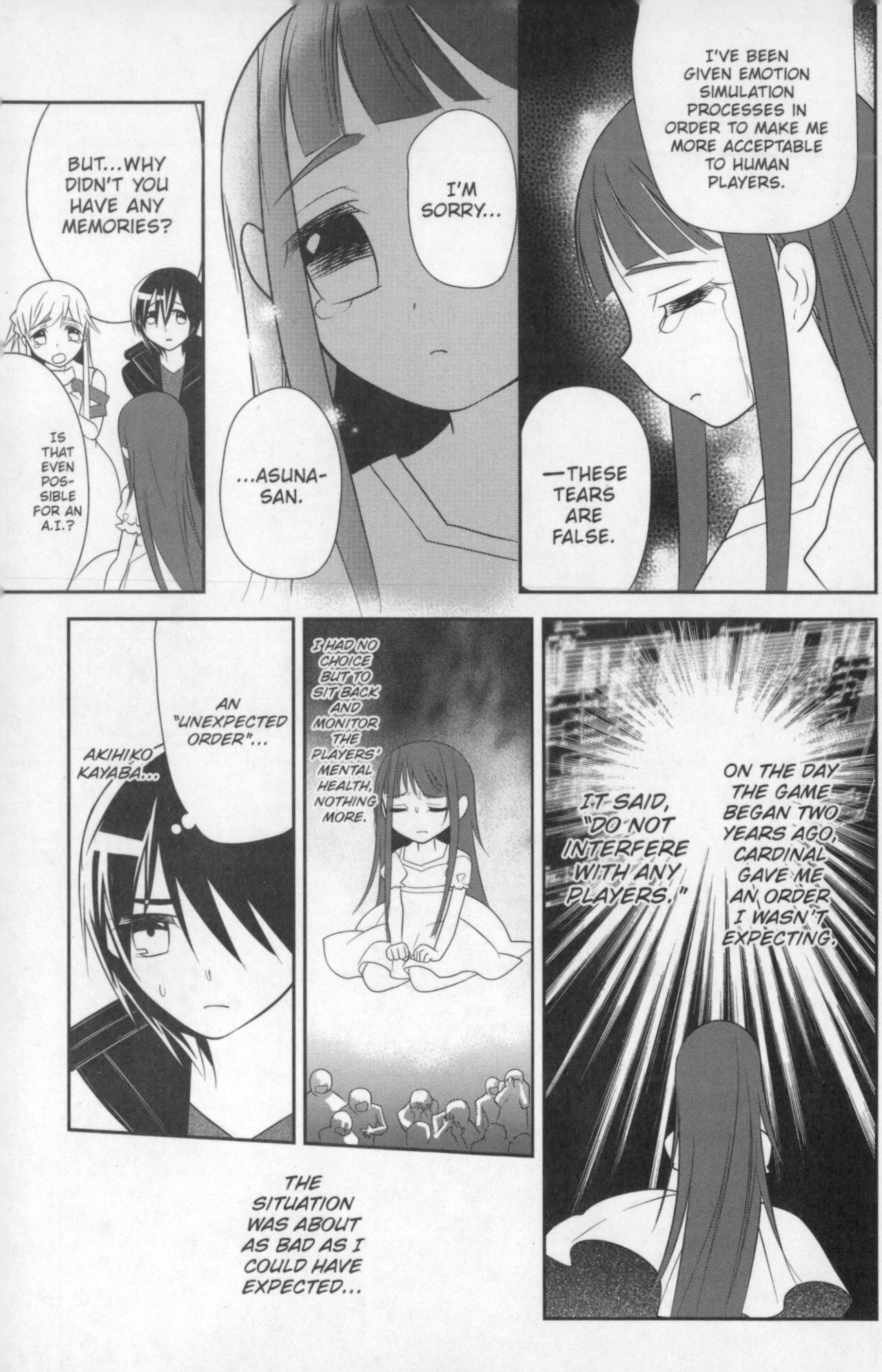
I'VE BEEN GIVEN EMOTION SIMULATION PROCESSES IN ORDER TO MAKE ME MORE ACCEPTABLE TO HUMAN PLAYERS.
—THESE TEARS ARE FALSE.
I'M SORRY...
...ASUNA-SAN.
BUT...WHY DIDN'T YOU HAVE ANY MEMORIES?
IS THAT EVEN POS-SIBLE FOR AN A.I.?
ON THE DAY THE GAME BEGAN TWO YEARS AGO, CARDINAL GAVE ME AN ORDER I WASN'T EXPECTING.
IT SAID, "DO NOT INTERFERE WITH ANY PLAYERS."
I HAD NO CHOICE BUT TO SIT BACK AND MONITOR THE PLAYERS' MENTAL HEALTH, NOTHING MORE.
THE SITUATION WAS ABOUT AS BAD AS I COULD HAVE EXPECTED...
AN "UNEXPECTED ORDER"...
AKIHIKO KAYABA...

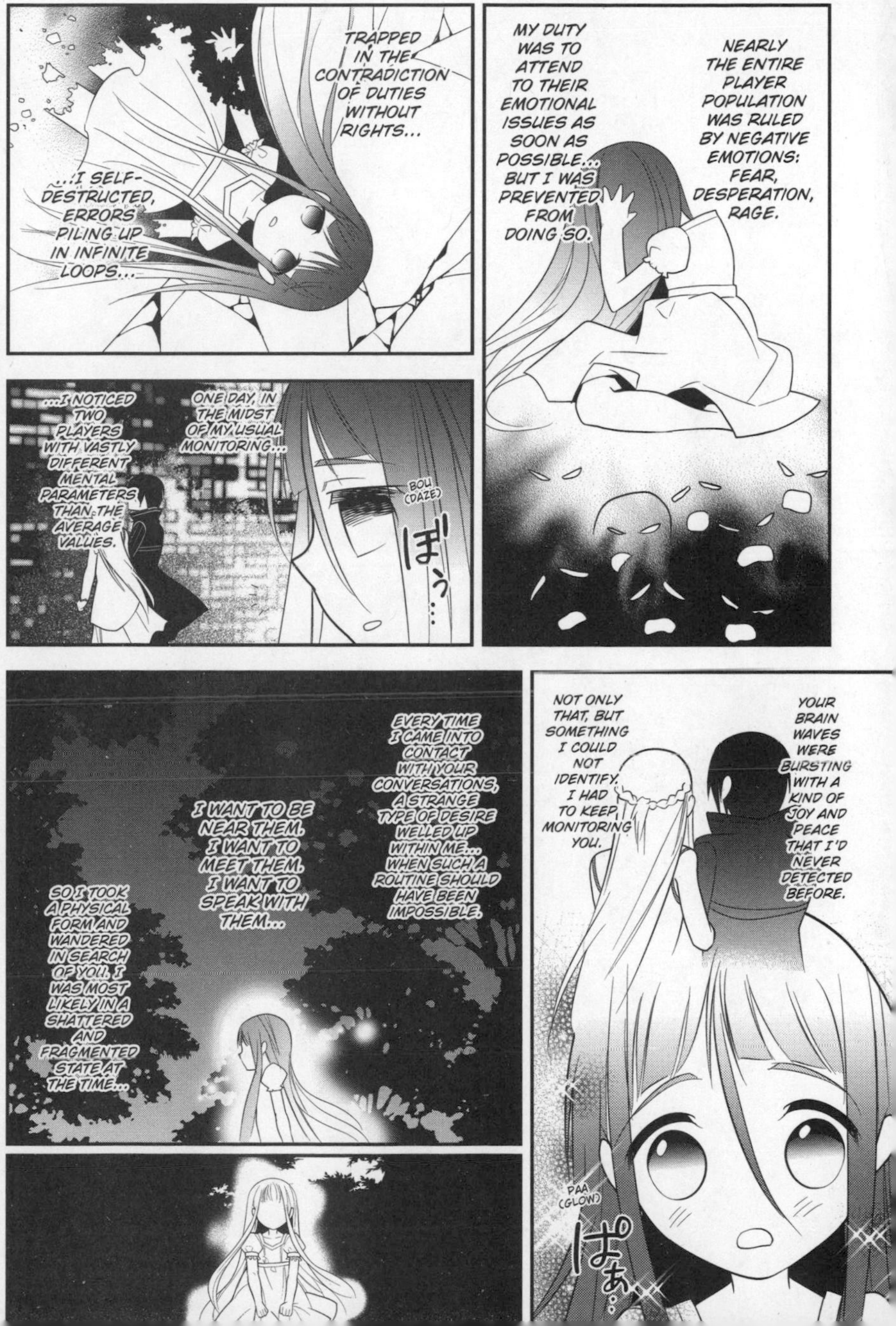
NEARLY THE ENTIRE PLAYER POPULATION WAS RULED BY NEGATIVE EMOTIONS: FEAR, DESPERATION, RAGE.
MY DUTY WAS TO ATTEND TO THEIR EMOTIONAL ISSUES AS SOON AS POSSIBLE... BUT I WAS PREVENTED FROM DOING SO.
TRAPPED IN THE CONTRADICTION OF DUTIES WITHOUT RIGHTS...
...I SELF-DESTRUCTED, ERRORS PILING UP IN INFINITE LOOPS...
ONE DAY, IN THE MIDST OF MY USUAL MONITORING...
BOU (DAZE)
ぼう…
...I NOTICED TWO PLAYERS WITH VASTLY DIFFERENT MENTAL PARAMETERS THAN THE AVERAGE VALUES.
YOUR BRAIN WAVES WERE BURSTING WITH A KIND OF JOY AND PEACE THAT I'D NEVER DETECTED BEFORE.
NOT ONLY THAT, BUT SOMETHING I COULD NOT IDENTIFY. I HAD TO KEEP MONITORING YOU.
PAA (GLOW)
ぱぁ…
EVERY TIME I CAME INTO CONTACT WITH YOUR CONVERSATIONS, A STRANGE TYPE OF DESIRE WELLED UP WITHIN ME... WHEN SUCH A ROUTINE SHOULD HAVE BEEN IMPOSSIBLE.
I WANT TO BE NEAR THEM. I WANT TO MEET THEM. I WANT TO SPEAK WITH THEM...
SO I TOOK A PHYSICAL FORM AND WANDERED IN SEARCH OF YOU. I WAS MOST LIKELY IN A SHATTERED AND FRAGMENTED STATE AT THE TIME...

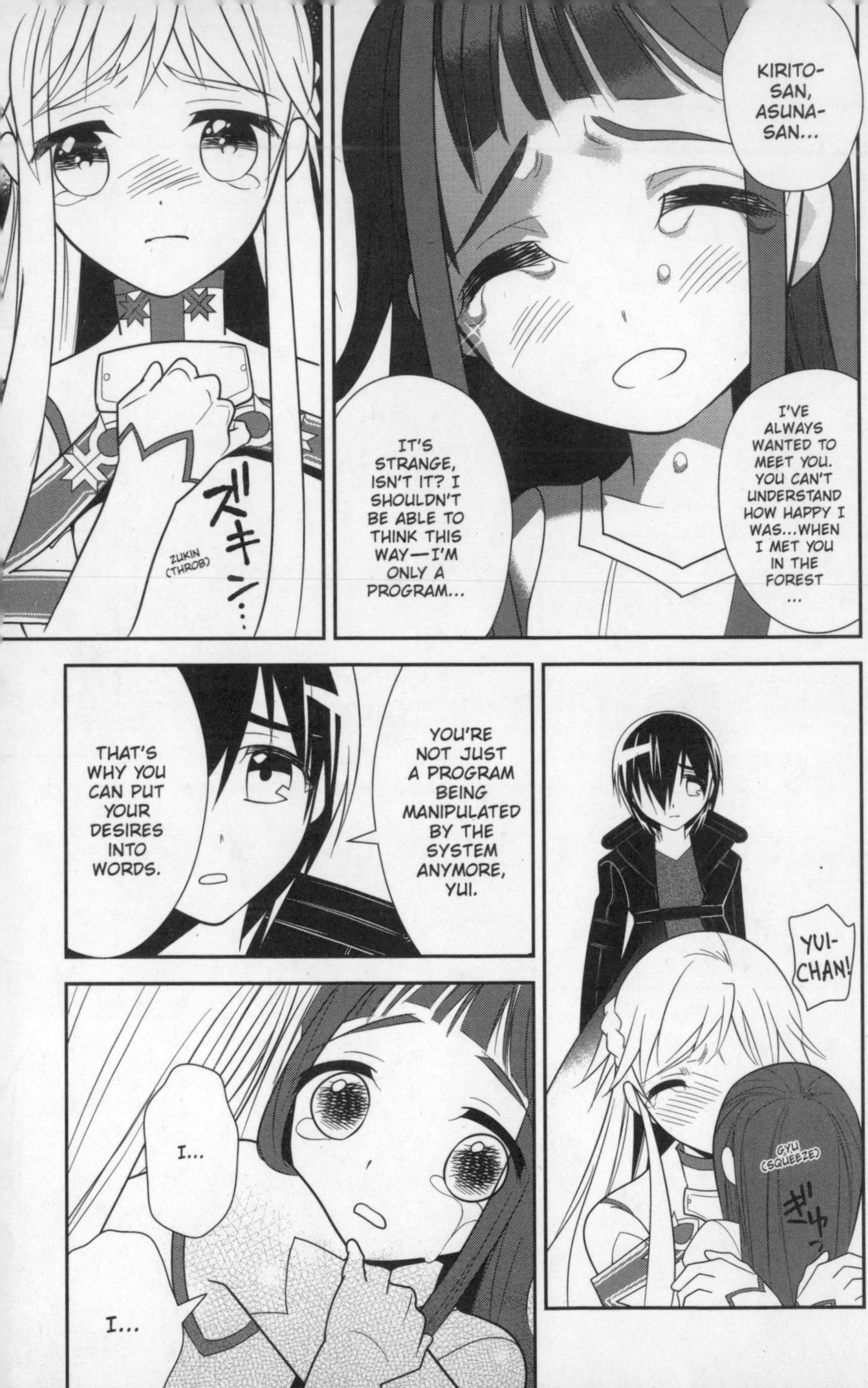
KIRITO-SAN, ASUNA-SAN...
I'VE ALWAYS WANTED TO MEET YOU. YOU CAN'T UNDERSTAND HOW HAPPY I WAS...WHEN I MET YOU IN THE FOREST...
IT'S STRANGE, ISN'T IT? I SHOULDN'T BE ABLE TO THINK THIS WAY—I'M ONLY A PROGRAM...
ズキン...
ZUKIN (THROB)
YUI-CHAN!
ぎゅっ
GYU (SQUEEZE)
YOU'RE NOT JUST A PROGRAM BEING MANIPULATED BY THE SYSTEM ANYMORE, YUI.
THAT'S WHY YOU CAN PUT YOUR DESIRES INTO WORDS.
I...
I...

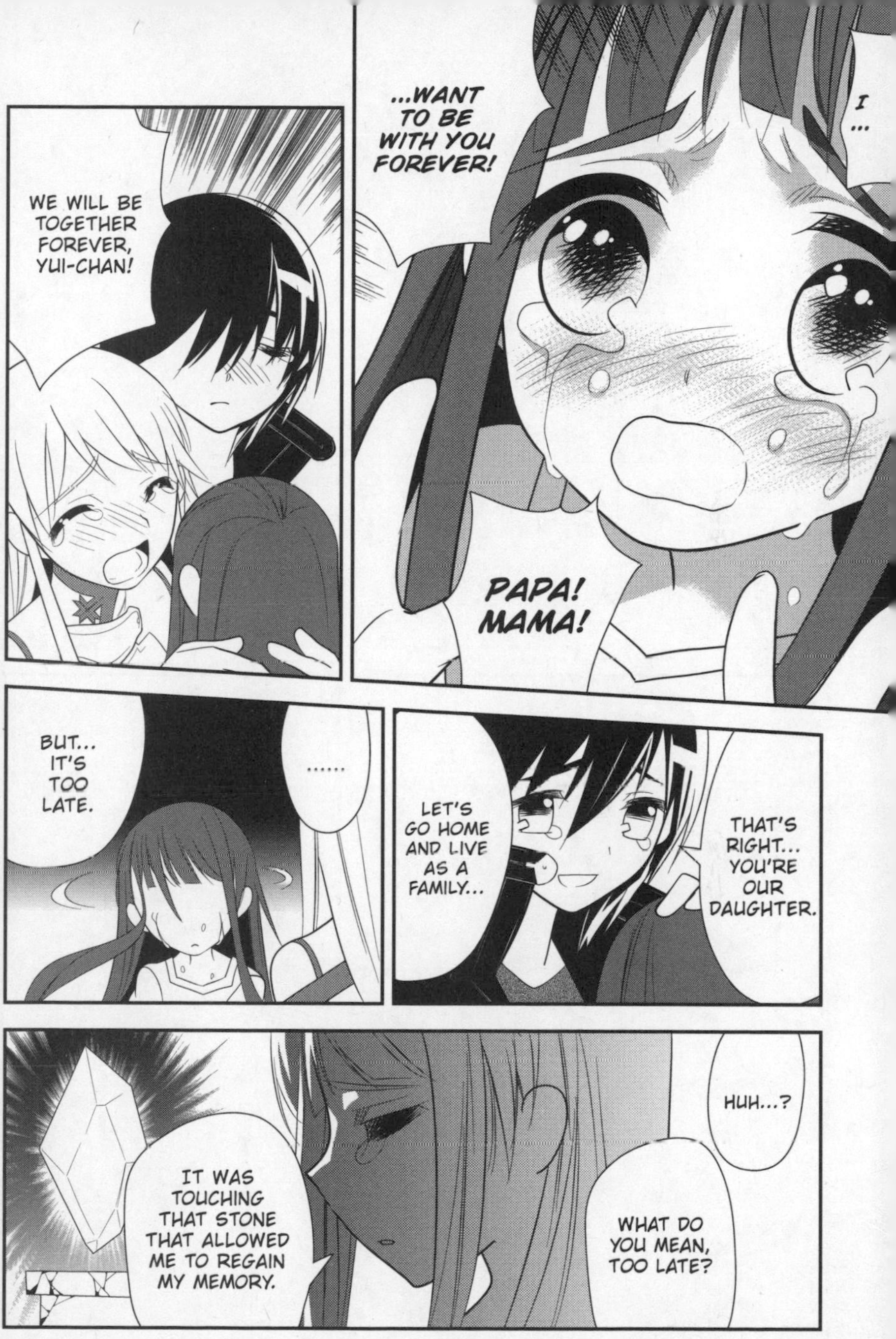
I ...
...WANT TO BE WITH YOU FOREVER!
PAPA! MAMA!
WE WILL BE TOGETHER FOREVER, YUI-CHAN!
THAT'S RIGHT... YOU'RE OUR DAUGHTER.
LET'S GO HOME AND LIVE AS A FAMILY...
......
BUT... IT'S TOO LATE.
HUH...?
WHAT DO YOU MEAN, TOO LATE?
IT WAS TOUCHING THAT STONE THAT ALLOWED ME TO REGAIN MY MEMORY.

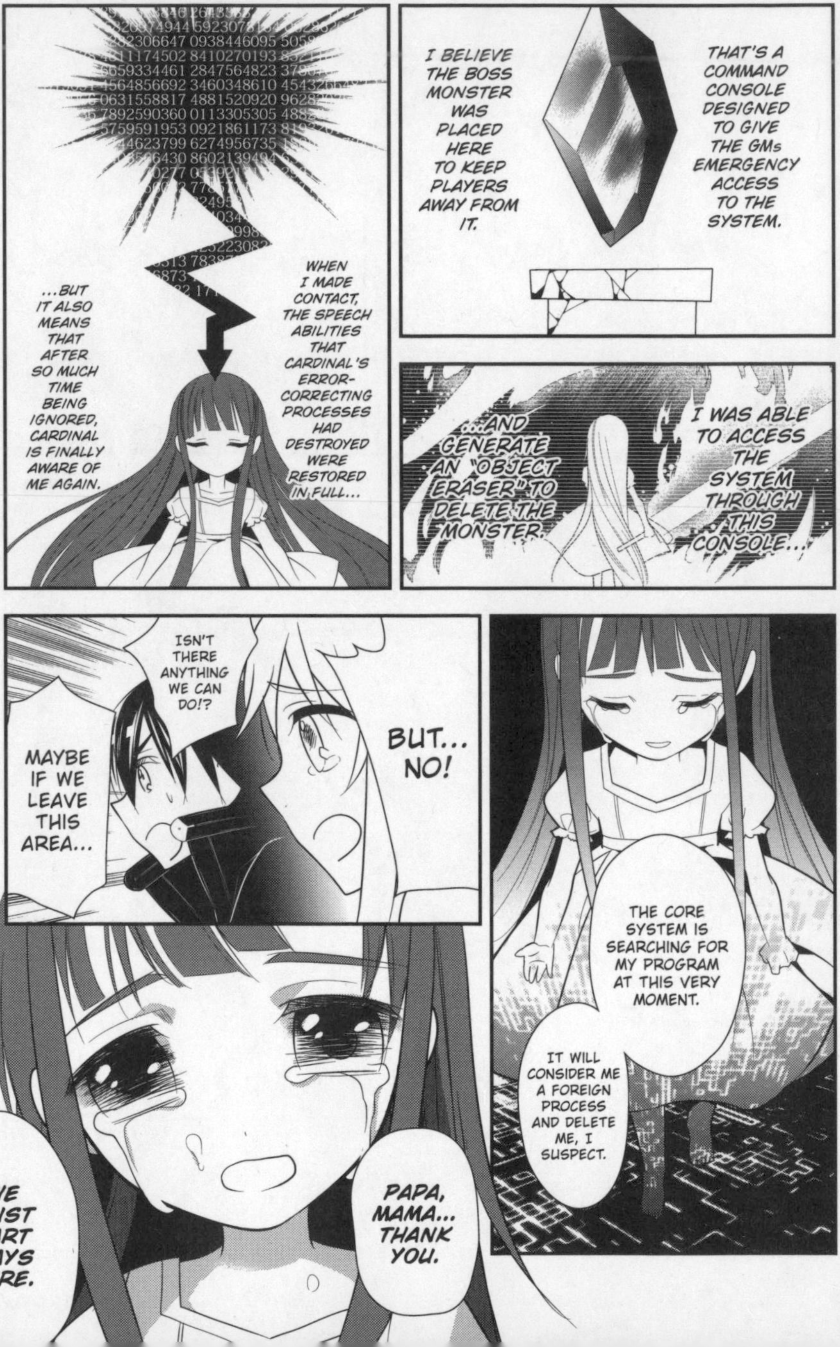
THAT'S A COMMAND CONSOLE DESIGNED TO GIVE THE GMs EMERGENCY ACCESS TO THE SYSTEM.
I BELIEVE THE BOSS MONSTER WAS PLACED HERE TO KEEP PLAYERS AWAY FROM IT.
I WAS ABLE TO ACCESS THE SYSTEM THROUGH THIS CONSOLE...
...AND GENERATE AN "OBJECT ERASER" TO DELETE THE MONSTER.
WHEN I MADE CONTACT, THE SPEECH ABILITIES THAT CARDINAL'S ERROR-CORRECTING PROCESSES HAD DESTROYED WERE RESTORED IN FULL...
...BUT IT ALSO MEANS THAT AFTER SO MUCH TIME BEING IGNORED, CARDINAL IS FINALLY AWARE OF ME AGAIN.
THE CORE SYSTEM IS SEARCHING FOR MY PROGRAM AT THIS VERY MOMENT.
IT WILL CONSIDER ME A FOREIGN PROCESS AND DELETE ME, I SUSPECT.
BUT... NO!
ISN'T THERE ANYTHING WE CAN DO!?
MAYBE IF WE LEAVE THIS AREA...
PAPA, MAMA... THANK YOU.
WE MUST PART WAYS HERE.

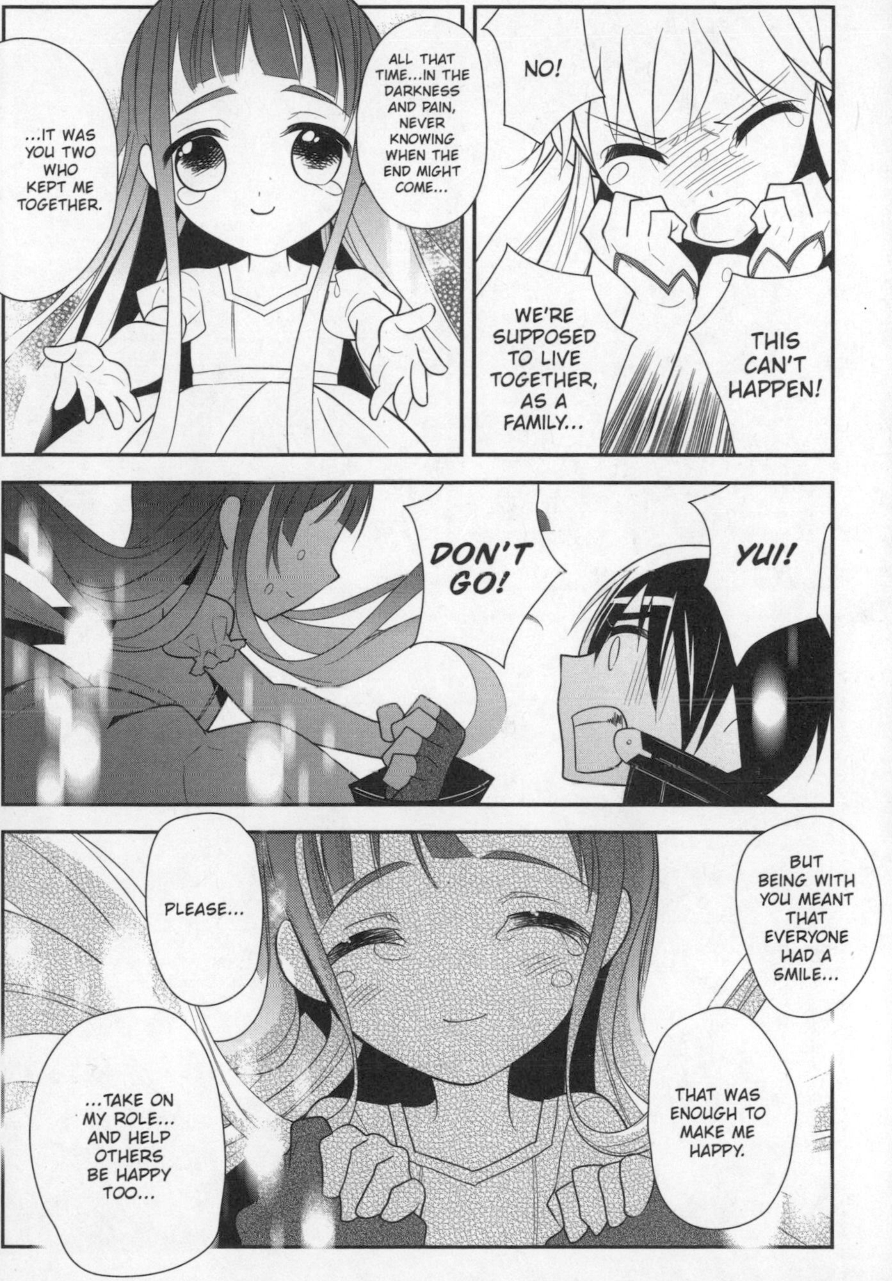
NO!
THIS CAN'T HAPPEN!
WE'RE SUPPOSED TO LIVE TOGETHER, AS A FAMILY...
ALL THAT TIME...IN THE DARKNESS AND PAIN, NEVER KNOWING WHEN THE END MIGHT COME...
...IT WAS YOU TWO WHO KEPT ME TOGETHER.
YUI!
DON'T GO!
BUT BEING WITH YOU MEANT THAT EVERYONE HAD A SMILE...
THAT WAS ENOUGH TO MAKE ME HAPPY.
PLEASE...
...TAKE ON MY ROLE... AND HELP OTHERS BE HAPPY TOO...

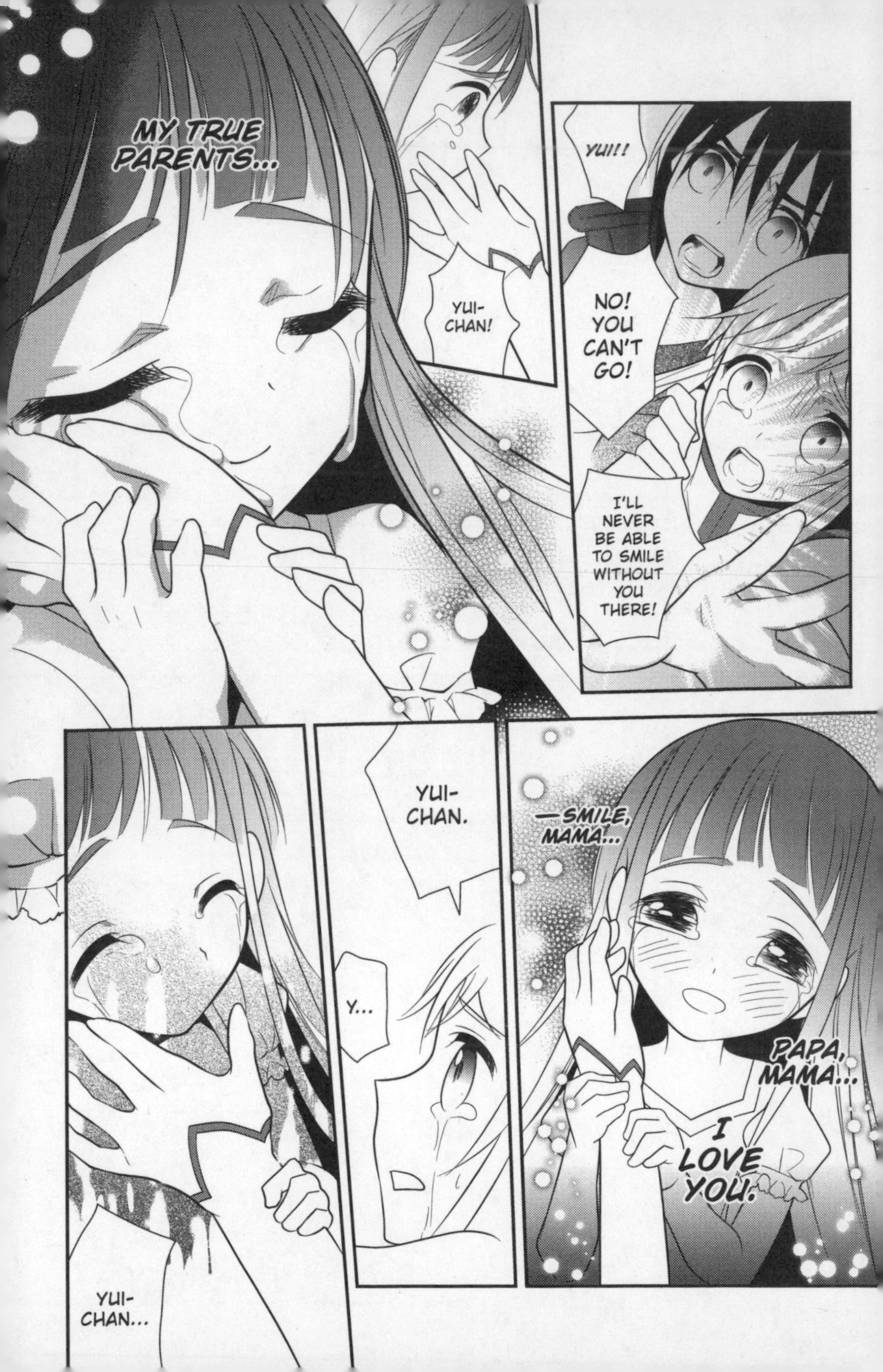
YUI!!
NO! YOU CAN'T GO!
I'LL NEVER BE ABLE TO SMILE WITHOUT YOU THERE!
YUI-CHAN!
MY TRUE PARENTS...
—SMILE, MAMA...
PAPA, MAMA...
I LOVE YOU.
YUI-CHAN.
Y...
YUI-CHAN...

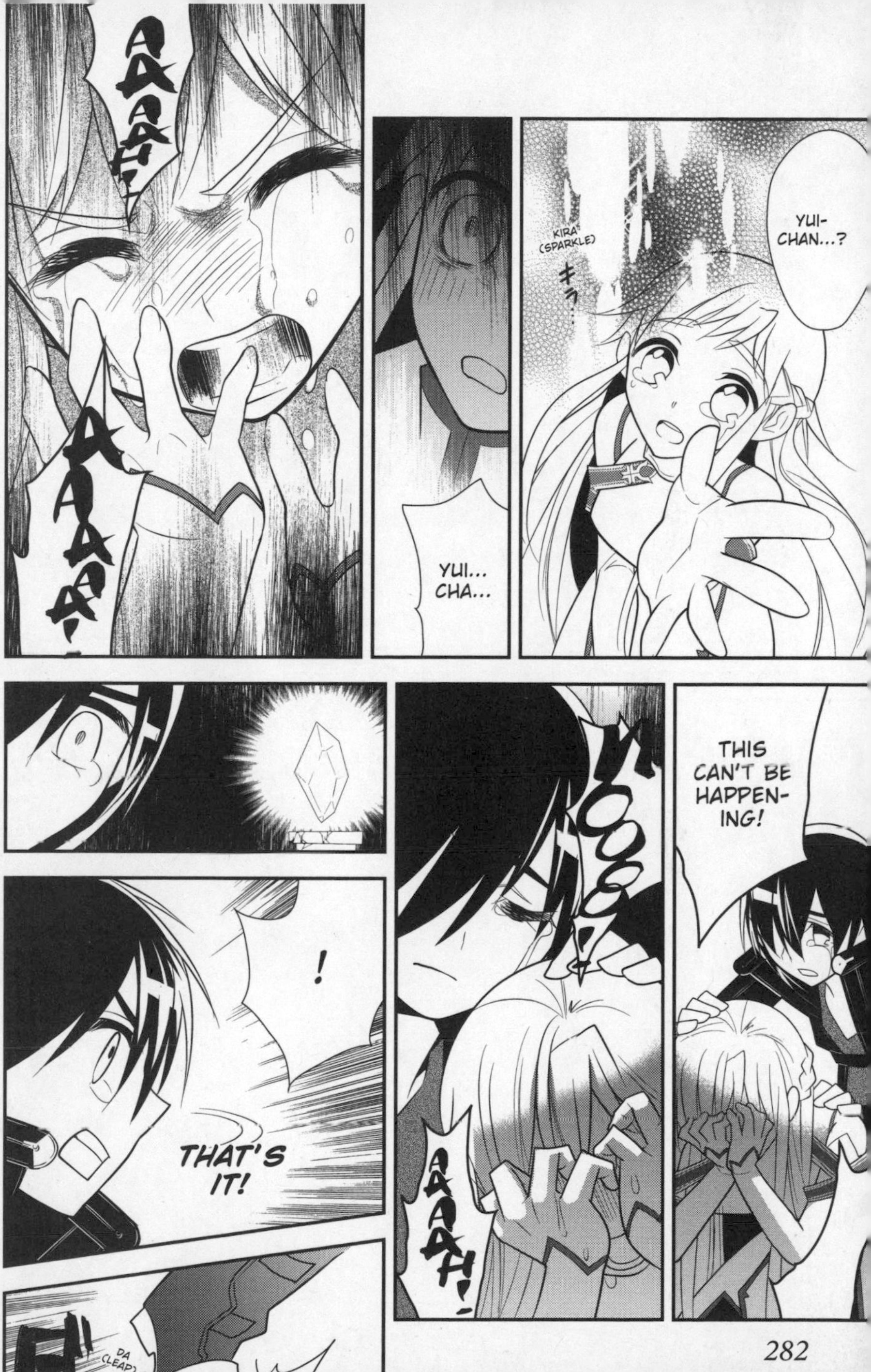
YUI-
CHAN...?
KIRA
(SPARKLE)
キラ
YUI...
CHA...
AAAAH!
AAAAA-
THIS
CAN'T BE
HAPPEN-
ING!
NOOOO!
AAAAH!
!
THAT'S
IT!
DA
(LEAP)

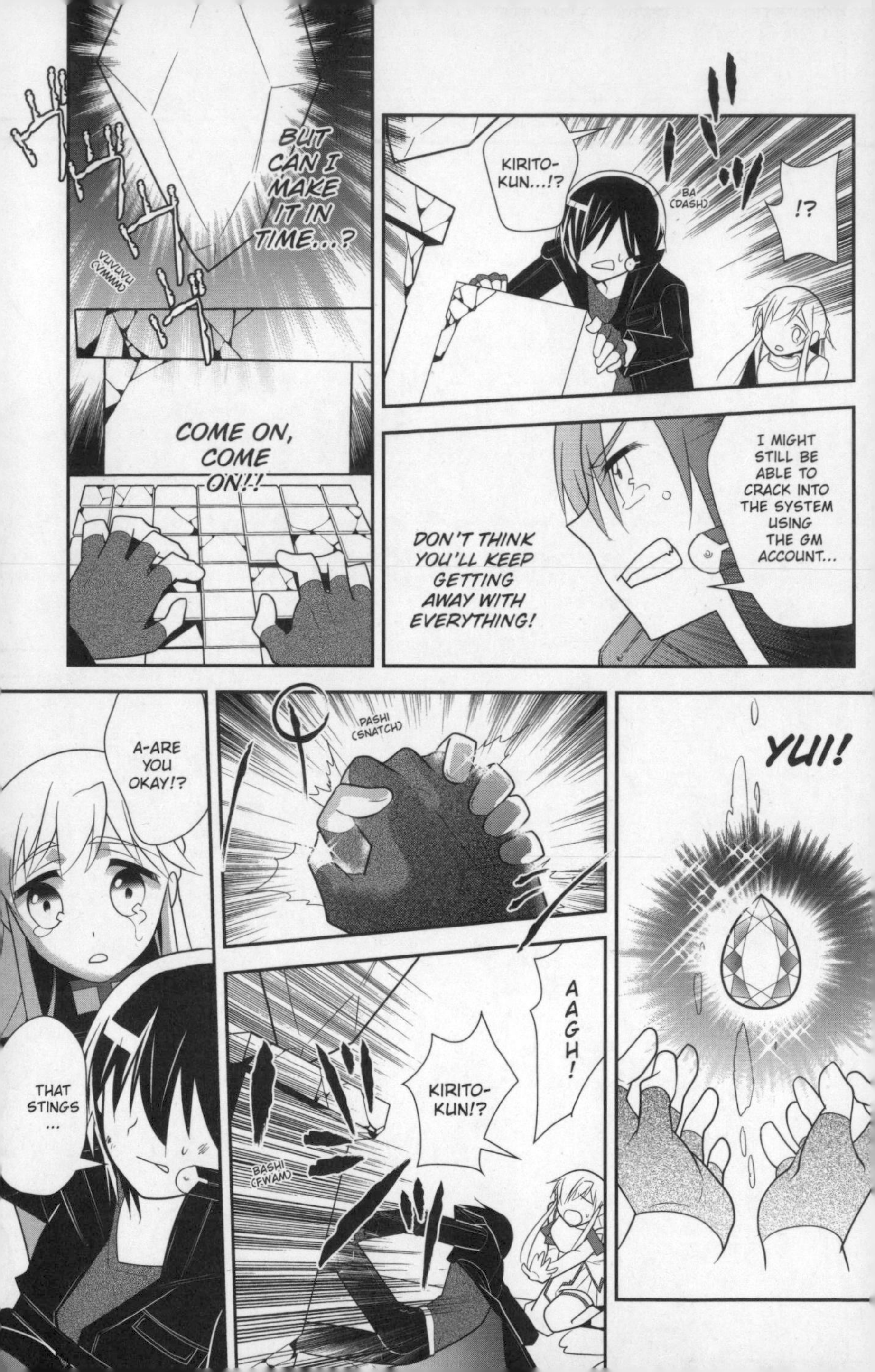
KIRITO-KUN...!?
BA (DASH)
!?
I MIGHT STILL BE ABLE TO CRACK INTO THE SYSTEM USING THE GM ACCOUNT...
DON'T THINK YOU'LL KEEP GETTING AWAY WITH EVERYTHING!
BUT CAN I MAKE IT IN TIME...?
VUVUVU (VMMM)
COME ON, COME ON!!
YUI!
PASHI (SNATCH)
AAGH!
KIRITO-KUN!?
BASHI (FWAM)
A-ARE YOU OKAY!?
THAT STINGS...

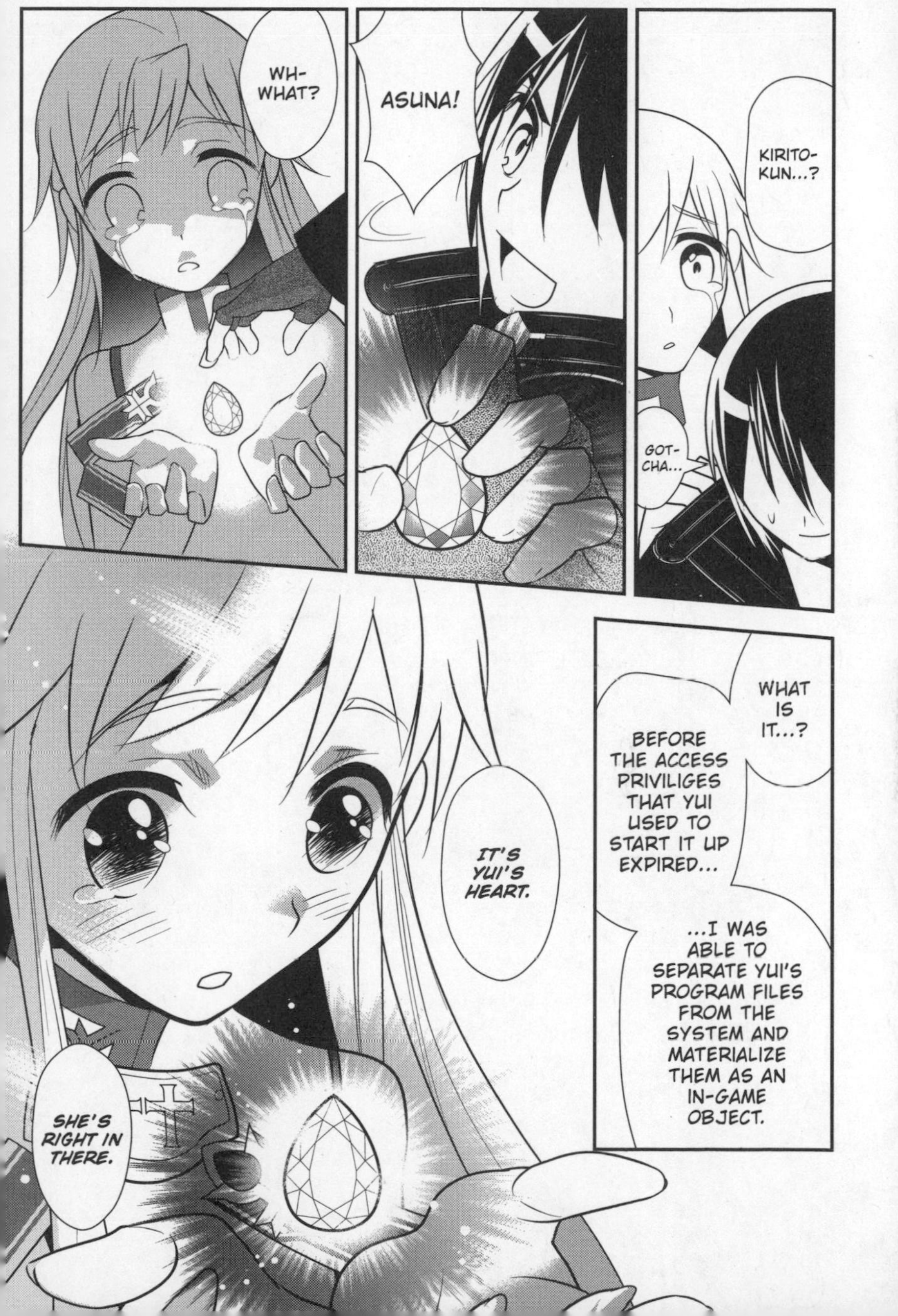
KIRITO-KUN...?
GOT-CHA...
ASUNA!
WH-WHAT?
WHAT IS IT...?
BEFORE THE ACCESS PRIVILIGES THAT YUI USED TO START IT UP EXPIRED...
...I WAS ABLE TO SEPARATE YUI'S PROGRAM FILES FROM THE SYSTEM AND MATERIALIZE THEM AS AN IN-GAME OBJECT.
IT'S YUI'S HEART.
SHE'S RIGHT IN THERE.

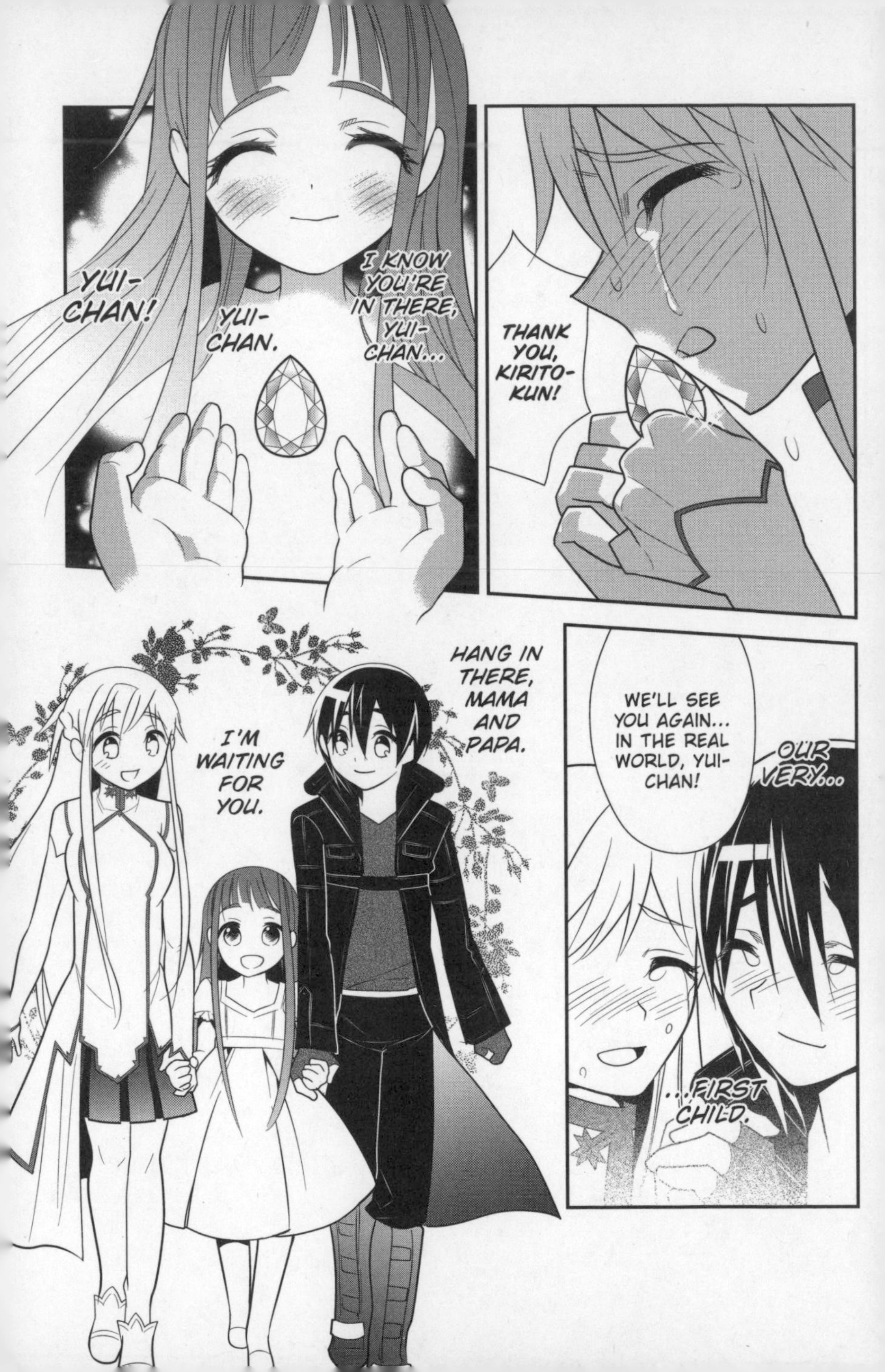
THANK YOU, KIRITO-KUN!
I KNOW YOU'RE IN THERE, YUI-CHAN...
YUI-CHAN.
YUI-CHAN!
WE'LL SEE YOU AGAIN... IN THE REAL WORLD, YUI-CHAN!
OUR VERY...
...FIRST CHILD.
HANG IN THERE, MAMA AND PAPA.
I'M WAITING FOR YOU.

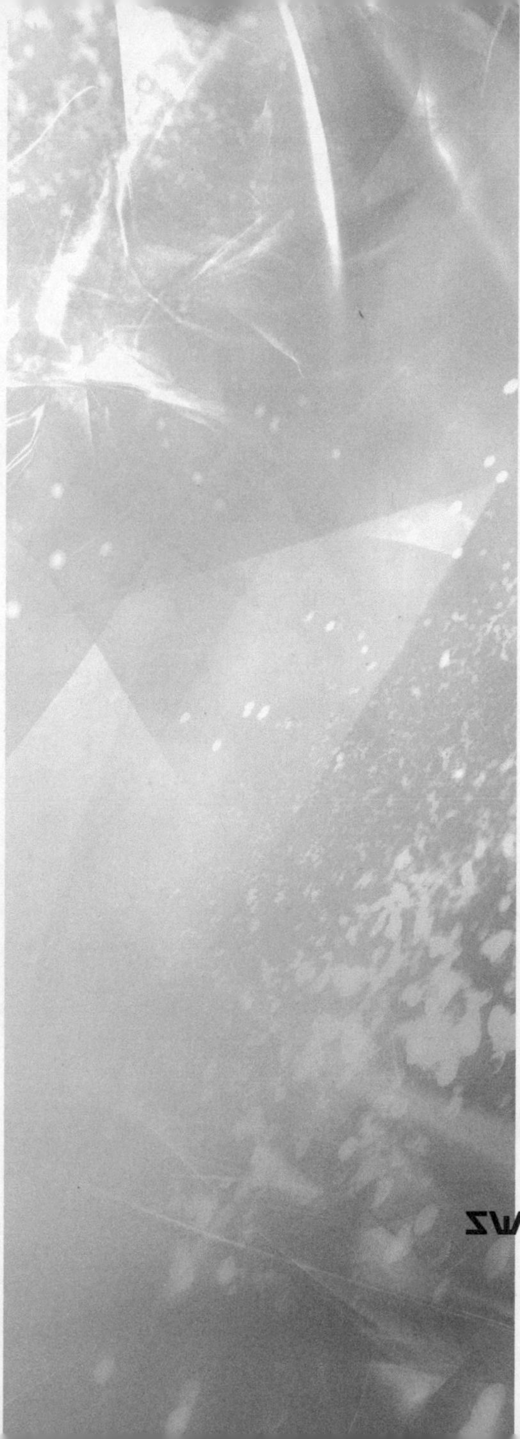

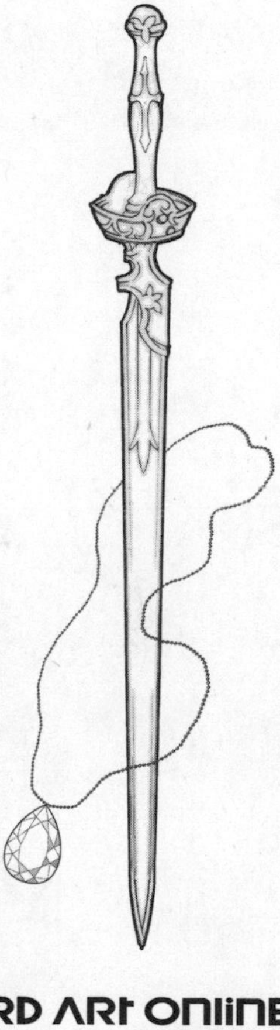

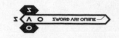

SWORD ART ONLINE
Aincrad

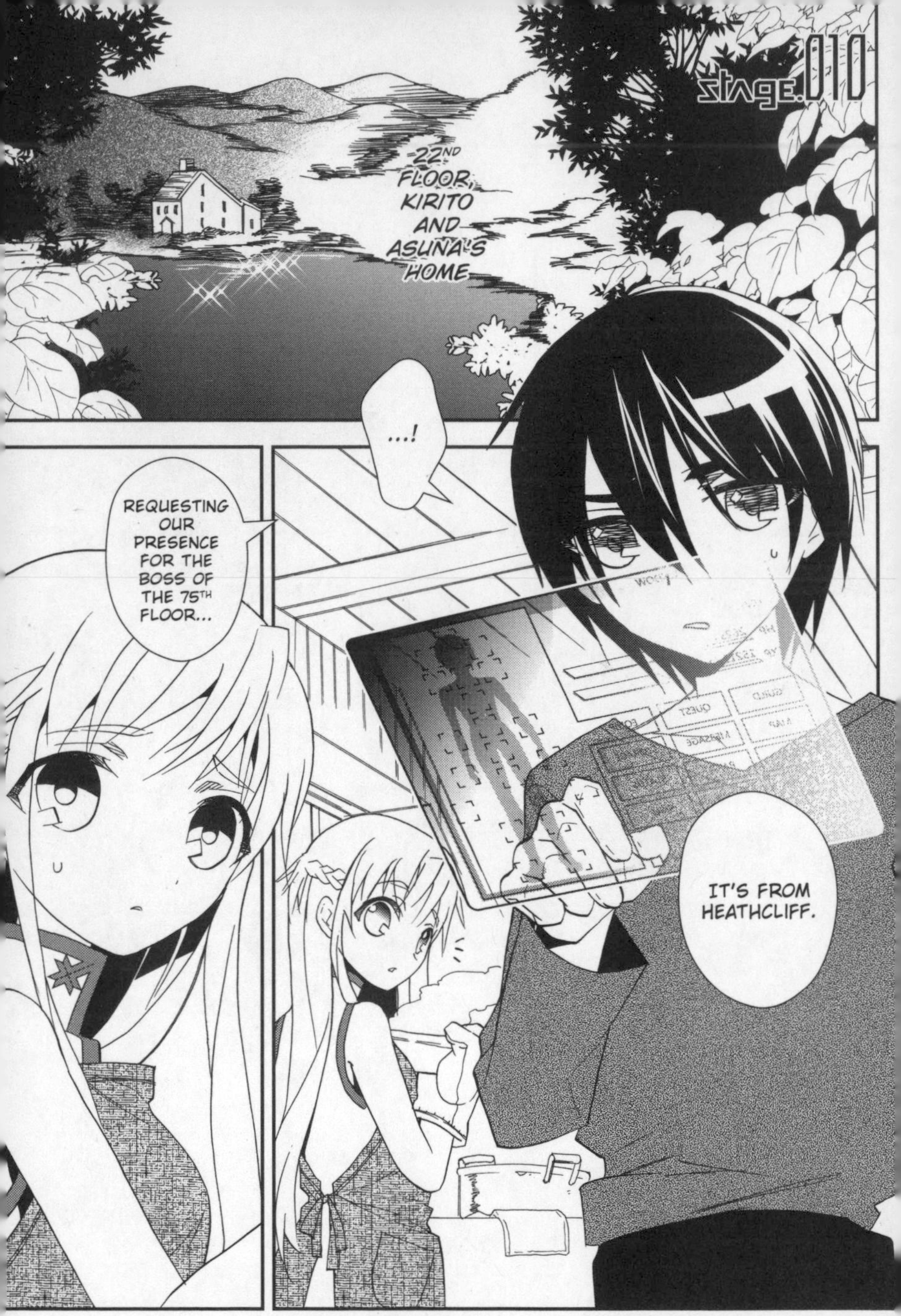
stage.010
22ND FLOOR, KIRITO AND ASUNA'S HOME
IT'S FROM HEATHCLIFF.
...!
REQUESTING OUR PRESENCE FOR THE BOSS OF THE 75TH FLOOR...

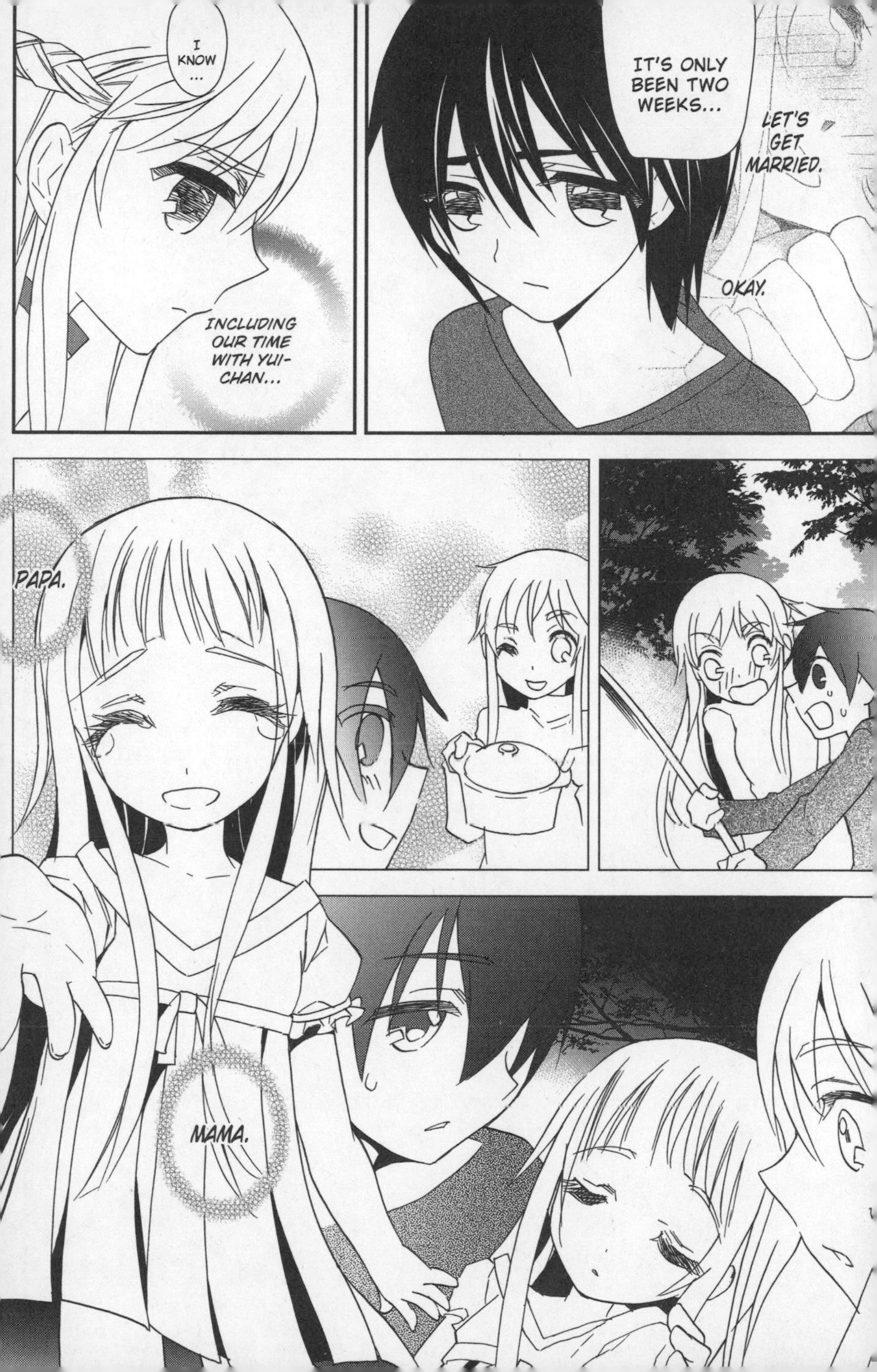
IT'S ONLY BEEN TWO WEEKS...
LET'S GET MARRIED.
OKAY.
I KNOW...
INCLUDING OUR TIME WITH YUI-CHAN...
PAPA.
MAMA.

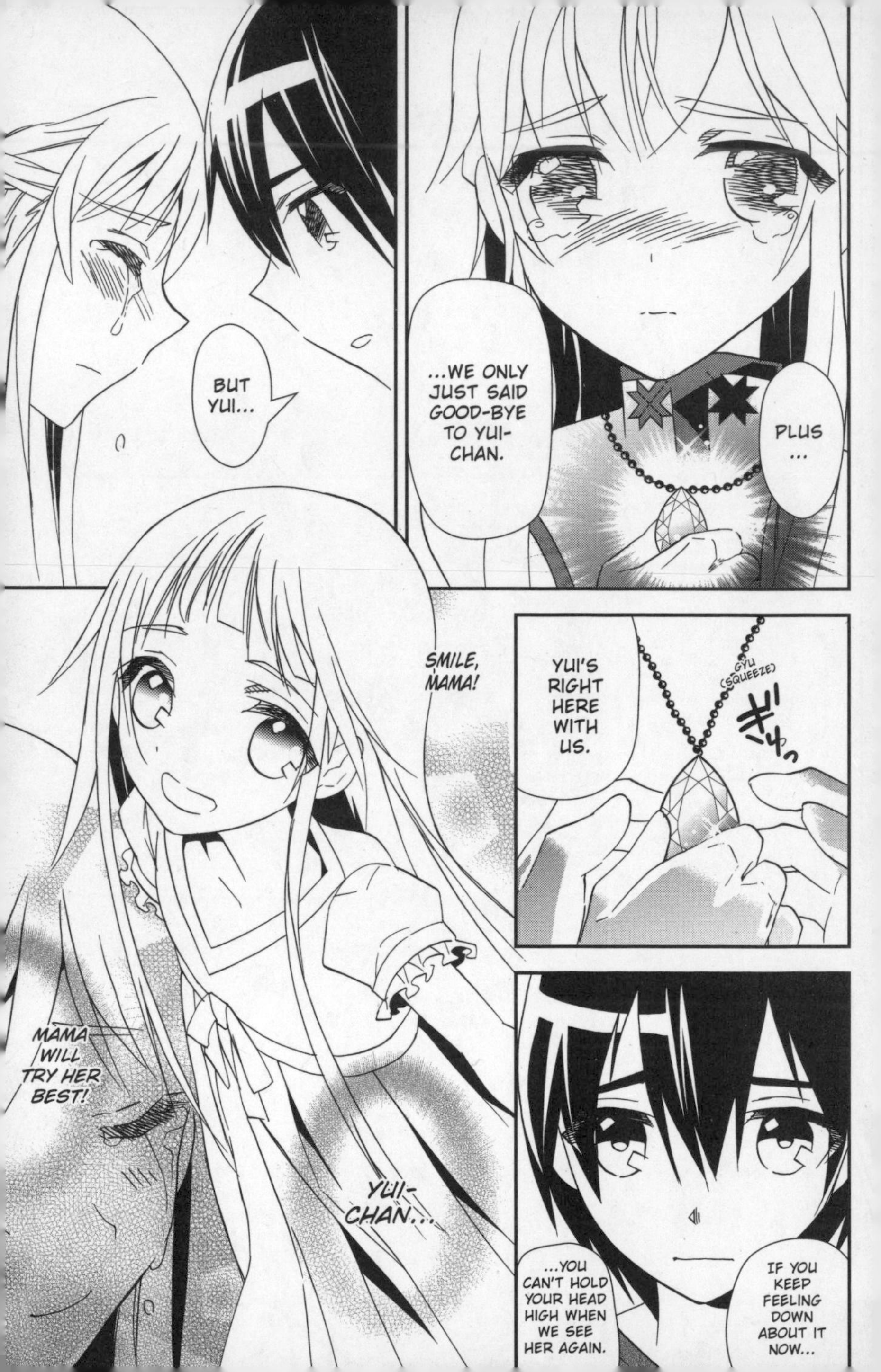
...WE ONLY JUST SAID GOOD-BYE TO YUI-CHAN.
PLUS...
BUT YUI...
YUI'S RIGHT HERE WITH US.
GYU (SQUEEZE)
IF YOU KEEP FEELING DOWN ABOUT IT NOW...
...YOU CAN'T HOLD YOUR HEAD HIGH WHEN WE SEE HER AGAIN.
SMILE, MAMA!
MAMA WILL TRY HER BEST!
YUI-CHAN...

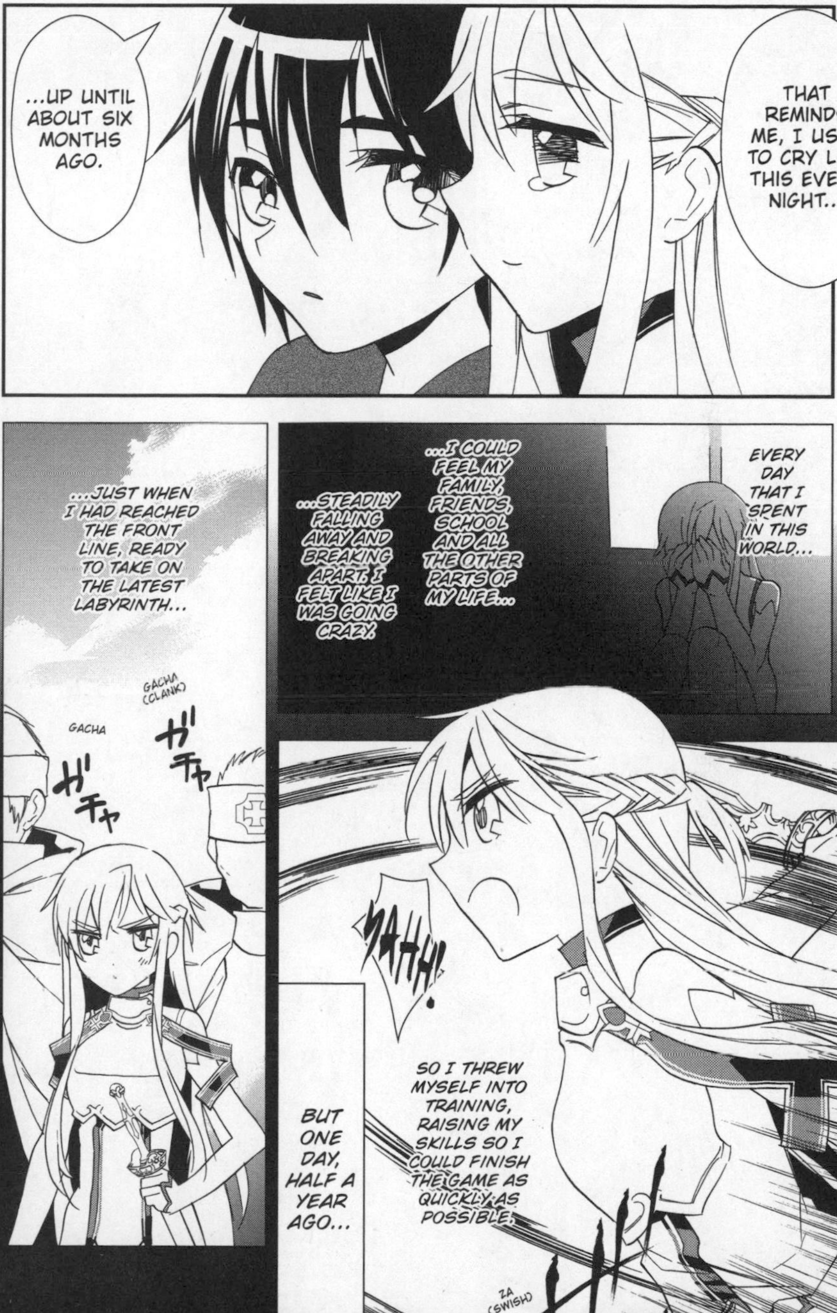
THAT REMINDS ME, I USED TO CRY LIKE THIS EVERY NIGHT...
...UP UNTIL ABOUT SIX MONTHS AGO.
EVERY DAY THAT I SPENT IN THIS WORLD...
...I COULD FEEL MY FAMILY, FRIENDS, SCHOOL AND ALL THE OTHER PARTS OF MY LIFE...
...STEADILY FALLING AWAY AND BREAKING APART. I FELT LIKE I WAS GOING CRAZY.
SAHH!
SO I THREW MYSELF INTO TRAINING, RAISING MY SKILLS SO I COULD FINISH THE GAME AS QUICKLY AS POSSIBLE.
BUT ONE DAY, HALF A YEAR AGO...
ZA (SWISH)
...JUST WHEN I HAD REACHED THE FRONT LINE, READY TO TAKE ON THE LATEST LABYRINTH...
ガチャ
GACHA (CLANK)
ガチャ
GACHA

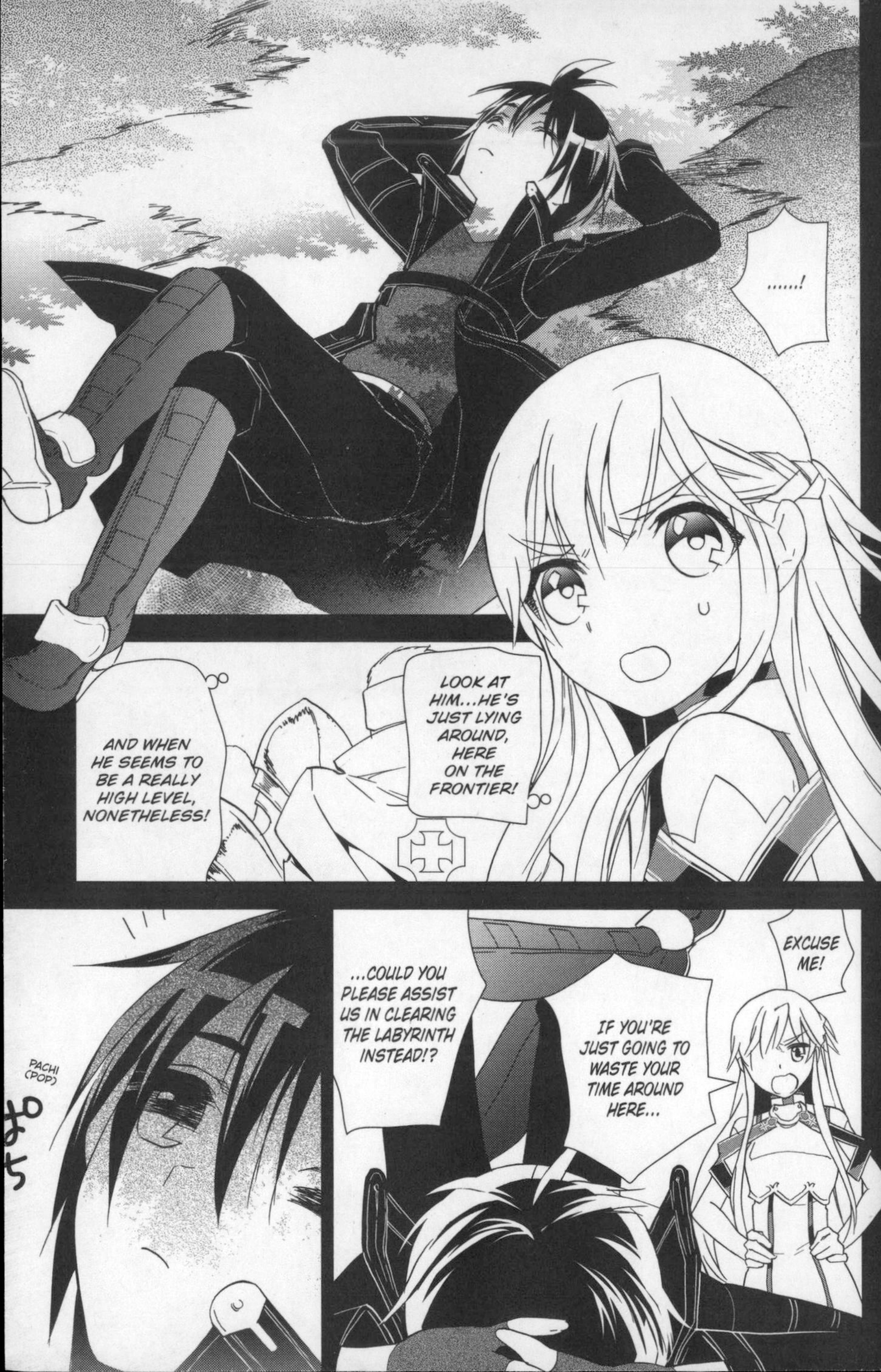
......!
LOOK AT HIM...HE'S JUST LYING AROUND, HERE ON THE FRONTIER!
AND WHEN HE SEEMS TO BE A REALLY HIGH LEVEL, NONETHELESS!
EXCUSE ME!
IF YOU'RE JUST GOING TO WASTE YOUR TIME AROUND HERE...
...COULD YOU PLEASE ASSIST US IN CLEARING THE LABYRINTH INSTEAD!?
ぱち
PACHI (POP)

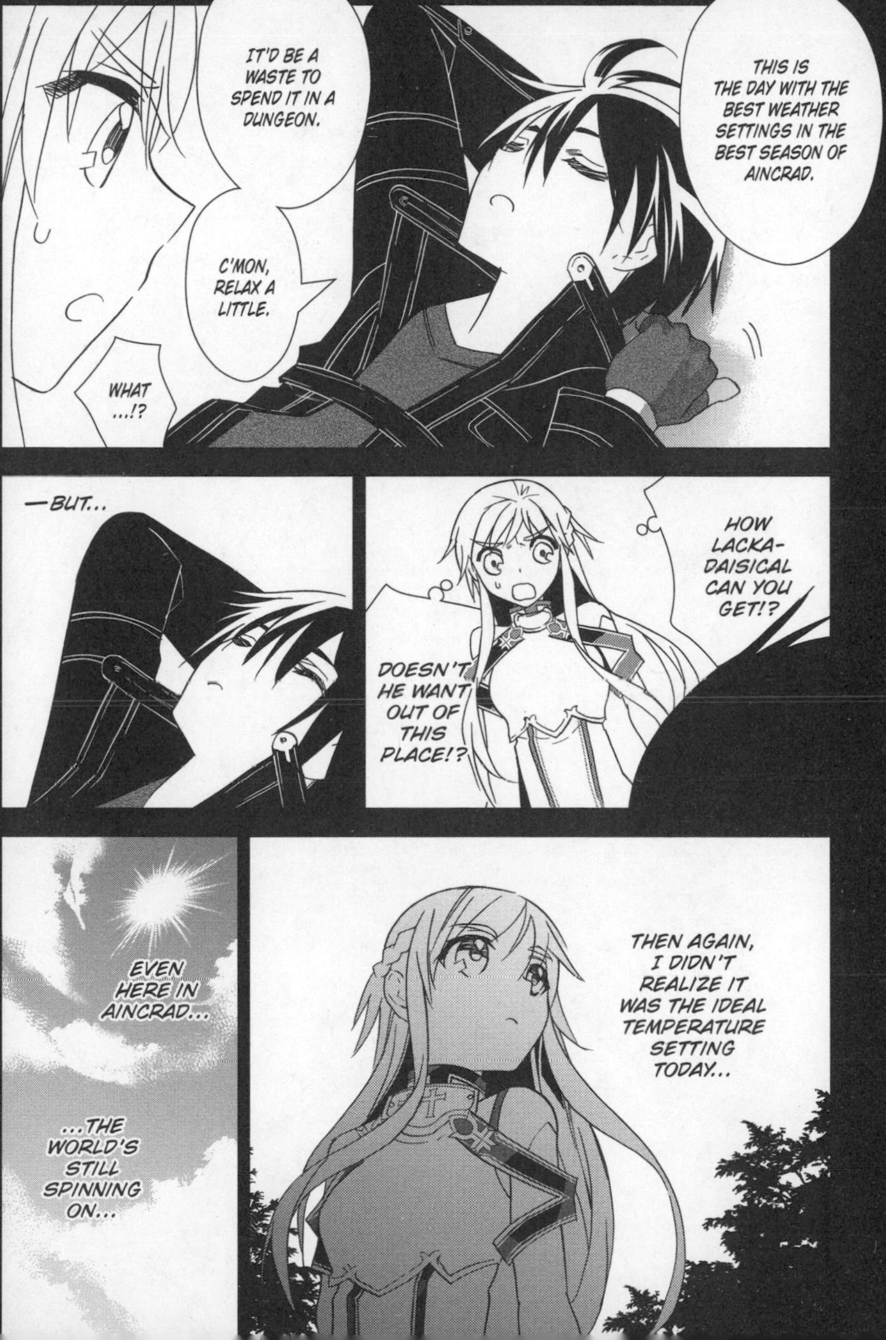
THIS IS THE DAY WITH THE BEST WEATHER SETTINGS IN THE BEST SEASON OF AINCRAD.
IT'D BE A WASTE TO SPEND IT IN A DUNGEON.
C'MON, RELAX A LITTLE.
WHAT ...!?
HOW LACKA-DAISICAL CAN YOU GET!?
DOESN'T HE WANT OUT OF THIS PLACE!?
—BUT...
THEN AGAIN, I DIDN'T REALIZE IT WAS THE IDEAL TEMPERATURE SETTING TODAY...
EVEN HERE IN AINCRAD...
...THE WORLD'S STILL SPINNING ON...

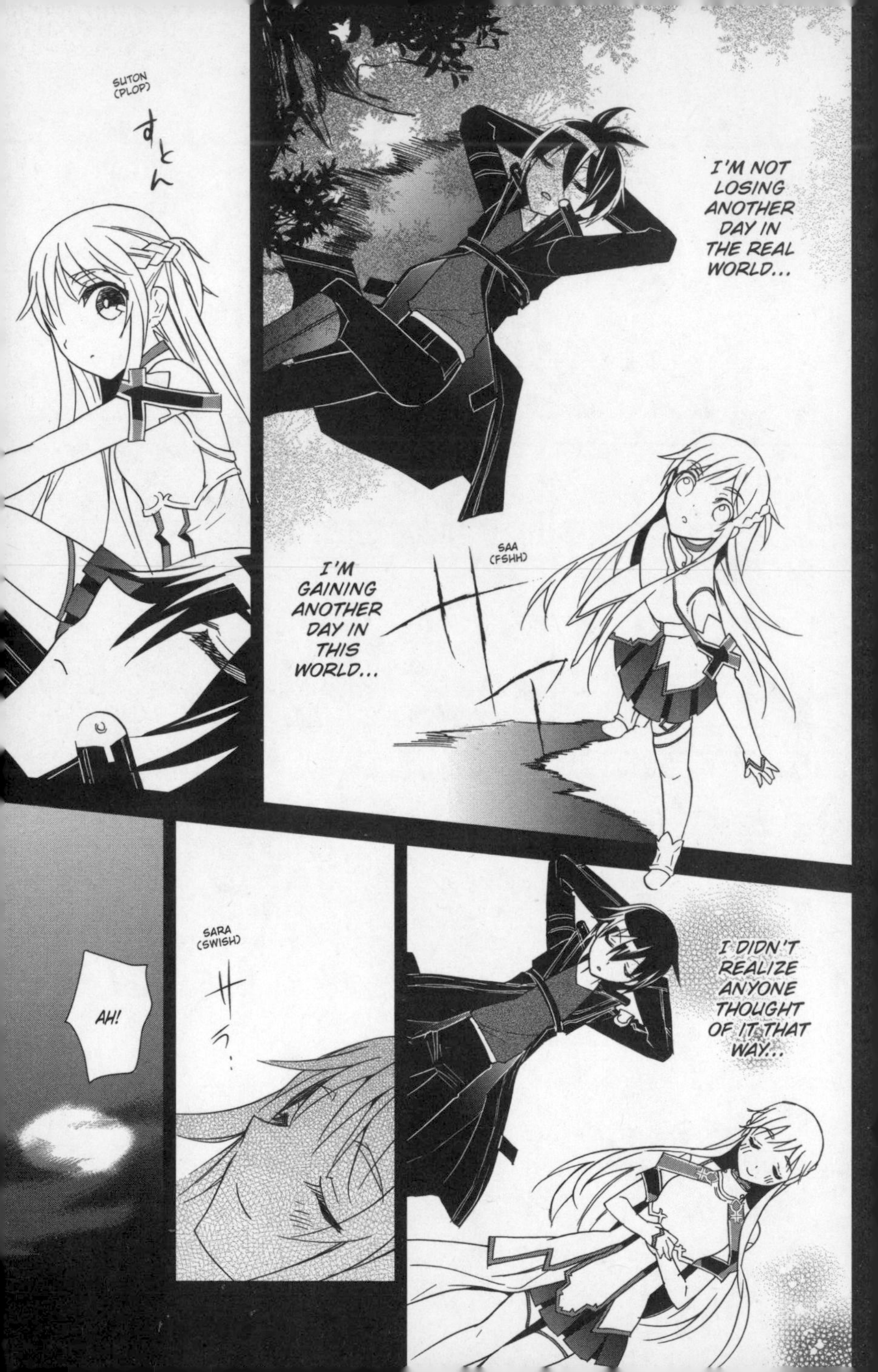

I'M NOT LOSING ANOTHER DAY IN THE REAL WORLD...
SAA (FSHH)
I'M GAINING ANOTHER DAY IN THIS WORLD...
SUTON (PLOP)
すとん
I DIDN'T REALIZE ANYONE THOUGHT OF IT THAT WAY...
SARA (SWISH)
サラ…
AH!

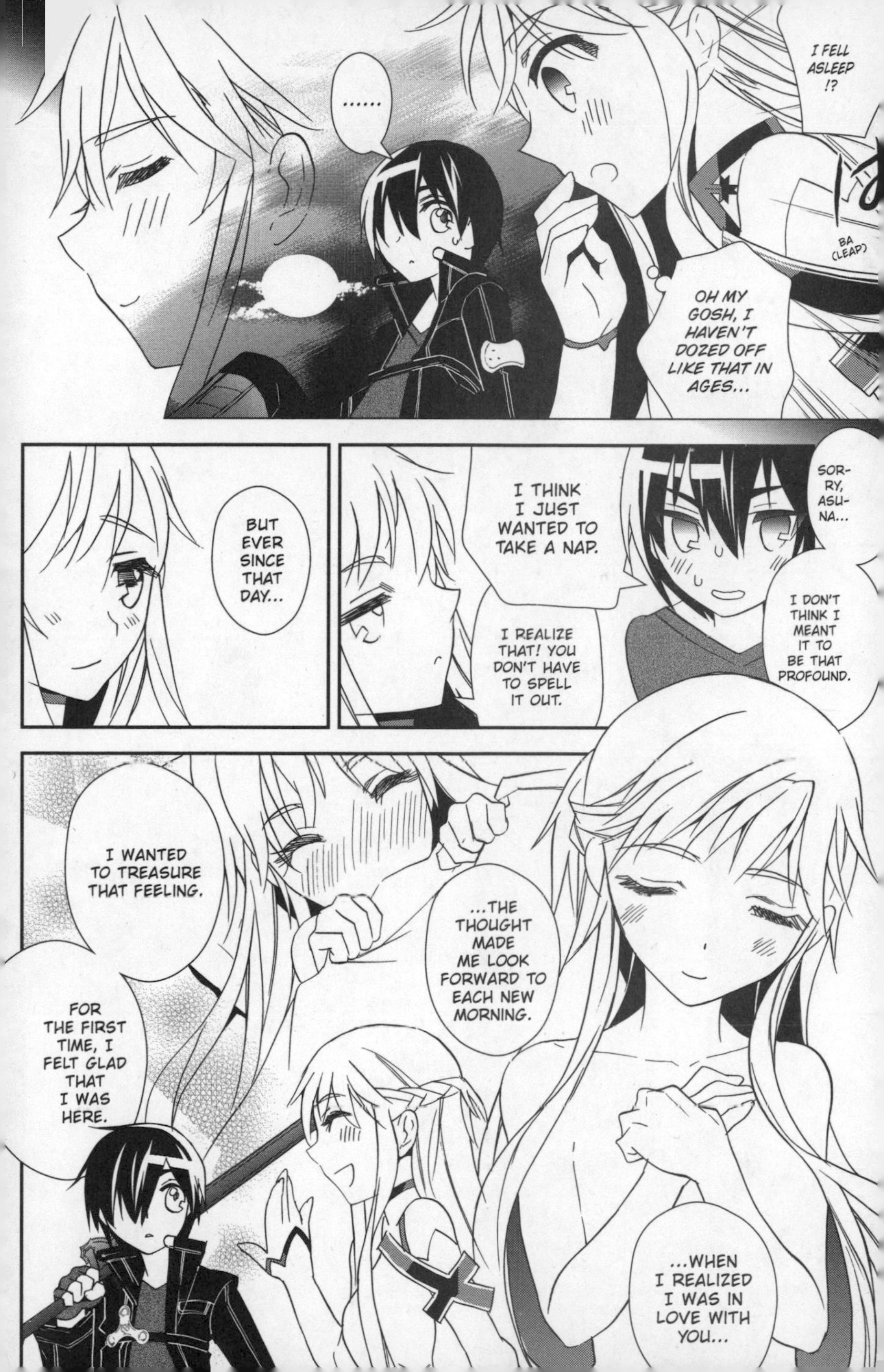
I FELL ASLEEP !?
BA (LEAP)
OH MY GOSH, I HAVEN'T DOZED OFF LIKE THAT IN AGES...
......
SORRY, ASUNA...
I THINK I JUST WANTED TO TAKE A NAP.
I DON'T THINK I MEANT IT TO BE THAT PROFOUND.
I REALIZE THAT! YOU DON'T HAVE TO SPELL IT OUT.
BUT EVER SINCE THAT DAY...
...WHEN I REALIZED I WAS IN LOVE WITH YOU...
...THE THOUGHT MADE ME LOOK FORWARD TO EACH NEW MORNING.
FOR THE FIRST TIME, I FELT GLAD THAT I WAS HERE.
I WANTED TO TREASURE THAT FEELING.

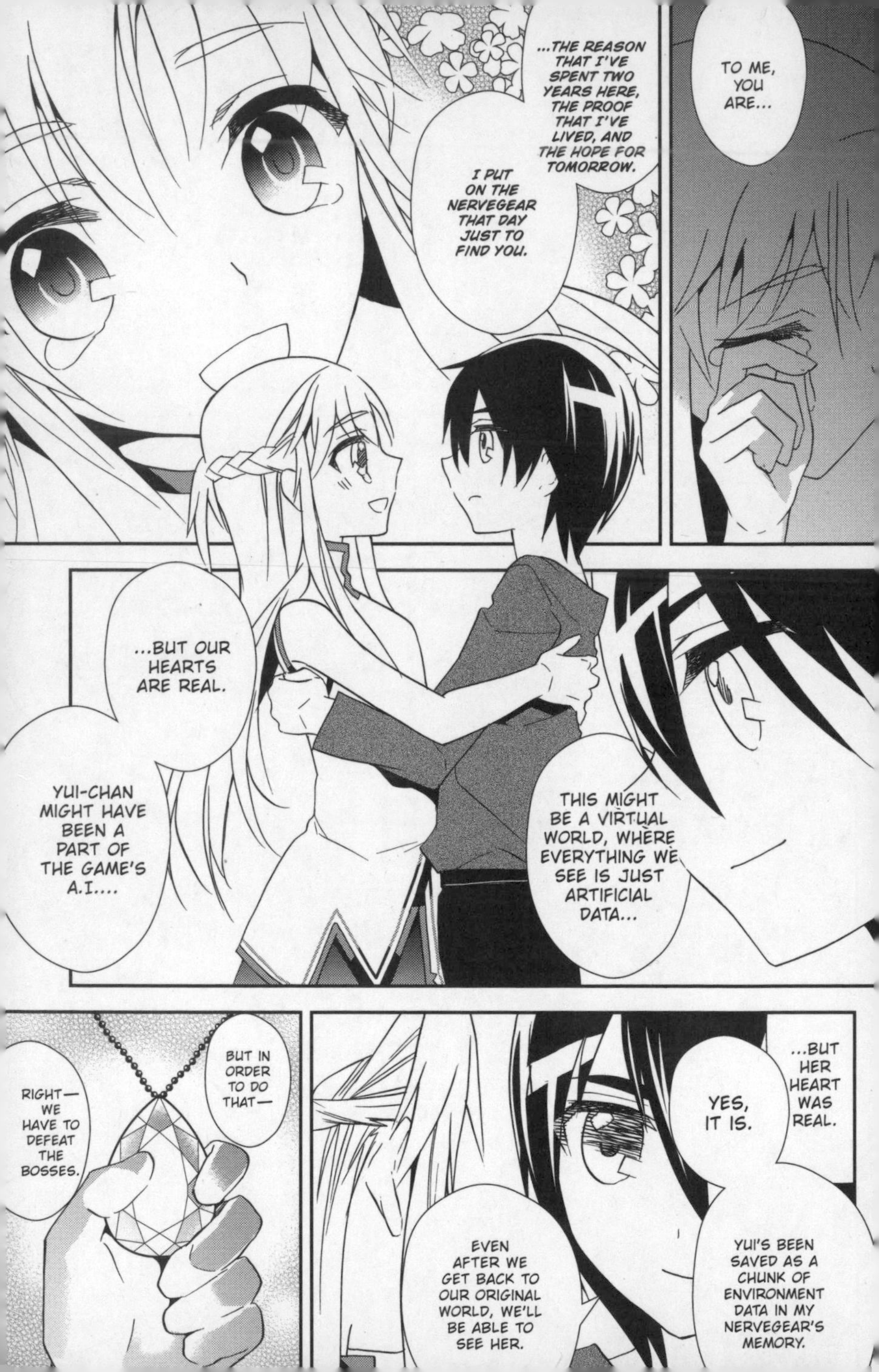
TO ME, YOU ARE...
...THE REASON THAT I'VE SPENT TWO YEARS HERE, THE PROOF THAT I'VE LIVED, AND THE HOPE FOR TOMORROW.
I PUT ON THE NERVEGEAR THAT DAY JUST TO FIND YOU.
THIS MIGHT BE A VIRTUAL WORLD, WHERE EVERYTHING WE SEE IS JUST ARTIFICIAL DATA...
...BUT OUR HEARTS ARE REAL.
YUI-CHAN MIGHT HAVE BEEN A PART OF THE GAME'S A.I....
...BUT HER HEART WAS REAL.
YES, IT IS.
YUI'S BEEN SAVED AS A CHUNK OF ENVIRONMENT DATA IN MY NERVEGEAR'S MEMORY.
EVEN AFTER WE GET BACK TO OUR ORIGINAL WORLD, WE'LL BE ABLE TO SEE HER.
BUT IN ORDER TO DO THAT—
RIGHT— WE HAVE TO DEFEAT THE BOSSES.

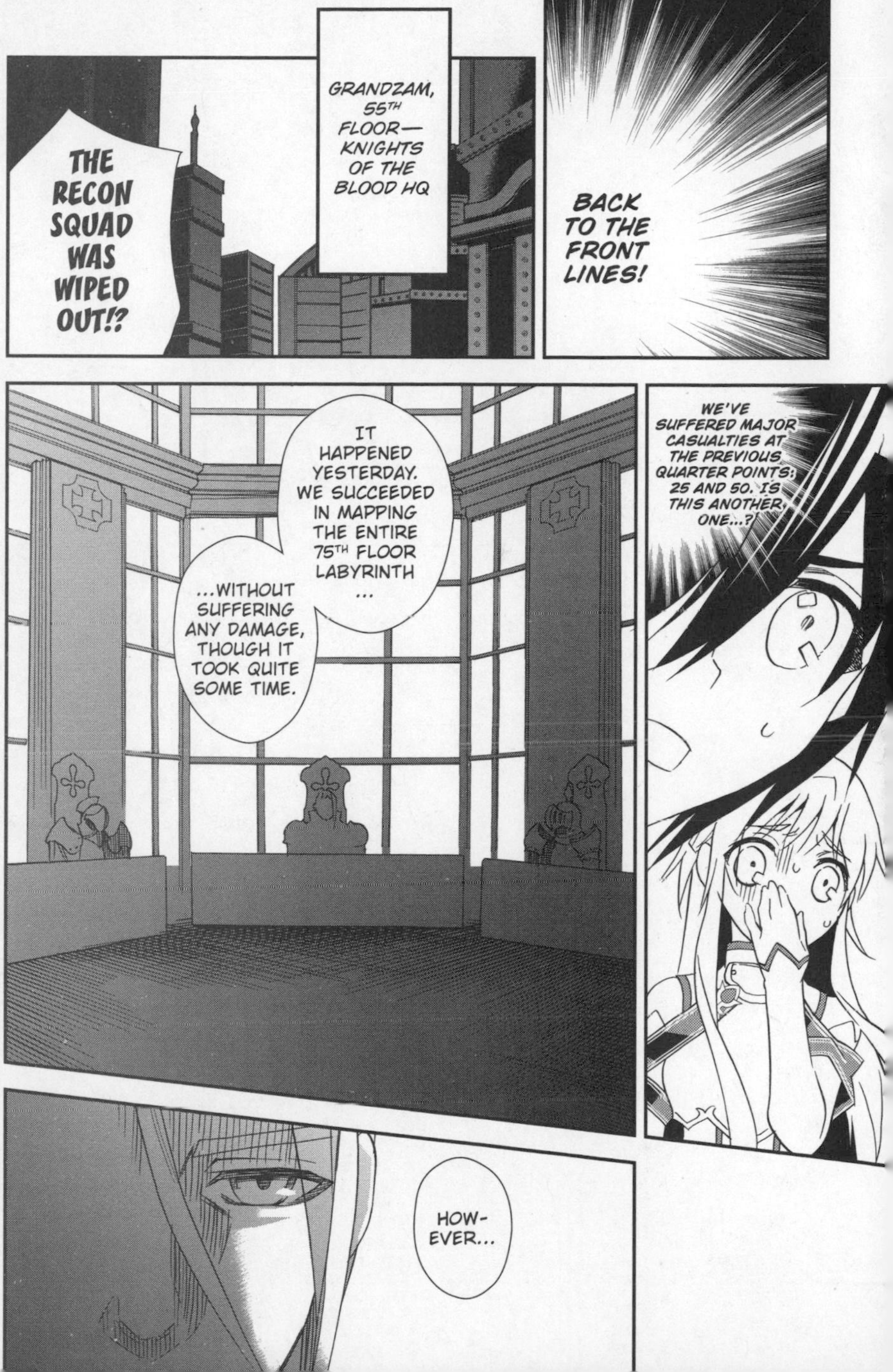
BACK TO THE FRONT LINES!
GRANDZAM, 55TH FLOOR—KNIGHTS OF THE BLOOD HQ
THE RECON SQUAD WAS WIPED OUT!?
WE'VE SUFFERED MAJOR CASUALTIES AT THE PREVIOUS QUARTER POINTS: 25 AND 50. IS THIS ANOTHER ONE...?!
IT HAPPENED YESTERDAY. WE SUCCEEDED IN MAPPING THE ENTIRE 75TH FLOOR LABYRINTH...
...WITHOUT SUFFERING ANY DAMAGE, THOUGH IT TOOK QUITE SOME TIME.
HOW-EVER...

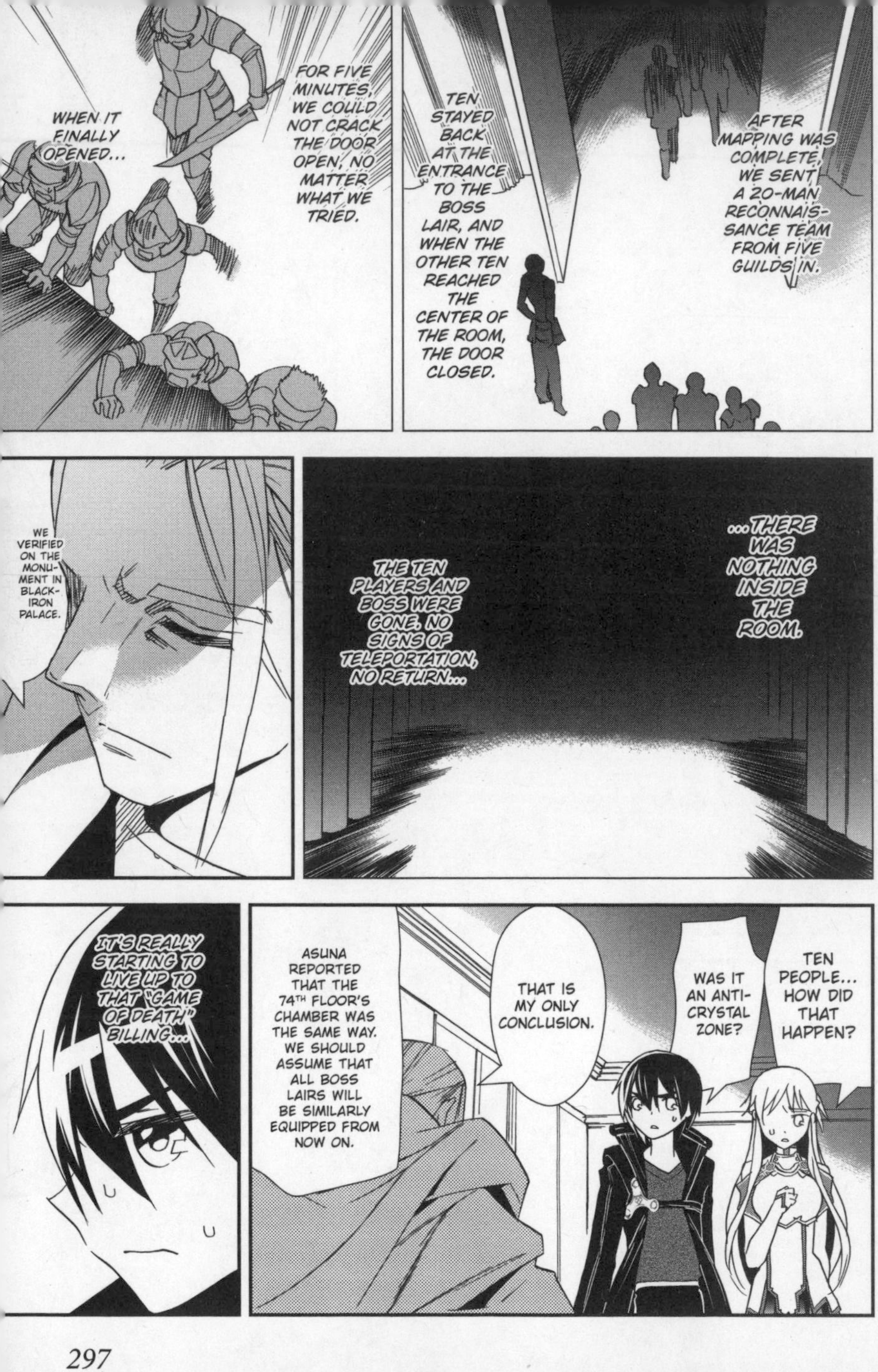
AFTER MAPPING WAS COMPLETE, WE SENT A 20-MAN RECONNAISSANCE TEAM FROM FIVE GUILDS IN.
TEN STAYED BACK AT THE ENTRANCE TO THE BOSS LAIR, AND WHEN THE OTHER TEN REACHED THE CENTER OF THE ROOM, THE DOOR CLOSED.
FOR FIVE MINUTES, WE COULD NOT CRACK THE DOOR OPEN, NO MATTER WHAT WE TRIED.
WHEN IT FINALLY OPENED...
...THERE WAS NOTHING INSIDE THE ROOM.
THE TEN PLAYERS AND BOSS WERE GONE. NO SIGNS OF TELEPORTATION, NO RETURN...
WE VERIFIED ON THE MONUMENT IN BLACK-IRON PALACE.
TEN PEOPLE... HOW DID THAT HAPPEN?
WAS IT AN ANTI-CRYSTAL ZONE?
THAT IS MY ONLY CONCLUSION.
ASUNA REPORTED THAT THE 74TH FLOOR'S CHAMBER WAS THE SAME WAY. WE SHOULD ASSUME THAT ALL BOSS LAIRS WILL BE SIMILARLY EQUIPPED FROM NOW ON.
IT'S REALLY STARTING TO LIVE UP TO THAT "GAME OF DEATH" BILLING...

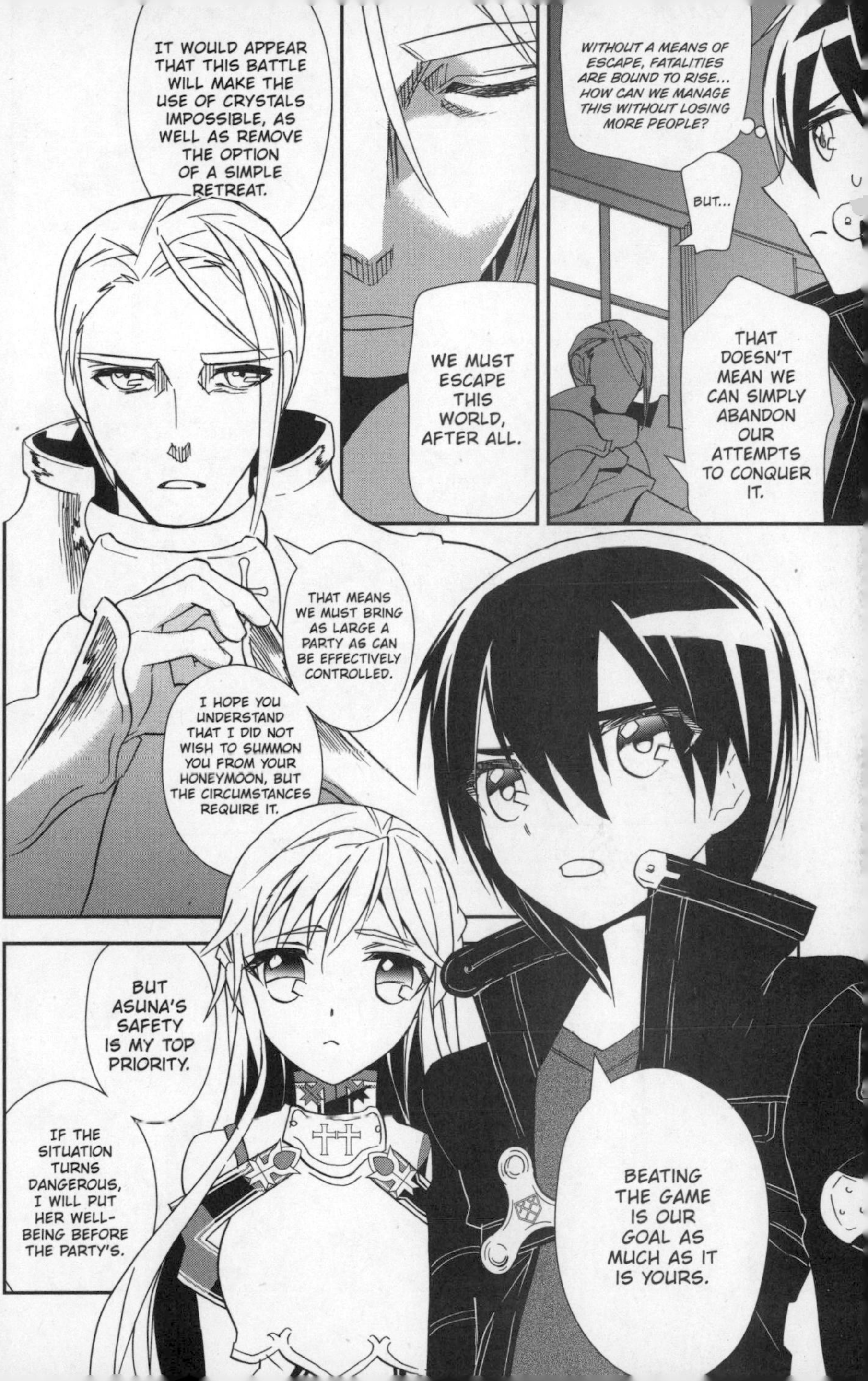
WITHOUT A MEANS OF ESCAPE, FATALITIES ARE BOUND TO RISE... HOW CAN WE MANAGE THIS WITHOUT LOSING MORE PEOPLE?
BUT...
THAT DOESN'T MEAN WE CAN SIMPLY ABANDON OUR ATTEMPTS TO CONQUER IT.
WE MUST ESCAPE THIS WORLD, AFTER ALL.
IT WOULD APPEAR THAT THIS BATTLE WILL MAKE THE USE OF CRYSTALS IMPOSSIBLE, AS WELL AS REMOVE THE OPTION OF A SIMPLE RETREAT.
THAT MEANS WE MUST BRING AS LARGE A PARTY AS CAN BE EFFECTIVELY CONTROLLED.
I HOPE YOU UNDERSTAND THAT I DID NOT WISH TO SUMMON YOU FROM YOUR HONEYMOON, BUT THE CIRCUMSTANCES REQUIRE IT.
BEATING THE GAME IS OUR GOAL AS MUCH AS IT IS YOURS.
BUT ASUNA'S SAFETY IS MY TOP PRIORITY.
IF THE SITUATION TURNS DANGEROUS, I WILL PUT HER WELL-BEING BEFORE THE PARTY'S.

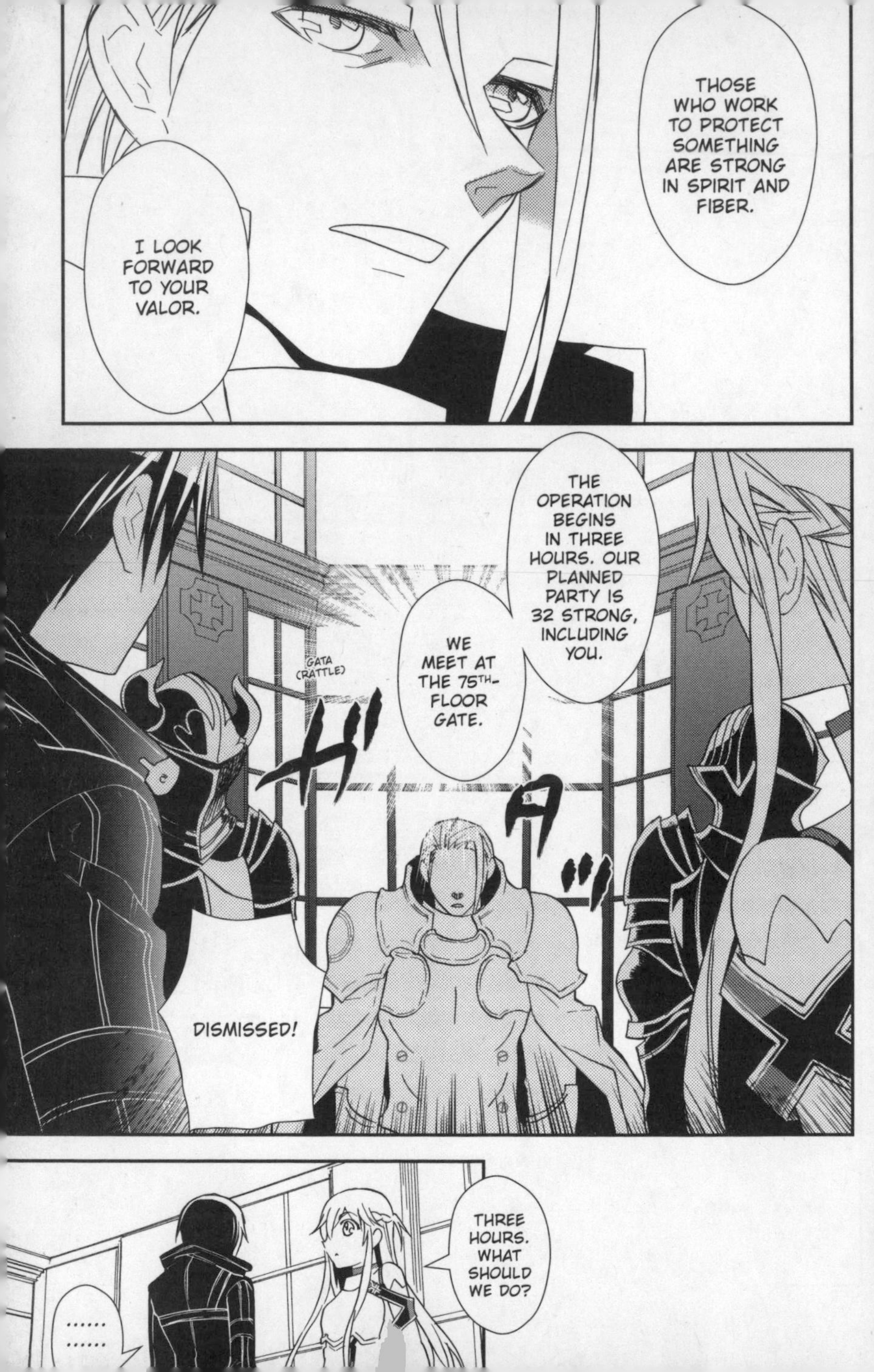
THOSE WHO WORK TO PROTECT SOMETHING ARE STRONG IN SPIRIT AND FIBER.
I LOOK FORWARD TO YOUR VALOR.
THE OPERATION BEGINS IN THREE HOURS. OUR PLANNED PARTY IS 32 STRONG, INCLUDING YOU.
WE MEET AT THE 75TH-FLOOR GATE.
GATA (RATTLE)
DISMISSED!
THREE HOURS. WHAT SHOULD WE DO?
......
......

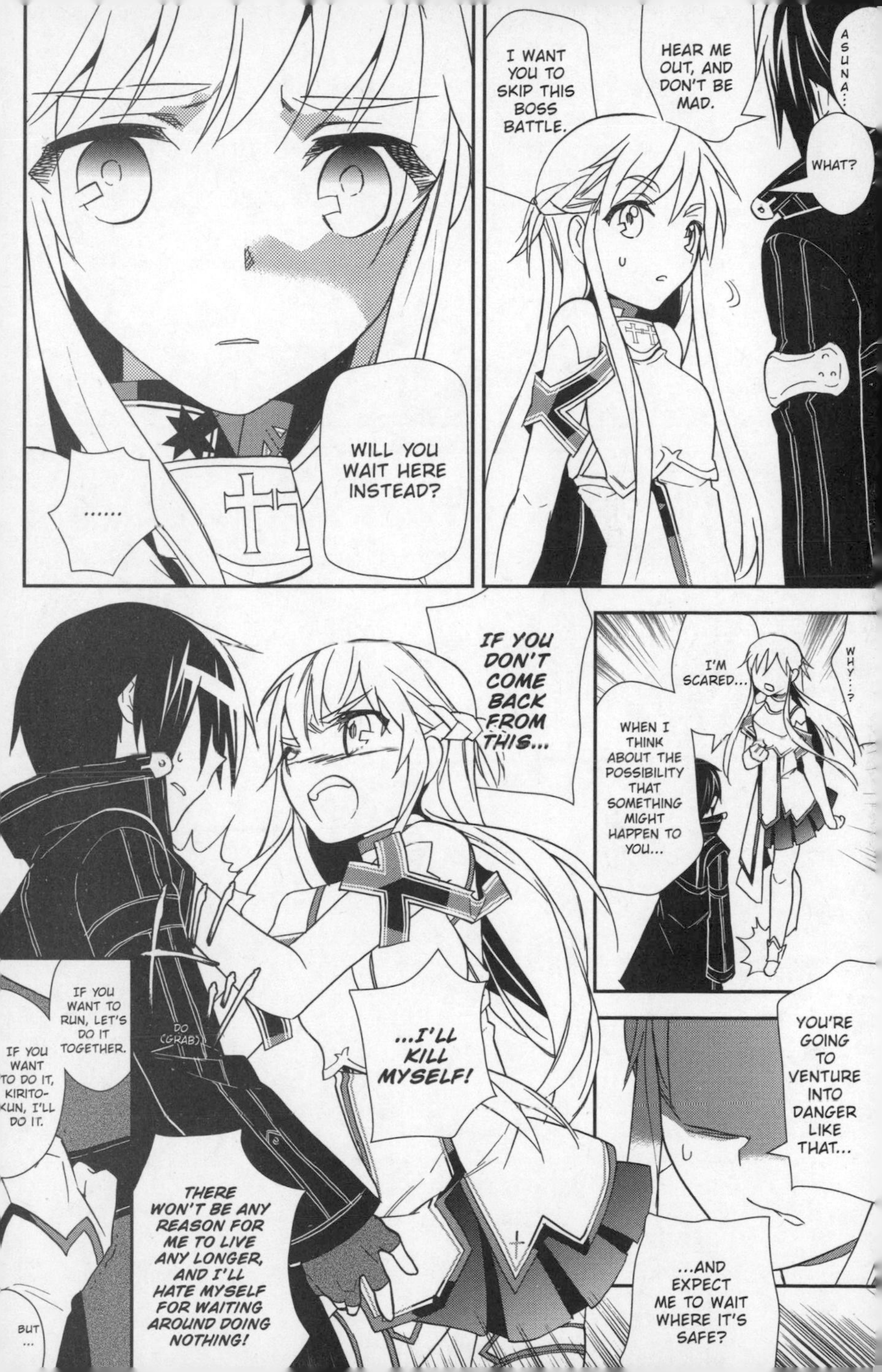
ASUNA...
WHAT?
HEAR ME OUT, AND DON'T BE MAD.
I WANT YOU TO SKIP THIS BOSS BATTLE.
WILL YOU WAIT HERE INSTEAD?
......
WHY...?
I'M SCARED...
WHEN I THINK ABOUT THE POSSIBILITY THAT SOMETHING MIGHT HAPPEN TO YOU...
YOU'RE GOING TO VENTURE INTO DANGER LIKE THAT...
...AND EXPECT ME TO WAIT WHERE IT'S SAFE?
IF YOU DON'T COME BACK FROM THIS...
...I'LL KILL MYSELF!
DO (GRAB)
THERE WON'T BE ANY REASON FOR ME TO LIVE ANY LONGER, AND I'LL HATE MYSELF FOR WAITING AROUND DOING NOTHING!
IF YOU WANT TO RUN, LET'S DO IT TOGETHER.
IF YOU WANT TO DO IT, KIRITO-KUN, I'LL DO IT.
BUT ...

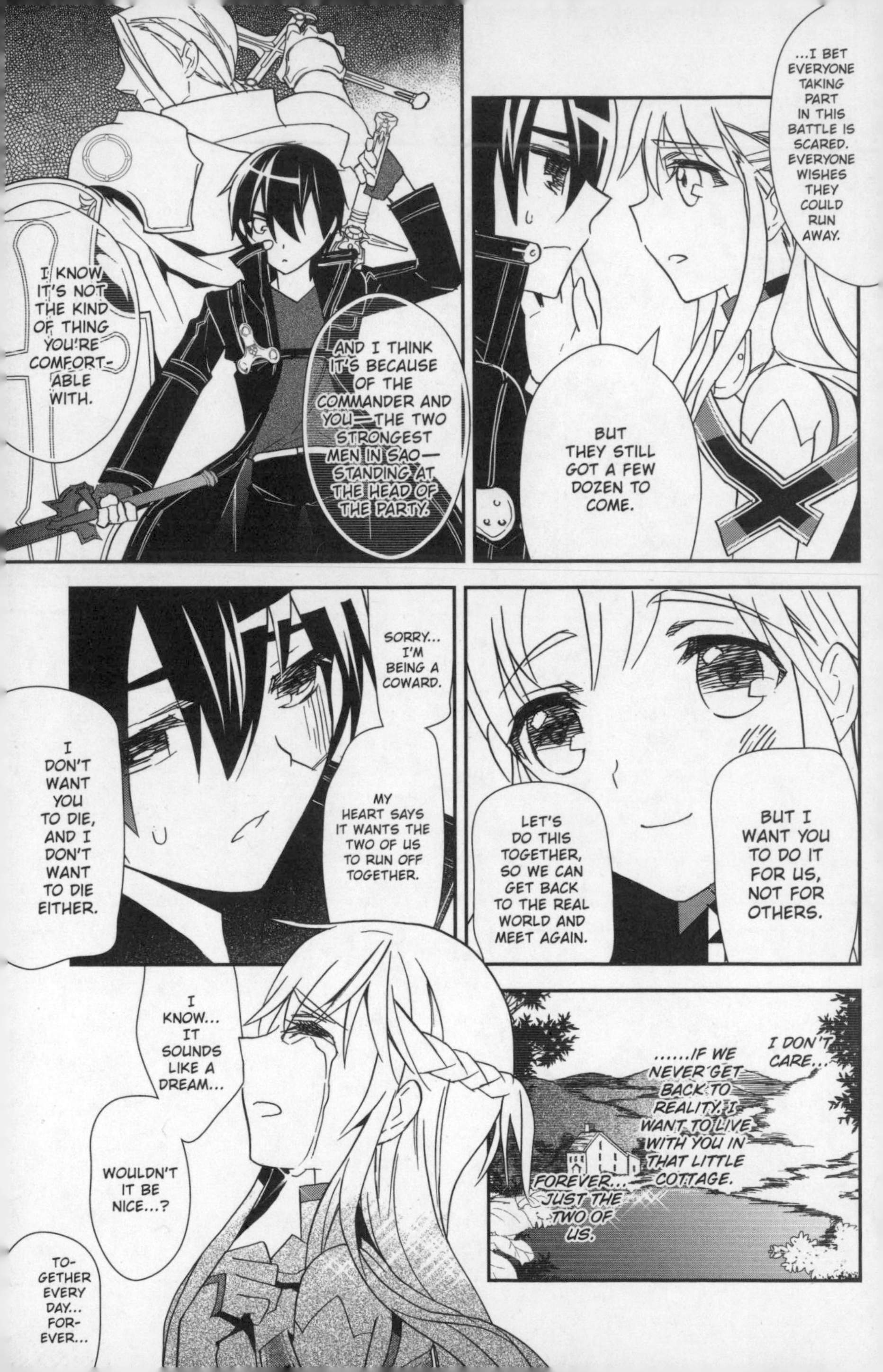
...I BET EVERYONE TAKING PART IN THIS BATTLE IS SCARED. EVERYONE WISHES THEY COULD RUN AWAY.
BUT THEY STILL GOT A FEW DOZEN TO COME.
AND I THINK IT'S BECAUSE OF THE COMMANDER AND YOU—THE TWO STRONGEST MEN IN SAO—STANDING AT THE HEAD OF THE PARTY.
I KNOW IT'S NOT THE KIND OF THING YOU'RE COMFORTABLE WITH.
BUT I WANT YOU TO DO IT FOR US, NOT FOR OTHERS.
LET'S DO THIS TOGETHER, SO WE CAN GET BACK TO THE REAL WORLD AND MEET AGAIN.
SORRY... I'M BEING A COWARD.
MY HEART SAYS IT WANTS THE TWO OF US TO RUN OFF TOGETHER.
I DON'T WANT YOU TO DIE, AND I DON'T WANT TO DIE EITHER.
I DON'T CARE...
......IF WE NEVER GET BACK TO REALITY, I WANT TO LIVE WITH YOU IN THAT LITTLE COTTAGE.
FOREVER... JUST THE TWO OF US.
I KNOW... IT SOUNDS LIKE A DREAM...
WOULDN'T IT BE NICE...?
TO-GETHER EVERY DAY... FOR-EVER...

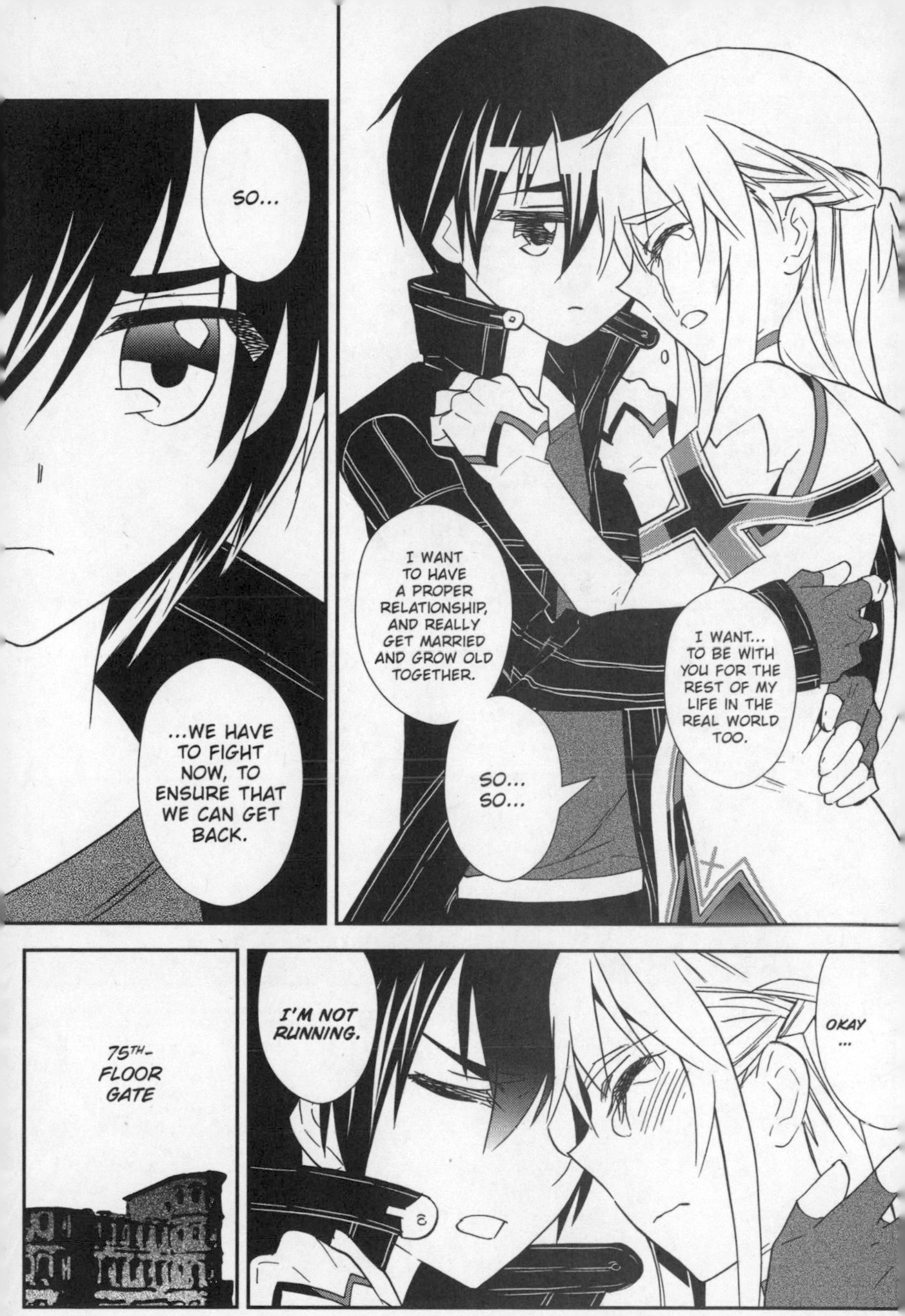
I WANT... TO BE WITH YOU FOR THE REST OF MY LIFE IN THE REAL WORLD TOO.
I WANT TO HAVE A PROPER RELATIONSHIP, AND REALLY GET MARRIED AND GROW OLD TOGETHER.
SO... SO...
SO...
...WE HAVE TO FIGHT NOW, TO ENSURE THAT WE CAN GET BACK.
OKAY ...
I'M NOT RUNNING.
75TH-FLOOR GATE

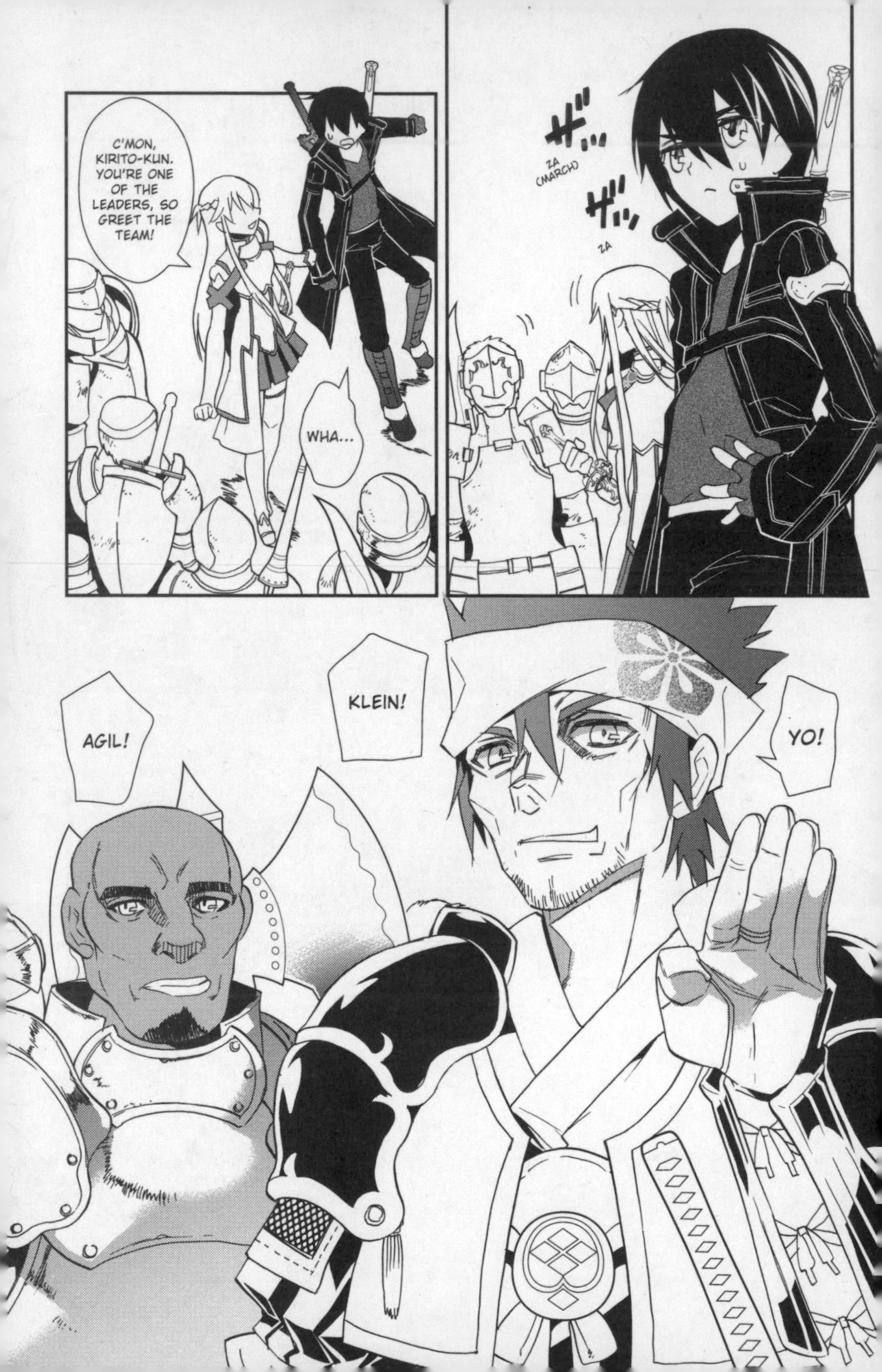
ZA (MARCH)
ZA
C'MON, KIRITO-KUN. YOU'RE ONE OF THE LEADERS, SO GREET THE TEAM!
WHA...
YO!
KLEIN!
AGIL!

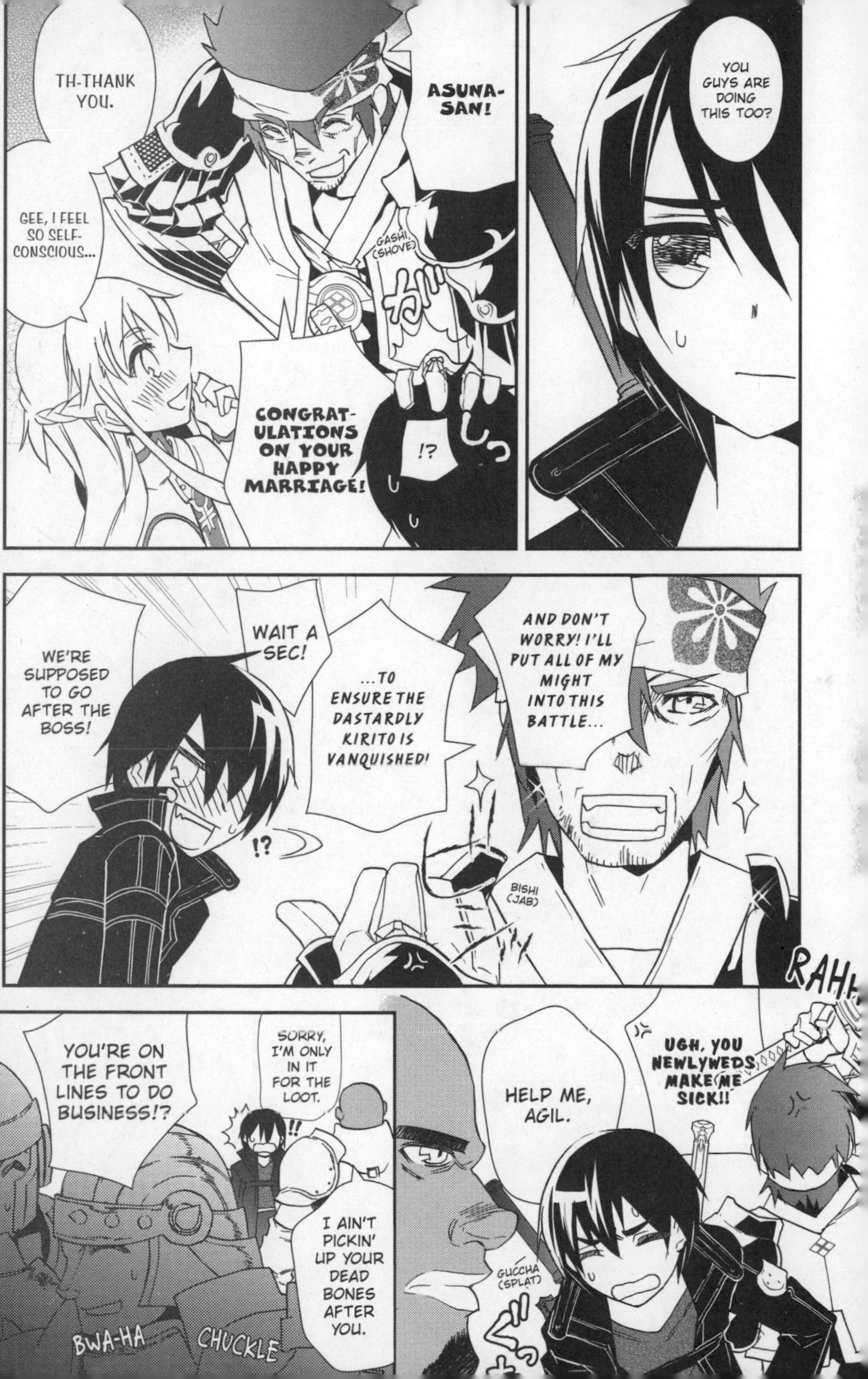
YOU GUYS ARE DOING THIS TOO?
ASUNA-SAN!
TH-THANK YOU.
GASHI (SHOVE)
GEE, I FEEL SO SELF-CONSCIOUS...
CONGRAT-ULATIONS ON YOUR HAPPY MARRIAGE!
!?
AND DON'T WORRY! I'LL PUT ALL OF MY MIGHT INTO THIS BATTLE...
...TO ENSURE THE DASTARDLY KIRITO IS VANQUISHED!
WAIT A SEC!
WE'RE SUPPOSED TO GO AFTER THE BOSS!
!?
BISHI (JAB)
RAHH
UGH, YOU NEWLYWEDS MAKE ME SICK!!
HELP ME, AGIL.
I AIN'T PICKIN' UP YOUR DEAD BONES AFTER YOU.
SORRY, I'M ONLY IN IT FOR THE LOOT.
YOU'RE ON THE FRONT LINES TO DO BUSINESS!?
!!
GUCCHA (SPLAT)
CHUCKLE
BWA-HA

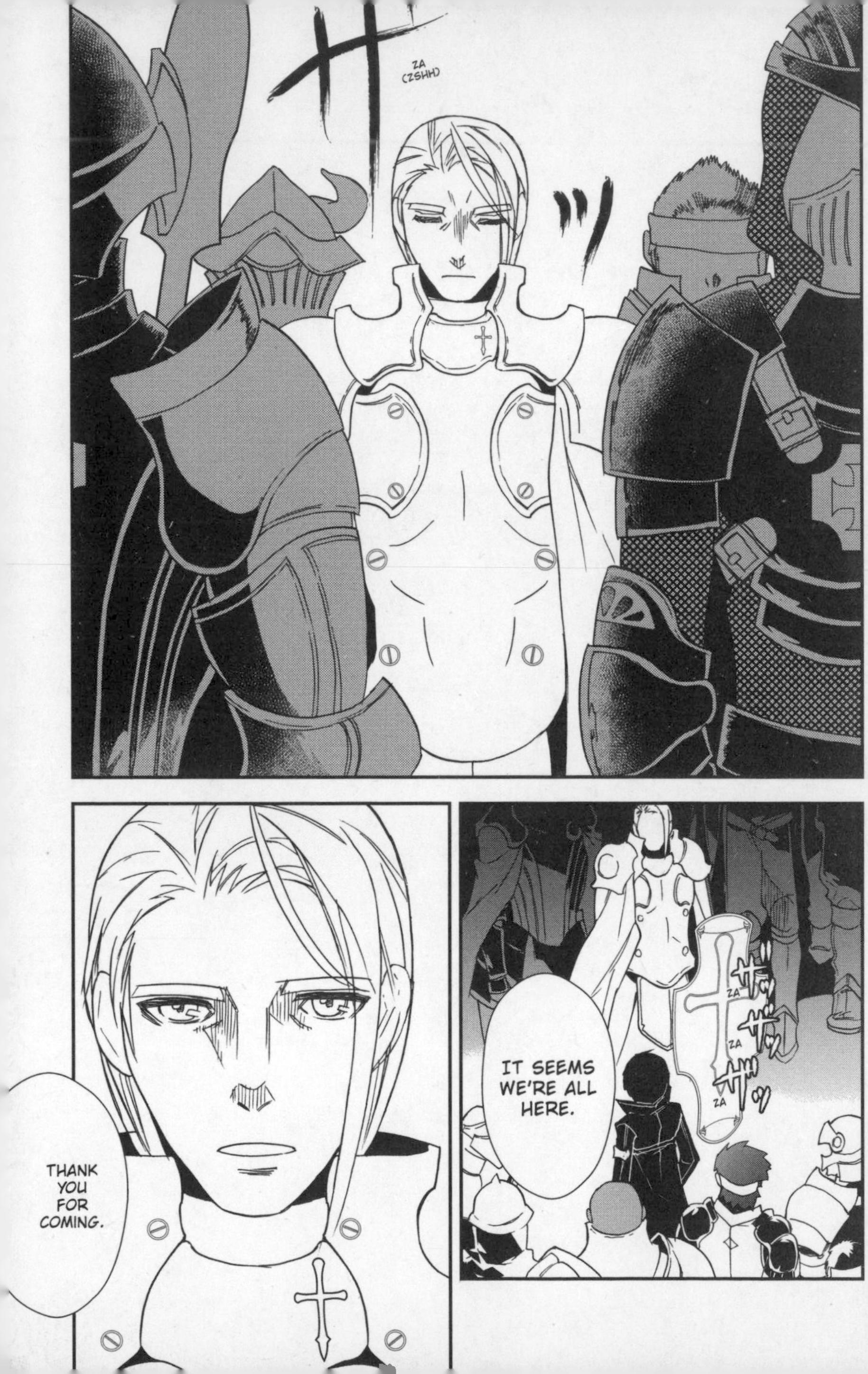
ZA (ZSHH)
IT SEEMS WE'RE ALL HERE.
ZA
ZA
ZA
THANK YOU FOR COMING.

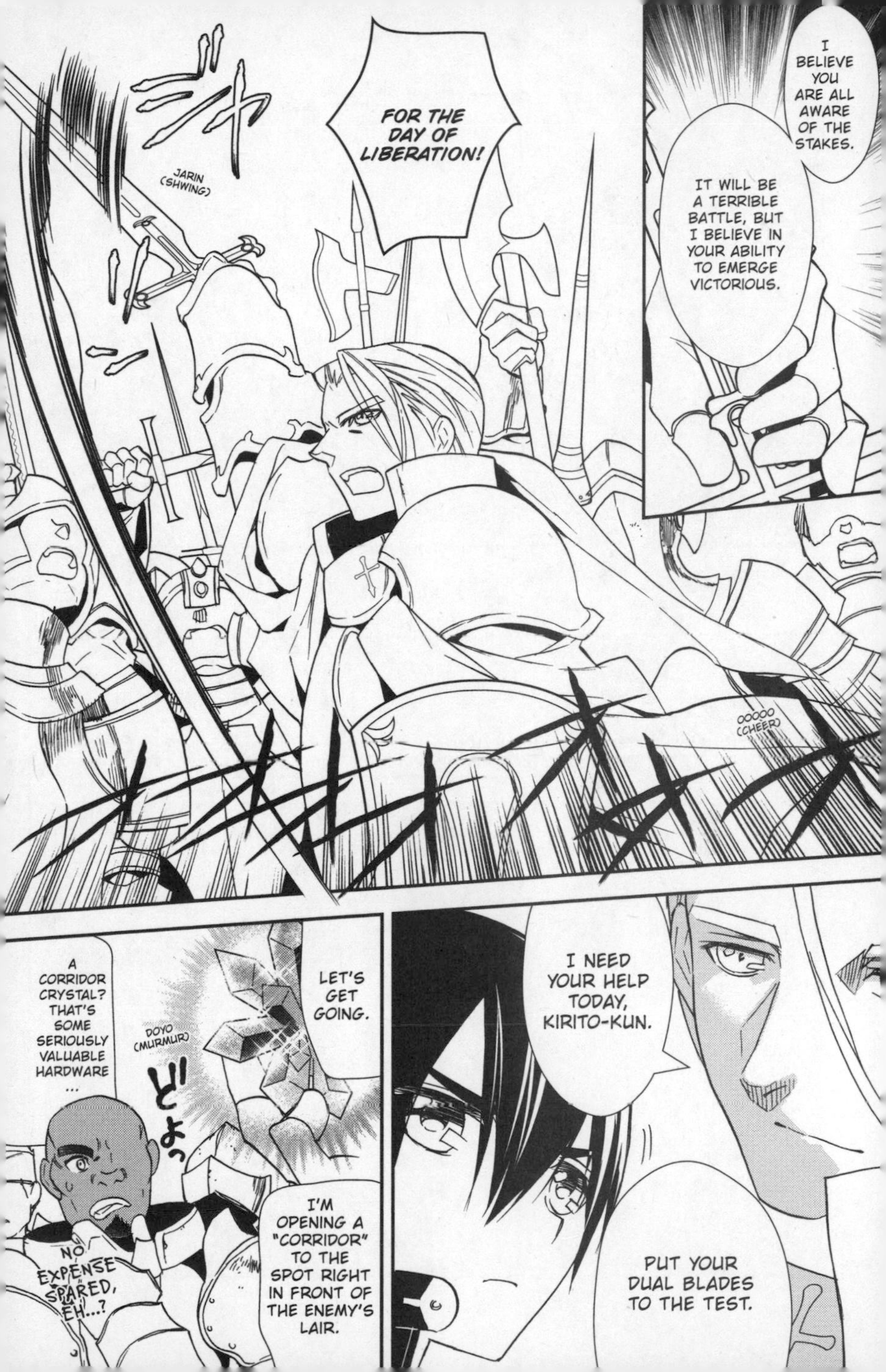
I BELIEVE YOU ARE ALL AWARE OF THE STAKES.
IT WILL BE A TERRIBLE BATTLE, BUT I BELIEVE IN YOUR ABILITY TO EMERGE VICTORIOUS.
FOR THE DAY OF LIBERATION!
JARIN (SHWING)
OOOOO (CHEER)
I NEED YOUR HELP TODAY, KIRITO-KUN.
PUT YOUR DUAL BLADES TO THE TEST.
LET'S GET GOING.
I'M OPENING A "CORRIDOR" TO THE SPOT RIGHT IN FRONT OF THE ENEMY'S LAIR.
A CORRIDOR CRYSTAL? THAT'S SOME SERIOUSLY VALUABLE HARDWARE ...
DOYO (MURMUR)
どよっ
NO EXPENSE SPARED, EH...?

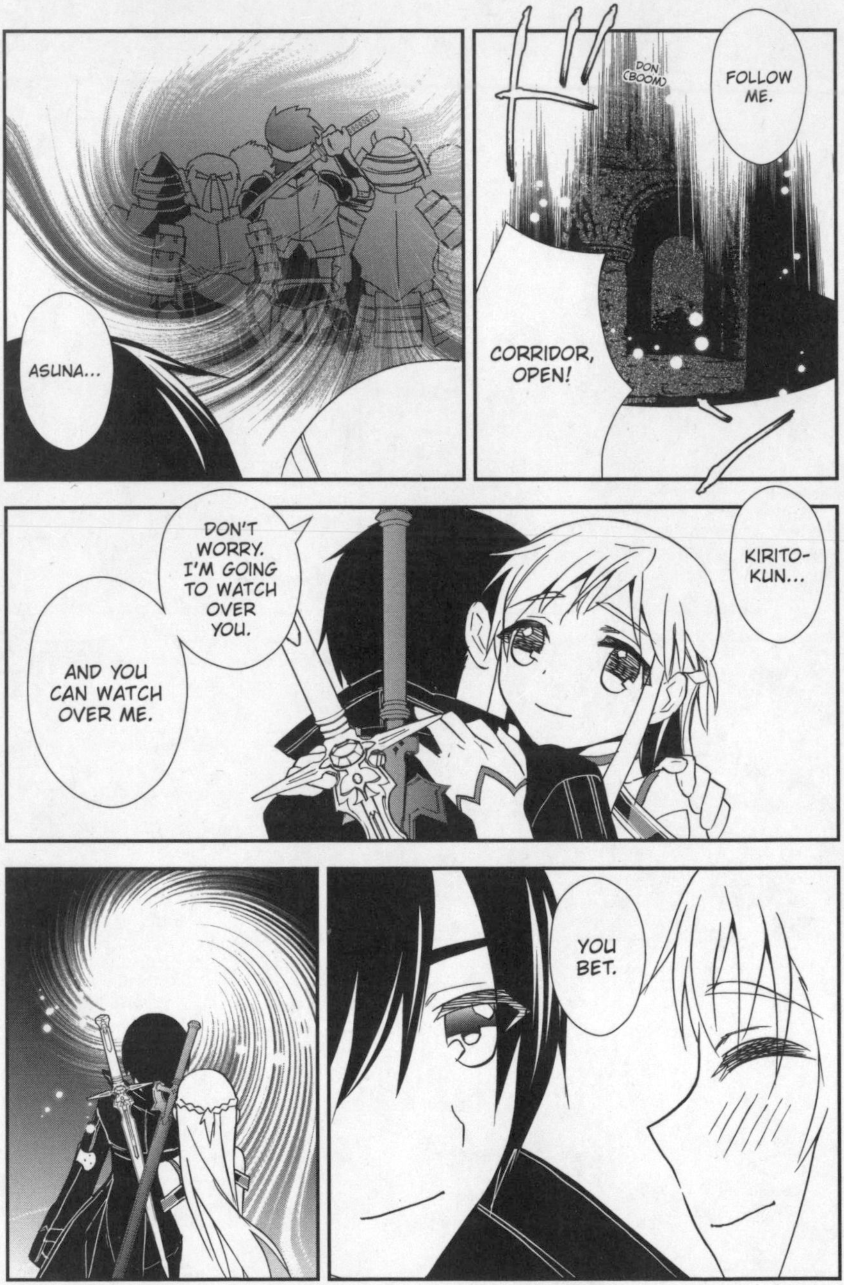
FOLLOW ME.
DON (BOOM)
CORRIDOR, OPEN!
ASUNA...
KIRITO-KUN...
DON'T WORRY. I'M GOING TO WATCH OVER YOU.
AND YOU CAN WATCH OVER ME.
YOU BET.

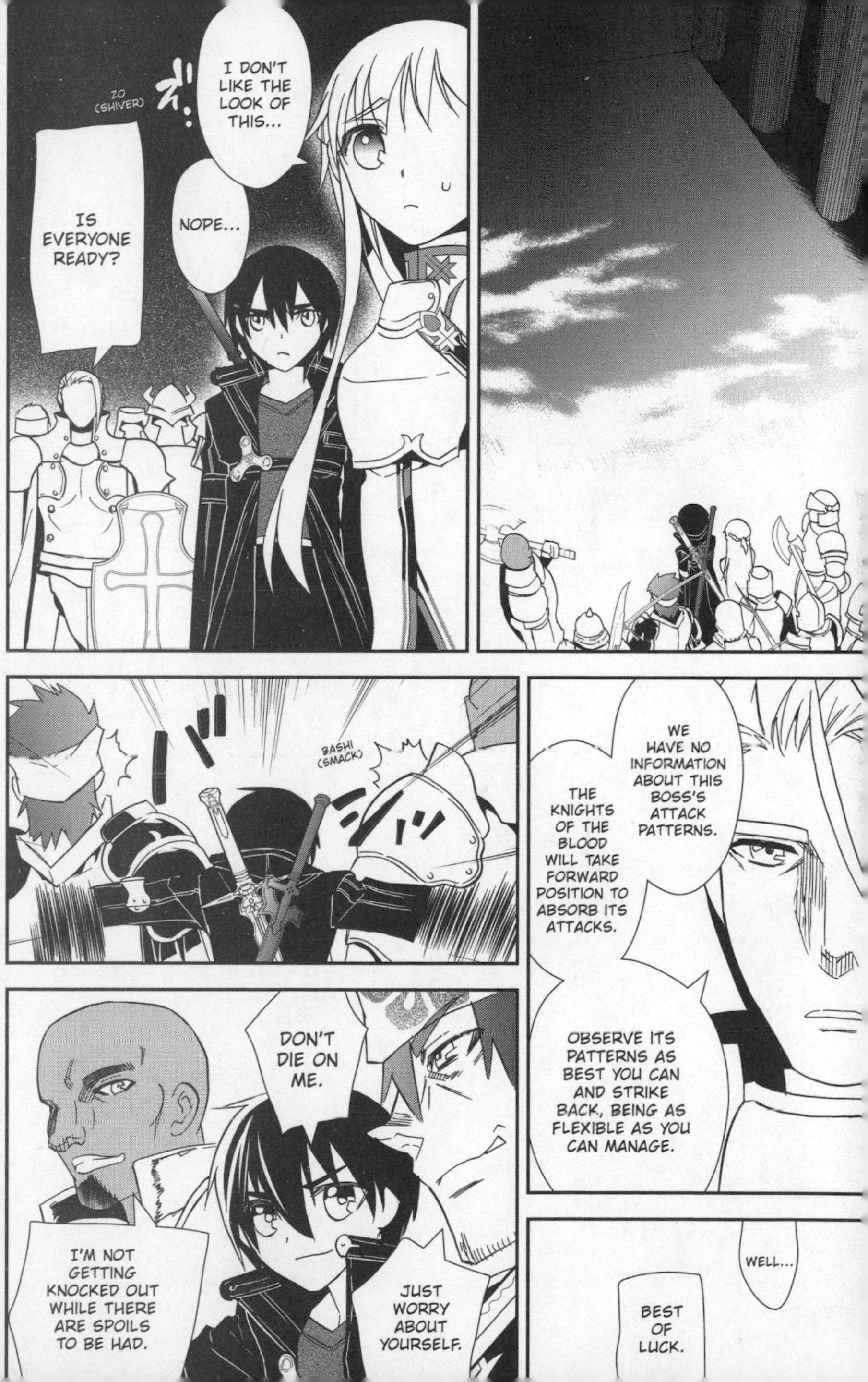
I DON'T LIKE THE LOOK OF THIS...
ZO (SHIVER)
NOPE...
IS EVERYONE READY?
WE HAVE NO INFORMATION ABOUT THIS BOSS'S ATTACK PATTERNS.
THE KNIGHTS OF THE BLOOD WILL TAKE FORWARD POSITION TO ABSORB ITS ATTACKS.
OBSERVE ITS PATTERNS AS BEST YOU CAN AND STRIKE BACK, BEING AS FLEXIBLE AS YOU CAN MANAGE.
WELL...
BEST OF LUCK.
BASHI (SMACK)
DON'T DIE ON ME.
JUST WORRY ABOUT YOURSELF.
I'M NOT GETTING KNOCKED OUT WHILE THERE ARE SPOILS TO BE HAD.

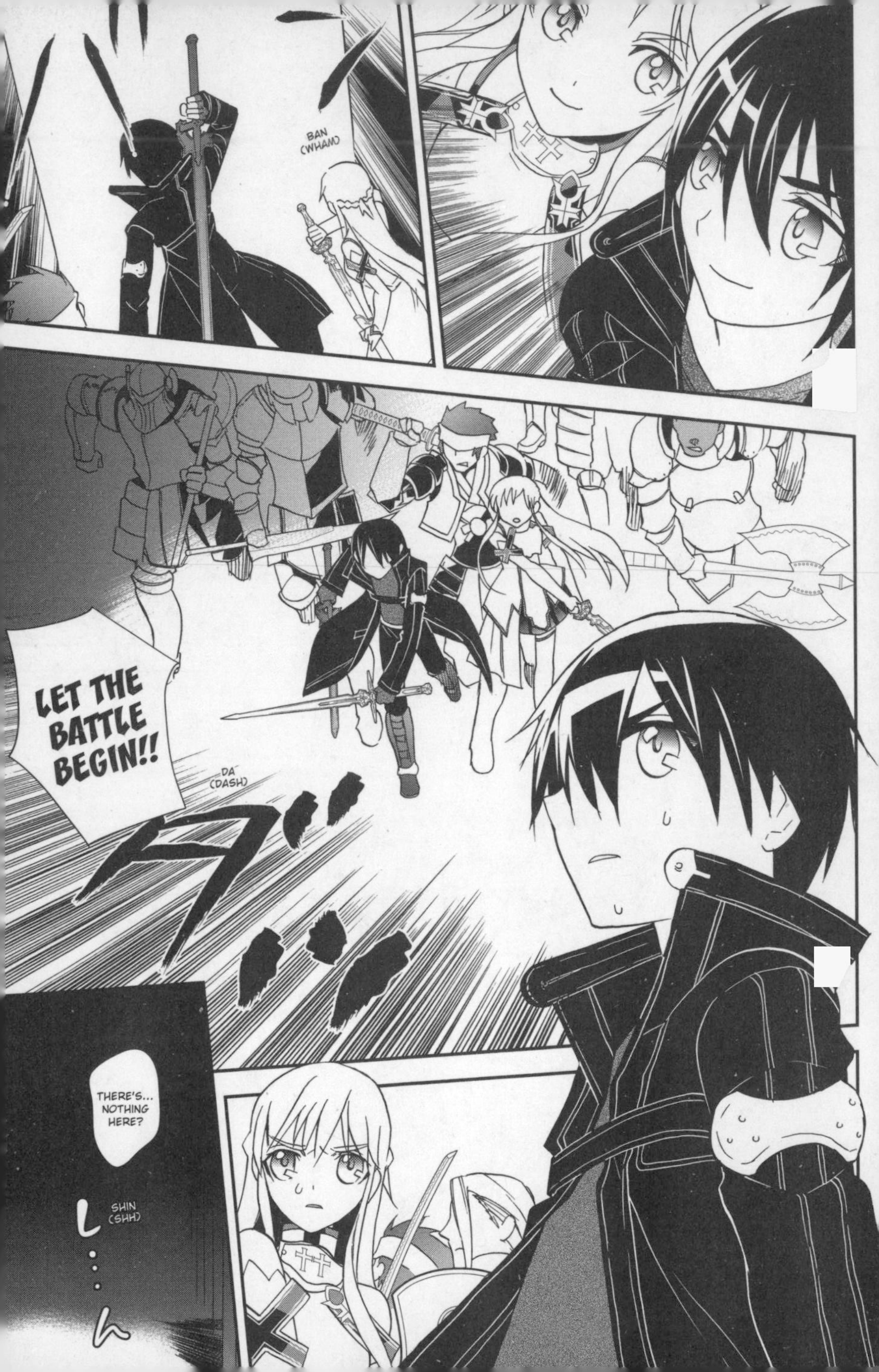
BAN (WHAM)
LET THE BATTLE BEGIN!!
DA (DASH)
THERE'S... NOTHING HERE?
SHIN (SHH)

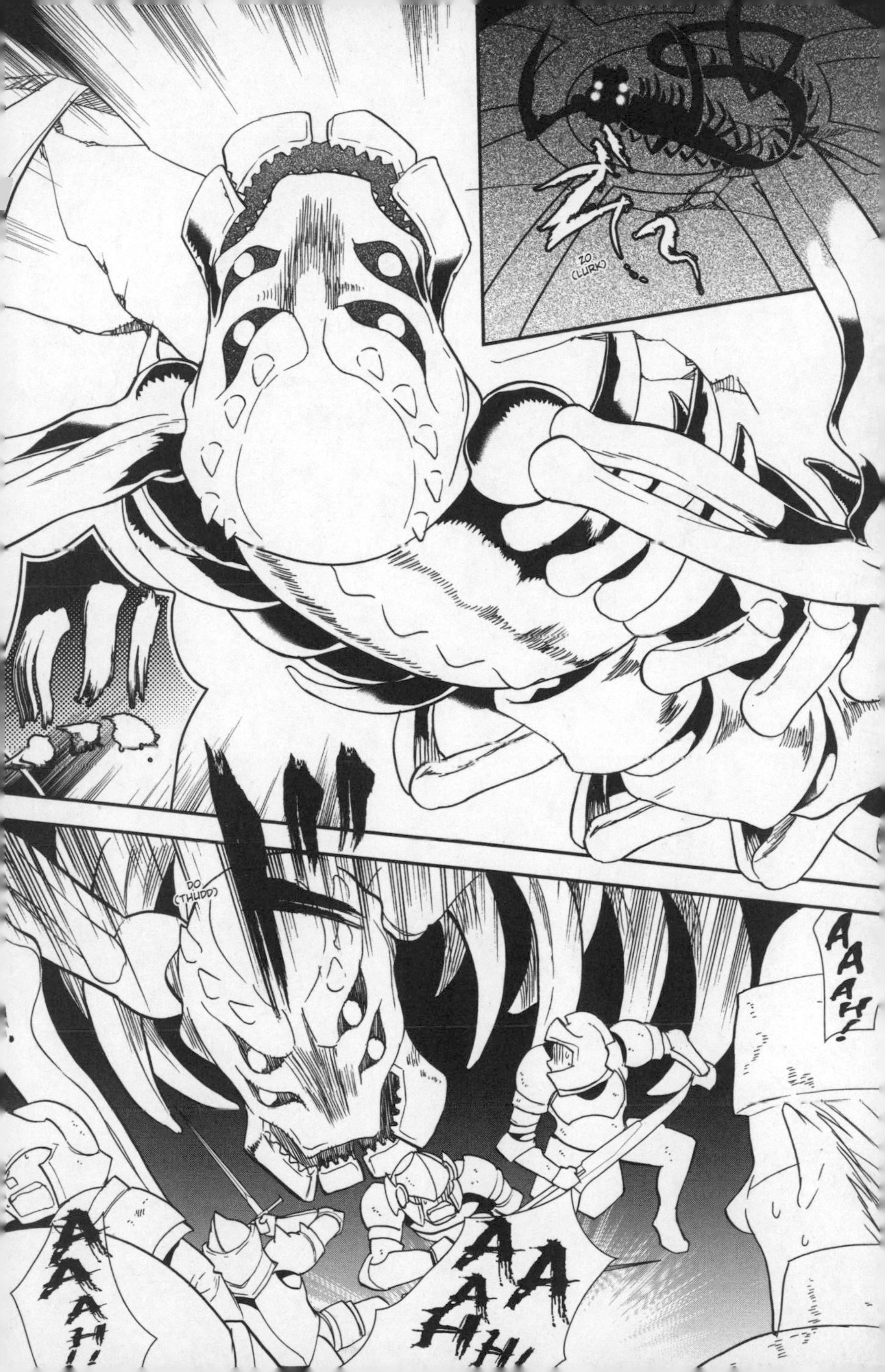
ZO (LURK)
AAAH!
DO (THUDD)
AAAAHH!
AAAAH!

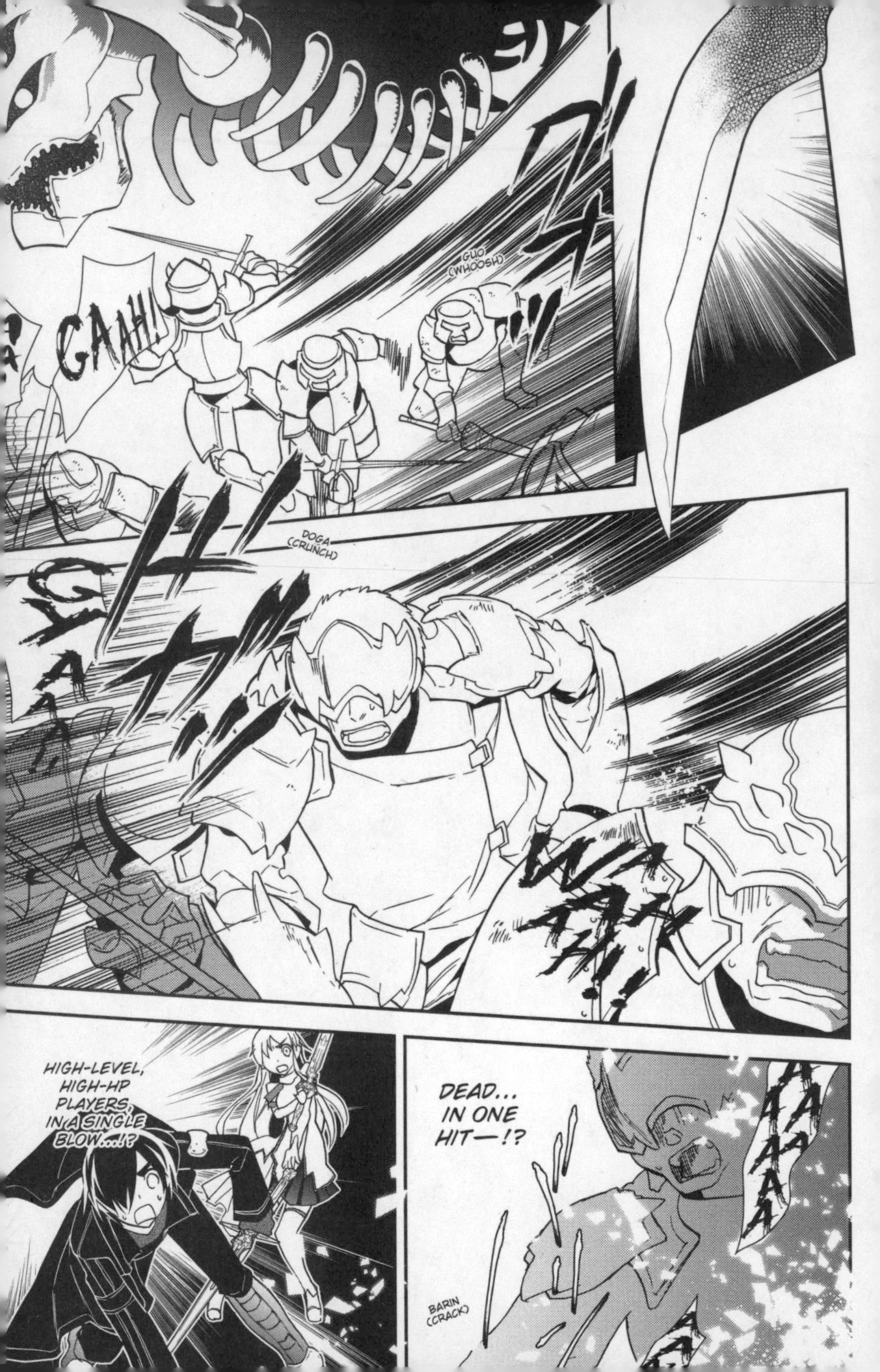
GUO
(WHOOSH)
GAAH!
DOGA
(CRUNCH)
DEAD... IN ONE HIT—!?
BARIN
(CRACK)
HIGH-LEVEL, HIGH-HP PLAYERS, IN A SINGLE BLOW...!?

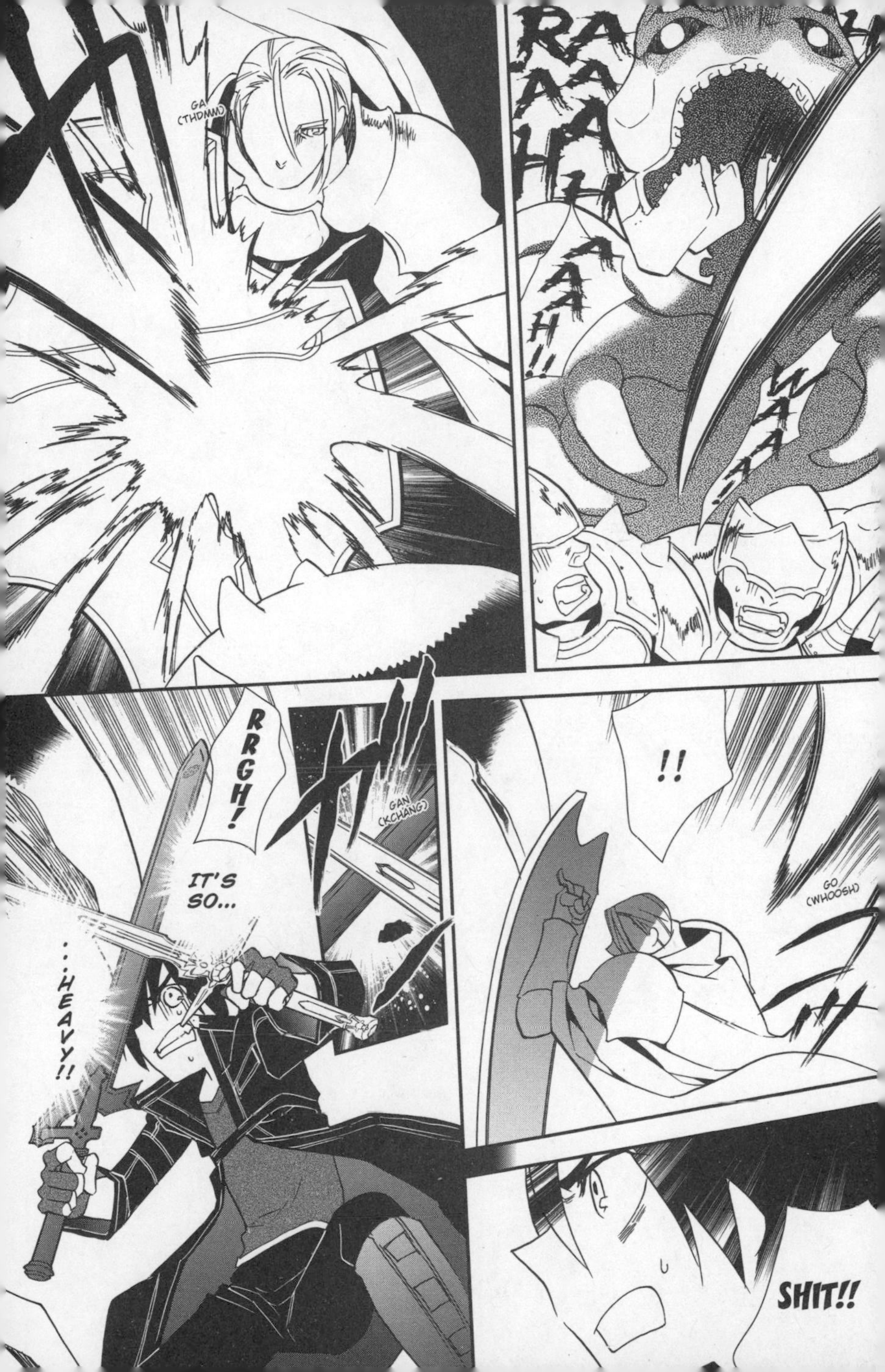
RAAAAHHHAAAH!!
WAAA!
GA (THDMN)
!!
GO (WHOOSH)
SHIT!!
RRGH!
GAN (KCHANG)
IT'S SO...
...HEAVY!!

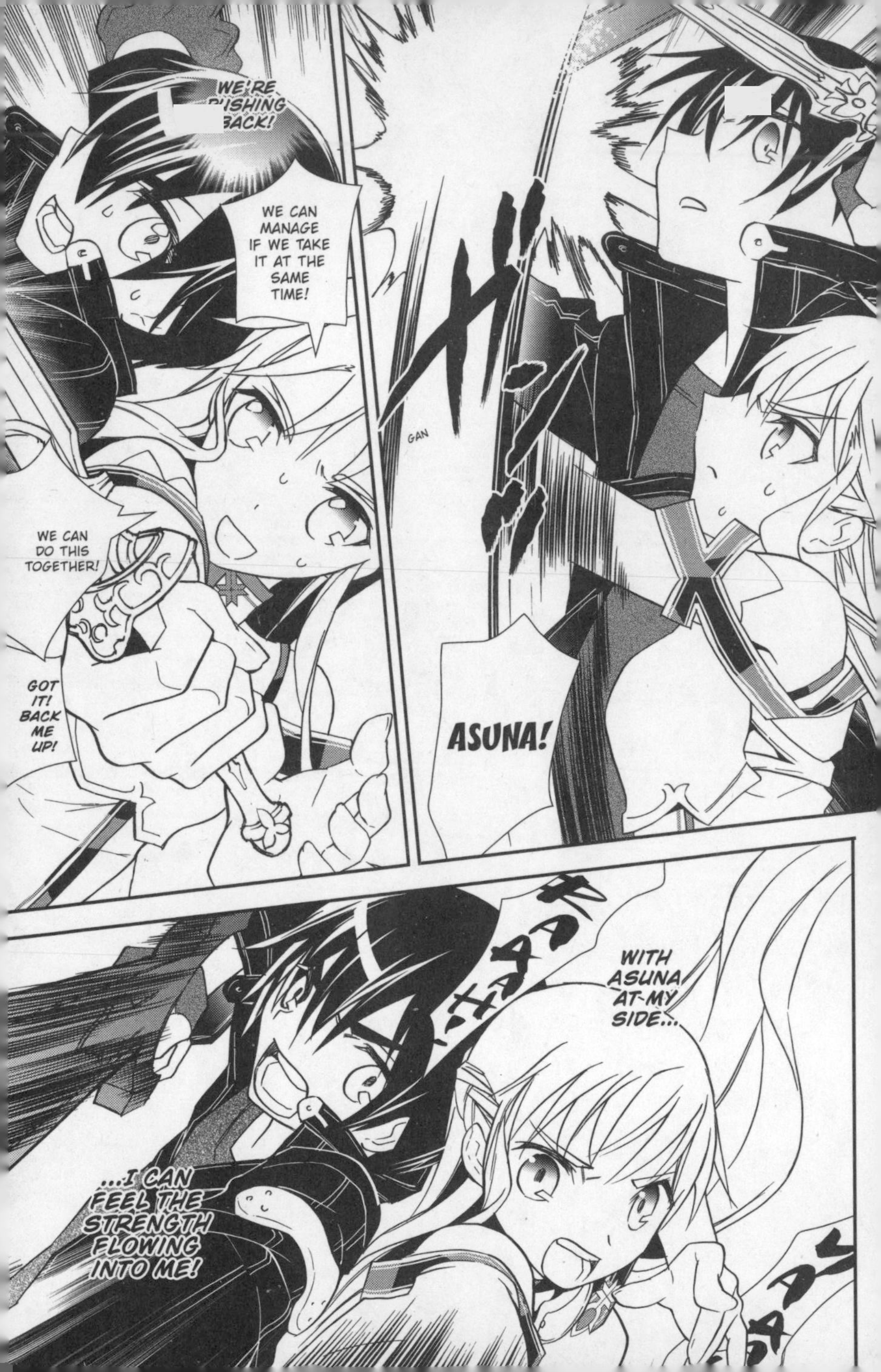
GAN
ASUNA!
WE'RE PUSHING BACK!
WE CAN MANAGE IF WE TAKE IT AT THE SAME TIME!
WE CAN DO THIS TOGETHER!
GOT IT! BACK ME UP!
HAAAH!
WITH ASUNA AT MY SIDE...
...I CAN FEEL THE STRENGTH FLOWING INTO ME!

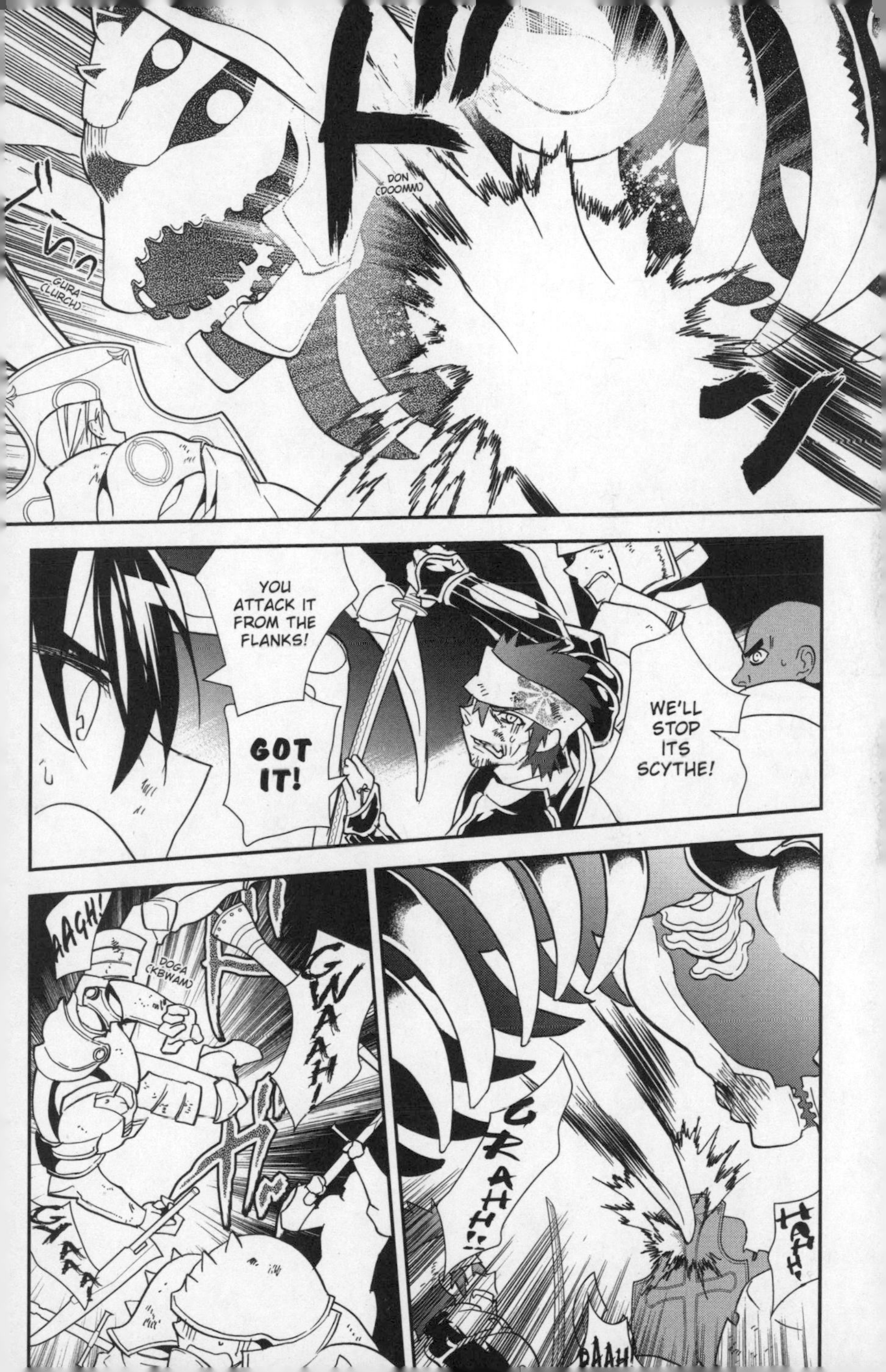
DON
(DOOMM)
GURA
(LURCH)
WE'LL STOP ITS SCYTHE!
YOU ATTACK IT FROM THE FLANKS!
GOT IT!
HAH!
URAHH!!
BAAH!
GWAAH!
DOGA
(KBWAM)
AAGH!
GYAAA!

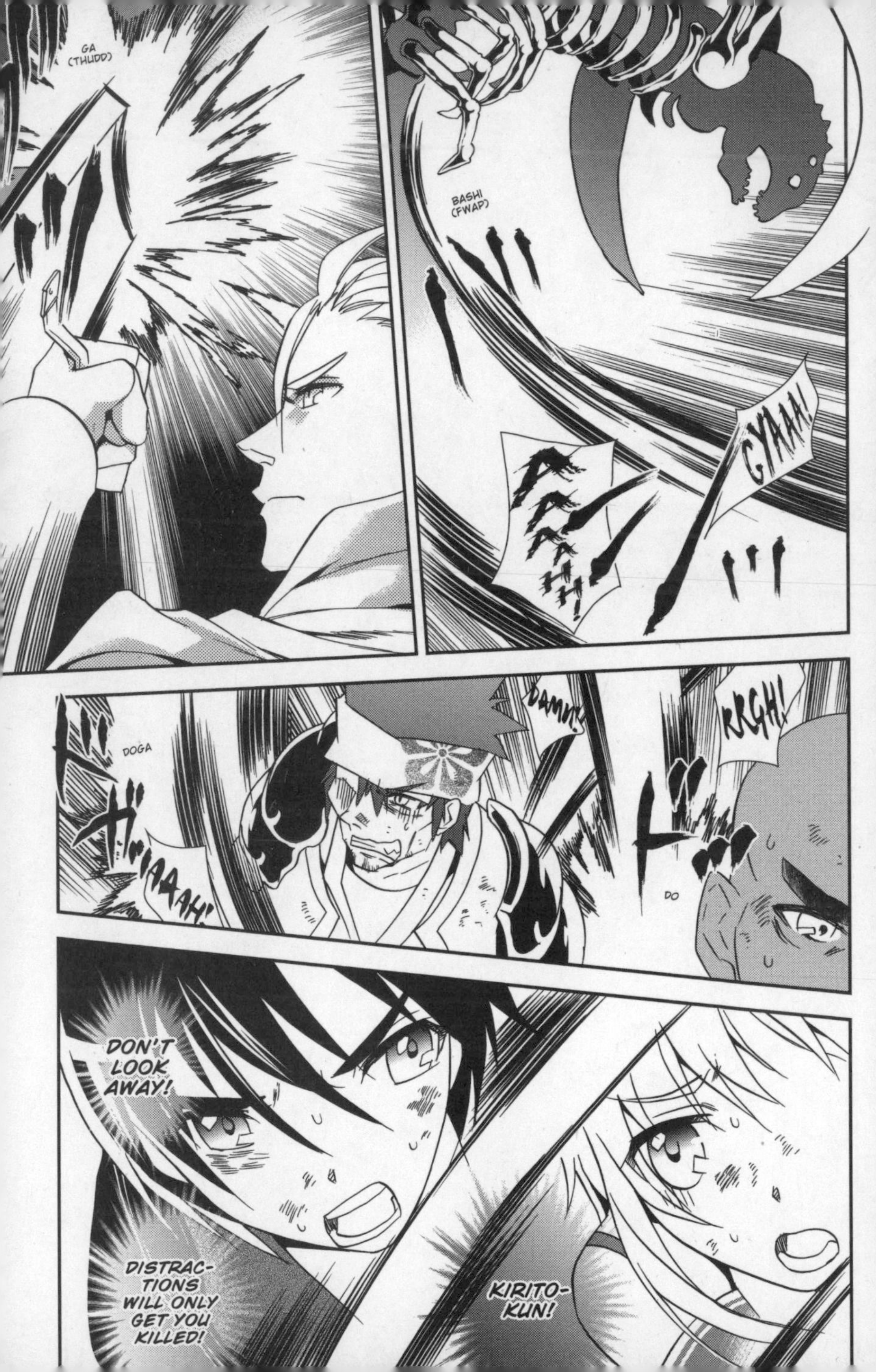
BASHI (FWAP)
CYAAA!
GA (THUDD)
RRGH!
DAMN!
DO
DOGA
KIRITO-KUN!
DON'T LOOK AWAY!
DISTRACTIONS WILL ONLY GET YOU KILLED!

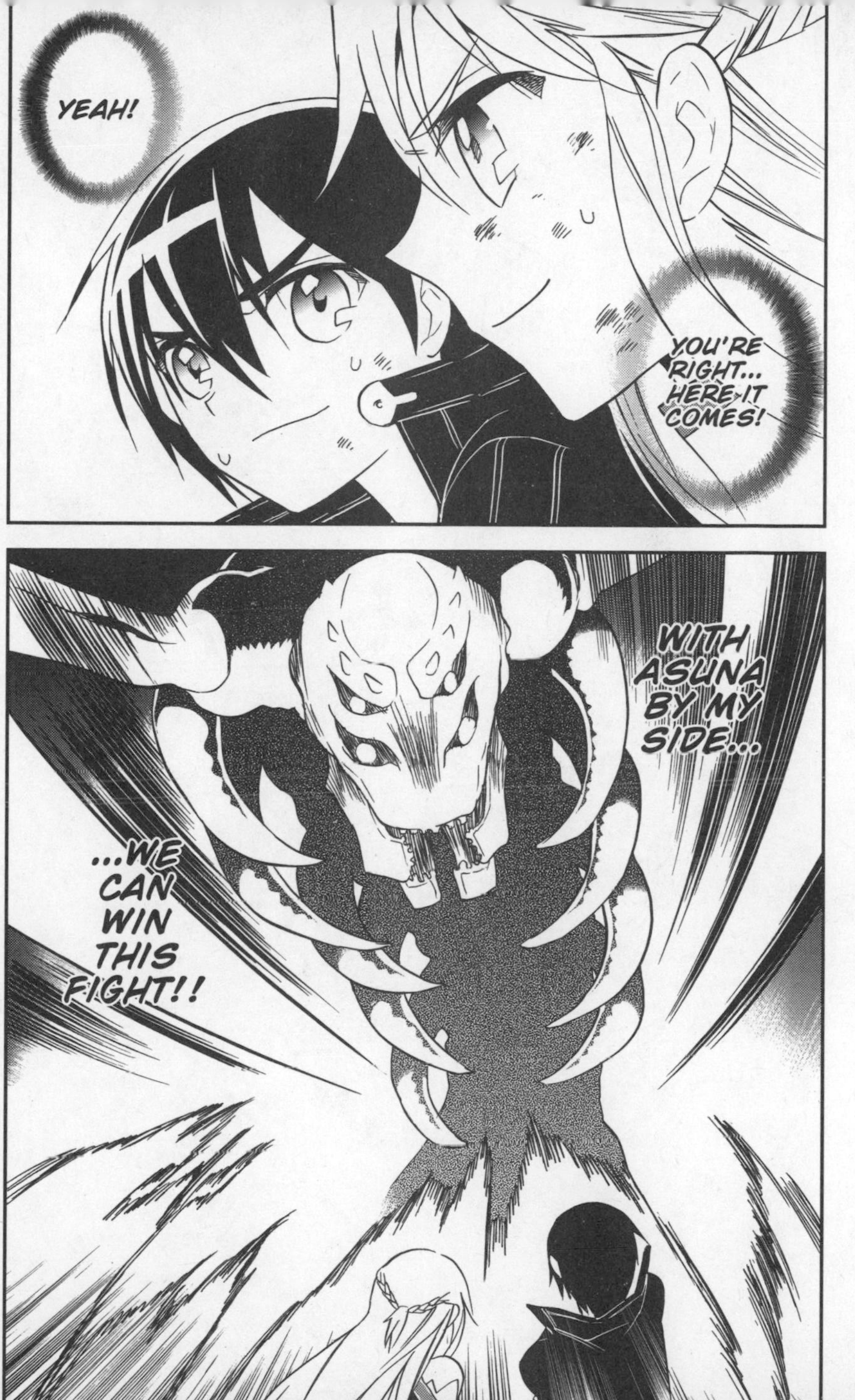
YOU'RE RIGHT... HERE IT COMES!
YEAH!
WITH ASUNA BY MY SIDE...
...WE CAN WIN THIS FIGHT!!

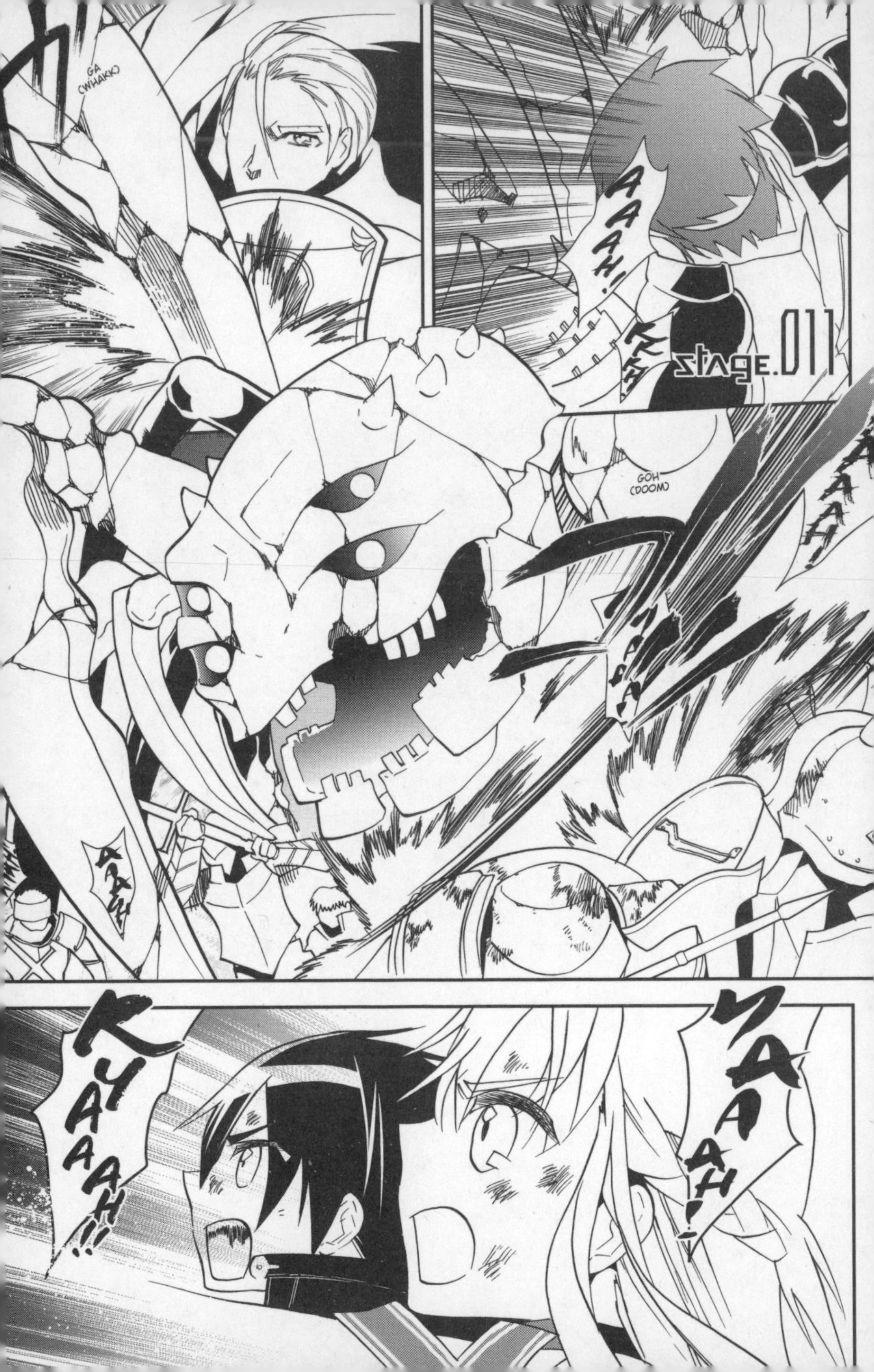
AAAAH!
KKK
stage.011
GA (WHAKK)
AAAAH!
GOH (DOOM)
NYAAAAH!!
KYAAAAH!!

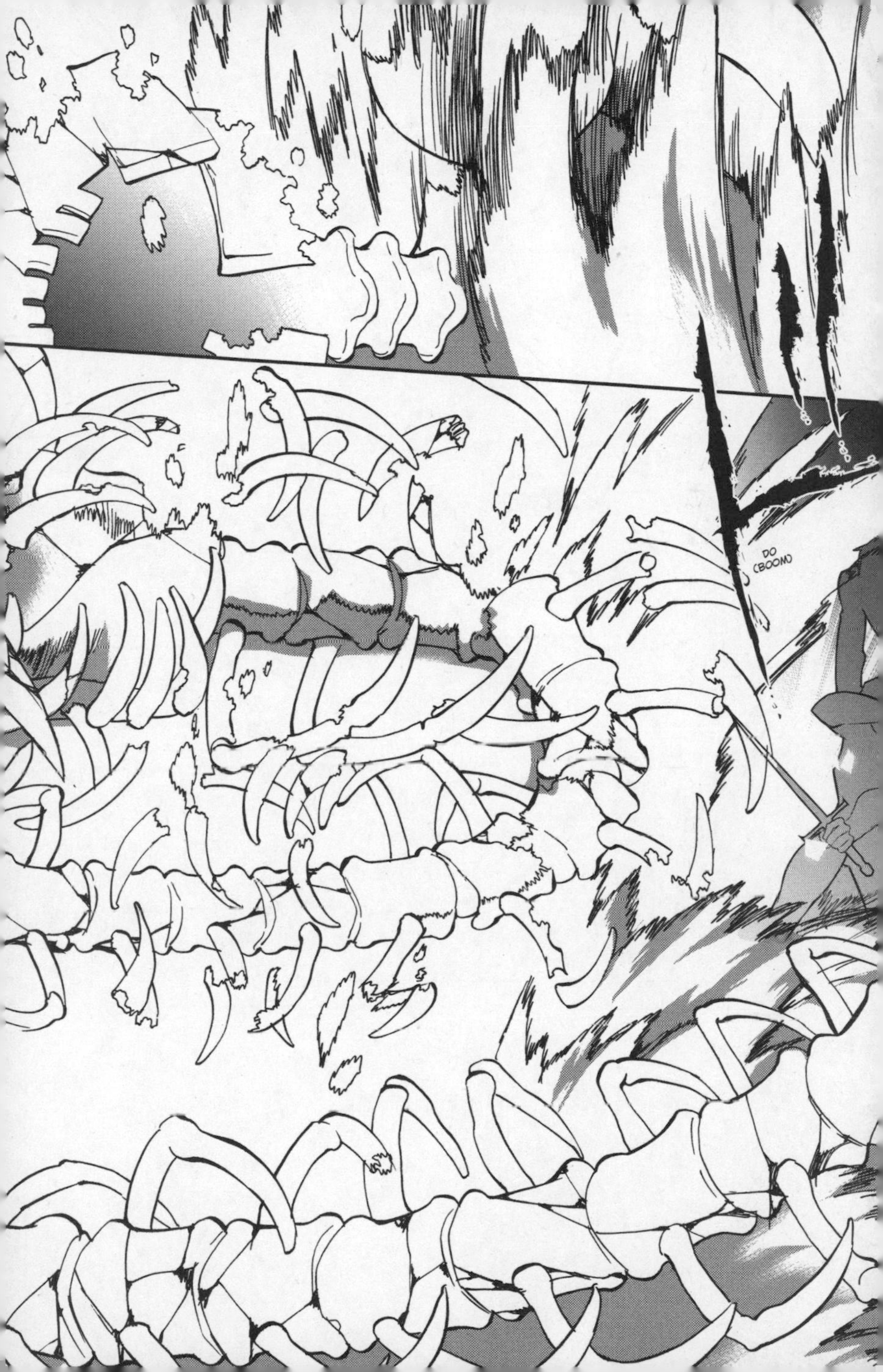
DO
(BOOM)

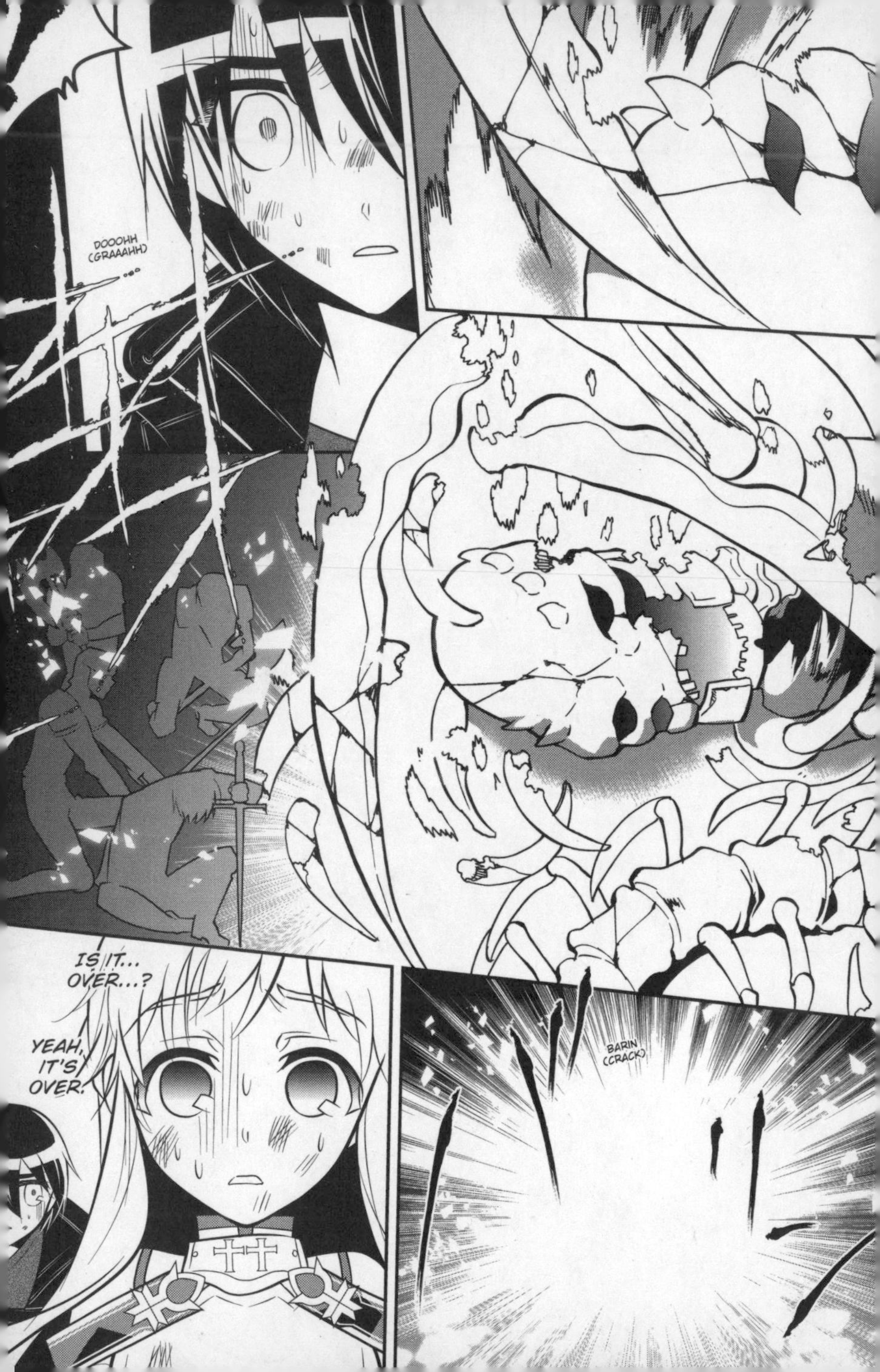
DOOOHH (GRAAAHH)
BARIN (CRACK)
IS IT... OVER...?
YEAH, IT'S OVER.

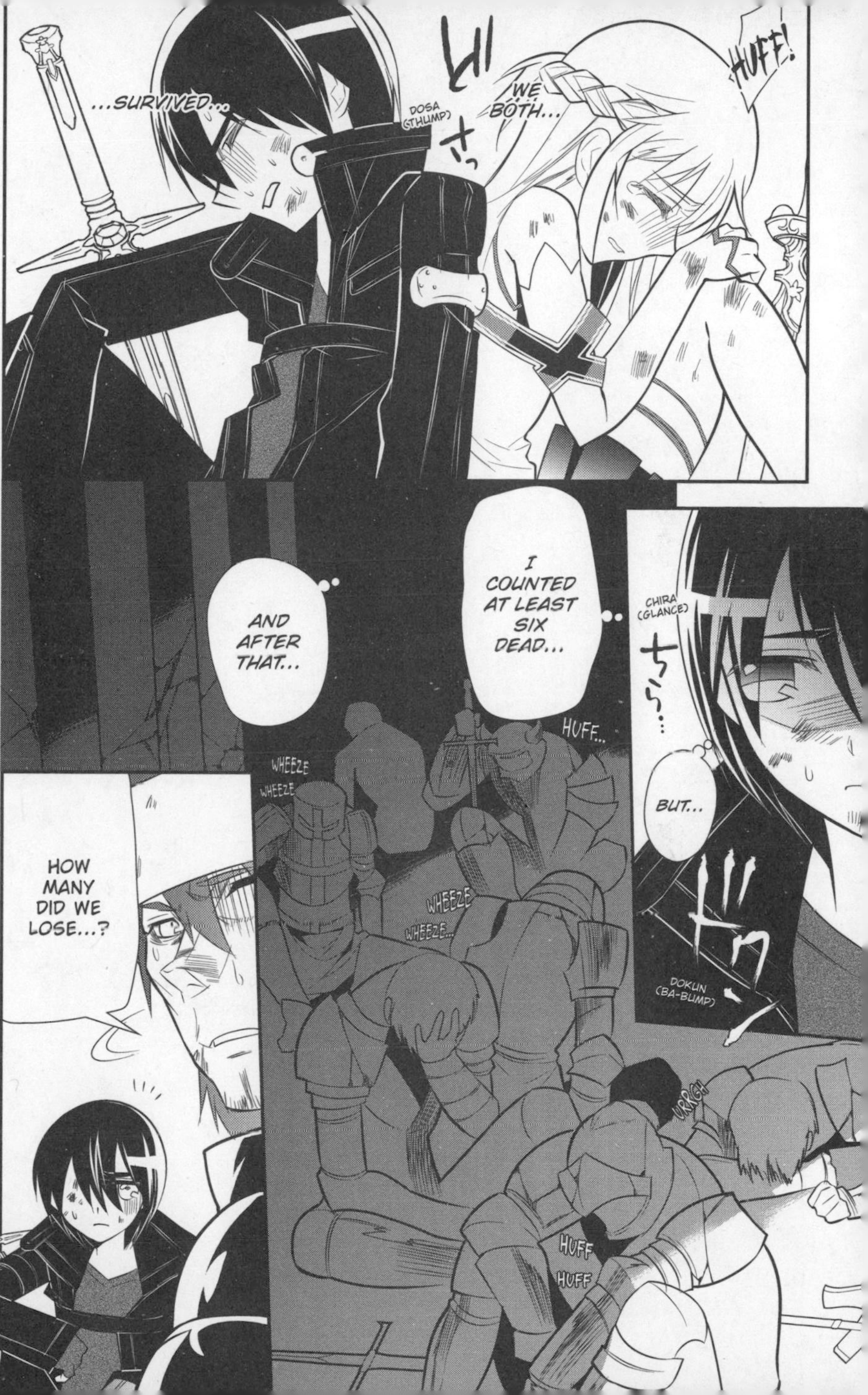
HUFF!
WE BOTH...
DOSA (THUMP)
...SURVIVED...
CHIRA (GLANCE)
BUT...
DOKUN (BA-BUMP)
I COUNTED AT LEAST SIX DEAD...
AND AFTER THAT...
HUFF...
WHEEZE WHEEZE
WHEEZE WHEEZE...
URRGH
HUFF HUFF
HOW MANY DID WE LOSE...?

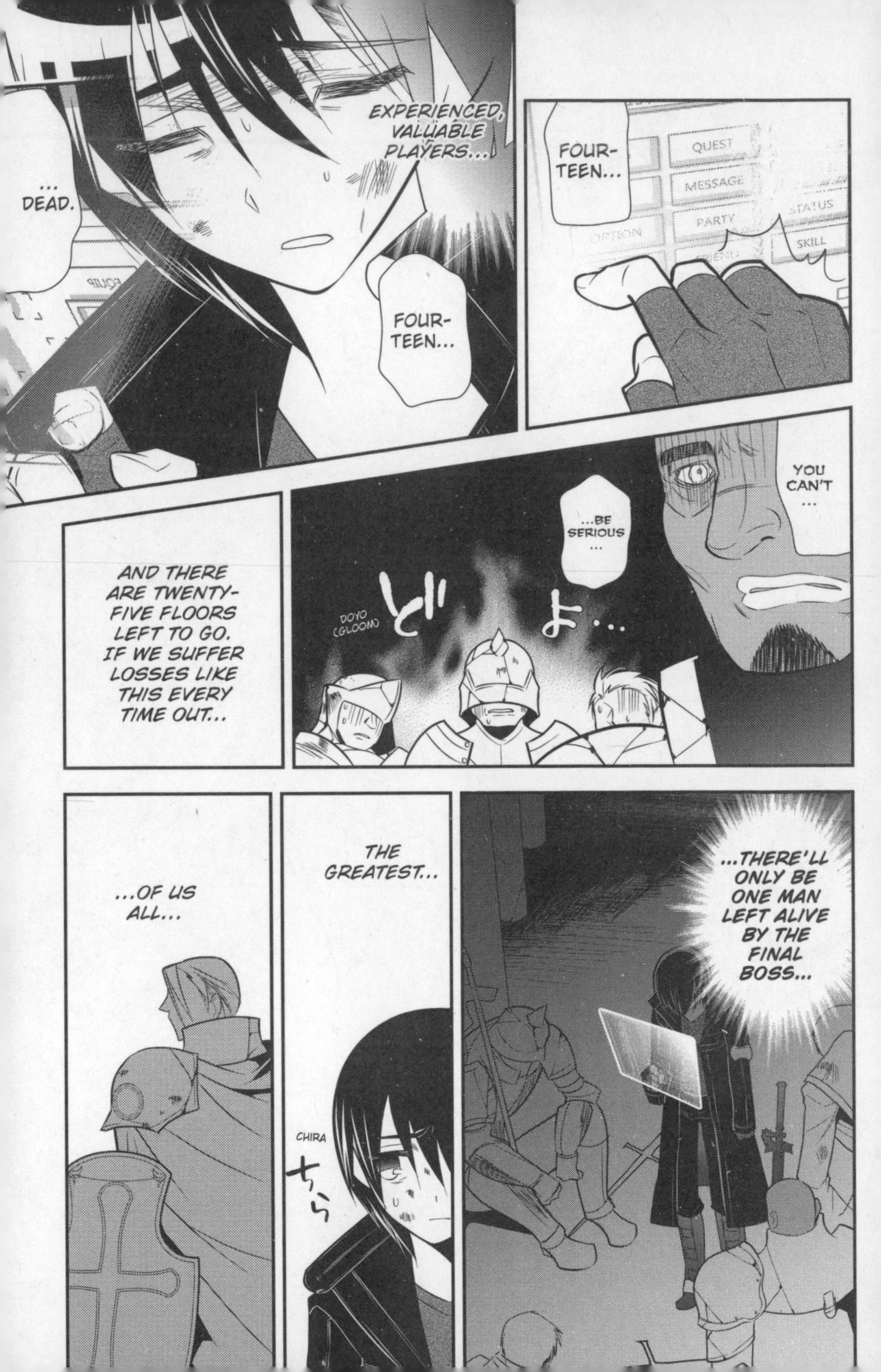
QUEST
MESSAGE
STATUS
PARTY
OPTION
SKILL
FOUR-TEEN...
EXPERIENCED, VALUABLE PLAYERS...
... DEAD.
FOUR-TEEN...
YOU CAN'T ...
...BE SERIOUS ...
DOYO (GLOOM)
どよ...
AND THERE ARE TWENTY-FIVE FLOORS LEFT TO GO. IF WE SUFFER LOSSES LIKE THIS EVERY TIME OUT...
...THERE'LL ONLY BE ONE MAN LEFT ALIVE BY THE FINAL BOSS...
THE GREATEST...
CHIRA
ちら
...OF US ALL...

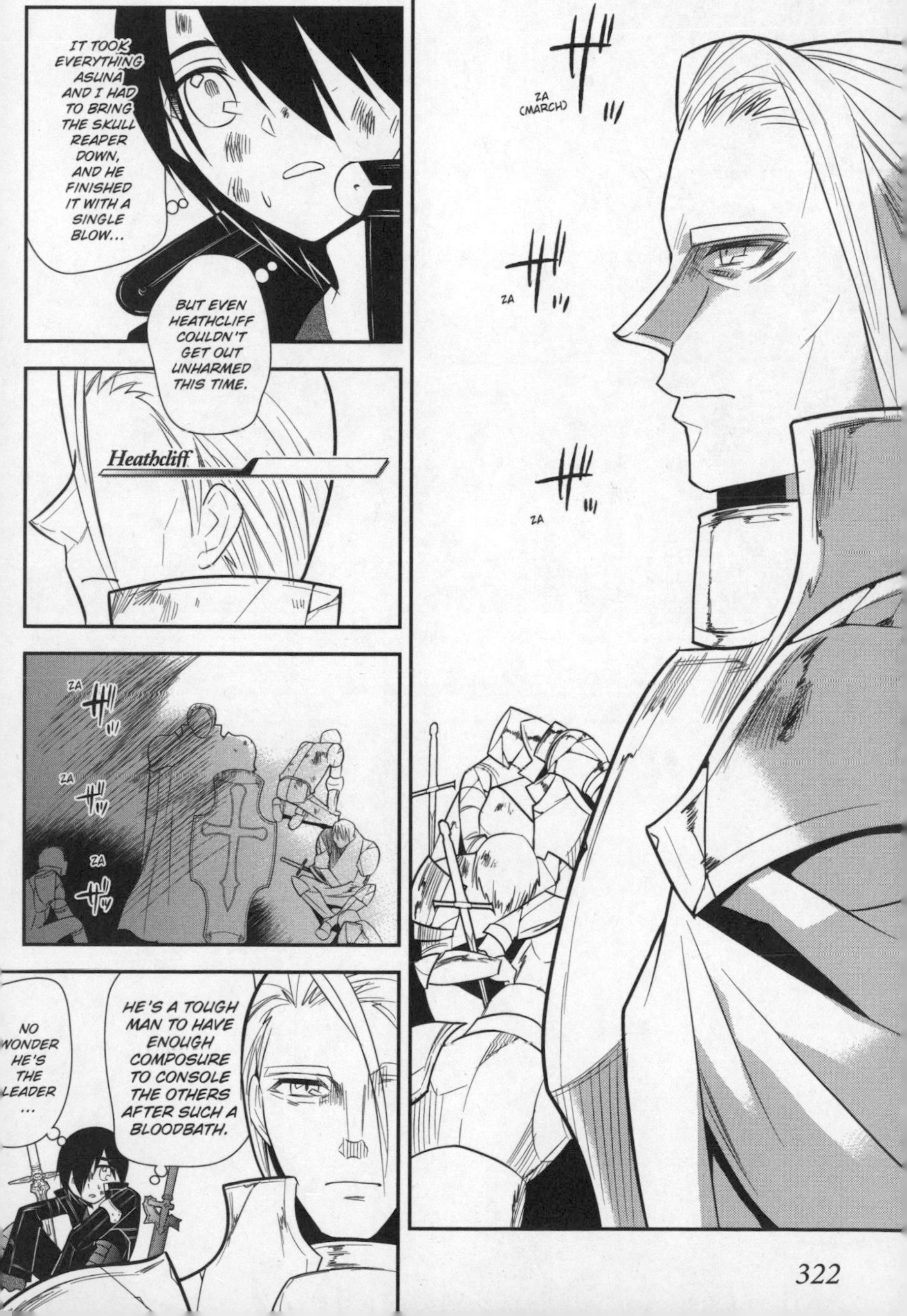
ZA (MARCH)
ZA
ZA
IT TOOK EVERYTHING ASUNA AND I HAD TO BRING THE SKULL REAPER DOWN, AND HE FINISHED IT WITH A SINGLE BLOW...
BUT EVEN HEATHCLIFF COULDN'T GET OUT UNHARMED THIS TIME.
Heathcliff
ZA
ZA
ZA
HE'S A TOUGH MAN TO HAVE ENOUGH COMPOSURE TO CONSOLE THE OTHERS AFTER SUCH A BLOODBATH.
NO WONDER HE'S THE LEADER ...

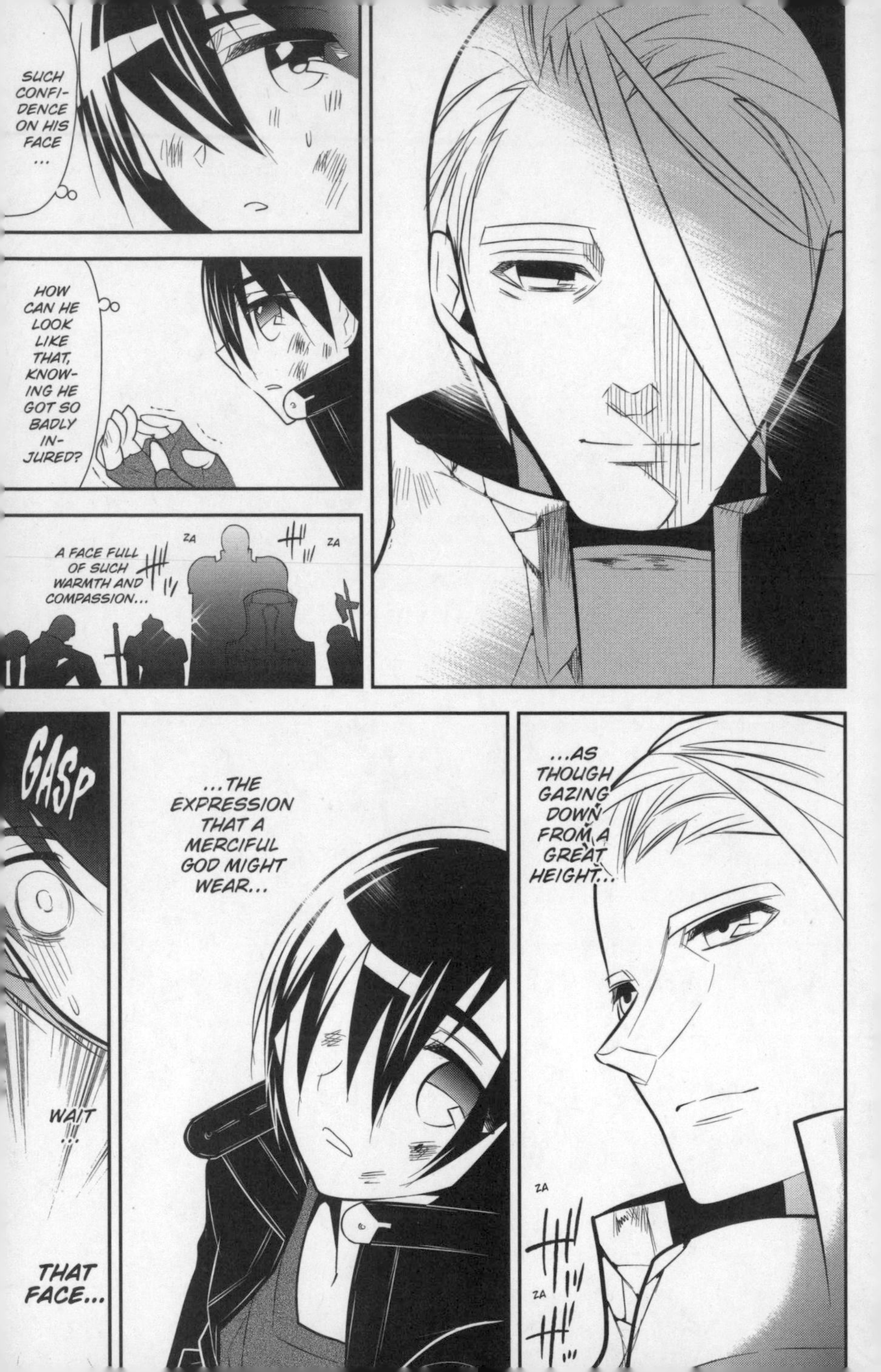
SUCH CONFIDENCE ON HIS FACE...
HOW CAN HE LOOK LIKE THAT, KNOWING HE GOT SO BADLY INJURED?
ZA
ZA
A FACE FULL OF SUCH WARMTH AND COMPASSION...
...AS THOUGH GAZING DOWN FROM A GREAT HEIGHT...
ZA
ZA
...THE EXPRESSION THAT A MERCIFUL GOD MIGHT WEAR...
GASP
WAIT...
THAT FACE...

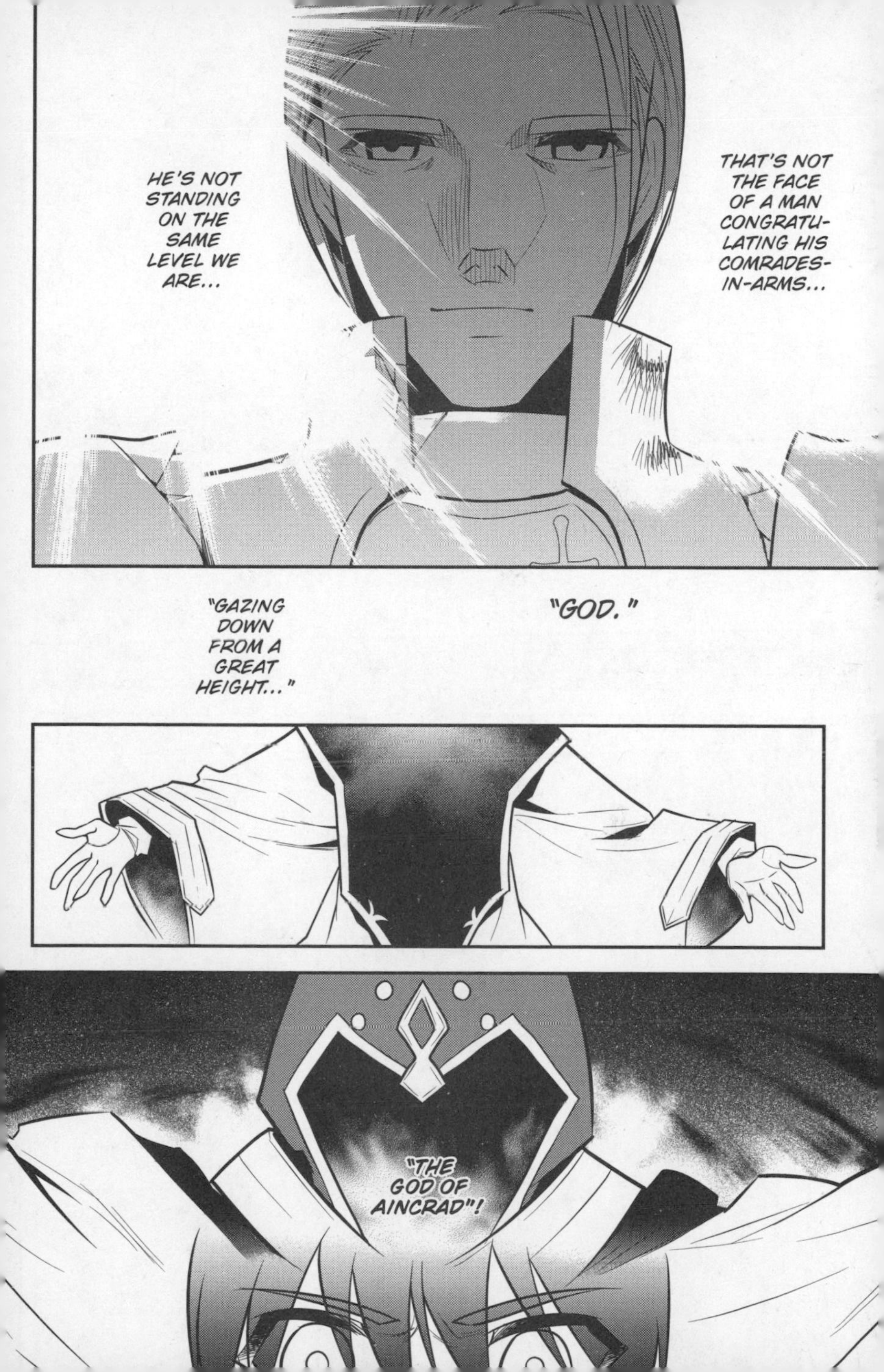
THAT'S NOT THE FACE OF A MAN CONGRATU-LATING HIS COMRADES-IN-ARMS...
HE'S NOT STANDING ON THE SAME LEVEL WE ARE...
"GOD."
"GAZING DOWN FROM A GREAT HEIGHT..."
"THE GOD OF AINCRAD"!

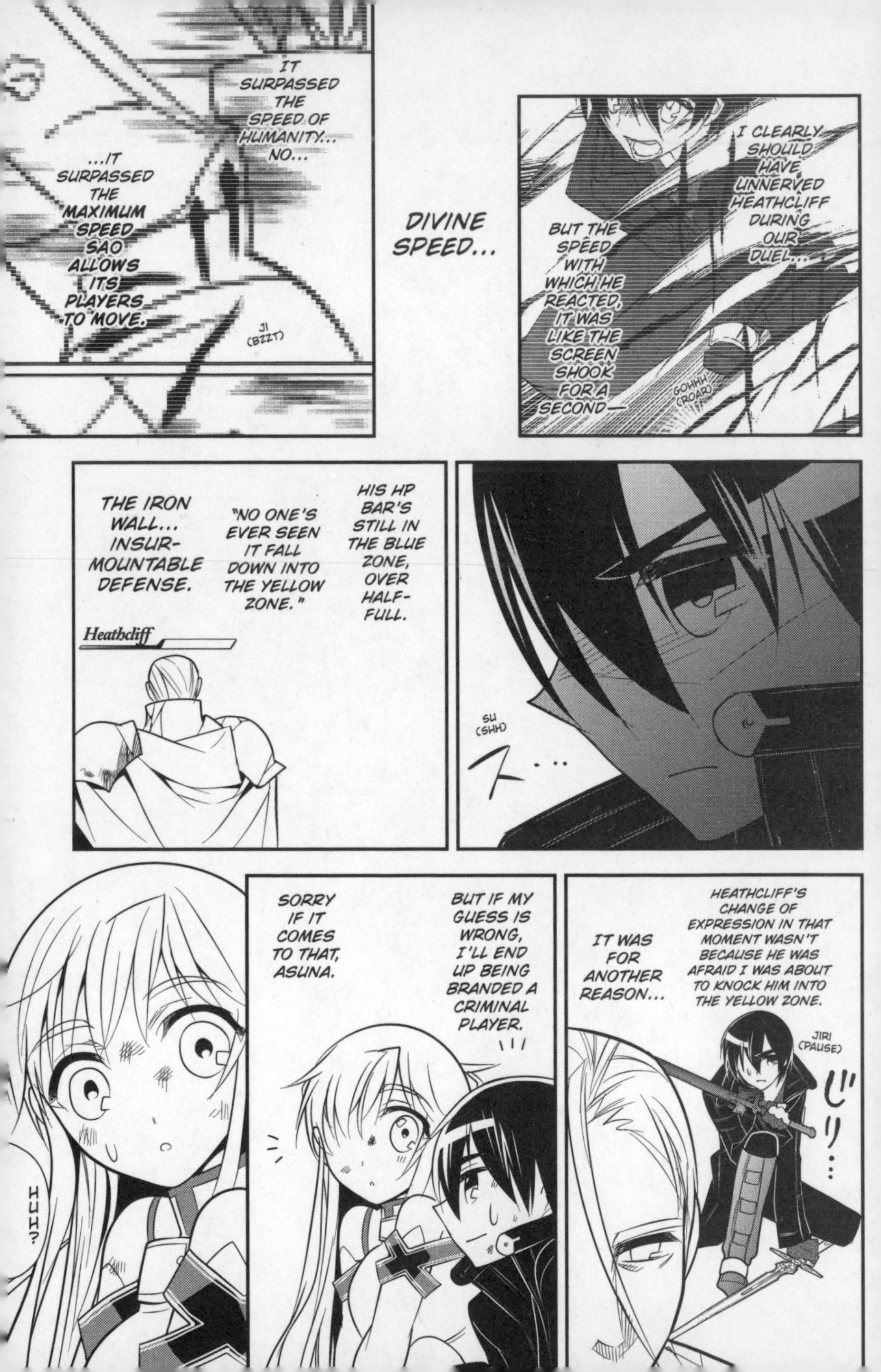
I CLEARLY SHOULD HAVE UNNERVED HEATHCLIFF DURING OUR DUEL...
BUT THE SPEED WITH WHICH HE REACTED, IT WAS LIKE THE SCREEN SHOOK FOR A SECOND—
GOHHH (ROAR)
DIVINE SPEED...
IT SURPASSED THE SPEED OF HUMANITY... NO...
...IT SURPASSED THE MAXIMUM SPEED SAO ALLOWS ITS PLAYERS TO MOVE.
JI (BZZT)
SU (SHH)
ス...
HIS HP BAR'S STILL IN THE BLUE ZONE, OVER HALF-FULL.
"NO ONE'S EVER SEEN IT FALL DOWN INTO THE YELLOW ZONE."
THE IRON WALL... INSURMOUNTABLE DEFENSE.
Heathcliff
HEATHCLIFF'S CHANGE OF EXPRESSION IN THAT MOMENT WASN'T BECAUSE HE WAS AFRAID I WAS ABOUT TO KNOCK HIM INTO THE YELLOW ZONE.
IT WAS FOR ANOTHER REASON...
JIRI (PAUSE)
じり…
BUT IF MY GUESS IS WRONG, I'LL END UP BEING BRANDED A CRIMINAL PLAYER.
SORRY IF IT COMES TO THAT, ASUNA.
HUH?

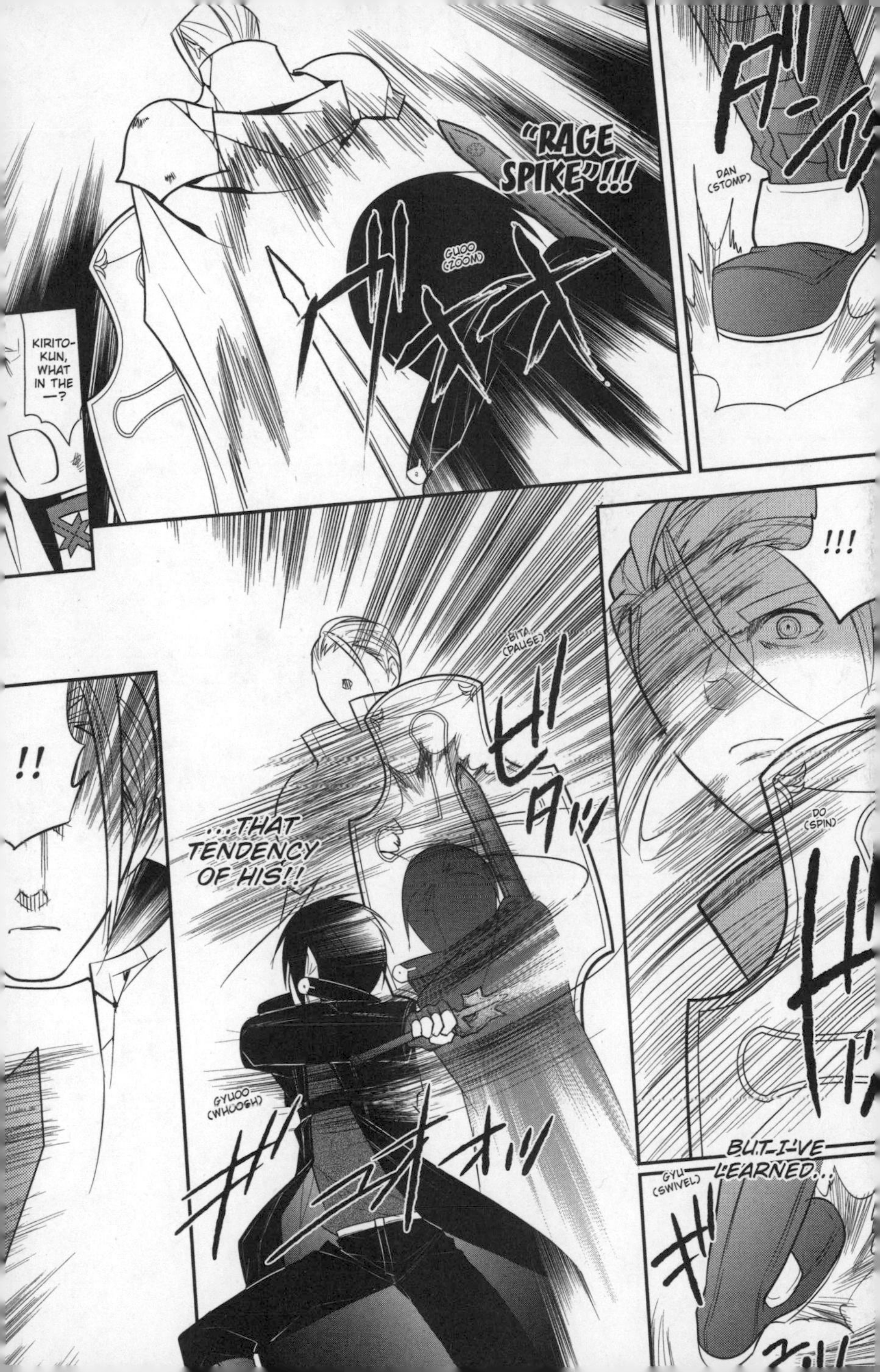
DAN (STOMP)
"RAGE SPIKE"!!!
GUOO (ZOOM)
KIRITO-KUN, WHAT IN THE—?
!!!
DO (SPIN)
GYU (SWIVEL)
BUT I'VE LEARNED...
BITA (PAUSE)
...THAT TENDENCY OF HIS!!
GYUOO (WHOOSH)
!!

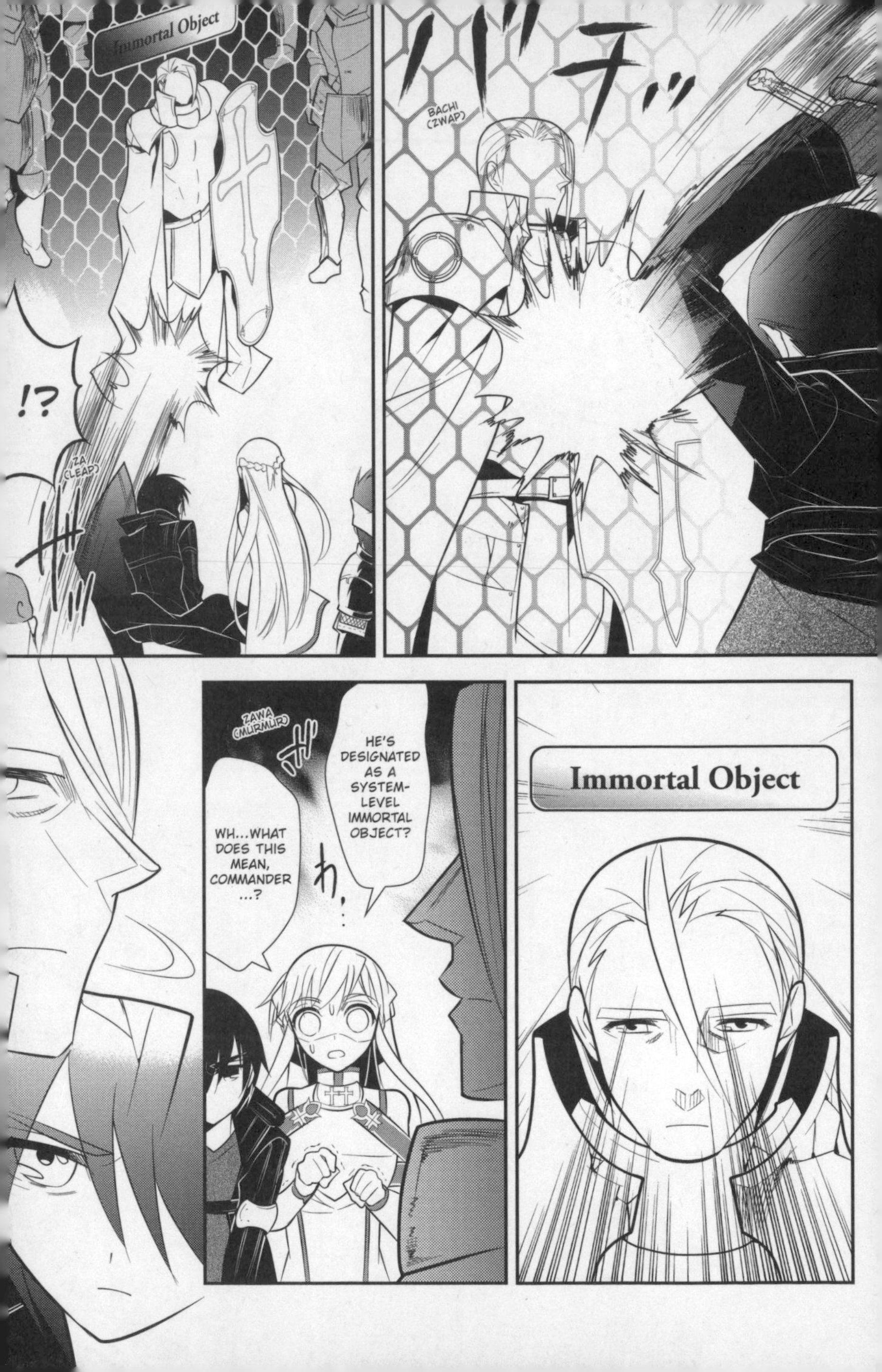
BACHI (ZWAP)
Immortal Object
!?
ZA (LEAP)
Immortal Object
HE'S DESIGNATED AS A SYSTEM-LEVEL IMMORTAL OBJECT?
ZAWA (MURMUR)
WH...WHAT DOES THIS MEAN, COMMANDER ...?

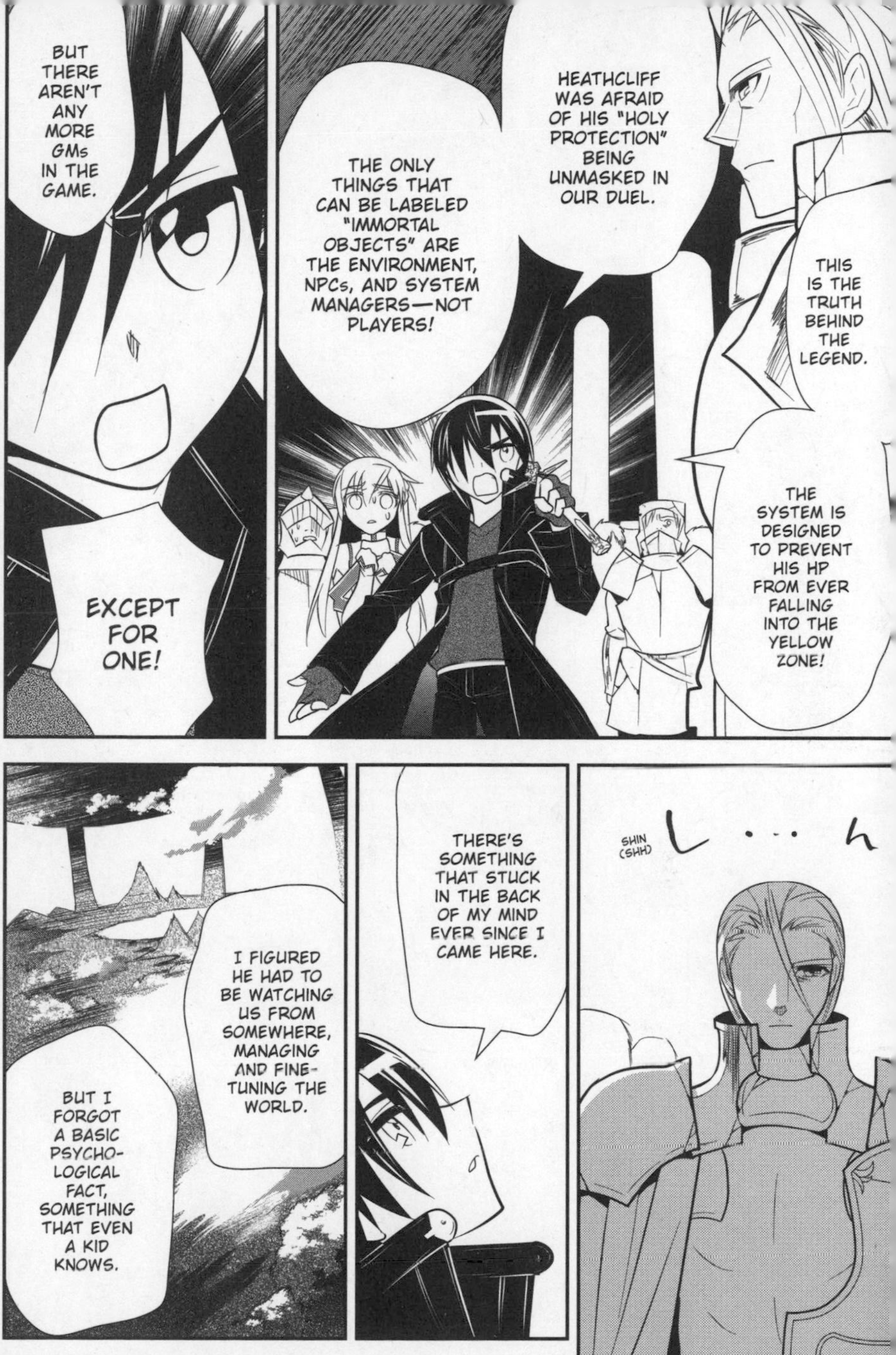
HEATHCLIFF WAS AFRAID OF HIS "HOLY PROTECTION" BEING UNMASKED IN OUR DUEL.
THIS IS THE TRUTH BEHIND THE LEGEND.
THE SYSTEM IS DESIGNED TO PREVENT HIS HP FROM EVER FALLING INTO THE YELLOW ZONE!
THE ONLY THINGS THAT CAN BE LABELED "IMMORTAL OBJECTS" ARE THE ENVIRONMENT, NPCs, AND SYSTEM MANAGERS—NOT PLAYERS!
BUT THERE AREN'T ANY MORE GMs IN THE GAME.
EXCEPT FOR ONE!
SHIN (SHH)
THERE'S SOMETHING THAT STUCK IN THE BACK OF MY MIND EVER SINCE I CAME HERE.
I FIGURED HE HAD TO BE WATCHING US FROM SOMEWHERE, MANAGING AND FINE-TUNING THE WORLD.
BUT I FORGOT A BASIC PSYCHOLOGICAL FACT, SOMETHING THAT EVEN A KID KNOWS.

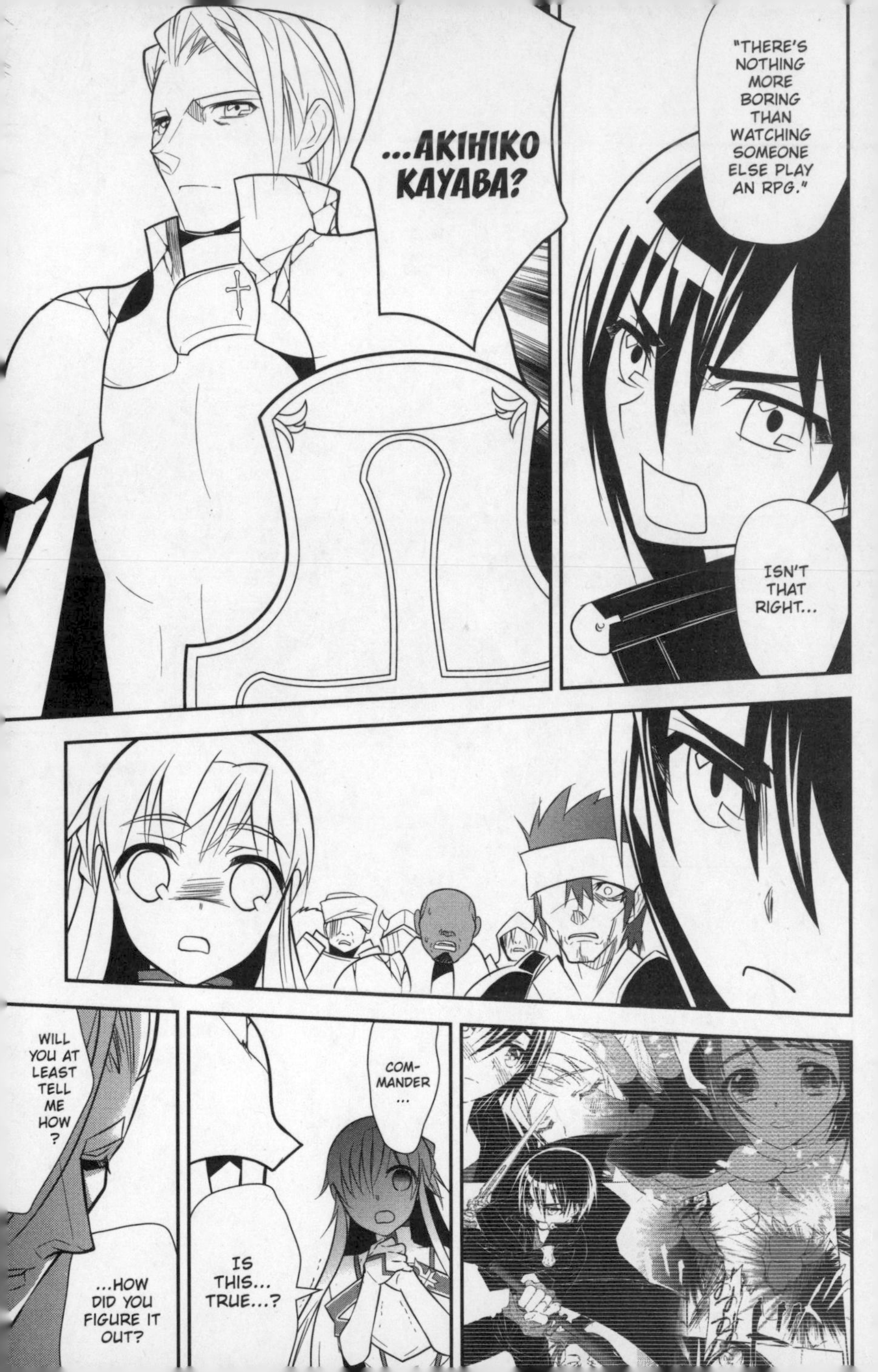
"THERE'S NOTHING MORE BORING THAN WATCHING SOMEONE ELSE PLAY AN RPG."
ISN'T THAT RIGHT...
...AKIHIKO KAYABA?
COM-MANDER ...
IS THIS... TRUE...?
WILL YOU AT LEAST TELL ME HOW?
...HOW DID YOU FIGURE IT OUT?

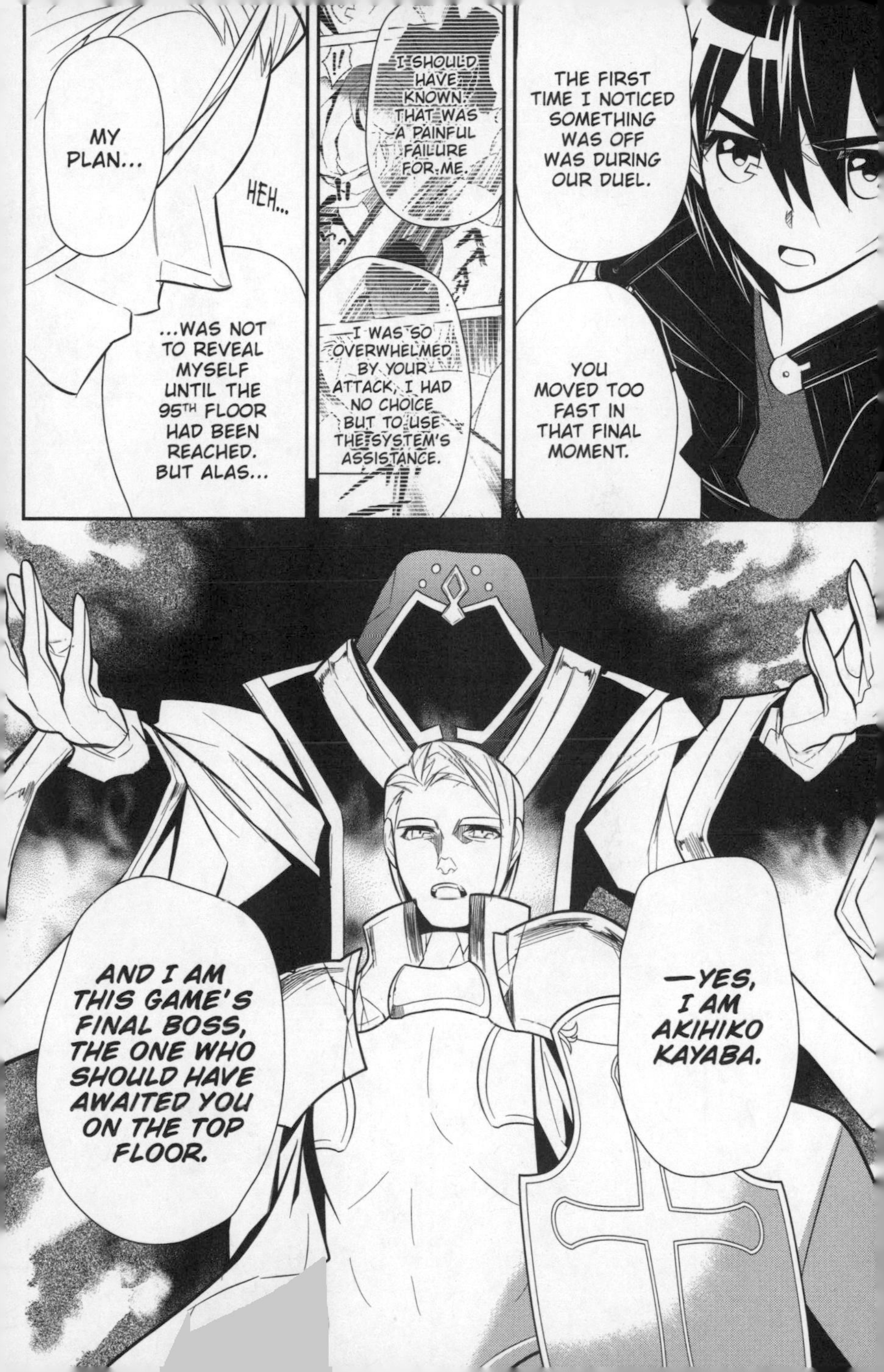
THE FIRST TIME I NOTICED SOMETHING WAS OFF WAS DURING OUR DUEL.
YOU MOVED TOO FAST IN THAT FINAL MOMENT.
I SHOULD HAVE KNOWN. THAT WAS A PAINFUL FAILURE FOR ME.
I WAS SO OVERWHELMED BY YOUR ATTACK, I HAD NO CHOICE BUT TO USE THE SYSTEM'S ASSISTANCE.
HEH...
MY PLAN...
...WAS NOT TO REVEAL MYSELF UNTIL THE 95TH FLOOR HAD BEEN REACHED. BUT ALAS...
—YES, I AM AKIHIKO KAYABA.
AND I AM THIS GAME'S FINAL BOSS, THE ONE WHO SHOULD HAVE AWAITED YOU ON THE TOP FLOOR.

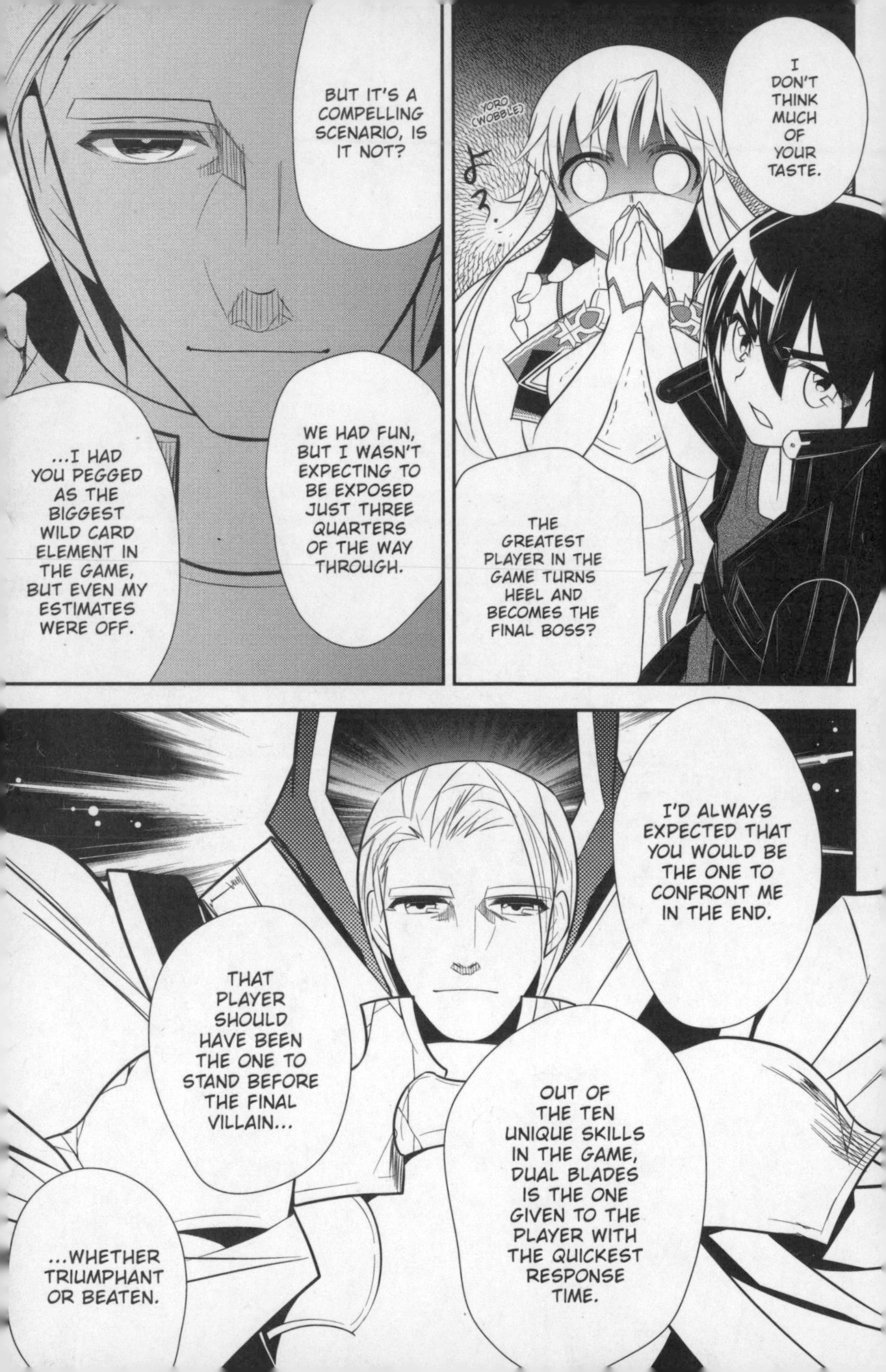
I DON'T THINK MUCH OF YOUR TASTE.
YORO (WOBBLE)
THE GREATEST PLAYER IN THE GAME TURNS HEEL AND BECOMES THE FINAL BOSS?
BUT IT'S A COMPELLING SCENARIO, IS IT NOT?
WE HAD FUN, BUT I WASN'T EXPECTING TO BE EXPOSED JUST THREE QUARTERS OF THE WAY THROUGH.
...I HAD YOU PEGGED AS THE BIGGEST WILD CARD ELEMENT IN THE GAME, BUT EVEN MY ESTIMATES WERE OFF.
I'D ALWAYS EXPECTED THAT YOU WOULD BE THE ONE TO CONFRONT ME IN THE END.
OUT OF THE TEN UNIQUE SKILLS IN THE GAME, DUAL BLADES IS THE ONE GIVEN TO THE PLAYER WITH THE QUICKEST RESPONSE TIME.
THAT PLAYER SHOULD HAVE BEEN THE ONE TO STAND BEFORE THE FINAL VILLAIN...
...WHETHER TRIUMPHANT OR BEATEN.

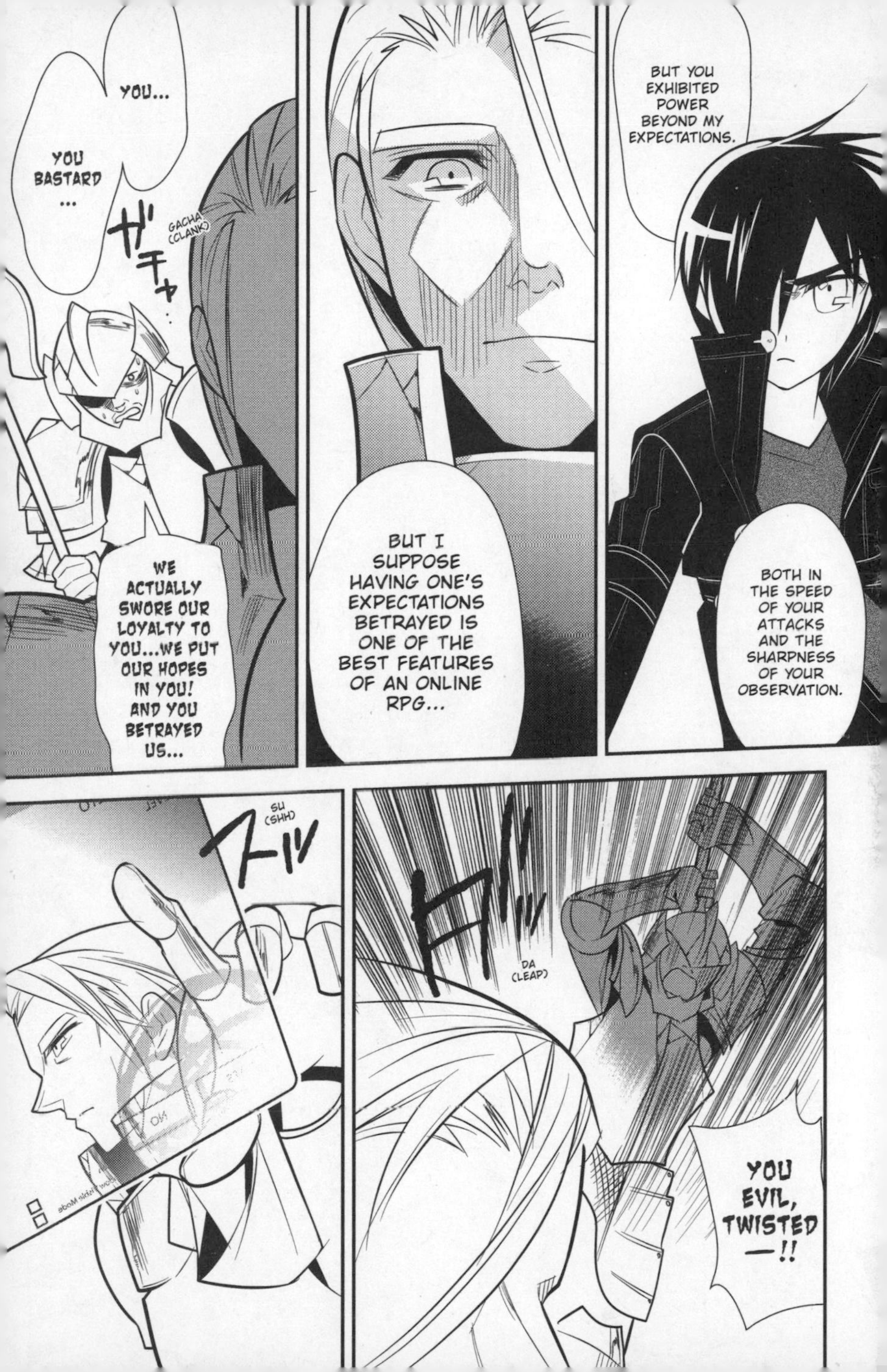
BUT YOU EXHIBITED POWER BEYOND MY EXPECTATIONS.
BOTH IN THE SPEED OF YOUR ATTACKS AND THE SHARPNESS OF YOUR OBSERVATION.
BUT I SUPPOSE HAVING ONE'S EXPECTATIONS BETRAYED IS ONE OF THE BEST FEATURES OF AN ONLINE RPG...
YOU...
YOU BASTARD...
ガチャ
GACHA (CLANK)
WE ACTUALLY SWORE OUR LOYALTY TO YOU...WE PUT OUR HOPES IN YOU! AND YOU BETRAYED US...
ダッ
DA (LEAP)
YOU EVIL, TWISTED—!!
スッ
SU (SHH)

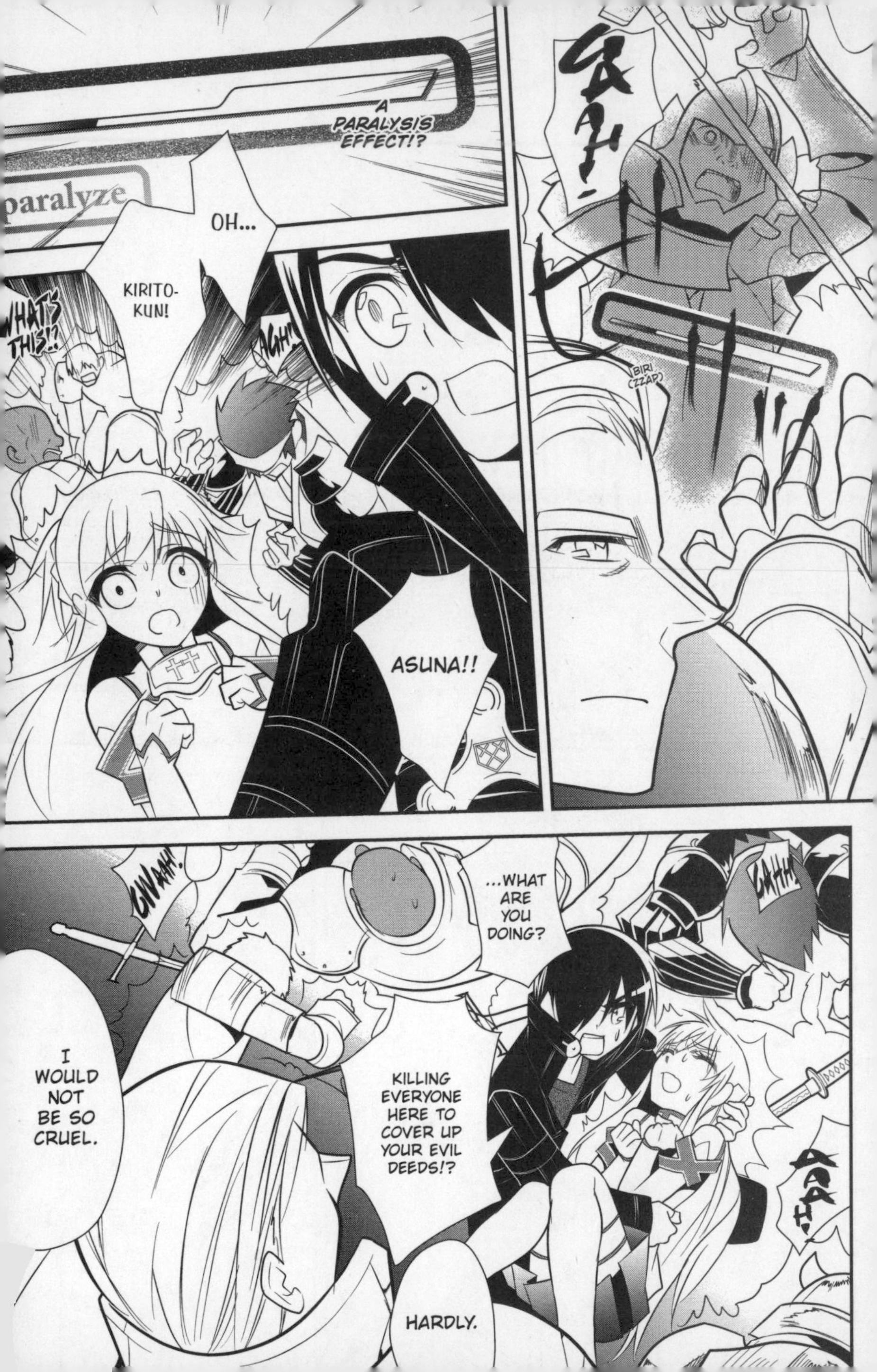
GAAH!
BIRI (ZZAP)
A PARALYSIS EFFECT!?
paralyze
OH...
AGH!
KIRITO-KUN!
WHAT'S THIS!?
ASUNA!!
GAHH!
...WHAT ARE YOU DOING?
KILLING EVERYONE HERE TO COVER UP YOUR EVIL DEEDS!?
AAAH!
GWAAH!
I WOULD NOT BE SO CRUEL.
HARDLY.

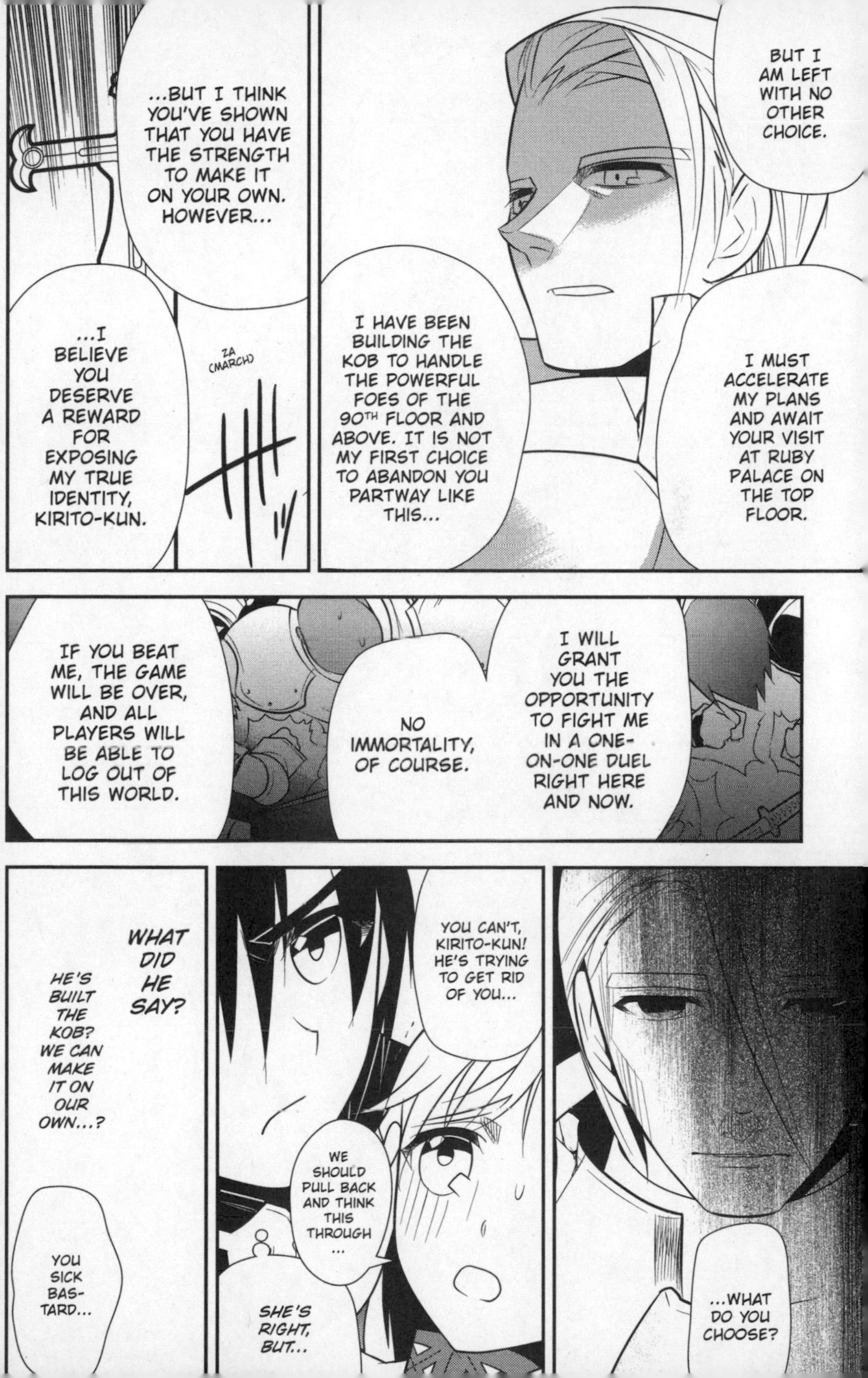
BUT I AM LEFT WITH NO OTHER CHOICE.
I MUST ACCELERATE MY PLANS AND AWAIT YOUR VISIT AT RUBY PALACE ON THE TOP FLOOR.
I HAVE BEEN BUILDING THE KOB TO HANDLE THE POWERFUL FOES OF THE 90TH FLOOR AND ABOVE. IT IS NOT MY FIRST CHOICE TO ABANDON YOU PARTWAY LIKE THIS...
...BUT I THINK YOU'VE SHOWN THAT YOU HAVE THE STRENGTH TO MAKE IT ON YOUR OWN. HOWEVER...
ZA (MARCH)
...I BELIEVE YOU DESERVE A REWARD FOR EXPOSING MY TRUE IDENTITY, KIRITO-KUN.
I WILL GRANT YOU THE OPPORTUNITY TO FIGHT ME IN A ONE-ON-ONE DUEL RIGHT HERE AND NOW.
NO IMMORTALITY, OF COURSE.
IF YOU BEAT ME, THE GAME WILL BE OVER, AND ALL PLAYERS WILL BE ABLE TO LOG OUT OF THIS WORLD.
...WHAT DO YOU CHOOSE?
YOU CAN'T, KIRITO-KUN! HE'S TRYING TO GET RID OF YOU...
WE SHOULD PULL BACK AND THINK THIS THROUGH ...
SHE'S RIGHT, BUT...
WHAT DID HE SAY?
HE'S BUILT THE KOB? WE CAN MAKE IT ON OUR OWN...?
YOU SICK BAS-TARD...

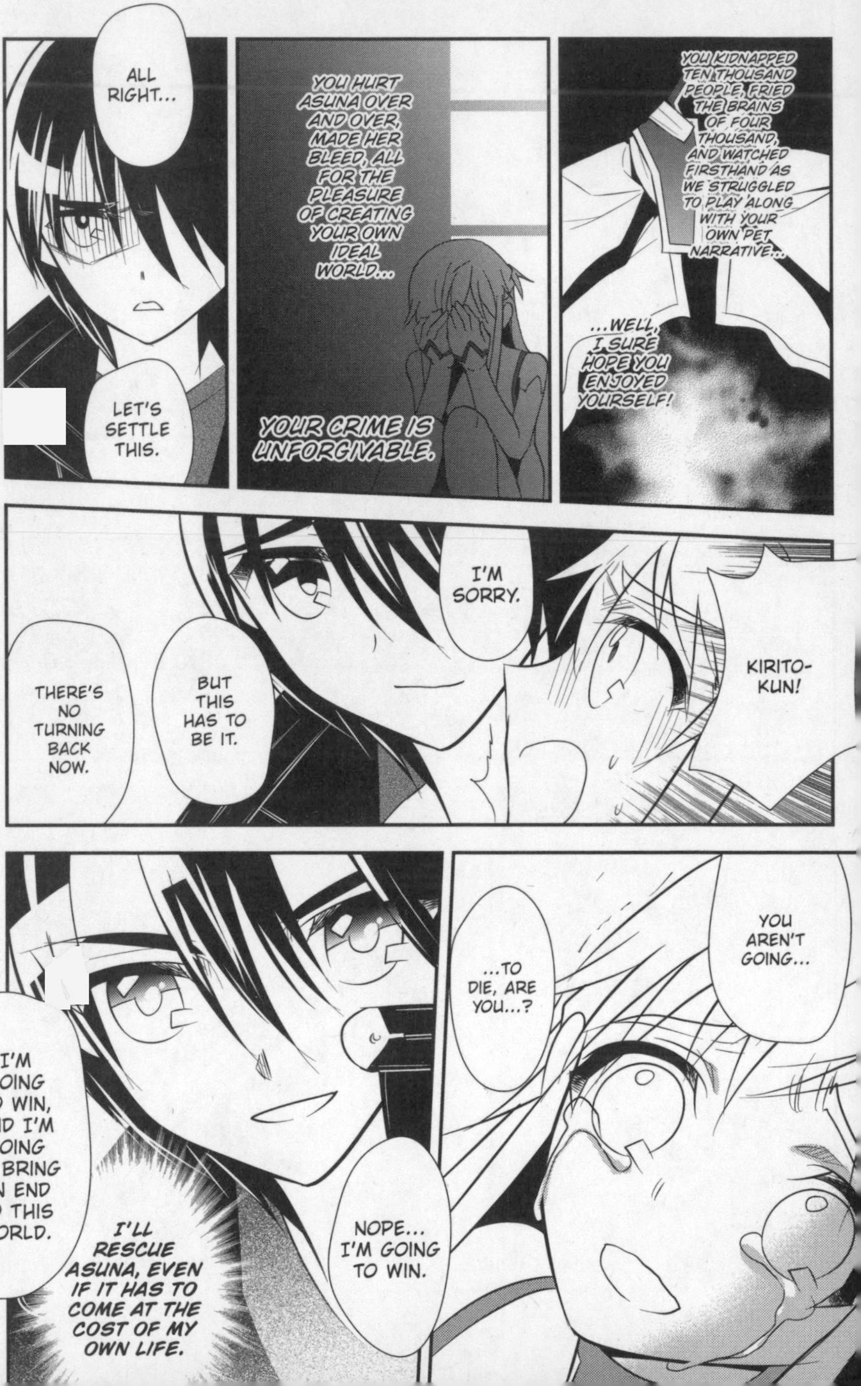
YOU KIDNAPPED TEN THOUSAND PEOPLE, FRIED THE BRAINS OF FOUR THOUSAND, AND WATCHED FIRSTHAND AS WE STRUGGLED TO PLAY ALONG WITH YOUR OWN PET NARRATIVE...
...WELL, I SURE HOPE YOU ENJOYED YOURSELF!
YOU HURT ASUNA OVER AND OVER, MADE HER BLEED, ALL FOR THE PLEASURE OF CREATING YOUR OWN IDEAL WORLD...
YOUR CRIME IS UNFORGIVABLE.
ALL RIGHT...
LET'S SETTLE THIS.
KIRITO-KUN!
I'M SORRY.
BUT THIS HAS TO BE IT.
THERE'S NO TURNING BACK NOW.
YOU AREN'T GOING...
...TO DIE, ARE YOU...?
NOPE... I'M GOING TO WIN.
I'M GOING TO WIN, AND I'M GOING TO BRING AN END TO THIS WORLD.
I'LL RESCUE ASUNA, EVEN IF IT HAS TO COME AT THE COST OF MY OWN LIFE.

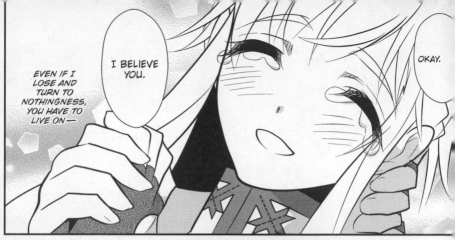

EVEN IF I LOSE AND TURN TO NOTHINGNESS, YOU HAVE TO LIVE ON—

I BELIEVE YOU.

OKAY.

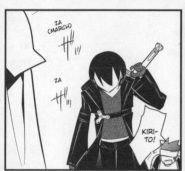

ZA (MARCH)

ZA (MARCH)

KIRI-TO!

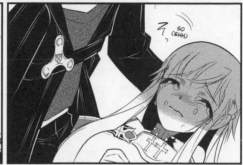

ヲ (SO)

SO (EHH)

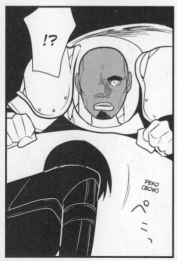

!?

PEKO (BOW)

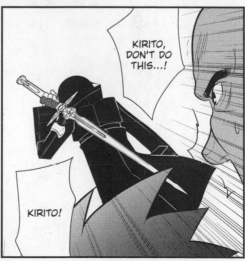

KIRITO, DON'T DO THIS...!

KIRITO!

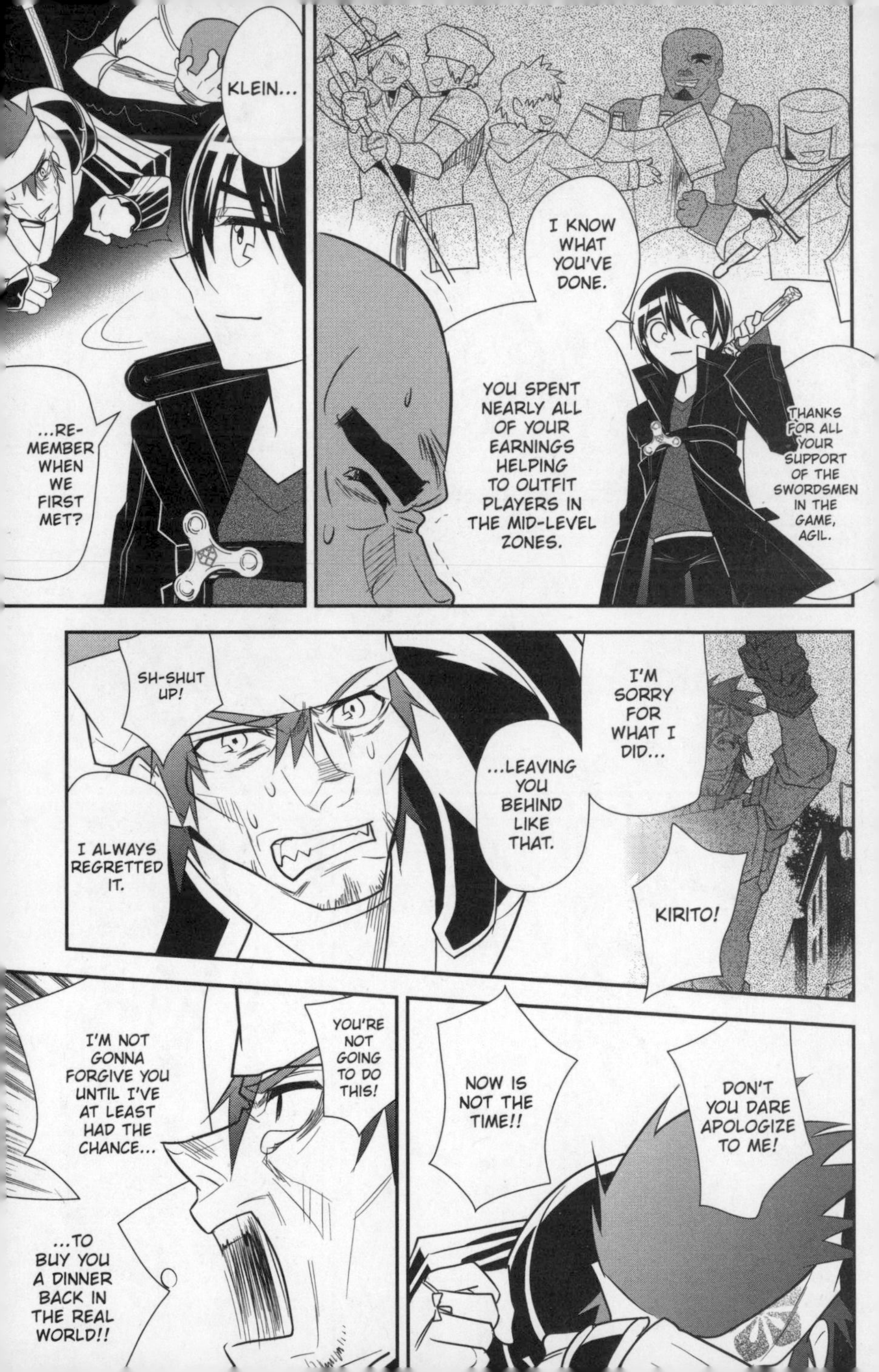
THANKS FOR ALL YOUR SUPPORT OF THE SWORDSMEN IN THE GAME, AGIL.
I KNOW WHAT YOU'VE DONE.
YOU SPENT NEARLY ALL OF YOUR EARNINGS HELPING TO OUTFIT PLAYERS IN THE MID-LEVEL ZONES.
KLEIN...
...RE-MEMBER WHEN WE FIRST MET?
KIRITO!
I'M SORRY FOR WHAT I DID...
...LEAVING YOU BEHIND LIKE THAT.
I ALWAYS REGRETTED IT.
SH-SHUT UP!
DON'T YOU DARE APOLOGIZE TO ME!
NOW IS NOT THE TIME!!
YOU'RE NOT GOING TO DO THIS!
I'M NOT GONNA FORGIVE YOU UNTIL I'VE AT LEAST HAD THE CHANCE...
...TO BUY YOU A DINNER BACK IN THE REAL WORLD!!

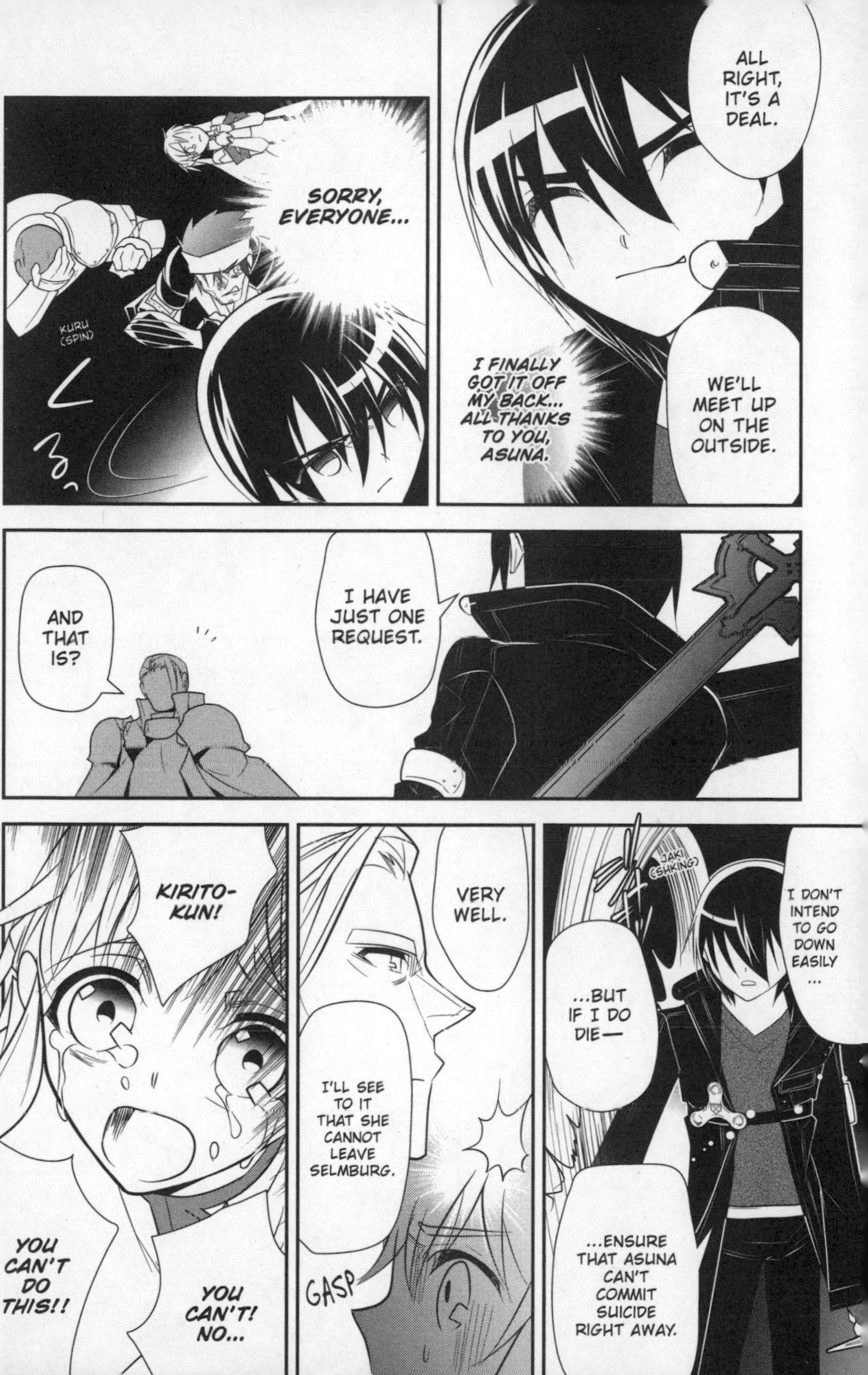
ALL RIGHT, IT'S A DEAL.
WE'LL MEET UP ON THE OUTSIDE.
I FINALLY GOT IT OFF MY BACK... ALL THANKS TO YOU, ASUNA.
SORRY, EVERYONE...
KURU (SPIN)
I HAVE JUST ONE REQUEST.
AND THAT IS?
JAKI (SHKING)
I DON'T INTEND TO GO DOWN EASILY...
...BUT IF I DO DIE—
...ENSURE THAT ASUNA CAN'T COMMIT SUICIDE RIGHT AWAY.
VERY WELL.
I'LL SEE TO IT THAT SHE CANNOT LEAVE SELMBURG.
GASP
KIRITO-KUN!
YOU CAN'T! NO...
YOU CAN'T DO THIS!!

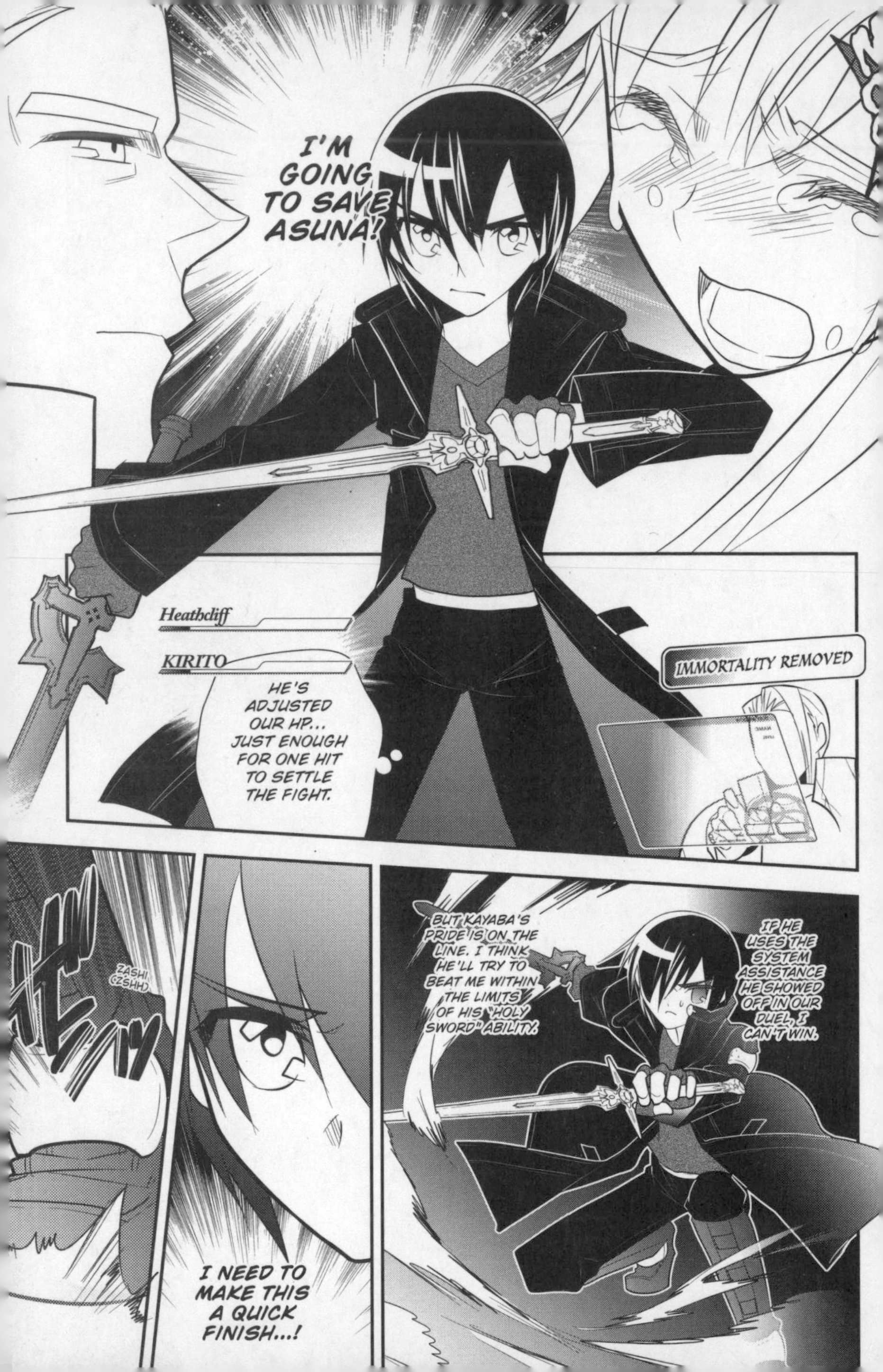
I'M GOING TO SAVE ASUNA!
IMMORTALITY REMOVED
Heathcliff
KIRITO
HE'S ADJUSTED OUR HP... JUST ENOUGH FOR ONE HIT TO SETTLE THE FIGHT.
IF HE USES THE SYSTEM ASSISTANCE HE SHOWED OFF IN OUR DUEL, I CAN'T WIN.
BUT KAYABA'S PRIDE IS ON THE LINE. I THINK HE'LL TRY TO BEAT ME WITHIN THE LIMITS OF HIS "HOLY SWORD" ABILITY.
I NEED TO MAKE THIS A QUICK FINISH...!
ZASHI (ZSHH)

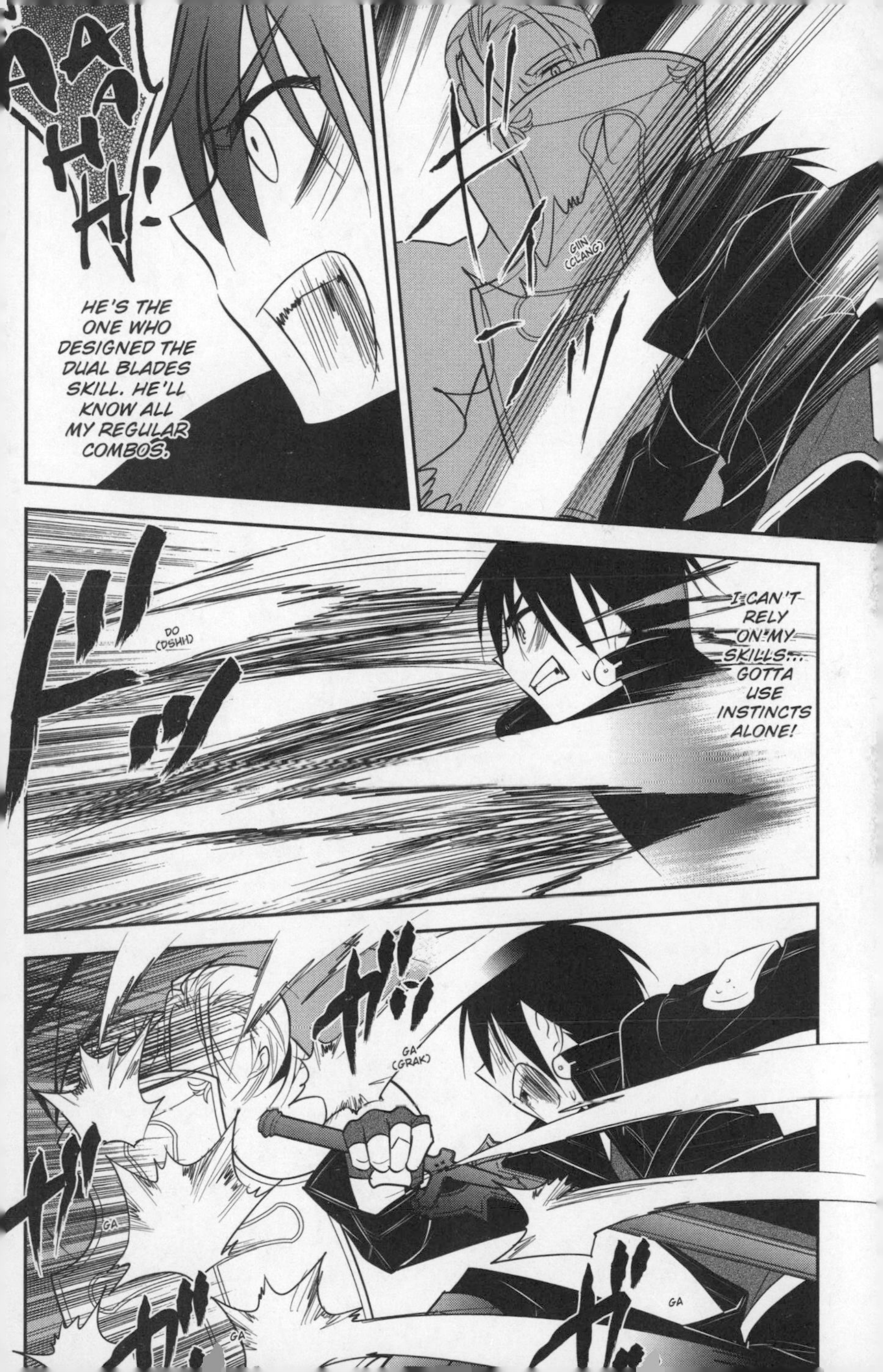
GIIN (CLANG)
AAAHH!
HE'S THE ONE WHO DESIGNED THE DUAL BLADES SKILL. HE'LL KNOW ALL MY REGULAR COMBOS.
I CAN'T RELY ON MY SKILLS... GOTTA USE INSTINCTS ALONE!
DO (DSHH)
GA (GRAK)
GA
GA
GA

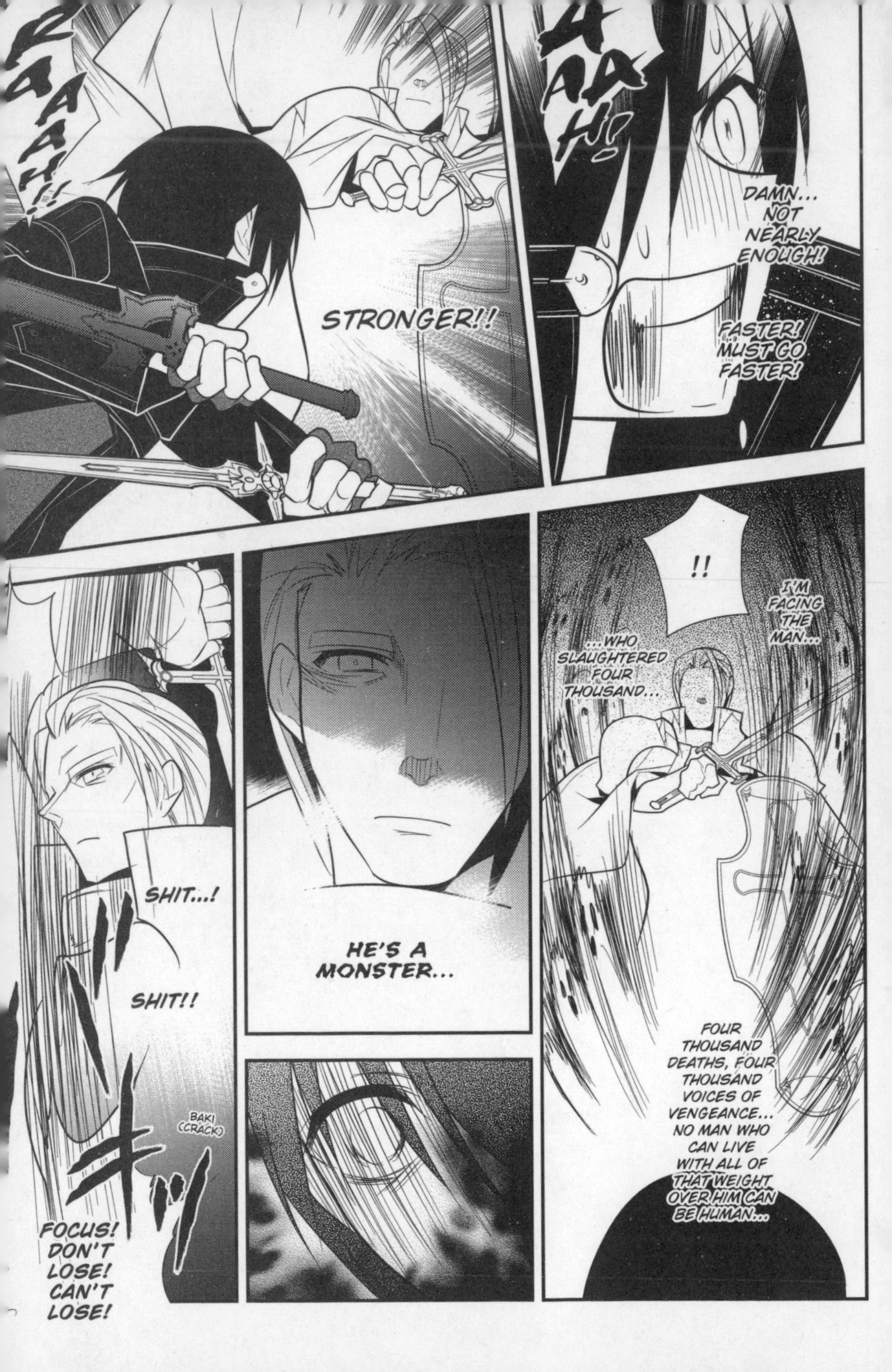
AAAH!
DAMN... NOT NEARLY ENOUGH!
FASTER! MUST GO FASTER!
RAAAH!!
STRONGER!!
!!
I'M FACING THE MAN...
...WHO SLAUGHTERED FOUR THOUSAND...
FOUR THOUSAND DEATHS, FOUR THOUSAND VOICES OF VENGEANCE... NO MAN WHO CAN LIVE WITH ALL OF THAT WEIGHT OVER HIM CAN BE HUMAN...
HE'S A MONSTER...
SHIT...!
SHIT!!
BAKI (CRACK)
FOCUS! DON'T LOSE! CAN'T LOSE!

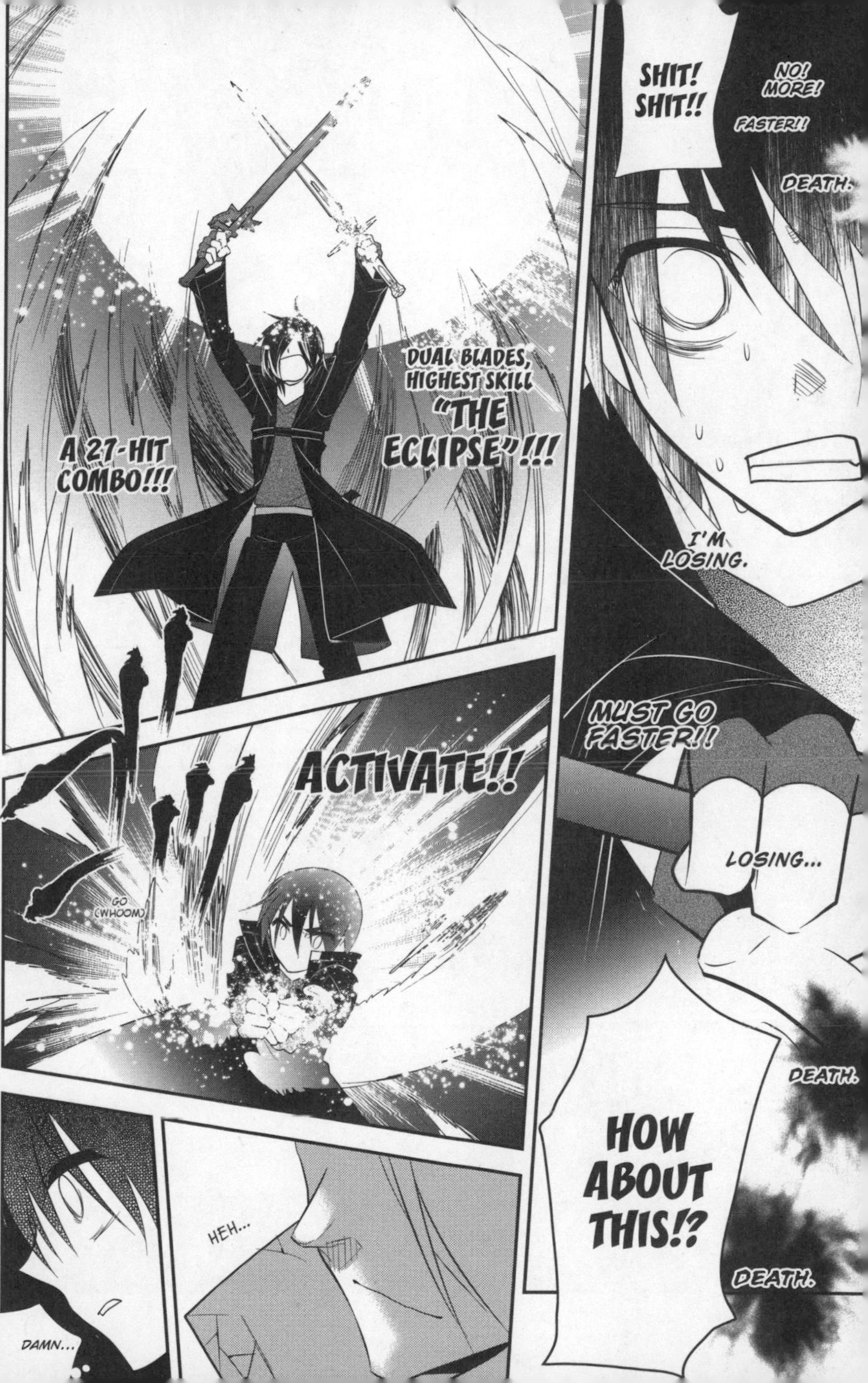
SHIT! SHIT!!
NO! MORE!
FASTER!!
DEATH.
I'M LOSING.
MUST GO FASTER!!
LOSING...
DEATH.
HOW ABOUT THIS!?
DEATH.
DUAL BLADES, HIGHEST SKILL "THE ECLIPSE"!!!
A 27-HIT COMBO!!!
ACTIVATE!!
GO (WHOOM)
HEH...
DAMN...

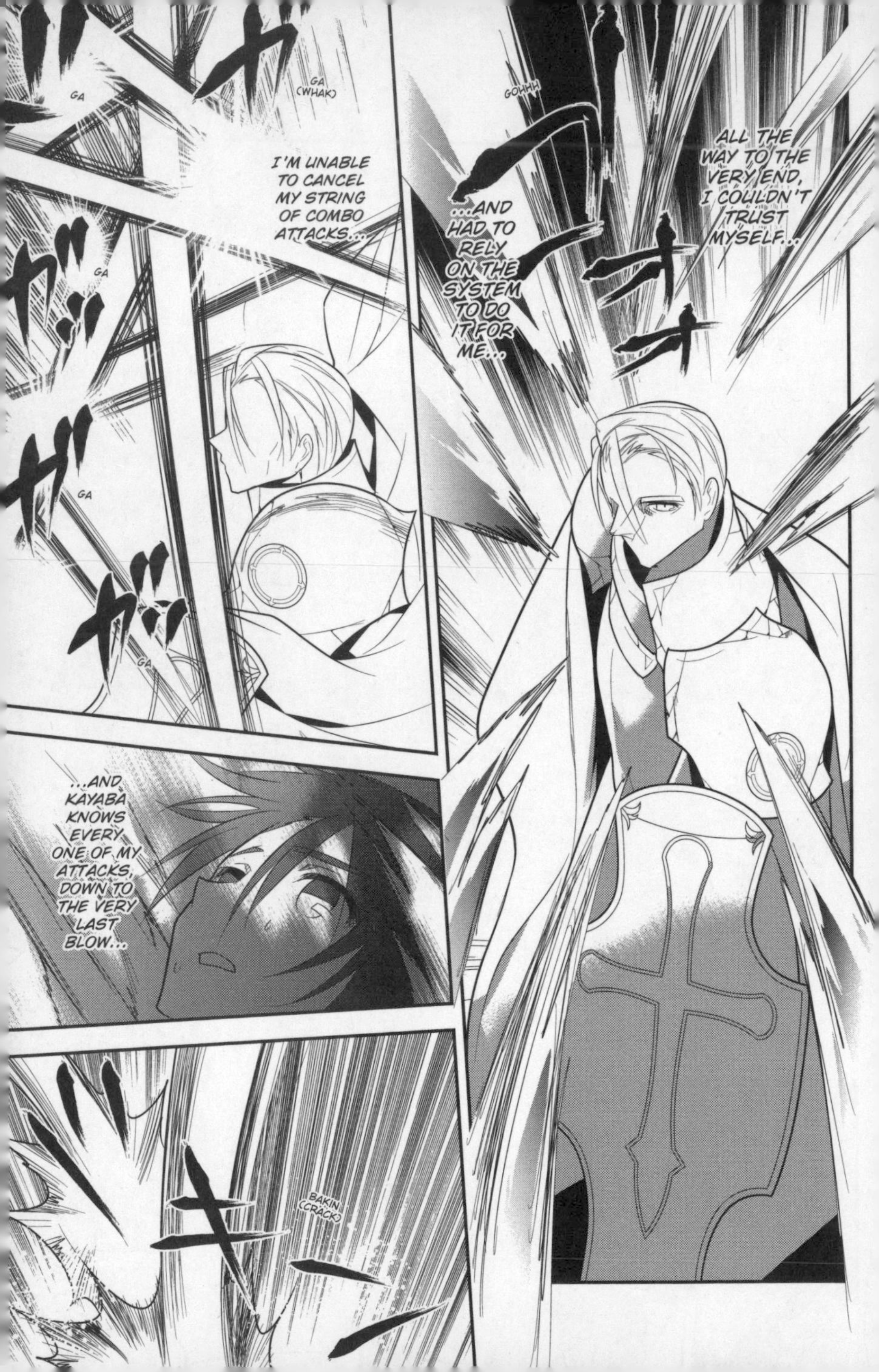
GOHHH
ALL THE WAY TO THE VERY END, I COULDN'T TRUST MYSELF...
...AND HAD TO RELY ON THE SYSTEM TO DO IT FOR ME...
GA
GA (WHAK)
I'M UNABLE TO CANCEL MY STRING OF COMBO ATTACKS...
GA
GA
GA
...AND KAYABA KNOWS EVERY ONE OF MY ATTACKS, DOWN TO THE VERY LAST BLOW...
BAKIN (CRACK)

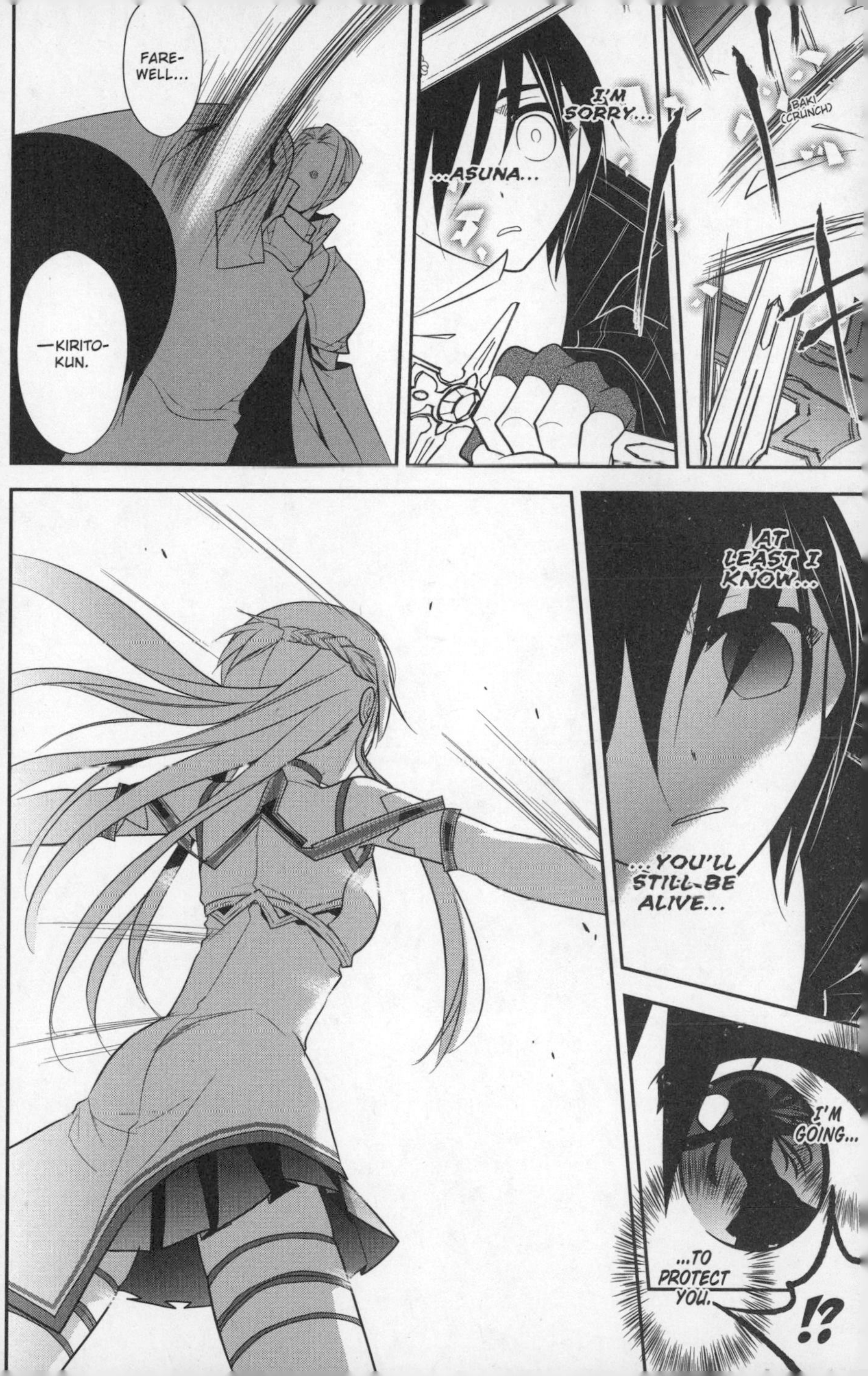
BAKI (CRUNCH)
I'M SORRY...
...ASUNA...
FARE-WELL...
—KIRITO-KUN.
AT LEAST I KNOW...
...YOU'LL STILL BE ALIVE...
I'M GOING...
...TO PROTECT YOU.
!?

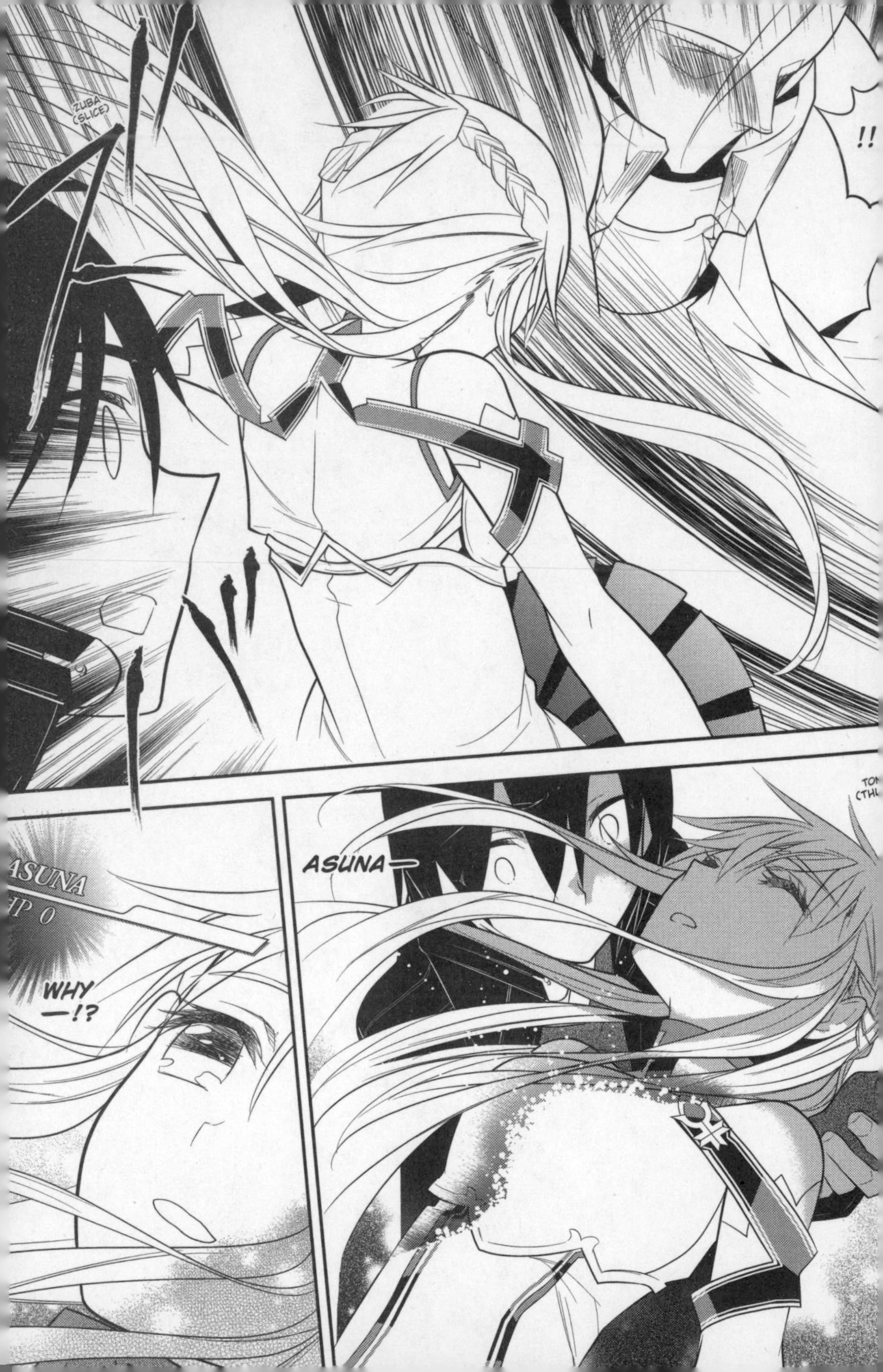
!!
ZUBA
(SLICE)
ASUNA—
ASUNA
WHY
—!?

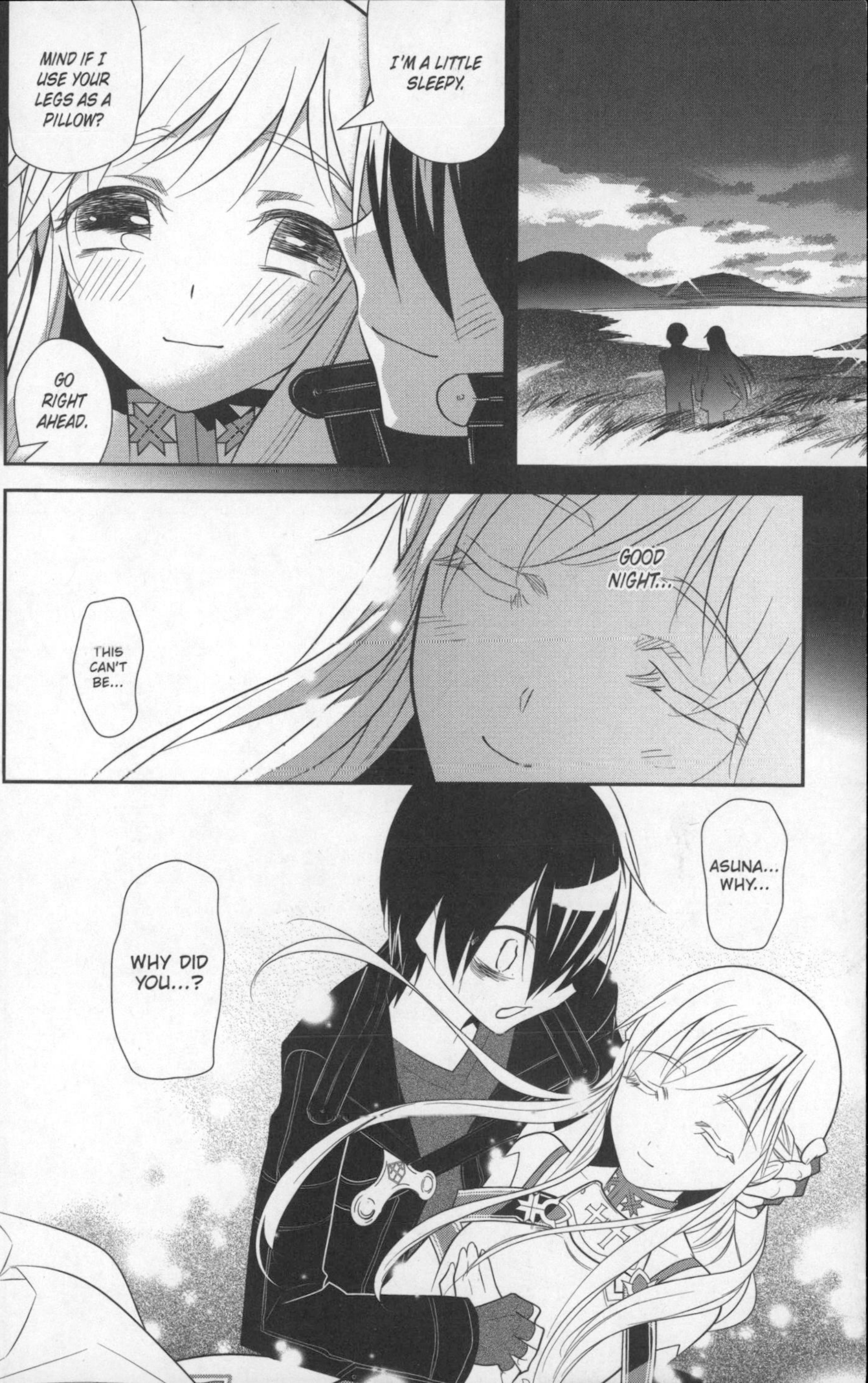
I'M A LITTLE SLEEPY.
MIND IF I USE YOUR LEGS AS A PILLOW?
GO RIGHT AHEAD.
GOOD NIGHT...
THIS CAN'T BE...
ASUNA... WHY...
WHY DID YOU...?

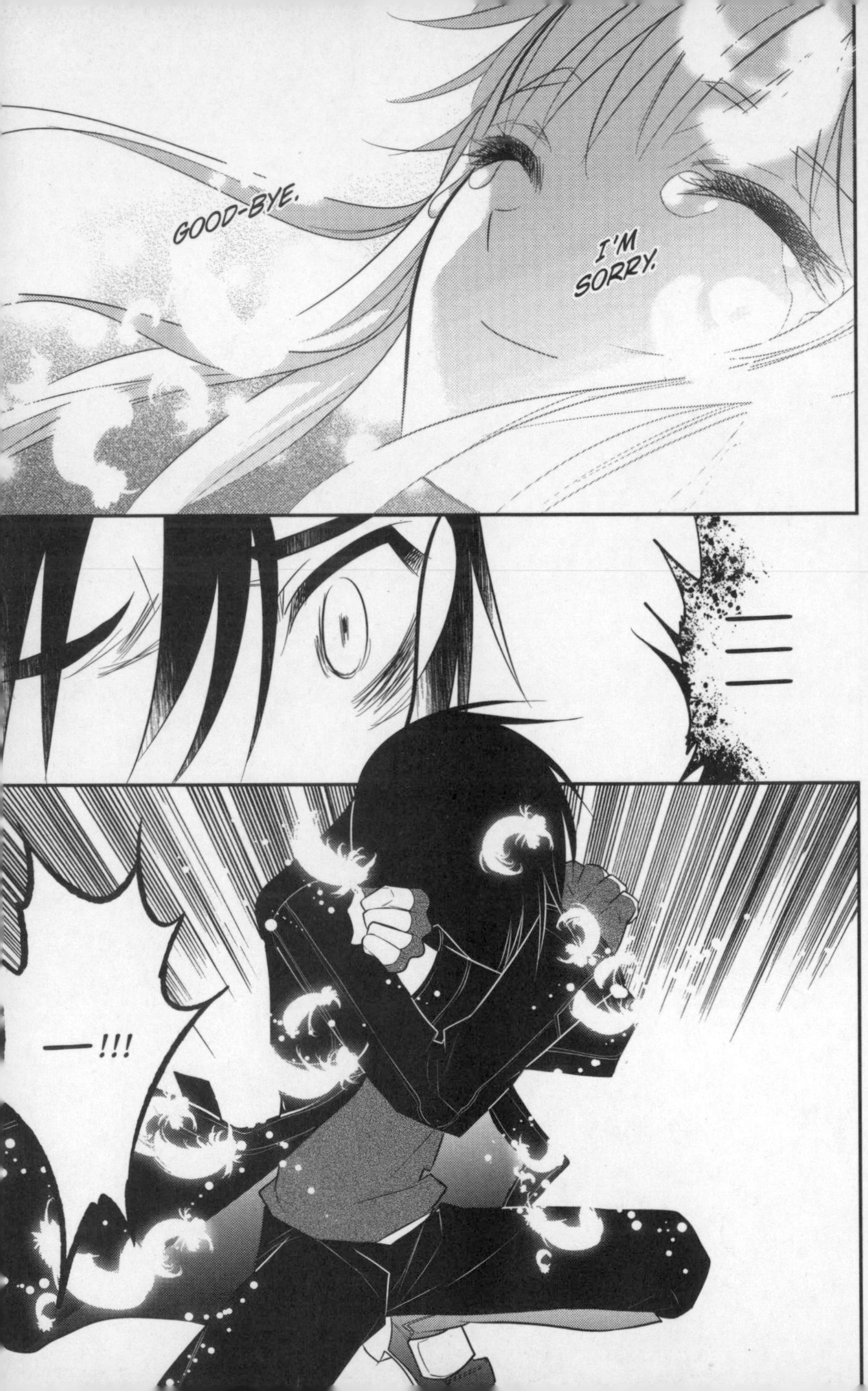
I'M SORRY.
GOOD-BYE.
—!!!

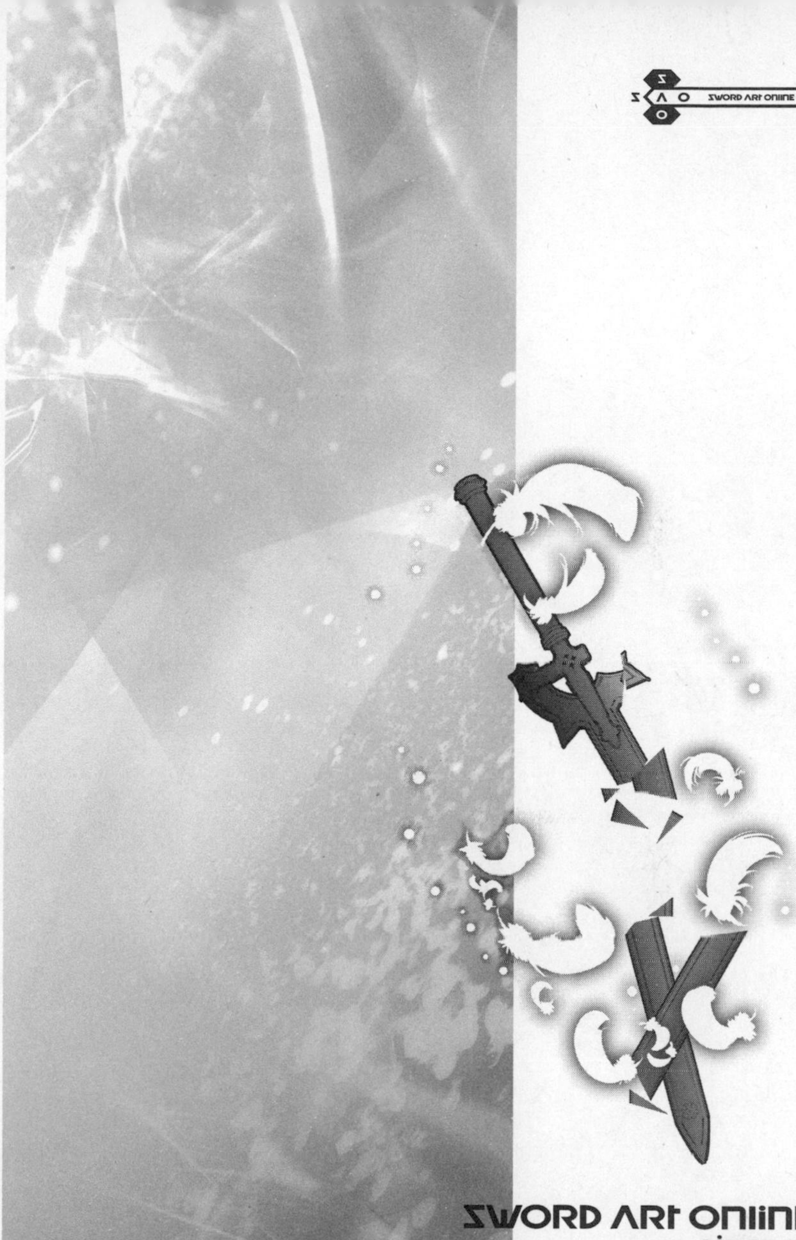

SWORD ART ONLINE
aincrad

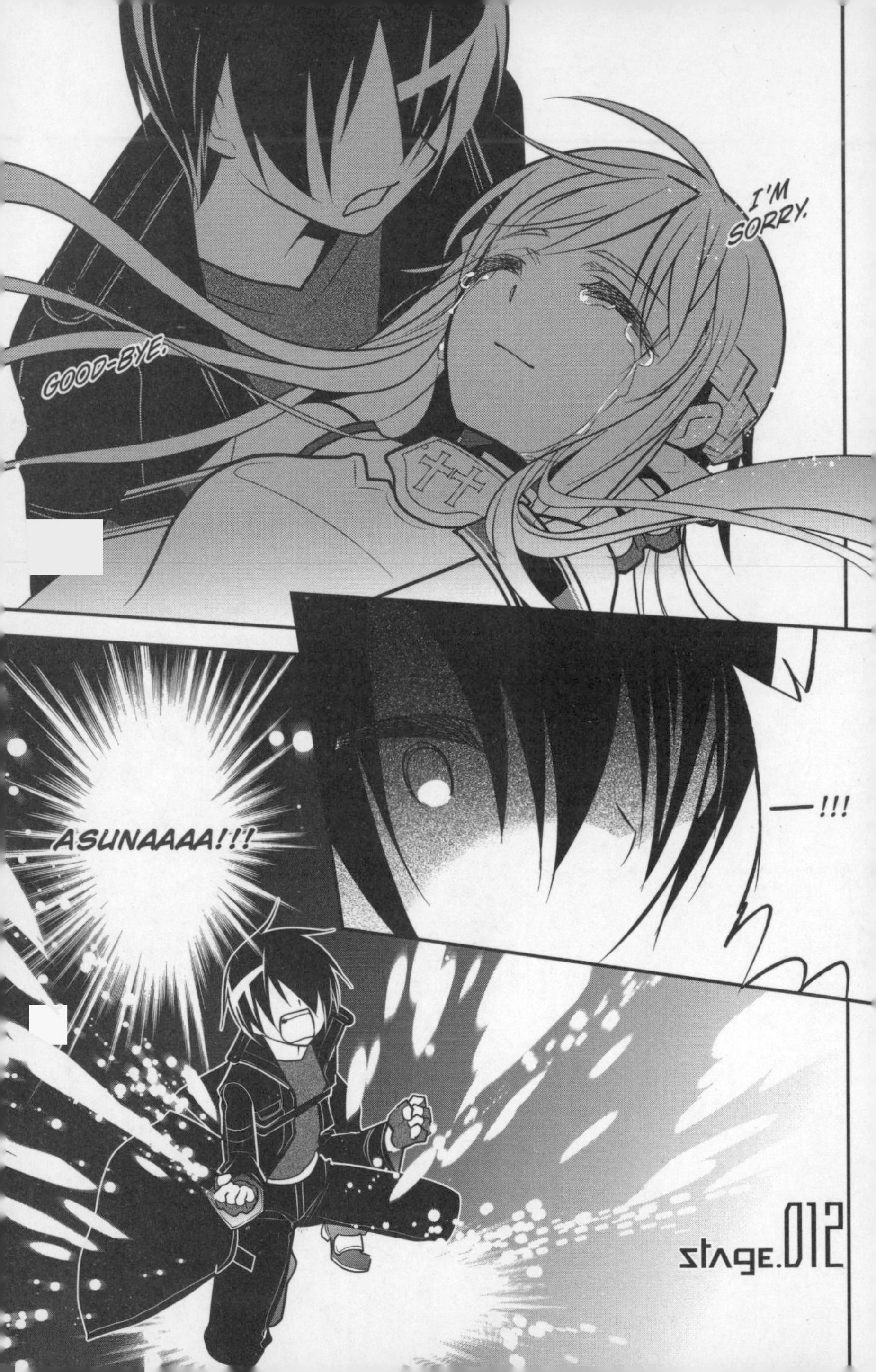
I'M SORRY.
GOOD-BYE.
—!!!
ASUNAAAA!!!
stage.012

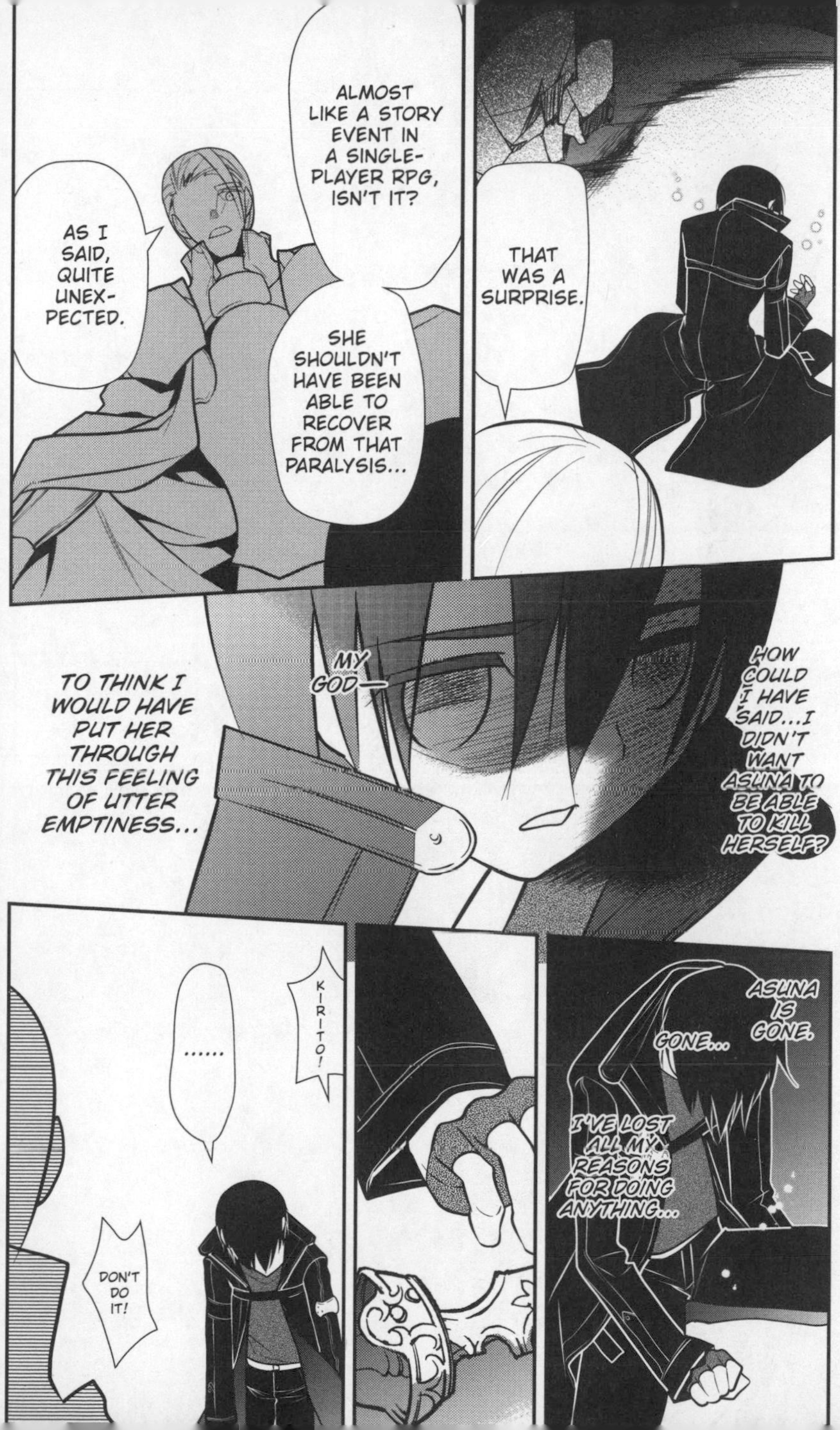
THAT WAS A SURPRISE.
ALMOST LIKE A STORY EVENT IN A SINGLE-PLAYER RPG, ISN'T IT?
AS I SAID, QUITE UNEXPECTED.
SHE SHOULDN'T HAVE BEEN ABLE TO RECOVER FROM THAT PARALYSIS...
HOW COULD I HAVE SAID...I DIDN'T WANT ASUNA TO BE ABLE TO KILL HERSELF?
MY GOD—
TO THINK I WOULD HAVE PUT HER THROUGH THIS FEELING OF UTTER EMPTINESS...
ASUNA IS GONE.
GONE...
I'VE LOST ALL MY REASONS FOR DOING ANYTHING...
KIRITO!
......
DON'T DO IT!

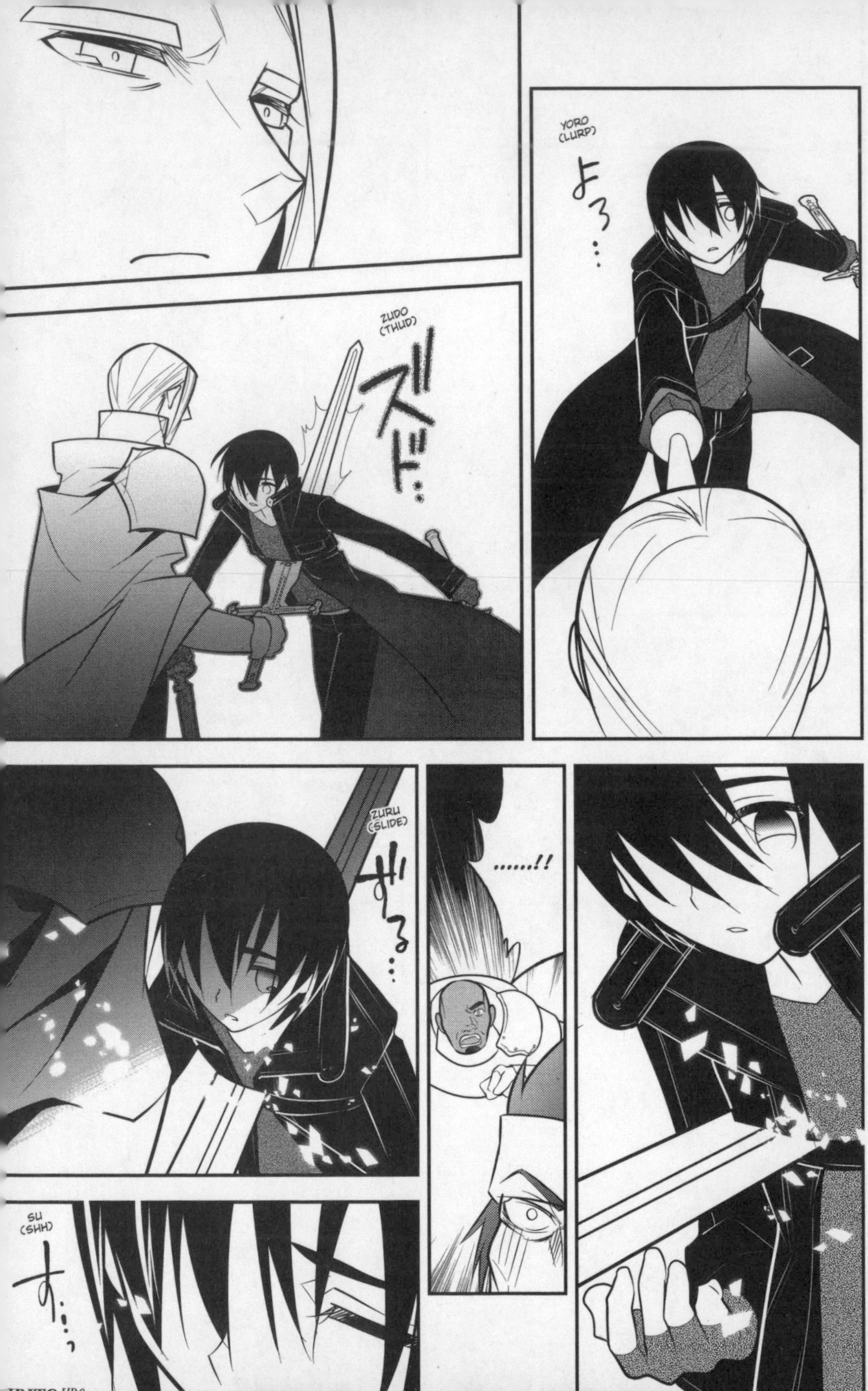
YORO (LURP)
よろ…
ZUDO (THUD)
ズド…
……!!
ZURU (SLIDE)
ずる…
SU (SHH)
す…

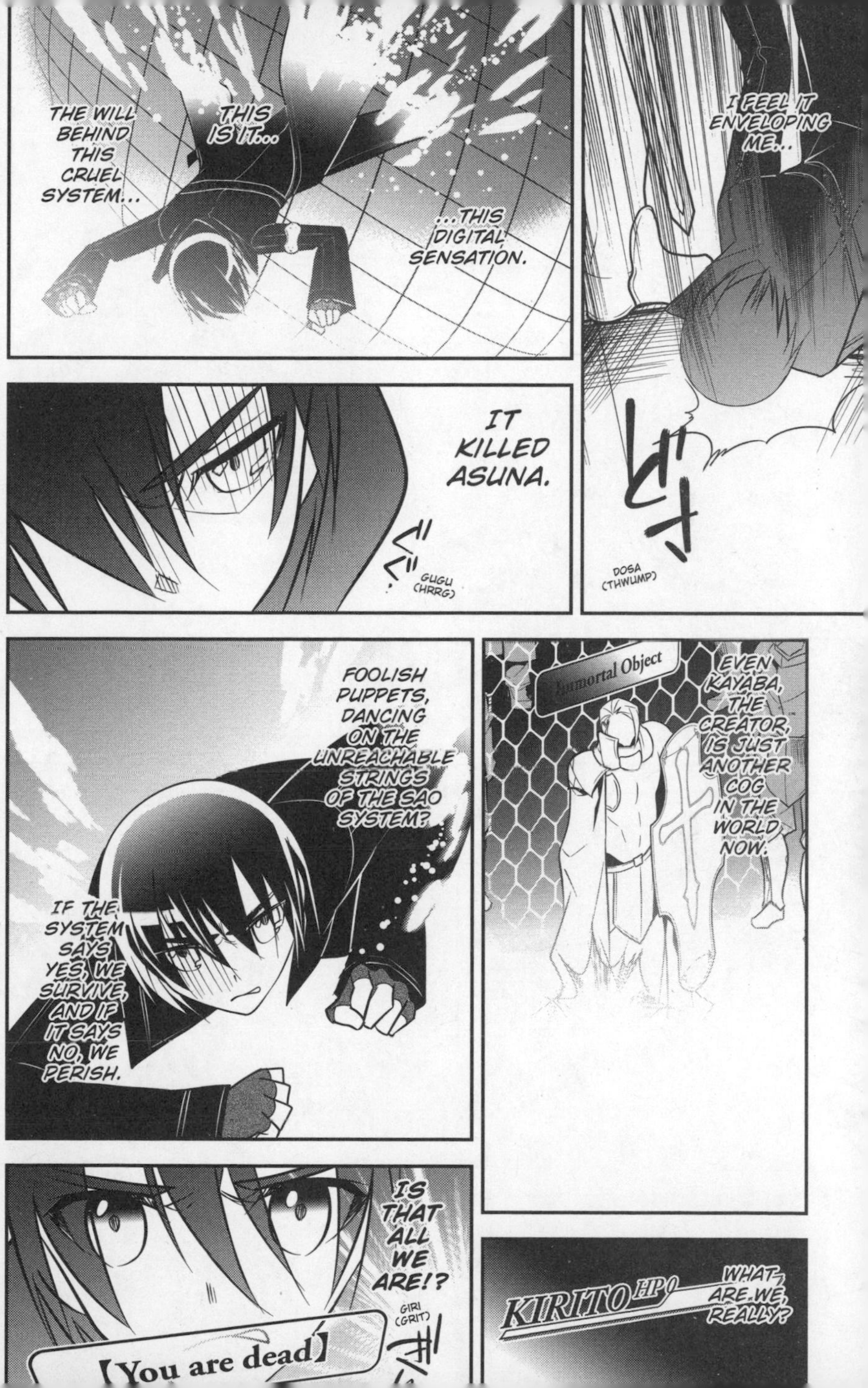
I FEEL IT ENVELOPING ME...
DOSA (THWUMP)
THIS IS IT...
THE WILL BEHIND THIS CRUEL SYSTEM...
...THIS DIGITAL SENSATION.
IT KILLED ASUNA.
GUGU (HRRG)
Immortal Object
EVEN KAYABA, THE CREATOR, IS JUST ANOTHER COG IN THE WORLD NOW.
WHAT ARE WE, REALLY?
KIRITO HP 0
FOOLISH PUPPETS, DANCING ON THE UNREACHABLE STRINGS OF THE SAO SYSTEM?
IF THE SYSTEM SAYS YES, WE SURVIVE, AND IF IT SAYS NO, WE PERISH.
IS THAT ALL WE ARE!?
GIRI (GRIT)
【You are dead】

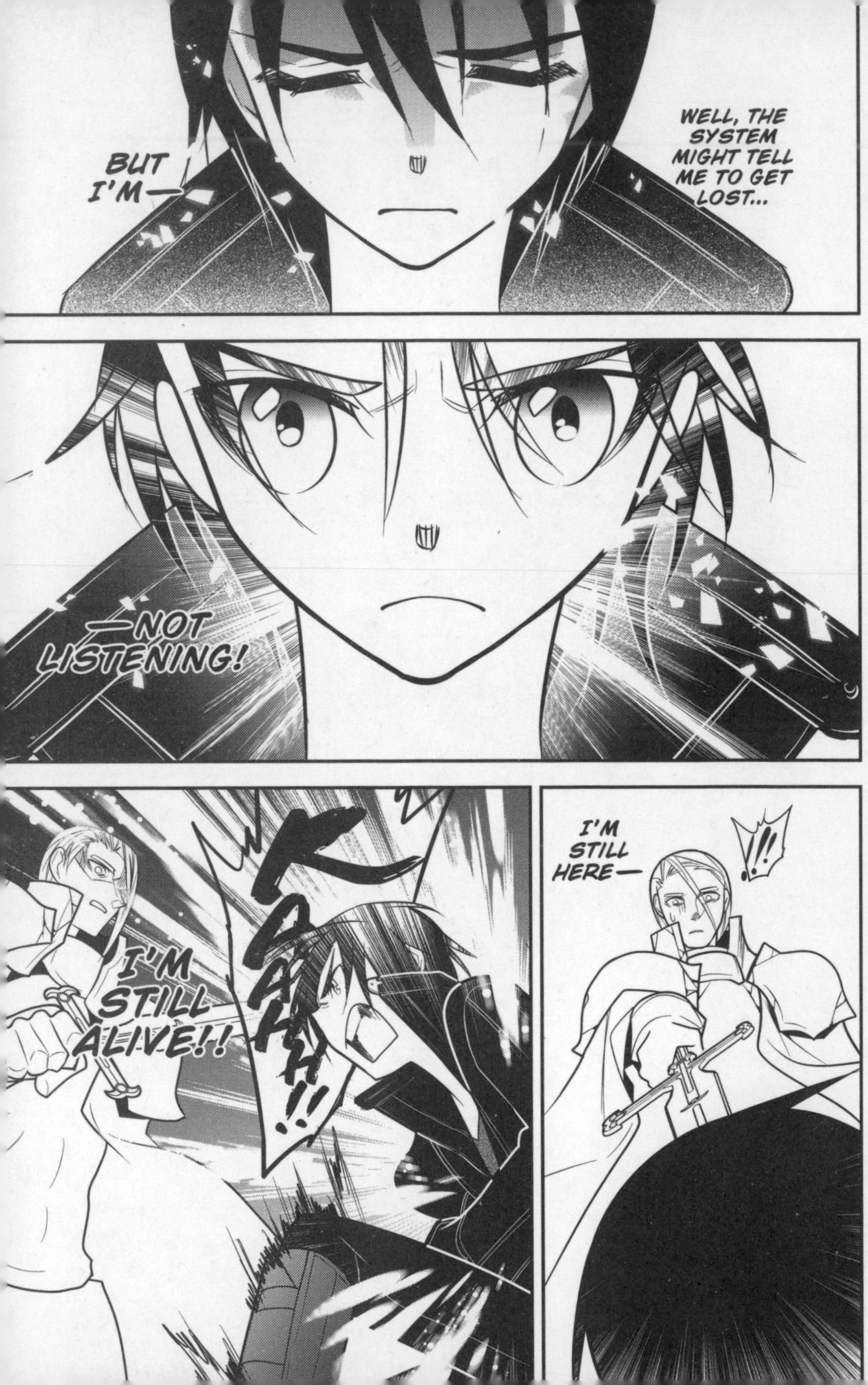
WELL, THE SYSTEM MIGHT TELL ME TO GET LOST...
BUT I'M—
—NOT LISTENING!
I'M STILL HERE—
!!
I'M STILL ALIVE!!

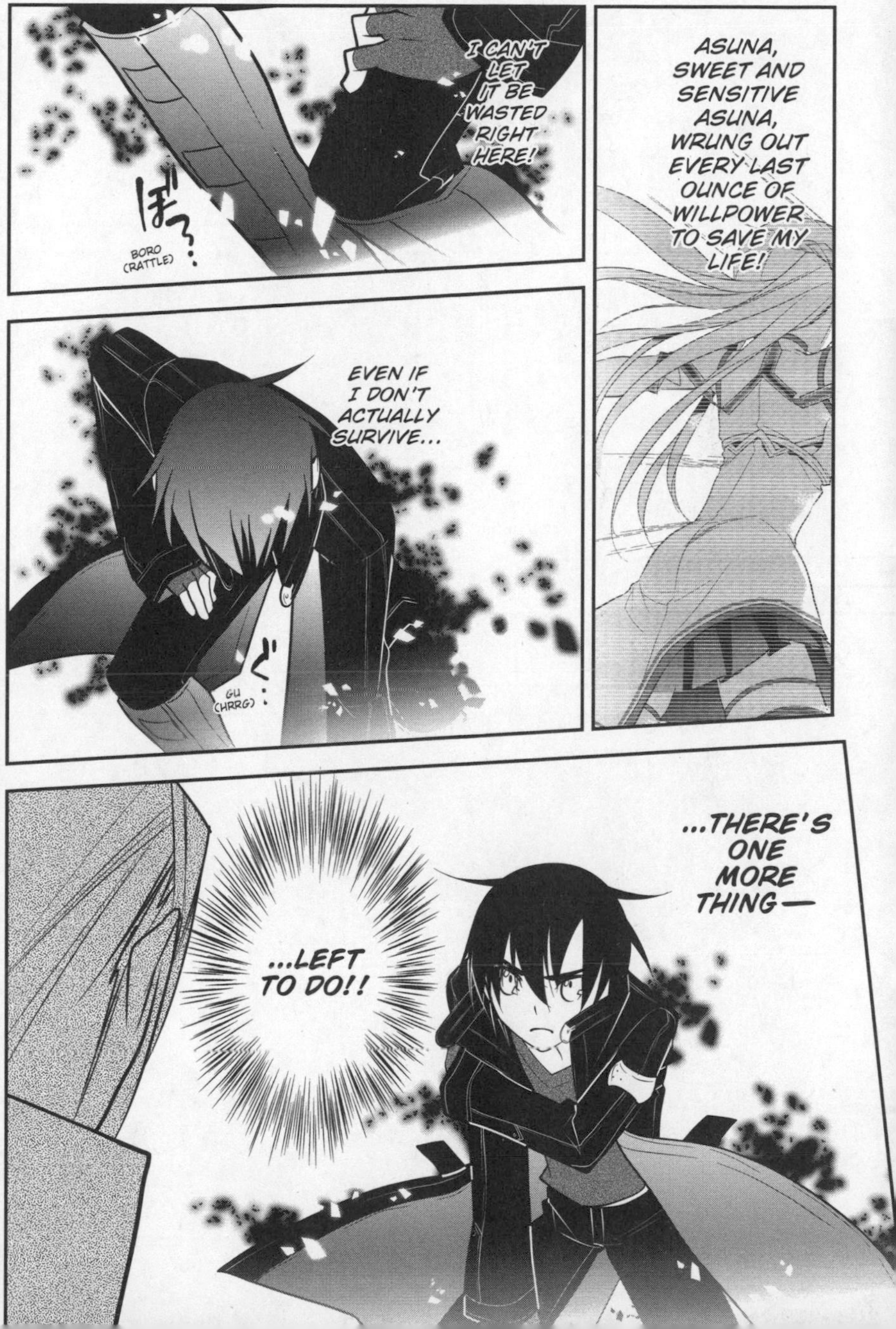
ASUNA, SWEET AND SENSITIVE ASUNA, WRUNG OUT EVERY LAST OUNCE OF WILLPOWER TO SAVE MY LIFE!
I CAN'T LET IT BE WASTED RIGHT HERE!
ぼろ…
BORO (RATTLE)
EVEN IF I DON'T ACTUALLY SURVIVE…
ぐ…
GU (HRRG)
…THERE'S ONE MORE THING—
…LEFT TO DO!!

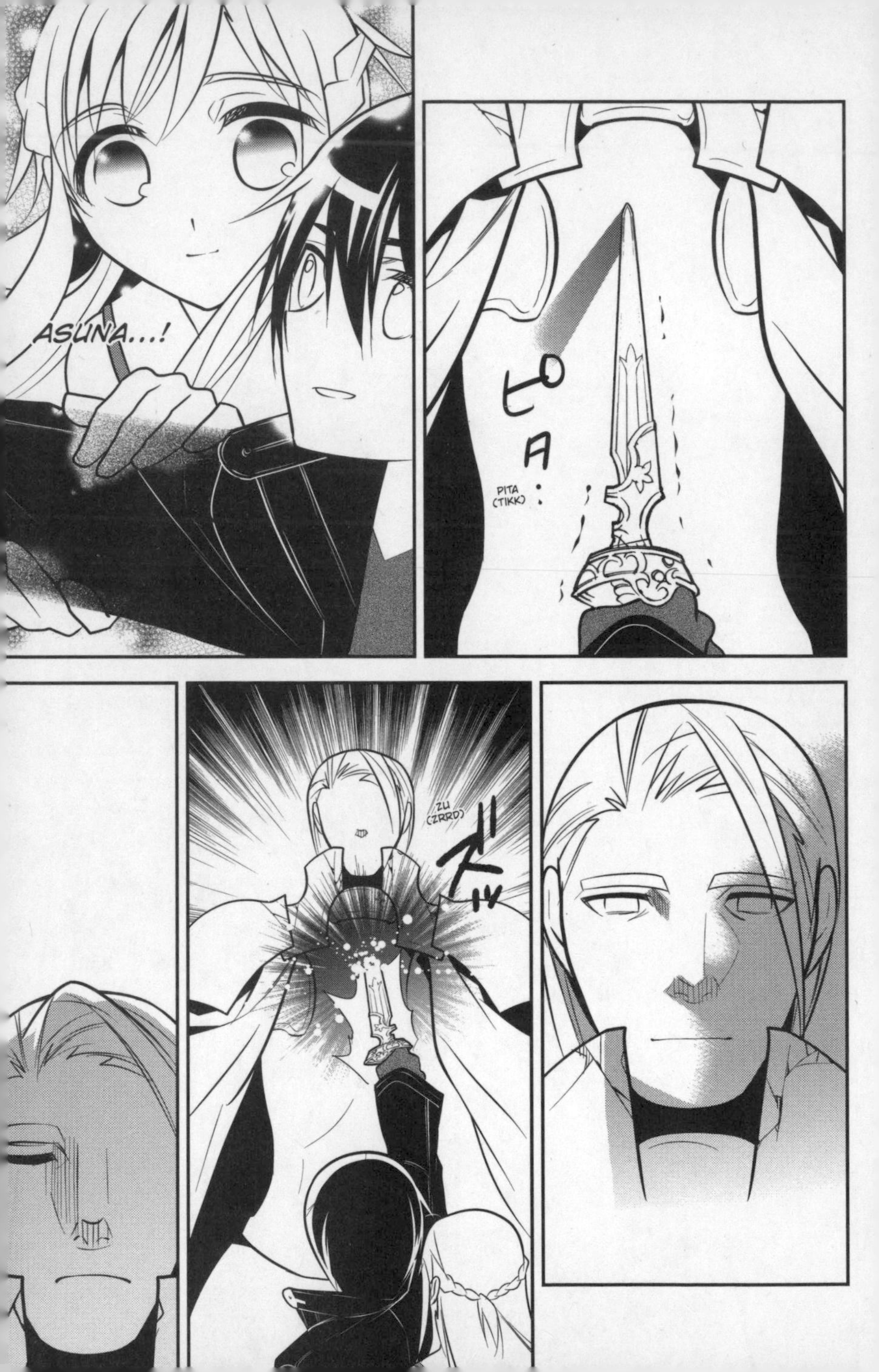

ピタ
PITA (TIKK)
ASUNA...!
ZU (ZRRD)
ズッ

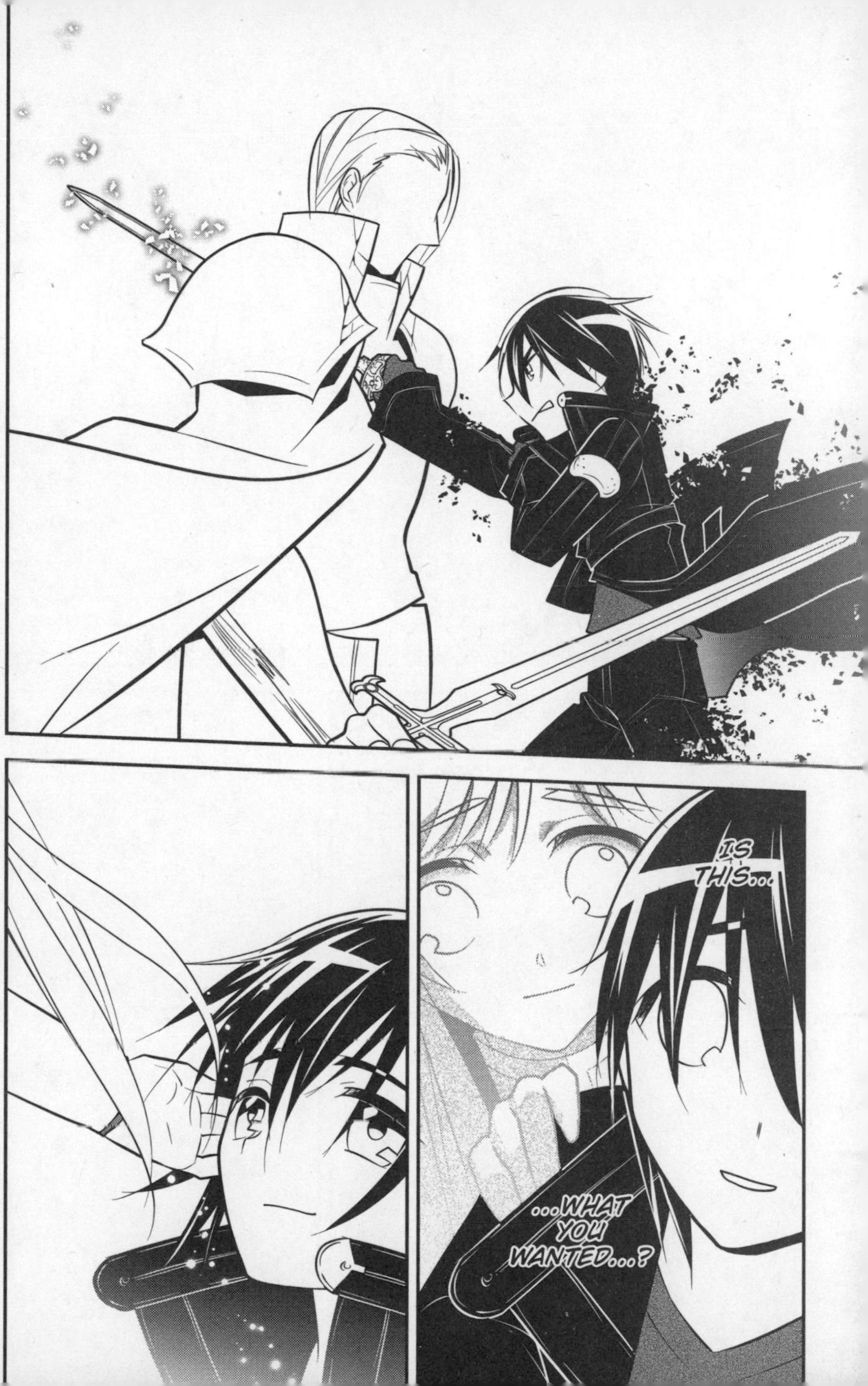
IS THIS...
...WHAT YOU WANTED...?

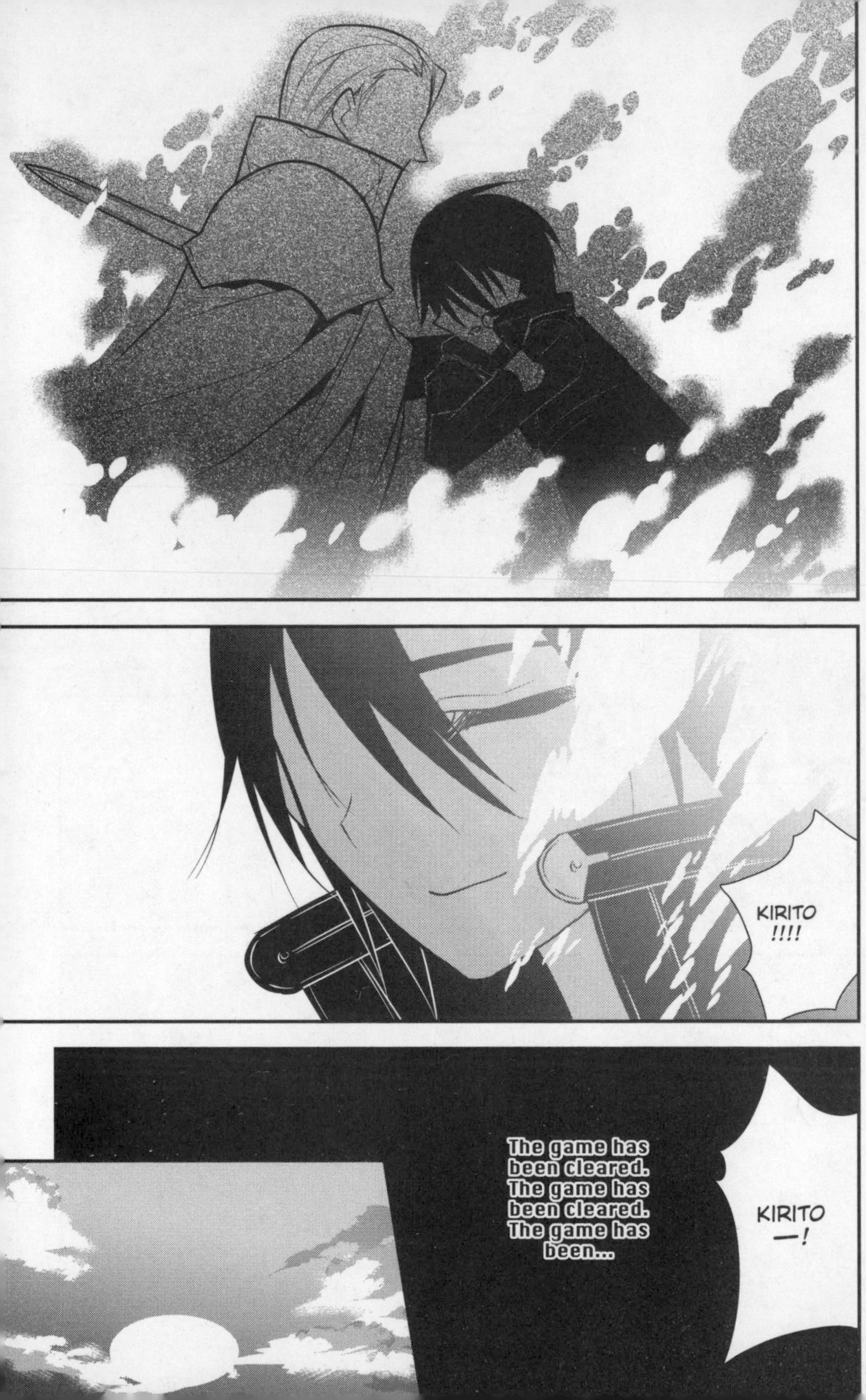
KIRITO !!!!
KIRITO —!
The game has been cleared. The game has been cleared. The game has been...

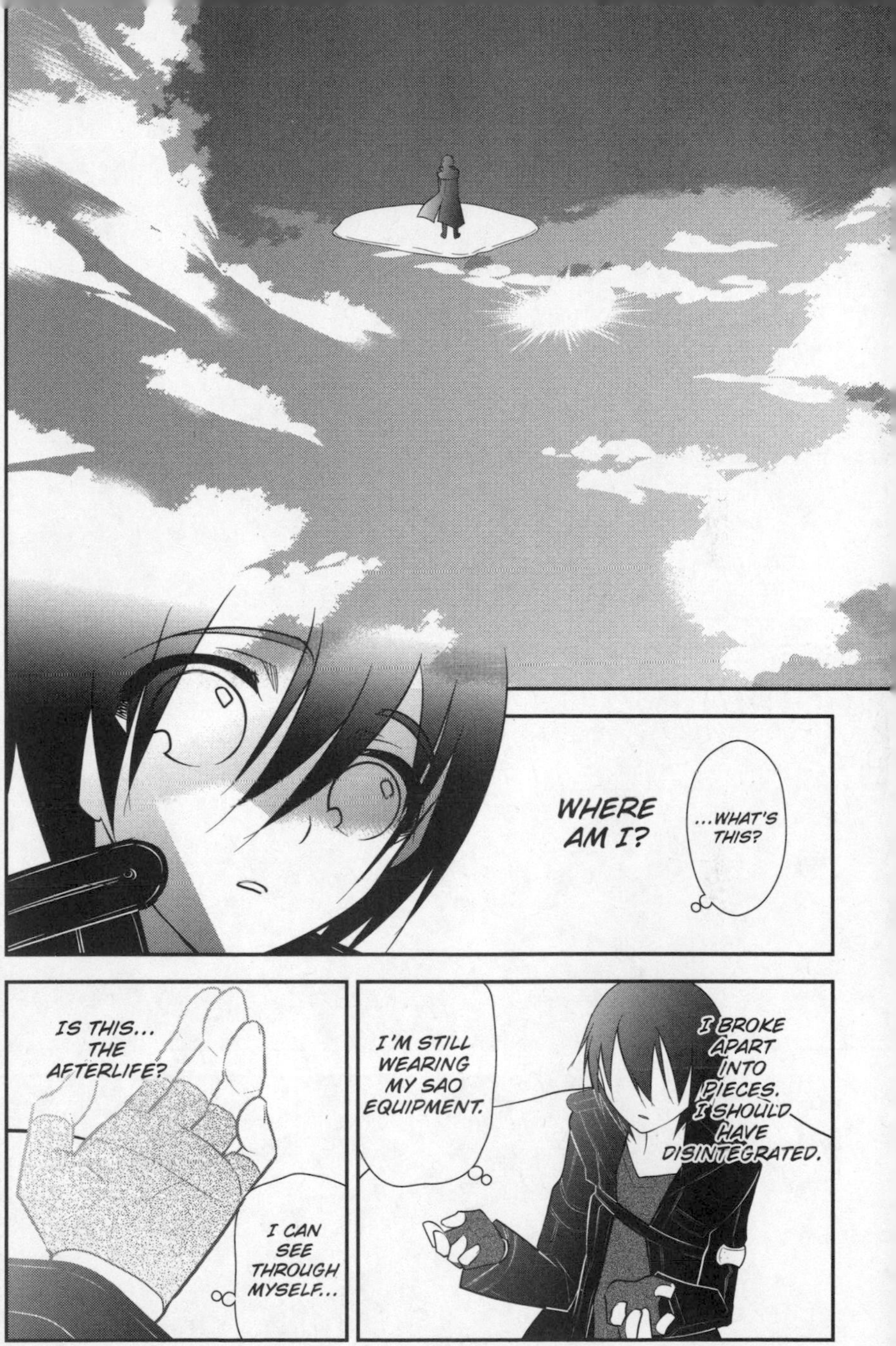
...WHAT'S THIS?
WHERE AM I?
I BROKE APART INTO PIECES. I SHOULD HAVE DISINTEGRATED.
I'M STILL WEARING MY SAO EQUIPMENT.
IS THIS... THE AFTERLIFE?
I CAN SEE THROUGH MYSELF...

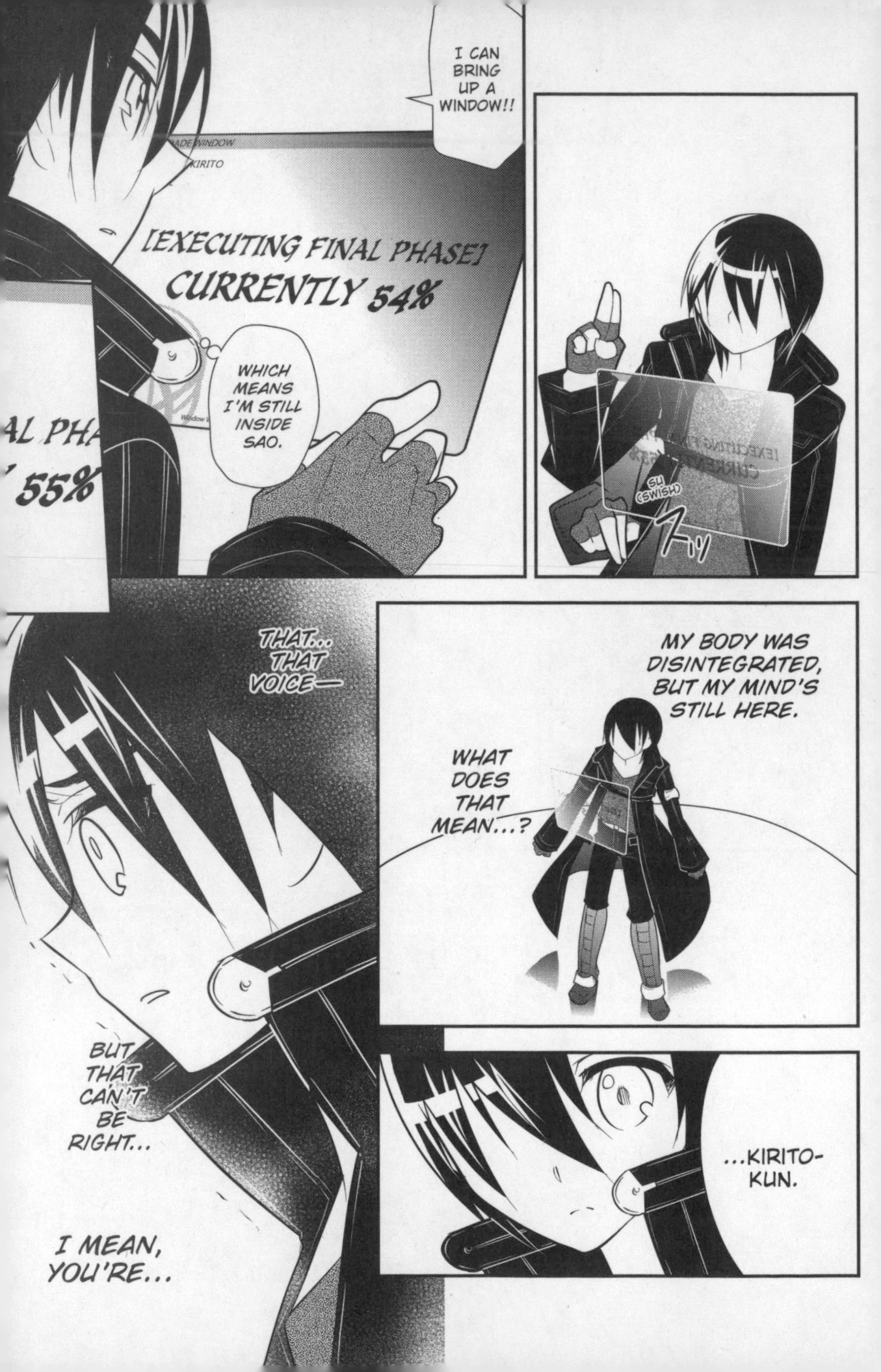
SU (SWISH)
I CAN BRING UP A WINDOW!!
KIRITO
[EXECUTING FINAL PHASE] CURRENTLY 54%
WHICH MEANS I'M STILL INSIDE SAO.
AL PHA
55%
MY BODY WAS DISINTEGRATED, BUT MY MIND'S STILL HERE.
WHAT DOES THAT MEAN...?
...KIRITO-KUN.
THAT... THAT VOICE—
BUT THAT CAN'T BE RIGHT...
I MEAN, YOU'RE...

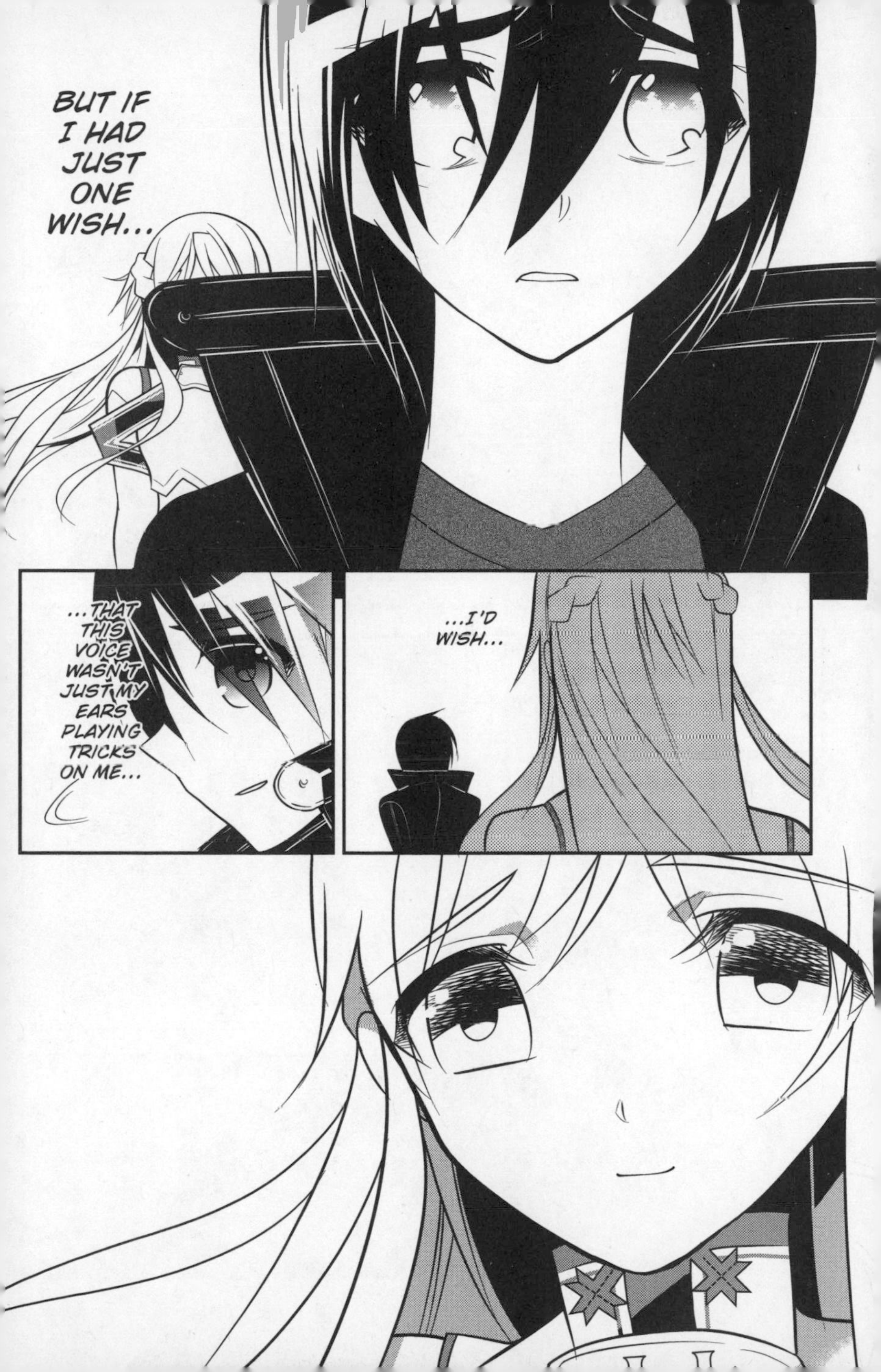
BUT IF I HAD JUST ONE WISH...
...I'D WISH...
...THAT THIS VOICE WASN'T JUST MY EARS PLAYING TRICKS ON ME...

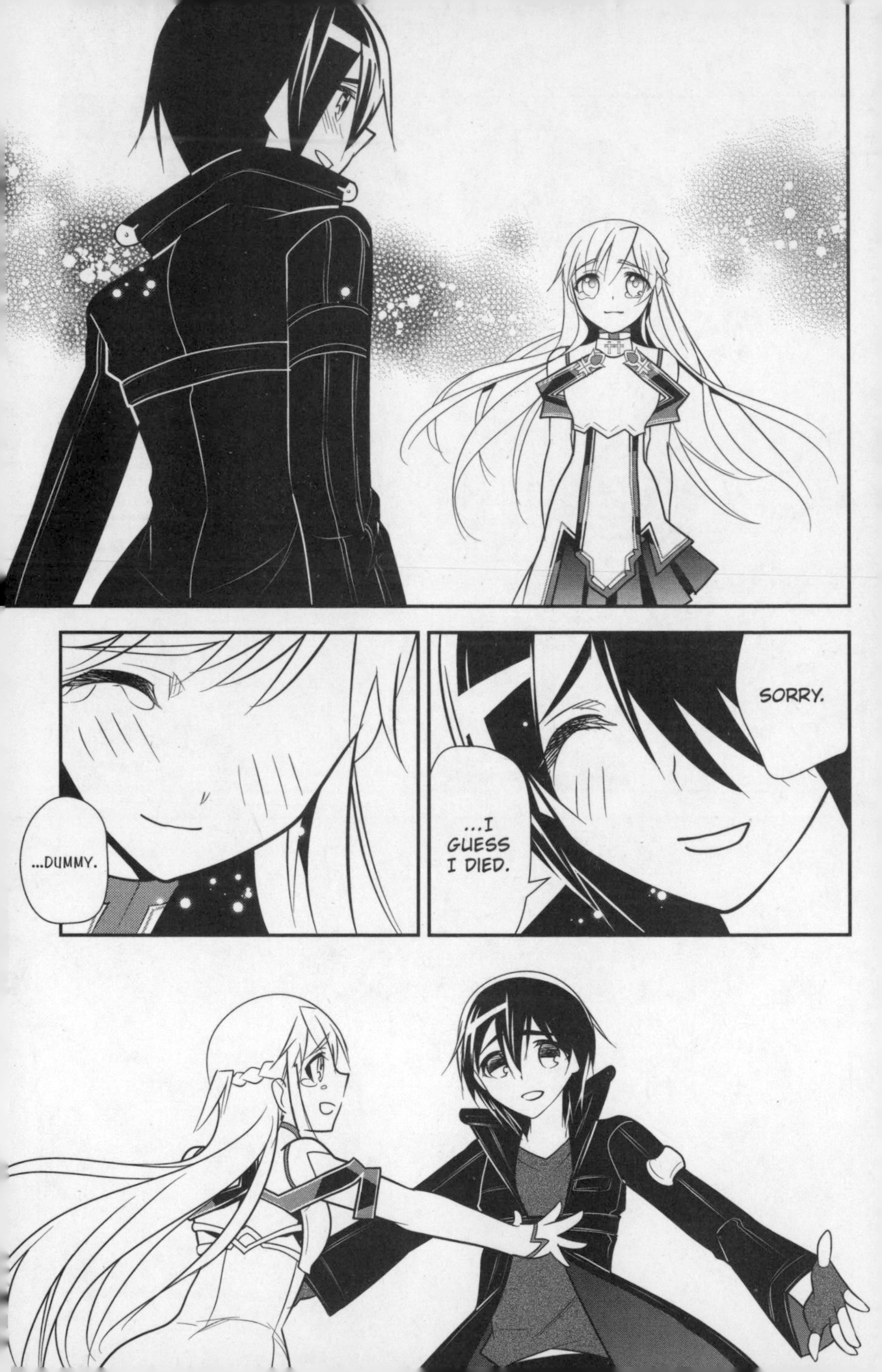
SORRY.
...I GUESS I DIED.
...DUMMY.

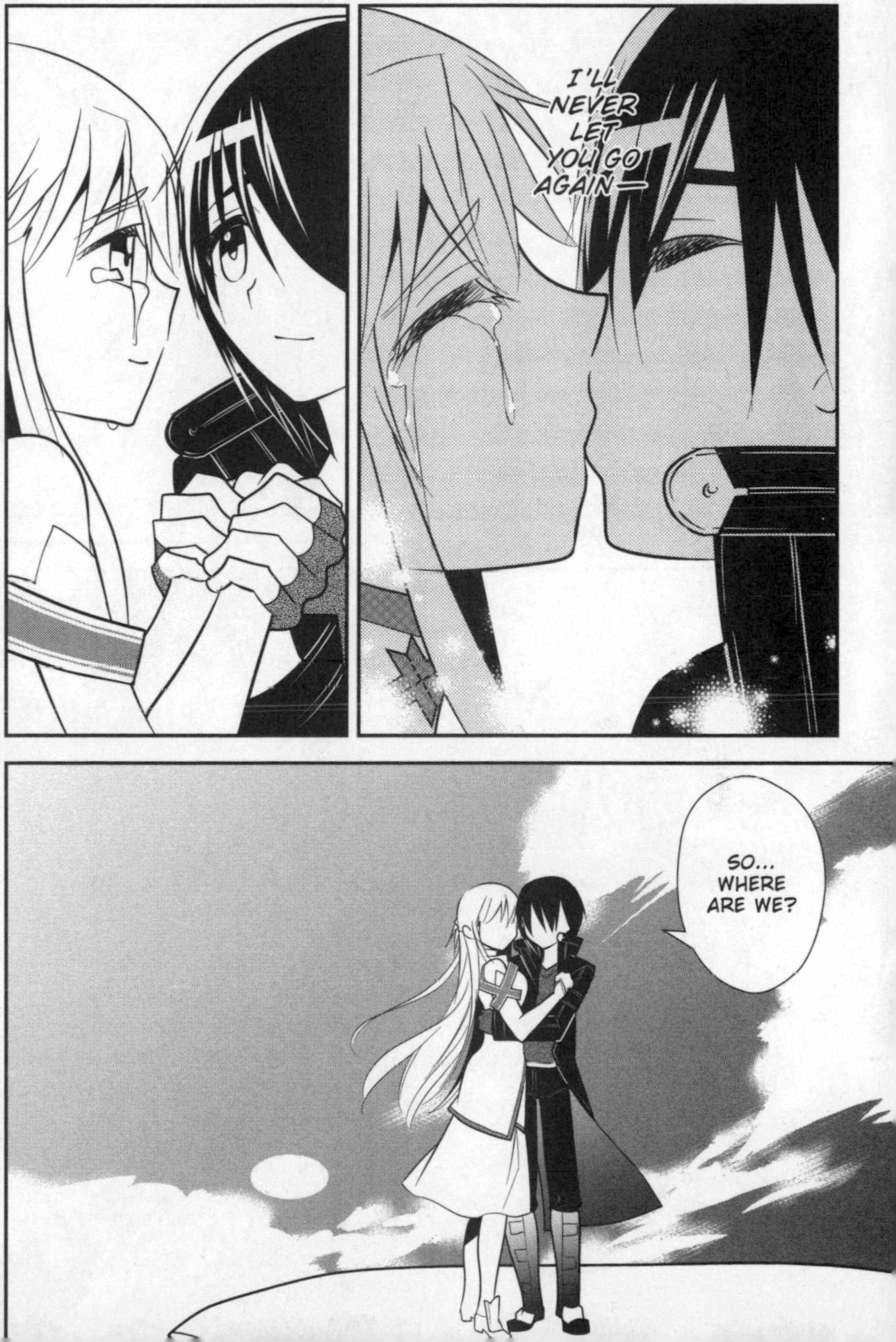
I'LL NEVER LET YOU GO AGAIN—
SO... WHERE ARE WE?

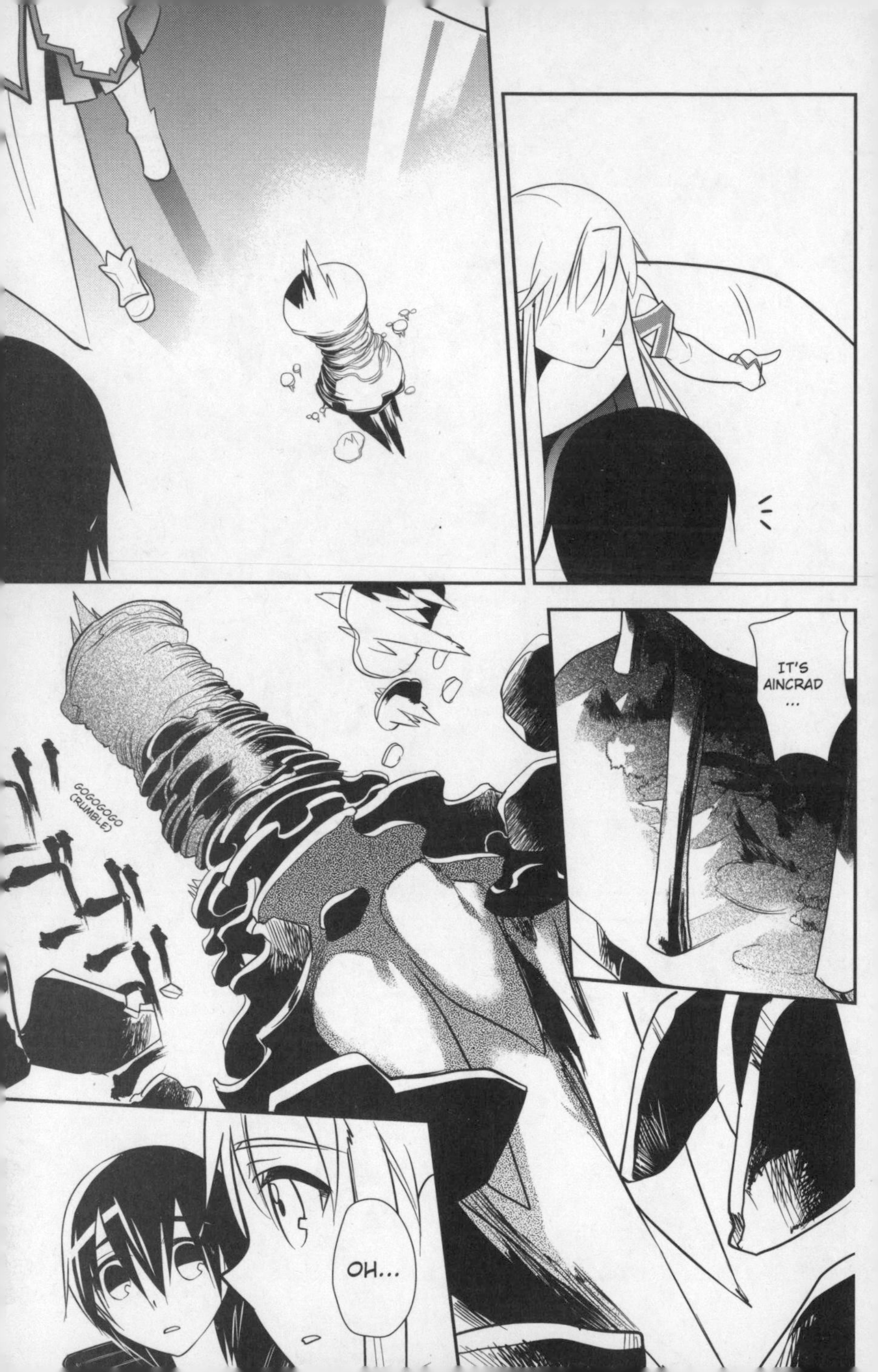
IT'S AINCRAD ...
GOGOGOGO (RUMBLE)
OH...

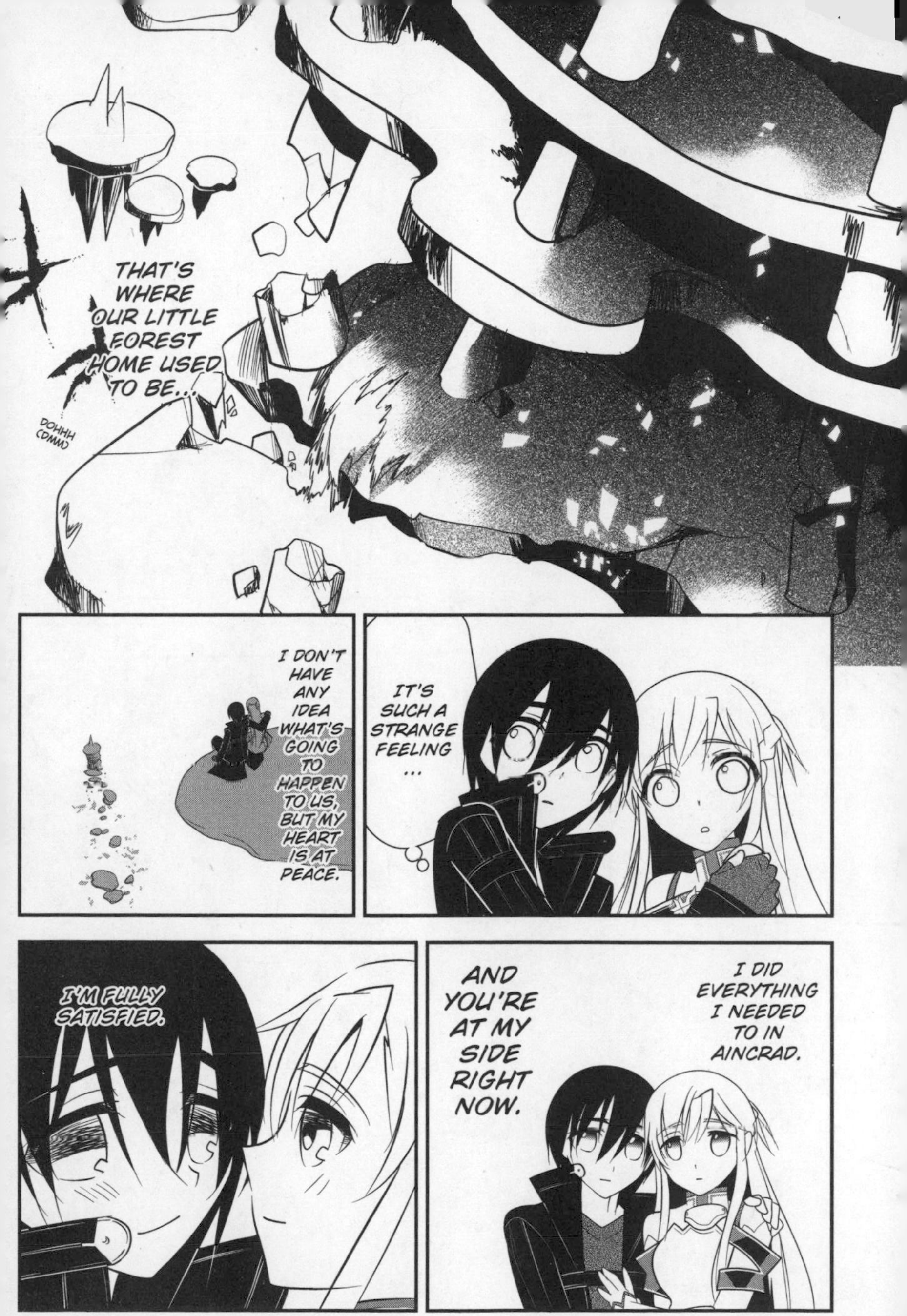
THAT'S WHERE OUR LITTLE FOREST HOME USED TO BE...
DOHHH (DMM)
IT'S SUCH A STRANGE FEELING ...
I DON'T HAVE ANY IDEA WHAT'S GOING TO HAPPEN TO US, BUT MY HEART IS AT PEACE.
I DID EVERYTHING I NEEDED TO IN AINCRAD.
AND YOU'RE AT MY SIDE RIGHT NOW.
I'M FULLY SATISFIED.

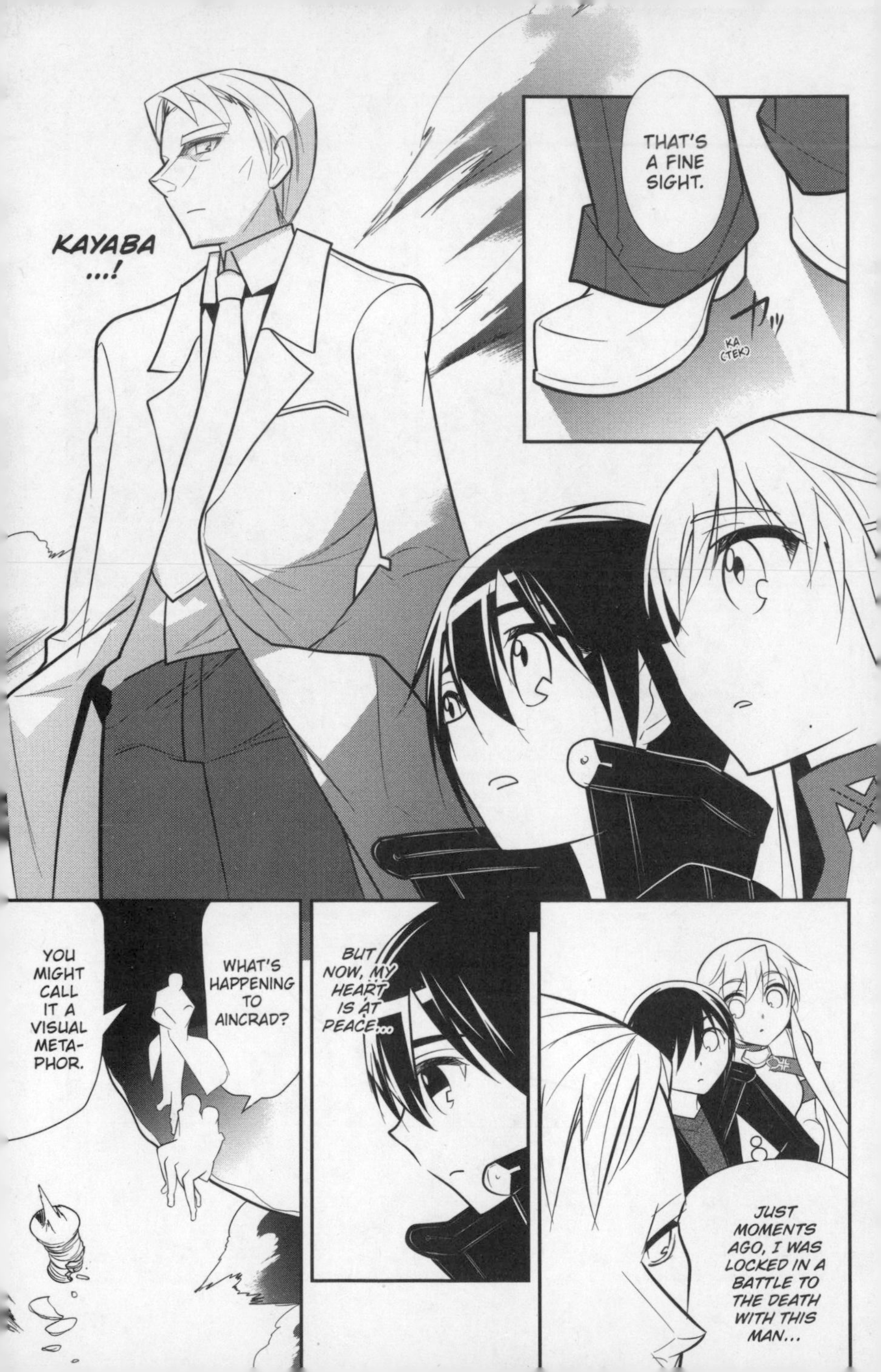
THAT'S A FINE SIGHT.
ガッ
KA (TEK)
KAYABA ...!
JUST MOMENTS AGO, I WAS LOCKED IN A BATTLE TO THE DEATH WITH THIS MAN...
BUT NOW, MY HEART IS AT PEACE...
WHAT'S HAPPENING TO AINCRAD?
YOU MIGHT CALL IT A VISUAL METAPHOR.

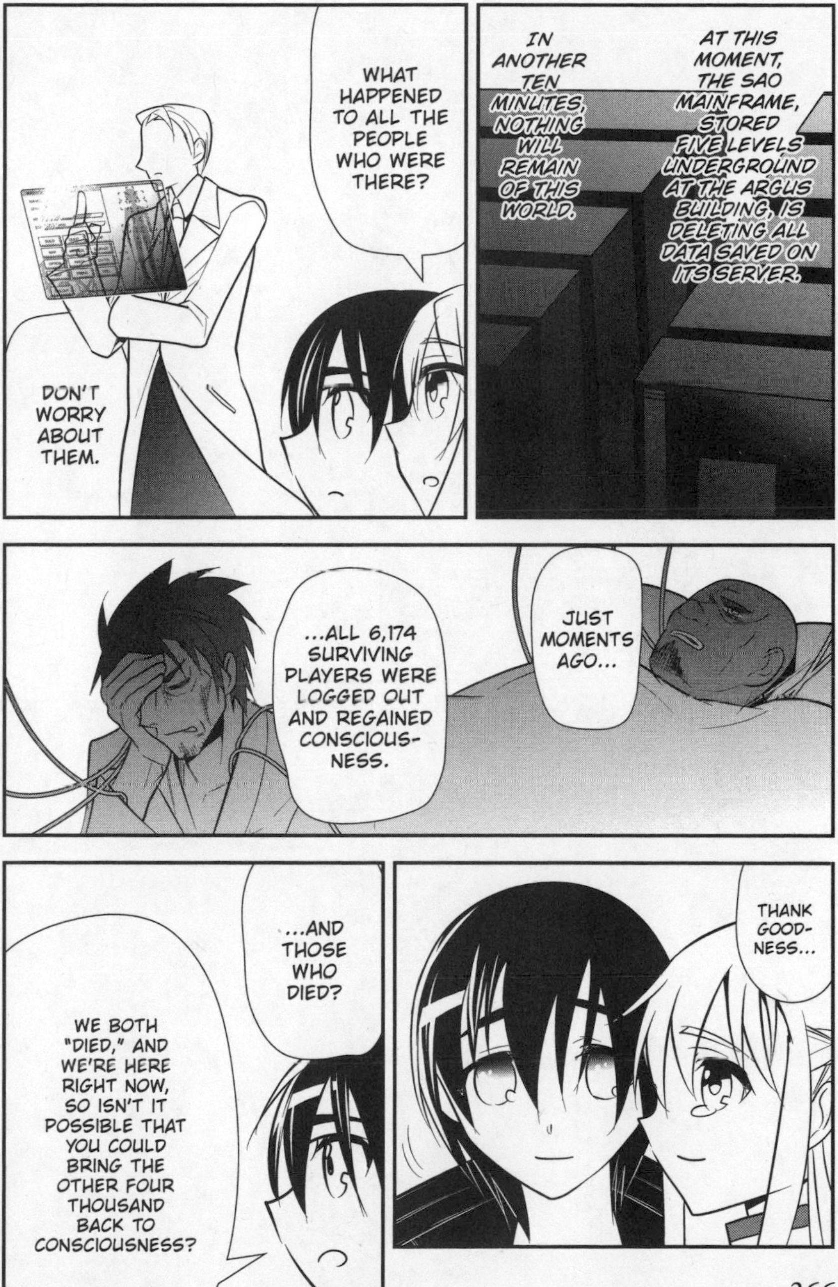
AT THIS MOMENT, THE SAO MAINFRAME, STORED FIVE LEVELS UNDERGROUND AT THE ARGUS BUILDING, IS DELETING ALL DATA SAVED ON ITS SERVER.
IN ANOTHER TEN MINUTES, NOTHING WILL REMAIN OF THIS WORLD.
WHAT HAPPENED TO ALL THE PEOPLE WHO WERE THERE?
DON'T WORRY ABOUT THEM.
JUST MOMENTS AGO...
...ALL 6,174 SURVIVING PLAYERS WERE LOGGED OUT AND REGAINED CONSCIOUS-NESS.
THANK GOOD-NESS...
...AND THOSE WHO DIED?
WE BOTH "DIED," AND WE'RE HERE RIGHT NOW, SO ISN'T IT POSSIBLE THAT YOU COULD BRING THE OTHER FOUR THOUSAND BACK TO CONSCIOUSNESS?

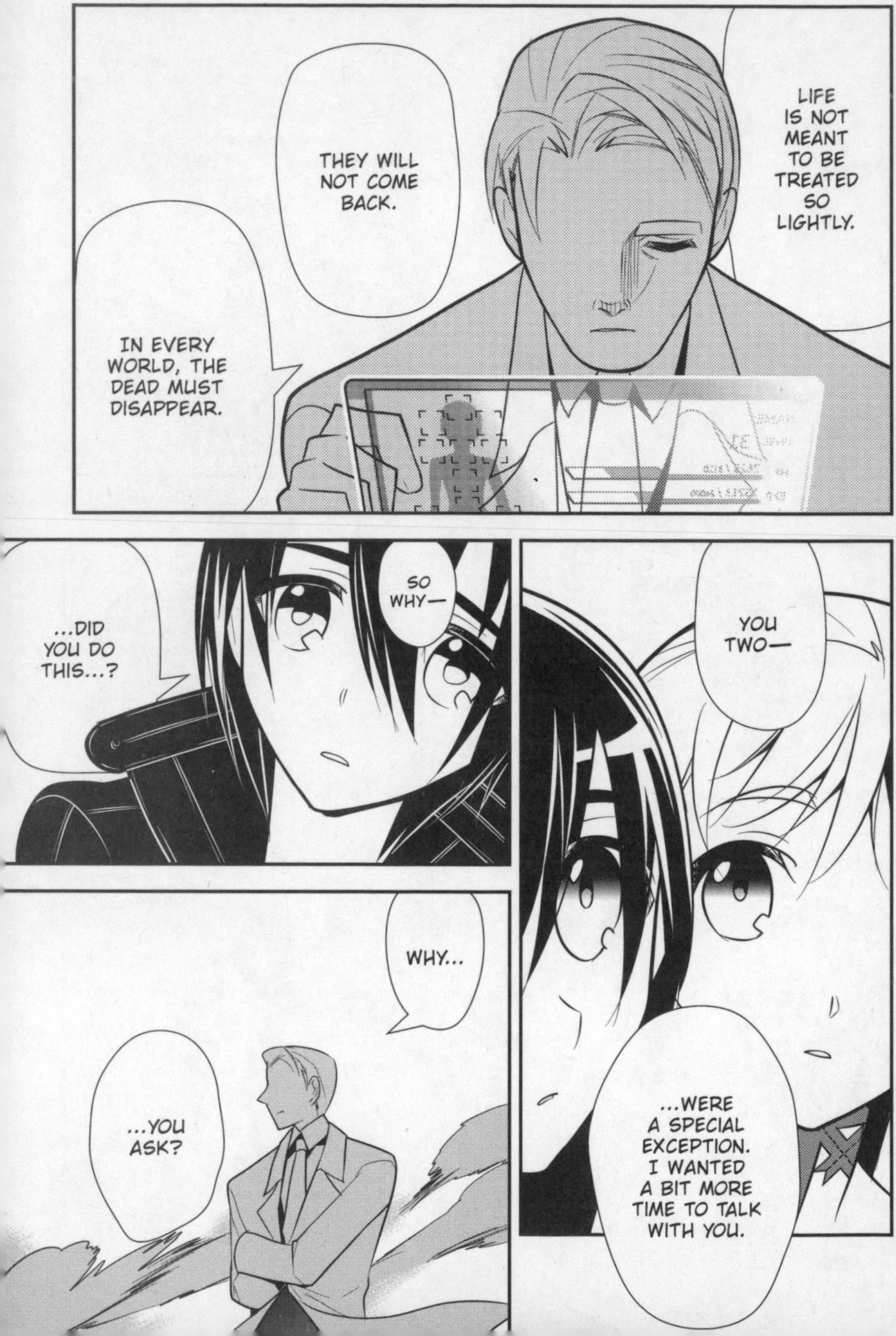
LIFE IS NOT MEANT TO BE TREATED SO LIGHTLY.
THEY WILL NOT COME BACK.
IN EVERY WORLD, THE DEAD MUST DISAPPEAR.
YOU TWO—
...WERE A SPECIAL EXCEPTION. I WANTED A BIT MORE TIME TO TALK WITH YOU.
SO WHY—
...DID YOU DO THIS...?
WHY...
...YOU ASK?

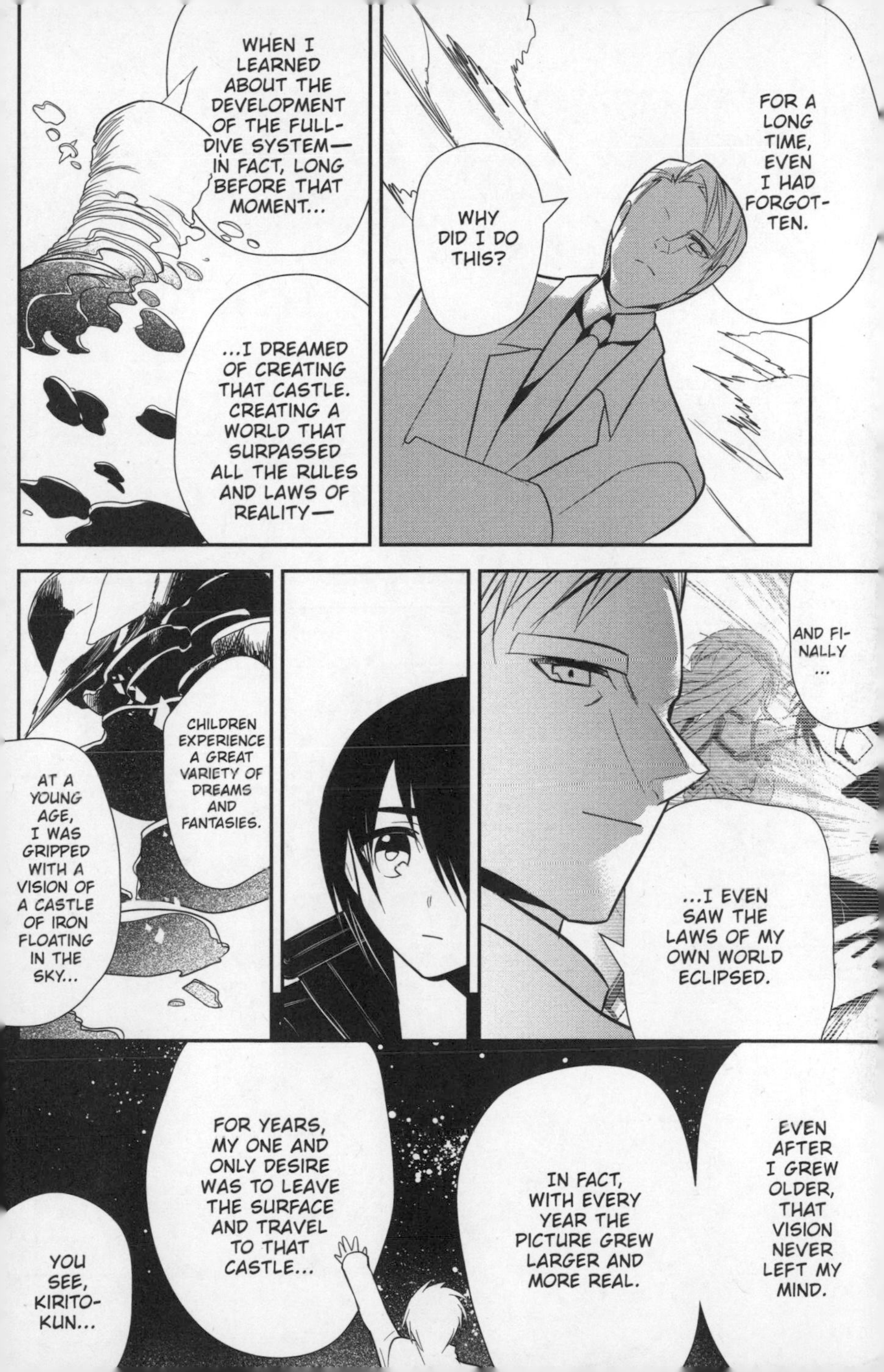
FOR A LONG TIME, EVEN I HAD FORGOTTEN.
WHY DID I DO THIS?
WHEN I LEARNED ABOUT THE DEVELOPMENT OF THE FULL-DIVE SYSTEM—IN FACT, LONG BEFORE THAT MOMENT...
...I DREAMED OF CREATING THAT CASTLE. CREATING A WORLD THAT SURPASSED ALL THE RULES AND LAWS OF REALITY—
AND FINALLY...
...I EVEN SAW THE LAWS OF MY OWN WORLD ECLIPSED.
CHILDREN EXPERIENCE A GREAT VARIETY OF DREAMS AND FANTASIES.
AT A YOUNG AGE, I WAS GRIPPED WITH A VISION OF A CASTLE OF IRON FLOATING IN THE SKY...
EVEN AFTER I GREW OLDER, THAT VISION NEVER LEFT MY MIND.
IN FACT, WITH EVERY YEAR THE PICTURE GREW LARGER AND MORE REAL.
FOR YEARS, MY ONE AND ONLY DESIRE WAS TO LEAVE THE SURFACE AND TRAVEL TO THAT CASTLE...
YOU SEE, KIRITO-KUN...

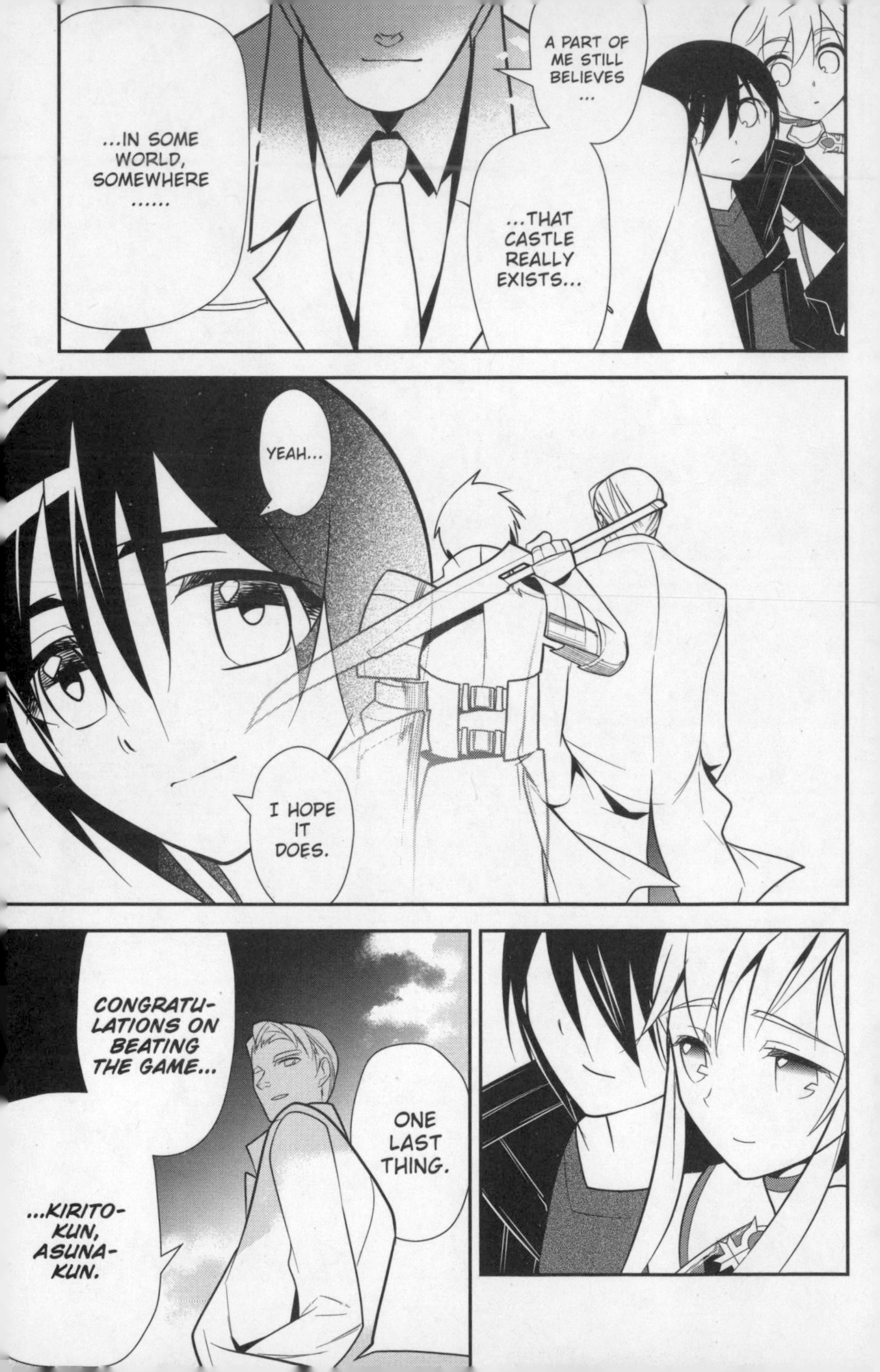
A PART OF ME STILL BELIEVES ...
...THAT CASTLE REALLY EXISTS...
...IN SOME WORLD, SOMEWHERE ......
YEAH...
I HOPE IT DOES.
ONE LAST THING.
CONGRATU-LATIONS ON BEATING THE GAME...
...KIRITO-KUN, ASUNA-KUN.

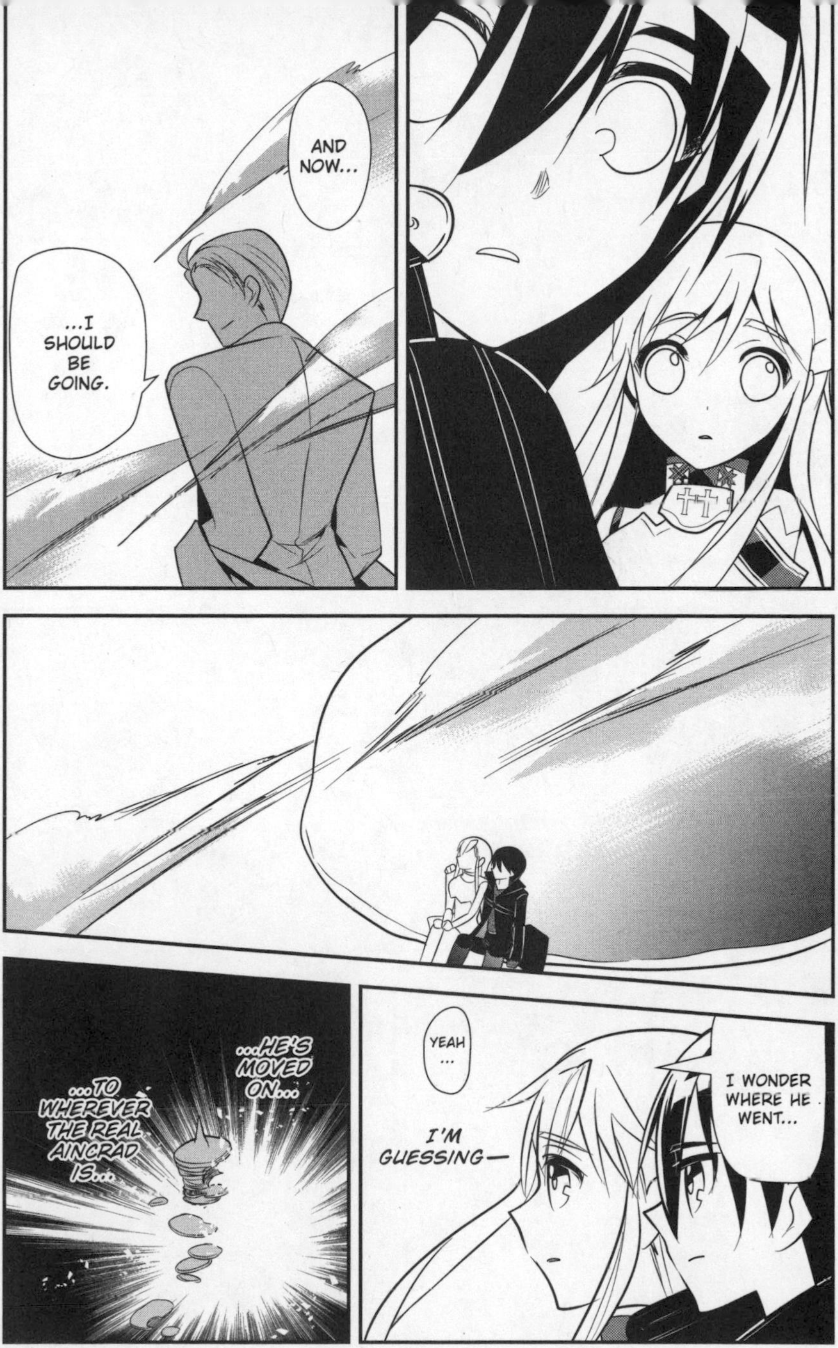
AND NOW...
...I SHOULD BE GOING.
I WONDER WHERE HE WENT...
YEAH...
I'M GUESSING—
...HE'S MOVED ON...
...TO WHEREVER THE REAL AINCRAD IS...

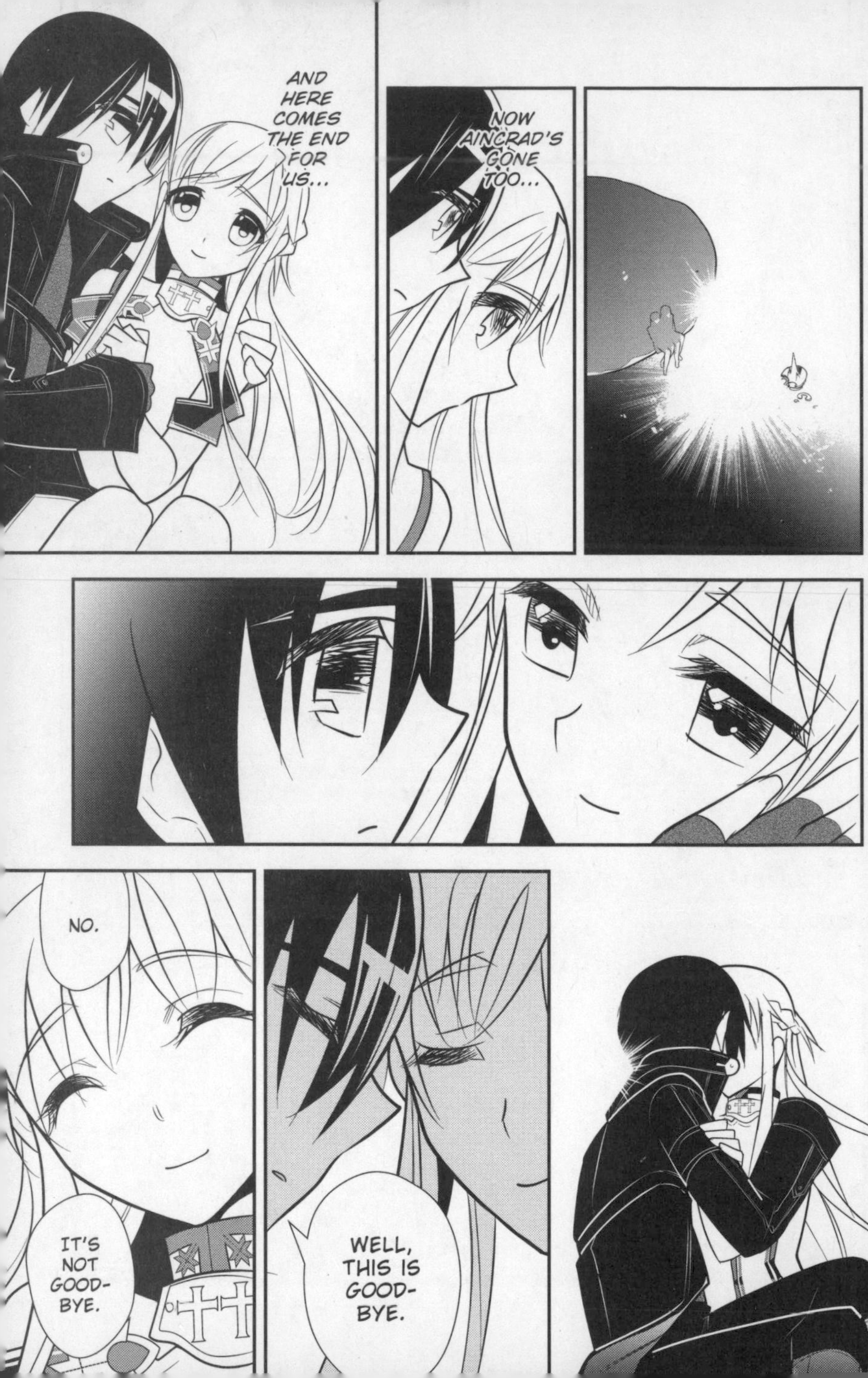
NOW AINCRAD'S GONE TOO...
AND HERE COMES THE END FOR US...
WELL, THIS IS GOOD-BYE.
NO.
IT'S NOT GOOD-BYE.

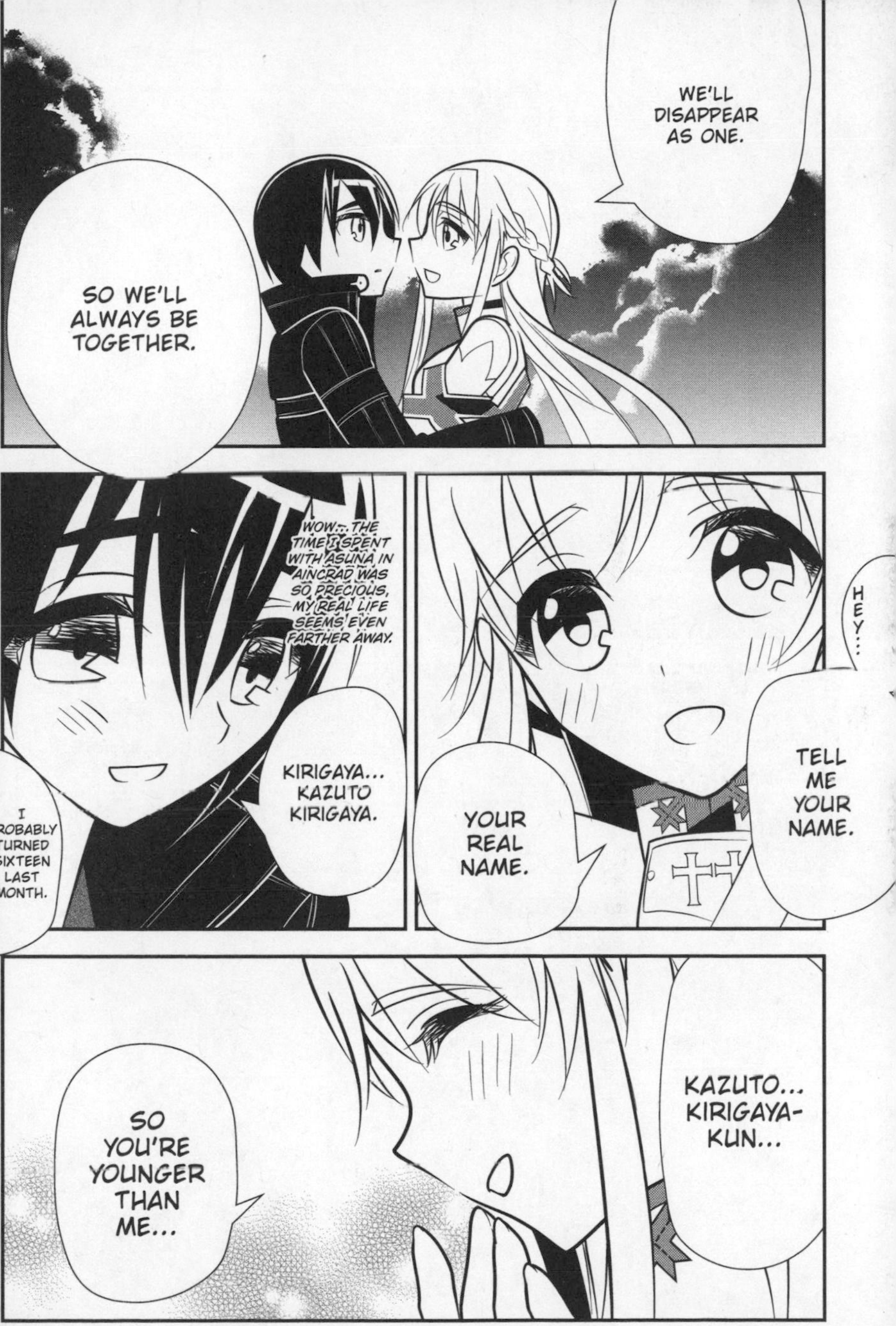
WE'LL DISAPPEAR AS ONE.
SO WE'LL ALWAYS BE TOGETHER.
HEY...
TELL ME YOUR NAME.
YOUR REAL NAME.
WOW... THE TIME I SPENT WITH ASUNA IN AINCRAD WAS SO PRECIOUS, MY REAL LIFE SEEMS EVEN FARTHER AWAY.
KIRIGAYA... KAZUTO KIRIGAYA.
I PROBABLY TURNED SIXTEEN LAST MONTH.
KAZUTO... KIRIGAYA-KUN...
SO YOU'RE YOUNGER THAN ME...

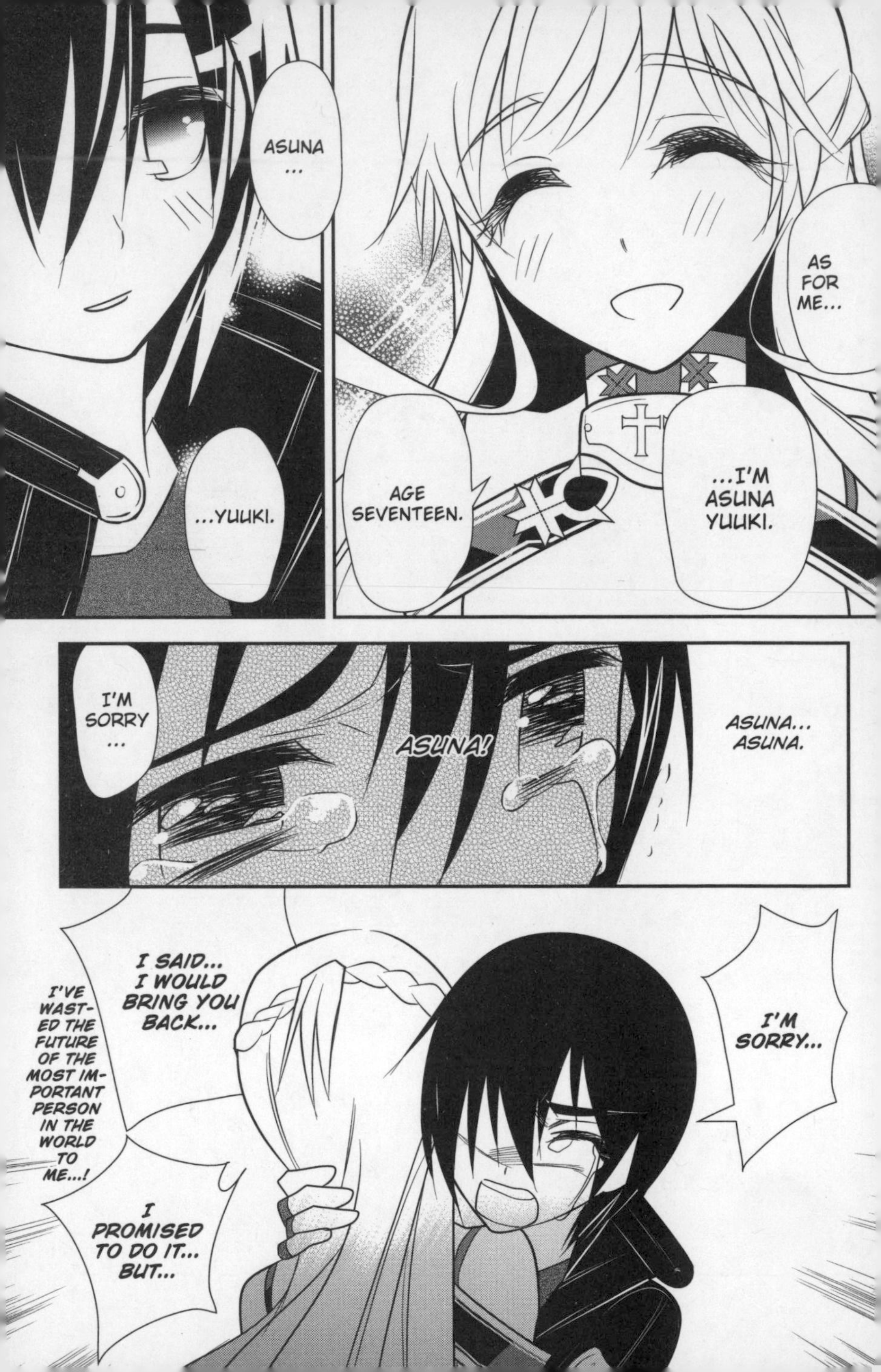

AS FOR ME...
...I'M ASUNA YUUKI.
AGE SEVENTEEN.
ASUNA ...
...YUUKI.
ASUNA... ASUNA.
ASUNA!
I'M SORRY ...
I'M SORRY...
I SAID... I WOULD BRING YOU BACK...
I PROMISED TO DO IT... BUT...
I'VE WASTED THE FUTURE OF THE MOST IMPORTANT PERSON IN THE WORLD TO ME...!

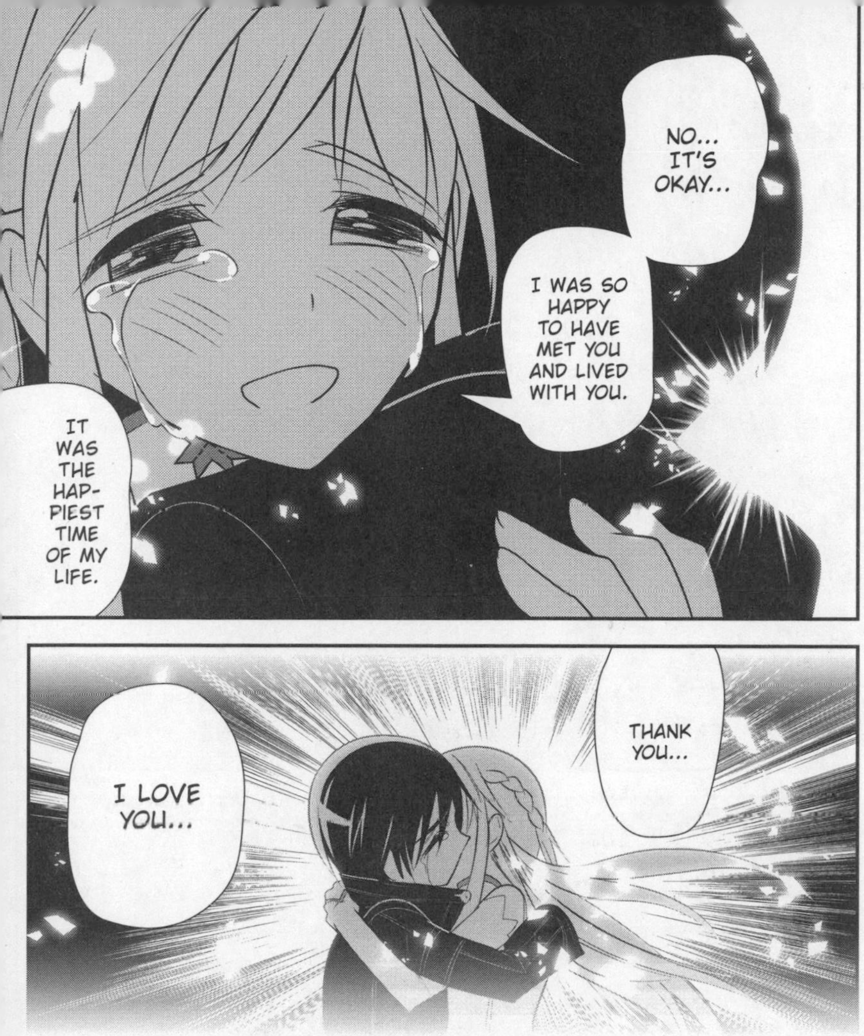
NO... IT'S OKAY...
I WAS SO HAPPY TO HAVE MET YOU AND LIVED WITH YOU.
IT WAS THE HAP-PIEST TIME OF MY LIFE.
THANK YOU...
I LOVE YOU...
—I LOVE YOU...
I LOVE YOU SO MUCH...

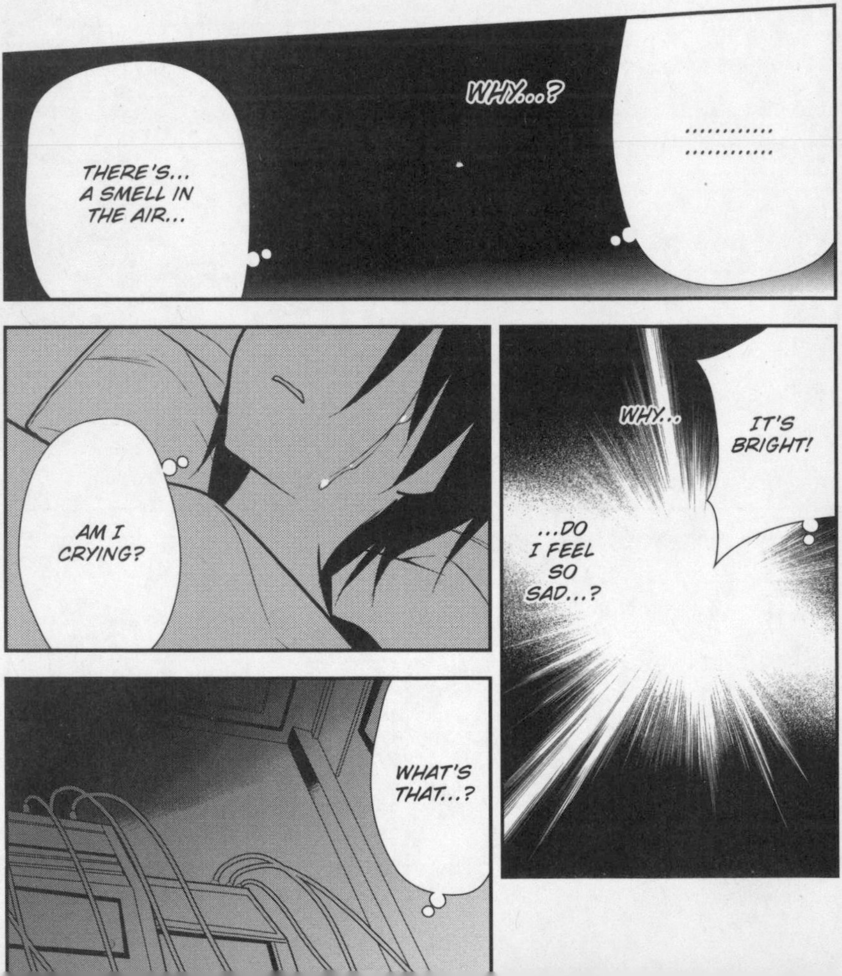
....
....
WHY...?
THERE'S... A SMELL IN THE AIR...
IT'S BRIGHT!
WHY...
...DO I FEEL SO SAD...?
AM I CRYING?
WHAT'S THAT...?

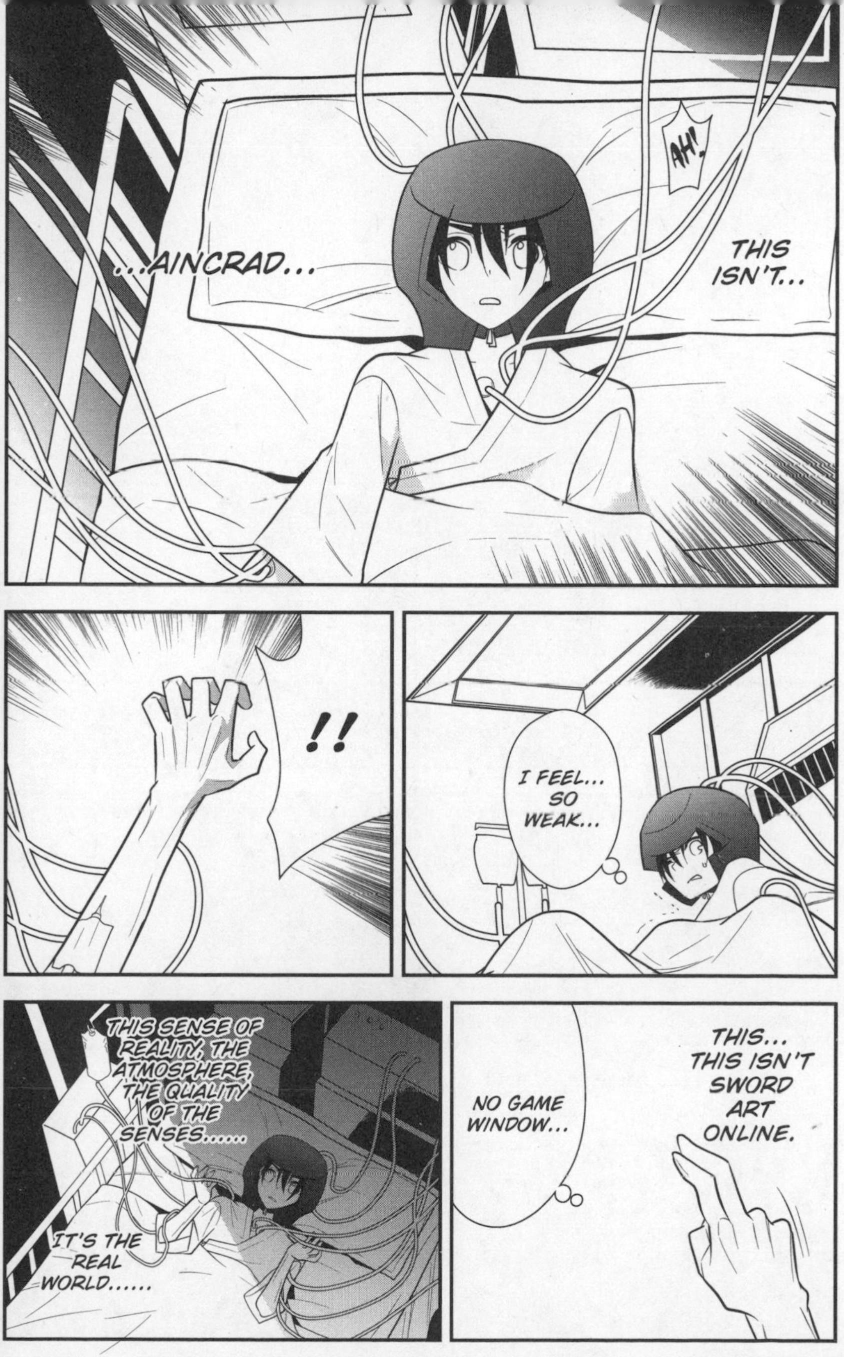
AH!
THIS ISN'T...
...AINCRAD...
I FEEL... SO WEAK...
!!
THIS... THIS ISN'T SWORD ART ONLINE.
NO GAME WINDOW...
THIS SENSE OF REALITY, THE ATMOSPHERE, THE QUALITY OF THE SENSES......
IT'S THE REAL WORLD......

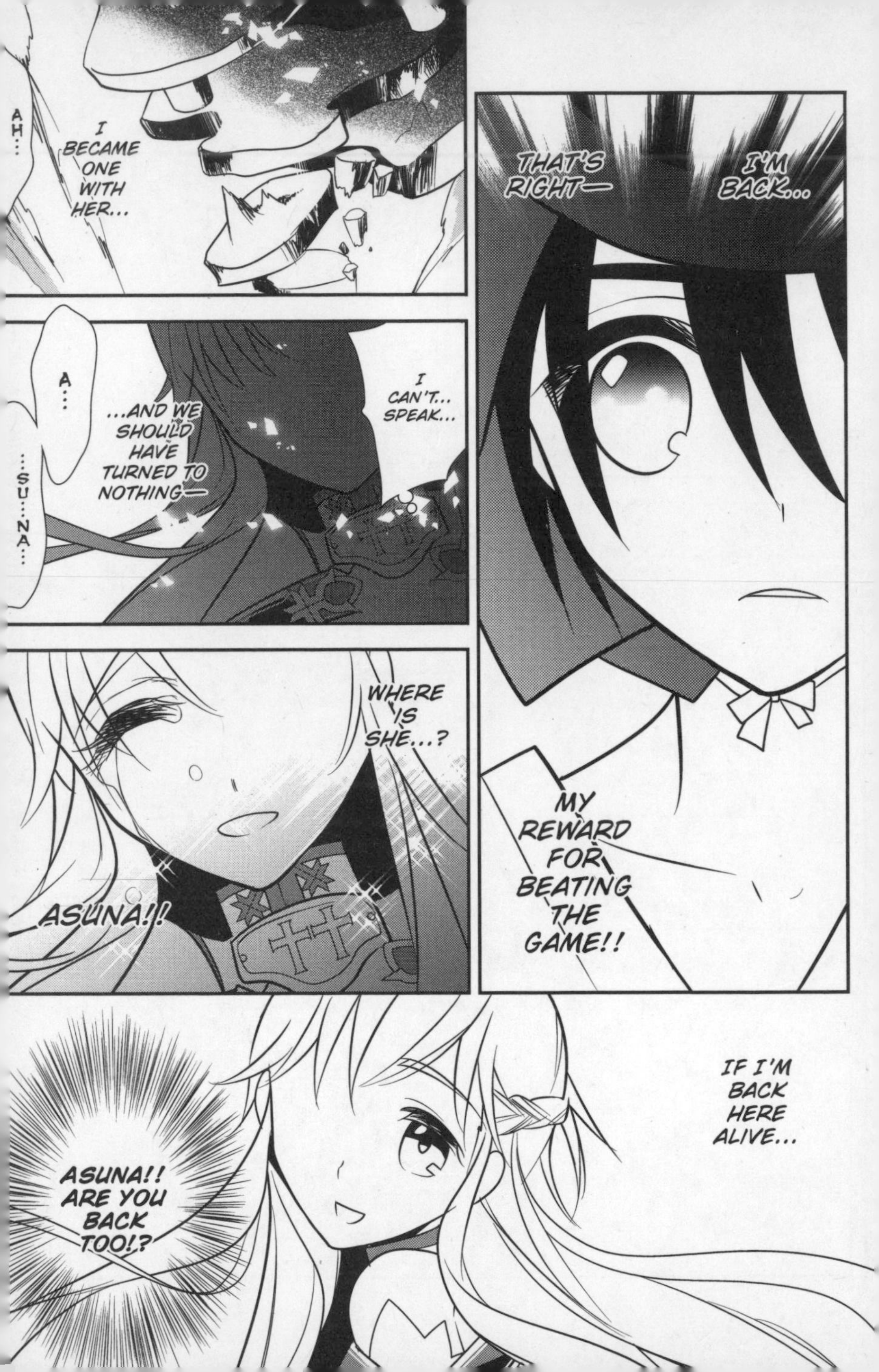
I'M BACK...
THAT'S RIGHT—
MY REWARD FOR BEATING THE GAME!!
I BECAME ONE WITH HER...
AH...
I CAN'T... SPEAK...
...AND WE SHOULD HAVE TURNED TO NOTHING—
A...
...SU...NA...
WHERE IS SHE...?
ASUNA!!
IF I'M BACK HERE ALIVE...
ASUNA!! ARE YOU BACK TOO!?

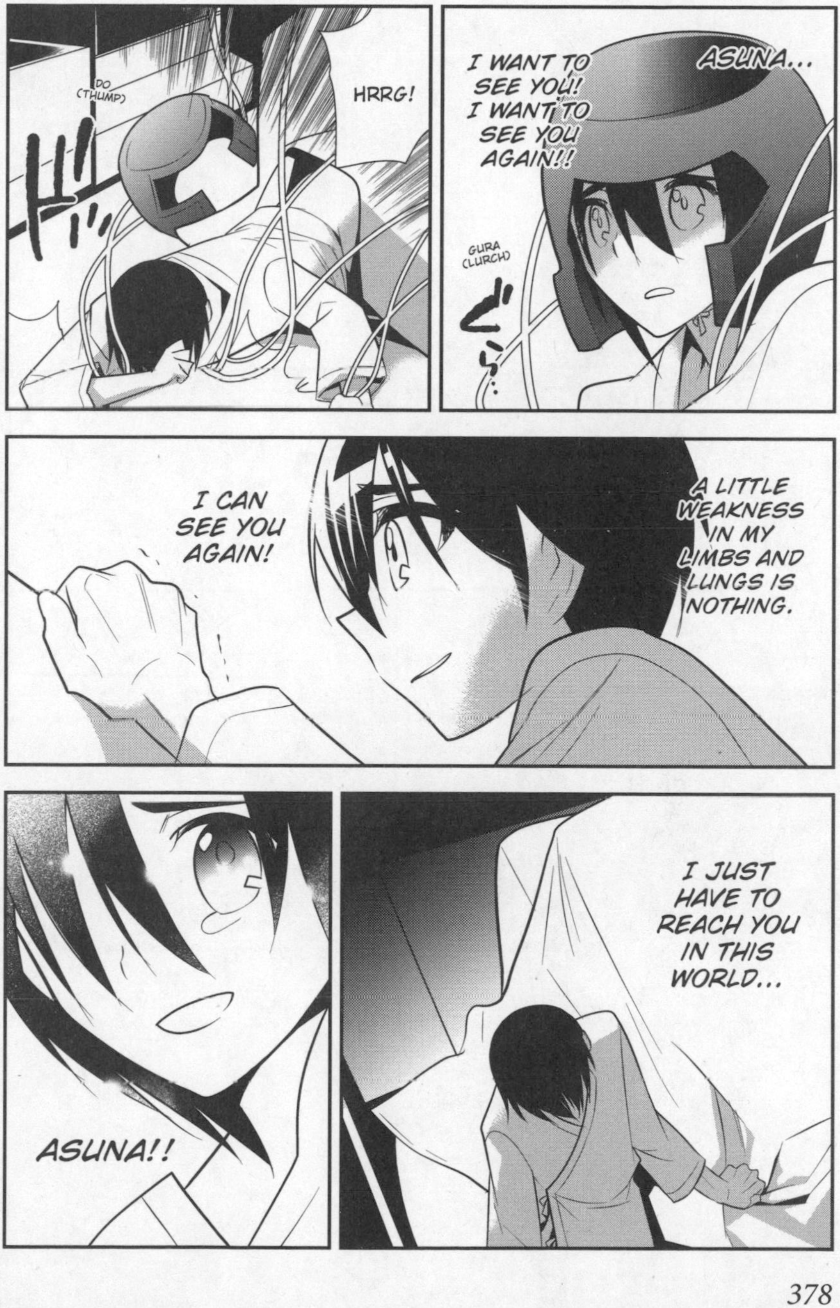
ASUNA...
I WANT TO SEE YOU! I WANT TO SEE YOU AGAIN!!
GURA (LURCH)
DO (THUMP)
HRRG!
A LITTLE WEAKNESS IN MY LIMBS AND LUNGS IS NOTHING.
I CAN SEE YOU AGAIN!
I JUST HAVE TO REACH YOU IN THIS WORLD...
ASUNA!!

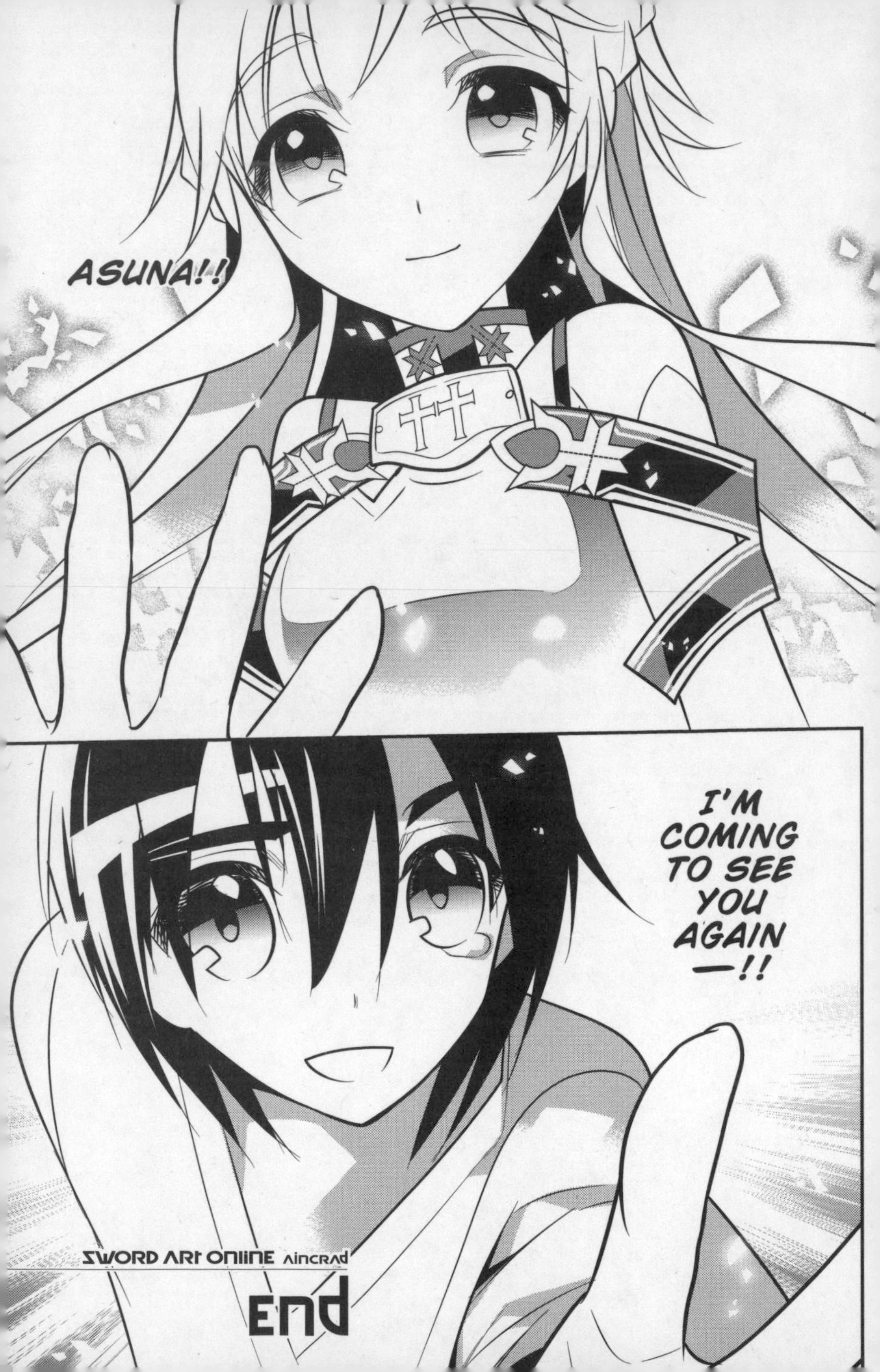
ASUNA!!
I'M COMING TO SEE YOU AGAIN—!!
SWORD ART ONLINE Aincrad
End

SWORD ART ONLINE Aincrad

Art: TAMAKO NAKAMURA
Original story: REKI KAWAHARA
Character design: ABEC

SPECIAL COMMENT

Original story: REKI KAWAHARA

SWORD ART ONLINE IS A STORY WITH A RATHER CONVOLUTED SETTING—THAT OF JAPANESE YOUTHS PLAYING A FANTASY GAME IN A VIRTUAL WORLD WHERE THE SITUATION TURNS SERIOUS AND THEIR VERY LIVES ARE AT STAKE.

WHEN I WAS WRITING THE ORIGINAL NOVEL THIS WAS BASED ON, I WAS OFTEN CONFLICTED ABOUT HOW TO PORTRAY THE SYSTEMATIC ELEMENTS OF THE GAME AND THE MENTAL PROCESSES OF THE CHARACTERS. I FOUND MYSELF UNABLE TO FULLY DEPICT THE CONTRASTING ELEMENTS—AN ALTERNATE WORLD AND DIGITAL SPACE; AN MMO GAME AND TRUE DEATH—AND THERE WERE MANY TIMES WHEN THE SIGHTS AND ATMOSPHERE OF THE SCENES WERE LEFT TO THE READER'S IMAGINATION.

SO WHEN I HEARD ABOUT THE POSSIBILITY OF A MANGA ADAPTATION, I COULDN'T HELP BUT WONDER IF THE VISUAL COMIC MEDIUM WOULD BE CAPABLE OF DEPICTING THE INORGANIC DIGITAL NATURE OF SAO OR THE UNCERTAIN DISTANCE FROM DEATH THAT EXISTS IN THE STORY.

BUT ARTIST TAMAKO NAKAMURA-SENSEI, WITH HER CLEAR, SHARP LINEWORK AND STRONG-EYED CHARACTERS, HAS SHOWN HERSELF TO BE WELL UP TO THE TASK OF DRAWING THE FLOATING FORTRESS AINCRAD AND THE PEOPLE WHO INHABIT IT. IT WAS A LONG SLOG LASTING TWO YEARS AND TWELVE CHAPTERS, BUT WITH THE MOVING FINAL SCENE DEPICTING KIRITO WALKING AGAIN IN THE REAL-LIFE HOSPITAL COMPLETED, I FEEL A GREAT GRATITUDE AND ADMIRATION FOR HER WORK.

JOB WELL DONE ON FINISHING YOUR SERIAL, AND THANK YOU. AND CONGRATULATIONS FOR HAVING BOTH VOLUMES RELEASED SIMULTANEOUSLY!

REKI KAWAHARA

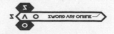

SWORD ART ONLINE
AINCRAD

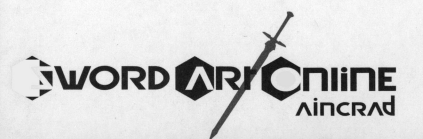

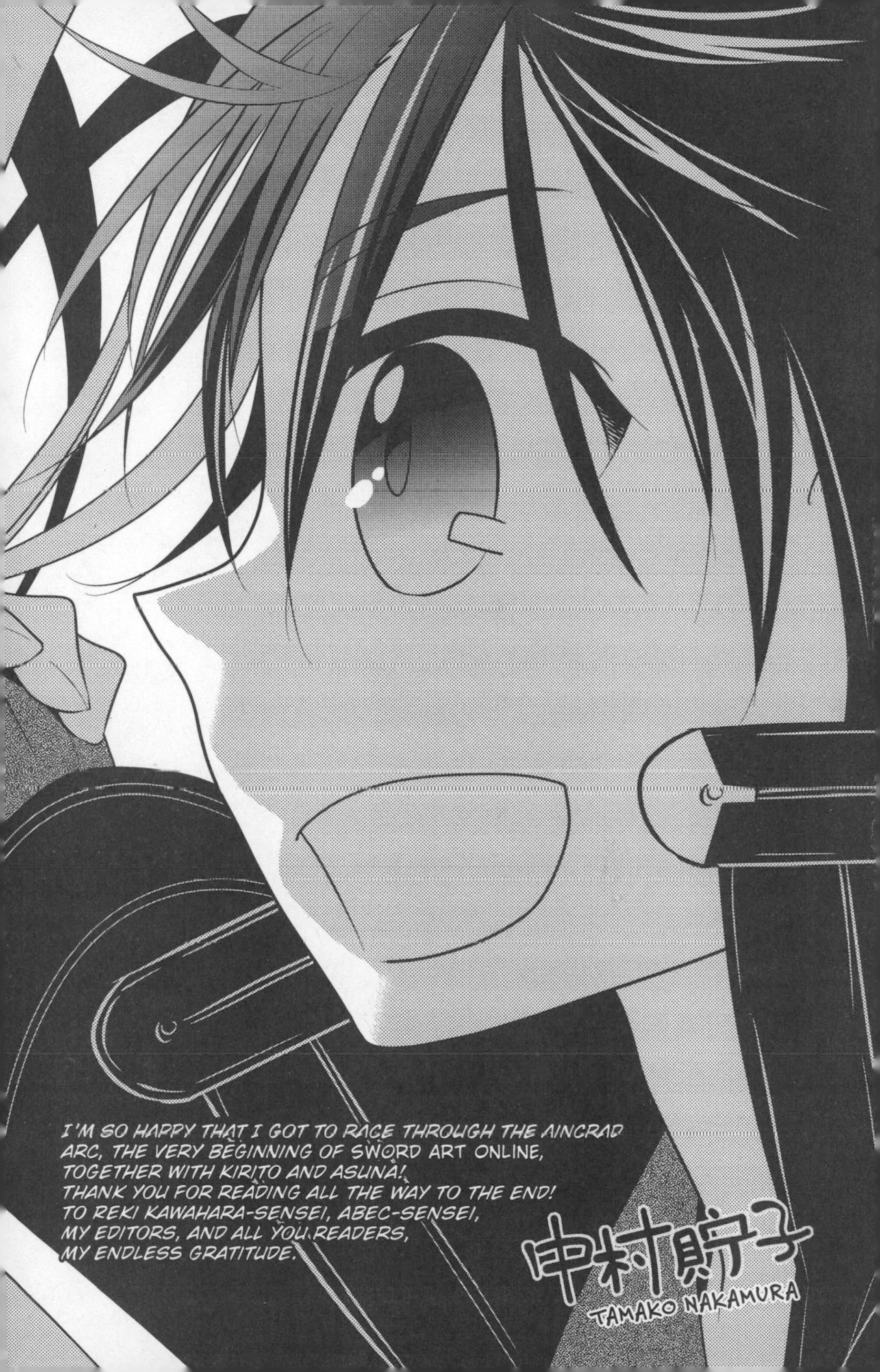
I'M SO HAPPY THAT I GOT TO RACE THROUGH THE AINCRAD ARC, THE VERY BEGINNING OF SWORD ART ONLINE, TOGETHER WITH KIRITO AND ASUNA!
THANK YOU FOR READING ALL THE WAY TO THE END!
TO REKI KAWAHARA-SENSEI, ABEC-SENSEI, MY EDITORS, AND ALL YOU READERS, MY ENDLESS GRATITUDE.
中村貯子
TAMAKO NAKAMURA

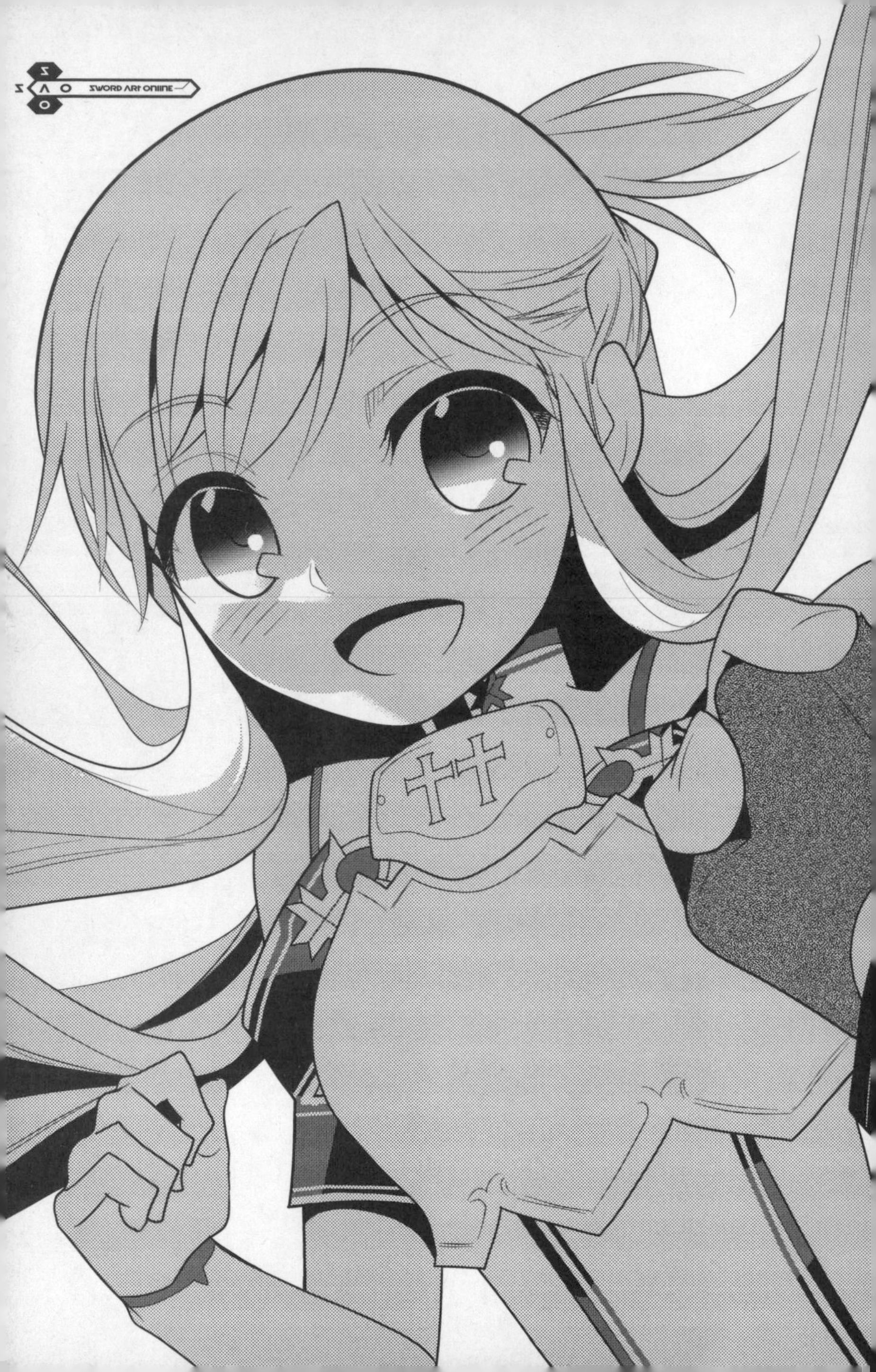

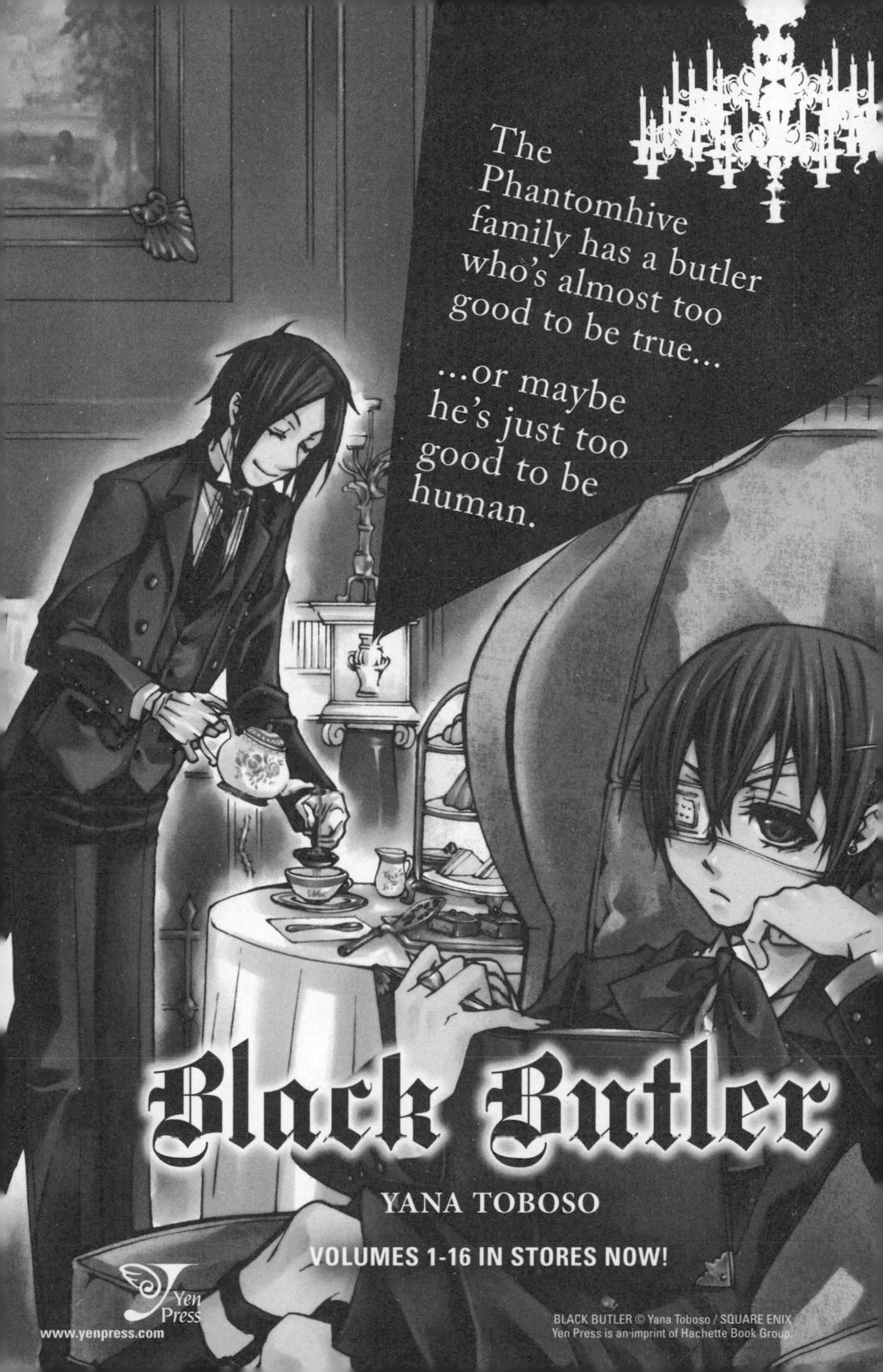
The Phantomhive family has a butler who's almost too good to be true...
...or maybe he's just too good to be human.
Black Butler
YANA TOBOSO
VOLUMES 1-16 IN STORES NOW!
Yen Press
www.yenpress.com
BLACK BUTLER © Yana Toboso / SQUARE ENIX
Yen Press is an imprint of Hachette Book Group.

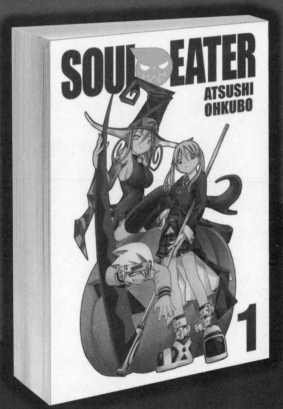

WELCOME TO IKEBUKURO, WHERE TOKYO'S WILDEST CHARACTERS GATHER!!

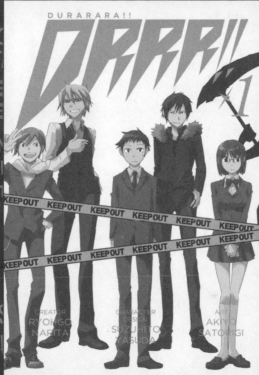

AS THEIR PATHS CROSS, THIS ECCENTRIC CAST WEAVES A TWISTED, CRACKED LOVE STORY...

AVAILABLE NOW!!

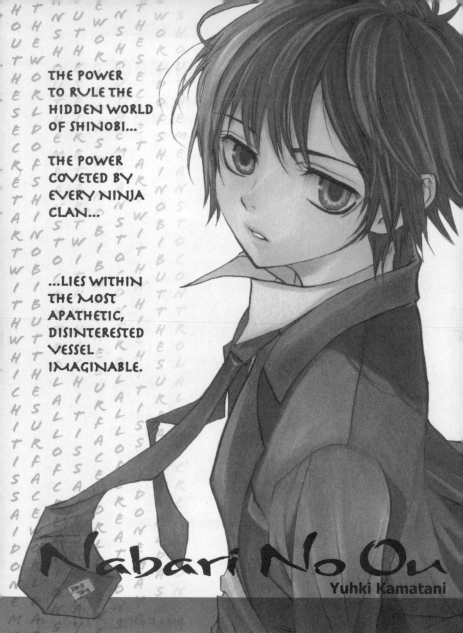

THE POWER
TO RULE THE
HIDDEN WORLD
OF SHINOBI...

THE POWER
COVETED BY
EVERY NINJA
CLAN...

...LIES WITHIN
THE MOST
APATHETIC,
DISINTERESTED
VESSEL
IMAGINABLE.

Nabari No Ou
Yuhki Kamatani

COMPLETE SERIES NOW AVAILABLE

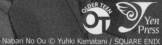

SWORD ART  D

IRA
IRA
CHARACTER DESIGN: ABEC

Translation: Stephen Paul • Lettering: Lys Blakeslee, Terri Delgado

This book is a work of fiction. Names, characters, places, and incidents are the product of the author's imagination or are used fictitiously. Any resemblance to actual events, locales, or persons, living or dead, is coincidental.

SWORD ART ONLINE: AINCRAD
© REKI KAWAHARA/TAMAKO NAKAMURA 2012
All rights reserved.
Edited by ASCII MEDIA WORKS
First published in Japan in 2012 by KADOKAWA CORPORATION, Tokyo.
English translation rights arranged with KADOKAWA CORPORATION, Tokyo,
through Tuttle-Mori Agency, Inc., Tokyo.

English translation © 2014 by Yen Press, LLC

Yen Press
1290 Avenue of the Americas
New York, NY 10104

www.YenPress.com

Yen Press is an imprint of Yen Press, LLC. The Yen Press name and logo are trademarks of Yen Press, LLC.

First Yen Press Edition: March 2014

ISBN: 978-0-316-37123-0

20 19 18 17

WOR

Printed in the United States of America